D1155249

DEVELOPMENT OF PROFESSIONAL EXPERTISE

Professionals such as medical doctors, airplane pilots, lawyers, and technical specialists find that some of their peers have reached high levels of achievement that are difficult to measure objectively. In order to understand to what extent it is possible to learn from these expert performers for the purpose of helping others improve their performance, we first need to reproduce and measure this performance. This book is designed to provide the first comprehensive overview of research on the acquisition and training of professional performance as measured by objective methods rather than by subjective ratings by supervisors. In this collection of articles, the world's foremost experts discuss methods for assessing the expert's knowledge and review how we measure professional performance and design-training environments that permit beginning and experienced professionals to develop and maintain their high levels of performance, using examples from a wide range of professional domains.

K. Anders Ericsson, PhD, is presently Conradi Eminent Scholar and Professor of Psychology at Florida State University. For the last 30 years he has studied the development of expert performance in domains such as music, chess, medicine, business, and sports and how expert performers attain their superior performance by acquiring complex cognitive mechanisms and physiological adaptations through extended deliberate practice. He has edited several books on expertise, including *Toward a General Theory of Expertise* (1991), *The Road to Excellence: The Acquisition of Expert Performance in the Arts and Sciences, Sports, and Games* (1996), and the influential *Cambridge Handbook of Expertise and Expert Performance* (2006). His research has been recently featured in *The New York Times*, *Scientific American*, *Fortune* magazine, *New Scientist*, and *Time* magazine. He is a Fellow of the American Psychological Association, the Association of Psychological Science, and the Center for Advanced Study in the Behavioral Sciences.

Development of Professional Expertise

TOWARD MEASUREMENT OF EXPERT
PERFORMANCE AND DESIGN OF OPTIMAL
LEARNING ENVIRONMENTS

Edited by

K. Anders Ericsson

Florida State University

CAMBRIDGE UNIVERSITY PRESS
Cambridge, New York, Melbourne, Madrid, Cape Town, Singapore, São Paulo, Delhi

Cambridge University Press
32 Avenue of the Americas, New York, NY 10013-2473, USA

www.cambridge.org
Information on this title: www.cambridge.org/9780521740081

First published 2009

Printed in the United States of America

A catalog record for this publication is available from the British Library.

Library of Congress Cataloging in Publication data
Development of professional expertise : toward measurement of expert performance
and design of optimal learning environments / edited by K. Anders Ericsson.
    p.   cm.
Includes bibliographical references and index.
ISBN 978-0-521-51846-8 (hardback) – ISBN 978-0-521-74008-1 (pbk.)
1. Expertise.   2. Professional employees.   3. Performance.   I. Ericsson, K. Anders
(Karl Anders), 1947–   II. Title.
BF431.D443   2009
153.9–dc22   2008054456

ISBN 978-0-521-51846-8 hardback
ISBN 978-0-521-74008-1 paperback

CONTENTS

FIGURES

TABLES

CONTRIBUTORS

ALISON L. ANTES
Department of Psychology
The University of Oklahoma
Norman, OK

EVA L. BAKER
University of California, CRESST
Los Angeles, CA

HERBERT H. BELL
Air Force Research Laboratory
Warfighter Readiness Research
  Division
Mesa, AZ

WINSTON BENNETT, JR.
Air Force Research Laboratory
Warfighter Readiness Research
  Division
Mesa, AZ

ROBERT A. BJORK
Department of Psychology
University of California
Los Angeles, CA

EDDY W. BOOT
TNO Defence, Security and Safety
Department of Training & Instruction
Soesterberg, The Netherlands

HENNY P. A. BOSHUIZEN
Open University of the Netherlands
Centre for Learning Sciences and
  Technology (Celstec)
Heerlen, The Netherlands

JOHN D. BRANSFORD
College of Education
University of Washington
Seattle, WA

JAY J. CAUGHRON
Department of Psychology
The University of Oklahoma
Norman, OK

RALPH E. CHATHAM
Technology and Training Consultant
Falls Church, VA

SUSAN E. F. CHIPMAN
Arlington, VA, and Boulder, CO

CHARLES M. COLEGROVE
Alion Science and Technology
Langley Air Force Base, VA

KEVIN P. CORRELL
Naval Undersea Warfare Center
  Division
Newport, RI

DAVE A. DAVIS
Association of American Medical
  Colleges
Washington, DC

DAVID W. ECCLES
The Learning Systems Institute
Florida State University
Tallahassee, FL

K. ANDERS ERICSSON
Department of Psychology
Florida State University
Tallahassee, FL

J. D. FLETCHER
Institute for Defense Analyses
Alexandria, VA

TAMARA L. FRIEDRICH
Department of Psychology
The University of Oklahoma
Norman, OK

DAVID A. GRESCHKE
General Dynamics Information
  Technology
Mesa, AZ

EARL B. HUNT
Department of Psychology
University of Washington
Seattle, WA

SUSAN S. KIRSCHENBAUM
Naval Undersea Warfare Center
  Division
Newport, RI

SUSANNE P. LAJOIE
Department of Educational and
  Counselling Psychology
McGill University
Montreal, Quebec, Canada

LAURA LANG
The Learning Systems Institute

Florida State University
Tallahassee, FL

JAMES W. LUSSIER
U.S. Army Research Institute
Fort Knox Research Unit
Fort Knox, KY

RICHARD E. MAYER
Department of Psychology
University of California
Santa Barbara, CA

SHELLEY L. MCINNIS
Naval Undersea Warfare Center
  Division
Newport, RI

MICHAEL D. MUMFORD
Department of Psychology
The University of Oklahoma
Norman, OK

RAY S. PEREZ
Office of Naval Research
Arlington, VA

ANTOINETTE M. PORTREY
Lockheed Martin
Mesa, AZ

JAN MAARTEN SCHRAAGEN
TNO Human Factors
Department Human in Command
Soesterberg, The Netherlands

BRIAN T. SCHREIBER
Lumir Research Institute
Grayslake, IL

DANIEL L. SCHWARTZ
Stanford University School of Education
Stanford, CA

SCOTT B. SHADRICK
U.S. Army Research Institute
Fort Knox Research Unit
Fort Knox, KY

BRETT VAN DE SANDE
School of Computer and
    Informatics
Arizona State University
Tempe, AZ

KURT VANLEHN
School of Computer and Informatics
Arizona State University
Tempe, AZ

JEROEN J. G. VAN MERRIËNBOER
Maastricht University, FHML
Department of Educational
    Development & Research
Maastricht, The Netherlands

PAUL WARD
Learning Systems Institute
Department of Psychology
Florida State University
Tallahassee, FL

The Measurement and Development of Professional Performance: An Introduction to the Topic and a Background to the Design and Origin of This Book

K. ANDERS ERICSSON, RAY S. PEREZ,
DAVID W. ECCLES, LAURA LANG, EVA L. BAKER, JOHN
D. BRANSFORD, KURT VANLEHN, AND PAUL WARD

Developments in technology and software engineering are making many types of traditional jobs, such as bookkeeping, accounting, routine design, and document indexing, virtually obsolete (Rasmussen, 2000). The rapid improvements in technology and automated work methods challenge even the traditional idea of stable job competence, as well as the ability to predict the length and the nature of current or future professional careers. Today's work conditions require ongoing adaptations by employees and entrepreneurs to new demands and competitive opportunities through continuing education and training. Technological innovations, such as the World Wide Web, broadband communication, and highly portable communication and work devices, have reduced the constraints of geography on work. Today, many services can be provided with an equivalent level of quality irrespective of whether the provider is in the office next door or on a different continent. It is, indeed, becoming an age of global consumerism in which one can "work with anyone, anytime, anywhere." Additionally, many specialized skills previously performed by human beings are now the purview of automated systems, and can often be conducted anywhere in the world at a fraction of the cost if carried out in Western Europe and North America. This technological revolution suggests that the competitive advantage of any country aspiring to economic prosperity is increasingly dependent on the capability of both its research and development groups and its skilled workforce, not only to create and develop new and improved products that are at the cutting edge, but also to quickly react and adapt to market forces. The shift from the industrial to the technological age clearly motivates increased efforts to support the development of existing and future professionals with these skill sets; to identify existing

Author Note: Generous support to the authors for the preparation of this article and the Development of Professional Performance conference described within it was provided by the US Office of Naval Research, grant # N00014-05-1-0785.

experts and high-performers; and to provide suitable learning environments that can position and maintain companies and nations ahead of the curve.

There are many recent books that address professional development and the need to foster and develop a company's personnel and skilled professionals. What makes this book unique and distinctive is its focus on measurable performance in representative activities that capture expertise in the associated domain, and its study of factors that promote the acquisition and development of superior professional performance. The commitment to focus on measurable performance comes from a desire to study superior professional achievement scientifically and is based on recent advances in the study of expert performance in more traditional domains of expertise, such as chess, music, sports, and medicine (Ericsson, Charness, Feltovich, & Hoffman, 2006). Recent research on reproducible superior performance has successfully challenged the popular myth that expertise and superior performance develop as inevitable, naturally emerging consequences of many years of experience in a domain. There is now ample evidence from many different domains that the number of years of experience is a poor predictor of objective professional performance (for more recent extensive reviews and a meta analysis supporting this claim, see Choudhrey, Fletcher, & Soumerai, 2005; Ericsson, 2004, 2006a; Ericsson, Whyte, & Ward, 2007). In fact, there is even evidence showing that the objective performance of medical professionals decreases as the number of years since graduation from initial professional education increases (Choudhry et al., 2005; Ericsson et al., 2007). For example, years of experience and age has been found to be negatively related to adherence of accepted standards for medical treatment. Even more importantly, survival of patients treated for heart problems has been found to decrease with number of years since graduation from medical school of the treating physician when other relevant variables were statistically controlled (Choudhry et al., 2005).

During the last five years an impressive number of scholarly books have been published on the topics of expertise, expert performance, high levels of skill, and excellence (Boshuizen, Bromme, & Gruber, 2004; Chaffin, Imreh, & Crawford, 2002; Ericsson, Charness, Feltovich, & Hoffman, 2006; Feist, 2006; Ferrari, 2002; Hoffman, 2007; Kurz-Milcke & Gigenrenzer, 2004; Montgomery, Lipshitz, & Brehmer, 2005; Runco, 2007; Simonton, 2004; Starkes & Ericsson, 2003; Sternberg & Grigorenko, 2003; Tetlock, 2005; Tsui, 2003; Weisberg, 2007; Williamon, 2005; Williams & Hodges, 2004). These books describe a wide range of methods used to study the structure and acquisition of high levels of achievement across a wide range of different domains of expertise, such as music, teaching, chess, sports, business, and medicine.

The study of expertise and expert performance has been conducted with several different approaches, but two approaches have been particularly dominant. The original theory of human expertise was developed by de Groot (1946/1978) and Simon and Chase (1973) and emphasized the importance of extended professional experience for the attainment of the expert level of achievement. Given the difficulties of measuring objective performance in most domains, this approach focused on how less accomplished individuals, such as novices and beginners, differed from experts, who were defined as individuals with extensive professional experience (typically over 10 years), or nominated by their peers as particularly accomplished professionals, or both (Chi, 2006). As mentioned above, experience was later found to be a poor predictor of objective performance and this finding led to proposals of an alternative approach, namely the *expert performance approach* (Ericsson & Lehmann, 1996; Ericsson & Smith, 1991). This approach focuses on objectively measurable superior performance on representative tasks that capture expertise in the domain (Ericsson, 2006a, 2006b; Ericsson & Smith, 1991). This approach to the measurement of expert performance avoids the problem of using questionable criteria that is based on professional experience and peer nomination to identify reproducibly superior performance. Throughout this book, we have encouraged contributors to cite research that used objectively measured performance to support claims about antecedents to increases in professional performance and, thus, professional development. Examinations of the changes in the nature of performance over extended periods of development have uncovered effective methods for enhancing many different aspects of performance, such as deliberate practice (e.g., Ericsson, 2006a; Ericsson, Krampe, & Tesch-Römer, 1993).

The unique perspective of this book on the study of professional development comes from the mission of a grant from the Office of Naval Research (Contract # N00014-05-1-0785) to convene a conference on the possibility of applying the expert performance approach to the development and maintenance of skilled and expert performance with Laura Hassler Lang as Principle Investigator and David Eccles and Anders Ericsson as co-Principle Investigators, and with Ray Perez as Contract Officer. The focus was on producing a review and an evaluation of state-of-the-art knowledge about instruction and training in the development and maintenance of professional skills, searching for research that emphasized *measurable objective performance.* The goal was to develop a synthesis of the knowledge of the structure and acquisition of expert performance in traditional domains, such as chess, music, and sports, recently summarized in the *Cambridge Handbook of Expertise and Expert Performance* (Ericsson et al., 2006) and relate it to knowledge about development of performance in a broader range of domains, namely professional performance. Consequently, the focus of this book is on research that has examined the performance of personnel involved in actual professional settings, including medicine, industry, and the military.

The primary focus of this book is on individual performance. While this will involve performance by individual members of teams, the invited contributors were encouraged not to emphasize team performance, which has received a great deal of research attention elsewhere (Bowers, 2006; Salas &

Fiore, 2004) and has been very difficult to measure with objective methods. Before we give more details about how the contributions to this book were produced and later revised, we will consider the history of research on measurement of professional performance and how earlier approaches differ from the expert performance approach and the invited contributions to this book.

A BRIEF HISTORY OF RESEARCH ON OBJECTIVE MEASUREMENT OF PROFESSIONAL PERFORMANCE

The 20th century saw impressive advances in psychometric theories and procedures for the development of tests of general and basic abilities. In contrast, the development of theories of the structure of professional performance and its associated measurement were largely neglected. In the early 1990s, Wigdor and Green (1991a) published a book commissioned by the National Research Council in which some of the most outstanding researchers in applied psychology summarized the past research as well as a new project on the development of "Performance Assessment for the Workplace." Wigdor and Green (1991a) argued that it has been much easier to develop sophisticated test instruments and associated statistical techniques "than to find adequate measures of performance to use as criteria in judging the relevance of the tests. For the most part, industrial and organizational psychologists and their institutional clients have used measures of convenience, such as training grades or supervisor ratings as a surrogate for job performance" (p. 22). Wigdor and Green exemplify these concerns by an extended description of a report by Captain John Jenkins on the selection of pilots during World War II. This report showed that psychometric tests were able to predict in advance which of the candidates would be eliminated from the accelerated training program due to poor flying performance, fear, or their own requests. However, an analysis of actual combat performance of successfully graduated pilots showed that none of the tests "gave evidence of predicting the combat criterion measures to any marked degree" (Jenkins's report, cited by Wigdor & Green, 1991a, p. 25). Their review concluded that prior use of selection tests had been validated against criteria based on successfully completing training, such as multiple-choice tests of knowledge at the end of the course, rather than actual job performance attained after some period of on-the-job experience. By designing the selection tests to predict performance *during* training rather than predicting subsequent performance on the job, the selection tests would be likely to screen out many individuals who would actually have very successful careers. The use of written selection tests that focus on predicting performance *during* the initial schoolhouse training resulted in the rejection of large segments of the population with low scores on the traditional types of psychometric tests. With the change into a volunteer military service in the United States, military recruiters were faced with the problem of what to do when there were not enough applicants who scored well on the selection tests used for recruitment. To what extent would individuals scoring below average on the selection tests be able to develop into average or above average performers on their military jobs? The first step to study this issue scientifically would require that applicants with a wide range of scores on the selection tests be admitted to training and their subsequent performance on the job evaluated by fair objective criteria. Instead of the typical measures of job performance, such as supervisor ratings or knowledge tests or both, Wigdor and Green (1991a) recommended "the criterion measure that comes closest to actual job performance, the hands-on job-sample test" (p. 30).

A group of scientists led by Wigdor and Green (1991a) gave scientific oversight to a massive project in the U.S. Department of Defense, namely the Joint-Service Job Performance Measurement/Enlistment Standards (JPM) project. In this project, several thousands of enlisted men and women were given selection tests at entry, such as variants of the Armed Services Vocational Aptitude Battery (ASVAB), and applicants with a wide range of scores on the selection tests were accepted for training. Later on, after several months of working, their performance was evaluated with various measures and tests of performance. The most innovative aspects of this project concerned the development of hands-on work-sample tests that would capture the actual behaviors necessary for executing particular job responsibilities for soldiers with a given occupational category, rather than testing soldiers by asking them to verbally describe procedure or answer multiple-choice questions about job-related knowledge. Wigdor and Green (1991a) define a hands-on *work-sample* as "an actual part of a job, chosen for its representativeness and importance to success on the job" (p. 59). For example, a work-sample test for a secretary might involve "a word-processing task, a filing task, and a form completion task" (p. 59). The work-sample methodology involved transforming these job activities into standardized hands-on tasks where all tested individuals can perform action sequences that can be checked for accuracy by trained observers.

Many of the findings from the JPM project with data from over 5,000 military personnel have been reported by Wigdor and Green (1991a, 1991b). One of the their general conclusions was that "it is possible to develop hands-on measures of job performance for a wide range of military jobs" (Wigdor & Green, 1991a, p. 183) and that hands-on performance on the work-sample tasks did not increase very much overall as function of length of work experience beyond the first year. Furthermore, the individual differences in hands-on performance attributable to cognitive abilities were reduced after the first year of service (Wigdor & Green, 1991a, p. 164). A part of the JPM study, referred to as Project A, was extended by the U.S. Army to include measurement of job performance immediately after training, and during the first and second 3-year tours of duty (Campbell, 2001; Campbell & Knapp, 2001). The focus of Project A (Campbell & Knapp, 2001) was not on identifying high levels of performance, but on developing tests for selecting recruits and assigning them to training for different military occupations where they would be able to exhibit an *acceptable* level of performance. In the work on identifying the latent variables underlying the large body of tests of different types of abilities as well as ratings and objective measures of job performance, the JPM project and Project A found that some of the different measures of job performance had low inter-correlations (for an extended discussion, see Knapp, Campbell, Borman, Pulakos, & Hanson, 2001). For example, observed correlations between the most valid measure of job performance, namely scores on the hands-on work-sample tests, correlated poorly with the job ratings of the soldiers' supervisors, with an average correlation coefficient of around 0.2 (Campbell, McHenry, & Wise, 1990; Wigdor & Green, 1991a). In the concluding chapter in a book on Project A, Campbell (2001) argued: "The efforts also convincingly show that a clear focus on the latent structure will illuminate the gaps as well as the strengths of our research knowledge. For example, the lack of research attention to the latent structure of 'job-relevant knowledge' and 'job-relevant skill' became painfully obvious" (p. 588). More generally, these studies on the selection of personnel uncovered several remaining obstacles for ultimate validation of the standardized objective tests for selecting and identifying individuals who would ultimately develop reproducibly superior performance under the target condition, namely performance under combat conditions. The developed tests of job performance focused primarily on assessment of reliable execution of standard procedures, rather than on assessment of skilled performance and high fidelity simulations of representative situations under combat conditions and real-time constraints. Even the most recent books (Bennett, Lance, & Woehr, 2006a) on performance measurement continue to argue that "the criterion problem continues to be one of the most vexing issues facing organization researchers and practitioners today" (Bennett, Lance, & Woehr, 2006b, p. 1). In their review of the progress on the development of criteria for job performance, Austin and Crespin (2006) described the emerging knowledge about motivational factors that are correlated with average productive performance across days and weeks. These factors included the effects of counterproductive work behavior (Miles, Borman, Spector, & Fox, 2002), the importance of contextual behaviors that support the social and motivational work situation (Motowidlo, Borman, & Schmit, 1997), and the differences between maximal performance during a test and the actual average performance measured on the job (Sackett, Zedeck, & Fogli, 1988). However, there has been less progress on the development of objective measures for job performance.

Is it possible to develop a methodology that can accurately capture and measure superior professional performance in critical situations, such as emergencies and other stressful task conditions? In the next section we will describe how the methods of the expert performance approach can be adapted toward the achievement of this goal.

THE EXPERT PERFORMANCE APPROACH TO THE STUDY OF SUPERIOR PERFORMANCE

The JPM project focused on basic performance and also found modest improvements in hands-on performance as a function of the length of experience on the job, suggesting that experience on the job may not dramatically improve this aspect of measured job performance. (See Mayberry & Carey, 1997, for an exceptionally large improvement in performance of helicopter repair technicians as a function of more experience even beyond the first year.) As noted earlier, experience on the job has not been found to relate closely to improvement in performance on representative tasks in domains such as the financial investment of clients' funds, treatment of patients with psychotherapy, and decision making in a wide range of situations involving prediction of behavior and events (Ericsson, 1996, 2004; Ericsson & Lehmann, 1996; Ericsson, Whyte, & Ward, 2007).

In the expert performance approach (Ericsson, 2006a, 2006b; Ericsson & Smith, 1991), investigators identify those individuals (expert performers) who exhibit superior performance on tasks that capture the essence of expertise in the critical domain. These studies encourage the identification of superior performers and specialists who are able to successfully deal with challenging and non-routine cases.

Once tasks with superior performance have been identified in everyday life, then the next step in the expert performance approach involves the design of tasks that can reproduce the superior expert performance in the laboratory. Repeated elicitation of the superior performance on representative tasks permits the application of standard cognitive methods to analyze the mechanisms that mediate experts' superior performance. The general paradigm pioneered by de Groot (1946/1978; Ericsson & Smith, 1991) started with an analysis of naturally occurring behavior, such as games between chess masters. He then identified key chess positions, where a chess move needs to be made, and where the best move can be determined after the fact. More generally, the expert performance approach involves the identification of critical situations, where an immediate action needs to taken, and where the correct action can be assessed after the fact. These critical situations can then be presented, for instance, as videos or simulations, with the requirement of immediate action to experts and less skilled performers to let them generate their best action. By presenting a sequence of these representative tasks and recording the speed and accuracy of generated actions, it has been possible to capture objective performance in different domains, such as chess, music, and the board game Scrabble, which is closely related to performance in tournaments and competitions (Tuffiash, Roring, & Ericsson, 2007; for a review, see Ericsson, 2006b). For example, in chess it is possible to take measures of these abilities with 10 to 20 minutes of testing that approach the validity of measures based on outcomes of chess games lasting 50 to 200 hours during tournament play (Ericsson & Williams, 2007; van der Maas & Wagenmakers, 2005).

Once the superior performance of experts can be repeatedly reproduced with representative tasks in the laboratory, it is possible to apply the entire toolbox of cognitive psychology and trace performance with process measures, such as latencies, eye movements, and concurrent or retrospective reports, and to design experiments to test hypotheses about the nature and structure of the mediating mechanisms (Ericsson, 2006b). Research on expertise, especially expert memory performance, has shown how protocols can identify complex mechanisms that can later be confirmed by specially designed experiments (Ericsson, 2006b). The expert performance approach, with its identification of mechanisms mediating consistently superior performance, has now been successfully applied to a wide range of activities, such as medical diagnosis, surgical procedures, music performance, writing, painting, Scrabble, darts, ballet, soccer, running, field hockey, volleyball, rhythmic gymnastics, and tennis (Ericsson, 2006a). The most interesting and exciting discovery from studying the superior performance of experts is that it has been directly linked to complex representations that are specific to the domain of expertise and, consequently, were developed as a result of extended exposure and practice (Ericsson, 2006b). For example, chess masters develop the ability to explore consequences of long sequences of chess moves mentally and are, in fact, able to play blindfold chess; that is, to play without seeing a physical chess board and pieces. Similarly, elite athletes, such as tennis and squash players, develop superior ability to anticipate the trajectory of future shots, as revealed by successful predictions of ball landing locations generated even before the opponent player has hit the ball with his/her racquet.

More experience does not automatically lead to increased engagement in dedicated and focused practice to reach the highest level of performance, such as wining international competitions (Ericsson, 2006a; Simon & Chase, 1973). More generally, diaries and retrospective estimates of weekly engagement in particular activities have demonstrated that not all domain-related activities are correlated with increases in performance. Ericsson, Krampe, and Tesch-Römer (1993) found that the total amount of domain-related activities for musicians was not associated with differences in attained levels of performance. The activity most closely related to level of performance was the amount of engagement in solitary practice as reflected by diaries and retrospective estimates. During solitary practice, musicians work on clear practice goals recommended by their teachers using methods designed to improve specific aspects of their individual performance. The improvements in performance are due to changes in performance linked to repetitions and refinements of processes with problem solving in response to feedback (deliberate practice). For example, piano students successfully master their assigned pieces of music by practicing and working on difficult sections by re-fingering transitions, repetitions, and speed work. Several researchers have reported a consistent association between the amount and quality of solitary activities meeting the criteria of deliberate practice and performance in different domains of expertise, such as chess (Gobet & Charness, 2006), darts (Duffy, Baluch, & Ericsson, 2004), music (Lehmann & Gruber, 2006), many types of sports (Ward, Hodges, Starkes, & Williams 2007; Williams, Ericsson, Ward, & Eccles, 2008), Scrabble (Tuffiash et al., 2007), and several other diverse domains (Ericsson, 2006a).

In sum, research within the expert performance framework has shown that individual differences in sustained activity and accumulated deliberate practice are correlated with attained performance in a wide range of domains of expertise.

THE PROCESS OF GENERATING THIS BOOK

Most of the authors of this chapter met in the spring of 2006 to design a conference on the objective measurement of professional performance and its development and acquisition in response to training and deliberate practice. We all agreed that we knew of no similar effort to organize a conference or produce an edited book on this topic.

We decided on a general approach that would maximize the chances that we would be able to identify published research on objective measurement of professional performance, and to stimulate discussion about related issues and their relation to training. We invited the most prominent and exciting researchers who had studied relevant issues to prepare chapters on how their domains of research related to the objective measurement of professional performance, and grouped them into four sections. To distill the most interesting ideas, we invited five eminent cognitive psychologists and educators to serve as discussants of the presentations within each section. The mere knowledge that one's chapter would be publicly discussed by eminent scientists should have motivated each group of authors to do their very best job. We selected eminent scientists who have served as editors for major journals and many books, expecting them to be able to critically review the presented material as well as extract and induce the key issues and fundamental empirical findings and connections to general theories in psychology and education. Hence, it was clear that the chapters and the resulting book would have to go through several iterations until we reached the final published form.

The first step was to generate a list of eminent scientists as well as key researchers who could present findings related to the key set of issues. We were grateful to find that everyone that we contacted was intrigued and willing to participate. By distributing abstracts for all of the presentations in the fall of 2006, we started a process for increased connections between chapters, exchange of relevant information, and greater integration of the contributions. In the spring of 2007, we planned a conference, organized under the leadership of Eccles, where the invited presenters gave brief summaries of their previously circulated chapters, followed by questions and most importantly a discussion by our invited eminent scientists. The conference, chaired by Eccles and Ward, was structured around four groups of presentations with their associated discussant, and was concluded by presentations from several individuals with broad perspectives on professional training. These individuals presented overviews focusing on the implications and applications of the presented ideas for future research and development of training devices. After the conference, held at the Westin Grand Bohemian Hotel on March 2–4, 2007, in Orlando, Florida, U.S.A., the plan then was that all presenters would revise their chapters, which were to be given to each of the group discussants, who then were to finalize the written version of their commentaries. Finally, all the written materials (chapters and written commentaries) were handed over to two general discussants to allow them to finalize their contribution.

While organizing a conference is always challenging, we encountered few unexpected complications with this conference and the subsequent completion of this edited volume. The fact that all invited participants made plans to attend our conference and viewed our project with interest and excitement certainly reflected positively on the experience, although not everything went entirely to plan. One presenter was snowed in for a couple of days in a large city in North America and was unable to catch a flight in time to attend even part of the conference. Another participant was forced at the last minute to stay home for a family emergency. Unexpected problems led to a few changes, but the published book is a refined and distilled version of the original plan generated in the spring of 2006, and thus the ideas and information presented at our conference in Orlando in 2007. In the next section we provide a summary of the content of the subsequent chapters of this book, with a focus on our goal to find and develop objective measures of professional performance and to identify the training and practice activities that lead to improvements and maintenance of this type of performance.

THE OUTLINE OF THIS BOOK

The first section of the book is concerned with general overviews of the challenges of objective measurements and training of professional performance in some of the major domains, and a review of the progress toward objective measurement.

In Chapter 2, Chatham describes the evidence for the role of skill acquisition and learning with feedback for the success of the armed forces. He discusses the evidence on effects of training on performance for representative tasks. One of the most striking and compelling examples of how representative training with feedback (deliberate practice) can improve performance under field conditions is provided by the U.S. Top Gun training program. This training program was designed to improve the probability that U.S. fighter pilots would survive their first mortal combat with enemy pilots during the Vietnam War. The Top Gun program trained pilots before their first mission against enemy pilots by simulated battles at a Navy air base in the United States. The pilots in training would embark on missions, during which they would encounter instructor pilots equipped and trained as enemy fighters with one noteworthy difference – the instructors were armed only with film cameras rather than lethal weapons. At the end of the mission the films would be reviewed and the pilots in training would be able to analyze all of their mistakes under the supervision of their teachers. They would then be able to go out on another mission the following day, practicing their new insights and tactics. This training program allowed inexperienced pilots to learn how to improve their performance on subsequent training missions without the risk of being killed or shot down. Participation in the Top Gun training prior to one's first encounter with enemy aircrafts led to a six-fold reduction in combat losses when compared to other pilots who did not participate in the training (see Chatham, Chapter 2).

In Chapter 3, Lajoie discusses one of the pioneering projects that applied the most promising methods of training from cognitive science, namely tutoring. This project for designing specialized training involved the elicitation of knowledge of a domain of expertise, namely electronic troubleshooting for aircraft repair, and building a computer program, SHERLOCK, that could train aspiring electronic technicians individually with a computer-based tutor. One of the exceptional aspects of this program is that it was fully implemented and evaluated with objective tests of performance. The redesigned training with tutoring led to more successful and rapid repair of malfunctioning equipment compared to traditional training. Lajoie also reports on her more recent extensions of these training methods to medicine with superior diagnostic performance.

In Chapter 4, the last of this section, Mumford and his colleagues (Mumford, Friedrich, Caughron, & Antes) review the research on leadership and report that the vast majority of research on leaders assesses performance from subjective ratings of supervisors and supervised employees, along with other socially determined variables such as salaries and promotions. They found that there is essentially no research on objective measurements of leader performance, where objective performance is defined as the leader's influence on the productivity of his/her respective group of supervised employees. They argue that a lack of objective validation raises fundamental problems in the measurement of leader development and assessment. In their chapter, they outline the nature of superior behavior of leaders and propose a model of leader behavior that emphasizes the important role of leaders' thought processes. Based on their new model of leadership, they develop an approach to the study of the development and assessment of leadership that relies extensively on the use of situational tests, where the leaders have to deal with presented management and leadership problems under controlled laboratory conditions.

In Chapter 5, Hunt offers reflections on some of the themes of the three chapters in this section. He begins by presenting a broad discussion of the central ideas of the three papers. He then reviews evidence for Chatham's (Chapter 2) argument for the importance of learning and training even outside the realm of the military and the effectiveness of activities involving negative feedback akin to the after-action review. He discusses the theoretical mechanisms assumed to mediate learning and forgetting, and the considerable knowledge in cognitive psychology based primarily on extensive studies in the laboratory. Next, Hunt gives an endorsement of the value of the computer-based tutors, such as the use of SHERLOCK for training electronic maintenance personnel, and discusses why these types of tutors were not more generally developed. He also raises concerns about the ability of these types of tutors to be sufficiently engaging and motivating to use, as well as their ability to facilitate learning of any form of skill, such as training soldiers to interact with non-English speaking civilians in Iraq. Following this, Hunt discusses the review by Mumford et al. (Chapter 4) of research on the effectiveness of training leadership and their model of mechanisms of leadership. Hunt discusses whether this model can explain extraordinary leaders, such as Abraham Lincoln, or whether one would need a richer model of leadership. In sum, Hunt provides a masterful discussion of Chatham's proposal (Chapter 2) for methods mediating effective training and shows how the chapters by LaJoie (Chapter 3) and Mumford et al. (Chapter 4) offer supporting evidence and identify some outstanding issues for future research on training.

The second section of the book is concerned with a review of the major approaches and general frameworks for training individuals in the necessary basic skills plus more complex skills, and for the continued education of professionals and maintenance of their skills during their careers. In Chapter 6, van Merriënboer and Boot review the developments in instructional design and instructional systems design over the last 25 years. In the beginning, instructional design approaches were simple and trained participants to attain one learning objective at a time in a sequential fashion. Over time there has been a realization of the need to conceive of real-world skills holistically given the complex organization of their dynamic and interacting mechanisms. The authors propose the need to develop instructional systems design and to create learning environments that allow the training of complex tasks using virtual reality and other forms of simulation of realistic situations and tasks.

In Chapter 7, Schraagen convincingly argues that task analysis is the most important activity in instructional systems design, and that effective task analysis should focus on the identification of cognitive processes of successful learners and expert performers. He demonstrates how an analysis of expert strategies and knowledge allowed his group of instructional designers to identify effective strategies and representations in electronic troubleshooting. In a training study, experienced troubleshooters were instructed in the use of these strategies and representations which were designed to help them structure their search space and reduce their workload. After a week of training, the troubleshooters were reliably superior to trainees receiving only traditional training when both groups were tested on representative tasks. In a subsequent step, Schraagen and his colleagues were able to redesign the existing troubleshooting training so that the same level of performance could be achieved with less than half the amount of training time.

In Chapter 8, the last of this section, Davis examines the evidence on continued education of fully trained performers with a focus on medicine, since the maintenance and improvement of medical treatment by doctors has received considerable attention and funding for several decades. Davis dispels the myth that doctors are able to assess their own performance by showing that the accuracy of medical doctors' self-assessments is generally poor and does not accurately identify need for improvements in professional performance. He describes how medical organizations attempt to exert control over their members' performance by requiring re-certification and yearly engagements in continued education, which predominantly involve a traditional classroom-based style of instruction such as attending lectures on new medical procedures and developments. Studies of this traditional approach indicate that it is essentially ineffective in causing change in actual performance. However, there are emerging opportunities for effective training with feedback via websites on the internet that would allow both the assessment of current level of performance and provide opportunities for engagement in deliberate practice to maintain and further improve clinical performance.

In his reflections on Chapters 6, 7, and 8, Mayer (Chapter 9) argues that design of effective instruction requires a clear specification of what students need to learn. He proposes that instructional design approaches have evolved from a tradition of teaching compartmentalized behaviors and knowledge that can easily be acquired, but can be developed into learning environments to promote the acquisition of more complex mental structures. Mayer shows that both van Merriënboer and Boot's (Chapter 6) and Schraagen's (Chapter 7) proposals for revisions of instructional design approaches can be described as directed toward making students acquire integrated knowledge, permitting them to engage in decision making, reasoning, and problem solving to deal with complex and even unfamiliar task situations. Mayer shows that Davis's (Chapter 8) argument that advanced students and professionals need to acquire mechanisms that permit them to assess the quality of their own skills and knowledge can be described as the generation of individualized knowledge. This metacognitive knowledge permits each learner to engage in appropriate self-directed learning to maintain and ideally improve his/her professional performance. In his concluding section, Mayer reviews the modest success of many instructional programs that designed technology-based learning environments to foster the acquisition of integrated and individualized knowledge. He invites researchers to develop deeper insights into how the acquisition of complex knowledge can be facilitated by appropriate learning activities and environments.

The third section of the book contains a discussion of the current and newly evolving methods for training skilled professionals, such as fighter pilots, officers leading combat units, and submarine officers. In the lead chapter, Chatham (Chapter 10) reviews the effectiveness of computer programs for training many aspects of professional performance, such as troubleshooting, convoy operations, and second-language acquisition. However, he also identifies limits of the current methodology for training professionals to handle successfully the demands of social and cultural interactions between individuals within their units but also primarily with external contacts made during their missions. He outlines a new type of virtual simulation that would allow trainees to experience these types of situations and scenarios in a safe and controlled environment with ample opportunities for feedback and repetition.

In the second chapter in this section, Schreiber and his colleagues (Schreiber, Bennett, Colegrove, Portrey, Greschke, & Bell, Chapter 11) review the history of the development of airplane simulators and the improved fidelity of the simulators to provide a realistic flying experience. They describe new simulation systems that can train the coordination of behavior of pilots, commanders, and recognizance officers in a large-scale war effort. However, they notice that the data showing improvements of objective performance have been restricted to "simple tasks representative of a small portion of a mission" and overall performance has almost exclusively been measured by ratings, which, as discussed earlier, have known sources of subjectivity and bias. Their chapter describes a new effort to develop objective measures of representative performance so that it will be possible to estimate the value of selection and training of pilots in terms of measurement of performance in actual everyday conditions that can be captured reliably in simulated environments.

In the next chapter, Kirschenbaum and her colleagues (Kirschenbaum, McInnis, & Correll, Chapter 12) examine the training of the two types of the most frequent specialist positions on a submarine, namely sonar operators and operators who analyze sparse target data for location and course. They describe the traditional training of these submarine specialists; like medical doctors, their training involves classroom instruction followed by apprentice training on a submarine where the students gradually get to perform increasingly complex tasks and eventually all of the jobs for which they have been trained. This training method creates a long delay between the school house and relevant on-the-job training, creating opportunities for forgetting. The new training, instituted in response to the U.S. Navy's Revolution in Training initiative, is quite different and has reduced the length of the initial school-house training phase and time to deployment to the submarine, and to their relevant on-the-job training. Additionally, school-house training is interspersed with short, intensive courses lasting only a few weeks. Kirschenbaum and her colleagues describe the new opportunities to use simulation and deliberate practice activities to enhance performance.

In the final chapter of this section, Shadrick and Lussier (Chapter 13) describe a very interesting project in which they use insights from the study of chess experts and the study of deliberate practice to design training for decision making by battlefield commanders. Using the analogy of how a chess master trains by attempting to identify the best moves for chess positions from previous games between grand masters, they present commanders in training with typical situations that require immediate action. Once the commanders have generated an action for a given tactical situation, they are presented with feedback so they can identify any key characteristic of the situation that they might have overlooked or misinterpreted. Shadrick and Lussier describe their recent work with the development of training programs involving representative decision-making situations and the validation of these training programs, which includes assessing the transfer and generalized effects of their training.

In his reflections on the themes in Chapters 10 to 13, Robert Bjork (Chapter 14), one of the most influential researchers in the study of memory and learning, starts by providing a careful review of laboratory studies on skill acquisition, memory, forgetting, transfer, and learning. He focuses especially on the evidence for an important distinction between observed performance (during training) and learning (the stable changes mediating subsequent performance tested after long or short delays and in altered task contexts – transfer). This distinction between learning and performance is very important in the military and industry, where the actual performance under field conditions is rarely measured and hardly ever used to optimize training. Instead training is often designed to maximize performance during training on less valid tests, such as multiple-choice items, which do not adequately capture the complexities of subsequent on-the-job performance. The focus of much of education has been on facilitating performance during training, often at the direct expense of performance during delayed and altered test conditions. In spite of the general problem with measurement of performance in the field

(Scheiber et al., Chapter 11; Shadrick & Lussier, Chapter 13), Bjork (Chapter 14) stresses that the military has also developed some innovative examples for providing measurement of behavior and immediate feedback in simulated field activities, such as the Top Gun training and after-action reviews (Chapman, Chapter 2; Hunt, Chapter 5). He also discusses the benefits of interweaving training and performance, where training, evaluation, and on-the-job performance can be coordinated and maintained to support career-long learning as illustrated by Kirschenbaum et al. (Chapter 12). In his discussion of Shadrick and Lussier's (Chapter 13) empirical studies, Bjork discusses how presenting decision scenarios randomly sampled from a large population of challenging tactical cases might be a useful simulation of the on-the-job environment. Training with these types of scenarios may capture the variability and spacing of tasks in a natural manner that presents desirable difficulties and mimics field conditions. Most importantly, Bjork (Chapter 14) discusses a number of important research issues, where future research on skill acquisition on traditional laboratory tasks and analysis of skilled professional performance using laboratory methods could jointly establish the potential and limits of our current theoretical understanding of learning during professional development.

The fourth and final section of the book focuses on how we can measure and describe the acquisition of skilled and expert performance. In the introductory chapter Baker (Chapter 15) provides a general overview of the role of assessment in learning and education. She proposes how an analysis of targeted achievement and skill can guide the design of assessment and thereby generate an integrated plan for the design of training and associated testing (cf. van Merriënboer & Boot, Chapter 6; Schraagen, Chapter 7). Baker argues that test design should draw on the literature of learning rather than simply the psychometric tradition. In particular, she suggests that test tasks be designed to support schema development and consequent transfer and generalization. She also discusses the role of the analysis of expertise as a method for inducing criterion level performance. Baker distinguishes simple cases where performance can be easily measured, such as accuracy of shots in archery, from complex skills where individuals need to master the concepts and activities in a complete domain, such as algebra. She provides examples for how one can describe complex domains with networks involving concepts and relations that represent mastery, and gives detailed illustrations from the domain of marksmanship and algebra. Finally, Baker discusses the identification and design of representative tasks involving simulations that will provide better measurement of attained performance than the traditional testing with many multiple-choice questions.

In the following chapter, VanLehn and van de Sande (Chapter 16) discuss conceptual expertise and examine its acquisition in the domain of introductory physics. They make a crucial distinction between being able to solve typical problems using standard equations in physics, on the one hand, and being able to solve conceptual problems and reason about laws and phenomena in physics on the other. They review evidence showing that the ability of college students to solve mathematical problems in physics develops much faster than their ability to answer conceptual problems correctly. In fact, they report that even graduate students in physics retain some misconceptions about physics. VanLehn and van de Sande (Chapter 16) propose a reason why the ability to solve mathematical problems develops faster than conceptual understanding and reasoning, and are able to propose different types of practice activities that focus on description of forces and other elements of problems, classification of conditions, and application conditions rather than traditional calculation of solutions to problems. These practice activities should increase the development of conceptual reasoning – the hallmark of genuine experts in physics. The development of representations for conceptual reasoning appears to be essential in most domains and does require appropriate types of practice activities for its efficient development.

In her chapter, Boshuizen (Chapter 17) reviews the history of professional education in law, business, and medicine with a special emphasis on the transformation of medical education. Traditionally, professional education consisted of lecture courses with theories and knowledge based on laboratory studies followed by apprenticeships, where individuals were supposed to learn how to apply their knowledge by observing and performing on the job. To bridge the gulf between these two types of learning, educators proposed problem-based learning (PBL) where abstract knowledge was introduced within the context of future professional problems. For example, medical students would learn about the anatomy of lungs and physiology of breathing in the context of studying typical problems of patients with related problems. Boshuizen also discusses how researchers have assessed the consequences of this change in training of medical students on the probability of completing education, proficiency in diagnosing problems and performing procedures, and in answering traditional tests of knowledge. Based on her review she concludes that the change toward a PBL curriculum has led to significant changes in job-related skills and performance without reliable decrements in traditional measures of knowledge. The changes due to the introduction of PBL are clearly positive and the most salient difference concerns increases in motivation during training, especially during the first years of medical school. She mentions a recent review that questions the favorable evidence for PBL (Colliver, Kucera, & Verhulst, 2008; see also Norman, 2008a) based on biased selection of medical students. Fortunately, the same year Koh, Khoo, Wong, and Koh, 2008 (see also Norman, 2008b) published a review that examined the effects of PBL in better controlled studies that focused on evaluations of physicians' competency after 1 to over 10 years after graduation. Koh et al. (2008) discarded findings based on the physicians' self ratings because of their poor validity shown in recent reviews (Davis, Chapter 8; Davis et al., 2006). When their review focused on ratings by supervisors, they found that physicians trained in PBL programs scored significantly higher on cognitive and social aspects of medical practice compared to graduates from traditional medical school programs. In spite of concerns about the variability in implementation of PBL curricula (Taylor & Miflin, 2009), this is a very important and promising finding.

In the last chapter of this section, Ericsson (Chapter 18) reviews research on the factors influencing the acquisition of experts' superior reproducible performance in traditional domains of expertise, using experts such as musicians, dancers, chess players, and athletes. In these domains, performance can be publicly observed and even objectively measured in open competitions and public performances. Past and current engagement in specially designed practice (deliberate practice) in these domains has been found to explain how the performance of experts is qualitatively different from enthusiastic amateurs. Ericsson describes how the theoretical framework of the expert performance approach has already been applied to these traditional domains and how it can be further extended to the study of the measurement and enhanced development of professional performance. One of the key issues is how some individuals restructure their professional activities so that the quality of their performance can be regularly evaluated in order that detailed and reliable feedback can be obtained for use in guiding deliberate practice in designed practice environments. Factors that promote and facilitate the engagement in deliberate practice in professional environments and the attainment and maintenance of high levels of performance are also discussed.

In their reflections on the themes in Chapters 15 to 18, Bransford and Schwartz (Chapter 19) note that the chapters in this book have gone beyond the classic comparisons of the behaviors of experts and novices (Chi, Feltovich, & Glaser, 1981) and focus on factors influencing the development of expert performance. Under the general theme of "it takes expertise to make expertise," they note that the contributions in this section discuss the instructional conditions (Boshuizen, Chapter 16; VanLehn & van de Sande, Chapter 17) and the contextual support for learning (Baker, Chapter 15; Ericsson, Chapter 18) that promote the development of expertise. They extract several points from the chapters about the role of feedback in learning. For example, they point to Baker's (Chapter 15) criticisms of high stakes testing as providing feedback to school administrators rather than to the individual students to facilitate their learning. They show how PBL in medicine (Boshuizen, Chapter 16) and computer-supported learning in physics (VanLehn & van der Sande, Chapter 17) guide students to encode knowledge to support their ability to reason and apply it in future situations. They also emphasize the importance for adults to engage in learning tasks that are challenging and where useful feedback is immediately available to gain improvements in performance (Ericsson, Chapter 18). Bransford and Schwartz (Chapter 19) give a very interesting discussion of the challenges to learning in domains of activity where the quality and immediacy of feedback after performance is virtually lacking, such as in psychotherapy, medical diagnosis, and education. They conclude with a discussion of how new directions in the assessment of performance successfully integrate testing and learning by providing informative feedback and opportunities for discovery and preparation for future learning.

In the final section of the book, two experts with extensive experience and knowledge about issues related to research on professional training make some general comments on how the findings reported in this book may be applied to further advance professional training and research on the associated theoretical issues. In the first chapter in this concluding section Fletcher (Chapter 20) comments on the evaluation of training in the military sector. His chapter addresses the crucial questions on the value of selection and training for any associated increases in performance of the members in groups and organizations in the military. First, he identifies a number of themes among the chapters in this book, such as deliberate practice, self-assessment and self-directed learning, agility, centrality of cognition, assessment of professional growth, and design of learning environments, and then summarizes some of the key findings about these themes. The main body of Fletcher's chapter reviews the evidence for reliable improvements in performance from selection of trainees and training for simulated tests, and, in particular, from operational experience and training in performance in field tests and in actual combat. Most interestingly, he discusses examples where the value of increased performance can be measured by the amount of money required to attain the same levels of performance by technical development of improved equipment. He reviews several efforts to measure increases in combat success due to operational experience and training, such as the earlier discussed Top Gun training of pilots in the Navy. For example, he provides a detailed analysis of the superior performance displayed in one remarkable battle success during the original liberation of Iraq and analyzes the superior training that made it possible. He summarizes the reviewed research in the military and how it relates and supports the earlier identified themes of the book. In conclusion, he argues that the value and costs of increases in on-the-job performance as the result of specific training interventions should be measured and quantified to demonstrate its superiority to the field performance attained by the traditional approach of investing in developing technical solutions and buying the newest equipment while preserving or even reducing training. Once the on-the-job performance is measurable, it will be possible to explore a wide range of training options to maximize the cost effectiveness of producing and maintaining a given level of the desired performance.

In her general commentary, Chipman (Chapter 21), one of the most influential grant administrators guiding research on training in the past decades, explores the limits of the approach taken in this book, namely the focus on *reproducibly superior individual performance*, and discusses the potential of studying expertise in the management of people. The principal method for training managers has relied on the learning from actual case descriptions with discussion supervised by teachers. Chipman examines the complex process of teaching and the difficulties of adapting instruction to the individual students and their mental models – much the same difficulties that a manager has in adapting his or her leadership behavior to supervise different individuals within a company. She discusses the virtual lack of scientific evidence for the dominant models in business for describing individual differences in personality, such as Myer-Briggs indicators, and questions the value of current managerial training in improving the performance of future managers. She concludes with a plea for establishing a new empirical foundation based on behavioral observation and proposes a more successful and scientific approach to the training and measurement of performance of managers.

RETROSPECTIVE COMMENTS

Looking back at the plans of our working group for the actual conference and for this book, it is fair to say that it has exceeded our expectations. The contributors generally had the sense that the synergy among all of the outstanding contributors led to a very interesting and important product. By bringing together scientists, applied researchers, and specialists that would not normally meet for discussions, we attained an exchange of information related to research findings and theoretical perspectives that is rarely seen in science. Perhaps more importantly, this book has pulled together much of our distributed knowledge about objective measurement of professional performance and its development. This book will provide the reader with insights into the challenges and prospects of future research on training and development of measurable performance of professionals. We hope that some of the readers will be excited and stimulated toward design of future studies by the ideas and issues presented in the chapters. Others may generate different ideas for projects and design research opportunities and collaborations. It is our hope that the excitement felt by the conference attendees about this evolving field of study will be successfully communicated in this book and that many readers will be similarly excited about the new frontier involving the study of expert professional performance and its acquisition.

REFERENCES

Austin, J. T., & Crespin, T. R. (2006). From "criterion problem" to problems of criteria in industrial and organizational psychology; progress, pitfalls, and prospects. In W. Bennett, C. L. Lance, & D. J. Woehr (Eds.), *Performance measurement* (pp. 9–48). Mahwah, NJ: Lawrence Erlbaum Associates.

Bennett, W., Jr., Lance, C. L., & Woehr, D. J. (Eds.). (2006a). *Performance measurement: Current perspectives and future challenges*. Mahwah, NJ: Lawrence Erlbaum Associates.

(2006b). Introduction. In W. Bennett Jr., C. L. Lance, & D. J. Woehr (Eds.), *Performance measurement: Current perspectives and future challenges* (pp. 1–5). Mahwah, NJ: Lawrence Erlbaum Associates.

Boshuizen, H. P. A., Bromme, R., & Gruber, H. (2004). *Professional learning: Gaps and transition on the way from novice to expert*. Dordrecht, The Netherlands: Kluwer Academic Publishing.

Bowers, C. A. (Ed.). (2006). *Creating high-tech teams: Practical guidance on work performance and technology*. Washington, DC: American Psychological Association.

Campbell, J. P. (2001). Implications for future personnel research and personnel management. In J. P. Campbell, & D. J. Knapp (Eds.), *Exploring the limits in personnel selection and classification* (pp. 577–580). Mahwah, NJ: Lawrence Erlbaum Associates.

Campbell, J. P., & Knapp, D. J. (Eds.). (2001). *Exploring the limits in personnel selection and classification*. Mahwah, NJ: Lawrence Erlbaum Associates.

Campbell, J. P., McHenry, J. J., & Wise, L. L. (1990). Modeling job performance in a population of jobs. *Personnel Psychology, 43*, 313–333.

Chaffin, R., Imreh, G., & Crawford, M. (2002). *Practicing perfection: Memory and piano performance*. Mahwah, NJ: Lawrence Erlbaum Associates.

Chi, M. T. H. (2006). Two approaches to the study of experts' characteristics. In K. A. Ericsson, N. Charness, P. Feltovich, & R. R. Hoffman (Eds.), *The Cambridge handbook of expertise and expert performance* (pp. 21–30). Cambridge, UK: Cambridge University Press.

Chi, M. T. H., Feltovich, P. J., & Glaser, R. (1981). Categorization and representation of physics problems by experts and novices. *Cognitive Science, 5*, 121–152.

Choudhry, N. K., Fletcher, R. H., & Soumerai, S. B. (2005). Systematic review: The relationship between clinical experience and quality of health care. *Annals of Internal Medicine, 142*, 260–273.

Colliver, J. A., Kucera, K., & Verhulst, S. J. (2008). Meta-analysis of quasi-experimental research: Are systematic narrative reviews indicated? *Medical Education, 42*, 858–865.

Davis, D. A., Mazmanian, P. E., Fordis, M., Van Harrison, R., Thorpe, K. E., & Perrier, L. (2006). Accuracy of physician self-assessment compared with observed measures of competence: A systematic review. *Journal of the American Medical Association, 296*(9), 1094–1102.

de Groot, A. (1978). *Thought and choice in chess*. The Hague: Mouton (Original work published 1946).

Duffy, L. J., Baluch, B., & Ericsson, K. A. (2004). Dart performance as a function of facets of practice amongst professional and amateur men and women players. *International Journal of Sport Psychology, 35*, 232–245.

Ericsson, K. A. (1996). The acquisition of expert performance: An introduction to some of the issues. In K. A. Ericsson (Ed.), *The road to excellence: The acquisition of expert performance in the arts and sciences, sports, and games* (pp. 1–50). Mahwah, NJ: Lawrence Erlbaum Associates.

(2004). Deliberate practice and the acquisition and maintenance of expert performance in medicine and related domains. *Academic Medicine, 79*, S70–S81.

(2006a). The influence of experience and deliberate practice on the development of superior expert performance. In K. A. Ericsson, N. Charness, P. Feltovich, &

R. R. Hoffman (Eds.), *The Cambridge handbook of expertise and expert performance* (pp. 685–706). Cambridge, UK: Cambridge University Press.

(2006b). Protocol analysis and expert thought: Concurrent verbalizations of thinking during experts' performance on representative task. In K. A. Ericsson, N. Charness, P. Feltovich, & R. R. Hoffman (Eds.), *The Cambridge handbook of expertise and expert performance* (pp. 223–242). Cambridge, UK: Cambridge University Press.

Ericsson, K. A., Charness, N., Feltovich, P., & Hoffman, R. R. (2006). *The Cambridge handbook of expertise and expert performance*. Cambridge, UK: Cambridge University Press.

Ericsson, K. A., Krampe, R. T., & Tesch-Römer, C. (1993). The role of deliberate practice in the acquisition of expert performance. *Psychological Review, 100*, 363–406.

Ericsson, K. A., & Lehmann, A. C. (1996). Expert and exceptional performance: Evidence on maximal adaptations on task constraints. *Annual Review of Psychology, 47*, 273–305.

Ericsson, K. A., Roring, R. W., & Nandagopal, K. (2007a). Giftedness and evidence for reproducibly superior performance: An account based on the expert performance framework. *High Ability Studies, 18*, 3–56.

(2007b). Misunderstandings, agreements, and disagreements: Toward a cumulative science of reproducibly superior aspects of giftedness. *High Ability Studies, 18*, 97–115.

Ericsson, K. A., & Smith, J. (1991). Prospects and limits in the empirical study of expertise: An introduction. In K. A. Ericsson & J. Smith (Eds.), *Toward a general theory of expertise: Prospects and limits* (pp. 1–38). Cambridge, UK: Cambridge University Press.

Ericsson, K. A., Whyte, J., & Ward, P. (2007). Expert performance in nursing: Reviewing research on expertise in nursing within the framework of the expert-performance approach. *Advances in Nursing Science, 30*, E58–E71.

Ericsson, K. A., & Williams, A. M. (2007). Capturing naturally-occurring superior performance in the laboratory: Translational research on expert performance. *Journal of Experimental Psychology: Applied, 13*, 115–123.

Feist, G. J. (2006). *The psychology of science and the origins of the scientific mind*. New Haven, CT: Yale University Press.

Ferrari, M. (Ed.). (2002). *The pursuit of excellence through education*. Mahwah, NJ: Lawrence Erlbaum Associates.

Gobet, F., & Charness, N. (2006). Chess. In K. A. Ericsson, N. Charness, P. Feltovich, & R. R. Hoffman (Eds.), *The Cambridge handbook of expertise and expert performance* (pp. 685–706). Cambridge, UK: Cambridge University Press.

Hoffman, R. R. (Ed.). (2007). *Expertise out of context: Proceedings of the sixth international conference on naturalistic decision making*. Mahwah, NJ: Lawrence Erlbaum Associates.

Hodges, N., Starkes, J., & MacMahon, C. (2006). Sports. In K. A. Ericsson, N. Charness, P. Feltovich, & R. R. Hoffman (Eds.), *The Cambridge handbook of expertise and expert performance* (pp. 587–611). Cambridge, UK: Cambridge University Press.

Knapp, D. J., Campbell, C. H., Borman, W. C., Pulakos, E. D., & Hanson, M. A. (2001). Performance assessment for a population of jobs. In J. P. Campbell & D. J. Knapp (Eds.), *Exploring the limits in personnel selection and classification* (pp. 181–234). Mahwah, NJ: Lawrence Erlbaum Associates.

Koh, G. C.-H., Khoo, H. E., Wong, M. L., & Koh, D. (2008). The effects of problem-based learning during medical school on physician competency: A systematic review. *Canadian Medical Association Journal, 178*, 34–41.

Kurz-Milcke, E., & Gigenrenzer, G. (2004). *Experts in science and society*. New York: Kluwer Academic/Plenum Publishers.

Lehmann, A. C., & Gruber, H. (2006). Music. In K. A. Ericsson, N. Charness, P. Feltovich, & R. R. Hoffman (Eds.), *The Cambridge handbook of expertise and expert performance* (pp. 685–706). Cambridge, UK: Cambridge University Press.

Mayberry, P. W., & Carey, N. B. (1997). The effects of aptitude and experience on mechanical job performance. *Educational and Psychological Measurement, 57*, 131–149.

Miles, D. E., Borman, W. E., Spector, P. E., & Fox, S. (2002). Building an integrative model of extra work behavior: A comparison of counterproductive work behavior with organizational citizenship behavior. *International Journal of Selection and Assessment, 10*, 51–57.

Motowidlo, S. J., Borman, W. C., & Schmit, M. J. (1997). A theory of individual differences in task and contextual performance. *Human Performance, 10*, 71–83.

Montgomery, H., Lipshitz, R., & Brehmer, B. (Eds.). (2005). *How professionals make decisions*. Mahwah, NJ: Lawrence Erlbaum Associates.

Norman, G. (2008a). The end of educational science? *Advances in Health and Science Education, 13*, 385–389.

(2008b). Problem based learning makes a difference. But why? *Canadian Medical Association Journal, 178*, 61–62.

Rasmussen, J. (2000). Human factors in a dynamic information society: Where are we headed? *Ergonomics, 43*, 869–879.

Runco, M. A. (2007). *Creativity theories and themes: Research development and practice*. Amsterdam, The Netherlands: Elsevier.

Sackett, P. R., Zedeck, S., & Fogli, L. (1988). Relations between measures of typical and maximum job performance. *Journal of Applied Psychology, 73*, 482–486.

Salas, E., & Fiore, S. M. (Eds.). (2004). *Team cognition: Understanding the factors that drive process and performance*. Washington, DC: American Psychological Association.

Simon, H. A., & Chase, W. G. (1973). Skill in chess. *American Scientist, 61*, 394–403.

Simonton, D. K. (2004). *Creativity in science: Chance, logic, genius, and zeitgeist*. Cambridge, UK: Cambridge University Press.

Starkes, J., & Ericsson, K. A. (Eds.). (2003). *Expert performance in sport: Recent advances in research on sport expertise*. Champaign, IL: Human Kinetics.

Sternberg, R. J., & Grigorenko, E. L. (Eds.). (2003). *The psychology of abilities, competencies and expertise*. Cambridge, UK: Cambridge University Press.

Taylor, D., & Miflin, B. (2009). Problem-based learning: Where are we now? *Medical Teacher, 30*, 742–763.

Tetlock, P. E. (2005). *Expert political judgment: How good is it? How can we know?* Princeton, NJ: Princeton University Press.

Tuffiash, M., Roring, R. W., & Ericsson, K. A. (2007). Expert word play: Capturing and explaining reproducibly superior verbal task performance. *Journal of Experimental Psychology: Applied, 13*, 124–134.

Tsui, A. B. M. (2003). *Understanding expertise in teaching: Case studies of ESL teachers*. Cambridge, UK: Cambridge University Press.

van der Maas, H. L. J., & Wagenmakers, E. J. (2005). A psychometric analysis of chess expertise. *American Journal of Psychology, 118*, 29–60.

Ward, P., Hodges, N. J., Starkes, J. L., & Williams, A. M. (2007). The road to excellence: Deliberate practice and the development of expertise. *High Ability Studies, 18*(2), 119–153.

Weisberg, R. S. (2007). *Creativity*. Hoboken, NJ: John Wiley & Sons.

Wigdor, A. K., & Green, B. F. (Eds.). (1991a). *Performance assessment for the workplace*, Vol. I. Washington, DC: National Academy Press.

(1991b). *Performance assessment for the workplace*, Vol. II. Technical issues. Washington, DC: National Academy Press.

Williamon, A. (Ed.). (2005). *Musical excellence: Strategies and techniques to enhance performance*. Oxford, UK: Oxford University Press.

Williams, A. M., Ericsson, K. A., Ward, P., & Eccles, D. W. (2008). Research on expertise in sport: Implications for the military. *Military Psychology, 20*, S123–S145.

Williams, A. M., & Hodges, N. J. (Eds.). (2004). *Skill acquisition in sport: Research, theory and practice* (pp. 231–258). London: Routledge.

SECTION 1

CHALLENGES IN PAST AND CONTEMPORARY EFFORTS TO MEASURE AND TRAIN THE OBJECTIVE PERFORMANCE OF PROFESSIONALS

The first section of the book is concerned with a review of the challenges of objective measurements of professional performance in different domains and a review of the progress toward objective measurement.

2

The 20th-Century Revolution in Military Training

RALPH E. CHATHAM

This chapter is about training as practiced by the United States military. In order to exercise some of the little we really know about learning, and in the spirit of the overworked phrase found at the start of almost every military course taught over the last four decades, I will begin this chapter by telling you what I intend to tell you, and then will proceed to tell it to you all over again in detail.

In the late 1970s the United States Army fostered a revolution in warfare training by institutionalizing group experiential learning with feedback. In doing so they changed the Army's culture such that even everyday actions are now routinely assessed and analyzed at all echelons up, as well as down the chain of command. The largest-scale use of these techniques trains brigade-sized units (3,500 soldiers) on huge training battlefields. The process is superbly effective, delivering in just weeks a measured order-of-magnitude increase in warfare proficiency in warfare areas as diverse as large-scale dismounted infantry operations and air-to-air combat. The revolution continues; it was recently adapted to train nonkinetic operations (everything that soldiers did not sign up to do) in large-scale events. This engagement simulation process is equally effective in non-military contexts, but its large-scale military applications are often expensive and episodic. Thus, it comes with a downside; it does not reach all our forces nor can it train those it does reach often enough

---

Author Note: I lifted much of the material in this chapter from an obscure technical report I wrote a number of years ago (Chatham, 1996). The aim of that report was to point out to the intelligence community that order-of-magnitude changes in proficiency made in a short time might be of some interest to them. Some of that flavor remains in the prose herein. I will be happy to send a copy of the ancient source to those who enjoy the archeology of technical reports.

Between 1998 and 2003, I was Co-Chairman of the Defense Science Board task forces on *Training Superiority and Training Surprise* and *Training for Future Conflicts*. I have been a submarine officer of the diesel persuasion, and remain a professional storyteller. As I wrote the first draft of this chapter, I was Program Manager for Training Superiority, Defense Advanced Research Projects Agency. Since then I have become a private consultant on technology for training and defense-related analyses. I also, long ago, earned a Ph.D. in experimental physics. However, not making house calls, I see no need to advertise this latter fact outside of these notes.

to prevent skill decay. Chapter 10 will discuss early steps to expand this revolution to reach more people, more of the time at a lower cost.

DECLARATION OF A REVOLUTION

Training Counts

Military performance is often far more dependent upon the proficiency of the warriors than upon the technology of the systems with which they fight. Numerous anecdotal examples can be found where a superior weapons system was beaten handily by inferior technology operated by a better-trained force. A certain kind of training can increase combat effectiveness for U.S. land and air forces by factors of 5 to 30 in periods as short, in some cases, as a few weeks.

The approach, sometimes called "engagement simulation," was discovered during what amounted to an unintended warfare experiment complete with control groups and large sample sizes. In 1969, new approaches to Navy training improved the exchange ratio in air-to-air combat over Viet Nam by a factor of 12 in a single year. At the same time, however, the U.S. Air Force continued to have one pilot shot down for every two MiGs killed (Gorman, 1990; You fight, 1974). The Air Force and the Army, especially, embraced this lesson and took it further with remarkable success.

It is important to compare military potential achieved through training with that attainable through the acquisition of new weapons systems, for failure to consider the human side of weapons systems often robs the gains hardware proponents claim for their expensive systems. The time needed to achieve training-driven proficiency gains is much less than the time required to acquire a new weapons system that might yield similar gains. Although I am about to tell you that training is expensive, it is almost always less costly per incremental increase in military proficiency than the purchase of high technology weaponry. There is a downside, however; training-derived proficiency can decay rapidly if warfare skills are not practiced for periods as short as three to six months. While weapons last longer than that, a culture of effective training can become even more enduring than hardware systems.

In this chapter, I will describe why training in the military is hard, and tell a story about how the United States Navy, Army, and Air Force invented a new way to develop competence through training that resulted in what I call the "first training revolution." I will make a case for why it is important. Then I will introduce and resolve a conundrum about military training; research persistently finds that large inputs of time and resources only deliver small, positive gains in proficiency, but engagement simulation seems to deliver huge gains for only a few weeks of effort.

I will then explore some of the implications and limitations of the first training revolution – why it doesn't get the attention it deserves, how it doesn't scale to reach many of our forces, how the high degree of proficiency gained can be lost quickly due to forgetting and personnel rotation – and then describe a general failure to assess value added by training. In Chapter 10 I will discuss some initial efforts I took at the Defense Advanced Research Projects Agency to bottle the first training revolution and export it electronically in order to scale the benefits to many more soldiers, more of the time and in many more places.

The Military Training Problem

The military has an almost insurmountable training problem. They must constantly train everyone in their workforce in the face of a continuing turnover of personnel, which results in a new person in every job every three years or so. Moreover, the tasks for which all these people must train and retrain do not remain static: they are constantly expanding. It is no longer enough to teach an Army unit and its soldiers, for example, that "Maneuver warfare is a way of life," a challenging prospect in itself. Today's missions now require that we also train each Soldier to be a little bit of a linguist, anthropologist, city manager, arbitrator, negotiator, engineer, contract specialist, ambassador, and a consummate bureaucrat within the Army system. As if that weren't enough, each soldier must be ready instantly to shift into a shooting mode and then an hour later calmly negotiate with the brother-in-law of the man he shot.

Military training also ranges across a spectrum of scales, from individual training to coordinated training of units with thousands of members. The sheer size of the task is as daunting as the costs. The four American military Services' huge array of technical schoolhouses is expensive to maintain. Moving the students or the units to and from fixed training sites costs billions of dollars each year. Moreover, schoolhouses are only part of the military training infrastructure; units, ships, aircraft – all of these need special spaces or ranges where students can practice. Creating and maintaining such areas is also expensive.

Many of these problems (rapidly changing technology, evanescent workforce, costs of schoolhouses) are common to industry and other post-secondary training. While my work has not considered civilian training explicitly, the processes and lessons are also applicable outside the military context. I challenge the reader to be looking for commercial parallels when reading what follows. I offer one example near the end of this chapter but I think savvy readers will be able to invent more.

A Revolution in Training

I have been admonished that the topic for this book is individual training, group training having been done to death. Nevertheless, I beg indulgence while I use this chapter to discuss what is mostly about group training to set the context for individual training issues discussed here and in Chapter 10. Moreover, if

I am to propose the possibility of a second training revolution, it is only fair that I should describe the first revolution. The late 20th-century discovery about the power of engagement simulation to change military performance, I claim, not only transformed Army training, but at the same time transformed Army culture. Today's Army is the only large organization that has institutionalized introspection at all levels and up and down echelons. If you are still with me by the end of the chapter, dear reader, I hope that you will see why this new group-training process cannot succeed without first training the individuals who make up the teams that are the base element of military performance today.[1]

A Story to Set Context

We return for a moment to the Navy's experiment in warfare. (I will give more numbers later in the chapter.) In 1968 the U.S. Navy found that over the previous nine months its air-to-air exchange ratio over Viet Nam (number of planes we shot down compared to the number of our planes they shot down) had dropped from an already unacceptable cumulative three-year ratio of two-to-one to less than one-to-one (see Braddock & Chatham, 2001; Chatham, 1996).

They decided to create a training program, the Navy Fighter Weapons School, which we now refer to colloquially as Top Gun. The training process had three key elements:

1. An instrumented range: the action was recorded and later displayed so that no longer would the winner be the first participant who got to the blackboard.
2. A better than real enemy: the best pilots were assigned to be the Red or Opposing Force (REDFOR or OPFOR). They flew in Soviet-like aircraft and were constrained to use Soviet doctrine, both of which were used by the North Vietnamese air forces. However, within those constraints the OPFOR could do anything they wanted to defeat the BLUEFOR, who were the next best pilots and had been sent to be trained at the school for two weeks. Very soon the OPFOR had a *lot* of experience defeating BLUEFOR.
3. No-holds-barred after-action reviews (AARs): after the BLUEFOR pilots were "shot down" (as they usually were), they were forced to confront what happened and be asked or ask themselves: What did you see? What were you thinking? What did you do? (No, you didn't do that. See the data from the range instrumentation.) What could you have done differently? By the end, they preferred to ask the questions of themselves rather than letting some instructor do so.

---

[1] Command Sergeant Major Ricky Pring told a handful of technologists, training experts, and me in June 2006 that even a simple interview with a storekeeper in the street must be a squad level action. Besides the security functions, each soldier should be looking around to see what else is happening. For example, if someone opens a window and looks out, and the storekeeper then stops talking and looks away, somebody in the squad should see it, report it, and try to understand its significance.

Then they went at it again. At the end of two weeks, the BLUEFOR pilots returned to their units to become squadron training officers and the REDFOR returned to defeating the next crop of trainees. After a year-long bombing halt, the Navy and the Air Force recommenced air-to-air combat over Viet Nam. The Air Force's exchange ratio continued at about two-to-one for the rest of the war. The Navy, however, achieved an exchange ratio of 12.5-to-one throughout the next three years.

After the war, the Air Force scraped the Navy-blue paint off the idea and created Red Flag exercises. These are large air operations in which the prime objective is to give the "blue four" (the novice pilot in a four fighter formation) a chance to get seven or eight combats under his or her belt so that he or she would not have to experience the dangerous part of the learning curve during real combat.

The Army watched this process evolve and in 1980, after a number of years exploring what might be trained in this way for large units and how (including inventing laser tag – MILES, the Multiple Integrated Laser Engagement System), they created the National Training Center (NTC) at Fort Irwin, California. There, in the Mojave Desert, a whole brigade (3,500 to 4,000 soldiers) moves to the desert and fights eight to ten simulated battles against a highly competent OPFOR. Everyone in the brigade is watched and, when possible, mentored by a corps of Observer Controllers (OCs). Each echelon participates in a host of AAR activities.

By the late 1980s the average unit came out of a three- to four-week rotation to the NTC having increased the odds of winning an offensive mission by 30:1 for light infantry platoons as measured over 237 trials, by 15:1 for combined arms teams as measured in 58 trials, and 5:1 for regiments or brigades (428 trials) (Gorman, 1995, citing Dr. R. H. Sulzen's chart presented in 1987).

Our Army's first battle in each war before NTC was a disaster. We won about half, but even the wins were Pyrrhic victories. The first test, however, of NTC-trained forces in war was so successful that there was no need for a second battle. The 100-hour Desert Storm victory, I assert in the face of the military technophiles, was largely due to the training done at NTC and not just superior hardware. Supporting my assertion, several generals of that era told me that, if they could have kept the NTC, they would have won even if they had traded equipment with the enemy. *This is the first training revolution*: an order-of-magnitude change in proficiency that can be instilled in *properly prepared* units in a few weeks.

The revolution was hard won. At its inception the leaders in the Army were divided equally into two camps. Half of the four-star generals thought the NTC and its engagement simulation process was vital to restoring the Army after Viet Nam; the other half felt the NTC would destroy the Army because it would, among other things, expose to the soldiers how bad their lieutenants were. General Jack Vessey, the Army Deputy Chief of Staff at the time, was sent to observe the first NTC rotation to try to find out which of these camps was right. He told me that he was "hunkering down" in the back of one of the first

AARs, trying to hide his shiny four stars, when a big sergeant stood up and said, "I got up over this hill and found that something was seriously [fouled] up." Then his Lieutenant stood up and said, "I know. I was listening to the wrong people and should have sent you to a different place. ... I am going to need some help." The sergeant replied, "That's OK Lieutenant, we'll fix it."

There are few other armies in the world where that offer would have been tolerated; there are, perhaps, no others where it would be accepted gladly – as it was here. There is some evidence that this is a unique characteristic of American culture and our approach to warfare. While I was visiting Nellis Air Force Base as co-chair of a Defense Science Board task force exploring training issues, one Red Flag OPFOR pilot told me that Kuwaiti pilots who learned how to fly from U.S. Air Force instruction could get value out of the AAR process, but those who had learned to fly from the French could not.

A Cultural Revolution, Too

The training revolution had consequences that reached deep within the Army. Until recently, the most important thing an Army unit did was to make the every-three-year pilgrimage to the NTC. Since this was the high point of the Army experience, the NTC process trickled down throughout the service. Twenty-five or so years after the institutionalization of the NTC process, the Army culture reflects this at all levels. For years I thought of the NTC as a glorious *experiment* in training since I had initially learned about it shortly after the NTC was created. Today's soldiers, on the other hand, can't imagine doing things any other way. Everything they do, large or small, they subject to the critical analysis process of the AAR – exactly as they learned to do during many rotations to the NTC, and everybody, high or low, is encouraged to participate.

The Army pamphlet, *Leader's Guide to After-Action Reviews* (Army Training Circular, 1993), describes ways to conduct AARs from formal to very informal. The cover sketch shows soldiers watching another soldier draw diagrams in the dirt with a stick, a process explicitly described and sanctioned. The result of this institutionalization of the AAR process is a force that constantly challenges itself to improve and whose people have insights into their performance, the like of which the world has never before seen. The creation and continued use of the NTC over 25 years has thus resulted in a cultural as well as a training revolution. Having, now, I hope, gotten your attention with the NTC story, I will proceed with some drier observations about why we should care about military training.

CONNECTING TRAINING TO MILITARY PROFICIENCY

The chief business of a military unit not at war is to prepare for war by training. When at war, training those sent in harm's way should be secondary only to the conduct of the war itself. A modern military force cannot be re-equipped in a year, but it can be re-trained in that time, and, as we have pointed out already, order-of-magnitude differences in military performance can be achieved with changes in training methods. Unfortunately, when we try to determine whether our, or somebody else's, military is up to performing some task, today's force assessment measures chiefly count people and parts rather than human proficiency in relevant tasks. Failure to put assessment of the effectiveness of training on an equal footing with the assessment of hardware capabilities can lead, and has led, us down some dangerous and unpleasant paths.

A Training Assessment Conundrum

Assessment of something done episodically after long periods of waiting, as opposed to measuring tasks done continuously, is never a simple task. In the military assessment case it is far easier to count weapons systems than to assess training effectiveness. Useful, quantifiable data are sparse. The data that *are* available about U.S. training appear contradictory. On the one hand, analyses correlating the U.S. Navy pilot's flying hours to such skills as bombing accuracy, carrier landing proficiency, and air-to-air combat performance suggests that a 20 percent change in flying hours would alter proficiency by the order of only 3 to 4 percent (Weis, 1994). This and other factors lead to the widely held assertion that "there are no quick-fix options for correcting training shortfalls" (Moore et al., 1995, p. xi). On the other hand, I have described order-of-magnitude changes in proficiency that were delivered in a few weeks. In the next few pages, I will suggest a resolution of this apparent conflict where training seems to work astoundingly well in some cases and, in others, where it seems to have little effect for a similar investment of effort.

Measuring Military Capability by Weapons Assessments

Counting Systems

In the era of high technology forces, when we assess the capability of armed forces (ours or others), we most often resort to a framework based upon the numbers and types of weapons systems in a country's inventories. We are driven to this metric for measuring military goodness, in part, because of a historical belief that revolutionary weapons systems win or have come close to winning wars: tanks in World War I, submarines in the Battle of the Atlantic, long bows at Agincourt.

Counting systems is also used as a measure of military performance because weapon costs are the major variable in military budgets. The yearly budgets for manpower or operating and maintenance of the U.S. Defense Department do not draw nearly the debate that procurement of ships or airplanes does. Budgets for operations, exercises, and training are viewed largely as fixed by the size of the forces we have and cannot be changed much. Procurement budgets, however, deal with a future about which decisions can be made. This continues to lead to thinking of our military in terms governed by the yearly debates: numbers of weapons systems owned or to be procured.

Weapon counting is also a seductive method of measuring the military of less-sophisticated countries because airplanes, tanks, and ships are showy. They are large, countable, and deliver a display of force for both external and internal audiences. They appear to provide a visible token of power for nations trying to assert their place among their neighbors. We tend to observe what the others value and to use their accounting.

When it comes time for the weapons systems to actually be used, however, the weapon-counting measure frequently fails to predict the outcome of a conflict. The quality of the operators is often far more important than the number and nature of the equipment they use (Gorman, 1990). By most measures of systems and certainly by the numbers, the Argentinean forces in the Falklands/Malvinas War were a far superior force than the British, but, particularly on the ground, the superior training and persistence of the U.K. soldiers made all the difference.

> An SAS [British special forces] officer remarked ... on the problem that afflicts many Third World armies, of concentrating on acquiring expensive technology rather than applying basic training and skills. On his own travels abroad, he said, he found again and again that his hosts disbelieved all that he told them about the achievements of the SAS being based on intensive, ceaseless, meticulous training and preparation: They all secretly believe that there is some pill you can take if only you will tell them what it is. (Hastings & Jenkins, 1983, p. 366)

In most cases they and we look for that pill in hardware (Braddock and Chatham 2001; Gorman, 1990). Counting systems is easy; measuring the quality of training is not. There can be a huge variability in force effectiveness among militaries with similar hardware counts, and capabilities can change in a very short time.

In a review of training and costs for NATO, Jesse Orlansky (1989) enumerated a series of findings:

1. Large increases in combat effectiveness can result from more effective training.
2. The time required to produce such increases is short compared to the development time of a new weapon capable of producing similar results.
3. The cost of improving training is less than the cost of developing a new weapon of comparable effectiveness.
4. [But] acquired skills decay faster than the rate at which weapons become obsolete.

Next I will discuss examples of performance variability due to training and explore some of the reasons for it. Then I will go on to consider the rate of learning and how it improves with additional investments in training, and finally show how learning is lost: which kinds of skills atrophy and at what rates.

Components of Readiness

General Paul Gorman, U.S. Army (retired), one of the principal architects of the NTC, holds that battle capability is a function of three variables: weapons, proficiency of personnel, and tactics (Gorman, 1990, 1995). He expresses this symbolically:

$$R = f(W, P, T)$$

Gorman points out that the weapons are only one readiness variable and "there is strong evidence to suggest that often others dominate."

> The P factor [as opposed to the weapons, W, factor] has a sizable, if less influential and well resourced proponency in most forces: the personnel management community, schools, centers, technical documenters, and unit commanders. ... most evaluations of "training" for readiness, [are] related to the P factor: selecting, training, and manning competently weapon systems within a given unit. Costs for P can be fairly well defined, but P effectiveness tends to elude sound quantification, being driven by a large number of variables, including time, some of which can not be observed, let alone measured.

Training for task-level proficiency is, however, the area where most attempts toward quantification of the effects of training on military effectiveness have been directed. Many of these analyses are motivated by a desire to understand how training resources should best be allocated. A frequent approach is to relate the investment in training to some measure of task performance. For example, analysts try to relate a pilot's flying hours to success at bombing, carrier landing grades, knob-ology errors, or air-to-air engagement performance. This has not been as fruitful an area of research as many analysts have hoped. "Everyone who develops a new regression tool tries to connect flight hours to readiness measures [but there has been little success]" (Brown, 1996).

The Learning Curve and Skills Training

One reason for this, I assert, lies in the character of the "learning curve" and at what time in the training process correlations between training investments and proficiency gains are observed. I show a notional learning curve in Figure 2.1. The curve, representing a performance gain as a result of some training investment, is S-shaped. The slope is shallow at first; background instruction and teaching of terms and concepts, while necessary for future learning, do not usually lead directly to task proficiency. Then the slope

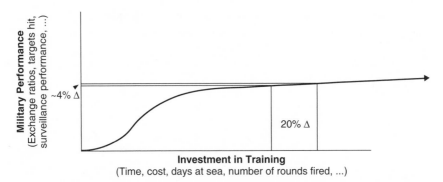

FIGURE 2.1. *A notional learning curve.* The horizontal axis represents investment in training and the dependent axis represents some quantitative measure of performance or proficiency. In general, after initial start-up costs, there is a rapid improvement in the trainee's proficiency followed by a plateau when additional investment in training *of the same kind* produces smaller and smaller changes in proficiency. In the case of a pilot's flight hours and performance of various flying tasks, most analyses are concerned with data taken from beyond the knee of the curve in an attempt to justify flying budgets. This results in the observation that large investments in training apparently result only in small changes in proficiency.

gets steeper; in the case of pilot training, for example, after ground school the trainee finally starts to fly and flying performance improves rapidly. Eventually, the curve flattens out; the trainee has learned about as much as possible under a particular syllabus.

Orlanksy (1989, p. xvii) notes: "Performance continues to improve with additional training but the amount of improvement with additional trials decreases and finally levels off. Thus, the point along this curve at which performance is measured has considerable influence on the values used to represent effectiveness, cost and military value." This results in an apparent trend in the literature that training investments seem to have only a small effect upon measured proficiency. I propose that this results from a selection effect in the choice of areas to investigate. Research is likely to be funded only in areas where there is concern about whether money is being spent wisely. The need for initial training, of pilots for example, is not a matter of contention and much of the costs for basic training are not hard to justify. Operational training and maintenance of skills are harder to account for and, therefore, are the subject of more research. Attempts to match proficiency to performance are therefore more likely to be focused upon the shallow final portion of the learning curve. Once past the knee of the learning curve, random factors frequently swamp the influence of recent training (e.g., Weis, 1994). For example, a monumental review of bombing performance of the U.S. Army Air Force in World War II found no consistent indicator that could be correlated with bombing proficiency (Brown, Brobst, & Fox, 1996).

Table 2.1. *Performance decreases expected as a result of a decrease of 10 percent in flying hours.*

Training performance measure	Loss in performance as a consequence of 10 percent cut in training/experience		
	Career flying hours	Recent flying hours	Career simulator hours
Unsatisfactory landings	6.9%	2.6%	–
Air-to-air combat			–
Probability red kills blue	6.3%	2.9%	–
Probability blue kills red	2.6%	2.2%	–
Marine bombing miss distance	1.2%	0.6%	0.3%
C-130 tactical airdrop miss distance			
Co-pilot	–	–	1.0%
Navigator	0.5%	2.3%	1.0%
TOTAL	0.5%	2.3%	1.0%

For example, the incidence of unsatisfactory carrier landings would increase by 6.9 percent if the career flying hours of Navy pilots were to be cut by 10 percent. A 10 percent cut in recent flying hours, however, would decrease landing proficiency by only 2.6 percent. Bombing miss distances would be only 1.2 percent worse if USMC pilots had 10 percent less training. Although the authors concluded that "training improves performance in a quantifiable way," it appears that U.S. pilots are well along on the learning curve: Large changes in ordinary flight hours will probably not make correspondingly large changes in proficiency.
(Adapted from a 1996 IDA briefing.)

A quantitative example of this phenomenon is shown in Table 2.1. A commonly used measure of training investments is flight hours (Hammon, 1990; Suess, 1994; Weis, 1994). An analysis correlating flying hours to proficiency (Hammon & Horowitz, 1996) reported that a 10 percent decrease in recent flying hours would increase the incidence of unsatisfactory carrier landings for patrol aircraft by 2.6 percent. Similar small correlations were established for other variables.

Once the shallow portion of the training curve is reached, inferences about the causes of good or bad performance are hard to draw from U.S. training experience and data. Such inferences are probably impossible to draw from the flat part of the curve when examining a foreign military's training investments. Measurements made in the steep part of the learning curve, however, yield more interesting correlations (Weis, 1994).

Figure 2.2 plots the performance increases that resulted from specialized air-to-ground combat training at the Navy's "Strike University." It shows that performance on specific tasks can be improved dramatically and rapidly with the right kind of training. These data, however, appear to contrast sharply with that for bombing miss distance shown in Table 2.1. In one case, a 10 percent change in recent flying hours made only a 0.6 percent change in accuracy, yet

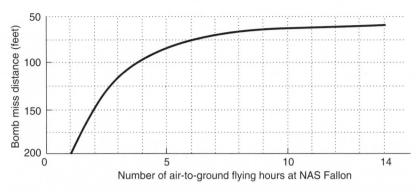

FIGURE 2.2. Training at the knee of the curve. The U.S. Navy's "Strike University" teaches air-to-ground warfare tactics. Center for Naval Analyses data (Newett, 1990) on 241 bombing runs conducted at Naval Air Station Fallon show classic learning curve behavior. The first four hours of training yield a factor of two improvement. The next 10 hours give much less. (The atrophy of these skills after the training ends is shown in Figure 2.3.).

in the case of training at NAS Fallon the *least productive single hour* of the 14 yielded a change in accuracy greater than 0.6 percent.

The resolution of this apparent contradiction lies in the nature of the flight hours counted. In Table 2.1, the flight hours indicated are general hours, not specifically related to any task. In Figure 2.2, however, the hours are dedicated to training on the task of accurate bombing. Generalized measures of training, therefore, do not necessarily correlate with specific measures of task performance. A second lesson is that some kinds of training directed toward specific military tasks can improve the proficiency *at that task* quickly. Here and elsewhere the time to reach the knee of the training curve appears to be the order of one to two weeks.

Training time is not, however, a universal constant. There appears to be a difference in the learning curve related to the sophistication of the weapons system being learned. In the late 1970s, during a series of well-measured, Air Force air-to-air engagement exercises called AIMVAL/ACEVAL, our most sophisticated fighter aircraft of the time, F-15s, were pitted against F-5s, smaller and less-sophisticated aircraft. It is hard to extract any unambiguous lessons from the exercises due to the multitude of constraints on the engagements. F-15 pilots, for example, complained that they could not use their prime advantage of beyond-visual-range engagement because they were not permitted to fire until visual contact had been established. One lesson, however, is somewhat less clouded than the others: F-5 pilots were able to learn to be the best they could be within a week; F-15 crews didn't peak until 30 days of flying in the exercises. The more complicated weapons systems took longer to master completely than the simpler ones (Sullivan, 1984).

This lesson does not make any statement about how much military performance and capability were gained from a fixed amount of training time by crews flying either system. It is probably the case that a partly optimum F-15 crew is more effective than an optimally trained F-5 pilot. What it does say is that it may take an adversary less time to achieve a modest competence with less sophisticated forces than it takes the United States to train our operators to be effective with our systems. We next consider how long such training-achieved performance gains are likely to last.

Skill Atrophy: The Unlearning Curve
A key finding of the analysis of F/A-18 bombing proficiency gained at NAS Fallon, however, was this: "Within at least 45 days after leaving the Fallon detachment, a pilot's bombing accuracy returns to the accuracy he had just before he reported to Fallon" (Weis, 1994, p. 34). This is supported by data later collected by the Defense Science Board task force on Training Superiority and Training Surprise (Chatham & Braddock, 2001). They found that engagement simulation-derived bombing accuracy degraded in the time it took Navy squadrons to move from the training range to the battlefield. At the start of training they hit 30 percent of their targets. Three weeks of training later they hit 70 percent, but three months after that, in combat over Iraq in 1998, their bombing accuracy had dropped to 40 percent. After three days of what I call "refresher training in combat," they could again hit 70 percent of their targets.

Army aviators lost basic instrument flight rules (IFR) flying skills with a similar time constant. An analysis of the value of refresher training versus minimal periodic proficiency flights showed that pilots who had not had significant flying experience for six months to a year fell below minimum acceptable skill levels. Even those who had performed "proficiency" flights of the order of one hour of flight time per month lost proficiency at almost the same rate as those who did not fly at all (only a 10 percent difference). Virtually all of the skill atrophy occurred within the first year; it took no longer to re-train pilots who had had periods of non flying of three years than it did pilots who had not flown for only a year. "The shape of the curves suggests that any training six months or more prior to resuming operational flying duties will have little value" (Wright, 1973). Wright concluded that, in order to maintain continued proficiency, refresher training would need to be performed every six months. This being too expensive, the implication of the work was that a single episode of refresher training of the order of 10 to 20 flight hours just before pilots were needed would be the most cost-effective method to return pilots to minimum flying competency.

The atrophy rate was faster for basic IFR flying skills than for Visual Flight Rules flying. This is a manifestation of a general principle that skills requiring intellectual content and memory fade faster and fall to lower levels than those requiring physical skills. The old saw about never forgetting how to ride a bicycle but quickly forgetting calculus is borne out by these data.

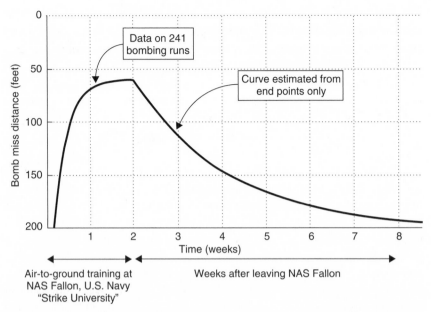

FIGURE 2.3. Skills atrophy. A further finding of the analysis portrayed in Figure 2.2 is that the skills attained by dedicated training may not last. We have added here a guess at a decay curve representing the loss of skills reported for F/A-18 pilots 45 days after the specialized, quality training ended and the aircrews returned to their squadrons.

Decay of competence in skills is not unique to attack aircraft pilots. The time scale for atrophy in newly taught skills is roughly the same for technicians being trained, for example, to become anti-submarine sonar operators. "If newly trained acoustic analysts are not provided with adequate practice and explicit feedback, their skills and knowledge are subject to substantial degradation within a relatively short period (1 to 3 months)" (Wetzel, Konoske, & Montague, 1983a). Data on the loss of knowledge and of various technical skills can be represented by curves quite similar to Figure 2.3 (Konoske, Wetzel, & Montague, 1983; Wetzel, Konoske, & Montague, 1983a, 1983b).

Skills relating to other military functions, such as training for naval warfare area commanders and their staffs, also seem to be subject to the same decay phenomenon at similar rates. The Center for Naval Analyses in exploring how training might correct persistent deficiencies in battle group performance in large-scale exercises noted that:

> The Anti Air Warfare Commander (AAWC) course ... has not had a recognizable impact on AAWC performance in fleet exercises. The fleet commanders suggested that timing of these courses during the work-up cycle is to blame. Between receipt of the AAWC course and the battle group exercise in the Pacific Fleet, the AAWC and his staff typically focus on functions other than AAW planning

and thus lost the skills taught several months before (Fox, 1990). This is probably not a consequence of personnel turnover because battle group staffs and crews are usually stabilized prior to an overseas deployment.

Orlansky (1989, pp. xvii–xviii) summarizes:

> The level of performance tends to decline as the amount of time without practice since the last training session increases. This is called forgetting and it is what military commanders try to overcome when they insist on frequent practice and field exercises. The amount of loss in performance per unit time decreases and finally levels off as [the] time since the last training session increases; the amount of loss before leveling off occurs appears to be greater for the retention of information and knowledge than for the retention of performance skills. Thus, similar to what was noted above for learning, the time after training when performance is measured will influence the cost-effectiveness relationship.

Summary: Skills Training and Individual Proficiency

The sparse data on training for military proficiency suggest that warfare skills can be substantially improved by dedicated training. For many tasks there appears to be a learning curve that shows rapid improvement at first and then a leveling off of the gain that comes from additional training of the same type. In well-documented situations, such as pilot performance, these curves can occasionally be quantified. In those cases it appears that the United States trains beyond the knee of the curve: up to, and then past the point where diminishing returns sets in. In cases where the skill being taught is one already partly held by the trainee – for example the bombing accuracy portrayed in Figures 2.2 and 2.3 – the knee of the curve can be reached in the order of two weeks of dedicated training. It may take longer to achieve proficiency in high-tech systems than in those with less sophisticated technology. Finally, these skills can atrophy if not exercised; frequently the decay time is as short as two or three months.

The kinds of training and kinds of skills described above are necessary (but as we will see below, not sufficient) to field a competent fighting force. They represent a set of minimum proficiencies needed to create effective military units. A good trainer will develop rules of thumb that define the knees of the task training curves. He or she will decide whether or not the force in question has dedicated resources sufficient to raise skills to a level where different kinds of training are required to make further substantial improvements in force readiness.

Warfare and Mission-Level Proficiency

This is not the whole story. Those quantifiable skills described above are usually only part-task competencies. The ability to land upon an aircraft carrier, to bomb accurately an unprotected target, to read a sonar "gram" may contribute to warfare proficiency, but they represent only single links in a whole chain of skills required to complete a warfare mission. Failure elsewhere in that chain can negate the value of the part-task training (Cohen & Gooch, 1990; Perrow, 1984; Sagan, 1993). To promote warfare competency, training must combine many part-tasks in more realistic situations where all or most of the whole task is simulated. Beyond that, training must focus on the reality of warfare: battles seldom occur in benign circumstances. Things go wrong. People are tired. The warrior's knowledge is imperfect. Finally, somewhere near the top of this hierarchy of training for whole-warfare tasks comes General Gorman's T variable: tactics and the proficiency of commanders.

You Fight Like You Train: A Personal Example

American submarines are divided into two major classes by primary mission: ballistic missile submarines (SSBN) and attack submarines (SSN). During the Cold War, an SSBN's mission was planned to revert to that of an attack submarine once she had launched her missiles and, therefore, for this reason and for self-defense, each SSBN crew received training in torpedo attacks as part of their regular training cycle. Each SSBN had (and still has) two crews that would alternately take possession of the ship. One crew would maintain and operate the ship for a period of about three months and then, after a short period to turn the boat over to the other crew, the first crew would return to shore and conduct off-ship training for the next three months. Two weeks of the off-crew training time were dedicated to torpedo training in a fairly high-fidelity simulator of the ship's control room, called an "attack trainer." Most of the situations were orchestrated to achieve a specific training goal, but usually one session would be devoted to free-play "fighting" an attack submarine crew in a neighboring trainer, without either crew's knowledge that they were engaged with a U.S.-like adversary. Despite the clear advantages held by the SSN in equipment and performance, and the fact that torpedo attacks were secondary missions for SSBNs, the ballistic missile submarine crews always won these encounters.[2]

The cause of this unexpected but consistent result was that the SSBN crew's only duties for two solid weeks were to develop torpedo-shooting tactical proficiency. The SSN crew, on the other hand, had all the distracting issues of manning, maintaining, and repairing a submarine in port. At least one-third of an SSN's crew had to remain on the ship at all times. More importantly, however, was that what training time they had available to spend in the simulators was used primarily to develop proficiency in missions related

---

[2]   This is based on my discussions with the Naval Submarine School, New London, Connecticut, attack trainer staff in 1979. I was the Operations Officer on a SSBN crew and noticed that some of the exercises were less well-structured than others – they seemed "mushy" and "less crisp." These were the exercises in which my crew was pitted against an SSN crew across the hall. I remarked that we seemed always to win these encounters. They replied that this was not unusual; in their experience, the SSBN crew always won when dueling with an SSN crew.

to peacetime operations, which emphasized the collection of intelligence, not violent attacks against submerged targets.

In this case, as for the Navy pilots exercising at NAS Fallon, recent training directed toward specific tasks was quite effective. The proficiency of tactical training in the SSBN case more than overcame substantial hardware disadvantages in speed, maneuverability, and sensor performance. The training time to achieve this proficiency for the SSBN crew was of the order of two weeks, the same calendar time that works well in NAS Fallon's Strike University or at the NTC.

There are two key training lessons to be derived from this example. First, training to promote *warfare* proficiency must be carried on at a higher level than that of teaching single skills. Sonar tracking, weapons preparation, periscope technique, ship control, are all valuable, necessary skills for a submariner. They were all taught and reviewed before the crew spent time in attack trainers. However, until exercised together in training *directed toward a specific mission area,* part-task proficiency did not make substantial changes to the *mission performance* of the submarine's crew.

I have already hinted at the second lesson but will now state it explicitly: the effect of training on proficiency is highly dependent upon the degree to which elements of that training are directed toward the essential elements of the mission to be performed. A submarine trained extensively to track other submarines is not necessarily a good shooter of subs.

A Hierarchy of Learning Curves

I have pointed out the apparent contradiction between data that imply small performance changes for substantial investments in flight hours, and anecdotal experience that the right kind of training can make enormous differences in performance. The "two weeks and that's the best you will get" impression given by Figure 2.2 and curves like it does not match experience that effective learning can occur over longer periods. I suggest that this can be resolved by postulating the existence of a hierarchy of learning curves.[3] Figure 2.1 represents part-task training, the teaching of one of the many individual skills needed to perform a warfare mission. It is not a good representation of the whole-task

---

[3]   Although this insight was discovered independently during a conversation between the author, then of Dynamics Technology, Inc., and Captain Wayne Thornton USN of the Office of Naval Intelligence, it had been described before.

   Fitts (1980, p. 126) shows a figure of training for the ECM operator. A series of learning curves with a bit of forgetting between one set is laid out on a notional graph. Performance rises rapidly and then levels out as a trainee goes from technical training, to OJT (on-the-job training), to continuation training, to combat.

   Sullivan (1981) shows the same kind of curves relating to cost/performance issues. Staging a new system (adding it onto an existing one, like a ground attack missile that replaces an unpowered bomb) extends the performance substantially beyond levels where the unaided system could go. One does not wish to waste resources working beyond the knee of a cost/performance curve, either for hardware development or for training.

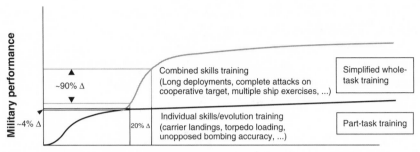

Investment in training

FIGURE 2.4. Two levels of a training curve family. Before one can work on the whole task, much part-task training must occur. "For any phase of training there is an initial period over which the increase in capability per training hour is very rapid. But after that point the capability increase per hour decreases and can only be increased by changing the type of training or its environment" (Fitts, 1980, p. 126). In this example, we suggest that an equal increase in training investment by 20 percent might either alter performance by 4 percent or by 90 percent, depending on which type of training is pursued.

training process required to perform a complicated mission. Figure 2.4, instead, represents two levels of training.

Although this curve is only a notional sketch, it suggests how a clever training system could avoid operating beyond the knee of a learning curve and thus wasting training investments; that is, move on to training on some broader task supporting some specific whole mission. Warfare success requires a combination of many interdependent skills. While many of those skills must be acquired separately, they do not contribute much to combat performance until tied together by whole-task training. In this way the next 20 percent of training investment can be applied to a steep portion of a higher-level learning curve.

For a naval vessel, simply taking the ship to sea for a period of time longer than a few days is a form of simplified whole-task training. Many things can be taught onshore, but the coordination of all those skills and a number of new ones is needed to ensure that a ship will survive on or under a hostile ocean. Sustained operations at sea are a foundation upon which combat performance must be built.

In submarine warfare, for example, sea time is necessary to achieve minimal proficiency in routine handling of torpedoes, surfacing and diving, charging batteries at sea, submerged ship control, sonar operation, communications with other ships and the shore, periscope technique, and target tracking to avoid collisions. All of these seagoing proficiencies, and a few more (such as setting weapon parameters), must be exercised together in order to learn to shoot successfully at even a cooperative target.

Once simple attacks can be completed with some ease, then more and more realism can be introduced into the training, as suggested by Figure 2.5.

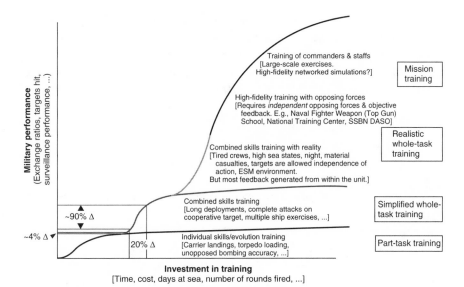

FIGURE 2.5. A hierarchy of learning curves. Warfare competence can be achieved by a set of training episodes, each one building upon the level below. While this curve is only notional, the performance axis has been scaled to match the one well-quantified case of training's effect upon performance in war: Top Gun schooling and Navy Air over Viet Nam. The keys to the higher levels of training and performance are simulation of the realities of war, measurement and feedback of performance, and independence of the opposing forces. Beyond unit training, there appears to be a great deal of leverage for improving wartime performance by training the commanders and their staffs. Such training, having a large intellectual component versus battlefield skills, would have to be repeated often or performed just before wartime operations in order for its lessons to be in the heads of the warriors when they are needed.

The unit must learn how to fight when wounded, when equipment fails, when the crew and commanders are tired, when the target has an opportunity to evade or fight back. There is still a level of unit training beyond this: engagement simulation with the essential ingredients of opposing forces, independent of the trainee command, which represent the expected enemy as closely as possible; an instrumented range that provides for detailed monitoring of the engagements; and a no-holds-barred, trainee-centered AAR.

This picture of a hierarchy of learning curves should not be taken for objective reality; it represents, instead, a framework for thinking about training issues. Orlansky (1989, p. xvii) observed that "examination of learning curves in military training is a largely unexplored issue." It remains so today. The hierarchy of learning curves we propose here is a conceptual step in the direction of mapping that territory. It helps explain the paradox of the relationships between training and performance: the slope depends upon what *kind* of performance is being measured and *where* on that training curve the trainee in question falls. The concepts point us in the direction both of looking for minimum performance criteria (below which a force is unlikely to be able to muster up much mission capability), and of looking for what actions move a force from one learning curve to the next. The framework provided by this hierarchy can also lead us in the direction of quantifying some of these relationships as we shall see in the next section.

Quantifying the Relationship Between Training Performance and Warfare Performance

THE MEASUREMENT PROBLEM

The question arises: Can training of the sort discussed above actually influence performance in war? Large improvements in unit performance *in simulators and exercises* have been documented, but there is a still a difference between the best simulator and actual warfare. Land combat simulation at the NTC, Fort Irwin, California, was said to be so real that the major difference between it and actual combat was that there were more Medal of Honor winners at Fort Irwin than in real battles (Starey, 1983). At the NTC soldiers know that enemy weapons won't kill them, so that difference may be critical. Given the extent to which training is not combat, we must be careful when using performance measured in simulators or exercises to predict actual combat performance.

There is, however, substantial anecdotal evidence, and centuries of tradition and military experience, to suggest that some kinds of training do correlate strongly with battle performance. The arguments, however, are confounded by the plethora of variables and conditions that also vie for the designation as the cause of the victory. General Gorman remarks, "There is no analysis that I know of which will resolve the central doubts about the validity ... of any training methods, other than actual battle" (Gorman, 1990, p. 59).

Unfortunately, even actual success in war cannot unambiguously validate a training program. Assigning reasons for performance in war is almost always confounded by its chaos; success may be sensitively dependent upon far too many things. War is a unique, continuous endeavor performed and influenced by many actors and many events that are unmeasured or unmeasurable. Captain Arthur Gallo, USN, provided a summarizing aphorism during my Defense Science Board training studies in 2002: "It is hard to sort out lucky from good." There are too few wars to allow an analyst to apply statistical procedures to filter out random factors. This measurement problem applies to both the identification and quantification of possible causative factors and to the assessment of performance in war. In this sense, study of war is study of history, and the admonitions of March, Sproull, and Tamuz (1991, pp. 7–8) in their article "Learning from Samples of One or Fewer" apply:

> The experimental design and sample sizes of history are inadequate for making inferences about it. ... Some of the processes by which history is produced may be genuinely stochastic. Understanding those processes

requires approximating the underlying distributions from which a realized event is drawn. The expected error in estimation can be decreased by aggregating over several events, but history limits the number of comparable events. ... [A] second kind of variability in estimation stems from the measurement and interpretation of historical events by observers. Measurement error, model misspecification, and system complexity introduce substantial noise into observations and interpretations. ... great organizational histories, like great novels, are written, not by first constructing interpretations of events and then filling in the details, but by first identifying the details and allowing the interpretations to emerge from them.

Lord Kelvin is attributed with saying that if you cannot measure a phenomenon and express it numerically, then you don't understand it.[4] The foregoing suggests that we are unlikely to be able to sort out cause and effect in warfare and training. We are left, therefore, with a conundrum: Everybody knows training counts, but how do we count training? How do we quantify it and thus subject it to analysis?

MEASURABLE WAR: AIR-TO-AIR COMBAT
AND THE EXISTENCE OF ACES

There is, fortunately, at least one warfare area where many of the above objections do not apply, one that lends itself to the kind of analysis denied us in most other engagements: this is air-to-air combat. It is quantized; there are numerous short, discrete, and countable engagements. Each engagement involves fewer people and fewer systems than most other battles, and thus there are fewer confounding variables. There is a simple and unambiguous measure of success in air battles: kill or be killed.[5] Careful records are kept of pilot flight history and of kills. In consequence, air-to-air combat has served as an analytical laboratory for warfare performance since Lanchester first applied numerical modeling to the subject early in the 20th century (Lanchester, 1914; Taylor, 1983).

---

4   Alan Ellinthorpe frequently reminds me of Kelvin's aphorism as I wander my hand-waving way through technical mazes. The actual quote is: "I often say that when you can measure what you are speaking about, and express it in numbers, you know something about it: but when you cannot measure it, when you cannot express it in numbers, your knowledge is of a meager and unsatisfactory kind: it may be the beginning of knowledge, but you have scarcely, in your thoughts, advanced to the stage of Science, whatever the matter may be" (William Thompson [Lord Kelvin] [1824–1907], *Popular Lectures and Addresses (1891–1894)*, p. xxx).

5   This is not to say that kill ratios are necessarily a good measure of performance in warfare. For example, the specific objective of an air battle might be to prevent the penetration of enemy forces into a specific airspace. If that objective is met, the number of aircraft shot down is of no immediate consequence. Kill ratios are, however, extremely easy to count when compared to other measures of warfare success. This simplicity of counting kills frequently leads people – from pilots to politicians – to erroneous conclusions about hardware and tactics. See, for example, Chatham (1990).

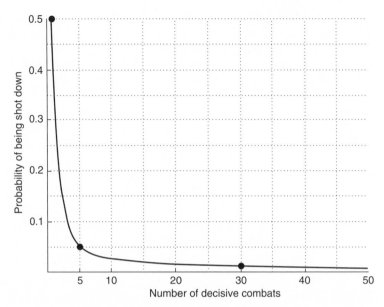

FIGURE 2.6. Pilot survivability in air-to-air combat: World War II and Korea. Pilots who survive a few engagements are vastly more likely to continue to survive and to kill adversaries. This figure is a plot of a pilot's actual performance based upon three quoted points. In the first decisive engagement (one in which some participant gets shot down), "Fewer than 15% of all pilots had a better than 50% chance of surviving" (Weiss, 1966, as quoted in Gorman, 1990). By the time a pilot has five kills under his belt, the pilot has decreased his likelihood of being killed to about 5 percent. By 30 kills, the risk to the pilot is something less than 1 in 100. The question arises: Is this learning or natural selection?

I have already mentioned, perhaps one too many times herein, the one striking instance where the "experimental design" of years of real air-to-air combat provided not only a clear test of training efficacy, but for which history has provided a "control group," one that fought in similar engagements against similar enemies at the same times, but did not have the same kind of training. Moreover, the sample size is large enough to justify drawing inferences from it. The consequences of this measurability and subsequent analyses have led to profound improvements in American military training methods.

Gorman outlines the history that led to this quantitative demonstration of the power of training. While analyzing the records of pilots in World War II and Korea, Weiss (1966) quantified what had been understood anecdotally before: Pilots who have survived a few decisive engagements are vastly more likely to survive the next engagement. Those who survived 30 air-to-air engagements were virtually invulnerable (Figure 2.6).

This kind of behavior seems to be common to other kinds of measurable combat. Gorman quotes an unpublished document by Weiss to the effect that in 373 decisive U.S. submarine engagements during World War II, "Once a commander had scored a kill, his chances of further success as opposed to his chances of losing his submarine appear to improve by a factor of *three*." Whether this vast change in performance was a case of survival of the fittest (the less capable pilots or submarine commanders get killed and the more capable survive to shoot again), or a case of learning could not be determined from the wartime data. Weiss leaned toward battlefield Darwinism. He recommended very careful selection procedures for choosing pilots for tactical aircraft.

Simulating Combat: Creating Aces Without Bloodshed

Top Gun and the Air War Over Viet Nam
(I promise this is the last time I will return to the Navy's unintentional warfare experiment. I do it this time only to satisfy an unnatural desire to deliver numbers and references in thus satisfying Lord Kelvin's admonition about numeracy.) In September, 1968, the Navy, looking for a way to improve unacceptable combat losses over Viet Nam, decided to give its pilots combat experience in a less lethal environment (You Fight, 1974). For the previous three years, their exchange ratio in air-to-air combat over Viet Nam had been little better than two to one. The Air Force experience had been similar.

The Navy's performance had declined until, in the first few months of 1968, the Navy lost 10 aircraft while shooting down only 9 MiGs and had fired over 50 air-to-air missiles in the previous 90 days without achieving one kill. The Navy then created the Navy Fighter Weapons School to train some of its aircrews by engagement simulation, what they called "a graduate course in dogfighting." Even though less than one-third of the Navy aircrews were able to attend the Top Gun school over the next four years, just over half of the 25 MiGs shot down by Navy pilots after its establishment were credited to Top Gun graduates (You Fight, 1974, p. 26). (See Figure 2.7 and Chatham, 1990.) In 1969 there were no planes shot down on either side due to a bombing halt. When the air war resumed, the Navy's kill ratio for the next three years was 12.5 to 1, while the Air Force's average fell slightly to 2.0 to 1.

These quoted exchange ratios are based upon the order of 100 enemy aircraft shot down in each of the two 3-year periods (110 kills by U.S. pilots for 1965 to 1968 and 74 for 1970 to 1973). Therefore, while there is some room to argue about details of aircraft types, weapons used, and personnel policy differences between the Navy and the Air Force, the sample size is large enough to yield a degree of confidence in drawing the conclusion that the change in kill ratios was real and that it was caused by the Navy delivering Top Gun trainees into the fleet.

Engagement Simulation and Training
The existence and performance of warfare "aces" appear, therefore, to be not just a result of battlefield Darwinism; they can be created by high-fidelity combat

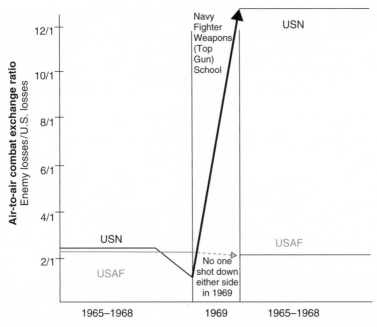

FIGURE 2.7. The influence upon combat proficiency of training by "simulated engagements." The Navy made a factor of 12 improvement in combat performance within the space of about one year. This dramatic change appears to be caused by personnel and training policies, including five weeks of Top Gun school for about 300 aircrews and "adversary" training of almost 1,000 more aircrews by Top Gun instructors in air combat maneuvering exercises against operational squadrons.

training. This lesson was not lost on the other organizations in the U.S. military. The Navy established the Strike University mentioned earlier. The Air Force created "Aggressor Squadrons" to participate in engagement simulations over new instrumented ranges in Red Flag exercises of their tactical squadrons. As General Gorman put it,

> [Tactical Air Command officers] cited Weiss' analyses, pointing out that the U.S. Air Force exhausted every recourse open to it in selecting fighting pilots, but that the USAF could ill afford not to provide for its pilots-to-be, however well selected, training aimed at optimum effectiveness in those early, vulnerable battle encounters. RED FLAG's stated objective was to enable each pilot to experience his first ten "decisive combats," and thereby make available to air commanders, on D-Day of any future war, the differential between 40 percent and 5 percent probability of pilot loss on sortie one, and the significant increase in pilots and aircraft that would be available for sorties two, or three or *n* (Gorman, 1990, pp. 5–6).

The U.S. Army's subsequent entry into the arena of large-scale, instrumented, combat simulation training at the NTC in Fort Irwin has already been covered (Gorman, 1990), but there is one more element that they added to the process that I tumbled to while trying to characterize the dramatic changes they made in the last few years in response to the war in Iraq; that is, *tailoring the training to the needs of each specific unit.* This element of the NTC process has been in place from the beginning but is easily obscured by the vision of a giant improvisational theater production in the desert. This theater involves a participating trainee audience of 4,000 soldiers and over 1,000 actors including, these days, 250 Arab Americans playing out coordinated parts in multiple, carefully scripted plot threads acting as Iraqi or Afghan civilians, insurgents, bankers, judges, storekeepers, mayors, drivers, hot-dog venders, Malaks, Sheiks, Imams, *etc.* Those plots and parts are all carefully and interactively tailored to the missions the unit will soon be expected to perform in the real world. They are also tailored to the state of that unit's training, that is, how well prepared the unit is when it first gets to the NTC.

A number of common features of the different Services' approaches to engagement simulation includes the following. The training is given to complete combat elements, not fragments of a group. The simulation is as realistic as possible with forces using the actual hardware they would in battle. The forces being trained fight complete engagements. Unless the arriving unit is severely deficient, they do not, for example, conduct artillery practice at the NTC; that is done before the units get there. During and after the battle there is a strong emphasis on feedback to and among the soldiers and their units. The state of mind of the trainees is explored with them; they are encouraged to ask themselves questions about what they knew and what they were thinking when they made decisions. Thus, the thought processes of battle are explored at all levels within the trained unit.

Another key element, which I discovered when reviewing unsuccessful attempts by other nations to imitate the U.S. successes, is the need to provide *independent* aggressor forces. The enemies (red forces) that the trainee units (blue forces) fight are equipped with the material that an expected red force would be likely to have. The aggressor force is trained to fight using red doctrine. They use red tactics. As a consequence of careful selection and of repeated engagements, they also become superbly capable warriors. They win the vast majority of the battles against the blue forces (Goldsmith, Grossman, & Sollinger, 1993).[6] They are independent of the units being trained, and are not judged by how good the trained forces look in the mock combat, but how well those units are trained. This independence is vital to their success, for when

---

[6] One sample taken to determine the effects of battlefield reconnaissance showed the blue forces being defeated on the order of 85 percent of the time (Goldsmith, Grossman, & Sollinger, 1993).

the opposing forces are subordinate to the commander of the trained unit, it is difficult to prevent unwanted influence being brought to bear upon the aggressor units. Such influence can drastically dilute the effectiveness of the training.[7]

Summary of Engagement Simulation

Although there is no independent "experimental control group" data with which to compare, there is little doubt that the U.S. Army's ability to maneuver and fight so effectively on the ground during Desert Storm and the maneuver warfare stages of the current Iraq war, was a result of a long process that changed the training methods for our Army. The most visible piece of that effort is the NTC where battalion-level units fight under the most realistic conditions against superbly skilled and motivated red forces, and where the results of those battles are measured, recorded, and fed back to the units involved. The Navy's air arm and the U.S. Air Force have similar training centers with similar philosophies. To paraphrase General Gorman, this kind of training center breeds battle-wise warriors bloodlessly.

The keys to the success of this engagement simulation training are:

1. The creation of an *independent* opposing force.
2. An ability to measure what actually happened.
3. The AAR; that is, objective feedback to the trainee unit that includes concentration on situation awareness, decision processes, and the state of mind of the players. The Army has gone much further by demanding that much of the feedback come from the trainees themselves, and by insisting on the participation of the trainees at all levels and up as well as down the chain of command. Feedback that comes only from the trainers often ends up in the form of "I'm OK, you're a fool." Even when it isn't meant that way, it is often so perceived by the recipient. When the trainee is forced to analyze his/her own actions, the lessons are much easier to take and much easier to remember.[8]
4. Dedication to making the simulation as real as necessary, but, in the interests of cost, not more so.

---

[7] Captain Bill Rohm, USN (retired) related, during July 1996 discussions held with the author to explore training and submarine proficiency, an incident which brought the need for independence clearly to the front. His ship, an older class of submarine (SSN-637), was pitted in a series of engagements against the newest class boat with a new and advanced sonar and combat system. The hidden purpose of the exercise was to show off the new capabilities. Captain Rohm was a tactician; the captain of the SSN-688 class boat was an engineer. Rohm's boat won all the engagements. He sent off a self-satisfied, after-action message, which his boss later described as setting the BSY-1 combat system back four years. The squadron commander didn't know whether to fire Rohm or give him a medal.

[8] Possibly worth noting is the trained unit has an expectation of failure. They know that the red force is almost certain to beat them.

5. An institutional commitment to fund and make frequent and comprehensive use of the facility.[9]
6. Tailoring the training for each unit's needs and to each unit's state of readiness. Each rotation is customized to help the unit experience the combat situation in the location they are likely to be deployed.

The process trains whole units in whole-unit warfare. Measurements made at the training centers show extraordinary improvements in combat performance after this type of training and, in one case, there is strong evidence of significant improvement in performance in actual combat.

IMPLICATIONS OF THE SUCCESS OF ENGAGEMENT SIMULATION

It Is Not Just About the Military

This process is applicable not only to soldier or pilot training. Dr. Joe Braddock, the co-chair with me on the recent Defense Science Board Training task forces, provided an anecdote concerning a bank that was anxious about how the introduction of the Euro would change the arbitrage business. With his help, they studied the NTC's engagement–simulation training process and built a similar kind of simulation of the economic "battlefield" for the exchange of currency. The bank created a team of OPFOR to take the sides of many other entities and other banks. Then they sent their team off to see if they could make money. For the first week, the team didn't. Finally the team discovered strategies to "defeat" the opponents. Although I cannot present specifics, the proof of the pudding was that the bank made a *lot* of money from the introduction of the Euro.

Training Surprise: Other Countries Could Use It, Too

The Defense Science Board's task force on Training Superiority and Training Surprise asked the following question and then set about to answer it (Braddock & Chatham, 2001, p. 21).

> Would it be possible for others to institute training programs that could yield the rapid proficiency changes our Combat Training Centers [CTCs] give us? In other words, should the U.S. be concerned about potential "training surprise" in the same way we have been watching for technological surprise?

---

[9] There is no consensus, at least for Top Gun School authorities, as to which element is the most important (Brown, 1996).

The [final] answer was yes: it had been done, but widespread use was impeded by cultural issues. The first answer we [the DSB task force] were given, however, was that the rest of the world is too destitute to do training well. We were left with the impression that, like the acquisition community, they did not view training as something that could make order-of-magnitude performance changes.

We later raised the issue with the National Intelligence Officer for Conventional Military Issues, and he convened a group of senior intelligence analysts, explicitly tasking them to examine the issue of possible training breakthroughs. They corroborated the DIA estimate that military training in most of our potential adversaries is poor.

They did point out that small groups of special forces in many countries are well trained and competent even though the bulk of their forces are not. None of the special forces use[s] the CTC approach to training, but by persistent and continual use of more conventional training they succeed in creating competent elite forces. North Korea's use of South Korea as a training ground for their commandos comes closest to the CTC paradigm, although, in this case, since the consequences of failure are more fatal than in a CTC, this comes closer to battlefield Darwinism.

The NIO's ad hoc group did, however, identify an additional instance of training surprise. (The U.S. experience with Top Gun and in Desert Storm are others, although the devastating consequences of those surprises were felt by our enemies, not by us.) This example occurred in the Croatian armed forces in 1993 and 1994. In the space of one year, with the help of a U.S. consulting firm, Military Professional Resources, Inc. (MPRI), with unusually strong political support from the top, and with adequate funding, the Croatians built a force that drove the Serbs out of their territory. They surprised not only their enemies but the rest of the world as well.

Croatia's success was a result of exceptional circumstances including not having an existing military to resist changes that made for effective training. Successes like this are likely to be rare.

The group assembled by the NIO *would* notice the implementation of a CTC-like training revolution in an adversary. We worry, however, that since they were assembled on a one-time basis, the focus raised by the NIO will fade with time. Nor were we convinced that the IC would recognize the implications of what we have called in this report the second training revolution. We recommend that, as a minimum, the Secretary of Defense should request a similar Training Surprise conclave annually to maintain the perspective in the IC that breakthroughs may be possible in training as well as in technology.

That recommendation was not accepted, which leaves me with the fear that it would be entirely possible for an adversary to use engagement simulation to change the proficiency of its forces and we would be surprised at the result.

LIMITATIONS

I have expended a lot of words extolling the value of the first training revolution. There are limitations as well.

The Process Doesn't Touch Everyone

Only some units have the opportunity to experience a rotation to a major combat training center. Those units receive training only every three or so years, and they must go to a distant, expensive-to-maintain training center to receive it. National Guard and Army Reserve units often do not get a chance to deploy to the NTC or its companion centers in Louisiana and Germany. None of the Marine Corps conducts the kind of training described above. Despite its protests that battle exercises at the USMC base at Twentynine Palms, California, are the same, essential features of the process are missing. My Navy, outside of its tactical air forces, has never heard of the process.

The Interdeployment Readiness Bathtub Curve

Learning decay is not the only way proficiency can be lost. Personnel turbulence takes a toll on unit proficiency as well. The gereral policy throughout the Defense Department is for people to change jobs at least every three years. Proficiency loss comes not only when trained people leaving a unit carry away their stores of knowledge. Equally debilitating is the loss of coordination skills and the practiced human networks that result when every six months or so a quarter of a submarine's crew, for example, is new to that boat. The Navy manages this by stabilizing a crew before a scheduled overseas deployment and holding the same crew on the ship throughout most of the deployed time. But when the lid is lifted near the end of the deployment, unit proficiency drops precipitously (Figure 2.8) and does not recover for a year or more. When the average unit proficiency sits halfway up this curve, one worries about come-as-you-are conflicts (Chatham & Braddock, 2003).

The Army, too, experiences the interdeployment readiness bathtub. Until we engaged in large-scale wars again, the peak in performance came at the end of a CTC deployment. Then the personnel system opened up and unit competence dropped dramatically within a few months. In an attempt to schedule around this effect, the Army instituted the Army Force Generation (ARFORGEN) process over the last few years to make the rises and falls of unit proficiency work in the more orderly fashion of the Navy's. The changing demands of the Iraq War, which force the re-deployment of units in as short a time as one year, have made it very difficult to institute the new policy.

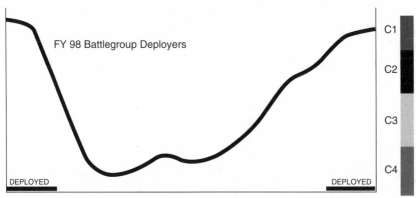

FIGURE 2.8. Readiness of the Navy in relation to its anticipated deployments. This chart shows an actual curve and points out that the Navy times its readiness to match expected deployments. Unexpected deployments are a different matter. The bar to the right provides a scale for the four levels of readiness designated by a self-reported "C" rating, where C1 is fully ready. A unit in the C4 category is unable to perform its mission. The horizontal scale measures months relative to the deployment date. (Adapted from the Defense Science Board Task Force, report on Training for Future Conflicts, 2003, p. 42.)

Training Counts but We Don't Count Training

This section's title quotes the last words of the Defense Science Board's Training Task Force in 2001. It describes two issues. The first is implied by all that I have laboriously covered above, but to make it explicit: if you describe training needs in terms of hours of instruction, or numbers of students and course throughput (colloquially "butts in seats"), you do not understand the problem. One needs to train to proficiency, not by the clock.

The second issue is that it is easier to count hardware than it is to assess how well that hardware will be used by real people. Given our national obsession with technology, it is hard to get the emphasis and resources to give training its proper seat in the mix of "man, equip, and train." Both these problems are distressingly common among those who fund the military and those who develop training within it.

CONCLUSIONS

Training Counts

Military performance is often far more dependent upon the proficiency of the warriors than upon the technology of the systems with which they fight. Numerous anecdotal examples can be found where a superior weapons system is beaten handily by inferior technology operated by a well-trained force. Unfortunately, there are little quantitative data to link gross measures of training to military performance.

Training versus Effectiveness Data Appear Contradictory

The data that are available appear contradictory. On one hand, analyses correlating the U.S. Navy pilot's flying hours to such skills as bombing accuracy, carrier landing proficiency, and air-to-air combat performance suggest that a 20 percent change in flying hours would alter proficiency by the order of only 3 to 4 percent. This and other factors lead to the widely held assertion that "there are no quick-fix options for correcting training shortfalls." At a basic skills level this is probably true. On the other hand, within one year, the establishment of the U.S. Navy Fighter Weapon (Top Gun) School appears to have changed the entire Navy air arm's air-to-air kill ratios over Viet Nam by more than a factor of 12, while the Air Force's effectiveness (without Top Gun–style training) remained unchanged. Here, relatively few hours of training made an enormous difference in military effectiveness, while elsewhere many more hours made little difference.

Resolving the Contradiction: A Hierarchy of Training

Military training can be directed toward goals on many levels. For example, a training program might be directed toward individual skills at performing specific evolutions such as loading torpedoes, identifying targets, or navigational proficiency. For these basic skills, at the lower level of the hierarchy, we can occasionally determine a quantitative learning curve that equates some measure of performance to some measure of the size of the investment in training. That curve is steep at first; a few more flying hours early on make a much better pilot. Then the curve starts leveling off; a pilot with 1,000 hours flying does not get that much better with a few more hours *of the same kind of practice.* When not exercised, skills frequently atrophy, with time constants of the order of several months. There are, therefore, minimum training rates that, if not met, will render a force relatively ineffective.

Military performance, however, is not only a function of individual skills. Those skills must be combined into mission tasks and those tasks must be merged in order to perform large-scale military operations. Training at each of these levels has a different impact upon performance. This can be viewed as a hierarchy of separate learning curves each riding upon the curve for the previous, lower, level of training. Once basic skills are acquired, training at the next level must commence or little additional military effectiveness will be added, even with large investments in training time. Thus, equal investment in training can yield unequal performance changes, depending upon what kind of training is conducted and where on the learning curve we take our measurements. Simple measures of training, such as numbers of rounds shot or hours spent at sea, have some predictive value for part-task rungs of this ladder of levels, but the quality of the training at the combined task levels can have an enormously greater influence upon the effectiveness of a military organization. It is training at these higher rungs of the ladder that win battles.

At the highest levels of unit training, a strong dose of realism is required to achieve additional performance benefits. Here the techniques used at the Army's NTC, the Navy Fighter Weapons School, and similar organizations can make vast differences in combat proficiency. A key ingredient in this kind of training is an *independent* opposing force that is rewarded for winning; special units that are evaluated upon how well they train others, not on whether they make a particular combat unit look good in the eyes of its superiors.

Beyond unit proficiency is the problem of training warfare commanders. When looking at the influence of exercises and training on total force effectiveness, the emphasis should shift to assessing the training of the senior officers and their staffs. Persistent deficiencies in U.S. military performance, both from a historical perspective (Depuy, 1989, as quoted in Gorman, 1990) and from naval exercise results, suggest that "training designed to provide key areas of focus for the … warfare commanders had the greatest impact on performance" (Fox, 1990, p. 31).

Intelligence Implications

Training deserves a place at the table when the intelligence community attempts to assess the military proficiency of foreign forces. If a military capability can be changed by factors of six to twelve *in one year* by changing the nature of the training process, then it is vital that the intelligence community be aware of that potential and have tools and methodologies to detect training changes and assess their importance. Improvements in mission performance through training can have a larger impact than changes in weapons systems. They can be achieved in a much shorter time and at a much lower cost than comparable performance changes arising from introduction of new weapons systems. Yet the improvements due to training can be lost more quickly if the training is not sustained. All these factors present strong incentives for the intelligence community to monitor and to analyze closely regional military training behavior.

Admonition to the Defense Department

The chief business of military units not at war is to prepare for war by training. Training should have equal standing with the purchase of military hardware. That it does not is a function of how hard it is to measure proficiency and the unfortunate truth that what you don't measure is easy to ignore. Assessment of the impact of training on military effectiveness has proven difficult in the past due, in part, to the variability in our own training data. The performance output seemed to have little correlation with the investment in training. Much of that variability can be explained by consideration of the learning and forgetting curves, as was suggested by Orlansky in 1989. It is worth the effort: The human in the loop is usually the limiting element in the combat effectiveness of the weapon. Funding the weapon is not sufficient. We must also fund the warrior.

REFERENCES

Army Training Circular (1993, 20 September) TC 25–20. Washington, DC: Headquarters, Department of the Army.

Braddock, J., & Chatham, R. (2001). *Training superiority and training surprise 2001*, Report of the Defense Science Board, Washington, DC. Retrieved from www.acq. osd.mil/dsb/reports.htm.

Brown, A. (1996). Interview on June 11, 1996, at Center for Naval Analysis' Operational Training Group.

Brown, A., Brobst, W., & Fox, C. (1996, 11 June). Meeting at Center for Naval Analyses with DTIs R. Chatham and S. Borchardt.

Chatham, R. E. (1990, September). Confuse the bastard. *Naval Institute Proceedings*, *116*, 54–59.

Chatham, R. (1996). *Training assessment: A critical intelligence deficiency. A report on the intelligence implications of relationships among training, exercises & military proficiency*. Dynamics Technology, Inc. Technical report DTW-9509.02–96001.

Chatham, R., & Braddock J. (2003) *Training for future conflicts*, Report of the Defense Science Board, Washington, DC. Retrieved from www.acq.osd.mil/dsb/reports. htm.

Cohen, E. A., & Gooch, J. (1990). *Military misfortunes, the anatomy of failure in war*. New York: The Free Press.

Fitts, R. E. (1980). *The strategy of electromagnetic conflict*. Los Altos, CA: Peninsula Publishing.

Fox, C. H. (1990). *Battlegroup training and readiness as seen in fleet exercises. Center for Naval Research Publication CNR 186*. Alexandria, VA: Center for Naval Research.

Goldsmith, M., Grossman, J., & Sollinger, J. (1993). *Quantifying the battlefield*. Santa Monica, CA: Rand Arroyo Center.

Gorman, P. F. (1990). *The military value of training*. Institute for Defense Analysis Paper P-2515.

——— (1995). Briefing to ARPA panel on small unit operations. Private communication.

Hastings, M., & Jenkins, S. (1983). *The battle for the Falklands*. London: Michael Joseph, Ltd.

Hammon, C. P. (1990). *Flying hours and aircrew performance*. Institute for Defense Analyses Reports Paper P-2379. Alexandria, VA: Institute for Defense Analyses.

Hammon, C. P., & Horowitz, S. A. (1996). *The relationship between training and unit performance for naval patrol aircraft*. Briefing at the Institute for Defense Analyses, Alexandria, VA.

Konoske, P. J., Wetzel, S. K., & Montague, W. E. (1983). *Estimating skill degradation for aviation antisubmarine warfare operators: Assessment of job training variables*. Navy Personnel Research and Development Center SR 83–28. San Diego, CA: Navy Personnel Research and Development Center.

Lanchester, F. W. (1914). Aircraft in warfare: The dawn of the fourth arm – No. V, The principle of concentration. *Engineering, 98*, 422–423. [Reprinted in J. Newman (Ed). (1956). *The World of Mathematics*, Vol. IV (pp. 2138–2141). New York: Simon and Schuster.]

March, J. G., Sproull, L. S., & Tamuz, M. (1991). Learning from samples of one or fewer. *Organization Science, 2*(1), 1–13.

Moore, S. C., Hanser, L. M., Rostker, B., Holroyd, S. M., & Fernandez, J. C. (1995). *A framework for characterization of military unit training status*. Santa Monica, CA: RAND National Defense Research Institute, MR-261-OSD.

Newett, S. W. *F/A-18 pilot proficiency vs. training resources: Fallon HARM analysis* (U). Center for Naval Research Memorandum 90–1994 (Secret). Alexandria, VA: Center for Naval Research Publications.

Orlansky, J. (1989). *The military value and cost-effectiveness of training*. NATO Defense Research Group Panel 7 on the Defense Applications of Operational Research: Research Study Group 15 on the Military Value and Cost-Effectiveness of Training, Final Report. Institute for Defense Analyses, Alexandria, VA, DIA Number AC/234 (Panel 7/RSG.15) D/4.

Perrow, C. (1984). *Normal accidents: Living with high risk technologies*. New York: Basic Books.

Sagan, S. D. (1993). *The limits of safety*. Princeton, NJ: Princeton University Press.

Starey, D. (1983). General, U.S. Army statement made during deliberations of the Defense Science Board Task Force on Technology for the Rapid Deployment Forces.

Suess, G. N. (1994). A look at navy flying hour requirements. *Center for Naval Research Memorandum CRM 94–77*. Alexandria, VA: Center for Naval Research.

Sullivan, L., Jr. (1981). *Q3: The quality/quantity quandary*. Briefing for an OSD panel on Quality vs. Quantity, Arlington, Virginia.

    (1984). Comments made by former Assistant Secretary of Defense for Program Analyses and Estimating to an OSD Quantity vs. Quality Workshop in the summer of 1984. [Notes taken by R. Chatham]

Taylor, J. G. (1983). *Lanchester models of warfare*. Arlington, VA: Operations Research Society of America.

Weis, T. D. (1994). *A review of the literature relating flying hours to readiness*. Center for Naval Analysis publication CIM 355, Alexandria, VA: Center for Naval Analysis.

Weiss, H. K. (1966). *Achieving system effectiveness*. New York: AIAA.

Wetzel, S. K., Konoske, P. J., & Montague, W. E. (1983a). Estimating skill loss throughout a navy technical training pipeline. *Navy Personnel Research and Development Center TR 84–7*. San Diego, CA: Navy Personnel Research and Development Center.

    (1983b). Estimating skill degradation for aviation antisubmarine warfare operators: Loss of skill and knowledge following training. *Navy Personnel Research and Development Center* SR 83–31. San Diego, CA: Navy Personnel Research and Development Center.

Wright, R. H. (1973). *Retention of flying skills and refresher training requirements: Effects of non-flying and proficiency flying*. Army Research Institute for the Behavioral and Social Sciences, HumRRO Technical Report 73–32. Fort Rucker, AL: Human Resources Research Organization.

You Fight Like You Train. (May, 1974). *Armed Forces Journal International*, 25–27.

3

Developing Professional Expertise with a Cognitive Apprenticeship Model: Examples from Avionics and Medicine

SUSANNE P. LAJOIE

One of the greatest challenges of assessment in the professions is the higher consequence of errors. In classrooms, there is a consequence to the individual learner if assessment errors are made, but the impact of such errors may not have large-scale consequences. However, when we certify trainees – be they in the military, in medicine, or professions in general – there can be consequences if the measures of proficiency are inadequate. Valid measures take on new meaning when the risks of improper assessments could endanger people's well-being. This paper will address the techniques used in the design and evaluation of Sherlock, an avionics tutor used by the U.S. Air Force to train technicians to troubleshoot problems pertinent to the F-15 aircraft (Lajoie & Lesgold, 1992a; Lesgold, Lajoie, Bunzo, & Eggan, 1992; Lesgold, Lajoie, Logan & Eggan, 1990). Sherlock presented airmen with realistic fault-isolation problems, similar to those they encounter when troubleshooting avionics equipment. The Sherlock trainees demonstrated improvements in their troubleshooting skills on a variety of measures, taken by Sherlock as training proceeded and via a post-training performance test (Lesgold et al., 1990; Lesgold et al., 1992;

Acknowledgments: Sherlock was very much a group effort led by Alan Lesgold as principal investigator. The lead programmer was Marilyn Bunzo and subject matter expert Gary Eggan. Joining us in the effort were Richard Eastman, Robert Glaser, Bruce Glymour, Linda Greenberg, Debra Logan, Maria Magone, Tom McGinnis, Arlene Weiner, Richard Wolf, and Laurie Yengo. Equally important were Sherrie Gott and the Air Force Human Resources Laboratory, Dennis Collins and other Air Force subject matter experts, and the personnel of the 1st and 33rd Tactical Fighter Wings, at Langley and Eglin Air Force Bases. The work was done as part of subcontracts with HumRRO and Universal Energy Systems, who were prime contractors with the Air Force Human Resources Laboratory.

The BioWorld research reported in this article was made possible through funding provided by the following granting agencies: the Canadian Social Sciences and Humanities Research Council, Network for Centres of Excellence, and Office of Learning Technologies. Many graduate students (former and current) have contributed to the work that is reported here. Special thanks to Gloria Berdugo, Sonia Faremo, Genevieve Gauthier, Claudia Guerrera, Nancy Lavigne, Carlos Nakamura, Solange Richard, Jeffrey Wiseman, M.D., Andrew Chiarella, and Marguerite Roy.

Nichols, Pokorny, Jones, & Gott, et al., in press). An analysis of Sherlock will be provided in terms of "what worked" or "lessons learned." Applications of these methods and extensions to these techniques are also provided for another domain, medical problem solving (Lajoie, 2007). The adaptations are at least one example of generalizability of methodology that can lead to innovations in assessment in other domains.

This chapter addresses professional competence in two domains, avionics troubleshooting and medical problem solving. Given that common proficiency dimensions have been identified in experts across domains (Chi, Glaser, & Farr, 1988), one would anticipate that professional proficiency would reflect these same dimensions of expertise. Examining competence or proficiency within a specific context is the first step in elaborating a model of thinking that can help the less competent become more proficient in a specific domain (Pellegrino, Chudowsky, & Glaser, 2001). Assessing professional competence within specialized contexts is a precursor to creating effective learning environments for the profession in question. Theories and methods used to support the identification of the cognitive competencies pertaining to a specific professional task are described, along with a mechanism for dynamically assessing the learners' strengths and weaknesses in the context of domain-specific problem solving. The mechanism is embedded in the design of computer-based learning environments to support the integration of instruction and assessment in authentic contexts. Additionally, this chapter discusses how cognitive apprenticeship models can be used to support instruction and assessment in avionics troubleshooting and medical problem solving.

ASSESSING PROFESSIONAL COMPETENCE

Contributions have been made to advances in the science of thinking and learning through the study of competence and developing expertise within specific areas of practice. Such advances can contribute to the identification of complex performance models that can inform the development of computer-based learning environments, some of which include interesting assessment options. These advances can inform the identification of proficiency in specific professions. A short summary of the literature findings pertaining to expertise is provided, followed by explicit applications in professional contexts.

The identification of cognitive processes in specific contexts has led to the discovery of common components of expertise (Alexander, 2003; Chi et al., 1988; Ericsson, 2002; Glaser, Lesgold, & Lajoie, 1987; Lajoie, 2003). One could argue that the nature of expertise research has changed over the years but the dimensions of expertise are reproducible, as are the methodologies for studying expert/novice differences. For instance, expertise has been studied in different contexts, chess (de Groot, 1946), physics (Larkin, McDermott, Simon, & Simon, 1980), and medicine (Ericsson, 2002; Patel, Arocha, & Kaufman, 1999;

Patel & Groen, 1991), and commonalities have been found among these experts. Experts demonstrate highly structured knowledge that helps them perceive meaningful patterns. When asked to describe such knowledge they reason using underlying principles of the domain in question. They are aware of what they know or do not know regarding specific situations, and thus are able to monitor themselves accordingly. Experts use their mental models to drive the selection of task strategies and are more efficient at problem-solving procedures. Experts also have faster access to contents of domain-specific memory. Recently, researchers have suggested that in addition to the routine experts just described, there are adaptive experts that demonstrate more flexibility and are more adaptive, innovative, and creative (Bransford, Brown, & Cocking, 1999; Hatano & Oura, 2003). Understanding these dimensions of proficiency can lead to domain-specific findings in new domains of professional competence. The methods employed to identify dimensions of expertise have been verbal protocol analyses (Chi, 1997; Ericsson & Simon, 1993) and cognitive task analyses (Crandall, Klein, & Hoffman, 2006; Schraagen, Chipman, & Shalin, 2000).

Throughout the generations of expertise research, there has been movement from examining problem solving in knowledge-lean to knowledge-rich contexts (Alexander et al., 2009). Knowledge-lean tasks (Holyoak, 1991) require general problem-solving skills that are not based on domain-specific information, as opposed to knowledge-rich tasks that require domain-specific knowledge to solve the problem, such as knowledge of chess, physics, etc. Research on professional competence can be seen at the higher end of the knowledge-rich continuum, since it involves complex problem solving in the real world.

Alexander et al. (2009) point to a third generation of expertise research, where researchers are committed to the development of expertise by considering the trajectory from novice to expert. Arguments have been made that models of expertise can serve to help learners attain higher levels of competence. The transition from student to expert professional can be accelerated when a trajectory for change is plotted and made visible to learners (Lajoie, 2003). Such trajectories or paths toward expertise are domain specific, and must first be documented and then used within instructional contexts to promote knowledge transitions. Assessing learners along this trajectory is essential in order to provide appropriate feedback to the less proficient.

A common assumption in expertise research is that identifying dimensions of expertise can lead to improvements in instruction that will ultimately result in helping learners become more competent. Instructional improvements are based on modeling these dimensions of expertise. The relevance of such modeling to learning is that learners deliberately practice the correct skills rather than practice indiscriminately (Ericsson, Krampe, & Tesch-Römer, 1993). The domain knowledge, the structure of the knowledge, and the strategies that lead to effective problem solutions can all be modeled for the learner. In addition to observing, individuals need opportunities to use such knowledge and interact with it with specific feedback. Better models of professional competence will lead to better feedback to those learners who are in transition. Furthermore, once we understand the components of professional competence, the easier it is to develop *deliberate practice* (Ericsson et al., 1993) environments. Examples of how such environments are designed are provided below.

COGNITIVE APPRENTICESHIP AS AN INSTRUCTIONAL MODEL

Apprenticeship settings have existed for centuries as ways to gradually introduce individuals to a professional trade, for example, apprenticing to become a tailor, where they learn skills in specific contexts (Lave & Wenger, 1991). Lave and Wenger (1991) documented the powerful aspects of participating in a community of practice whereby individuals learn from each other and engage in the overall activity of the community at skill levels in which they are ready to engage. All members legitimately participate in an activity such as tailoring, but participate at different levels, where novices are at the periphery where they learn to hem a pair of pants before they design a suit pattern. Apprentices learn by observing those who have mastered tasks and by talking with members of their group. The advantage of a natural apprenticeship is that learning is situated in the context of a concrete activity where physical skills are observable. However, cognitive skills are not readily observable and adaptations to such an apprenticeship model are necessary to support education more broadly.

Collins, Brown, and Newman (1989) saw the value of apprenticeship as an instructional framework and defined an original instructional model termed "cognitive apprenticeship." The model provides a template for connecting abstract and real-world knowledge by creating new forms of pedagogy based on a model of learners, the task, and the situation in which learning occurs. Cognitive apprenticeship speaks to types of content knowledge, pedagogical methods, sequence of instruction, and the sociology of learning in instructional settings. The value of this model is that it encompasses the learner, the teacher, the context of instruction, and assessment. The teacher can be viewed as a master, where students are apprentices. Consequently, the teacher decides what to model, how to scaffold or assist, and when to fade assistance based on the individual learner. Computer coaches can assist students as well when designed with representations of what students should know and understand. These representations have been called "student models." Student models can be updated based on student actions. Consequently, the computer can assess students dynamically and provide scaffolding or help based on an individual's performance and competency level. Content knowledge can be modeled for learners by providing them with examples of strategies used by competent learners. Sequencing instruction can also be controlled via technology based on student models of performance that would provide the computer tools to adapt to individual differences. A learning culture can be supported when learners share their experiences in the context of complex tasks.

The most defining characteristic of a cognitive apprenticeship model is the externalization of expert knowledge. Verbal protocol methods are used to delineate the cognitive and metacognitive processes that embody the tacit knowledge of experts. Expert knowledge is then made explicit for learners to observe, enact, and ultimately practice. Collins et al. (1989) described cognitive apprenticeship success stories in math (Schoenfeld, 1985), reading (Palincsar & Brown, 1984), and writing (Scardamelia & Bereiter, 1985). For instance, mathematics teachers externalize their knowledge when they respond to student-generated problems, and demonstrate that problem solving can be recursive and may take more than one effort to reach a solution (Schoenfeld, 1985). The teacher's ability to think out loud and make the contents of their thinking visible to students sensitizes learners to details of expert performance as the basis for making incremental adjustments in their own performance.

Williams (1992) reviews the problem-based learning (PBL) literature in medicine and the case-based research in law as partial exemplars of the cognitive apprenticeship model. For instance, scaffolding is a central component in PBL in medical schools (Barrow, 1988): Teachers gauge students' current abilities with respect to what they are expected to do to solve problems, and base their feedback to students by breaking down an activity into manageable tasks. In medical PBL classrooms, students ask more questions and construct more explanations (Hmelo-Silver, 2003). Teachers provide metacognitive guidance and scaffold collaboration by asking questions pertaining to the construction of explanations. These questioning strategies are withdrawn as students internalize them.

Given that cognitive apprenticeship models incorporate models of expertise in their instructional approach, it seems appropriate to consider this model in terms of assessment of professional competence. This chapter provides two examples of developing professional competence using a cognitive apprenticeship framework, one in avionics and one in medicine.

Avionics Troubleshooting

The Air Force identified a training dilemma in the mid 1980s. They found that some trainees who did well in technical school were not able to apply such skills on the job. Specifically, the trainees who scored well on tests of electronics circuit tracing and declarative knowledge of electronics were not effective in troubleshooting the Manual Avionics Test Station for the F-15 aircraft. Such observations are not limited to the Air Force. In fact, transfer from school learning to professional environments is often problematic. Much of what is learned in school remains inert (Whitehead, 1929) since it is not used in contexts other than recalling information at exam time. Students who test well on schooled facts and concepts fail to use such concepts on appropriate occasions. When schooled knowledge is not used or applied in some way, it does not transfer to real-world skills.

Sherlock, a computer-coached practice environment, was designed for airmen who had completed their technical school training and had started to apprentice in their assigned avionics shops (Lajoie & Lesgold, 1992a; Lesgold et al., 1992). Sherlock was designed to help trainees become proficient at avionics troubleshooting by providing an intelligent, coached, practice environment that would respond to their requests in the context of troubleshooting. Extensive field testing demonstrated that Sherlock was effective: Trainees demonstrated improvements in their troubleshooting skills on a variety of measures, taken by Sherlock as training proceeded, as well as on post-test performance (Lesgold et al., 1988). After 24 hours of practice with Sherlock, first-term airmen, who had been on the job for 6 months, demonstrated proficiency in their ability to troubleshoot test station failures at a level comparable to airmen who had been on the job for four years (Nichols et al., in press). Sherlock can be considered a success story. The following sections provide insight regarding some of the reasons for its success, as well as some guiding principles for generalizing these results to new domains.

Sherlock can be seen as an example of cognitive apprenticeship (Lajoie & Lesgold, 1992a). Designing a system like Sherlock forces the designers to be explicit about what to teach, how to teach it, when to model specific types of knowledge, and when to fade assistance. Sherlock uses explicit models of student competence to drive coaching and fading of instruction, and provides different levels of help according to the student's current level of achievement, when and where help is needed.

Background

Sherlock was developed to provide job-situated training for the F-15 Manual Avionics technician. People in this job repair electronic navigation equipment from F-15 aircraft, using a test station to isolate the sources of failures. The equipment that is malfunctioning (the unit-under-test) is attached to the test station by a cable (called the test package). When the test station is functioning appropriately, diagnoses are simple, and trainees have no problem learning their basic job. However, the test station itself fails frequently. Given that the test station is composed of 40 to 100 square feet of discrete electronic components soldered to printed circuit cards, diagnosing the test station is complex. Sherlock was designed to teach technicians to troubleshoot the more difficult task of diagnosing a fault that lies in the test station. Modeling the most difficult troubleshooting tasks provides opportunities to identify, teach, and assess, the critical concepts and procedures needed for job proficiency.

Sherlock is designed for airpersons who have completed their technical school training and have started to apprentice in the F-15 Manual Avionics shop. Technical school training provides trainees with basic skills needed for the job, but does not provide hands-on problem-solving skills with real test stations. Instead, troubleshooting is taught by focusing on basic principles underlying the electronics devices in question. Once technicians are on the job, they are expected to apprentice and learn troubleshooting skills by observing experts diagnose and repair faults. However, natural apprenticeships are not necessarily excellent instructional settings, given that there is a job to be accomplished in a safe and timely manner. Experts do not always have time to explain their actions when they are problem solving, and it would be difficult to recap their strategies over a multi-day period of troubleshooting. Furthermore, there is not a set of standard problems that technicians see routinely. Some problems are rare and diverse, and an airman might not see certain problems.

The Solution

Sherlock provides a computer simulation of the job environment and trainees practice their skills in the context of troubleshooting realistic problems. The work environment matches the real shop. The test station is presented with all its drawers, and every drawer, such as the digital multi-meter (DMM), can be accessed and operated by setting up the dials according to the technical orders specified in the shop. Technical orders are available on-line, and trainees search them to find the appropriate procedures to run on specific devices. Schematic diagrams are also accessible and trainees indicate the pins they would measure, with which equipment, and with which specific setups. Coaching is available at all times for all aspects of troubleshooting (Figure 3.1).

Sherlock embodies a cognitive apprenticeship model in that it provides a practice environment for professionals to acquire knowledge in the context of realistic troubleshooting activity. Examining competency or proficiency within a specific context is the first step in elaborating a model of thinking that can help the less competent become more proficient in a specific domain (Pellegrino et al., 2001). A cognitive task analysis of the avionics troubleshooting domain (Gitomer, 1984; Lesgold et al., 1986; Lesgold et al., 1990) provided information about the nature of troubleshooting proficiency. The analyses served to identify the types of tasks to tutor and what content to cover, as well the types of cognitive models to externalize to scaffold learners along the proficiency trajectory. The analyses also revealed how performers solve such problems and served to identify the cognitive competencies that differentiate performers.

Our analyses revealed that both skilled and less skilled trainees performed discrete knowledge tasks well, and that differences became apparent when such skills had to be used in the context of a troubleshooting problem. Consequently, Sherlock sharpened skills in the context of solving real problems, rather than

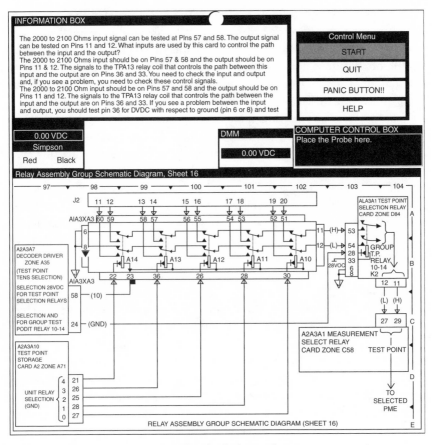

FIGURE 3.1. The Sherlock interface.

tutoring learners on one skill until they were proficient at it. Rather than give
a set of problems that are designed to tune the learners' comprehension of one
skill, such as how to trace a signal on a circuit diagram, troubleshooting problems are presented where the specific skill of tracing signals is required in the
context of locating a specific fault in the test equipment. Thus, a specific skill,
such as signal tracing, becomes sharpened in the context of the procedural task
of electronics troubleshooting. Trainees must be able to self-monitor when
specific skills are required, and allocate appropriate cognitive resources to perform them appropriately. For instance, the skill of knowing *which* equipment
to use may be necessary at one point in the problem, and knowing *how* to use
the equipment may be necessary at another point. Our pedagogical approach
is dependent upon a dynamic assessment of the learners' competency of such
specific skills in the context of their troubleshooting performance. If procedural
performance is impaired by poor declarative skills, these later skills are reme-
diated in the context of how it affects overall troubleshooting performance for
a specific problem (Lajoie & Lesold, 1992a). Trainees learn by doing the whole

activity and receive scaffolding on specific components when needed. Skills are not taught in isolation. Trainees learn concepts and skills in multiple situations in multiple problems, so that transfer of knowledge occurs. An underlying instructional principle is that individual differences exist in terms of prior knowledge and mental models. Consequently, assessment is used to inform the coach regarding what a student knows or does not know, and only then is help provided based on an individual's needs.

The results of the cognitive task analysis informed Sherlock's curriculum design. As mentioned above, the instructional strategy was to sharpen specific skills in the context of the overall task of electronics troubleshooting. Given there are multiple "best" paths or sequences for solving troubleshooting problems, Sherlock was designed to allow trainees to follow a number of solution paths and to receive coaching in the context of their chosen paths. Given such flexibility, each problem had an underlying structure called the effective problem space (EPS). A problem space refers to a node graph that indicates a start state, a goal state, and a set of problem-specific operations that can be performed. The problem space can be represented schematically by a problem behavior graph in which nodes represent partial solution states for a problem and links represent actions that move the solution process from one partial solution state to another (Ernst & Newell, 1969). In the course of solving a problem, one "traverses" the problem space via a path that represents the sequence of problem solution steps taken. An overarching EPS was created for the Sherlock problems that represented the domain of troubleshooting activities, including the types of plans and actions that could be accomplished to solve problems. By having both expert and novice paths planned ahead of time, it is possible to specify coaching for different levels of skill as well as for the specific nodes in the problem space. Each specific problem had its own subset of goals and actions that were appropriate to its solution. Each node in the problem space was a potential place for coaching.

The help was based on the appropriate actions, test outcomes, conclusions, and best next-moves for the specific EPS node where the trainee requested assistance. Thus, the help was based on an up-to-date assessment of skills based on the trainee's competence and performance models. The student competence model included all of the curriculum issues that pertained to the cognitive components of troubleshooting. Each node in the problem space had specific curriculum issues that were pertinent to traversing the node, and these competencies were assessed as unlearned, perhaps learned, probably learned, or strong. Performance models were assessed as bad, satisfactory, and good. Actions related to performances would be assessed and the quality of the performance would be used to update the competency levels for specific curriculum issues relevant to that performance. Coaching, when requested, would be driven by the level of performance. In other words, a trainee that demonstrated good performance on a test-taking curriculum issue and asked for help would get less assistance than a poor performer.

The content of the coaching was based on the domain expertise of the Sherlock team domain expert Gary Eggan, who was both a subject matter expert as well as a pedagogical expert. He served as both technician and supervisor in the Manual Avionics F-15 shop. His domain knowledge was instrumental in helping design the problem sequencing from less complex to more complex, as well as creating the type and depth of hints for specific problems. Consequently, the coaching included articulate guidance based on complex models of the test station, tests and measurements, and tracing strategies. His pedagogical expertise was evident in his ability to forecast where trainees were likely to have learning impasses.

The cognitive task analysis helped to inform several aspects of the cognitive apprenticeship model, including the design of instructional content with regard to the components of troubleshooting proficiency. The domain expert also provided assistance with elaborating the content knowledge by identifying the heuristics and strategies that experts use so that appropriate models could be provided when coaching trainees in the context of troubleshooting. Given this analysis, we knew what to teach and we chose to model, coach, scaffold, and fade assistance based on the trainees' competence and performance models when trainees asked for assistance. Sherlock adapted to individual differences by providing the appropriate level of help.

Much of Sherlock's coaching is designed to stimulate a trainee's thinking by asking questions rather than generating answers for what the trainee should do next. A minimal hinting approach was selected in order to encourage active construction of problem-solving knowledge by the trainee (Lajoie & Lesgold, 1992a). Thus, each time a trainee asked for help, the first hint was a structured rehearsal of what the trainee had already done on that problem, so the trainee could reflect on his/her plans and actions. Further, when the trainee requested additional help, the trainee received a trace of the hints received previously. More elaborate hints supported the trainee's problem solving much as a shop supervisor might. The content of these hints was specific to the current work environment and to the state of the trainee's knowledge.

All trainees received the same sequence of problems (from least to most complex) that gradually built upon trainees' conceptual understanding of troubleshooting. However, each individual experienced these problems differently, given there was flexibility in how learners could traverse the problem space and assistance was generated based on individual needs. Every individual had a different learning trajectory facilitated by the coaching mechanism that was based on dynamic forms of assessment. Sherlock facilitated the development of emerging competence by supporting overall troubleshooting performance and embedding assistance in the context of problem solving. For example, a trainee may have excellent measurement-taking skills but not be allowed to demonstrate such skills if the trainee did not traverse the plan that would allow such knowledge to be revealed. If assistance had not been provided at the planning level, trainees would not have had the opportunity to demonstrate what they do know or do not know about measurement taking. Sherlock provides bridging information that enables assessment of a trainee's knowledge that would be inaccessible in a testing environment that terminated a performance when an impasse occurs. This assessment strategy is modeled after Vygotsky's (1978) zone of proximal development, where feedback is used in the assessment process to encourage the development of competence rather than assessment that looks at learning as an end product. Sherlock's hinting structure provides trainees with experiences that would be just beyond their reach without coaching.

Evidence of Effectiveness

There were two separate evaluations of Sherlock, one by the Air Force and one by our research team. The Air Force evaluation indicated that trainees who were on the job for six months and spent 20 to 25 hours working with Sherlock were as proficient in troubleshooting the test station as technicians who had been on the job four years (Nichols et al., in press). Our evaluation of Sherlock's effectiveness consisted of both quantitative and qualitative measures (Lesgold et al., 1986). The quantitative evaluation was performed on matched experimental and control groups of airmen at two Air Force F-15 bases. The experimental group spent an average of 20 hours working through Sherlock's 34 problems. Tutoring sessions were conducted in 2- to 3-hour blocks that spanned an average of 12 working days. The control group subjects went about their daily activities in the manual avionics shop. Structured interviews were administered as pre- and post-tests of troubleshooting to 32 trainees. These tests consisted of problems based on actual failures encountered in the shop rather than on Sherlock problems, and Air Force technical orders were used rather than Sherlock's modified technical orders. There were no significant differences between the experimental and control groups at pre-testing [$X^2(1, N=63)=0.00, p=1.00$], but on post-test performance [$X^2(1, N=62)=10.29, p < .001$], the tutored group solved significantly more problems (mean = 30) than the control group (mean = 21).

Qualitative analyses of the pre- and post-test data revealed that the experimental group was significantly different from the control group on several factors that reflected emerging competence. Individual trainee's computer trace data revealed the troubleshooting steps taken for each problem. The domain expert coded the troubleshooting steps as expert, good, redundant, or inappropriate. Analyses of covariance were performed, examining performance differences between the two groups on post-test criteria variables while controlling for the qualitative pre-test variables. The tutored group displayed more expert-like problem-solving steps (mean = 19.33) in the post-test than the control group (mean = 9.06) [$F(1,27) = 28.85, p < .000$], and made fewer inappropriate or bad moves (mean = 1.89) [$F(1,27) = 7.54$, $p < .01$], than the control group (mean = 4.19). Sherlock trainees became more expert-like in their solutions.

Analyses revealed that trainee performance improved with practice, regardless of aptitude levels. Three problems – one early, one middle, and one late in the tutor sequence – were scored to see whether there was a change in expertise over the course of the tutored practice. A repeated measures analysis of variance examined the effects of aptitude (high, low) and time spent in the tutoring environment (early, middle, and late tutor problem) on types of moves (deviation from expert path scores and total steps to solution). There was a significant main effect due to time spent in the tutoring environment [$F(2,42) = 4.19$, $p < .02$] on the trainee's deviation scores and steps to solution. The more problems the trainee solved using Sherlock, the closer the trainee's troubleshooting solution processes were to expert troubleshooting solution processes, and the fewer steps were taken to reach a solution. With practice on Sherlock, trainees became more expert-like and efficient. Both the high- and low-ability trainees responded in the same manner, with the low-ability individuals showing slightly more improvement than the high-ability group.

Sherlock improved troubleshooting proficiency, and it is effective for trainees of various aptitudes. In addition, Sherlock's student modeling indicates that improvements occurred in every major category of knowledge that was targeted for training, which is confirmed by the analyses of post-test performance. Both quantitative and qualitative measures supported these findings.

Reasons for Success

The Sherlock research was designed to enhance troubleshooting proficiency, which it did effectively. The research did not address which aspects of design led to specific learning gains. Future research could isolate instructional features and test their effectiveness or replicate the key features that led to Sherlock's success in another system. Some of the key features that led to Sherlock's success are:

1. Cognitive task analysis of the most complex thinking tasks provided critical information needed to represent the avionics troubleshooting domain. The analysis served to identify the critical concepts and procedures situated within the job and to help situate explanations and guidance.
2. A cognitive apprenticeship model helped craft the instructional and assessment framework. Instruction and assessment are interwoven and this intersection most likely contributes to Sherlock's success. The instructional setting was an authentic, simulated work environment where trainees could practice the skills needed in the manual avionics shop. Their learning was situated in specific troubleshooting contexts. The underlying theoretical premise is that learners learn complex cognitive procedures

by doing them rather then learning about them in an abstract manner. When trainees encounter difficulty in the context of the overall task, they are supported through the parts they cannot handle but are still engaging in completing the task. The instructional content was based on a cognitive task analysis that revealed the cognitive components of avionics troubleshooting. Sherlock's curriculum was designed based on this analysis and, consequently, design decisions supported trainees' self-monitoring skills by making key aspects of mental model building visible to them. The instructional methods consisted of modeling, coaching, and fading assistance, and Sherlock could do this automatically through the dynamic assessment of student performance and competence.

3. Dynamic assessment provides a mechanism for developing expertise along individual trajectories of competence. When students reach an impasse they get assistance that helps them move closer to their goals rather than being stopped in midstream while problem solving. Assistance is situated in specific contexts where learners can examine their strategies compared to experts. For a system to be able to shape performance toward expertise, it must reflect, in its coaching, the expertise of real workers who have learned to do the job, not just the designer's model of the work environment. There are several dimensions that underlie proficiency in any domain, and dynamic forms of assessment should consider learning transitions in these dimensions as indicators of emerging competence (Glaser, Lesgold, & Lajoie, 1987). These dimensions are derived from research on expert/novice differences that provide a theoretical framework for measuring achievement in various domains. Systems like Sherlock offer an able means for providing dynamic forms of assessment of such dimensions. The dimensions of expertise can be directly mapped to the assessment of troubleshooting proficiency (Lajoie & Lesgold, 1992b). For example, one dimension of expertise pertains to knowledge organization. As efficiency increases in a domain, elements of knowledge become more interconnected so that proficient individuals access coherent chunks of information versus fragmented knowledge. Assessment should consider the degree of fragmentation, structuredness, and accessibility to interconnected chunks of knowledge. Systems like Sherlock can assess knowledge organization unobtrusively by monitoring the plans and actions trainees entered via the forced-choice, menu-driven computer interface. If the learner demonstrates random switching of plans without taking the necessary actions to confirm a plan, then the result is a measure of knowledge fragmentation. If the learner constrains the problem by systematically evaluating each plan in terms of the mental model of a problem, we have a measure of knowledge structuredness. By monitoring student data in this way, Sherlock provides a means to measure transitions in proficiency in knowledge organization, as well as to give advice on this basis. See

Lajoie and Lesgold (1992b) for how Sherlock does or does not address other dimensions of emerging competence. For instance, more research is needed on how to automate the labor-intensive coding of expert-like steps and changes in mental models.

4. Sherlock provides adaptive instruction based on individual differences. It has been clear for some time that there is not one form of instruction that is appropriate for all, since individuals differ in the ways they learn (Cronbach & Snow, 1977). Part of Sherlock's success can be attributed to the flexibility it provides learners in traversing the problems, as well as on-demand, individualized-feedback based on an assessment of their competence.

EXTENDING SHERLOCK'S SUCCESS TO NEW DOMAINS: FROM AVIONICS TROUBLESHOOTING TO MEDICAL PROBLEM SOLVING

This section describes extending some of the guiding principles behind Sherlock's design to computer-based learning environments in medicine. In this context, various aspects of Sherlock's design have been replicated, in particular, the cognitive apprenticeship approach.

Professional competence is domain specific but there are parallels that can be made between avionics troubleshooting and medical problem solving. Some medical schools suffer the same training dilemma identified by the Air Force. Schooled knowledge does not translate into on-the-job skills. Medical students often take years of basic science prior to working with patients, much like the Air Force trainee who reads about test stations but does not interact with them until they are on the job. Both avionics troubleshooting and medical problem solving are complex. In both scenarios, trainees are presented with a symptom(s) and need to determine what the problem is so that it can be fixed. However, locating the problem and what caused it may take an extended amount of time given the enormous amount of electronic or human circuitry that needs to be traced. In both situations, in order to make a diagnosis and prescribe a treatment plan, trainees need to collect and interpret evidence, generate and test diagnostic hypotheses, and consult additional sources of information such as more experienced staff, guides, and manuals. Broader assessment methods are needed to capture cognitive competencies in complex tasks.

The following section describes which relevant attributes of Sherlock's design were used to develop computer-based learning environments for medical problem solving. The first parallel was the use of cognitive task analysis to construct a cognitive model of medical problem solving. In developing a model of diagnostic reasoning, it was important to model the different types of cognitive processes that individuals engage in while diagnosing a case. There are different types of knowledge representations that are part of the overall problem-solving task. For instance, there is declarative knowledge (factual knowledge pertaining to a particular disease), conceptual knowledge (what one understands), and procedural knowledge (knowledge of what procedures or skills are necessary to test hypotheses and reach a final diagnosis). The overall cognitive model encompasses all of these competencies including contextual knowledge (knowing when to use and apply knowledge) and meta-knowledge (knowing what one knows or does not know). Given that effective problem solving requires the ability to orchestrate various types of knowledge and skills in specific contexts, it is important to study knowledge in situ.

In constructing a cognitive model of diagnostic reasoning, we start with selecting a task or case that represents the complexity of the domain. As in any cognitive task analysis, working with subject matter experts in identifying difficult and significant problems to solve is crucial. Experts help us construct a task that parallels what they do in the real world. We then examine how individuals with varying levels of expertise perform. At one end of the spectrum, we study how experts solve such problems to get a sense of their plans, mental models, and strategies that guide their performance. In establishing expert benchmarks, we can see how novices or intermediates vary in their knowledge or the misconceptions that exist. Documenting such problem spaces provides ideas of how we might tutor individuals in their problem-solving and decision-making strategies. Models of expertise can assist us in determining what to monitor, how to assess, and where to scaffold learners to help them become independently proficient in their chosen fields (Lajoie, 2003).

Using Cognitive Models in the Design of Computer-Based Learning Environments

Developing computer-based learning environments from cognitive task analyses can validate performance models by demonstrating that learning does occur in the predicted manner, and that providing feedback based on such performance models can lead to greater proficiency. As with Sherlock, a cognitive apprenticeship model was used to design BioWorld, a computer-based learning environment that was designed to promote scientific reasoning in high school students. BioWorld provides students with a realistic environment to learn about diseases through solving specific patient cases (Lajoie, Lavigne, Guerrera, & Munsie, 2001). This environment is currently being redesigned for medical students. The cognitive apprenticeship model speaks to situating learning in contexts where students use their knowledge and where instruction and assessment are interwoven. Instructional methods are based on modeling, coaching, and fading assistance when help is no longer needed. In BioWorld, students are provided with a way to learn about diseases

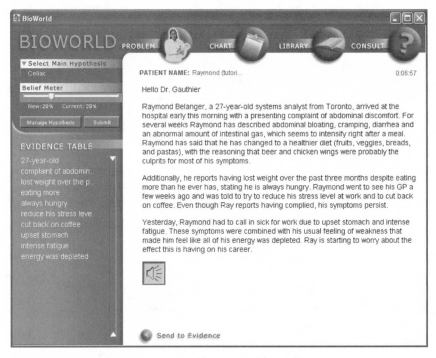

FIGURE 3.2. The BioWorld interface.

by solving patient cases. In determining what to model, we asked medical experts to solve the patient cases designed for BioWorld, in an attempt to get a robust expert model of problem solving for each case. By identifying what experts know, we developed assessment genres for examining transitions in learning in novice performers. Expert problem-solving traces were monitored and collected dynamically, as were verbal protocols. These data determined the unique profiles of experts in terms of plans, strategies, and actions within BioWorld, demonstrating different clusters of competencies that served to establish benchmarks of performance (Lajoie, Greer, Munsie, Wilkie, Guerrera, & Aleong, 1995).

Just as Sherlock had a valid work environment simulation, BioWorld simulates the medical environment (Figure 3.2). Learners read a patient case and can enter and revise their hypotheses and confidence levels at any point in the problem-solving exercise. Collecting patient histories is an essential part of diagnostic reasoning, which consists of knowing what information is pertinent to making an accurate diagnosis. BioWorld supports this task by allowing students to collect relevant information from the case history and store it in an evidence palette for future reference. In essence, the evidence palette provides a mechanism for learners to monitor what they thought was important to the solution process. Metacognition and reflection on the problem-solving processes is supported at the completion of the problem as well. Students can compare their prioritized list of evidence to that of an expert. Background knowledge about a specific disease also plays a role in problem solving; hence, to support learners with varying levels of declarative knowledge, an on-line library can be accessed that provides information on diseases and diagnostic tests. In addition to having a hypothesis about a disease, the learner must test to see whether the hypothesis is valid or invalid. Diagnostic tests help confirm or rule out specific diseases and BioWorld provides the platform for these diagnostic tests by allowing the student to write an order on the patient's chart. The consult button was designed to model expertise in the form of feedback. Finally, reflection on problem-solving processes was supported at the completion of a problem where students looked at their evidence and compared it to an expert's prioritized evidence list.

Dynamic assessment is a critical element in moving students forward toward competence. BioWorld currently supports learners in the context of problem solving but there is more research to be done on learning trajectories. We have started to use BioWorld cases with different cohorts in an effort to document specific learning trajectories for diagnostic reasoning along a learning continuum (high school, medical students, residents, and physicians). In particular, we are examining the types of data collected, the types of hypotheses formed, and the differences in planning when individuals view case history information, conduct physical exams, and order diagnostic tests. In analyzing the cognitive processes involved in diagnostic reasoning, it is possible to represent the knowledge levels and qualitative differences in argumentation and reasoning patterns for high school and undergraduate cohorts. Our goal is to document the transitions in learning processes across age groups, providing some evidence of how knowledge evolves in this domain. Our pattern analysis reveals definite cohort differences. High school students needed more scaffolding of basic knowledge, connecting hypothesis generation to case history information with the information they collected through on-line library searches and diagnostic testing. Novice and intermediate-level medical personnel had some proficiency in terms of linking domain knowledge to diagnostic hypotheses, but their planning about how to proceed with a case (e.g., linking hypotheses to actions) was minimal when compared to medical experts (Faremo, 2004). We concluded that they would probably benefit from assistance in working with hypotheses to develop diagnostic plans. Even when medical students identified some of the same information as experts as relevant, they did not engage in the same systematic planning and evidence evaluation as experts. This type of in-depth analysis of diagnostic reasoning across cohorts can eventually lead to robust models of problem solving that can extend the use of BioWorld to higher education classrooms and complete the picture of emerging expertise in this domain.

In terms of using BioWorld to adapt to individual differences, we are currently exploring ways in which individuals can interact with their own

knowledge representations as a way to validate their problem-solving processes, as well as compare their thinking with that of experts (Gauthier, in
preparation; Gauthier & Lajoie, 2007; Lajoie, Gauthier, & Richard, 2007). This
tool will support the individuals in their metacognitive ability as well as foster
change in their own thinking. Our intent is to demonstrate that enhancing
metacognitive ability by promoting the bi-directionality of internal to external
representations will lead to deeper understanding.

LESSONS LEARNED AND FUTURE DIRECTIONS

Numerous professional domains complain that graduates are not prepared for
the workforce. One's performance at work is not necessarily proportional to
one's previous performance at school. Often, individuals have difficulty in applying (or transferring) the knowledge they acquired in school to the situations (or
problems) they encounter in their jobs. The examples from avionics and medicine presented in this chapter illustrate how computer systems can better train
individuals for their chosen professions. Part of this success is due to the nature
of their training when it is based on a cognitive apprenticeship framework. This
framework helps researchers and designers consider issues pertaining to the
content knowledge (what to teach), the method of instruction (how to teach,
model, scaffold, fade, etc.), the sequencing of instruction, and the sociology of
learning. This framework is supported by cognitive task analyses that are used
to develop the appropriate models of proficiency. Without the appropriate models, it is difficult to determine what to instruct and what to assess. Integrating
instruction and assessment around representative tasks is the key principle in
making learning effective and ultimately improving performance.

Technology-rich environments can be designed to dynamically assess
learning in the context of real-world situations. The learning environments
described in this chapter provide examples of different proficiency assessments, in particular, assessing differences in knowledge structuring, procedural efficiency on domain specific tasks, accessing relevant declarative
information through on-line resources, and depth of metacognitive awareness
in the problem-solving processes.

In conclusion, I see a balance between the contributions and limitations of
the cognitive apprenticeship approach for developing professional competence.
On the positive side, the approach works and can result in enormous training
savings when one considers that a system such as Sherlock can reduce training by years, not days, and result in proficient professionals. Furthermore, the
approach is generalizable, as demonstrated in the work with BioWorld in science and medicine, and with the cognitive apprenticeships in reading, writing,
and arithmetic (as described by Collins et al., 1989), and in medicine and law
(Williams, 1992). The possibilities for extending this approach to other professional domains are endless. In fact after presenting my work in this area, I have

been approached by colleagues in engineering, dentistry, nursing, veterinary schools, mental health, and management. Government agencies as well as pharmaceutical companies and industry have also approached me about training. Needless to say I could not say yes to each request but I could definitely see the possibilities of using this approach in these domains.

Although cognitive apprenticeship approaches are generalizable, well-structured domains are easier to model than ill-structured domains. For example, using a space-splitting heuristic, avionics technicians were able to use a diagnostic test to rule out problems in half of the test station. Unfortunately, one medical diagnostic test cannot rule out the diseases in half of the human body. Thus, the difficulty level increases when developing a cognitive apprenticeship model for ill-structured professional tasks. The difficulty level is also influenced by the nature of the knowledge itself. In particular, is the knowledge fixed or flexible? In electronics, for example the rules are somewhat fixed, that is, ohms, voltages, etc., do not change their definition. However, medical knowledge is dynamic; new discoveries and changing methodologies are announced each day. In the latter case, more investment must be made in maintaining and updating training systems where knowledge is constantly evolving. Another consideration is the complexity of the professional environment itself. Some professional domains are more complex than others. In both the avionics and medical examples provided herein, there is a great deal of equipment that needs to be modeled or simulated, since trainees must attend to information when acting on information. Part of the complexity of the environment entails the sociology of the environment. For instance, does the domain require team approaches to problem solving or independence?

In conclusion, a fine balance exists between the contributions and limitations of the cognitive apprenticeship approach for enhancing professional competence. If one has both the financial and manpower resources, then the payoffs are high. In order to achieve this payoff, there are several things to consider: the complexity of the domain in terms of what needs to be modeled in the environment besides expertise, the type of knowledge being modeled (well-structured being easier than ill-structured problems), who is being modeled (an individual or team of individuals), and how to model activities in an authentic manner.

Much of the complexity of cognitive task analyses and verbal protocol analyses are due to the qualitative coding procedures that are designed and applied to the protocols. A future action point is to develop methods that can serve to semi-automate coding procedures to facilitate the assessment of different levels of proficiency over time. Given that dimensions of proficiency exist across domains, the identification of core coding routines may help to craft more global schemes to assist in coding domain-specific expertise. Once such templates are constructed, technology could be used to better track emerging competence. A specific template can be seen in Sherlock, where a human expert helped create scoring rubrics that demonstrated different depths of expert-like performance. Individual learners' problem-solving trace files were then coded for such expert-like performance and changes in their performance were examined at different times during practice with Sherlock. Similarly, scoring rubrics are being designed to assess proficiency differences in diagnostic reasoning to assist in the automation of such important assessments (Gauthier & Lajoie, 2007; Lajoie, Gauthier, & Richard, 2007). If technology could later incorporate production rules based on such proficiency rubrics, it would be easier to monitor and assess trainee performance, and assessing professional competence would become more efficient and more effective.

Once the work in developing sophisticated systems for professional domains is expended, maintaining and altering such systems with new problems or cases to solve needs to become more seamless. Authoring tools can be developed to involve subject matter experts, trainers, and instructors in the process of designing new test beds of problems. Chatham (this volume) adds a further dimension to authoring, including students and trainees in developing cases for others to solve based on their own personal experiences. Given the rapid changes that professional communities face daily, it is important to involve the trainees in the training, since their experience in the field may be quite different than what was current prior to developing the training system.

In closing, cognitive apprenticeship models can be used to support the development of professional competence. Using a theory-driven approach to professional training can lead to effective technology-rich environments that result in better-trained individuals.

REFERENCES

Alexander, P. A. (2003). Development of expertise: The journey from acclimation to proficiency. *Educational Researcher, 32*(8), 10–14.

Alexander, P. A., Murphy, P. K., & Kulikowich, J. M. (2009). Expertise and the adult learner: A historical, psychological, and methodological exploration. In M. C. Smith & N. DeFrates-Densch (Eds.), *The handbook of research on adult learning and development* (pp. 484–523). New York: Routledge.

Barrow, H. S. (1988). *The tutorial process.* Springfield: Southern Illinois University Press.

Bransford, J. D., Brown, A. L., & Cocking, R. R. (1999). *How people learn: Brain, mind, experience, and school.* Washington, DC: National Academy Press.

Chi, M. T. H. (1997). Quantifying qualitative analyses of verbal data: A practical guide. *The Journal of the Learning Sciences, 6*(3), 271–315.

Chi, M. T. H., Glaser, R., & Farr, M. (1988). *The nature of expertise* (pp. xv–xxxvi). Hillsdale, NJ: Lawrence Erlbaum Associates.

Collins, A., Brown, J. S., & Newman, S. E. (1989). Cognitive apprenticeship: Teaching the craft of reading, writing, and mathematics. In L. B. Resnick (Ed.), *Knowing, learning, and instruction: Essays in honor of Robert Glaser* (pp. 453–494). Hillsdale, NJ: Lawrence Erlbaum Associates.

Crandall, B., Klein, G., & Hoffman, R. (2006). *Working minds: A practitioner's guide to cognitive task analysis*. Cambridge, MA: MIT Press.

Cronbach, L. J., & Snow, R. E. (1977). *Aptitudes and instructional methods: A handbook for research on interactions*. New York: Irvington.

de Groot, A. D. (1946). *Het denken van den schaker [Thought and choice in chess]*. Amsterdam: North-Holland.

Ericsson, K. A. (2002). Attaining excellence through deliberate practice: Insights from the study of expert performance. In M. Ferrari (Ed.), *The pursuit of excellence in education* (pp. 21–55). Hillsdale, NJ: Lawrence Erlbaum Associates.

Ericsson, K. A., Krampe, R. Th., & Tesch-Römer, C. (1993). The role of deliberate practice in the acquisition of expert performance. *Psychological Review, 100*(3), 363–406.

Ericsson, K. A., & Simon, H. A. (1993). *Protocol analysis: Verbal reports as data*. Cambridge, MA: MIT Press.

Ernst, G. W., & Newell, A. (1969). *GPS: A case study in generality and problem solving*. New York: Academic Press.

Faremo, S. (2004). *Problem solving and post-problem reflection in BioWorld*. Unpublished doctoral dissertation, McGill University, Montreal, Canada.

Gauthier, G. (in preparation). *Visualization and validation of expert teachers solution process in ill-defined problem solving*. Unpublished doctoral dissertation, McGill University, Montreal, Canada.

Gauthier, G., & Lajoie, S. P. (2007, April). *Using multi-layered decision trees in the context of diagnostic reasoning*. Paper presented at the annual conference of the American Educational Research Association, Chicago, Illinois.

Gitomer, D. H. (1984). *A cognitive analysis of a complex troubleshooting task*. Unpublished doctoral dissertation. Pittsburgh, PA: University of Pittsburgh.

Glaser, R., Lesgold, A., & Lajoie, S. P. (1987). Toward a cognitive theory for the measurement of achievement. In R. Ronning, J. Glover, J. C. Conoley, & J. C. Witt (Eds.), *Nebraska Symposium on Measurement: Vol. 3. The Influence of Cognitive Psychology on Testing* (pp. 41–85). Hillsdale, NJ: Lawrence Erlbaum Associates.

Hatano, G., & Oura, Y. (2003). Commentary: Reonceptualizing school learning using insight from expertise research. *Educational Researcher, 32*(8), 26–29.

Hmelo-Silver, C. E. (2003). *Facilitating collaborative knowledge construction*. Paper presented at the 36th Annual Hawaii International Conference on System Sciences (HICSS'03), Big Island, Hawaii.

Holyoak, K. J. (1991). Symbolic connectionism: Toward third-generation theories of expertise. In K. A. Ericsson, & J. Smith (Eds.), *Toward a general theory of expertise: Prospects and limits* (pp. 301–335). Cambridge, UK: Cambridge University Press.

Lajoie, S. P. (2007). Developing computer based learning environments based on complex performance models. In B. Shuart, W. Spaulding & J. Poland (Eds.), *Nebraska Symposium on Motivation. Modeling complex systems: Vol. 52* (pp. 123–144) Lincoln: University of Nebraska Press.

(2003). Transitions and trajectories for studies of expertise. *Educational Researcher, 32*(8), 21–25.

Lajoie, S. P., Gauthier, G., & Richard, S. (2007). *Computer tools to support medical problem solving*. Presented at the European Association for Research on Learning and Instruction conference. Budapest, Hungary.

Lajoie, S. P., Greer, J. E., Munsie, S. D., Wilkie, T. V., Guerrera. C., & Aleong, P. (1995). Establishing an argumentation environment to foster scientific reasoning with BioWorld. In D. Jonassen & G. McCalla (Eds.), *Proceedings of the International*

Conference on Computers in Education (pp. 89–96). Charlottesville, VA: Association for the Advancement of Computing in Education.

Lajoie, S. P., Lavigne, N. C., Guerrera, C., & Munsie, S. (2001). Constructing knowledge in the context of BioWorld. *Instructional Science, 29*(2), 155–186.

Lajoie, S. P., & Lesgold, A. (1992a). Apprenticeship training in the workplace: A computer-coached practice environment as a new form of apprenticeship. In M. Farr & J. Psotka (Eds.), *Intelligent instruction by computer: Theory and practice* (pp. 15–36). New York: Taylor & Francis.

(1992b). Dynamic assessment of proficiency for solving procedural knowledge tasks. *Educational Psychologist, 27*(3), 365–384.

Larkin, J. H., McDermott, J., Simon, D. P., & Simon, H. A. (1980). Expert and novice performance in solving physics problems. *Science, 208*, 1335–1342.

Lave, J., & Wenger, E. (Eds.). (1991). *Situated learning: Legitimate peripheral participation*. Cambridge, UK: Cambridge University Press.

Lesgold, A., Lajoie, S. P., Bajpayee, J., Bunzo, M., Eastman, R., Eggan, G., et al. (1988). *A computer coached practice environment for the manual test station shop: Sherlock's influence on trainee job performance* (contract no. F33615–84-c-0058). Alexandria, VA: Human Resources Research Organization.

Lesgold, A., Lajoie, S. P., Bunzo, M., & Eggan, G. (1992). SHERLOCK: A coached practice environment for an electronics troubleshooting job. In J. H. Larkin & R. W. Chabay (Eds.), *Computer assisted instruction and intelligent tutoring systems: Shared goals and complementary approaches* (pp. 201–238). Hillsdale, NJ: Lawrence Erlbaum Associates.

Lesgold, A., Lajoie, S. P., Eastman, R., Eggan, G., Gitomer, D., Glaser, R., et al. (1986). *Cognitive task analysis to enhance technical skills training and assessment*. Technical Report. University of Pittsburgh, the Learning Research and Development Center. April, 1986.

Lesgold, A., Lajoie, S. P., Logan, D., & Eggan, G. M. (1990). Cognitive task analysis approaches to testing. In N. Frederiksen, R. Glaser, A. Lesgold, & M. Shafto (Eds.), *Diagnostic monitoring of skill and knowledge acquisition* (pp. 325–350). Hillsdale, NJ: Lawrence Erlbaum Associates.

Nichols, P., Pokorny, R., Jones, G., Gott, S. P., & Alley, W. E. (in press). *Evaluation of an avionics troubleshooting tutoring system*. Technical Report, Armstrong Laboratory, Human Resources Directorate, Brooks AFB, TX.

Palinscar, A. S., & Brown, A. L. (1984). Reciprocal teaching of comprehension-fostering and monitoring activities. *Cognition and Instruction, 1*, 117–175.

Patel, V. L, Arocha, J. F, & Kaufman, D. R. (1999). Medical cognition. In F. T. Durso (Ed.), *Handbook of applied cognition* (pp. 663–693). Hoboken, NJ: Wiley.

Patel, V. L., & Groen, G. (1991). The general and specific nature of medical expertise: A critical look. In K. A. Ericsson & J. Smith (Eds.), *Towards a general theory of expertise: Prospects and limits* (pp. 93–125). New York: Cambridge University Press.

Pellegrino, J., Chudowsky, N., & Glaser, R. (2001). *Knowing what students know*. National Academy of Science.

Scardamalia, M., & Bereiter, C. (1985). Fostering the development of self-regulation in children's knowledge processing. In S. F. Chipman, J. W. Segal, & R. Glaser (Eds.), *Thinking and learning skills: Research and open questions* (pp. 563–577). Hillsdale, NJ: Lawrence Erlbaum Associates.

Schoenfeld, A. H. (1985). *Mathematical problem solving*. New York: Academic Press.

Schraagen, J. M., Chipman, S. F., & Shalin, V. L. (2000). *Cognitive task analysis*. Mahwah, NJ: Lawrence Erlbaum Associates.

Vygotsky, L. S. (1978). *Mind in society.* Cambridge, MA: Harvard University Press.

Whitehead, A. N. (1929). *The aims of education and other essays.* New York: Macmillan Press.

Williams, S. M. (1992). Putting case-based instruction into context: Examples from legal and medical education. *The Journal of the Learning Sciences, 2,* 367–427.

4

Leadership Development and Assessment: Describing and Rethinking the State of the Art

MICHAEL D. MUMFORD, TAMARA L. FRIEDRICH,
JAY J. CAUGHRON, AND ALISON L. ANTES

When one mentions the word "professional," images come to mind of lone doctors or lawyers pursuing their practice as they see it. Romantic as this image may be, in the 21st century professionals typically practice in an organizational setting (Mumford, Scott, Gaddis, & Strange, 2002). In these settings, leadership of the organization is a critical influence on the productivity of professionals (West, Borrill, Dawson, Brodbeck, Shapiro, & Haward, 2003). This rather straightforward observation has an important, albeit often overlooked, implication. To ensure the productivity of professionals, one must also ensure that they are *led* effectively.

Over the course of the last century the study of leader effectiveness has come to preoccupy, if not obsess, the social sciences (Bass, in press; Yukl, 2002). Broadly speaking, this research has given rise to two major approaches that have sought to enhance performance of those who lead other professionals. More specifically, one might 1) select to employ effective leaders or 2) seek to train or develop current employees into effective leaders (Bray & Howard, 1988; Day, 2000). These two approaches implicitly assume that differences in leadership performance can be measured objectively in terms of the output of the group or system. Over the years, a host of techniques have been proposed for leader development and leader assessment – techniques ranging from assessment centers (Byham & Thornton, 1986) to classroom instruction (Fiedler, 1996) to real-world experience (McCauley, Ruderman, Ohlott, & Morrow, 1994). It is evident in two meta-analyses (Burke & Day, 1986; Collins & Holton, 2004), however, that, although on the whole these leader interventions appear beneficial to leader performance, they have rarely been validated by objective measurements of system performance. Additionally, only a small number of studies that were part of these meta-analyses included measures of

Acknowledgments: We thank Sam Hunter and Katrina Bedell for their contributions to the present effort. Correspondence should be addressed to Dr. Michael D. Mumford, Department of Psychology, The University of Oklahoma, Norman, Oklahoma 73019 or mmumford@ou.edu.

objective performance and evaluated the productivity of the supervised units; these studies had equivocal results.

The majority of studies evaluating leadership training has instead focused on measurement of increases in knowledge and perceived expertise by their employees and their supervisors. If one looks at the literature on leader development, one finds techniques being employed that range from network creation (Ragins & Cotton, 1999) to action learning (Senge, 1990). Training programs may seek to enhance the decision-making process (Vroom & Yetton, 1973), or seek to develop self-awareness and self-integration (Shamir & Eilam, 2005). Leader assessment might focus on social intelligence (Connelly, Gilbert, Zaccaro, Threlfall, Marks, & Mumford, 2000) or, alternatively, tacit knowledge (Hedlund, Forsythe, Horvath, Williams, Snook, & Sternberg, 2003).

The diversity of these programs and their lack of objective validation points to the fundamental problem confronting those of us interested in measurement of leader development and assessment. Consequently, there is not a coherent framework to guide the construction of effective leader development and assessment programs. Accordingly, in this chapter we will begin by describing the nature of superior leader behavior. Based on our analysis we will present an integrative model of leader behavior that stresses the fundamental importance of leader thought. We will then consider some of the implications of this model of leader thought for the development and assessment of leaders.

WHAT DO LEADERS DO?

Leader Behavior

To formulate a general model of leader behavior one must first have an understanding of exactly what it is that superior leaders must be able to do. Over the years, the behavior of leaders has been defined in different ways by different investigators (Fleishman, Mumford, Zaccaro, Levin, Korotkin, & Hein, 1991; Yukl, 2002). Although, broadly speaking, leadership is thought to involve the exercise of social influence, influence may be exerted in a number of ways. Thus, Mintzberg (1973) describes leadership of organizations as involving many different kinds of activities, such as dissemination and monitoring of information, negotiating and monitoring of resources, among other dimensions. Tornow and Pinto (1976) argued that managerial roles involve supervising, planning, decision making, controlling, representing, coordinating, consulting, and administering. Clearly, even in the one domain of organizational leadership, a variety of roles or behaviors have been proposed to attain effective exercise of influence.

An alternate approach that intended to define what superior leaders are able to do identifies the conditions under which the actions of leaders make a difference for their organization (Hunt, Boal, & Dodge, 1999; Mumford, Zaccaro,

Harding, Jacobs, & Fleishman, 2000). In one study along these lines, Mumford and his colleagues (Connelly et al., 2000; Mumford, Marks, Connelly, Zaccaro, & Reiter-Palmon, 2000; Zaccaro, Mumford, Connelly, Marks, & Gilbert, 2000) proposed that the actions of leaders make a difference when the organization, or social system, is confronting complex, ill-defined problems. They argued that the leadership would depend on both creative problem-solving skills, such as problem construction, information gathering, conceptual combination, and idea evaluation; social judgment skills, such as reflection, objectivity, and solution fit; and expertise, as reflected in the complexity and organization of relevant knowledge structures.

A similar logic was at the core of a study by Hunt et al. (1999), which examined charismatic, or visionary, leadership. They proposed that a crisis, as opposed to a no crisis condition, resulted in visionary leaders being perceived as more effective than other leader types. Other studies by Bligh, Kohles, and Meindl (2004) and Halverson, Holladay, Kazma, and Quinones (2004) also point to the importance of leadership under conditions of crisis or change.

If leadership makes a difference in social systems undergoing novel crises or change events, then skills underlying intelligence (Lord, DeVader, & Alliger, 1986) and creative thinking (Connelly et al., 2000) may contribute to individual differences in leader performance. By the same token, however, the Connelly et al. (2000) study reminds us of another point. The nature of the social system operating in organizations and the conditions giving rise to a crisis or change event must be considered in any examination of leader performance.

Organizations, and leaders as the occupants of formal or informal roles in the organization, operate in a distinctly social setting. The necessary social skills of leaders may be quite complex, involving communication skills (Emrich, Brower, Feldman, & Garland, 2001; Fiol, Harris, & House, 1999), interaction skills, such as individualized consideration (Mumford, Dansereau, & Yammarino, 2000), and political skills (Treadway, Hochwater, Ferris, Kacmar, Douglas, Ammeter, & Buckley, 2004).

In any complex social system, problems cannot be addressed solely by a leader acting alone. Consequently, a leader must work together with other individuals by creating a context that motivates the efforts of other individuals. Leaders, moreover, may create the conditions that induce intrinsic motivation in others – for example, by articulating followers' sense of self-identity (Shamir, House, & Arthur, 1993).

Measurement

The most common method of describing individual differences in leadership involves subjective ratings conducted by superiors or subordinates. Ratings by supervisors or subordinates are error prone and may be biased by differing perspectives and ultimate goals of the stakeholders. To illustrate, a superior may be more concerned with task accomplishment and will focus more on task-related behaviors, whereas a subordinate may be more focused on consideration or distribution of responsibilities (Salam, Cox, & Sims, 1997). Evaluation from multiple perspectives, however, may provide a more global picture of a leader's strengths and weaknesses (Tornow, 1993). The 360-degree performance rating method is the most well-known way of conducting such evaluations (Alimo-Metcalfe, 1998; Brett & Atwater, 2001; Conway & Huffcutt, 1997; Tornow & London, 1998). This method involves not only subordinate and supervisor ratings of performance, but also peer ratings and the leader's rating of him- or herself. Salam, Cox, and Sims (1997) found that ratings do, in fact, differ depending on who is doing the rating; however, this may actually provide added diagnostic value with regard to the target leader's performance.

Another individual level measurement method for leadership performance has been rate of advancement (Bray, Campbell, & Grant, 1974). This measure is likely to have been primarily based on subjective evaluations for the purpose of promotion.

These subjective perceptions of leader behaviors do not provide objective measures of the effects of leaders on the performance of their units. Objective measures of leader performance are typically more difficult to obtain and must measure the performance of the group or organization. The nature of leadership is to motivate *others* to accomplish goals that in turn can ultimately be measured. Work done by Riggio, Riggio, Salinas, and Cole (2003) included the evaluation of leadership behaviors and group performance, and demonstrated the disparities found between subjective and objective performance measures, particularly across different types of tasks.

Specifically, Riggio, Riggio, Salinas, and Cole (2003) conducted one study that evaluated leaders and their groups working on two tasks – ranking items needed on a deserted island, and an assembly task. Leader effectiveness was assessed by ratings of relationship-oriented behaviors (e.g., does the leader establish rapport with group members?) and task-oriented behaviors (e.g., does the leader delegate responsibility?); objective group production (e.g., number of correctly assembled components); and team member assessments of the leaders using the leadership behavior description questionnaire (LBDQ), a survey requiring followers to indicate the degree to which leaders engage in different person-focused and task-focused behaviors. Leaders that had more social skills were rated by subordinates as more effective, particularly in the deserted island task, a task that requires more discussion. There were no differences found, however, in objective group performance. As this study demonstrates, there are often differences between subjective ratings of leaders, usually by subordinates, and objective measures of performance.

Group level measures tend to focus on observable outcomes that are relatively easy to measure (e.g., changes in productivity). On the other hand, individual differences in leader behaviors that cause these differences in outcomes are likely to be mediated by less-visible specific cognitive processes, such as knowledge or skills. Given that it would be very difficult to study the leaders' thought processes and behaviors during weeks and months of interactions with subordinates during the real-world operations, relatively new developments have identified methods to study leaders in the laboratory. The second approach applied in leader assessment is based on a low-fidelity simulation strategy (Motowidlo, Dunnette, & Carter, 1990). One variant on this approach, a situational judgment strategy, presents a series of decision-making tasks likely to be encountered by leaders. Assessment is based on the viability of the decision options selected. The other variant on this approach may be found in assessment centers (Bray & Howard, 1988). In assessment centers, leaders typically complete a battery of standard psychological tests and then are asked to work on three to seven simulation exercises, such as an "in-basket" or a leaderless group discussion, where leaders' performance on these exercises is assessed by judges with respect to dimensions such as judgment, decision making, and participation.

Both situational judgment tests and assessment center ratings have proven to be valid predictors of ratings of performance for a wide range of jobs, including managerial positions. A recent meta-analysis by McDaniel, Hartman, Whetzel, and Grubb (2007) demonstrated that situational judgment tests consistently contributed incremental validity beyond general intelligence and personality in predictions of performance. Additionally, another recent meta-analysis conducted by Arthur, Day, McNelly, and Edens (2003) demonstrated the criterion-related validity of assessment center dimensions (e.g., communication, organization, and planning). Specifically, the authors found that four general assessment dimensions – problem solving, influencing others, organizing and planning, and communication – explained 20 percent of the variance in measures of supervisors' ratings of performance. Again, however, no information is provided with regard to thought processes of managers and leaders.

These observations regarding leader assessment point to the critical problem confronting those of us interested in the topic. Virtually all strategies used to assess leadership view leadership as a performance – often, although not always, as an undifferentiated performance. Moreover, none of these strategies provides assessment of the specific constructs held to underlie leader thought. Because both leader assessment and the evaluation of training programs intended to improve leader thought (Goldstein & Ford, 2002) require assessments of specific components of leader thought, we will, in this section, examine the implications of our model of leader thought with respect to both knowledge and process-based assessments.

Researchers of leader assessment and development are faced with a problem. Should they search for cases where individual differences among leaders lead to reliable differences in objective performance of their respective groups or organizations? Or should they develop measures of individual differences of leaders and then go out to find correlates of these differences in objective measures of performance? Given the lack of research finding generalizable differences in leader characteristics with large reproducible differences in objective performance of their units or groups, we have decided to study individual differences in leaders' thought processes. We will propose a model and then discuss the empirical evidence related to that model.

MODEL OF INDIVIDUAL DIFFERENCES OF LEADERS' THINKING

According to our model, leadership is reflected in the identification of potential influence attempts. In this section we will examine the knowledge structures and processes that allow leaders to identify viable influence strategies in identifying and responding to change events.

Knowledge Structures

All people, including leaders, have and apply multiple alternative knowledge structures as they work through their day-to-day tasks. Knowledge comes in several forms such as schematic (Holyoak & Thagard, 1997), associational (Estes, 1991), and case based (Kolodner, 1997). The type of knowledge being applied, of course, influences how people work with this knowledge in generating actions. Of the knowledge structures that might be applied in identifying and resolving the issues arising from change events, it seems likely that leaders' thinking, more often than not, rely on case-based knowledge.

Most of the work supporting these ideas are based on presenting undergraduates with management tasks. For example, in one recent study, Scott et al. (2005) asked undergraduates to assume the role of principal (the leader) of a new experimental high school. These undergraduates were asked to formulate a new curriculum for the high school, where curriculum plans were evaluated for quality and originality. As students worked through this problem they were given instructions intended to encourage the application of effective strategies for working with case-based knowledge – specifically, identify critical case features, list the strengths and weaknesses of the case, forecast the outcomes of case implementation, and revise. It was found that the effective application of these strategies was strongly related to the quality and originality of solutions obtained to the leadership problem. Other work by Berger and Jordan (1992) and Strange and Mumford (2005) has shown that case-based knowledge also underlies the formation of influence attempts and the creation of leader vision statements. Moreover, it appears that, when confronted with crises, people are especially likely to apply case-based knowledge as a basis for understanding and coping with the implications of a change event (Bluck & Staudinger, 2000; Pillemer, 1998; Taylor & Schneider, 1984).

Case-based, or autobiographical, knowledge is commonly thought to be organized in a "library" system (Bluck & Habermas, 2001). These case libraries are held to include prototypic case exemplars along with cases that represent significant variations on this prototype. These variations may be organized on a number of bases including situation, time, affect, key contingencies, and restrictions. Generally, however, case-based knowledge, as it is applied by leaders, tends to be organized around critical causes influencing the attainment of select goals. In keeping with this proposition, Marcy and Mumford (in press) have shown that training people in the analysis of causes, for example identifying causes that have large effects or that have direct effects, improves the quality and originality of solutions to leadership problems.

In fact, a variety of evidence accrued in studies of managerial cognition suggests this cause–goal organization of case-based knowledge, as bounded by the situation, provides an underlying structure guiding the thinking of leaders. For example, Calori, Johnson, and Sarnin (1992) conducted a content analysis of 20 chief executives' responses to interview questions about their operating environment. They found that leaders organized their understanding of the organization's operations in the form of a set of cause–goal linkages organized into a mental model (Johnson-Laird, 1983). Similar findings have been obtained by Barr, Stimpert, and Huff (1992), and Cossette and Audet (1992). The content of these mental models, moreover, appears to depend on both the functional experience of the leader and the nature of the problem being addressed (Daniels, Johnson, & deChernatony, 1994; Frankwick, Walker, & Ward, 1994).

Processes

Application of mental models and case-based knowledge by leaders in identifying and resolving change events depends, of course, on how leaders work with relevant information. Figure 4.1 provides an overview of the processes by which leaders work with mental models and case-based knowledge in formulating influence attempts. In this model, it is assumed that ongoing scanning of both the internal and external environment by leaders gives rise to the identification of potential change events. In fact, the available evidence indicates that the intensity of scanning activities, especially external scanning, is related to leader performance (Keisler & Sproull, 1982; Lant & Milliken, 1992; March & Olsen, 1976).

Here, however, what should be noted is that scanning of the internal and external environment is not unconstrained. Both the internal and external

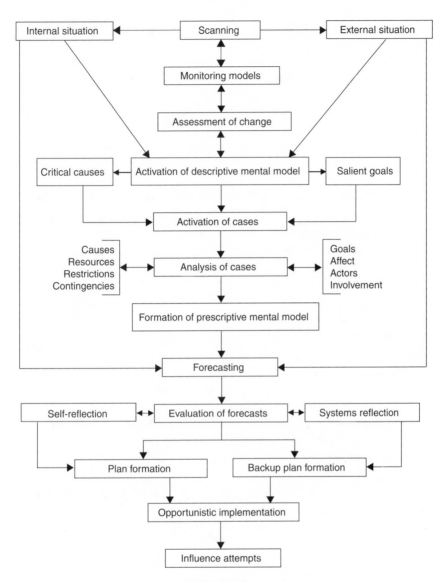

FIGURE 4.1. Model of leader cognition.

environments provide a wide array of information – information that is often costly to gather. As a result, leaders selectively seek certain types of information in scanning, basing their search activities on monitoring models abstracted from prior experience. These monitoring models will call attention to certain sources of information bearing on central issues – especially those issues relevant to threats and opportunities. Leaders, in scanning, will typically attend more to outcome relevant information due to its salience. Nonetheless, leaders will also attend to familiar, frequently encountered information, especially information of high visibility in the social network of the leader (Mitra, 2000).

Based on these scanning activities, leaders will identify anomalies – potential disruptions in current operations (Kiesler & Sproull, 1982). The significance of an anomaly as a potential change event, however, arises from the interpretation the leader places on the anomaly. Typically, an anomaly will be treated as a change event if it implies a change in the status of the leader's descriptive mental model of the social system given the internal and external events under consideration. Thus, change events are identified and understood in the context of the leader's understanding of the social system and the nature of its operations. Events that imply either risk (loss) or gain (enhancement) will be those that relieve the attention of leaders. The descriptive mental model applied by leaders will then be used to identify likely causes of the event and salient goals that might be influenced by the event (Dukerich & Nichols, 1991). The abstraction of key causes and goals will then serve to activate relevant cases in the leader's library of cases. Typically, leaders will work with prototypical cases that evidence similar goals and causes within the situation at hand. However, unusual causes or unique potentialities may result in leaders applying a wider range of cases in thinking about the change event.

With activation of a set of cases that might be used to understand the change event, a more detailed and more thorough analysis of these cases will begin. Analysis of activated cases will typically involve a twofold process (Fleishman, 1953; Fleishmann et al., 1991). One part of this process will focus on an objective response to the change event with causes, contingencies, resources, and restrictions all being addressed. The other part of the process will consider socio-emotional aspects of the case including goals, affect, actor roles, and involvement. Subsequent combination and reorganization of these case elements will be used by the leader to formulate a prescriptive mental model for understanding and responding to the change event (Mumford & Strange, 2002).

With regard to this model of leader thought, four critical points should be noted. First, the cases applied in thinking may be garnered either through direct experience or observation. Second, the success of leaders in working through change events will depend – strongly depend – on both the nature and extent of forecasting and the evaluative criteria applied to these forecasts. Third, the formulation of plans does not lock a leader into a set of action steps, but rather planning permits the formation of a range of intentions guiding opportunistic responses to emerging opportunities or blockages (Mumford, 2002). Fourth, and finally, within this model the influence exerted by the leader is embedded in how they make sense of the change events. The leaders exert influence in part through sense-making activities in which they convey their plan and prescriptive mental model to followers (Weick, 1995).

Support for the Model

Although this model indicates that leader thinking is a highly complex phenomenon, it does find some support in the literature. Perhaps the most obvious implication of this model arises from the apparent complexity of leader thought. More specifically, it cannot be expected that people will invest the kind of extended active processing described above to all change events or crises. What may be lost sight of, however, is that cases, once activated, do not always require extensive processing. Instead, leaders may, at times, simply apply the best available case as a basis for plans and actions. In fact, Nutt (1984), in an analysis of managerial decisions, found that leaders frequently apply relevant case models in a wholesale fashion.

Another implication of this model is that leaders, in thinking about influence attempts, will attend to select aspects of the information provided by cases. Some support for this conclusion has been provided by Strange and Mumford (2005). They asked undergraduates to assume the role of principal of a new high school and to prepare a speech to be given to students, parents, and teachers describing their vision for the school. Prior to starting work on these vision statements, participants were exposed, through a consultant's report, to either good (successful) or bad (unsuccessful) cases where they were asked to analyze either goals or causes. It was found that analysis of goals and causes contributed to the production of stronger vision statements.

Studies of real-world leaders also tend to provide support for this model. For example, Thomas and McDaniel (1990) conducted a survey study of corporate executives who were asked to describe the basis for their decisions. It was found that, in formulating decisions, executives typically focused on a limited number of key controllable causes. In another study along these lines, Isenberg (1986) contrasted experienced and novice managers. He found that experienced managers, in contrast to novices, tended to formulate simpler plans; however, their plans tended to be built around a limited set of critical causes.

In a qualitative study of leadership activities occurring during the development of a new airplane, Drazin, Glynn, and Kazanjian (1999) found, in accordance with this model, that leadership emerged in crisis or change events. However, the impact of the leader on crisis resolution seemed as closely linked to sense-making, the formation of a prescriptive mental model for understanding the crisis, as the leader's actual influence attempts. In fact, leaders often exercised influence by framing influence attempts around the prescriptive mental model used in sense-making.

Taken as a whole these experimental and field studies indicate that the model of leader thought presented above is, in fact, plausible. Indeed, evidence bearing on the plausibility of this model is available from studies examining errors in leader performance. For example, leaders have been shown to err either by applying the wrong cases in thinking about a crisis (Finkelstein, 2002) or by failing to consider complex, non-linear dependencies among causes and resources (Dorner & Schaub, 1994; Langholtz, Gettys, & Foote, 1995).

Let us now use the model of leader thought as a framework for discussing research on leader assessment and development.

LEADER ASSESSMENT

Attempts to measure leader knowledge have been few and far between. In a study examining knowledge assessment, Mumford and colleagues (Connelly et al., 2000; Mumford, Marks, et al., 2000) presented 70 common leadership tasks to over 2,000 army officers. These leaders were then asked to group these tasks into categories. These task groupings were then assessed with regard to organization, principles, coherence, theoretical correctness, and number. It was found that not only did knowledge increase as a function of experience (e.g., lieutenants versus colonels) but that these knowledge measures were positively related – *strongly* positively related – to various indices of leader performance. A mixture of objective and subjective indices of leader performance was used. The first measure was a self-report of career achievements that could be objectively verified (e.g., medals won). The second was an assessment of the quality and originality of solutions to hypothetical military problems as rated by expert judges, and the third was a self-report of "best performance" examples for four dimensions of leadership behavior that were subsequently rated by expert judges.

Leader knowledge involves descriptive and prescriptive mental models as well as cases. A number of studies have sought to assess leader mental models (e.g., Barr, Stimpert, & Huff, 1992; Frankwick, Walker, & Ward, 1994). Although these mental models have typically been identified through qualitative analysis, it is possible that a more systematic set of procedures might be developed to assess leaders' mental models (Snow & Lohman, 1993). For example, in assessments of descriptive mental models, leaders might be presented with a list of causes and goals. They would then be asked to diagram the relationships among causes and/or the impact of causes on goals. These mental model diagrams might be scored based on fit to either expert mental models or theoretical models. Alternatively, leaders might be presented with an idealized mental model and then asked to answer a series of open- or closed-ended questions about key characteristics of the model. For example, what contingencies would be associated with attempts to influence a given cause? Or, alternatively, if an action was taken on a cause, what would be the likely effects on follower involvement?

Although it seems clear that descriptive mental models can be assessed, the assessment of the prescriptive mental model may be more difficult, in part because prescriptive mental models are local constructions to address a change event. Here, however, viable approaches might involve presentation of a change event and a set of cases that might be used to understand this change event. Leaders could then be presented with a series of questions bearing on the relevance of different cases for addressing the change event. For example, what would be the key resources needed to exercise an influence attempt? A variation of this strategy might ask leaders to identify the weaknesses apparent in presented cases for addressing the change event.

Processes

Is it possible to develop an assessment of the key processes involved in leader thought? In an initial study along these lines, Connelly et al. (2000) presented army leaders with a complex and novel problem scenario. As they worked through the scenario, they were asked to provide short answers to a series of probe questions intended to elicit certain processes; for example, what information would you need to gather (information gathering), or what do you see as the critical problem facing your unit (problem construction). Judges' evaluations of the effectiveness of answers to these probe questions were found to produce correlations of .40 with indices of leader performance with these processing skills showing growth across leaders' careers (Mumford, Marks, et al., 2000). Measures of leader performance included a self-report of verifiable (and thus more objective) career achievements, along with ratings by expert judges of the quality and originality of solutions provided to hypothetical leadership problems.

Other work by Marta, Leritz, and Mumford (2005) has focused on the assessment of one set of leadership processing skills specified in our model of leader thought. Specifically, they sought to develop a measure of leader planning skills. Individual participants were presented with abstracts of a business case and, subsequently, they were presented with five events that might arise in this case where these events reflected different aspects of planning (e.g., opportunistic implementation). Subsequently, participants were asked to select the best 3 response options from 12 options of varying quality with respect to the particular aspect of planning being assessed. The undergraduate study participants then engaged in a group task – a simulated consulting task. Leaders were identified as those individuals that group members indicated, through a series of questions, as the emergent leader. It was found that the planning skills of the emergent leaders, as assessed by their performance on the initial planning measure, were related to subsequent performance in work on the group task – a simulated business task in which the group was asked to serve as a team of consultants hired to solve a hypothetical company's decline in market share.

The Marta et al. (2005) study is, of course, of interest because it suggests that viable measures can be developed to assess planning skills. However, it does seem feasible to develop assessment measures to evaluate most of the other process measures indicated by the model of leader thought under consideration. For example, this model stresses the importance of forecasting. Viable measures of forecasting skills, however, might be developed by presenting a leadership case involving a change event and describing the influence attempts being contemplated by this leader. Those being assessed could be asked to pick, from a list of alternatives, the outcomes most likely to occur as a result of the leader's influence attempt. Indeed, this kind of assessment might be extended to capture common errors in forecasting such as over-optimism.

Along related lines, it seems plausible to develop viable assessments of scanning, evaluation, and analysis. One way scanning skills might be assessed is by asking from what sources a leader typically seeks information and what information is derived from these sources. Scoring of this type of assessment measure might be based either on analysis of experts or a priori theoretical models. Evaluation skills might be appraised by presenting leaders with hypothetical products, of varying quality, produced by followers. Leaders might then be presented with a list of potential criticisms or, alternatively, a list of feedback recommendations. The quality of criticisms and the viability of feedback recommendations selected from this list might be used to assess evaluation skills (Lonergan et al., 2004). Indeed, extensions of this approach – for example, where leaders were asked to identify potential systems implications or potential implications for themselves as a leader – might be used to take into account systems reflection and self-reflection.

Analysis of cases, although a complex topic, is also amenable to assessment. For example, leaders might simply be presented with cases of varying quality and asked to indicate potential problems that might arise from the case. Alternatively, leaders might be presented with two or three cases and asked to identify various elements such as shared critical causes or unique contingencies applying to one case but not to others.

Of course, we do not wish to speak for the validity of either the measures of processing skills described above, or the measures of knowledge we have suggested. Rather, these examples seem sufficient to make a key point. It does, in fact, appear possible to develop viable assessment measures of the knowledge structures and processes held to underlie leader thought. Not only might such measures prove valid but they might provide a basis for assessing the effectiveness of various leader development interventions as a basis for enhancing leader thought.

LEADER DEVELOPMENT

Although the available evidence indicates that leadership development programs produce differences in various indices of knowledge and perceived expertise (Burke & Day, 1986; Collins & Holton, 2004), these programs do not allow detailed assessment of the induced changes. Training of leaders is administered in many different forms. For example, "classroom" training programs may be short courses targeted on training toward a particular model of leadership, or, alternatively, these courses may be far longer sessions, involving substantial real-world experience (Fulmer, 1997; Hamilton & Bean, 2005). Developmental interventions may stress mentoring, or, instead, apply 360-degree feedback (Day, 2000). The diversity of these programs, of course, broaches the fundamental question – exactly what is it that is being developed?

In this section we will attempt to provide a provisional answer to this question. More specifically, we will examine the implication of these developmental programs with respect to two key aspects of the model of leader thought presented earlier – examining the implications of these developmental programs with respect to 1) knowledge and 2) the skills involved in application of this knowledge. We will, in examining knowledge and skills, examine both what is being done effectively, and what is being done ineffectively, vis-à-vis the model of leader thought under consideration.

Knowledge

A key proposition underlying our model of leader thinking is that leadership is ultimately grounded in experiential or case-based knowledge. In fact, most leadership training presents cases with leadership problems (Yukl, 2002). Although these cases may either be presented by the trainer or elicited from participants, virtually all case discussions focus on the goals and outcomes of the case as well as the critical causes of these outcomes. Given the role of causes and goals in the activation and application of case-based knowledge, this instructional method seems likely to lead to relevant learning especially when the cases presented are tied to the problems confronting leaders at that point in their careers (Jacques, 1976). The effectiveness of case-based instruction may, however, be limited by three considerations: 1) limitations on case content, 2) development of case libraries, and 3) application of appropriate cases.

Case-based instruction, like most other forms of instruction, requires adequate depth of analysis. One aspect of depth, of course, is the articulation of multiple causes and goals. Unfortunately, it is unclear the extent to which most leadership development programs seek to describe and encourage that analysis of various causes vis-à-vis the goals under consideration. To complicate matters further, cases reflect not only information about causes and goals, but also include information about resource restrictions, contingencies, and key actions. Frequently, however, these less obvious, but still significant, aspects of case-based knowledge are given little, or no, attention in instruction, thereby undermining, or limiting, the transfer of training to everyday work situations.

The presentation of cases in leadership development programs stresses the need to consider objective constraints (e.g., causes, resources, restrictions, and contingencies). Leadership thought, however, also calls for thinking about the social implications of actions. In other words, leaders must think about the affect, involvement, and identity of followers among other elements of the *social* system. In fact, the success of some leadership development programs – for example, Vroom's program (Vroom & Jago, 1988) – may in part lie in the fact that it calls leader's attention to issues of participation and involvement in the decision-making process. Nonetheless, case presentation often discounts the importance of these socio-emotional issues (James & Arroba, 2005; Uhl-Bien, 2003). This lack of interactional context in the cases used in leadership development may, at times, especially when instruction does not involve discussion of real-world experiences (Conger, 1993), act to undermine the effectiveness of leadership development programs.

Although limited coverage of "objective" and socio-emotional case attributes represents a significant problem in leadership development efforts, a more important and more serious problem arises from the organization of case material. More specifically, leadership development programs typically present and encourage the analysis of a limited number of prototypic cases. Although valuable, the limited number of cases does not constitute a viable case library (Kolodner, 1997). Failure to provide alternative cases displaying distinctive features or attributes will ultimately limit the effectiveness of instruction. And, as a result, it would seem that leadership development programs might be improved by providing multiple cases differing with regard to critical attributes, or features, giving rise to the application of a case.

The issue of development of case libraries points to a broader issue arising in leadership instruction. Within the model of leader thought presented earlier, it was apparent that case activation was not simply dependent on a situation – a case-attribute matching model. Instead, case activation was held to depend in part on the descriptive mental models used by leaders to understand the situation at hand. Unfortunately, although techniques are available for identifying mental models applied by leaders to understand their work (Walsh, 1988), most leadership development programs do not seek to articulate these descriptive mental models and embed cases within these models. The notable exception to this rule of thumb, an exception that has proven effective in leadership development, may be found in action learning techniques (Conger & Toegel, 2003). In action learning, a real-world organizational problem is presented, with teams being asked to provide a solution to this problem to more senior executives. Feedback is provided both during solution development and presentation. It is expected that these real-world, organizationally based problems, through peer interaction and feedback, will give rise to the development of viable mental models (Senge, 1990).

Our observations about descriptive mental models, of course, also point to the importance of prescriptive mental models. In fact, our model of leader thought argues that prescriptive models are crucial for identifying and generating actions for change events. Unfortunately, leadership development programs typically provide little, or no, guidance for the construction of prescriptive models. Given their importance to leadership, this gap may represent one of the most serious deficiencies in current leadership development programs.

Processes

Our model of leader thought under consideration points to five processing activities likely to have a marked impact on leader performance: 1) scanning, 2) analysis, 3) forecasting, 4) evaluation and reflection, and 5) planning.

The initiation of leader thought is, within this model, contingent on identification of a crisis or change event. Although crises or change events are sometimes obvious, quite often they are more subtle. Moreover, the conditions under which leaders operate, conditions of stress and fragmentation, may cause leaders to ignore or discount cues signaling a change event. An illustration of these kinds of scanning interventions may be found in the training program developed by Fiedler and colleagues (Fiedler, 1996; Fiedler, Bell, Chemers, & Patrick, 1984). This training program is based on the notion that leaders differ in their personality with certain personality types proving effective under certain conditions. Training, accordingly, attempts to instruct leaders in scanning for the conditions that promote their preferred strategy for the exercise of influence.

Identification of a change event, coupled with activation of a prescriptive mental model and relevant cases, permits leaders to begin analysis of the cases bearing on a change event. Analysis of case-based knowledge has received little attention in the literature, both as a phenomenon of interest in its own right and as a key aspect of leader thought. Nonetheless, the available evidence suggests that five key problems are likely to arise in leaders' analyses of cases. First, leaders, like people in general, will tend to minimize active investment in analysis (Hogarth & Makridakis, 1981). Second, only a limited number of cases will be considered, typically only prototypic cases, that may not be relevant to the change event at hand (Hershey, Walsh, Read, & Chulef, 1990). Third, the aspects of these cases that are considered in analysis will be limited, with causal and goal relevant information receiving more attention than information bearing on contingencies, resources, restrictions, involvement, and follower identity (Langholtz, Gettys, & Foote, 1995). Fourth, interrelationships among case attributes, especially negative, inhibitory, or contingent relationships, will receive limited attention (Dorner & Schaub, 1994). Fifth, and finally, unique case elements will not be given adequate attention with respect to the situation at hand (Mumford, Schultz, et al., 2002).

It is, of course, possible to develop training programs that might offset all of these analytic errors. And, in fact, it appears that many leadership training programs are implicitly designed in such a way as to encourage application of more effective strategies in case analysis (Conger, 1993). In this regard, however, two points should be borne in mind. One concern is that we lack evidence bearing on the most crucial elements of leader analysis to be addressed in training. The other concern is that analytic skills may develop in part as a function of real-world events suggesting that training must be linked to systematic developmental initiatives, such as mentoring and action learning, if it is to prove effective.

Assuming leaders can identify a viable idea for addressing a change event, they must formulate a plan for exercising influence. In fact, the available evidence does indicate a number of factors that influence the successful development and execution of these plans. To begin with, while leader thought may be complex, plans prove most effective when boiled down to a limited number of key controllable causes (Thomas & McDaniel, 1990). Moreover, plans appear more effective when they provide frameworks for the exercise of influence rather than a detailed sequence of influence attempts (Mumford et al., 2002). The value of plans also increases when plans are executed in an opportunistic fashion and the base plan is accompanied by a series of backup plans (Hayes-Roth & Hayes-Roth, 1979; Patalano & Seifert, 1997; Xiao, Milgram, & Doyle, 1997).

CONCLUSIONS

The evidence for individual differences in generalizable leader performance defined as causal influences of their units' or organizations' superior objective performance and productivity is essentially lacking. This chapter proposed that it is possible to develop a model of leadership thought that can be assessed and trained and ultimately related to future findings with objective leadership performance. Certainly, there is more to leadership than the leader's performance in thinking about change and crises (Bass, in press; Yukl, 2002). Leadership is related to attractiveness, trust, and dyadic exchange characteristics (Graen & Uhl-Bien, 1998). Moreover, we know that personality characteristics such as extraversion and integrity are related to leader emergence and performance (McCall & Lomabardo, 1983). Nonetheless, how leaders think about the problems broached by crises or change events (Hunt, Boal, & Dodge, 1999) would seem to be related to differences in objective measures of leadership performance. If that were the case, leadership development and assessment efforts may benefit – and benefit greatly – from a more explicit focus on the cognitive mechanisms that allow leaders to craft viable solutions to the change or crisis events where leader performance is known to make a difference.

Our model of leader thought holds that, ultimately, leader cognition is founded in case-based knowledge and mental models abstracted from this knowledge. These cases and descriptive mental models allow leaders to formulate the prescriptive mental models that provide a basis for influence attempts (Strange & Mumford, 2005). However, these knowledge structures, while providing a basis for leader thought, are not unto themselves sufficient to allow leaders to formulate viable responses to change events. Instead, leaders must work with this information through five key processing operations: 1) environmental scanning, 2) case analysis, 3) forecasting, 4) idea generation, and 5) planning.

Development of this model is noteworthy in part because it points to a number of strategies that might be used in leader development. For example, presenting leaders with cases from large collections or case libraries should provide opportunities for learning as long as the cases have known outcomes, so that the correctness of proposed solutions can be evaluated objectively. On the other hand, without informative feedback about proposed solutions, merely encountering cases would not lead to improvements in performance as shown in recent reviews of the weak effects of professional experience (Ericsson, 2006; Ericsson, Whyte, & Ward, 2007). Along similar lines, one might seek to design training programs to develop viable mental models through action learning strategies. Moreover, it appears that the key processes used by leaders in working with this knowledge can be developed. Thus, scanning might be improved by providing leaders with diagnostics, while other processes might be improved through classroom instruction and real-world practice exercises focusing on common errors that arise in leader evaluations of current situations.

Although it appears feasible to apply this model to guide the design of leader development interventions, it should be recognized that leader thought is a complex – in fact, a highly complex – phenomenon. One implication of the complex nature of leader thought is that leadership cannot be developed through a single, short-term intervention. Rather, what will be required is a progressive and sequential series of interventions.

A second implication of the complex, sequential nature of leader development concerns the timing and design of various developmental interventions (Goldstein & Ford, 2002). Traditional leader assessment measures lack sufficient specificity with regard to relevant knowledge structures and processes. Our chapter reviewed some evidence that suggested it is possible to develop assessment measures targeted on critical aspects of knowledge and information processing proposed to underlie leader thought.

Our observations with regard to leader development and assessment, however, point to broader implications of the present effort. Leader development and assessment efforts, although often effective in changing knowledge and perceived expertise (Bray & Howard, 1988; Burke & Day, 1986; Collins & Holton, 2004), do provide a systematic framework for guiding the design of these interventions.

Our development of a model of leader thought might have several benefits. Our model should allow investigators to search for everyday situations where individual differences in leader thought would be large and thus likely to be associated with objective performance differences of their units', groups', or organizations' performance and productivity. Secondly, our work should permit the analysis of the mechanisms of reliable differences in objective leader performance, once they have been discovered.

REFERENCES

Alimo-Metcalfe, B. (1998). 360-degree feedback and leadership development. *International Journal of Selection and Assessment, 6,* 35–44.

Arthur, W., Day, E. A., McNelly, T. L., & Edens, P. S. (2003). A meta-analysis of the criterion-related validity of assessment center dimensions. *Personnel Psychology, 56,* 125–154.

Barr, P. S., Stimpert, J. L., & Huff, A. S. (1992). Cognitive change, strategic action, and organizational renewal. *Strategic Management Journal, 13,* 15–36.

Bass, B. M. (in press). *Handbook of leadership.* New York: The Free Press.

Berger, C. R., & Jordan, J. M. (1992). Planning sources, planning difficulty, and verbal fluency. *Communication Monographs, 59,* 130–148.

Bligh, M. C., Kohles, J. C., & Meindl, J. R. (2004). Charisma under crisis: Presidential leadership, rhetoric, and media responses before and after the September 11th terrorist attacks. *Leadership Quarterly, 15,* 211–239.

Bluck, S., & Habermas, T. (2001). Extending the study of autobiographical memory: Thinking back about life across the life span. *Review of General Psychology, 5,* 135–147.

Bluck, S., & Staudinger, U. M. (2000). *Looking back and looking ahead: The role of the past and future in present life evaluations.* Unpublished manuscript.

Bradbury, H., & Lichtenstein, B. (2000). Relationality in organizational research: Exploring the space between. *Organization Science, 5*(5), 551–564.

Bray, D. W., Campbell, R. J., & Grant, D. L. (1974). *Formative years in business: A long-term AT&T study of managerial lives.* New York: Wiley.

Bray, D. W., & Howard, A. (1988). *Managerial lives in transition.* New York: The Guilford Press.

Brett, J. F., & Atwater, L. E. (2001). 360-degree feedback: Accuracy, reactions, and perceptions of usefulness. *Journal of Applied Psychology, 86,* 930–942.

Burke, M. J., & Day, R. R. (1986). A cumulative study of the effectiveness of managerial training. *Journal of Applied Psychology, 71*(2), 232–245.

Byham, W. C., & Thornton, G. G. (1986). Assessment centers. In R. A. Berk (Ed.), *Performance assessment: Methods and applications.* Baltimore, MD: Johns Hopkins University Press.

Calori, R., Johnson, G., & Sarnin, P. (1992). French and British top managers' understanding of the structure and the dynamics of their industries: A cognitive analysis and comparison. *British Journal of Management, 3,* 61–78.

Collins, D. B., & Holton, E. F. (2004). The effectiveness of managerial leadership development programs: A meta-analysis of studies from 1982 to 2001. *Human Resource Development Quarterly, 15*(2), 217–248.

Conger, J. A. (1993). The brave new world of leadership training. *Organizational Dynamics, 21,* 46–58.

Conger, J., & Toegel, G. (2003). Action learning and multi-rater feedback as leadership development interventions: Popular but poorly deployed. *Journal of Change Management, 3,* 332–348.

Connelly, M. S., Gilbert, J. A., Zaccaro, S. J., Threlfall, K. V., Marks, M. A., & Mumford, M. D. (2000). Exploring the relationship of leadership skills and knowledge to leader performance. *Leadership Quarterly, 11*, 65–86.

Conway, J. M., & Huffcutt, A. I. (1997). Psychometric properties of multi-source performance ratings: A meta-analysis of subordinate, supervisor, peer, and self-ratings. *Human Performance, 10*, 331–360.

Cossette, P., & Audet, M. (1992). Mapping of an idiosyncratic schema. *Journal of Management Studies, 29*, 325–347.

Daniels, K., Johnson, G., & de Chernatony, L. (1994). Differences in managerial cognitions of competition. *British Journal of Management, 5*, 21–30.

Day, D. V. (2000). Leadership development: A review in context. *The Leadership Quarterly, 11*, 581–613.

Dörner, D., & Schaub, H. (1994). Errors in planning and decision-making and the nature of human information processing. *Applied Psychology: An International Review, 43*, 433–453.

Drazin, R., Glynn, M. A., & Kazanjian, R. K. (1999). Multilevel theorizing about creativity in organizations: A sense-making perspective. *Academy of Management Review, 24*, 286–307.

Dukerich, J. M., & Nichols, M. L. (1991). Causal information search in managerial decision making. *Organizational Behavior and Human Decision Processes, 50*, 106–122.

Emrich, C. G., Brower, H. H., Feldman, J. M., & Garland, H. (2001). Images in words: Presidential rhetoric, charisma, and greatness. *Administrative Science Quarterly, 46*, 527–557.

Ericsson, K. A. (2006). The influence of experience and deliberate practice on the development of superior expert performance. In K. A. Ericsson, N. Charness, P. Feltovich, and R. R. Hoffman (Eds.), *Cambridge handbook of expertise and expert performance* (pp. 685–706). Cambridge, UK: Cambridge University Press.

Ericsson, K. A., Whyte, J., & Ward, P. (2007). Expert performance in nursing: Reviewing research on expertise in nursing within the framework of the expert performance approach. *Advances in Nursing Science, 30*, 58–71.

Estes, W. K. (1991). Cognitive architectures from the standpoint of an experimental psychologist. *Annual Review of Psychology, 42*, 1–28.

Fiedler, F. E. (1996). Research on leadership selection and training: One view of the future. *Administrative Science Quarterly, 41*, 241–250.

Fiedler, F. E., Bell, C. H., Chemers, M. M., & Patrick, D. (1984). Increasing mine productivity and safety through management training and organizational development: A comparative study. *Basic and Applied Psychology, 5*, 1–18.

Finkelstein, S. (2002). Planning in organizations: One vote for complexity. In F. J. Yammarino & F. Dansereau (Eds.), *The many faces of multi-level issues* (pp. 73–80). Oxford: Elsevier Science/JAI Press.

Fiol, C. M., Harris, D., & House, R. J. (1999). Charismatic leadership: Strategies for effecting social change. *Leadership Quarterly, 10*, 449–482.

Fleishman, E. A. (1953). Leadership climate, human relations training, and supervisory behavior. *Personnel Psychology, 6*, 205–222.

Fleishman, E. A., Mumford, M. D., Zaccaro, S. J., Levin, K. Y., Korotkin, A. L., & Hein, M. B. (1991). Taxonomic efforts in the description of leadership behavior: A synthesis and functional interpretation. *Leadership Quarterly, 2*, 245–287.

Frankwick, G. L., Walker, B. A., & Ward, J. C. (1994). Belief structures in conflict: Mapping a strategic marketing decision. *Journal of Business Research, 31*, 183–195.

Fulmer, R. M. (1997). The evolving paradigm of leadership development. *Organizational Dynamics, 25*, 59–72.

Goldstein, I. L., & Ford, J. K. (2002). *Training in organizations: Needs assessment, development, and evaluation* (4th ed.). Belmont, CA: Wadsworth/Thomson Learning.

Graen, G. B., & Uhl-Bien, M. (1998). Relationship based approach to leadership: Development of Leader-Member Exchange (LMX) theory of leadership over 25 years: Applying a multi-level multi-domain perspective. In F. Dansereau and F. J. Yammarino (Eds.), *Leadership: The multi-level approaches: Contemporary and alternative*. Stamford, CT: Elsevier Science/JAI Press.

Halverson, S. E., Holladay, C. C., Kazma, S. M., & Quinones, M. A. (2004). Self-sacrificial behavior in crisis situations: The competing roles of behavioral and situational factors. *Leadership Quarterly, 15*, 211–240.

Hamilton, F., & Bean, C. (2005). The importance of context, beliefs and values in leadership development. *Business Ethics: A European Review, 14*, 336–347.

Hayes-Roth, B., & Hayes-Roth, F. (1979). A cognitive model of planning. *Cognitive Science, 3*, 275–310.

Hedlund, J., Forsythe, G. B., Horvath, J. A., Williams, W. M., Snook, S., & Sternberg, R. (2003). Identifying and assessing tacit knowledge: Understanding the practical intelligence of military leaders. *Leadership Quarterly, 14*, 117.

Hershey, D. A., Walsh, D. A., Read, S. J., & Chulef, A. S. (1990). Effects of expertise on financial problem-solving: Evidence for goal-directed, problem-solving scripts. *Organizational Behavior and Human Decision Processes, 46*, 77–101.

Hogarth, R. M., & Makridakis, S. (1981). Forecasting and planning: An evaluation. *Management Science, 27*, 115–138.

Holyoak, K. J., & Thagard, P. (1997). The analogical mind. *American Psychologist, 52*, 35–44.

Hunt, J. G., Boal, K. B., & Dodge, G. E. (1999). The effects of visionary and crisis-responsive charisma on followers: An experimental examination of two kinds of charismatic leadership. *Leadership Quarterly, 10*, 423–448.

Isenberg, D. J. (1986). Thinking and managing: A verbal protocol analysis of managerial problem solving. *Academy of Management Journal, 29*, 775–788.

Jacques, E. (1976). *A general theory of bureaucracy*. London: Heinemann.

James, K. T, & Arroba, T. (2005). Reading and carrying: A framework for learning about emotion and emotionality in organizational systems as a core aspect of leadership development. *Management Learning, 36*, 299–316.

Johnson-Laird, P. N. (1983). *Mental models: Towards a cognitive science of language, inference and consciousness*. Cambridge, UK: Cambridge University Press.

Kiesler, S., & Sproull, L. (1982). Managerial response to changing environments: Perspectives on problem sensing from social cognition. *Administrative Science Quarterly, 27*, 548–570.

Kolodner, J. L. (1997). Educational implications of analogy: A view from case-based reasoning. *American Psychologist, 52*, 57–66.

Langholtz, H., Gettys, C., & Foote, B. (1995). Are resource fluctuations anticipated in resource allocation tasks? *Organizational Behavior and Human Decision Processes, 64*, 274–282.

Lant, T. K., & Milliken, F. J. (1992). The role of managerial learning and interpretation in strategic persistence and reorientation: An empirical exploration. *Strategic Management Journal, 13*, 585–608.

Lonergan, D. C., Scott, G. M., & Mumford, M. D. (2004). Evaluative aspects of creative thought: Effects of idea appraisal and revision standards. *Creativity Research Journal, 16*, 231–246.

Lord, R.G., DeVader, C.L., Alliger, G.M. (1986). A meta-analysis of the relation between personality traits and leadership perceptions: An application of validity generalization procedure. *Journal of Applied Psychology, 71,* 402–410.

March, J.G., & Olsen, J.P. (1976). *Ambiguity and choice in organizations.* Oslo: Scandinavian University Press.

Marcy, R.T., & Mumford, M.D. (in press). Social innovation: Enhancing creative performance through causal analysis. *Creativity Research Journal* (Eds.), *The Relationship Between Creativity, Knowledge, and Reason.* Cambridge, UK: Cambridge University Press.

Marta, S., Leritz, L.E., & Mumford, M.D. (2005). Leadership skills and the group performance: Situational demands, behavioral requirements, and planning. *Leadership Quarterly, 16,* 591–615.

McCall, M., & Lombardo, M. (1983). What makes a top executive? *Psychology Today, 17,* 26–31.

McCauley, C.D., Ruderman, M.N., Ohlott, P.J., & Morrow, J.E. (1994). Assessing the developmental components of managerial jobs. *Journal of Applied Psychology, 79,* 544–560.

McDaniel, M.A., Hartman, N.S., Whetzel, D.L., & Grubb, W.L. (2007). Situational judgment tests, response instructions, and validity: A meta-analysis. *Personnel Psychology, 60,* 63–91.

Mintzberg, H. (1973). *The nature of managerial work.* New York: Harper and Row.

Mitra, J. (2000). Making corrections: Innovation and collective learning in small businesses. *Education & Training, 42,* 228–237.

Motowidlo, S.J., Dunnette, M.D., & Carter, G.W. (1990). An alternative selection procedure: The low-fidelity simulation. *Journal of Applied Psychology, 75,* 640–647.

Mumford, M.D., Dansereau, F., & Yammarino, F.J. (2000). Followers, motivations, and levels of analysis: The case of individualized leadership. *Leadership Quarterly, 11,* 313–340.

Mumford, M.D. (2002). Social innovation: Ten cases from Benjamin Franklin. *Creativity Research Journal, 14,* 253–266.

Mumford, M.D., Lonergan, D.C., & Scott, G. (2002). Evaluating creative ideas: Processes, standards, and context. *Inquiry: Critical Thinking Across the Disciplines, 22,* 21–30.

Mumford, M.D., Marks, M.A., Connelly, M.S., Zaccaro, S.J., & Reiter-Palmon, R. (2000). Development of leadership skills: Experience and timing. *Leadership Quarterly, 11,* 87–114.

Mumford, M.D., Schultz, R.A., & Osburn, H.K. (2002). Planning in organizations: Performance as a multi-level phenomenon. In F.J. Yammario & F. Dansereau (Eds.), *Research in multi-level issues: The many faces of multi-level issues* (pp. 3–25). Oxford, UK Elsevier.

Mumford, M.D., Scott, G.M., Gaddis, B., & Strange, J.M. (2002). Leading creative people: Orchestrating expertise and relationships. *Leadership Quarterly, 13,* 705–750.

Mumford, M.D., & Strange, J.M. (2002). Vision and mental models: The case of charismatic and ideological leadership. In B.J. Avolio & F.J. Yammarino (Eds.), *Charismatic and Transformational Leadership: The Road Ahead* (pp. 109–142). Oxford, UK Elsevier.

Mumford, M.D., Zaccaro, S.J., Harding, F.D., Jacobs, T.O., & Fleishman, E.A. (2000). Leadership skills for a changing world: Solving complex social problems. *Leadership Quarterly, 11,* 11–36.

Nutt, P.C. (1984). Types of organizational decision processes. *Administrative Science Quarterly, 29,* 414–450.

Patalano, A. L., & Seifert, C. M. (1997). Opportunistic planning: Being reminded of pending goals. *Cognitive Psychology, 34*, 1–36.

Pillemer, D. B. (1998). *Momentous events, vivid memories: How unforgettable moments help us understand the meaning of our lives.* Cambridge, MA: Harvard University Press.

Ragins, B. R., & Cotton, J. L. (1999). Mentor functions and outcomes: A comparison of men and women in formal and informal mentoring relationships. *Journal of Applied Psychology, 84*, 529–550.

Riggio, R. E., Riggio, H. R., Salinas, C., & Cole, E. J. (2003). The role of social and emotional communication skills in leader emergence and effectiveness. *Group Dynamics: Theory Research and Practice, 7*, 83–103.

Salam, S., Cox, J. F., & Sims, H. P. (1997). In the eye of the beholder: How leadership relates to 360-degree performance ratings. *Group and Organization Management, 22*, 185–209.

Scott, G. M., Lonergan, D. C., & Mumford, M. D. (2005). Contractual combination: Alternative knowledge structures, alternative heuristics. *Creativity Research Journal, 17*, 21–36.

Senge, P. M. (1990). *The fifth discipline.* London: Century Business.

Shamir, B., & Eilam, G. (2005). "What's your story?" A life-stories approach to authentic leadership development. *The Leadership Quarterly, 16*, 395–417.

Shamir, B., House, R. J., & Arthur, M. B. (1993). The motivational effects of charismatic leadership: A self-concept based theory. *Organizational Science, 4*, 577–594.

Snow, R. E., & Lohman, D. F. (1993). Cognitive psychology, new test design, and new test theory: An introduction. In N. Frederiksen, R. J. Mislevy, & I. Bejar (Eds.), *Test theory for a new generation of tests* (pp. 1–17). Hillsdale, NJ: Lawrence Erlbaum Associates, Inc.

Strange, J. M., & Mumford, M. D. (2005). The origins of vision: Effects of reflection, models and analysis. *Leadership Quarterly, 16*, 121–148.

Taylor, S. E., & Schneider, S. K. (1984). Coping and the stimulation of events. *Social Cognition, 7*, 174–194.

Thomas, J. B., & McDaniel, R. R. (1990). Interpreting strategic issues: Effects of strategy and the information-processing structure of top management teams. *Academy of Management Journal, 33*, 286–306.

Tornow, W. W. (1993). Perceptions or reality: Is multi-perspective feedback a means or an end? *Human Resource Management, 32*, 221–230.

Tornow, W. W., & London, M. (1998). *Maximizing the value of 360-degree feedback: A process for successful individual and organization development.* San Francisco, CA: Jossey-Bass Publishers, Inc.

Tornow, W. W., & Pinto, P. R. (1976). The development of a managerial job taxonomy: A system for describing, classifying, and evaluating executive positions. *Journal of Applied Psychology, 61*, 410–418.

Treadway, D. C., Hochwater, W. A., Ferris, G. R., Kacmar, C. J., Douglas, C., Ammeter, A. et al. (2004). Leader political skill and employee reactions. *Leadership Quarterly, 15*, 493–513.

Uhl-Bien, M. (2003). Relationship development as a key ingredient for leadership development. In S. E. Murphy and R. E. Riggio (Eds.), *The future of leadership development.* Mahwah, NJ: Lawrence Erlbaum Associates.

Vroom, V. H., & Yetton, P. W. (1973). *Leadership and decision making.* Pittsburgh, PA: University of Pittsburgh Press.

Vroom, V. H., & Jago, A. G. (1988). Managing participation: A critical dimension of leadership. *Management Learning, 36*, 299–316.

Walsh, J. P. (1988). Selectivity and selective perception: An investigation of managers' belief structures and information processing. *Academy of Management Journal*, *31*, 873–896.

Weick, K. E. (1995). *Sensemaking in organizations.* Thousand Oaks, CA: Sage.

West, M. A., Borrill, C. S., Dawson, J. F., Brodbeck, F., Shapiro, D. A., & Haward, B. (2003). Leadership clarity and team innovation in health care. *Leadership Quarterly 14*(4–5), 393–410.

Xiao, Y., Milgram, P., & Doyle, D. J. (1997). Capturing and modeling planning expertise in anesthesiology: Results of a field study. In C. E. Zsambok & G. Klein (Eds.), *Naturalistic decision making* (pp. 197–205). Hillsdale, NJ: Lawrence Erlbaum Associates.

Yukl, G. (2002). *Leadership in organizations.* Upper Saddle River, NJ: Prentice-Hall.

Zaccaro, S. J., Mumford, M. D., Connelly, M. S., Marks, M. A., & Gilbert, J. A. (2000). Assessment of leader problem-solving capabilities. *Leadership Quarterly*, *11*, 37–64.

5

Revolutions, Leaders, and Diagnosticians: Reflections on the Themes in Chapters 2–4

EARL B. HUNT

My task is to comment on three papers delivered to a conference on the development of expertise, and included herein. One, by Ralph Chatham, outlines changes in U.S. military training in the late 20th century (Chapter 2). I will also make brief mention of a second paper by Chatham (Chapter 10 in this book), which deals with computer-based training systems. Susan Lajoie (Chapter 3) describes Sherlock, an intelligent tutoring system developed for the U.S. Air Force in the 1980s, and then remarks on some medical intelligent tutoring systems that are now under development, which she regards as follow-ons from the Sherlock project. The third paper, by Michael Mumford and colleagues (Friedrich, Caughron, & Antes), presented as Chapter 4 in this book, reviews and analyzes leadership training. While these papers do not have a common theme, they are somewhat complementary. Chatham lays out a comprehensive set of issues and examples related to learning, training, and retention of skills in the armed services. Are these the right issues? Can psychology help? To what extent do Lajoie and Mumford address the issues Chatham raises? I will try to organize my review around these three questions. In the process I will make some comments that I hope will be useful in thinking about how expertise may be acquired and used, both in the armed services and elsewhere.

At the outset, though, I should say that it may be hard to find a common theme in my own critiques. I will range from historical examples, including some minutiae about a minor historical figure, to an application of mathematical psychology. I hope these widely varying references do lead to a coherent critique.

This is a commentary on papers delivered at an ONR sponsored conference on the development of professional expertise, at Orlando, Florida, in January, 2007. I would like to thank those members of the conference who discussed with me the verbal presentation on which this chapter is based, and Susan Chipman for calling my attention to some military references. I especially thank Ralph Chatham for his very useful comments on an earlier draft of this chapter. Naturally any errors of fact or poorly reasoned opinions are my responsibility alone.

CHATHAM'S "FIRST REVOLUTION" IN MILITARY TRAINING: (HOPEFULLY) SOME CONSTRUCTIVE COMMENTS

Chatham begins with a complimentary discussion of the National Training Center and after-action reviews (AARs). He rightly stresses the importance of skilled personnel, relative to technological prowess, in winning wars. He then discusses "notional" learning and forgetting curves for unit and individual proficiency, and draws some conclusions from these curves.

Chatham's stress on the importance of trained personnel is not a new message. The decision makers in American society, including but by no means limited to military decision makers, seem firmly committed to not hearing it. Let me put this in a historical context.

In 1588 the Spanish Armada, the largest naval task force ever assembled up until that time, was utterly and totally defeated by a smaller English force. Control of the sea, with all that it implied for the colonization of the New World, shifted to the English. The English ships were somewhat better than the Spanish ships. The English sailors, especially the officers, were very much better seafarers. In agreement with Chatham's analysis, they were much better practiced than their Spanish opponents, for an English sea captain of that day might have just a tinge of piracy in his past.

About four hundred years later, in Desert Storm, U.S.-led, NATO-trained forces attacked Saddam Hussein's Soviet-equipped Iraqi forces. The Iraqis were dug in in defensive positions. A Soviet field marshal was asked to predict what would happen. He said "The Americans will ride like cowboys over the skies of Iraq." They did, on both air and ground. Not since the Spanish Armada had there been such a one-sided victory in a battle between two forces with approximately equivalent technology. The difference? Training and discipline.

In between, the United States lost the Viet Nam War. About 20 years after the Vietnamese war ended, *The New York Times* interviewed the then-retired commander of the Vietnamese forces, Vo Nguyen Giap. After speaking with respect about the American commander, General Westmoreland, Giap said that wars are won by men and equipment and that of the two, men are more important and that was what Westmoreland forgot.

Wars, and many other endeavors, are won by people who are motivated, trained, confident, and have adequate equipment. Three of those qualities are psychological. You can make a lot of money selling the fourth to the military, which may explain why the message about training does not get heard amid the hype for new weapons systems. We cannot do anything about that, however, for there is little money to be made reading and writing essays like this. So one does what one can. Let us look at what psychology has to say about the first three qualities, especially training, in the light of Chatham's analysis.

Chatham stresses the importance of AARs, where there is a frank discussion of what went right and wrong. AARs are a form of negative feedback. It is a basic principle of systems analysis that any system that interacts with its environment must have a negative feedback mechanism or it will drift out of control (Weiner, 1948). This is as true of systems made up of humans as it is of systems made up of electronic components. Positive feedback systems are inherently unstable. No matter what teachers and clinical psychologists tell you, *unfettered positive feedback is a bad thing.* You do not want to be told that you are okay when you are not.

Previous armed forces have utilized negative feedback mechanisms. Peter the Great, the 17th–18th-century Tsar who modernized Russia, regularly sought critical review of both his military and civil ventures (Hughes, 2002). During the Napoleonic wars whenever a ship was lost or suffered major damage, Royal Navy captains appeared at court-martials to conduct what amounts to a review of the case. Merely convening the court did not imply indictment of the officers involved.

In modern times, reviews similar to AARs are conducted after transportation incidents, among weather forecasters who routinely discuss the differences between the forecast and actual weather (and, as a result, are among the best calibrated of all forecasters, in spite of their popular reputation), and in medicine via grand rounds and the analysis of incidences, to name only a few examples. There are also a number of feedback mechanisms that operate in society but are not part of the organization performing the action. The press is one of them.

Chatham makes the important point that in an AAR, people at all ranks are encouraged to speak out. This is a place where the modern AAR is unusual, especially in a hierarchical society such as the military, and not all that common in less formally organized social systems. All participants are encouraged to speak out, without following the usual rules of command and deference to rank. This is extremely important, because negative feedback is most effective when incidents are reviewed from all perspectives. Interestingly, the fact that an organization can encourage free-form feedback of this sort is not a sign of weak discipline; it is just the opposite. Appropriate discipline has to be maintained, both in the military and in civilian organizations, because decisions have to be made with a reasonable expectation that the concomitant orders will be carried out. The organization can only temporarily suspend the trappings of discipline, such as deference to rank, if the organization's leaders are sure that there is sufficient solidarity so that the day-to-day chain of command remains intact. The American armed services are sufficiently confident of themselves so that they can utilize the AAR.

Both historically and in contemporary times, other, weaker militaries have not had such confidence. Chatham (personal communication) has pointed out to me that the 18th–19th-century Royal Navy court-martials could, and sometimes did, fail in their review purposes because the Admiralty was afraid that any breakdown in deference and custom would lead to revolt. Their concern was realistic. Sailors at that time could be pressed (i.e., kidnapped) into service, and held in conditions very close to imprisonment. This discouraged the courts from soliciting frank statements from military personnel other than officers and from making certain unacceptable conclusions (e.g., that Admiral Lord X_____ really was incompetent).

Did this just happen long ago? In 2007, the cartoon strip "Dilbert," a wry commentary on software engineering, depicted a situation in which one of the programmers, Alice, reported to the boss that the product was not working. The boss pointed out to Alice that her own salary depended upon sales of the product. I know of situations in modern companies (names withheld to protect the guilty) where I am strongly suspicious that frank feedback resulted in firing.

To take a better documented, more historic case, in the 1920s the U.S. "battleship admirals" resolutely refused to realize that their majestic warships were sitting ducks without air cover. General "Billy" Mitchell was court-martialed for insubordination when he pointed out, caustically and publicly, that these results and other facts about air power were being ignored.

I will not use examples from more contemporary warfare to avoid political controversy, but I can think of a few. Instead, I ask why there is resistance to the use of negative feedback. Here are four psycho-social phenomena that I believe are major inhibitors of the learning process.

1. *Attributing the results to the person:* Walter Mischel (2004) has shown that people tend to attribute success or failure to the persons involved rather than the situation or system effects. It is not clear to me whether this is a fact about American/European society or about humanity in general, but that is not germane here. To the extent that a review of actions may result in sanctions against the persons involved, those in charge quite realistically should be concerned about anything like an AAR. The problem is that in most complicated cases [e.g., friendly fire incidents (Snook, 2000)] there may well be both personal and system failures.

2. *The fishbowl: Systems within systems:* In our society all the systems and most of the people who might usefully expose themselves to self-criticism live in a very snoopy larger system. Mechanisms like the press and attorneys are, on the whole, a very good thing. They keep democracies from spinning out of control. If you want a counter-example, suppose that a free, investigative press had existed in Iraq in 1990. If there had been public review of the actual state of the Iraqi army at that time, would Saddam Hussein have been able to convince his generals to challenge American forces to a tank-and-air campaign in an open desert? But all that said, there is a disadvantage to openness. Reviews intended to provide negative feedback within the local system are likely to leak out into the larger system. Once the cat is out of the bag, it can deliver nasty scratches.

3. *The culture of self-esteem:* I have already pointed out that tolerating open negative feedback requires confidence. Confidence should not be confused with a fear of bruising one's self-esteem, which is a risk you have to take in order to benefit from negative feedback. Our educational system seems to be overly concerned about bruises, to point of denying the facts. American parents are evidently well satisfied with their children's progress in mathematics, and send this message to their children by regarding the amount of homework as just right, and not terribly important. Chinese and Japanese parents are quite concerned about their children's performance, and stress the children's need to work harder. Japanese and Chinese students exceed U.S. students in their mathematics skill (Stevenson, Lee, & Stigler, 1986). To the extent that U.S. students are brought up to feel that life is supposed to be a series of successes due to their personal skills (or rights), frank negative feedback can be extremely threatening. There is a difference between saying "You made a mistake," and "You made a mistake, stupid!" Children who are shielded from the first message may, when they grow older, be unable to distinguish between the first and second message.

4. *Shooting the messenger:* It is worth remembering that Billy Mitchell was court-martialed. On a more prosaic front, professors who grade severely are likely to get poor teaching ratings from students (Greenwald & Gilmore, 1997). If salaries are partly determined on the basis of teaching ratings, then we have a positive feedback mechanism ... a very bad thing. Refer to point 3 about the culture of self-esteem.

Chatham is correct that negative feedback is essential, both for personal and organizational learning. I worry that psychological and social factors in our society make such feedback hard to get.

Now let us turn to learning. This is a point where I will fault Chatham (and by implication, many, many government decision makers) for failing to consider a voluminous psychological literature on learning and memory. This failing has a very important implication for organizational policies that are supposed to develop expertise. (Besides, the government paid for most of this research. They might try using it.)

Chatham is concerned with two things, the extent to which further investment in training promotes more learning (i.e., higher tested performance), and the problem of retention of trained skills over time. These are serious issues for the military and many other organizations, because there is often a considerable length of time between the end of training and the presence of an operational requirement to demonstrate the skills and knowledge acquired during training. Everyone should learn to perform cardiac resuscitation, but very few of us pull a swimmer out of the water within 30 minutes of our graduation from the Red Cross training session.

In order to investigate learning, Chatham (see Figure 2.2 in Chapter 2) presents a sigmoid "notional learning curve," and argues that it is rational to invest resources into training while the trainees are on the steep part of the curve, because the marginal return on investment, in terms of trained proficiency, is greatest at that point. He then presents another "notional curve" for forgetting, and worries that there will be substantial forgetting after training.

These are legitimate issues. The problem is that Chatham has treated learning and forgetting as separate phenomena. They are not.

The forms for learning and forgetting curves have been the topic of intense investigation for more than 150 years (Hunt, 2002). Remarkable regularities have been discovered, in situations ranging from the training of machine operators (including pilots) to sophomores learning paired associates, and including studies involving monkeys, dogs, rats, and mice. The fact that these regularities occur over such a wide range of situations suggests strongly that they are due to properties of the mammalian neural system. To widen the field, it has been observed that some of the same properties are found in inorganic systems, such as libraries (Schooler & Anderson, 1997). This suggests that the form of the learning curve may be due to environmental constraints.

I do not want to be misunderstood as saying that the mechanisms of learning and forgetting are completely understood. My point is that certain descriptive phenomena are very well known, and that in many situations, policy makers responsible for allocating training resources and/or estimating recall do not need anything more than this. Here are some relevant facts.

A very wide number of learning phenomena can be described by the *power law of learning* (Newell & Rosenbloom, 1981). This can be expressed in terms of the time it takes to do a task:

$$L(P) = A + BP^{-c} \qquad (1)$$

where $L(P)$ is the latency after P practice trials, A is the minimum time in which the task could be done, B is the difference between the time required to do the task initially and the minimum time, and c $(c > 0)$ is a learning rate parameter. An analogous equation holds for the probability that a task can be completed at a time interval, T, after the completion of training:

$$\Pr(T) = \Pr(0)T^{-d} \qquad (2)$$

where $\Pr(0)$ is the probability of correct execution upon completion of training and d $(d > 0)$ is the decay rate. There is a lively controversy over whether power functions are the best functions to describe learning and forgetting, but the debate is not germane here.[1] Power functions are close enough to be a

---

[1]   There are two aspects to this controversy. One is over whether or not the power function is the most accurate function that can be found. Since all the functions suggested have the general form of the power function, this argument, although important to theories

The relation of memory strength to training experiences

FIGURE 5.1. An illustration of the power law relation between memory strength to occasions of learning (both in arbitrary units).

considerable improvement over "notional curves" as predictors of the benefits of training and the costs of disuse.

The reason that this is important is because of what comes next. Anderson and colleagues (Anderson, Fincham, & Douglass, 1999) have pointed out that power functions for both learning and forgetting can be derived from a single notion of "strength of memory." The idea is that every experience produces a "trace strength" in memory. Trace strength begins to decay, in accordance with a power function, immediately after the experience. A subsequent training experience will produce a second trace strength. The overall strength of the memory will be the sum of the strengths of all traces in memory, after allowing for the decay of each of them. One need not accept all of the details of Anderson's model to appreciate the gist of the argument. All that has to be accepted is that the model is reasonably close to reality, which it certainly is. We can then apply the model to the important cases considered by Chatham.

Figure 5.1 shows the strength of memory (in arbitrary units) as a function of the number of training trials. This function is a reasonable approximation of a very wide range of psychological data, including people learning rules, apes

of learning, is not germane here. The second argument is over whether or not the power function fits individual data or is produced by the amalgamation, across cases, of learning and retention functions that are not themselves power functions. Again, this argument is important to theories of learning but is not germane to the present discussion. The reason is that decision makers charged with establishing training principle will almost always be concerned with the expected performance of a randomly chosen learner, not the performance of specified individuals.

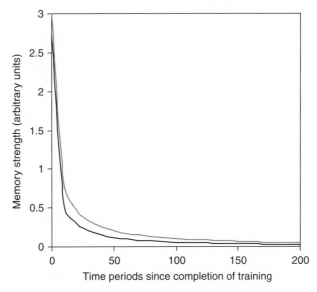

FIGURE 5.2. An illustration of the power law relation between memory strength and the number of time periods between cessation of training and testing.

and monkeys learning discrimination tasks, rats running mazes, and pigeons pressing levers for food. As Chatham notes, there is a diminishing return for fixed amounts of training as training progresses. A person who followed this argument might cease training at about 20 trials (half the number of trials shown), on the grounds that the next 20 trials would only result in a 10 percent increment in memory strength.

The situation changes when we turn to retention. Figure 5.2 shows the retention curve predicted by Anderson's model. The form of the retention curve is consistent with Chatham's ideas, and with a great deal of psychological data. Figure 5.2 also illustrates something Chatham does not consider, the effects of overlearning. The two curves in Figure 5.2 illustrate the fall-off in retention, across various periods of disuse, following 20 or 40 learning trials. The 40 trial curve is above the 20 trial curve at every point. The difference is even more dramatic if we plot the ratio $S_{40}(t)/S_{20}(t)$, where $S_x(t)$ is the strength of learning after x training trials and t periods of disuse. This is shown in Figure 5.3. Doubling the number of training trials produces a 10 percent improvement in performance immediately after training. However, it produces almost 100 percent improvement in retention after a long period of time. More generally, it can be shown that for any two training periods of length x and y, the asymptotic ratio of retained memory strengths will be x/y and this ratio does not depend upon the decay rate, although the absolute amount of the memory strength does.

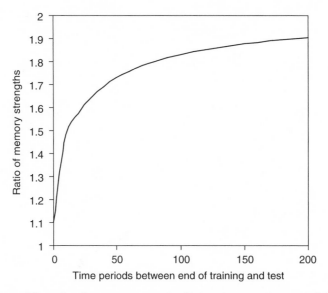

FIGURE 5.3. The ratio of memory strengths during the retention period, shown for the case in which one training period is twice the length of the other.

Does this exercise in mathematical psychology have any relevance to actual training situations? I think it does, for several reasons. Anderson's model of memory strength has been used as an illustration, but the general point being made does not depend upon accepting this particular model. Any reasonable model of memory and learning must produce curves similar to these in order to be in accord with the massive literature on the topic. Power functions are good approximations to the data in a wide variety of situations involving learning and retention of both skills and declarative knowledge. Logically, these functions can be derived from models of learning that assume that learning consists of acquiring micro-rules (*productions* in the jargon of cognitive science) for responding to situations (Newell and Rosenbloom, 1981). This model of learning is behind many intelligent tutoring systems.

Overlearning occurs in important learning situations outside the laboratory. Chatham says that you never forget how to ride a bicycle, but you forget calculus quickly. I know of no experimental study of retention of calculus in particular, but there has been a study of the retention of mathematical skills over a 30-year period (Bahrick and Hall, 1991). They are not lost all that quickly, some are never lost, and overlearning is very important. As a rule of thumb, you remember mathematics up to the class just below the highest class you took. If you took calculus you will not forget algebra. I speculate that if you took differential equations you will remember a good bit of your calculus.

Training programs should not be judged by the performance of trainees immediately after the end of the program. They should be judged by their effect on the performance of trainees in the field, sometimes months or even years after training has ceased. The economics of training to end-of-course performance and the economics of training to performance in the field may be quite different.

This is all very well in theory, but in practice the assessment of performance varies from being trivial to being very difficult. The general rule is that the more tightly defined the job, the easier the assessment. The warehouse discount store Costco records the number of transactions per hour completed by check-out clerks. Traditionally, examples like this have been dismissed as being relevant only to precisely defined occupations. However, the times may be changing. More and more electronic records are being generated, even by upper-class, white-collar, professional, and managerial personnel. Consider some of the following examples. Schools keep electronic records of student performance and of teacher characteristics, such as level and source of degree and years of experience teaching. Insurance companies and government agencies have detailed records of diagnoses, treatments, prescriptions, and, in some cases, outcomes of treatments of patients. These can be related to physician characteristics, which are similarly recorded. (In at least one case, they are. Pathology findings are related to radiologists' diagnoses, making it possible to conduct signal-detection analyses of the performance of the radiologists.) Electronic records exist of the number of contacts, length of appointments, and sales records of individual salespersons. And to close, bringing my examples close to home, electronic records exist of professorial performance. These include papers, grants, student ratings, and student performance.

It is not easy to make sense of these masses of data. From the management standpoint, there is a very real danger that executives might start to "manage the computer," thus missing important variables that were not in the digital record. This could have deleterious effects. In the professorial example, for instance, the use of present-day electronic records would probably bias managers toward emphasizing short-term performance, even though the mission of the university is supposed to be to encourage people who think about difficult long-term issues. Furthermore, there are non-trivial issues about the use of such information in personnel decisions. Various teachers' unions have made it quite clear what they think of using performance as a basis for establishing salaries.

There is likely to be much less resistance to proposals to use these records for the evaluation of training programs than there will be to use the records for evaluation (and paying and promoting) individuals. A teachers' union that would be on the picket line if student performance records were used to establish pay raises might be quite indifferent to a program that used the same records to evaluate the relative effectiveness of teachers trained at different universities, as long as the focus was on comparison of the universities and not the individual teachers. There is a potential for using electronic performance records to assess the relationship between training and performance. The task will not be trivial, but that is what makes research interesting.

To summarize, Chatham's reviews of the first training revolution in the armed services (Chapter 2) and his speculation about a coming revolution (Chapter 10) define some of the issues involved in training for high-level performance. Up to this point I have tried to relate his comments on lessons from the first training revolution to well-known principles established by decades of research in psychology and related sciences. I now turn to the Lajoie and Mumford et al. chapters, and attempt to show how they fit into the discussion initiated by Chatham.

SHERLOCK AND ITS HEIRS

Lajoie (Chapter 3) describes the very long-lived Sherlock project, in which some of the best ideas about cognitive science in education were deployed to create a tutor on how to repair a complicated piece of equipment used in the maintenance of F-15 fighter jets. She goes on to sketch how the same general approach used in the Sherlock project is being used to create a similar tutoring system for medical diagnostics. Sherlock has been around for some time; it was sufficiently developed to undergo (favorable) evaluation in 1988, 19 years before the date of the conference on which this volume was based (Lesgold et al., 1988). Why is it that Chatham does not mention Sherlock in either of his two papers, even though the second of these is concerned with the application of computer-controlled tutoring to military situations? I discussed this with Chatham as I was preparing this paper. He stressed the fact that certain key bureaucrats decided not to try to emulate Sherlock widely. I am not so sure that that was the case. At the microscopic level, decisions are made by individuals. At the macroscopic level, what seems to be a decision dependent on personalities can often be seen as the result of particular players running through a script that was written by larger, more impersonal, forces. I think that the problem is the characteristics of the tutorial system itself.

Sherlock is one of a class of several tutorial systems that are now operating in training and education. In addition to the medical system being developed by Lajoie and colleagues, there are similar programs intended to teach aspects of introductory physics (especially mechanics), mathematics, and biology. I am sure that there are others that I do not know about. Following the Navy's tradition, I will refer to them, collectively, as Sherlock class tutors.

Sherlock class tutors are characterized by careful analyses of the information and skills to be imparted, followed by construction of a program that analyzes the trainee's current skills and then presents information and/or problems that move the trainee toward a higher level of expertise. As Lajoie has pointed out with respect to Sherlock, and as has been shown in other fields, these systems work quite well both in controlled environments and in the field. However they are not, nor were they intended to be, the answer to all the diverse training problems encountered in both military and civilian settings. This class of tutoring systems works in some places and not in others.

Sherlock class systems depend upon the existence of a well-defined body of knowledge that can be programmed, using conventional programming techniques. Let us call this the *encapsulated knowledge* criterion. In designing the system, one or more experts are asked to place their capsules of knowledge into the tutor. Interestingly, this knowledge does not have to be correct. The goal is to program the reasoning of a current expert, not an ultimate expert. If a Sherlock class program for prenatal care had been constructed in the 1950s, it would have advised prescribing thalidomide for morning sickness, because the teratogenic effects of the drug were unknown at the time. It is worth keeping this example in mind. Unless we are dealing with a tutorial program for a constructed world (as Sherlock did, but as medical tutors do not), encapsulated knowledge changes over time.

Knowledge is not always encapsulated. In some cases, what the trainee needs to learn is how to generate knowledge from experience. This is particularly the case when the trainee is trying to learn how to interact with other humans. Chatham (Chapter 2) offers a good example, the use of skilled opposition forces (OPFOR) in training exercises. A good OPFOR commander is not told how to act; he or she is told to follow the general doctrine of a potential enemy, amplified by ingenuity. More generally, in some areas of expertise, the role of the expert is to interact with other humans. I will return to this point later when I discuss the chapter by Mumford et al. on leadership, where I think encapsulated knowledge is difficult to find. For the moment I turn to two issues related to the adoption of Sherlock class programs.

It takes years to develop them. The biggest bottleneck seems to be the difficulty of extracting and codifying expert knowledge, although the programming step is also significant. This is not a problem when the goal is to integrate trained experts who will work on a very large project, such as a major weapons system. Sherlock appears to have taken roughly 10 years to develop. So what? The F-15 aircraft first flew in 1972, and as of 2007 the Air Force still had over 400 F-15s in operation. Presumably medical training will continue for a very long time. On the other hand, in early 2003 the U.S. military had no plan to have large numbers of U.S. troops in close contact with Iraqi civilians. By 2004, such contact was part of a major mission. As Chatham describes, there is a place for rapid development of training programs for missions that appear quickly and may be of intense but limited duration. Chatham (personal communication) kindly allowed me to examine one such program, *Tactical Iraqi*. It is a combination of an automated phrase-book with computer game–like vignettes intended to allow U.S. personnel to engage in simple, mission-relevant conversations with speakers of Arabic. It also does some training in how to avoid social gaffes.

Tactical Iraqi and similar programs are intended to establish minimal competence. They have to be designed quickly. It is not clear to me that the lessons learned from constructing Sherlock class programs have very much relevance to the development of this sort of training aid.

Computer-based training programs belong to that large class of devices, including diets, birth control pills, and the Bible, that only provide a benefit if one uses them. Motivation is important. It can come from one of two sources. The student/trainee may be intensely motivated to master the material (*extrinsic* motivation) or the process of interacting with the program may itself be enjoyable (*intrinsic* motivation). The designers of the most successful Sherlock class programs, including Sherlock itself, have been able to assume extrinsic motivation. Senior aviation technicians and medical students understand exactly why they want to know what the computer program is supposed to teach. Human computer interface (HCI) issues are important in order to minimize the time needed to learn how to use the program, but HCI designers are not asked to make using the program fun.

Chatham (Chapter 10) argues that the many training programs for military personnel, in general, do have to provide intrinsic motivation. The same thing is certainly true for programs designed to teach students in the K–12 system. If the experience of interacting with the program is not a rewarding one, trainees may simply decline to log in. Understandably, Lajoie ignores this issue because it arises very little, if at all, in the aircraft maintenance and medical education worlds. In other worlds, it can be crucial. For example, Graesser and colleagues have shown that attention to the design of natural conversations with human-appearing avatars can have a beneficial effect for undergraduate students learning academic topics, even within the Sherlock class of tutors (Graesser, McNamara, & VanLehn, 2005).

Students/trainees can be conceptualized as being on a dimension stretching from the dedicated professional who knows why he or she wants to know the material, to the student taking a required course for rather opaque reasons (high school trigonometry class, perhaps?). To the extent that the reason for studying poses problems in both course design and student motivation. Course design can be handed over to technical experts, such as the master technician who consulted on Sherlock. But what about establishing motivation? This is a task for a leader, not a computer program.

Which brings us to the paper on leadership by Mumford and colleagues (Chapter 4).

IS LEADERSHIP A NATURAL KIND?

Mumford et al. (Chapter 4) begin by analyzing the literature showing that a variety of leadership training programs work. A puzzling finding is that the training programs that they review take quite different approaches to the problems of training leaders, but they all seem to work. As a result, although we know that in leadership something works, we hesitate to say that anything works and we are not quite sure what the something is. Next, Mumford et al. stress the importance of a leader being able to articulate a plan, and then, as the plan is being executed, being able to identify circumstances under which the plan had to be changed, in the jargon of Mumford et al., a *change event*.

I do not claim any particular expertise in the training of leaders, so it would be presumptive of me to criticize Mumford and colleagues' review of the literature. Accepting their review and reflecting on some personal experiences while either being a leader or being led (or being a consultant to others who were leading) has led me to speculate a bit on why such a variety of training methods seems to work. These speculations will lead me to critique something that is implicit in the argument posed by Mumford et al., the assumption that there is a general trait/skill of leadership.

Certain ways of being a bad leader generalize across situations. These include, but are not limited to, failing to have a plan, failing to realize that the plan is not working (remember Chatham's remark about the value of AARs in Chapter 2?), and doing things that alienate the people upon whom the leader depends to get the plan executed. I start with an example of a principle for avoiding bad leadership, and an example of a failure of that principle in modern business.

Years ago, and for all I know today, lieutenants and sergeants in the U.S. Marine Corps were told, in their respective schools, that there were three principles the Marines lived by. The third was "Officers eat last."[2] This remark, with all that it implies, does not just apply to military organizations. At the start of the 21st century, U.S. airlines had a great deal of labor trouble. The airlines had a serious financial problem, and needed to seek salary concessions from their employees. Everyone agreed with this, including leaders of the pilots' and mechanics' unions. Union attitudes hardened when it was found that the airline executives were simultaneously asking the employees to take pay cuts and awarding themselves large bonuses. Indeed, the day that I wrote these words, airline pilots picketed the United Airlines ticket counter at my home airport precisely about this issue. Officers were not eating last, and there was Hell to pay.

Being a unit commander in the Marines and being the CEO in a modern airline are very different jobs. The point of this example is that there may be a great deal of commonality in ways to be a *bad* leader. These ways are surprisingly easy to fall into. Leadership training can increase competence, albeit not really imparting expertise, by showing leader trainees how to avoid common mistakes. Some methods of training may do a good job in stamping

---

[2] The first was "We never leave anyone behind." The second, which I shall not repeat, was an uncomplimentary remark about the United States Navy.

out mistake A, while others stamp out mistake B. This would lead to precisely the situation Mumford et al. describe. Lots of different approaches seem to work reasonably well. However, our present leadership training methods have not produced Napoleons, Henry Fords, or Abraham Lincolns. Nor has anyone ever claimed they do. This brings me to my second speculation.

In their chapter (and, I think, somewhat more in the public presentation on which the chapter is based), Mumford et al. place great emphasis on a leader's creating a plan, monitoring the execution of a plan, and deciding when plans need to be changed. This is certainly part of leadership, especially in a business context. I am struck, though, by the fact that in many situations the tasks of planning and observing the situation are relegated to staff; the operations and intelligence officers in a military context and the production and marketing departments in business. The role of the leader is to outline the goals of the plan, approve it, make sure that there are channels of information that will inform the leader about the change event, and then, in the act that separates the leader from the staff, *motivate other people to carry out the plan.* This in itself may require substantial attention to training, organization, and acquiring knowledge of the strengths and weaknesses of key people.

The abilities needed to handle these positive aspects of leadership may depend upon the situation. Thus, while bad leaders are pretty much all of a kind, and often can be made acceptable by training, good and even expert leadership differs greatly from situation to situation. If I am correct, there cannot be any "one size fits all" training program to produce expert leaders.

To buttress my point, I now present a "case study" of two people with a record of successful leadership, blemished by some conspicuous failures. They were both expert leaders but there was no common theme to their strengths and weaknesses. I ask readers to consider whether the recommendations of Mumford et al. or, for that matter, any one coherent program of leadership training, could have produced both these leaders.

My first example is Abraham Lincoln. He is familiar to us all.[3] My second example is a less familiar figure – the Napoleonic era Royal Navy officer, Vice Admiral William Bligh, RN, FRS. I briefly state some facts about his career.[4]

Unlike most highly ranked Royal Navy officers of the time, Bligh had essentially no familial political influence. As a teenager and young man he served on merchant ships and then entered the Royal Navy as a midshipman. He proved a very competent sailor, serving as sailing master for Captain James Cook on Cook's final voyage of exploration. After a brief return to the merchant service, he was appointed Lieutenant Commanding (and hence by courtesy "Captain") of HMS Bounty, bound for Tahiti on a scientific mission. There

---

[3]   There have been many biographies and accounts of Lincoln and his time. I have relied heavily on Goodwin (2005).

[4]   I rely on MacKanness (1936) for my information about Bligh.

followed a mutiny and an amazing voyage in which Bligh took a group of loyal officers and men 3,000 miles in an open boat without a single casualty. After the subsequent court-martial (in which Bligh was completely exonerated of blame), he returned to service in the Napoleonic Wars. He was twice singled out for heroism and competence in battle, the equivalent of receiving a decoration today. One of his awarders was Admiral Lord Nelson.

When the Napoleonic Wars ended, Bligh was appointed Governor-General of the New South Wales colony in Australia. Upon arrival he found a colony that most historians today agree was corrupt, in no small part due to exploitation of convict labor and other misdeeds by the officers of the New South Wales regiment. Bligh developed excellent plans for correcting the situation, but in attempting to execute them, he rode roughshod over both the officers of the regiment and politically important colonists. In modern parlance, he was not a people person. The New South Wales Regiment mutinied and Bligh was exiled to Tasmania. The mutiny was suppressed by a newly appointed governor general, Lachlan Macquarie, who brought his own troops with him. Macquarie then proceeded to execute many of Bligh's plans, but with much more tact. Bligh returned home, where he was again exonerated, and promoted to Rear Admiral. After some shore duties he was given a retirement rank of Vice Admiral, the rank he held when he died.

Lincoln will probably be famous as long as there is a United States, and maybe long afterwards. Bligh was moderately well known in his time. Two books[5] and three movies (to date) made his 15 minutes of fame last for 200 years. Unfairly, the lasting fame is for a fictional Bligh, and not the real man.

Both Bligh and Lincoln were, by and large, successful leaders. Both had their moments of failure. The situations in which they led and the leadership traits they displayed were very different. We may learn something about producing leaders by combining some of the remarks by Mumford et al. about leadership training with an analysis of the differences between Bligh and Lincoln.

Lincoln was notoriously reflective. He seldom made a decision immediately upon being presented with a problem, preferring to hear arguments pro and con. He then produced a reasoned decision, usually compromising between arguments on one side and those on another. This is often a good thing for a very high-level policy maker, as Lincoln was. At times his deliberate approach frustrated and even enraged his supporters. His policy on slavery

---

[5] *Mutiny on the Bounty* and *Men Against the Sea,* both by Charles Nordhoff and James Norman Hall. Although Nordhoff and Hall were novelists, they appear to have been exceptionally careful in their research. The first book is a fictionalized account of the voyage of the Bounty in a way that is, to say the least, unsympathetic to Bligh. The movies are based on this story. The second book, also fiction, tells the story of Bligh's voyage in the open boat. It paints a very different picture of a short-tempered, insensitive, extremely competent, courageous leader.

is a good example. Very early in his career Lincoln determined that slavery was evil and should go. He was also sensitive to the economic problems that slaveholders would face, believed that their property rights should be recompensed, and, when he became president, appreciated the need for support for the Union by the border states, where slavery was legal but belief in the Union was strong. Abolitionists in the cabinet and in Congress were furious at what they regarded as temporizing with a moral evil.

Bligh did not have the luxury of reflection. When an 18th–19th-century warship was caught in a storm, the sails had to be set *now*. Challenges to authority had to be met immediately. To the consternation of his Secretary of War, Lincoln temporized when the commander of the Army of the Potomac, General McClellan, was publicly insubordinate. Lincoln waited to remove McClellan until he had calculated the political effect such a removal would have. At one point on the voyage in the open boat, Bligh's leadership was challenged. He picked up one of the two cutlasses aboard and dared the challenger to pick up the other. (He did not.)

These were not isolated incidents. Throughout his career, Lincoln was troubled by subordinates who felt they could challenge him without repercussions. In spite of the reputation of the fictional Bligh, the real Bligh was not thought of as a notoriously cruel captain by the standards of the time. But everyone knew that insubordination would have repercussions.

There is another side to this issue. After all, Bligh did endure two mutinies, and few of the people who worked with him found him a comfortable person to be around. Most of the people who worked with Lincoln became intensely loyal to him as a person. The best example is his Secretary of State, William Seward. In 1860 Seward felt that he was better qualified than Lincoln to be president and that, in justice, he ought to have the Republican nomination for the services he had done to the party. A good case can be made that Seward was right. After 1860, no one served Lincoln more loyally than Seward did. Compare this to the actions of the First Lieutenant of the *Bounty,* Fletcher Christian, after being rebuked in public by Bligh. Why such a difference?

When Lincoln had a policy disagreement with someone, he was careful to attack the idea, not the person. In the one court action in his career where he was found guilty, Bligh received a reprimand from a board of senior officers for his intemperate language toward junior officers and crews. During the Napoleonic Wars, being known as the most profane captain in the Royal Navy was an honor not won lightly.[6]

I offer one more contrast, and then turn to an important point of agreement in the histories of these two very different leaders. Bligh was very well

---

[6] Surprisingly, it appears that when Bligh was ashore he was a loving husband and father. Perhaps this is a dramatic case of Mischel's argument that we too often attribute situation-specific behavior to a person-specific trait.

versed in the technical details of navigation. Cook, one of the greatest navigators of all time, would hardly have chosen him for sailing master if this had not been true. He also knew the principles of naval warfare, as fought at the time, and the ins and outs of the Royal Navy. He knew these things from direct experience, having been at sea and often in command since he was a teenager.

When Lincoln took office he was not similarly conversant with the Federal government. At the outset of the Civil War he unwisely enmeshed himself in the details of dispensing Federal appointments to loyalists,[7] to the detriment of the urgent business of preparing for war. This is not surprising. He had only two years' experience in Federal office, as a congressman from Illinois, and he had never had "command experience" of anything larger than a law office with, at most, three or four partners.

But, and a most important but, Lincoln knew reasoning, he knew how to strike compromises, and he knew how to work through other people. As a successful lawyer, he had a great deal of experience in making arrangements for business that would be carried out far from his supervision. He had learned how to earn the respect of judges and colleagues who would be with him on one case and against him on another. When he turned to politics he had a huge case library (Mumford and colleague's term) dealing with how to get your way through logical reasoning and persuasion. This was very useful when Lincoln, as president, had to get people to carry out his policies when they were well out of his direct observation and control. When Bligh came to New South Wales, he had built himself a case library dealing with the exercise of direct command and highly technical situation analysis and planning. On board a Napoleonic era warship most of the captain's orders were executed only yards away from the quarterdeck. He had the wrong case library for his new situation.

Had Bligh had Lincoln's case library I think that the New South Wales colony would have been reformed without a mutiny. Where does this place us in terms of training leaders?

Leaders have to have the opportunity to build up a case library. Mumford et al. put this very well. This library will consist of two sub-libraries: technical expertise appropriate to the field and interpersonal experiences, also appropriate to the field. These libraries can certainly be acquired through experience and analysis – Chatham's battle simulations and AARs again. However, experience, though the best teacher, has two drawbacks. It takes a career and the tuition is high. Can leadership training shortcut the process of career growth?

With respect to technical expertise the answer is yes. Games to simulate at-sea refueling, battlefield tactics, air traffic control, and the analysis of weather patterns exist today. Whether these and other such trainers should be patterned on the Sherlock class programs or the more rough and ready approach

---

[7] This was the common practice at the time. The present Civil Service did not appear in the United States until more than 30 years after Lincoln's death.

taken by *Tactical Iraqi* depends upon the circumstances, the time and money available, and the level of expertise desired. Field-appropriate technical expertise is an important part of leadership. But, in the last analysis, what separates the commander from the operations officer, and the CEO from the long-term planning office, is the ability to lead people.

I am very hesitant to say that computers cannot be made to do x, no matter what x is. But if x is training people to lead other people, I think we are more than a little ways away. As he often did, Shakespeare summed up the problem.

KING HENRY THE IVTH, PART 1: *The rebel English leader, Harry Hotspur, is talking with the Welsh chieftain, Own Glendower. They are reviewing the forces they can bring to bear against King Henry.*

GLENDOWER: I can call spirits from the vasty deep.
HOTSPUR: Well, so can I, so can any man. Will they come?[8]

If they don't come, you aren't a leader.

SUMMARY

These three chapters, on their face so varied, actually do complement each other. Chatham has given us a big picture of military training and set questions about the teaching of technical and organizational expertise. Lajoie described an approach that addresses some of Chatham's questions but leaves others unanswered. Mumford and colleagues also address some of Chatham's questions, but in doing so they leave us wondering whether it is a good idea to treat leadership as a unitary skill. These are the big issues. Subsequent sections of this book deal with the skills necessary for high levels of individual performance in a variety of fields in both the civilian and military sector with a focus on professionals, such as physicians (Boshuizen, Chapter 17; Davis, Chapter 8), sonar operators (Kirschenbaum, McInnis, & Correll, Chapter 12), musicians (Ericsson, Chapter 18), and pilots (Schreiber, Bennett, Colegrove, Portrey, Greschke, & Bell, Chapter 11). With a few exceptions, high-level performance is seldom solely a matter of individual and technical performance. Experts have to operate in social contexts and often are expected to be leaders and to guide and/or direct members of their teams while commanding a military combat unit (Shadrick & Lussier, Chapter 13), conducting surgery (Ericsson, Chapter 18), or teaching introductory physics (VanLehn & van de Sande, Chapter 16). I worry that this focus on measurable individual performance may have missed some important aspects of typical expertise. I suggest that as the reader looks through the following chapters, he or she asks how the proposed training techniques and examples deal with the social aspects of team and organizational performance.

---

[8] *King Henry IV*: Part I. Act III, Scene I.

REFERENCES

Anderson, J. R., Fincham, J. M., & Douglass, S. (1999). Practice and retention: A unifying analysis. *Journal of Experimental Psychology: Learning, Memory, and Cognition, 25*(5), 1120–1136.

Bahrick, H. P., & Hall, L. K. (1991). Lifetime maintenance of high school mathematics content. *Journal of Experimental Psychology: General, 120*(1), 20–33.

Goodwin, D. K. (2005). *Team of rivals: The political genius of Abraham Lincoln.* New York: Simon & Schuster.

Graesser, A. C., McNamara, D. S., & VanLehn, K. (2005). Scaffolding deep comprehension strategies through Point&Query, AutoTutor, and iSTART. *Educational Psychologist, 40*(4), 225–234.

Greenwald, A. G., & Gillmore, G. M. (1997). Grading leniency is a removable contaminant of student ratings. *American Psychologist, 52*(11), 1209–1217.

Hughes, L. (2002). *Peter the Great: A biography.* New Haven, CT: Yale University Press.

Hunt, E. (2002). *Thoughts on thought: A discussion of formal models of cognition.* Mahwah, NJ: Lawrence Erlbaum Associates.

Lesgold, A., Lajoie, S. P., Bajpayee, J., Bunzo, M., Eastman, R., Eggan, G., et al. (1988). *A computer coached practice environment for the manual test station shop: Sherlock's influence on trainee job performance (contract no. F33615-84-c-0058).* Alexandria, VA: Human Resources Research Organization.

Mackaness, G. (1936). *The life of vice-admiral William Bligh, R.N., F.R.S.* New York: Farrar & Rihehart.

Mischel, W. (2004). Toward an integrative science of the person. *Annual Review of Psychology, 55,* 1–22.

Newell, A., & Rosenbloom, P. S. (1981). Mechanisms of skill acquisition and the law of practice. In J. R. Anderson (Ed.), *Cognitive skills and their acquisition* (pp. 1–56). Hillsdale, NJ: Lawrence Erlbaum Associates.

Schooler, L. J., & Anderson, J. R. (1997). The role of processes in the rational analysis of memory. *Cognitive Psychology, 32*(3), 219–250.

Snook, S. A. (2000). *Friendly fire: The accidental shootdown of U.S. Black Hawks over Northern Iraq.* Princeton, NJ: Princeton University Press.

Stevenson, H. W., Lee, S-Y, & Stigler, J. W. (1986). Mathematics achievement of Chinese, Japanese, and American Children. *Science, 231*(4739), 693–699.

Weiner, N. (1948). *Cybernetics.* New York: Wiley.

SECTION 2

PAST AND CONTEMPORARY EFFORTS TO DESIGN INSTRUCTION, TRAIN, AND MAINTAIN PROFESSIONAL PERFORMANCE

The second section of the book is concerned with a review of the major approaches and general frameworks for training individuals to acquire necessary basic skills, more complex skills, and the continued education of professionals and maintenance of their skills during their careers.

6

Research on Past and Current Training in Professional Domains: The Emerging Need for a Paradigm Shift

JEROEN J. G. VAN MERRIËNBOER AND
EDDY W. BOOT

About 25 years ago, the computer was introduced in education and training. More than any other tool, it shaped the development of the field of educational technology. There are many similarities between the developments in the general educational field and professional training, but also important differences. This chapter focuses on professional training. The main questions are how did professional training develop since the early 1980s, what is the current state of affairs, and what are necessary future developments?

The structure of this chapter is five-part. First, we discuss how the goals of professional training have been changing – and still are changing – at all levels of the organizations involved (e.g., business and industry, government, military) in order to cope with new societal and technological demands. Second, we show how the changing goals of professional training are connected to the way training is developed, that is, to instructional systems design (ISD). Third, we demonstrate how these changing goals are connected to the use of new learning technologies. Fourth, we discuss the developments in technology enhanced learning environments (TELEs), in which ISD and the use of learning technologies meet in concrete training applications. In the fifth and final section, we discuss future implications of our analysis. The claim is made that ISD approaches in professional training are often outdated, making the development of TELEs more and more technology driven. A paradigm shift is needed, where traditional ISD is replaced by a holistic approach to the development of highly integrated TELEs, in which authentic tasks drive the learning process.

THE CHANGING GOALS OF PROFESSIONAL TRAINING

During the last decades, professional training has been based on a systems approach or ISD. Uniform training requirements and assessments are established in a task, condition, and standard (TCS) paradigm: Which tasks should be executed, under which complicating conditions, and by which objective standards (Brown, 2003; Scales, 2006)? This TCS paradigm allows for training employees in their professional or occupational specialties uniformly and efficiently. Complex content and tasks are reduced into simpler elements, and are transferred to the learners through presentation, practice, and feedback.

However, professional training is currently transforming, instigated by fast societal and technological changes. In modern society, knowledge quickly becomes obsolete and new technologies are developed at an ever-increasing speed. Professionals must be highly flexible, both in the sense that they must be able to deal with unfamiliar situations and must act as lifelong learners who continuously update their competencies. Military training may serve as a good example, because before and after executing operational missions, the military is primarily a training organization. Training has always been an intrinsic, integral part of each military job, and the armed forces is the largest single training organization with a standardized policy (Bratton-Jeffery, Hoffman, & Jeffery, 2006). In military training, an increasing shift of responsibility over task performance down the command chain can be observed. Providing commanders and soldiers on lower operational levels with more possibilities, information, and responsibilities should make it possible to deal better with the current, complex (battlefield) situations and agile opponents (Chatham, Chapter 10; Dixon, Allen, Burgess, Kilner, & Wchweitzer, 2005). This is necessary because of the following changes:

- Military operations have changed from large-scale, international, and national conflicts to missions in (regional and local) complex situations known as "three-block wars," in which soldiers are conducting full-scale military actions, peacekeeping operations, and assisting in humanitarian relief in confined space and time. This increases the need for creative solutions in constantly changing situations, as well as considerable cultural awareness (e.g., knowledge of local language and customs).

- More and more independent services operate jointly (e.g., the Air Force with the Army) and/or in international combinations (e.g., in the context of NATO and/or the U.N.), requiring close collaboration among soldiers from different backgrounds and nationalities. Again, cultural awareness and flexibility in behavior are extremely important to reach an acceptable level of performance.

- New generations of integrated ICT systems are introduced in the military, which (in due time) distribute information just in time, just in place, and with the content and presentation of that content adapted to the profile of the user and the characteristics of the particular (mobile) device. It provides soldiers – especially those close to action – with shared situational awareness and ad hoc resources. This enables, for example, an individual Special Force soldier to direct B-52 strikes in Afghanistan.

For military training to respond to these changes, the original TCS paradigm needs to be changed. Moreover, this change should occur at all chain-of-command levels in the organization, because it not only affects the performance of soldiers in the field but also executive functions. Thus, it affects basic military training, advanced training (e.g., military occupational specialties), as well as (non-commissioned) officer training (e.g., military academies and staff colleges). Analogous developments can be observed in other professional domains, such as business and industry, governmental organizations, health care, and so forth.

In this chapter, we will explore the consequences of the changing goals of professional training given the way training is designed and implemented in TELEs using different learning technologies. In any case, cultural awareness and knowledge that can be flexibly applied under unpredictable conditions become more and more important. This challenges the traditional compartmentalization of professional training in distinct sets of skills, knowledge, and attitudes – as well as its focus on procedural rather than social and problem-solving skills. As a related issue, it is becoming impossible to specify all goals of training in highly specific learning objectives, because effective behaviors often involve integrated objectives or even extend beyond them. This challenges the fragmentation of training in independent pieces that cover separate learning objectives. Finally, training should not only be directed toward what to do under familiar situations, but especially what to do in new, unfamiliar, and unforeseen situations. This indicates that transfer of learning is at least equally important as the direct learning outcomes. Finally, professional training should be more directed at decision making, creativity, imagination, and problem solving in dealing with unexpected situations. Employees will need to learn to share and find information from multiple sources and then use that information to plan and make decisions, assisted by network-based information management and decision support tools.

INSTRUCTIONAL SYSTEMS DESIGN

ISD is sometimes characterized as a "soft" technology (Jonassen, 2004) because it focuses on the pedagogical methods and techniques (i.e., how to educate) rather than on the hard technology of equipment, media, and software used. Dick (1987), Olsen and Bass (1982), Reiser (2001a, 2001b), and Reiser and Dempsey (2002) provide a historical overview of educational technology from a North American perspective. Most authors pinpoint its beginning during the Second World War when thousands of soldiers were trained in a very short period of time through "teaching machines" and instructional films – usually based on behavioral principles (Skinner, 1954). In 1956, Benjamin Bloom introduced his taxonomy of learning objectives and the "mastery learning" principle, characteristic for the central notions that various learning objectives required various educational methods, and that well-designed education had to lead the learner step-by-step to his chosen learning goals. This, in combination with the *General Systems Theory* of Ludwig von Bertalanffy (1976) led to the ISD approach for the development of instruction. In a review article, Robert Glaser (1962) introduced the term "instructional design" to refer to the use of theoretically founded instructional design rules within ISD, Robert Mager (1975) refined the system to specify and formulate learning objectives, and Robert Gagné (1965) introduced a systematic approach to organize learning content with the learning hierarchy of intellectual skills in his book *The Conditions of Learning.*

The I(S)D approach continued to develop up to the start of the 1990s. A key development related to expanding the flexibility of the linear-cyclical approach, regarded by many designers as a straitjacket. Approaches like "rapid prototyping" (Tripp & Bichelmeijer, 1990) are better geared to gradual prototype development based on user tests, while "layers of necessity" (Tessmer & Wedman, 1990) enable phases or sub-phases to be skipped. Another development related to automating parts of the design process ("courseware engineering"; Tennyson, 1994). Originally, tools were mainly developed for the production and realization phase (Authorware, Toolbook, and many others; Nantel, 2004), but soon tools also were created to support instructional designers in performing the design phase (ISD Expert, Instructional Design Environment, Designer's Edge). In a military context, for example, systems developed in the Advanced Instructional Design Advisor (AIDA) project (Muraida & Spector, 1993; Spector, Muraida, & Marlino, 1991) included the Guided Approach to Instructional Design Advising (GAIDA), which guided the design of courseware lessons based upon Gagné's nine events of instruction, and the Experimental Advanced Instructional Design Advisor (XAIDA), which used the instructional transaction theory of Merrill, Li, and Jones (1991, 1992) as a framework to encapsulate context-specific knowledge. In the late 1980s and 1990s, however, the influence of the ISD approach declined due to the rise of constructivism.

Social-Constructivist Design

The rising social-constructivist paradigm took off against the dominant educational-technological notions, amid a heated debate raging largely within the United States that was termed "constructivism versus objectivism" (Jonassen, 1991; Wilson, 1997). Characteristic of ISD at that time was its atomistic approach. Complex learning contents are analyzed in increasingly smaller entities such as learning objectives. According to the "conditions of learning," different types of objectives are best reached with different methods for presentation, practice, and feedback. So, a piece of instruction is developed for each separate objective and the pieces of instruction are put together in larger instructional units. These principles are known as objectivist, since they appear to presume that knowledge of the world is objectively available and that this "objective" knowledge can be transferred to learners. Constructivists reject this transfer model, claiming that knowledge is always the result of a highly personal process of knowledge construction. A radical form of constructivism (e.g., Bednar, Cunningham, Duffy, & Perry, 1991) suggests that we know no objective reality since our perception of reality is always a construction. In education, learning is approached as an interactive process and "negotiation of meaning" helps to build up a – more or less – shared interpretation of the world. The ISD approach is rejected on three grounds: 1) *epistemology*: knowledge cannot be transferred but can only be constructed; 2) *learning theory*: learning is deriving meaning on the basis of (mediated) social interaction processes rather than an associative process of linking information elements together; and 3) *didactic approach*: meaningful tasks in an authentic context drive learning rather than pieces of instruction aimed at distinct learning objectives.

What does the social-constructivist approach substitute for ISD? Building on the cultural-historical ideas of Vygotsky (1978) and Piaget's ideas of socio-cognitive conflict (1950), a central position was given to the interaction of the learner with the world and with others. In the interaction with the world, tools and cultural artifacts play a key role. A research line around *cognitive tools* emerged (Kommers, Jonassen, & Mayes, 1992). Such tools support and stimulate conceptualization and learning processes and may have various forms, from domain-specific expert systems and microworlds, to general applications (e.g., spreadsheets, word processors) and knowledge representation tools (e.g., concept mapping, flowcharting). The use of tools in the form of construction kits is crucial to "learning by design," an educational technology approach based on the suitability of constructive design activities for facilitating knowledge construction.

In addition to interaction with the world, interaction with others is crucial to the social-constructivist approach, and reference is often made to Vygotsky's assertion: "The mind grows through interaction with other minds." Collaborative learning is enjoying a renewed focus, especially in the form of computer-supported collaborative learning (CSCL), defined as learning in a computer-based network that supports groups through a shared interface in collaborating on common learning tasks (Kirschner, 2004).

Social constructivism does offer a designer a number of basic principles that a "good" educational design must fulfill. It entails creating a learning environment for collaboration on complex, authentic tasks and drawing out the required behavior ("affordances") with adequate support ("scaffolding") to prevent too much trial-and-error behavior. It does *not*, however, provide a real design science with a systematic engineering approach such as ISD. This is why social-constructivist design never became dominant in professional training.

Whole-Task Design Models

Over the past 10 years a cautious synthesis has taken place between systematic ISD approaches and social-constructivist approaches (Dijkstra, 1997; Vrasidas, 2000; Wilson, 1997). The notion here is that emphasizing antitheses is usually ineffective and that different approaches, such as regarding light as both waves and particles, or the application of both qualitative and quantitative research methods, can often bear fruit when used together. Merrill (2002; see also Collis & Margaryan, 2005) discusses a number of design theories, each of which tries to arrive at a synthesis of systematic designs and social-constructivist principles. A critical analysis brings Merrill (2002) to the conclusion that five "first principles of instruction" lie at the basis of all these recent models:

1. Learning is promoted if students work on "whole tasks" or problems that are related to their daily lives or their future professions.
2. Learning is promoted if prior knowledge is activated as a seed bed for new knowledge.
3. Learning is promoted if new knowledge is demonstrated to students.
4. Learning is promoted if students have to apply new knowledge.
5. Learning is promoted if new knowledge is integrated into the world of the students.

Three developments characterize current design approaches. First, an emphasis on *realistic, whole tasks* as the "engine" for learning, which leads to a different starting point for design. Traditionally the design has been based on content along with the corresponding presentation methods, after which assignments and feedback are coupled to the learning materials presented earlier. Recent approaches, in contrast, begin by shaping the learning environment with realistic learning tasks or scenarios and only then provide the relevant information in a more or less structured manner. In addition to feedback, all other kinds of supervision, support, and scaffolding have acquired a central role in channeling learning using complex, realistic tasks. This "topling" of the design approach can be found in recent theories as well as in new computer-supported design tools (for examples, see van Merriënboer & Martens, 2002).

Second, more attention is paid to the position of the learner. *Personalization* of education takes student's prior knowledge (including competencies gained elsewhere), needs, and interests explicitly into account. Assessments of performance on realistic tasks and (electronic) development portfolios offer a basis for personalization (see, in this volume, Baker, Chapter 15, and Lajoie, Chapter 3; van Merriënboer, Sluijsmans, Corbalan, Kalyuga, & Tattersal, 2006). Demand-driven and other flexible forms of education offer students more and more possibilities to shape their own learning trajectories.

The third development is closely related to the greater flexibility of education (Brown, 2003). Learners need to possess a diversity of *higher-order skills* to be able to adequately shape their own learning processes and trajectories; that is, planning of new learning activities, monitoring of task performance, assessing the quality of their own learning process and the results of it, and so forth. This means that current ID-models pay more attention to the development of higher-order processes that enable self-regulation, independent learning, and learning-to-learn. So the question here is how the teaching of higher-order skills can be integrated into the teaching of first-order skills or professional competencies (see, for example, Masui & de Corte, 1999).

State of the Art and Outlook

The traditional ISD approach was, until now, quite popular in professional settings, probably because the systematic, engineered approach connects well with a goal-oriented method of working and a focus on efficiency (i.e., cost effectiveness). However, ISD is becoming less and less suitable to reach the new goals of professional training. Following social-constructivist approaches is more likely to fulfill these new learning goals, but is rarely adopted due to a lack of practical and unequivocal design principles. The current synthesis between both approaches, in the form of design models geared to "whole tasks," fits the new learning goals and is also based on a systematic, engineered approach. Therefore, we expect that this synthesis of both approaches might be successfully applied in future professional training.

LEARNING TECHNOLOGIES

Whereas ISD can be seen as a "soft" technology, the term learning technologies is typically used to refer to the "hard" aspects of educational technology. Many authors (e.g., Hawkridge, 1999) date the start of learning technologies to the early 20th century when radio was first used for educational purposes. Publications quickly noted the educational use of the radio and its effects on school results (Ross, 1930). Especially in areas where large distances have to be bridged, like Australia, Canada, and the United States, radio was used with some success (Beagles-Roos & Gat, 1983). After the Second World War, educational use of the radio was replaced by the television, which offered a richer medium (text and moving pictures on top of audio), though production and user costs were much higher. Publications on the use of television in education and the effects on learning results first appeared in the 1950s (see, e.g., McKeachie, 1952, on the teaching of psychology via television). Both radio and television were initially enthusiastically received in the field of education because they appeared to offer potential opportunities for pedagogical improvement. But in the end, the advantage of television appeared to be not pedagogical but largely organizational: Large groups of students could be reached in remote areas (Spector, 2001). Radio and television have not drastically altered education and are nowadays used only to a limited extent. Our review, therefore, begins with the successor of the radio and the television: the computer.

The Computer

At the beginning of the 1980s, the (micro)computer made significant progress as a new medium. The possibilities of using the computer in education were quickly recognized, and roles emerged for the computer as tutor, tool, and tutee. First, the computer as *tutor* was expected to realize "teacher-free instruction" by taking over all the functions of the teacher and thus make education less expensive, with the computer presenting the learning material, setting assignments, and providing feedback on errors. Second, the computer as *tool* was expected to support the learning process. In language teaching, the computer was used as a word processor; in mathematics it was used as a calculator (e.g., spreadsheet programs), and in various other subjects it was used as a medium for storing and processing data (e.g., in labs for physics, chemistry, and biology). Calculators that replaced slide rules and, later, graphic calculators that replaced working with ruler and compass are also examples of the "computer" as tool in education. Third, the computer as *tutee* was expected to replace constructive educational tools. One of the first exponents of this approach was Logo Turtle Graphics: Students could program the computer to allow a simple robot, the Turtle, to draw geometric figures. One of the key arguments was that the students would be able to use programming to better develop their problem-solving skills (Papert, 1982). This notion returns in later developments such as "learning by design," where students do not so much program in the narrow sense of the word but develop all kinds of models and artifacts.

The Internet

In the mid 1990s, the computer as an independent medium was replaced more and more by the computer as a link to the Internet, and the emphasis shifted toward the communication and information search possibilities that became available. Originally, the Internet was mainly seen as a new possibility to offer education independent of time and place; that is, as an alternative for the "correspondence model" in distance learning. Just as with radio and television, the computer now offered information to "remote" students as well as the possibility of time-independent education since students could consult continually updated information at any moment, as well as communicate with their teacher and each other via asynchronous means of communication like e-mail and discussion lists. The value of the Internet in realizing distance learning appears evident, but the Internet also opened up new possibilities for traditional education especially in terms of access to seemingly infinite amounts of information, and facilities for communication and collaboration.

With respect to information, three types of use can be distinguished. First, the World Wide Web developed extremely fast into an unlimited collection of data where all kinds of relevant (and irrelevant!) information can be found. The Web thus became an extension of the (school) library and a link with the world outside the school or training organization. In all kinds of resource-based learning (RBL) (Hill & Hannafin, 2001) attention focuses on the information literacy of students and their capacity to find information systematically, assess the value of this information, and synthesize it into a coherent report. Second, the Internet started to be used more and more for traditional contact education to make course information available to students, originally via bulletin boards but later with increasing use of special electronic learning environments like Blackboard, ThinQ, and SABA. Third, the Internet offered new possibilities to provide students or employees in the workplace information "just-in-time" to enable tasks to be properly performed (Goodyear, 1995). In recent years further developments took place especially in the area of mobile technology (PDAs, smart phones, MP3 players, and podcasting) to provide learners with the necessary information "just-in-time."

With respect to communication and collaboration, various forms of Internet use can be distinguished. Asynchronous communication like e-mail, listservs, and threaded discussions offer students the possibility of contacting their teachers outside of office hours, exchange information with fellow students, and continue discussions that begun face-to-face in a structured fashion. Synchronous communication like chats, instant messaging, and various forms of videoconferencing offer the possibility for students to take part in learning activities with each other at the same time, outside their own physical educational setting. These new communication possibilities have led to renewed interest in collaborative learning. In professional training settings, Internet use for communication and information provision is growing rapidly, but major doubts still exist whether this type of use is desirable given security issues for sensitive information (e.g., in R&D-intensive industries) and/or the strict hierarchical structure of some organizations (e.g., the military).

Learning Objects and Standards

The technology of the computer and the Internet makes it possible, in principle, to reuse and share educational content. The basic notion for reuse of educational content is *modularization*: If content is divided into small modular units, developers can repeatedly combine these units for new courses. The modular units tend to be referred to as "learning objects," digital information units with an educational objective. The underlying principle is the building block method: Each learning object can be combined with every other learning object. Ackermann (1996) compares such software objects with LEGO blocks, whereby each block – independent of color, shape, or size – can be combined with every other block. Very different designs can be made with the same blocks and building with blocks is relatively easy, requiring no specific technical expertise.

Standards should facilitate reuse of the learning objects through the realization of "interoperability" (the coupling of different systems) and "portability" (use of the same learning objects for different systems) (Hamel & Ryan-Jones, 2002). Many organizations and initiatives are developing such standards, including official standards organizations (ISO, CEN/ISSS, ANSI, NEN) and consortia of sellers, publishers, and educational institutions (including the IMS Global Learning Consortium and the Dublin Core Metadata Initiative). Recent initiatives also focus on standardizing how the educational methods can be specified. Koper and Manderveld (2004; also see Koper, Olivier, & Anderson, 2002) describe a generic modeling language for this as the basis for a standard now known as IMS learning design.

Standardization should ultimately produce a "learning object economy," in which learning objects are widely available and can be easily used in different educational systems and for various objectives (Polsani, 2003). Many commercial developers believe that an open market for the exchange of learning objects would benefit both the suppliers ("created once, sold many") and buyers ("bought once, used many"). Non-commercial developers, too, who target learning objects available as "open source," also benefit from far-reaching standardization. However, it still has to be seen how much learning objects and standards will change the educational landscape of the future. Until now, the level of reuse of materials has remained very limited and it seems to be difficult to achieve with the development of innovative educational forms in which meaningful, complex learning tasks are at the heart of the educational program. Even more importantly, the use of learning objects in these innovative forms of education will, according to some researchers, generate fundamental problems (van Merriënboer & Boot, 2005).

State of the Art and Outlook

If anything is clear from the analysis above, it is that each description of the current state of affairs is cursory. Educational technology is not only a young field but one in which the developments in hardware (Internet infrastructure) and software (search algorithms like Google) are changing the research topics in a more rapid tempo each year. Hardware, software, and standards follow each other so rapidly that technology-driven research is a non-starter. An average doctorate takes four to five years, which means that the results of research into new technology are often out of date at the moment of publication. Research geared toward the development of TELEs should therefore, in our opinion, not be driven by new technologies but by a clear vision on teaching and learning that is reflected in a suitable ISD approach. The next section will discuss, in historical order, TELEs used in professional training.

TECHNOLOGY ENHANCED LEARNING ENVIRONMENTS

The soft and the hard aspects of educational technology meet each other in TELEs. Here we focus on the characterization of particular TELEs, the research conducted on them, and the theoretical contributions from this research, rather than on stressing research *comparing* different TELEs. However, the "media versus method" debate cannot be fully ignored. Clark (1983, 1994) claims that specific media (radio, television, computer, etc.) have no differential effects on learning. He compares them with grocery trucks: It is not the kind of truck but the food it is bringing (i.e., the instructional method) that makes the difference. Thus, according to Clark, using the same method with different media has the same effect. This does not mean that all media are interchangeable: Some methods can be used with some media and cannot be used with other media and, under particular conditions, some media may be more cost-effective than other media. For example, demonstrating a procedure with the medium "television" will be equally effective as demonstrating it with the medium "computer." But demonstrating it with the medium "book" is impossible and the medium "television" is preferable to the medium "computer" if the learners have access to television but no access to computers.

Kozma (1991, 1994), in contrast, claims that one medium might elicit other learning activities than other media, yielding different learning outcomes. In his view, Clark assumes a direct relationship between method and learning outcomes, whereas the outcomes are actually mediated by the medium. Thus, media and methods are interdependent, and particular media-method combinations may have an added value that should be taken into account when designing instruction. For instance, learners may learn less from the demonstration of a procedure with the medium "television" than from exactly the same demonstration with the medium "computer," because they associate the television with relaxation (stretched out on the couch) and the computer with investing effort (working on the keyboard). In line with Clark, this section will not discuss media comparison studies (Are computers better than books? Is educational television better than classroom instruction?), but will discuss instructional methods that optimize the use of a particular medium, although the possibility that particular media-method combinations have added value is not excluded. In the next sections, different TELEs are discussed in roughly historical order.

Computer-Based Training

Early applications of the computer in education and training in the 1970s and early 1980s were referred to as computer-assisted instruction (CAI), computer-based instruction (CBI), or computer-based training (CBT). CBT was mainly used to present subject matter, including general information (concepts, procedures, principles) and concrete examples; to provide practice on naming objects, performing procedures, and applying principles; and to test simple knowledge and skills. In general education, example applications are basic arithmetic, spelling, and topography; in professional training, example applications are naming the parts of complex technical systems, performing maintenance procedures, and applying principles for basic troubleshooting tasks. Most CBT is characterized by a "drill-and-practice" approach, with ample repetition and corrective feedback. Branching offers limited possibilities to take individual differences into account: Students who make errors are sent back to previously presented information, receive specific feedback on their errors, or receive additional practice items.

Drill-and-practice CBT proved its instructional value: These programs belong to the most successful computer applications in education and training. Sometimes the computer is abused for its use of drill-and-practice, but often these criticisms are unfounded. They compare drill on simple practice items with meaningful learning from authentic learning tasks, but they seem to forget that *additional* drill-and-practice on routine aspects of tasks may improve performance and facilitate learning of precisely those authentic learning tasks (van Merriënboer & Kirschner, 2007). If it comes to learning routine aspects of complex behaviors, the computer is a highly suitable medium because it can make drill effective and appealing by giving procedural support; compressing simulated time so that more exercises can be done than in real time; giving knowledge of results (KR) and immediate feedback on errors; and using multiple presentations, gaming elements, sound effects, and so on. Whereas new terms such as e-learning and web-based training replaced the term CBT, this kind of computer application is still widely used in professional training, although they no longer have the form of stand-alone applications but are now typically distributed to learners over the Internet.

Intelligent Tutoring Systems

Research on intelligent tutoring systems (ITS) is fully in line with earlier CBT research. The main assumption is that the computer can replace the instructor (i.e., teacher-free instruction) and so make training more cost-effective. Furthermore, techniques from the field of artificial intelligence are used in an effort to make the computer just as smart as a human instructor in one-to-one tutoring. SCHOLAR (Carbonell, 1970) is typically seen as the first forerunner of ITS. This system uses the Socratic dialogue to teach the geography of South America. Both the student and the system may ask questions such as "Which language is spoken in Argentina?," "Where is Chili located in relation to Venezuela?," and "Is it hot in Asunción?" The system analyzes the dialogue in order to diagnose and remediate the student's misconceptions. The main components of SCHOLAR can also be found in the vast majority of later ITSs:

1. *A domain or expert model*: This model contains a representation of the knowledge and skills taught to the student. Often, this model does not only contain a model of "correct" or effective knowledge and skills, but also of "incorrect" or ineffective knowledge (misconceptions) and skills (malrules) so that it can properly react to student errors and suboptimal behaviors.

2. *A student or learner model*: This model contains a representation of what the student (already) knows and is able to do, does not yet know and is not able to do, which misconceptions and malrules the student possesses, and so forth. Often, the student model is tightly linked to the domain model, of which it is then said to be an "overlay."

3. *An instructional or pedagogical model*: This model contains the instructional rules or principles that are applied by the system. In SCHOLAR, these are the rules for carrying out a Socratic dialogue, but ITSs greatly differ in the contents of their instructional models (Dijkstra, Krammer, & van Merriënboer, 1992).

4. *An evaluation or diagnosis model*: This model diagnoses the student's behavior, adjusts the student model, and uses the instructional model to take actions (e.g., provide feedback, give explanations or examples, present new tasks or problems etc.) that promote learning.

Like the research on artificial intelligence, research on ITSs did not meet the extremely high-running expectations of two decades ago. Nevertheless, important progress has been achieved. First, research on ITSs yielded a wealth of "pedagogical content knowledge," because the specification of domain and student models requires an in-depth analysis of the problem-solving approaches, heuristics or rules-of-thumb, typical errors, and misconceptions in a particular domain. Obviously, this knowledge is not only relevant to the development of ITSs but also to the optimization of traditional instructional methods. Second, ITS research yielded several generic approaches that are now widely used. A good example is "model tracing," where a rule-based system tracks a student's behavior step-by-step and does not interfere as long as the student's behavior can be explained by correct rules, but provides error information and hints for how to continue if the behavior can be explained by incorrect rules or malrules. Model tracing is used in a family of ITSs based on the ACT*-model of John R. Anderson, a model which describes the performance and acquisition of cognitive skills (1993). (For an overview of ACT*-tutors, see Anderson, Douglass, & Qin, 2004.) Third, knowledge resulting from ITS research (including model tracing) is nowadays used in intelligent *pedagogical agents*, which are applied in a wide variety of TELEs, including multimedia and hypermedia environments, computer-based simulations, and virtual reality environments. Whereas ITSs have never been applied on a wide scale in general education, they have always been popular in professional training settings dealing with large numbers of trainees (e.g., military training), probably because their promise of cost-effective, one-on-one tutoring better fits a professional training model than a classroom-based educational model. The same is true for new applications of artificial intelligence research in computer-based simulation and virtual reality, as will be discussed in a later section.

Dynamic Visual Representations and Animations

In the 1980s, the computer was mainly seen as a machine that could take over the role of instructors and teachers. In the 1990s, however, more and more researchers claimed that the main added value of computers in education and training would be to provide learning experiences that could *not* be provided by other media. Dynamically presenting complex processes and activities that would otherwise not be observable, in an insightful and interactive fashion, is one of those added values. Examples are the dynamic visualization of chemical processes where new molecules are formed from existing molecules, taking different perspectives on how the planets turn around the sun, or, in an industrial setting, animating the working of complex pieces of new equipment that are not yet operational. The fast increase in the multimedia capabilities of computers made it possible to visualize such processes on the computer screen and to combine them with spoken text and/or audio effects. Despite the high expectations, research provided evidence that learning from dynamic visualizations is certainly not always better than learning from static visualizations such as pictures in a book (for a review, see Plötzner & Lowe, 2004). Sometimes, dynamic visualizations must be greatly simplified to facilitate learning or must be combined with options for user interaction to be effective, for instance, giving learners the opportunity to stop, replay, zoom in or out, or take different perspectives on the visualization.

Two influential theories explain many of the findings for learning from dynamic visualizations and animations: Mayer's (2002) *cognitive theory of multimedia learning* and Sweller's (1999) *cognitive load theory* (Paas, Renkl, & Sweller, 2003; van Merriënboer & Sweller, 2005). Both theories claim that dynamic visualizations might easily overload novice learners' working memory, with negative effects on learning. This is caused by the fact that dynamic visualizations often contain a large amount of interacting information elements (i.e., high element interactivity) and, moreover, these information elements continuously disappear from the visualization (i.e., they are "transient") and new information elements come in as the process unrolls. The learner, however, must keep the disappearing information elements active in working memory to be able to understand the whole process. The cognitive theory of multimedia learning and cognitive load theory describe a number of principles to decrease non-effective (i.e., extraneous) cognitive load and to improve learning and transfer. If dynamic visualizations are accompanied by texts, these texts should be spatially and temporally integrated with the visualization (the split attention principle) and better yet, they should be spoken texts rather than written texts (the modality principle). For the dynamic visualization itself, it might be effective to lower the learner's cognitive load by splitting up the demonstrated process in functional parts (segmentation), slowing it down (pacing), or focusing the learner's attention on the most important information elements (cueing). In addition, both theories assume that adding options for user interaction might have a positive effect on learning and transfer, especially for more experienced learners. For experienced learners, the risk of cognitive overload is relatively small so that increased interactivity might help them to process the newly presented information more deeply, with positive effects on learning outcomes.

Hypertext and Hypermedia

The computer and early Internet technologies not only lead to a new perspective on visualizations, but also to a new perspective on learning from text. Hypertext refers to the use of texts containing *hyperlinks* that refer to (link to) other texts, which again contain hyperlinks that refer to other texts, and so forth. Thus, the linear presentation of study texts in a book can be replaced by a non-linear presentation, in which the learner can find his or her own way by clicking on the hyperlinks. Nowadays the Web is the most familiar example of a hypertext system; however, the term hypermedia is actually more appropriate because Web information is not limited to texts, but also includes pictures, movies, music files, and so forth (Burton, Moore, & Holmes, 1995; Dillon & Gabbard, 1998). Hypertext applications began to appear in the field of education and training shortly after Apple introduced the very popular application *Hypercard* to the market in 1987. The non-linear nature of hypertext nicely fitted the constructivist ideas that came into vogue by that time. A well-known metaphor used by constructivists to describe learning from hypertext originates from Wittgenstein (1953), who described the study of complex information as "a traveler criss-crossing a landscape." Thus, the learner is compared to a hiker who chooses his own way, gets ever-different perspectives on the world around him, and sees a new landscape looming up after each new hill.

Cognitive flexibility theory (CFT; Spiro, Feltovich, Jacobson, & Coulson, 1992) is explicitly concerned with learning from hypertext and hypermedia. This theory emphasizes the presentation of information from different viewpoints ("multiple perspectives") and the use of case studies that show a great variation on all dimensions that are also different in the real world. It is critical that students are given the opportunity to construct new knowledge, which, according to the theory, can be reached by having the learners actively *explore* a hypertext or hypermedia system. CFT is mainly concerned with experienced learners in complex and ill-structured domains, for instance, students in medicine who are practicing diagnostic skills. For novice learners in a domain, learning from large hypertext systems is difficult and demands great effort: They miss the prior knowledge that is necessary to navigate effectively in the system.

In professional training, there has been only limited interest in CFT and multiple viewpoints, probably because constructivist approaches to design never became dominant due to a lack of unequivocal instructional design methodologies and guidelines. But hypertext has been and still is used to make large amounts of information easily accessible in a modular fashion. For instance, technical information pertaining to complex machinery, diagnostic information pertaining to medical disorders, and juridical information pertaining to legal cases can be made accessible in hypertext systems consisting of self-contained units (i.e., the given information is comprehensible by itself), which have hyperlinks to other self-contained units, and so forth. Principles from minimalism (Carroll, 1998) are often used to design such information systems, which might provide just-in-time information, instruction, and help to employees performing, for instance, maintenance, troubleshooting, and repair tasks.

Computer Simulations and Virtual Reality

A logical next step following research on dynamic visual representations is research on computer-based simulation and, more recently, virtual reality (VR). A high level of interactivity allows learners to perform actions in a simulated world, to be confronted with the results of those actions, and to study those results in order to plan further actions. Computer-based simulations offer learners a "safe" environment in which they can sometimes do things that would be out of the question in the real world. There are two types of simulations: 1) simulations of conceptual domains (de Jong & van Joolingen, 1998), which are aimed at the acquisition of conceptual knowledge, and 2) simulated task environments (van Merriënboer & Kirschner, 2007), which are aimed at the development of complex skills. Examples of the first type of simulation are "microworlds" and "discovery worlds," which students can study in a more or less systematic fashion. In one extreme, learners explore the simulation without any guidance; in the other extreme, learners are guided to conduct a carefully designed sequence of experiments to discover the principles and laws that are illustrated in the simulated domain. Research on this type of simulation mainly yielded knowledge on methods and techniques that make (guided) discovery learning into an attractive and effective type of instruction.

In contrast to simulations of conceptual domains, simulated task environments (Gray, 2002; van Merriënboer & Kester, 2005) have always been popular in professional training because they offer a cost-effective alternative for training based on physical simulators. As with role play or physical simulators, "learning by doing" in a relatively safe environment is the driving force for learning. The (physical) fidelity of the task environment might be relatively low, for instance, such as in medical training when a decision must be made on the basis of a textual description of a patient and the medical history presented on a computer screen, or high, when the same decision must be made and actions taken on the basis of a simulated patient in virtual reality. The use of simulated task environments nicely fits current instructional design ideas on the importance of "whole" tasks, based on real-life tasks (Merrill, 2002; Winn, 2002). On the one hand, simulated task environments may not yield the degree of physical fidelity offered by physical simulators or on-the-job performance, but on the other hand, there may be good reasons to use lower levels of fidelity (Table 6.1). Recent developments in computer-simulated task environments concern, as example, the combination of simulated elements with reality or "augmented reality," where reality is extended with task-related elements projected on VR goggles, and team training (e.g., for first responders such as police and firefighters), where learners cooperate in a joint mission in simulated task environments that often apply principles from multi-user gaming. Closely related to these developments is the use of mobile technologies for learning. Such technologies make it possible for learners to perform their tasks in real, professional settings, while task-related information is made accessible just-in-time through their mobile phones, PDAs, or other mobile devices. The tested and approved connectivity of computer systems is becoming more and more critical to the success of simulation exercises (Mangum, 2000).

State of the Art and Outlook

Obviously, there is a parallel between the historical use of TELEs in professional training and in general education. But there are also some clear differences. First, some TELEs are regularly used in general education but are not often used in professional training. Three examples are 1) constructionist learning environments, 2) CSCL environments, and 3) electronic learning environments (ELEs) supporting traditional classroom teaching. Constructionist learning environments are rooted in the LEGO movement (Papert, 1982), with Boxer (di Sessa, 2000) and LEGO Mindstorms as successors. A relevant theory here is *learning by design* (Kolodner, Crismond, Fasse, Gray, Holbrook, Ryan, & Puntambekar, 2003), but its focus on productive thinking and the development of general problem-solving skills found little response in professional training. CSCL environments use the computer as mediator for collaborative instructional methods, such as peer tutoring, reciprocal teaching,

Table 6.1. *Reasons for using a simulated rather than real task environment.*

Reasons	Example
Gain control over the sequence of learning tasks offered to learners.	Give learners increasingly more demanding clients (i.e., tasks) in a simulated shopping store rather than being dependent on the arbitrary clients walking into a real store.
Better opportunity to add support and guidance to learning tasks (i.e., change their format).	Give learners tasks to make strategy decisions in a management game, with the opportunity to consult experts and peers, rather than making these decisions in the boardroom of a real company.
Prevent unsafe and dangerous situations while performing the learning tasks.	Give medical students tasks to perform surgical operations on corpses rather than on real patients.
Speed up or slow down the process of performing the learning tasks.	Give learners tasks to steer a large vessel in a time-compressed simulator rather than to steer a real vessel in open sea.
Reduce the costs of performing the learning tasks.	Give learners tasks to shut down a simulated nuclear power plant rather than letting them shut down a real plant.
Create learning tasks that rarely occur in the real world.	Give pilot trainees tasks to deal with emergency situations in an aircraft simulator rather than waiting for these situations to happen in a real aircraft.
Create learning tasks that would otherwise be impossible due to limited materials or resources.	Give student dentists tasks to fill holes in porcelain molars rather than to fill holes in the teeth of real clients.

(Adapted from van Merriënboer & Kirschner, 2007.)

project-based learning, and so forth (Kreijns, Kirschner, & Jochems, 2003). A relevant theory here is *distributed cognition* (Moore & Rocklin, 1998), but the idea that knowledge construction is the – largely unpredictable – result of interactions among learners, the environment, and the available technological artifacts (e.g., in "learning communities"; Wenger, 1999) also made no headway in professional training. Finally, ELOs that support traditional classroom teaching (e.g., Blackboard, ThinQ, SABA) also did not fit the requirements for the field of professional training.

Furthermore, different aspects of TELEs are often emphasized in professional training and in general education. With regard to CBT and ITS, professional training has been and still is a much more important field of application than general education, probably because the promise of cost-effective, one-to-one tutoring better fits the dominant training model in, for instance, industry and the military. With regard to hypertext and hypermedia, professional training focused on their structured use in minimalist documentation rather than their constructive use in open-ended learning environments. With regard to dynamic visualizations, animations, and simulations, professional training paid relatively little attention to learning about conceptual domains, and paid much more attention to the acquisition of complex, professional skills in computer-simulated task environments.

In summary, TELEs in professional training have always shown a strong focus on procedural learning and actual task performance, but new developments stress the importance of authentic learning tasks to drive the learning process in simulated task environments, which more and more take the form of networked computer systems and mobile technologies. In our opinion, the prevailing soft technology of traditional ISD cannot properly support the new developments needed. A clear risk is that the development of TELEs becomes more and more technology driven: They have particular characteristics because new learning technologies allow for that – *not* because they facilitate learning. In the next section, we plead for a paradigm shift where a *holistic* approach is taken to instructional design, and where *integrated* technological learning environments sustain the performance of rich learning tasks, give part of the responsibility for the learning process to the learners, and allow for the development of higher-order skills next to professional skills.

THE EMERGING NEED FOR A PARADIGM SHIFT

As discussed in the previous sections, the goals of professional training are drastically changing. New goals refer to decision making, creativity, imagination, and problem solving for dealing with unexpected situations. The traditional TCS paradigm and ISD approach are not apt to develop TELEs aimed at those new goals. In such TELEs, learning should be driven by meaningful authentic learning tasks, learners are primarily responsible for their own learning process, and attention is paid to both the development of professional competencies and higher-order and interpersonal skills. The lack of a clear vision on training design, and the absence of a suitable ISD approach easily leads to a suboptimal "technology-driven" development of TELEs in professional training. TELEs then make ample use of new technologies but lose sight of what really counts, namely, the quality of the learning process.

In our view, a paradigm shift is necessary in the field of professional training. The TCS paradigm must – finally – be replaced with a whole-task ISD approach that offers new approaches to task analysis (e.g., Clark, Feldon, van Merriënboer, Yates, & Early, 2008; Schraagen, Chapter 7) and also helps to integrate different TELEs in such a way that complex learning is promoted. van Merriënboer (1997; van Merriënboer, Clark, & de Croock, 2002) describes a four-component instructional design model that is exemplary for a whole-task approach; van Merriënboer and Kirschner (2007) further developed this four-component model into an ISD model with 10 main steps:

1. *Design learning tasks (component 1).* Learning tasks provide concrete experiences, based on real-life tasks, to learners. Learners receive ample support and guidance for new tasks, but support and guidance diminishes in a process of "scaffolding" as their expertise increases.
2. *Identify task classes.* Learning tasks are ordered in classes of equivalent tasks, which can be performed on the basis of the same body of knowledge. Learners start to work on tasks from the easy-task classes, and only continue to work on tasks from more difficult task classes if they master the tasks from easier classes.
3. *Set performance objectives.* Performance objectives set the standards for acceptable performance for all the different aspects of behavior. They make it possible to assess complex performance and provide feedback to learners.
4. *Design supportive information (component 2).* Supportive information helps learners to perform the problem-solving and reasoning aspects of learning tasks. It concerns cognitive strategies (How do I approach problems in this domain?) and mental models (How is this domain organized?)
5. *Analyze cognitive strategies.* Cognitive strategies are analyzed into systematic approaches to problem solving or SAPs. They describe phases and subphases in the problem-solving process as well as rules-of-thumb that may help to successfully complete the phases.
6. *Analyze mental models.* Mental models are analyzed into domain models, including conceptual models (answering the question: "What is this?"), structural models (answering the question: "How is this built or organized?"), and causal models (answering the question: "How does this work?").
7. *Design procedural information (component 3).* Procedural information helps learners to perform the routine aspects of learning tasks. It concerns just-in-time information displays that provide how-to information.
8. *Analyze cognitive rules.* Cognitive rules are analyzed into if–then rules or procedures. They provide an algorithmic description of how to perform routine aspects of a complex task.
9. *Analyze prerequisite knowledge.* Prerequisite knowledge is analyzed into facts and concepts that must be mastered in order to be able to apply cognitive rules.
10. *Design part-task practice (component 4).* Part-task practice helps learners to reach a very high level of automaticity for routine aspects of the task. Compare the drilling of multiplication tables or musical scales.

Table 6.2. *The four components coupled to learning processes and suitable media.*

Learning processes	Component	Suitable media
Schema construction		
Induction	Learning tasks	Real or simulated task environments
Elaboration	Supportive information	Hyper- and multimedia systems
Schema automation		
Compilation	Procedural information	EPSS, on-line help systems
Strengthening	Part-task practice	Drill-and-practice CBT

In addition to its focus on whole tasks as the driving force for complex learning, these 10 steps allow for adaptation and personalization. For instance, lower-ability learners may work on many learning tasks with sizeable support and guidance before they progress from one task class to another task class (i.e., start to work on more difficult tasks), while higher-ability learners may work on only a few learning tasks without support and guidance before they progress to the next level task class. Furthermore, self-directed learning can easily be implemented by having learners select the learning tasks they work on. Then, the learners select the next tasks from a database with tasks that differ in difficulty, available support, and guidance, and all other dimensions that also differ in the real world. A carefully designed system for self-directed learning helps learners to develop higher-order skills, such as planning learning activities and monitoring and evaluating their own performance, which are also critical for the development of lifelong learning skills.

With regard to the integration of TELEs, van Merriënboer and Kester (2005) describe how the four components put constraints on the selection and combination of media. This is due to the fact that the four components are connected to four fundamental learning processes, and particular media are suitable to sustain particular learning processes but not other learning processes (Table 6.2). Learning tasks and supportive information help learners to construct cognitive schemas. If learners work on learning tasks, they primarily construct schemas in a process of inductive learning. They can only do so in a real or simulated task environment. If learners study supportive information, they construct schemas in a process of elaboration in which new information is connected to what they already know. Hyper- and multimedia systems are suitable to support this process. Procedural information and part-task practice help learners to automate cognitive schemas. If learners receive procedural information, they may automate schemas because the how-to information they are given is transformed into cognitive rules in a process of knowledge compilation. Electronic performance support systems (EPSSs), on-line help systems, or mobile devices that provide just-in-time information during task performance help facilitate this process. Finally, if learners perform part-task practice, they build routines for familiar task aspects in a process of strengthening. Drill-and-practice CBT might help do so. This way, it becomes possible to develop an integrated TELE (Jochems, van Merriënboer, & Koper, 2003), in which all components necessary for complex learning are combined. Ideally, a learning management system (LMS) is used to integrate and distribute all components and to monitor the progress of individual learners (e.g., Gunzelman, 2000).

In conclusion, the greatest challenge for professional training is to bid farewell to an atomistic ISD approach that served the field for more than 25 years, and replace it with a holistic but yet systematic ISD approach that is more suitable to reach the new 21st-century goals of professional training. In distinct professional domains, a clear vision on its new goals and on how to reach those goals will make the technology-driven development of TELEs, which use the latest technologies but do not promote learning in the best possible way, less likely. In some domains, such as medical training, the paradigm shift from atomistic ISD to whole-task approaches has begun (Janssen-Noordman, van Merriënboer, van der Vleuten, & Scherpbier, 2006; Maran & Glavin, 2003); in other domains, however, such as basic military training, the first steps have yet to be taken.

REFERENCES

Ackermann, P. (1996). *Developing object-oriented multimedia software.* Heidelberg, Germany: Verlag für Digitale Technologie GmbH.

Anderson, J. R. (1993). *Rules of the mind.* Hillsdale, NJ: Lawrence Erlbaum Associates.

Anderson, J. R., Douglass, S., & Qin, Y. (2004). How should a theory of learning and cognition inform instruction? In A. Healy (Ed.), *Experimental cognitive psychology and its applications.* Washington, DC: American Psychological Association.

Beagles-Roos, J., & Gat, I. (1983). Specific impact of radio and television on children's story comprehension. *Journal of Educational Psychology, 75,* 128–137.

Bednar, A. K., Cunningham, D., Duffy, T. M., & Perry, J. D. (1991). Theory into practice: How do we link? In G. Anglin (Ed.), *Instructional technology: Past, present, and future.* Denver, CO: Libraries Unlimited.

Bloom, B. S. (1956). *Taxonomy of educational objectives: Cognitive domain.* New York: David McKay.

Bratton-Jeffery, M. F., Hoffman, S. Q., & Jeffery, A. B. (2006). Instructional design opportunities in military education and training environments. In R. Reiser & J. Dempsey (Eds.), *Trends and issues in instructional design and technology* (2nd Ed., pp. 185–196). Old Tappan, NJ: Merrill/Prentice-Hall.

Brown, F. J. (2003). Three revolutions: From training to learning and team building. *Military Review,* July–August, 54–61.

Burton, J. K., Moore, D. M., & Holmes, G. A. (1995). Hypermedia concepts and research: An overview. *Computers in Human Behavior, 11,* 345–369.

Carbonell, J. R. (1970). AI in CAI: Artificial Intelligence approach to Computer Assisted Instruction. *IEEE Transactions on Man-Machine Systems*, *11*, 190–202.

Carroll, J. M. (1998). *Minimalism beyond the Nurnberg funnel*. Cambridge, MA: MIT Press.

Clark, R. E. (1983). Reconsidering research on learning from media. *Review of Educational Research*, *53*, 445–459.

(1994). Media will never influence learning. *Educational Technology, Research and Development*, *42*, 21–29.

Clark, R. E., Feldon, D. F., van Merriënboer, J. J. G., Yates, K. A., & Early, S. (2008). Cognitive task analysis. In J. M. Spector, M. D. Merrill, J. J. G. van Merriënboer, & M. Driscoll (Eds.), *Handbook of research on educational communications and technology* (3rd Ed., pp. 577–593). Mahwah, NJ: Lawrence Erlbaum Associates.

Collis, B., & Margaryan, A. (2005). Design criteria for work-based learning: Merrill's first principles of instruction expanded. *British Journal of Educational Technology*, *36*, 725–739.

de Jong, A. M., & van Joolingen, W. R. (1998). Scientific discovery learning with computer simulations of conceptual domains. *Review of Educational Research*, *68*, 179–201.

Dick, W. (1987). A history of instructional design and its impact on educational psychology. In J. A. Glover & R. R. Ronning (Eds.), *Historical foundations of educational psychology* (pp. 183–202). New York: Plenum Press.

Dijkstra, S. (1997). The integration of instructional systems design models and constructivistic design principles. *Instructional Science*, *25*, 1–13.

Dijkstra, S., Krammer, H. P. M., & van Merriënboer, J. J. G. (Eds.). (1992). *Instructional models in computer-based learning environments*. Heidelberg, Germany: Springer Verlag.

Dillon, A., & Gabbard, R. (1998). Hypermedia as an educational technology: A review of the quantitative research literature on learner comprehension, control, and style. *Review of Educational Research*, *68*, 322–349.

di Sessa, A. A (2000). *Changing minds: Computers, learning, and literacy*. Cambridge, MA: MIT Press.

Dixon, N. M., Allen, N., Burgess, T., Kilner, P., & Wchweitzer, S. (2005). *Company Command: Unleashing the power of the army profession*. West Point, NY: Center for the Advancement of Leader Development & Organizational Learning.

Gagné, R. M. (1965). *The conditions of learning* (1st Ed.). New York: Holt, Rinehart, & Winston.

Glaser, R. (1962). Psychology and instructional technology. In R. Glaser (Ed.), *Training research and education*. Pittsburgh, PA: University of Pittsburgh Press.

Goodyear, P. (1995). Situated action and distributed knowledge: A JITOL perspective on electronic performance support systems. *Educational and Training Technology International*, *32*, 45–55.

Gray, W. D. (2002). Simulated task environments: The role of high-fidelity simulations, scaled worlds, synthetic environments, and microworlds in basic and applied cognitive research. *Cognitive Science Quarterly*, *2*, 205–227.

Gunzelman, K. J. (2000). From TFS to KALT: Evolution of military learning. *Military Review*, November–December, 25–31.

Hamel, C. J., & Ryan-Jones, D. (2002). Designing instruction with learning objects. *International Journal of Educational Technology* [on-line], *3*(1). Retrieved June 16, 2003, from, http://www.ao.uiuc.edu/ijet/v3n1/hamel/index.html.

Hawkridge, D. (1999). Thirty years on, BJET! And educational technology comes of age. *British Journal of Educational Technology*, *30*, 293–304.

Hill, J. R., & Hannafin, M. J. (2001). Teaching and learning in digital environments: The resurgence of resource-based learning. *Educational Technology, Research and Development, 49,* 37–52.

Janssen-Noordman, A. M. B., van Merriënboer, J. J. G., van der Vleuten, C. P. M., & Scherpbier, A. J. J. A. (2006). Design of integrated practice for learning professional competences. *Medical Teacher, 28*(5), 447–452.

Jochems, W., van Merriënboer, J. J. G., & Koper, R. (Eds.). (2003). *Integrated E-learning: Implications for pedagogy, technology, and organization.* London: Routledge.

Jonassen, D. H. (1991). Objectivism vs. constructivism: Do we need a philosophical paradigm shift? *Educational Technology, Research and Development, 39,* 5–14.

Jonassen, D. H. (Ed.). (2004). *Handbook of research for educational communications and technology: A project of the Association for Educational Communications and Technology.* Mahwah, NJ: Lawrence Erlbaum Associates.

Kirschner, P. (2004). Design, development, and implementation of electronic learning environments for collaborative learning. *Educational Technology, Research and Development, 52,* 39–46.

Kolodner, J. L., Crismond, D., Fasse, B. B., Gray, J. T., Holbrook, J., Ryan, M., & Puntambekar, S. (2003). Problem-based learning meets case-based reasoning in the middle-school science classroom: Putting a Learning-by-Design curriculum into practice. *Journal of the Learning Sciences, 12,* 495–548.

Kommers, P., Jonassen, D. H., & Mayes T. (Eds.). (1992). *Cognitive tools for learning.* Heidelberg, Germany: Springer-Verlag.

Koper, E. J. R., & Manderveld, J. M. (2004). Educational Modeling Language: Modeling reusable, interoperable, rich, and personalized units of learning. *British Journal of Educational Technology, 35,* 537–552.

Koper, E. J. R., Olivier, B., & Anderson, T. (2002). *IMS learning design information model: Final.* Boston, MA: IMS publication.

Kozma, R. (1991). Learning with media. *Review of Educational Research, 61,* 179–211.

(1994). A reply: Media and methods. *Educational Technology, Research and Development, 42,* 11–14.

Kreijns, K., Kirschner, P. A., & Jochems, W. (2003). Identifying the pitfalls for social interaction in computer-supported collaborative learning environments: A review of the research. *Computers in Human Behavior, 19,* 335–353.

Mangum, R. S. (2000). Training imperatives for reserve forces. *Military Review,* November–December, 17–24.

Mager, R. (1975). *Preparing instructional objectives* (2nd Ed.). Belmont, CA: Lake Publishing Co.

Maran, N. J., & Glavin, R. J. (2003). Low- to high fidelity simulation: A continuum of medical education? *Medical Education, 37,* 22–28.

Masui, C., & de Corte, E. (1999). Enhancing learning and problem solving skills: Orienting and self-judging, two powerful and trainable learning tools. *Learning and Instruction, 9,* 517–542.

Mayer, R. E. (2002). *Cambridge handbook of multimedia learning.* New York: Cambridge University Press.

McKeachie, W. J. (1952). Teaching psychology on television. *American Psychologist, 7,* 503–506.

Merrill, M. D. (2002). First principles of instruction. *Educational Technology, Research and Development, 50*(3), 43–59.

Merrill, M. D., Li, Z., & Jones, M. K. (1991). Instructional transaction theory: An introduction. *Educational Technology, 31*(6), 7–12.

(1992). Instructional transaction shells: Responsibilities, methods, and parameters. *Educational Technology, 32*(2), 5–26.

Moore, J. L., & Rocklin, T. R. (1998). The distribution of distributed cognition: Multiple interpretations and uses. *Educational Psychology Review, 10*, 97–113.

Muraida, D. J., & Spector, J. M. (1993). The advanced instructional design advisor. *Instructional Science, 21*, 239–253.

Nantel, R. (2004). *Authoring tools 2004: A buyer's guide to the best e-learning content development applications* (executive summary). Retrieved February 12, 2004, from, http://www.brandon-hall.com.

Olsen, J. R., & Bass, V. B. (1982). The application of performance technology in the military: 1960–1980. *Performance and Instruction, 2*(6), 32–36

Paas, F., Renkl, A., & Sweller, J. (Eds.). (2003). Cognitive load theory and instructional design: Recent developments. *Educational Psychologist, 38*, Whole Special Issue.

Papert, S. (1982). *Mindstorms: Children, computers, and powerful ideas.* New York: Basic Books.

Piaget, J. (1950). *The psychology of intelligence.* London: Routledge.

Plötzner, R., & Lowe, R. (Eds.). (2004). Dynamic visualisations and learning. *Learning and Instruction, 14*, Whole Special Issue.

Polsani, P. R. (2003). Use and abuse of reusable learning objects. *Journal of Digital Information, 3*(4), article # 164.

Reiser, R. A. (2001a). A history of instructional design and technology – Part I: A history of instructional media. *Educational Technology, Research and Development, 49*, 53–64.

(2001b). A history of instructional design and technology – Part II: A history of instructional design. *Educational Technology, Research and Development, 49*, 57–67.

Reiser, R. A., & Dempsey, J. V. (2002). *Instructional design and technology.* Upper Saddle River, NJ: Pearson Education.

Ross, V. R. (1930). A preliminary investigation of the effect of radio reception on school achievement. *Journal of Applied Psychology, 14*, 456–464.

Scales, R. H.(2006).The second learning revolution. *Military Review,* January–February, 37–44.

Skinner, B. F. (1954). The science of learning and the art of teaching. *Harvard Educational Review, 24*, 86–97.

Spector, J. M. (2001). An overview of progress and problems in educational technology. *Interactive Educational Multimedia, 3*, 27–37.

Spector, J. M., Muraida, D. J., & Marlino, M. R. (1991). *Modeling user interactions with instructional design software.* Paper presented at the Annual Meeting of the American Educational Research Association, Chicago, IL.

Spiro, R. J., Feltovich, P. J., Jacobson, M. J., & Coulson, R. L. (1992). Cognitive flexibility, constructivism and hypertext: Random access instruction for advanced knowledge acquisition in ill-structured domains. In T. Duffy & D. Jonassen (Eds.), *Constructivism and the technology of instruction.* Hillsdale, NJ: Lawrence Erlbaum Associates.

Sweller, J. (1999). *Instructional design in technical areas.* Camberwell, Australia: ACER Press.

Tennyson, R. D. (Ed.). (1994). *Automating instructional design, development, and delivery* (NATO ASI Series F, Vol. 119). Berlin, Germany: Springer-Verlag.

Tessmer, M., & Wedman, J. F. (1990). A layers-of-necessity instructional development model. *Educational Technology, Research and Development, 38*, 77–85.

Tripp, S. D., & Bichelmeijer, B. (1990). Rapid protoyping: An alternative instructional design strategy. *Educational Technology, Research and Development, 38*, 31–44.

van Merriënboer, J. J. G. (1997). *Training complex cognitive skills*. Englewood Cliffs, NJ: Educational Technology Publications.

van Merriënboer, J. J. G., & Boot, E. W. (2005). A holistic pedagogical view of learning objects. In J. M. Spector, S. Ohrazda, P. van Schaaik, & D. A. Wiley (Eds.), *Innovations in instructional technology: Essays in honor of M. David Merrill* (pp. 43–64). Mahwah, NJ: Lawrence Erlbaum Associates.

van Merriënboer, J. J. G., Clark, R. E., & de Croock, M. B. M. (2002). Blueprints for complex learning: The 4C/ID-model. *Educational Technology, Research and Development, 50*(2), 39–64.

van Merriënboer, J. J. G., & Kester, L. (2005). The four-component instructional design model: Multimedia principles in environments for complex learning. In R. E. Mayer (Ed.), *The Cambridge handbook of multimedia learning* (pp. 71–93). New York: Cambridge University Press.

van Merriënboer, J. J. G., & Kirschner, P. A. (2007). *Ten steps to complex learning*. Mahwah, NJ: Lawrence Erlbaum Associates.

van Merriënboer, J. J. G., & Martens, R. (Eds.). (2002). Computer-based tools for instructional design. *Educational Technology, Research and Development, 50*, Special Issue.

van Merriënboer, J. J. G., Sluijsmans, D. A., Corbalan, G., Kalyuga, S., & Tattersal, C. (2006). Performance assessment and learning task selection in environments for complex learning. In J. Elen & R. E. Clark (Eds.), *Handling complexity in learning environments: Theory and research* (pp. 201–220). Oxford: Elsevier Science.

van Merriënboer, J. J. G., & Sweller, J. (2005). Cognitive load theory and complex learning: Recent developments and future directions. *Educational Psychology Review, 17*, 147–177.

von Bertalanffy, L. (1976). *General system theory: Foundations, development, applications*. New York: George Braziller.

Vrasidas, C. (2000). Constructivism versus objectivism: Implications for interaction, course design, and evaluation in distance education. *International Journal of Educational Telecommunications, 6*(4), 339–362.

Vygotsky, L. S. (1978). *Mind in Society*. Cambridge, MA: Harvard University Press.

Wenger, E. (1999). *Communities of practice: Learning, meaning and identity*. Cambridge, MA: Cambridge University Press.

Wilson, B. (1997). Reflections on constructivism and instructional design. In C. R. Dills & A. Romiszowski (Eds.), *Instructional development paradigms* (pp. 63–80). Englewood Cliffs, NJ: Educational Technology Publications.

Winn, W. (2002). Research into practice – Current trends in educational technology research: The study of learning environments. *Educational Psychology Review, 14*, 331–351.

Wittgenstein, L. (1953). *Philosophical investigations*. New York: Macmillan.

7

Designing Training for Professionals Based on Subject Matter Experts and Cognitive Task Analysis

JAN MAARTEN SCHRAAGEN

Instructional design (ID) is a field of both applied research and development activities that aims at formulating, executing, and testing theoretically sound solutions for instructional problems in real-life situations. ID focuses on the analysis and design phases that usually occur before the actual development/ production and implementation of training systems. As such, ID is part of the more encompassing instructional systems development or design process (ISD). In a traditional ISD approach, every ID will incorporate a task or content analysis. The purpose of the task and content analysis is to organize the content to be taught by analyzing a job to be performed (task analysis) or the content domain that represents the information to be learned (content analysis) (Tennyson & Elmore, 1997). According to Jonassen, Tessmer, and Hannum (1999, p. 3), "task analysis is probably *the* most important part of the ISD process, and it has been thought so for some time."

Notwithstanding its alleged importance, Jonassen, Tessmer, and Hannum also state that task analysis is the most often misconstrued, misinterpreted, poorly executed, or simply ignored component of the ID process. This complaint has been voiced not only in the development of training systems, but also in the design of computer systems to support human work (Diaper & Stanton, 2004a, 2004b). The reasons are manifold: Task analysis requires a lot of time, effort, and expertise; it is more of an art than a science; and its usefulness is frequently doubted, which has resulted in a gulf between the outcomes of task analysis and systems design (Schraagen, 2006; Schraagen, Chipman, & Shalin, 2000). Designers are often not convinced that task analysis is worth the effort.

Hence, task analysis is viewed by some as the most important step in the design process, while others think very little of the process. Before being able to reach some kind of consensus between these camps, it is best to look into the reasons behind each position and to ask ourselves *why* task analysis, according to some, is such a useful tool, and *why*, according to others, we should *not* use it. After having reached a consensual view on the importance of task analysis,

I will then proceed to a discussion of the use of domain experts in ID, and the way cognitive task analysis may be used here. Next, I will illustrate these theoretical notions with a case study on the design of a set of training courses in troubleshooting. This should give the reader an understanding of how particular methods of task analysis were applied, how they fit into the larger scheme of ID, and what the impact of this research effort has been.

THE ADVANTAGES OF TASK ANALYSIS

Task analysis, viewed as a decomposition of a complex task into a set of constituent subtasks, provides an overview of the target task that has to be learned or supported, and therefore serves as a reminder for the designer to include every subtask in the design. So, the first advantage of task analysis is the assurance that nothing is forgotten in our training design. This function of task analysis is to inventory or describe tasks, rather than analyze them.

A second function of task analysis is to identify sources of actual or potential performance failure or identify training needs. As emphasized by Annett (2000), task analysis, as opposed to task description, should be a way of producing answers to questions. Task analysis should always be undertaken with some purpose in mind. If the purpose is to design instruction, then the analyst needs to select tasks for training based on the priorities assigned to training objectives. The priorities may be derived from observations of trainees before and after a training course. Observations before the training course provide an idea of what trainees already know (and, hence, need not be taught); observations after the training course provide an idea of what trainees have and have not learned from the course (and hence what needs to be emphasized more during the course). The second advantage of task analysis therefore, is to provide input to the instructional designer as to what content should be taught (specified at an abstract level) and what should not be taught.

A third function of task analysis is to list the knowledge, skills, and attitudes that are required for performing each (sub)task. This function has varied the most over the course of history, and is dependent on the particular scientific, technological, economical, political, and cultural developments that together constitute the social constraints with which the task analyst is working (Schraagen, 2006). Several "long waves" of economic development have been distinguished by Perez (2002).

1. *The age of steel, electricity, and heavy engineering.* Leading branches of the economy are electrical equipment, heavy engineering, heavy chemicals, and steel products. Railways, ships, and the telephone constitute the transport and communication infrastructure. Machines are manually controlled. This period, during which industrial psychology emerged (e.g., Viteles, 1932), lasted from approximately 1895 to 1940. Task analysis

mainly consisted of time and motion study in order to determine how manual labor could be carried out more efficiently.

2. *The age of oil, automobiles, and mass production.* Oil and gas allow massive motorization of transport, civil economy, and war. Leading branches of the economy are automobiles, aircraft, refineries, trucks, and tanks. Radio, motorways, airports, and airlines constitute the transport and communication infrastructure. A new mode of control emerged: supervisory control, characterized by monitoring displays that show the status of the machine being controlled. The "upswing" in this period lasted from 1941 until 1973 (oil crisis). The "downswing" of this era is still continuing. Task analysis techniques began to focus on the unobservable cognitive activities, such as state recognition, fault finding, and scheduling. Hierarchical task analysis (HTA), developed in the 1960s by Annett and Duncan, is a primary example of these task analysis techniques (Annett & Duncan, 1967).

3. *The age of information and telecommunications.* Computers, software, telecommunication equipment, and biotechnology are the leading branches of the economy. The Internet has become the major communication infrastructure. Equipment is "cognitively" controlled, in the sense that users need to draw on extensive knowledge of the environment and the equipment. Automation gradually takes on the form of intelligent cooperation. This period started around 1970 with the emergence of "cognitive engineering," and still continues. During the Age of Information Processing (1973 to the present), cognitive control, or rather the "joint cognitive system" (Hollnagel, 2003) is the predominant form of control and cognitive task analysis the main form of task analysis (Schraagen, Chipman, & Shalin, 2000).

In conclusion, it is clear that this function of task analysis differed over the years, as the definition of what constitutes a task has varied over the years. We are rapidly moving toward a situation where computers take over more and more tasks that were formerly carried out by humans. Humans are relegated to a supervisory role or no role at all, and their training for these roles needs to be dictated by the knowledge, skills, and attitudes that are required to successfully fulfill these roles. The third advantage of task analysis is therefore to inform the instructional designer exactly what should be taught.

THE DISADVANTAGES OF TASK ANALYSIS

The main reasons why task analysis is not applied as widely as some believe it should have to do with its perceived usefulness, lack of rigor, complexity, and costliness in terms of time and effort. To start with the usability of the products of task analysis, Diaper (2001) has argued that, since the beginning of the

1990s, a gulf exists between task analysis and traditional software-engineering approaches. When designing systems, software engineers rarely use the task-analysis techniques advocated by psychologists. This may have to do with differences in background and training between software engineers and cognitive psychologists. The same may be the case with ID, although there seems more overlap here than in the field of human–computer interaction, both in terms of background and training of the groups of analysts, as well as in content between the outcomes of task analysis and the instructional products.

As long as task analysis defines itself as a collection of isolated techniques largely derived from mainstream cognitive psychology, it is doomed to have little or no impact on ID practice, just as it has had little impact on the field of human–computer interaction. Mainstream cognitive psychology invents its techniques and tasks for a particular purpose, namely to test a theory on the nature of the representations and processes used by humans in particular situations. It is a mistake to isolate these techniques from their theoretical context and present them as "knowledge elicitation techniques" [Cooke (1994) listed over 70 of them!], or task analysis methods. Task analysis is an applied activity and its outcomes should be of direct utility to the practitioners that design training systems or interfaces or tests. This means that task analysis methods should deliver results in a format that is directed by the end users of the task analysis results.

The perceived lack of rigor of task analysis methods may also be more of a problem within the software engineering field than in the ID field. Software engineers have their own formalisms that often bear little resemblance to the outcomes of task analyses, although recently there has been some work on integrating task analysis with standard software engineering methods such as the Universal Modeling Language (Diaper & Stanton, 2004a, 2004b; Part IV). Interestingly, with ID moving into computer-assisted instruction and intelligent tutoring systems, the distinction from traditional software engineering becomes more and more blurred and therefore also the gulf with task analysis. In other words, as ID becomes more formalized and computerized, task analysis will be seen as having less and less to offer. Again, it will be up to the task analysis community to adapt itself to the requirements of the instructional designers.

Task analysis is often viewed as complex, filled with uncertainty and ambiguity. However, task analysis does not seem to be any more complex than, say, learning the intricacies of the Universal Modeling Language (which usually takes a couple of hundred pages to explain). Task analysis may be somewhat ambiguous, but this is more often than not a reflection of the state of the world it is trying to capture, and not an inherent feature of its method. At any rate, more formalized methods are also complex and must deal with uncertainty and ambiguity as well.

Finally, a perceived disadvantage of task analysis is that it is very time consuming and therefore expensive. Yes, it is cheaper, in the short term, to skip a task analysis altogether. And it may also be cheaper, even in the long term, to skip a task analysis if it does not yield any usable results. However, given that a task analysis yields usable results, the argument of cost should be countered by pointing to its tangible results. The design of computer programs has also evolved from the attitude of "I just sit there and type code" to a highly evolved and structured approach to programming based on extensive up-front analysis and specification. The latter approach is much more expensive than the former, but it pays dividends when programs have to be changed or debugged. Of course, the benefits and cost-effectiveness increase as programs become more critical. A simple program that has little impact on society at large may not need a structured and documented approach to programming. By analogy, the more important the training system one has to design, the more important becomes the up-front task analysis on which it is based, no matter what its cost may be.

TASK ANALYSIS FOR INSTRUCTIONAL SYSTEMS DEVELOPMENT: A CONSENSUAL VIEW

After having described the reasons behind the respective positions on the advantages and disadvantages of task analysis, I now proceed to a consensual view that strikes a compromise between both positions. If the advantages of task analysis as listed are correct, then we may conclude that task analysis is indispensable in ID. This is because it provides an overview of all tasks to be trained, provides input as to what should be taught and what should not be taught, and specifies the details of what should be taught (in terms of, for instance, knowledge, skills, and attitudes, or whatever one's theoretical predilection may specify). On the other hand, task analysis is only indispensable if it delivers results in a format that is directed by the end users of the task analysis results. Therefore, rather than starting with reading books on task analysis methods for ID, the task analyst should first and foremost talk to the instructional designers themselves in order to find out what they need. It is then up to the analyst to deliver the format required by the instructional designer.

This is easier said than done and it will almost never be the final story. For instance, what happens when instructional designers base their learning objectives on existing documentation, as we have observed in the case of troubleshooting that will be discussed later? Existing factory documentation of systems to be maintained was used by the instructional designers as the basis for their training courses. This is suboptimal, as this tends to promote an orientation on hardware rather than functions; moreover, describing how a system is put together is fundamentally different from troubleshooting a system. In this case, we convinced the instructional designers to change the content of their training courses, while at the same time abiding by the general format they prescribed. In general, the format an instructional designer needs may leave open the details of what should be taught, and may therefore still allow room for innovation.

COGNITIVE TASK ANALYSIS AND THE USE OF SUBJECT-MATTER EXPERTS

In the early 1970s, the word "cognitive" became more acceptable in American academic psychology, though the basic idea had been established at least a decade earlier by George Miller and Jerome Bruner (see Gardner, 1985; Hoffman & Deffenbacher, 1992; Newell & Simon, 1972, for historical overviews). Neisser's *Cognitive Psychology* had appeared in 1967, and the scientific journal by the same name first appeared in 1970. It took one more decade for this approach to receive broader methodological justification and its practical application.

In 1984, Ericsson and Simon (1984) published *Protocol Analysis: Verbal Reports as Data*. This book reintroduced the use of think-aloud problem-solving tasks, which had been relegated to the historical dustbin by behaviorism, even though it had some decades of successful use in psychology laboratories in Germany and elsewhere in Europe up through about 1925. In 1983, Card, Moran, and Newell published *The Psychology of Human–Computer Interaction*. This book helped lay the foundation for the field of cognitive science and presented the GOMS model (goals, operators, methods, and selection rules), which is a family of analysis techniques and a form of task analysis that describes the procedural, how-to-do-it knowledge involved in a task (see Kieras, 2004, for a recent overview). Task analysis profited substantially from the developments in artificial intelligence, particularly in the early 1980s when expert systems became commercially interesting (Hayes-Roth, Waterman, & Lenat, 1983). Since these systems required a great deal of expert knowledge, acquiring or "eliciting" this knowledge became an important topic (see Hoffman & Lintern, 2006). Because of their reliance on unstructured interviews, system developers soon viewed "knowledge elicitation" as the bottleneck in expert-system development, and they turned to psychology for techniques that helped elicit that knowledge (Hoffman, 1987). As a result, a host of individual techniques was identified (see Cooke, 1994), but no single overall method for task analysis that would guide the practitioner in selecting the right technique for a given problem resulted from this effort.

However, the interest in the knowledge structures underlying expertise proved to be one of the approaches to what is now known as cognitive task analysis (Hoffman & Woods, 2000; see Hoffman & Lintern, 2006; Schraagen, Chipman, & Shalin, 2000). With artificial intelligence coming to be a widely used term in the 1970s, the first ideas arose about applying artificial intelligence to cockpit automation. As early as 1974, the concepts of adaptive aiding and dynamic function allocation emerged (Rouse, 1988). Researchers realized that as machines became more intelligent, they should be viewed as "equals" to humans. Instead of Taylor's "designing the human to fit the machine," or the human factors engineering's "designing the machine to fit the human," the maxim now became to design the joint human–machine system, or, more aptly phrased, the joint cognitive system (Hollnagel, 2003). Not only are cognitive tasks everywhere, but humans have lost their monopoly on conducting cognitive tasks, as noted by Hollnagel (2003, p. 6). Again, as in the past, changes in technological developments were followed by changes in task-analysis methods. In order to address the large role of cognition in modern work, new tools and techniques were required "to yield information about the knowledge, thought processes, and goal structures that underlie observable task performance" (Chipman, Schraagen, & Shalin, 2000, p. 3). Cognitive task analysis is not a single method or even a family of methods, as are HTA or the critical incident technique. Rather, the term denotes a large number of different techniques that may be grouped, for instance, by the type of knowledge they elicit (Seamster, Redding, & Kaempf, 1997) or the process of elicitation (Cooke, 1994; Hoffman, 1987). Typical techniques are observations, interviews, verbal reports, and conceptual techniques that focus on concepts and their relations.

Apart from the expert-systems thread, with its emphasis on knowledge elicitation, cognitive task analysis has also been influenced by the need to understand expert decision making in naturalistic, or field, settings. A widely cited technique is the critical decision method (CDM) developed by Klein and colleagues (Klein, Calderwood, & Macgregor, 1989; see Hoffman, Crandall, & Shadbolt, 1998, for a review; and see Hoffman & Lintern, 2006; Ross, Shafer, & Klein, 2006). The CDM is a descendent of the critical incident technique developed by Flanagan (1954). In the CDM procedure, domain experts are asked to recall an incident in detail by constructing a time line, assisted by the analyst. Next, the analyst asks a set of specific questions (so-called cognitive probes) about goals, cues, expectancies, and so forth. The resulting information may be used for training or system design, for instance, by training novices in recognizing critical perceptual cues.

Instructional systems design employs domain experts as a source of accurate information on how specific tasks should be conducted (Amirault & Branson, 2006). Put simply, the goal of instruction is to transform a novice into an expert. From the early 1980s onward, the emphasis was placed more and more on the underlying knowledge and strategies required for expert performance. For instance, in "intelligent tutoring systems," a distinction was made between "student models" and "expert models," and the discrepancy between the two drove the instructional interventions. For a more detailed view on changes in military training during the past 25 years, and its relation to ID and ISD, see van Merriënboer and Boot (this volume).

As an example in the area of troubleshooting, consider the impressive work carried out by BBN Laboratories in the 1980s on the MACH-III tutoring system to support the training of novices in troubleshooting complex electronic devices (see the chapters by Tenney & Kurland, 1988; Kurland & Tenney, 1988; Massey, De Bruin & Roberts, 1988). They started out by a cognitive task analysis of novices, intermediates, and experts who were asked to explain during an interview how a radar works. The participants' explanations were corroborated with drawings of the radar that they made. This was an attempt to see how the mechanics' views, or mental models, of the radar changed as they acquired experience. The results of this study showed that novices focused on power distributions and the physical layout of the radar, whereas experts had a better functional understanding of the flow of information. They concluded that an important aspect of training was to help the student map the functional aspects of the radar onto the physical machinery (Tenney & Kurland, 1988).

In a second study, Tenney and Kurland looked at the troubleshooting behavior of the same participants. They found that the novice followed the Fault Isolation Manual literally, but needed lots of help with reasoning and procedures. They concluded that a tutoring system should teach the novice the kind of reasoning the expert uses in deciding what faults are possible, what fault possibilities have been eliminated, and when all but one possibility has been ruled out. They demonstrated the close ties between a trainee's mental model of the radar system and troubleshooting performance. More specifically, a functional model of the radar is a necessary condition for good troubleshooting.

Based on these expert–novice differences in troubleshooting, Kurland and Tenney (1988) concluded that the HAWK intelligent tutoring system should focus on both the representations and the strategic troubleshooting skills of novices. As far as representations are concerned, the tutoring system should provide summary views varying in detail and emphasis for each functional circuit. This would reduce the information overload novices have to cope with and would result in more structured troubleshooting. In addition, the system should include a simulation of the way an expert would reason about the radar, both to explain its working and predict its behavior, and to show how to troubleshoot the radar (Massey, De Bruin, & Roberts, 1988). Obviously, an intelligent tutoring system provides the possibility of extensive practice with practical problem solving, which remedies a problem frequently encountered in education: a lack of opportunity for hands-on experience.

An evaluation study of the MACH-III carried out by the U.S. Department of the Army in 1990 compared two groups (Acchione-Noel, Saia, Willams, & Sarli, 1990). Both had equal amounts of hands-on training with the actual radar. But one group alternated training on the radar with training on the MACH-III, while the other alternated training on the radar with training using a paper-based troubleshooting method (which depended on asking questions of students who were working on the radar and waiting for their answers).

Acchione-Noel et al. (1990) found an advantage for students trained with the MACH-III in the speed with which they completed problems in a troubleshooting test on the actual radar. There was no difference in number of solutions, just in speed of completion on actual radar problems, favoring the MACH-III training. As the investigators point out, the additional speed could have been due to either to the MACH-III group's exposure to more problems during training (which might have allowed them to remember and use solutions on the radar test), or to their having learned more methodical troubleshooting strategies. The experiment did not differentiate between these two possibilities.

One thing that might have prevented stronger findings in favor of MACH-III (e.g., the investigators found that students trained on the MACH-III did not do better on written and oral tests of radar functionality), was that the students in the MACH-III group were not required to read the explanations provided by the tutor. They were trained in a mode where they could see a critique of what they did at the end, but there is no evidence that they paid attention to that, as opposed to moving right on to the next problem. When reading is not required, there is a tendency for students to play a game of "swap the parts and see if it solves the problem." Lajoie (this volume) describes another research effort aimed at enhancing troubleshooting skill by providing a practice environment for professionals to acquire knowledge in the context of realistic troubleshooting activity.

The MACH-III system is a prime example of how to use experts in the design of instruction. Note that the system was not focused on duplicating the observable behavior of experts (the physical behaviors associated with performing tests and replacing components), but rather with the cognitive processes that support effective troubleshooting. As such, it is also in line with numerous expert–novice studies carried out in other domains. These studies have all found that expertise involves functional, abstracted representations (see Feltovich, Prietula, & Ericsson, 2006, for a review).

TRAINING STRUCTURED TROUBLESHOOTING: A CASE STUDY

I will now turn to a discussion of a study conducted by my colleagues and I during the 1990s for the Royal Netherlands Navy, in particular the Weapon Engineering Service. In the beginning of the 1990s, complaints started to emerge from the operational Dutch fleet concerning the speed and accuracy of weapon engineers. The Royal Netherlands Navy asked TNO Human Factors to look at these complaints and suggest possible solutions to the problem. One possible solution that we considered early on was the use of a knowledge-based system to support the technician (Schaafstal & Schraagen, 1991). As this turned out to be too daunting a task, and the root cause, being inadequate training, remained unaffected, we turned our attention to the innovation of the training courses given by the Weapon Engineering School.

We started by carrying out a cognitive task analysis consisting of a number of preliminary observational studies on troubleshooting in which technicians with varying levels of expertise participated. The results of these observational studies were interpreted in the context of the literature and previous studies on expert–novice differences in the area of problem solving in general and troubleshooting in particular. Our observations of experts and novices while they troubleshooted faults planted in a radar system is summarized as follows:

1. We observed a gap between theory and practice: a theory instructor for the radar course had great difficulties troubleshooting in practice.
2. There was not much functional thinking.
3. The training courses were component oriented instead of functionally oriented. Hence, we observed little transfer from one radar system to the other.
4. Beginners were very unsystematic in their approach to troubleshooting, partly as a result of the component-oriented nature of the training course, but partly also as a result of lack of practice in actual troubleshooting.
5. Some experts exhibited a general troubleshooting strategy in the absence of domain knowledge.
6. Problems were mainly solved by recognition of a similarity to a previous problem. This is a rather brittle basis for a training philosophy, as we would like trainees to be able to handle novel faults as well as previously encountered faults.

We were able to quantify these qualitative observations in later studies, with larger samples, ratings of think-aloud protocols, scores on a knowledge test, and number of problems solved (see Schaafstal, Schraagen, & Van Berlo, 2000, for a review). The results of these studies showed that on average: 1) only 40 percent of the problems were solved accurately, 2) students were not very systematic in their reasoning process (2.6 on a scale from 1 to 5), and 3) they did not have a high degree of functional understanding (2.9 on a scale from 1 to 5). In addition, only a small correlation was found between the knowledge test and troubleshooting performance (Pearson $r = .27$). This confirmed the results of the radar study, showing a gap between theoretical knowledge and the application of this knowledge in real-life situations.

Research in the domain of papermaking (Schaafstal, 1991) and integrated circuit design (Ball, Evans, Saint, Dennis, & Ormerod, 1997) has shown that expert troubleshooters use a structured approach to troubleshooting consisting of a number of steps they take in a particular order, deviating only a small degree from a normatively optimal top-down and breadth-first method. For the generic class of troubleshooting problems, we posited that the following steps constitute the systematic approach that experts follow: make a problem description (list both normal and abnormal cues); generate possible causes; test possible causes; repair the cause of the problems; evaluate. The function of this approach is primarily memory management. Particularly with novel faults – that is, ones not previously encountered – the control strategy is essential for preventing working memory overload. Working memory overload occurs when students have lost track of where they are in the problem-solving process because they encountered unforeseen problems while troubleshooting. For example, in testing, students may encounter a problem in interpreting a signal, leaving them wondering whether or not they used the measurement tools correctly or measured at the right place. This may result, for example, in taking measurements at various places or recalibrating measurement tools to make sure the original measurement was correct. If this process takes some time, there is a fair chance that the students will have forgotten why and what they were measuring at all, resulting in having to back up in the troubleshooting process. Novice troubleshooters, lacking a good control strategy, do not see the forest for the trees. Based on our observations of expert troubleshooters and the problems trainees have, we hypothesized that explicit training in a structured, systematic approach to troubleshooting would be beneficial for novices.

The systematic approach by itself will not be sufficient, however, in solving all problems. Schraagen (1993) has shown how highly experienced researchers may exhibit a structured approach in designing an experiment in an area with which they are unfamiliar. However, the result may be as poor as that of a beginner. Experienced researchers know what it means to design an experiment, and they will start by trying to fill in the slots of their design schemata in a systematic way. When confronted with research questions outside their area of expertise, they lack the necessary domain knowledge to adequately fill in the slots. Beginners, therefore, need to draw upon structured domain knowledge. In the area of troubleshooting, almost all researchers have found that a functional representation of systems is a necessary condition for good troubleshooting. Where they differ is whether this is a sufficient condition. Kurland and Tenney (1988) seem to imply that it is: Once novices are equipped with a functional model of a system, the structured approach to troubleshooting will follow automatically. We take a different approach and argue that strategic, or metacognitive, knowledge constitutes a separate layer and needs to be taught separately yet integrated with functional domain knowledge (see Mettes, Pilot, & Roossink, 1981, for evidence of the effectiveness of teaching a structured approach to problem solving separately).

In an earlier experiment, described in detail in Schraagen and Schaafstal (1996), we tried to teach the strategy for troubleshooting independent of the context of a particular system, the rationale being that a context-free strategy may well be trained independently of a particular context. The results were somewhat disappointing: The students trained explicitly on a strategy for diagnosis did not outperform trainees trained in the regular way. In hindsight, differences might have been found if we had taken finer-grained measures, but we wanted to have a real impact on troubleshooting success itself. We concluded that our inconclusive findings were caused by the limited time we had available for practicing with the general strategy for troubleshooting (4 hours). Therefore, in consultation with the Royal Netherlands Navy, we decided to implement the interaction between the proposed strategy for troubleshooting and models of the system into a one-week training course, added on to the existing function course, as a first step. If this proved successful, the Navy agreed to completely modify the existing course according to our principles, and the modified course would also be evaluated empirically. The interaction between the strategy for troubleshooting and system models will henceforth be referred to as structured troubleshooting (ST). I will now turn to a description of how the courses were modified based on a thorough task analysis; the instructional objectives; the instructional materials used; how practical exercises, written questions, and tests were designed; and how we developed the curriculum.

STRUCTURED TROUBLESHOOTING
AS A ONE-WEEK ADD-ON

When developing the one-week add-on course, we followed the following principles:

1. Instruction needs to be developed based on a thorough task analysis. On the basis of the task analysis, one is able to identify which knowledge and skills are required for adequate task performance. This will prevent education from becoming too detailed at some points, while showing gaps at others. After the knowledge and skills have been identified, one will determine what knowledge and skills are considered present at the start of the course. Finally, one needs to determine which parts are better dealt with in theory and which parts in practice sessions, and what the most suited exercises are. This will prevent education from being grounded too much on existing documentation of systems and personal experiences of instructors. This documentation is mostly written by system developers and is not always suitable to serve as educational material. A trainee needs to troubleshoot until he or she reaches the Line Replaceable Unit (LRU) level and only a certain level of detail of system knowledge is required for this. Technical documentation presents too much detail and goes well beyond the LRU level. This is not to say that technical documentation should play no part during the training courses – students need to learn how to use the

documentation, as this is the primary reference source onboard ships. But the current practice that we encountered was that instructional materials were selected *before* the instructional goals were formulated, rather than the other way around. This is what we tried to alter.

2. Theory and practice need to be tuned to each other, both in content and in timing. Current practice within the Royal Netherlands Navy was to develop theory lessons supported by practical lessons. We advocate the opposite: practice lessons supported by theoretical lessons. What is learned in theory should be practiced as soon as possible directly afterward. In order to tune theory and practice to each other, the methods for developing both types of lessons should be integrated. Preferably, both theory and practice need to be taught by the same instructor, and not by different instructors as was the case in the past.

3. Cognitive skills can only be acquired by practicing. This implies that students need to have the opportunity to troubleshoot themselves using the actual system or a simulation. It used to be the case that practice lessons degraded into theory lessons even while sitting in front of the equipment.

4. A systematic approach to troubleshooting needs to be acquired in the context of a specific system.

The one-week course was developed by a team of two TNO researchers and one engineer from the Weapon Engineering School. The TNO researchers delivered the task analysis, methods for the analysis of knowledge and skills, and the way instructional goals needed to be achieved, whereas the naval engineer provided the knowledge and skills required for the specific system that was being taught (a computer system). During a period of 10 weeks, the team met once a week for a full day to discuss progress.

It should come as no surprise that the first step, the task analysis, started out with the structured approach to troubleshooting characteristic for expert behavior. The standard task decomposition for corrective maintenance (1.1) was defined as follows:

1.1.1 Establishes problem description
1.1.2 Generates possible causes
1.1.3 Tests possible causes
1.1.4 Repairs possible cause
1.1.5 Checks for correct functioning

Subtask 1.1.1 was further decomposed into:

1.1.1.a: Establishes problem description at system level
1.1.1.b: Establishes problem description at functional level
1.1.1.c: Establishes problem description at deeper level

Subtask 1.1.1.a was further decomposed into:

1.1.1.a.1: Recognize normal behavior at system level
1.1.1.a.2: Identify abnormal behavior

At the lowest level of a subtask, we arrive at the skills and attitudes required for carrying out the subtask. To execute a skill requires knowledge, and therefore the knowledge elements are always represented below the skills. Knowledge elements that represent "normal behavior" are, for instance:

1. 24V DC BAT LED on
2. 115V / 60 Hz ACH-lamp burns
3. Lamp X during 10 seconds on, then off
4. TTW prints "application"
5. CSR rewinds

Knowledge of normal behavior is essential, as it is the starting point for the technician to start troubleshooting. Only when abnormal behavior is perceived does the engineer start with troubleshooting. Moreover, knowledge of normal behavior also leads to conclusions of what still functions correctly. Hence, these functions do not need to be taken into account any longer, which reduces the search space enormously right at the start.

During the subtask of "Generates possible causes," the trainee draws upon knowledge of system functioning at several levels of abstraction. For the computer system under consideration here, we developed the following three levels of abstraction:

1. At the highest level, the computer system is decomposed into four functional blocks:
   a. Power supply
   b. CPIO
   c. Memory
   d. Peripheral equipment
2A. The block "power supply" is further decomposed into four blocks; the blocks CPIO, memory, and peripheral equipment are also further decomposed.
2B. Level "2 plus" contains no new functional blocks, but does add the electrical signals between blocks. This level is required for testing purposes.
3. Level 3 are the "electric principle schemata" that already exist in the system documentation. This level is required if one wishes to know how the signals at level "2 plus" are generated.

Hence, for educational purposes, we developed the levels 1, and 2A and 2B. Level 1 is primarily used in classroom exercises to teach students that troubleshooting can take place at different levels of abstraction, and that with particular faults at level 1, complete functional blocks may be eliminated (for instance, if the translator is defective, there is no connection with the peripheral equipment; the power supply is not defective, however, because the system can be turned on). Levels "2" and "2 plus" are actually used during troubleshooting. For instance, when a fault manifests itself only in one particular type of peripheral equipment (as it usually does), it becomes necessary to distinguish among various types of peripheral equipment. This is what level "2" does.

Space prohibits presenting the complete task decomposition with its constituent knowledge, skills, and attitudes. I will therefore move on to the next step we took in developing the one-week add-on course: *formulating instructional goals*. The instructional goals should be derived from the task analysis and the analysis of the knowledge and skills required. Our philosophy in formulating instructional goals may be summarized in the following three points:

1. ST should be taught in parts. Therefore, separate goals were formulated for establishing a problem description, generating causes, testing, repairing, and evaluating.
2. Instructional goals were established in which troubleshooting was connected to the different levels of abstraction. Separate goals were formulated in which the trainee had to troubleshoot faults at levels 1 and 2. Goals involving level "2 plus" were related to the testing of possible causes.
3. Goals were established that explicitly referred to the skill of troubleshooting, for example, "To be able to find a number of faults in the computer system and its peripheral equipment by applying the fault finding method." These goals emphasize the importance of learning by doing.

The next step was to establish how these instructional goals should be achieved during instruction. The resulting methodology is meant as a manual for the instructor. The following didactic principles were followed:

1. The trainee must troubleshoot on his or her own. In the beginning, this will not always be successful, and the instructor will be tempted to assist. There is nothing wrong with that, as long as the instructor does not take over completely, and the trainee is put into a passive role. The instructor should ask a few questions, and then give the initiative back to the trainee.
2. Faults should be ranked from easy (day 1) to difficult (day 4).
3. Faults should be adapted to the instructional goals. We developed faults to explain the different levels and to practice measurement skills.
4. Knowledge acquired on a particular day will be tested at the end of the day with a number of "control questions." These questions serve to consolidate the knowledge better. The answers to the control questions are discussed first thing the following morning with the instructor.

5. Troubleshooting does not always need to take place with the real system present. The instructor can play the role of the system and the trainee can ask the instructor/system questions. This serves to remind the trainee that troubleshooting is more a matter of thinking than of measuring. Generally, the instructional goals emphasizing knowledge should be taught in a classroom setting, whereas all skills and attitudes should be taught with a simulated or actual installation to practice upon.

6. In order to force the students to follow the structured method of troubleshooting with each fault, a so-called "troubleshooting form" was developed. The purpose of this form was to teach students a systematic approach to troubleshooting. It also serves as a memory aid, given that students often forget what they measured and why they measured at all. The form follows the five main tasks in corrective maintenance and asks the student to write down during (not after!) troubleshooting:

   a. The incorrect *and* correct attributes
   b. What functional blocks function incorrectly, *and* what functional blocks still work correctly
   c. What test is being used, what the expected results are, what the actual results are, and which blocks function correctly after testing
   d. What LRU needs to be replaced, repaired, or adjusted
   e. Whether the incorrect attributes have disappeared after the LRU has been replaced, repaired, or adjusted.

The final step was to arrange the instructional goals across the five days. We chose to successively extend the skills of the students. Day 1, therefore, dealt with the theme of problem descriptions and generating causes of some simple faults at level 1. Day 2 extended this to faults at level 2. On day 3, the transports were taught at the level of "2 plus" and the theme of "testing" was addressed. On day 4, faults at the "2 extra level" were presented and the student was required to more or less independently find these faults and repair them. Finally, day 5 consisted of a practice test, during which the students had to work completely independently on a number of faults.

To obtain an objective assessment of the effect of this training innovation compared with the previous training situation, we performed an experimental evaluation of the new course (for more details, see Schaafstal, Schraagen, & Van Berlo, 2000). The participants were 21 corporals, 10 of whom had passed the regular function course (control group). The remaining 11 participants took the one-week add-on course described above. Before starting troubleshooting, participants were asked to take a test to measure their theoretical knowledge. Next, participants were asked to diagnose four faults and were asked to think aloud while troubleshooting. The verbal protocols were transcribed literally and rated blindly by two expert troubleshooters on three aspects: quality of solution (on a scale from 0 to 1 with five increments), systematicity of reasoning, and functional understanding of the system (both on a scale from 1 to 5). A problem was considered to be "solved," when the quality of the solution was .75 or higher. Finally, participants in the ST group were asked, after having finished the extra week but before the experiment started, to fill out an anonymous evaluation form about their experience with the extra week of training.

The results showed that the ST group solved 86 percent of the problems, while the control group solved 40 percent of the problems, a highly significant difference, $F(1,19) = 26.07, p < .01$. The ST group displayed higher systematicity of reasoning than the control group (4.64 versus 2.60; $F(1,19) = 77.57, p < .01$), and more functional understanding (4.59 versus 2.87; $F(1,19) = 43.00, p < .01$). The ST group did not score higher on the knowledge test than the control group (63 percent versus 55 percent, respectively; $F(1,10) = 2.36, p = .14$). The course was judged to be "useful" and "very good" by the ST group; they felt it was more practice oriented and provided a better and faster troubleshooting method. Regarding the latter point of faster troubleshooting, we did not formally test this, as we had set a 1-hour time limit on troubleshooting and participants in the control condition frequently had not solved their problem within one hour. Given that ST participants often solved at least the first three problems within 30 minutes, and sometimes even within 5 to 10 minutes, we feel confident that a reduction of 50 percent in time to solution can be achieved when someone has been trained according to the ST principles.

Based on these successful results, the Royal Netherlands Navy asked us to completely modify the existing function course and come up with a new course fully grounded on ST principles. This would also address a possible objection to the impressive results obtained, namely that these results were due to the extra week of instruction, and not so much to the ST principles as such.

MODIFYING EXISTING COURSES BASED ON STRUCTURED-TROUBLESHOOTING PRINCIPLES

The regular computer course lasted for six weeks. We modified this course according to the principles described above in the development of the one-week add-on course. The modification resulted in a course with a duration of four weeks instead of six weeks, a 33 percent reduction. This reduction was achieved in the following way. The theory no longer went beyond the level of line replaceable units. This implied that a lot of unnecessary detail was eliminated. The functional decomposition takes less time to convey to students than does component-oriented training, which may be because the former provides a better context for memorizing materials (more top-down and hierarchically structured instead of a more list-oriented approach, which was the structure of component-oriented training).

The shortened course was also evaluated, along the same lines as described above. This time, 95 percent of the malfunctions were correctly identified (score of .75 or higher on "quality of solution"), the systematicity of reasoning was 4.84, and the functional understanding was 4.77. These scores are all significantly higher than the control group scores; they do not differ significantly from the scores obtained by the group with 6 + 1 weeks of training, except for "quality of solution" (average of 0.86 for the 6 + 1 week group, and 0.97 for the 4 week group, $F(1,20) = 4.63$, $p = .04$). Scores on the knowledge test again did not differ among the three groups (control: 53%; 6 + 1 weeks: 63%; 4 weeks: 65%). A spearman rank order correlation between "quality of solution" and "score on knowledge test" for all three groups on all four problems was calculated. The correlation was .26, meaning that knowledge of the theory is hardly predictive of actual troubleshooting performance, a result frequently reported in the troubleshooting and process control literature (see Morris and Rouse, 1985, for a review).

CONCLUSIONS

The practical implication of the present results for the training of troubleshooting in technical systems is that training designed and given according to the principles of ST results in an enormous performance improvement and faster troubleshooting. In his foreword to the book *Intelligent Tutoring Systems: Lessons Learned*, Lt. Col. Kenneth H. Rose wrote:

> We are not interested in applying new technology just because it is new technology. Benefits must be clear. They must be expressed in terms of effectiveness, material covered, time, and costs. Of course, a sure winner would be a system that offers more training that is more effective in less time for less cost. (p. xxii)

We believe that with ST we have a sure winner. We offer more training in the sense that trainees finish the course with a more structured approach to troubleshooting and a deeper, more principled knowledge of the systems they have to maintain. It is likely that this knowledge will transfer to other systems as well. The training we provided is more effective because at the end of their training, students solve more than twice the number of problems than they did in traditional training and in about 50 percent of the time. We offer shorter training programs, because courses modified along the principles of ST are shortened on average by 25 percent to 35 percent. Finally, we offer training for less cost because courses are shorter and demand less instructor time, and the nonavailability of trainee technicians for operational service due to education goes down. Effectiveness, material covered, time, and costs are not compensatory: increasing one does not lead to a decrement in the other. For this reason, the Naval Weapon Engineering School has taken this method as the basis for the design of all its function courses (including the technical management courses), resulting in a more practice-oriented and job-oriented training with less emphasis on the detailed functioning of an installation and its components, and more emphasis on the actual skill of troubleshooting.

The ID approach we took to modifying the naval courses started with a cognitive task analysis using subject matter experts. However, added value was provided by introducing a quasi-experimental manipulation – for example, by using experts with different perspectives, backgrounds, or areas of expertise, and by contrasting expert with novice performance. In our radar observation study, for instance, we observed both theory and practice instructors as well as experts with varying familiarity with a particular radar system. This study yielded the important insights that possessing theoretical knowledge was not sufficient for good troubleshooting and that, presumably because of training practices, there was no such thing as "general radar knowledge." In this broad sense of task analysis, the analyst frequently gains more insight into the domain studied, the problems and opportunities present, and hence may use this insight to design novel instructional concepts.

In a more restricted sense, task analysis is required for the actual content of the course one designs. Our observations of expert troubleshooting behavior have led us to a generic task structure that formed the basis for all our modified courses in corrective maintenance. The generic task structure is, first of all, used to derive the knowledge, skills, and attitudes required for effective maintenance. Second, it is used to formulate and segment the instructional goals. For each component of the generic task structure, a particular instructional goal was formulated. Third, it inspired us to develop a support tool for the trainee, the "troubleshooting form." The form is an external representation of the structured approach to troubleshooting displayed by experts. We use it as a normative instructional tool to guide students through the complexities of their task, serving both as a memory aid and a reminder of how the general task of troubleshooting should be carried out.

In the opening paragraphs of this chapter, I described the advantages and disadvantages of task analysis for ISD. I concluded that the outputs of a task analysis should be directed by the end users of the task analysis results. In the case study of ST presented here, there was less of a distinction between the analysts and the instructional designers than I described. The project team we had formed at the time consisted of "believers" in the new approach to training troubleshooting. This team had the persuasive power, backed by empirical data, to convince management of the need to change the traditional approach to ID. In other words, the end users in some cases may be too conservative and need to be convinced, by task analysis or other means, that things need to change.

Of course, there are examples of task analyses that were less successful than the one reported here (see Schraagen, 2006, for an example in the area of pilotage). Determining when a particular task analysis method is cost-effective, or just effective, depends on a host of factors. First, at the level of individual methods, Hoffman and Lintern (2006) claim that knowledge elicitation methods differ in their relative efficiency. The think-aloud problem-solving task combined with protocol analysis has uses in the psychology laboratory but is relatively inefficient in the context of knowledge elicitation. Concept mapping is arguably the most efficient method for the elicitation of domain knowledge (Hoffman, 2002). Yet, elicitation is rarely something that can be done easily or quickly. In eliciting weather-forecasting knowledge for just the Florida Gulf Coast region of the United States, about 150 concept maps were made (Hoffman & Lintern, 2006). Second, whether a task analysis method is effective, that is, delivers results that are useful for the end users, is determined to a large extent by knowing exactly what the end users want. The analyst therefore needs to be clear from the outset about the end users' requirements and subsequently needs to attune his or her methods to these requirements. It pays to be somewhat opportunistic in one's choice of methods, and it certainly pays to always rely on more than one single method. This is because the method depends on the exact circumstances, including the nature of the expertise to be elicited, the expert's personality and communication skills, the time and budget available, and, of course, the desired end results. Third, the analyst needs to be aware of the political issues involved. In carrying out a task analysis, one always needs to ask oneself: What is my role in the multitude of conflicting interests (experts, sponsors, academic versus commercial interests, etc.)? For instance, do sponsors really value the expert's knowledge, or do they want to capture the knowledge and make the experts redundant? When developing instructional systems, is the primary goal to further academic knowledge, the students' abilities to learn, or the school management's interests? In the end, these organizational and sometimes political issues may be the decisive factors that lead to successful or unsuccessful applications.

REFERENCES

Acchione-Noel, S. C., Saia, F. E., Willams, L. A., & Sarli, G. G. (1990). *Maintenance and Computer HAWK Intelligent Institutional Instructor Training Development Study.* Final Report. Department of the Army, December 1990.

Amirault, R. J., & Branson, R. K. (2006). Educators and expertise: A brief history of theories and models. In K. Anders Ericsson, N. Charness, P. J. Feltovich, & R. R. Hoffman (Eds.), *The Cambridge handbook of expertise and expert performance* (pp. 69–86). New York: Cambridge University Press.

Annett, J. (2000). Theoretical and pragmatic influences on task analysis methods. In J. M. Schraagen, S. F. Chipman, & V. L. Shalin (Eds.), *Cognitive task analysis* (pp. 25–37). Mahwah, NJ: Lawrence Erlbaum Associates.

Annett, J., & Duncan, K D. (1967). Task analysis and training design. *Occupational Psychology, 41,* 211–221.

Ball, L. J., Evans, J., Saint, B. T., Dennis, I., & Ormerod, T. C. (1997). Problem-solving strategies and expertise in engineering design. *Thinking and Reasoning, 3,* 247–270.

Card, S. K., Moran, T. P., & Newell, A. (1983). *The psychology of human-computer interaction.* Hillsdale, NJ: Lawrence Erlbaum Associates.

Chipman, S. F., Schraagen, J. M., & Shalin, V. L. (2000). Introduction to cognitive task analysis. In J. M. Schraagen, S. F. Chipman, & V. L. Shalin (Eds.), *Cognitive task analysis* (pp. 3–23). Mahwah, NJ: Lawrence Erlbaum Associates.

Cooke, N. J. (1994). Varieties of knowledge elicitation techniques. *International Journal of Human-Computer Studies, 41,* 801–849.

Diaper, D. (2001). Task analysis for knowledge descriptions (TAKD): A requiem for a method. *Behavior and Information Technology, 20,* 199–212.

Diaper, D., & Stanton, N. (Eds.). (2004a). *The handbook of task analysis for human-computer interaction.* Mahwah, NJ: Lawrence Erlbaum Associates.

(2004b). Wishing on a sTAr: The future of task analysis. In D. Diaper & N. Stanton (Eds.), *The handbook of task analysis for human-computer interaction* (pp. 603–619). Mahwah, NJ: Lawrence Erlbaum Associates.

Ericsson, K. A., & Simon, H. A. (1984). *Protocol analysis: Verbal reports as data.* Cambridge, MA: MIT Press.

Feltovich, P. J., Prietula, M. J., & Ericsson, K. A. (2006). Studies of expertise from psychological perspectives. In K. A. Ericsson, N. Charness, P. J. Feltovich, & R. R. Hoffman (Eds.), *The Cambridge handbook of expertise and expert performance* (pp. 41–67). New York: Cambridge University Press.

Flanagan, J. C. (1954). The critical incident technique. *Psychological Bulletin, 51,* 327–358.

Gardner, H. (1985). *The mind's new science: A history of the cognitive revolution.* New York: Basic Books.

Hayes-Roth, F., Waterman, D. A., & Lenat, D. B. (Eds.). (1983). *Building expert systems.* Reading, MA: Addison-Wesley.

Hoffman, R. R. (1987). The problem of extracting the knowledge of experts from the perspective of experimental psychology. *AI Magazine, 8,* 53–67.

(2002, September). An empirical comparison of methods for eliciting and modeling expert knowledge. In *Proceedings of the 46th Meeting of the Human Factors and Ergonomics Society* (pp. 482–486). Santa Monica, CA: Human Factors and Ergonomics Society.

Hoffman, R. R., Crandall, B. W., & Shadbolt, N. R. (1998). A case study in cognitive task analysis methodology: The critical decision method for elicitation of expert knowledge. *Human Factors, 40,* 254–276.

Hoffman, R. R., & Deffenbacher, K. (1992). A brief history of applied cognitive psychology. *Applied Cognitive Psychology, 6,* 1–48.

Hoffman, R. R., & Lintern, G. (2006). Eliciting and representing the knowledge of experts. In K. A. Ericsson, N. Charness, P. J. Feltovich, & R. R. Hoffman (Eds.), *The Cambridge handbook of expertise and expert performance* (pp. 203–222). New York: Cambridge University Press.

Hoffman, R. R., & Woods, D. D. (2000). Studying cognitive systems in context: Preface to the special section. *Human Factors, 42,* 1–7 (Special section on cognitive task analysis).

Hollnagel, E. (2003). Prolegomenon to cognitive task design. In E. Hollnagel (Ed.), *Handbook of cognitive task design* (pp. 3–15). Mahwah, NJ: Lawrence Erlbaum Associates.

Jonassen, D. H., Tessmer, M., & Hannum, W. H. (1999). *Task analysis methods for instructional design.* Mahwah, NJ: Lawrence Erlbaum Associates.

Kieras, D. (2004). GOMS models for task analysis. In D. Diaper & N. A. Stanton (Eds.), *The handbook of task analysis for human-computer interaction* (pp. 83–116). Mahwah, NJ: Lawrence Erlbaum Associates.

Klein, G. A., Calderwood, R., & Macgregor, D. (1989). Critical decision method for eliciting knowledge. *IEEE Transactions on Systems, Man, and Cybernetics, 19,* 462–472.

Kurland, L. C., & Tenney, Y. J. (1988). Issues in developing an intelligent tutor for a real-world domain: Training in radar mechanics. In J. Psotka, L. Dan Massey, & S. A. Mutter (Eds.), *Intelligent tutoring systems: Lessons learned* (pp. 119–180). Hillsdale, NJ: Lawrence Erlbaum Associates.

Massey, L. Dan, De Bruin, J., & Roberts, B. (1988). A training system for system maintenance. In J. Psotka, L. Dan Massey, & S. A. Mutter (Eds.), *Intelligent tutoring systems: Lessons learned* (pp. 369–402). Hillsdale, NJ: Lawrence Erlbaum Associates.

Mettes, C. T. C. W., Pilot, A., & Roossink, H. J. (1981). Linking factual and procedural knowledge in solving science problems: A case study in a thermodynamics course. *Instructional Science, 10,* 333–361.

Morris, N. M., & Rouse, W. B. (1985). Review and evaluation of empirical research in troubleshooting. *Human Factors, 27,* 503–530.

Newell, A., & Simon, H. A. (1972). *Human problem solving.* Englewood Cliffs, NJ: Prentice-Hall.

Perez, C. (2002). *Technological revolutions and financial capital: The dynamics of bubbles and golden ages.* Cheltenham: Edward Elgar.

Ross, K. G., Shafer, J. L., & Klein, G. (2006). Professional judgments and "naturalistic decision making." In K. A. Ericsson, N. Charness, P. J. Feltovich, & R. R. Hoffman (Eds.), *The Cambridge handbook of expertise and expert performance* (pp. 403–419). New York: Cambridge University Press.

Rouse, W. B. (1988). Adaptive aiding for human/computer control. *Human Factors, 30,* 431–443.

Schaafstal, A. M. (1991). *Diagnostic skill in process operation: A comparison between experts and novices.* Unpublished doctoral dissertation, Groningen University, Netherlands.

Schaafstal, A. M., & Schraagen, J. M. C. (1991). Diagnosis in technical environments: A theoretical framework and a review of the literature (Tech. Rep. 1991 A–37). Soesterberg: TNO Institute for Perception.

Schaafstal, A., Schraagen, J. M., & van Berlo, M. (2000). Cognitive task analysis and innovation of training: The case of structured troubleshooting. *Human Factors, 42,* 75–86.

Schraagen, J. M. (1993). How experts solve a novel problem in experimental design. *Cognitive Science, 17,* 285–309.

Schraagen, J. M. C. (2006). Task analysis. In K. A. Ericsson, N. Charness, P. J. Feltovich, & R. R. Hoffman (Eds.), *The Cambridge handbook of expertise and expert performance* (pp. 185–201). New York: Cambridge University Press.

Schraagen, J. M. C., Chipman, S. F., & Shalin, V. L. (Eds.). (2000). *Cognitive task analysis.* Mahwah, NJ: Lawrence Erlbaum Associates.

Schraagen, J. M. C., & Schaafstal, A. M. (1996). Training of systematic diagnosis: A case study in electronics troubleshooting. *Le Travail Humain, 59,* 5–21.

Seamster, T. L., Redding, R. E., & Kaempf, G. L. (1997). *Applied cognitive task analysis in aviation.* London: Ashgate.

Tenney, Y. J., & Kurland, L. C. (1988). The development of troubleshooting expertise in radar mechanics. In J. Psotka, L. Dan Massey, & S. A. Mutter (Eds.), *Intelligent tutoring systems: Lessons learned* (pp. 59–83). Hillsdale, NJ: Lawrence Erlbaum Associates.

Tennyson, R. D., & Elmore, R. L. (1997). Learning theory foundations for instructional design. In R. D. Tennyson, F. Schott, N. M. Seel, & S. Dijkstra (Eds.), *Instructional design: International perspectives* (Vol. 1: Theory, research, and models) (pp. 55–78). Mahwah, NJ: Lawrence Erlbaum Associates.

Viteles, M. S. (1932). *Industrial psychology*. New York: W.W. Norton & Company.

8

How to Help Professionals Maintain and Improve Their Knowledge and Skills: Triangulating Best Practices in Medicine

DAVE A. DAVIS

> The greatest importance of education, formal and informal, lies not primarily in the intrinsic value of the activity to the physicians, but in how these activities benefit patients.
> (Jon C. Nelson, M.D., President, AMA, 2004–2005)

This chapter is about the difficulties faced by professionals to keep up-to-date with their domain knowledge and practical skills, and the frequent gap between professionals' actual practice and the best possible practice. In this chapter this gap and the associated processes are viewed primarily through the lens of the physician and his or her participation in continuing medical education (CME). This chapter considers the best evidence and clinical practice, as well as the current system of monitoring and maintaining clinical competence captured as CME credits. It proposes a model of how the best evidence can be translated and transformed into practice so that we may measure and optimize the professionals' observable performance.

To understand these issues more fully, it is necessary to understand how physicians – and indeed most professionals – keep themselves up to date. Described by Nowlen's seminal book (1988) nearly 20 years ago, the individual passes through a series of steps in education, licensure, and certification on the road to the status of a professional. These steps include: demonstrated achievement in a pre-professional program generally leading to a degree, such as Medical Doctor (M.D.) or Bachelor of Science in Nursing (Bsc.N.); demonstrated mastery by passing all tests required by the profession for certification; and finally acceptance by a regulatory body in their respective state and country that permits them to start practicing their profession (licensure). In addition, many professions, especially those in medicine, have established criteria for a review of their professional competence by re-licensure or re-certification at regular intervals during their professional career. While re-licensure in many domains is often linked to participation in formal continuing education activities, re-certification, at least for physicians, has become more rigorous, requiring not only participation in continuing education but also some form of performance reviews, such as demonstrated achievements in periodic tests of their competency.

Following these steps, the individual is then free – in Nowlen's (1988) terms – to participate in three broadly shaped routes to maintain his or her competence. First, the professional may engage in formal continuing education courses, conferences, symposia, and meetings. These activities are widespread, are frequently "accredited" or approved by a sponsoring agency or body representing the profession, and are counted toward the professional continuing education credit requirement set by many professional member organizations or for re-licensure in a professional body. Second, the individual may undertake self-directed learning activities, done on his or her own time, including reading texts or journals, undertaking on-line learning programs, actively seeking out advice from expert colleagues, and other educational activities to increase knowledge and clinical skills relevant to a type of task or problem. Finally, the individual may be exposed to a wide variety of learning opportunities in the course of normal practice and life. These learning events are triggered by encounters with clients or patients, colleagues, or casual reading and experience, and are termed "informal" by Nowlen (1988) and many adult educators.

Nowlen (1988) further characterizes adult education and continuing professional development across the professions and business as three models:

1. *The update model:* The major goal of this model is to generate activities that provide participants with knowledge about new findings in their professions. Beginning in the 1950s with farmers' interest in improving their knowledge of new seeds, the model has grown exponentially in response to the steady development of new laws or regulations (prominent in the legal and accounting professions), new theories (key to learning among many scientific fields), or new scientific discoveries (prominent in medicine and other health disciplines).

2. *The competence model:* The major goal of this model is to generate learning activities that lead to changes in the professional's skills. Examples of this might include learning new surgical techniques for dentists, learning to fly new aircraft in cockpit simulators for pilots, or acquiring new procedures for cognitive behavioral therapy for psychotherapists and others.

3. *The performance model:* Nowlen (1988) recognizes that the educational activities leading to updates of knowledge and development of proficiencies will not by themselves be enough to guarantee that best practices are conducted in the workplace. In this model, the primary goal of these activities is to take into account the elements of the practice setting, the culture in which the practitioner works, and other means to achieve the implementation of best practices in everyday work activities.

Gaps in learning remain despite extensive and well-elaborated formal and informal activities among professionals in many disciplines. In the health-care arena these gaps are well documented by studies. The focus of this chapter is on these gaps, their causes, and the means to measure and improve performance in order to correct them.

THE GAP IN CLINICAL CARE: FROM BEST EVIDENCE TO BEST PRACTICE

When doctors fail to apply the best evidence on treatment effectiveness and provide suboptimal care to their patients, it is referred to as the clinical care gap or a "quality chasm," as described by The Institute of Medicine (2001). Examples abound and may be described as instances of misuse, underuse, and overuse (Chassin & Galvin, 1998). For example, "[A]voidable complications of surgery and medication use are important examples of misuse" (p. 1002); "[M]issing a childhood immunization of measles would be an example of underuse" (p. 1002); "[P]rescribing an antibiotic for a viral infection like a cold, for which antibiotics are ineffective, constitutes overuse" (p. 1002). In the United States, Asch and colleagues describe failures to deliver adequate treatment of high blood pressure (hypertension control) (Asch et al., 2005), which is an important but smaller example of widespread inadequacies in health-care delivery in the United States (Schuster, McGlynn, & Brook, 1998). Furthermore, the problems are not limited to the United States. In Canada, gaps occur in the management of elderly diabetic patients so that a considerable proportion of patients do not meet their treatment targets (Shah, Mamdani, & Kopp, 2003) and the number of appropriate early referrals reduces efficacy of therapeutic interventions (Buhrmann, Assaad, Hux, Tang, & Sykora, 2003). Doctors over-prescribe tranquilizers, such as benzodiazepines, to the elderly, "which leads to adverse outcomes including increased risk of falls and fractures, motor vehicle accidents and cognitive impairment" (Pimlott, Hux, Wilson, Kahan, Li, & Rosser, 2003, p. 835).

CAUSES OF THE GAP BETWEEN CURRENT AND BEST PRACTICES

Why do such gaps exist? There are many multidisciplinary lenses that provide different perspectives. For example, the educator examines the role of the clinicians' learning styles, motivations, and educational resources and formats (Davis, Barnes, & Fox, 2003). The health-care system identifies performance indicators by which the outcome of systems and performance of clinicians may be measured. Researchers involved in evaluation of health-care systems examine the effects and outcomes of the overall system (Grol, Baker, & Moss, 2004).

The clinical epidemiologist determines best evidence for recommended practice. Finally, the clinician, health-care system administrator, patients and their families, among many others, contribute their perspectives.

There are as many causes for the gap as there are perspectives. For the purposes of this chapter, the reasons for the practice gap may be clustered in four areas. First, there are problems with the information or evidence that supports adoption of new or modified methods. The adoption of innovations in our society is influenced by several different factors (Rogers, 2003). Some successful innovations, such as cell phones and video games, are demonstrated regularly in public and thus highly observable. Successful innovation should be better than the alternatives (relative advantage) and simpler (low complexity) to learn to use. It should be possible to test them on a limited basis (trialability) before an interested individuals needs to make a commitment, such as a purchase (Rogers, 2003). Other authors have added other aspects of innovations as they apply to changes in methods of medical practice. Cluzeau and colleagues (Cluzeau, Littlejohns, Grimshaw, Feder, & Moran, 1999) had raters judge new guidelines for medical treatments with respect to how the evidence was selected and employed to portray convincingly that the new treatments were superior to old methods and how well they described what patient groups would benefit. Grilli and Lomas (1994) found that the complexity and trialability of the proposed guidelines affected the implementation of recommended treatments. Second, there are problems in implementing adoptions of new methods at the level of the health-care system as well as at the level of patients. It is well established that care varies, from the macrolevel (e.g., regional variation: Wennberg et al., 1996) to the microlevel of the clinician's office or hospital setting. This finding has given rise to attempts to explain variation in the adoption of recommended treatment guidelines based on principles of system management and the role of local opinion leaders. Differences in implementation of new methods are sometimes dictated by health-care plan coverage (Dombkowski, Cabana, Cohn, Gebremariam, & Clark, 2005). In addition, there are problems at the level of individual patients in the areas of their compliance with taking medications regularly, their motivation to change their lifestyle, and the system for payment and reimbursement. Third, there are problems with the successful communication of information about new methods and guidelines to the clinicians. Studies of CME and professional development have shown that non-interactive methods, such as lectures and presentations, have essentially no demonstrable effects on the physicians' performance in the clinical realm, or in improving health outcomes (Davis et al., 1999; Davis, Thomson, Oxman, & Haynes, 1992, 1995; Grimshaw et al., 2004), yet these methods of teaching remain the primary mode of most formal CME and professional development efforts.

Fourth and finally, there are problems concerning the clinician as a learner. Among others, Cabana and colleagues (Cabana, Rand, Becher, & Rubin, 2001) have identified barriers to physicians' adherence to clinical practice guidelines, identifying awareness, agreement, self-efficacy, and outcome expectancy as key elements in their adherence to best practices. Barriers to adherence of practice guidelines include lack of awareness of practice guidelines; lack of familiarity with guidelines and procedures; lack of agreement with the value of the proposed guideline given risks for patients; lack of self-efficacy or confidence in successfully implementing the recommended interventions, such as changing patients' eating habits; lack of outcome expectancy in, for example, preventing alcohol abuse, and the inertia of old practice habits (Cabana et al., 1999). In summary, the problems with physicians may be characterized by three main issues that will be the focus of the remaining sections of this chapter. First, there are problems with physicians' abilities to monitor their competence through self-assessment. Second, there are problems with the clinicians' updated knowledge about effective practices or attitudes toward implementing the recommended effective practice. Finally, the clinician may exhibit suboptimal clinical performance.

THE ITERATIVE GOAL OF APPROACHING "BEST MEDICAL CARE"

In light of the barriers and obstacles that confront the physicians and the health-care system, how can we improve current practices and eventually adopt "best practices"? This section examines how it might be possible to improve physician performance, and close the clinical care gap. The key to improvement concerns measurement and assessment, and we will first discuss the potential for self-assessment and self-directed efforts for improving performance.

SELF-ASSESSMENT

Self-assessment is the cornerstone of self-directed learning, the hallmark of a self-regulating profession. In this chapter I define self-assessment as the ability of the professional to determine his or her own gaps between best and currently administered clinical care, and thus assess need for learning and changes in practice. The successful process of continued professional education can be viewed as a chain connecting several elements. The emphasis on self-directed lifelong-learning with the accumulation of CME credits for medical re-licensure, accreditation, and ongoing certification relies on the ability of physicians and trainees to assess their own performance so they can determine their own learning needs and meet them. In this process, a central question is: Can physicians accurately assess their own performance?

Davis et al. (2006) reviewed studies that compared physicians' self-assessment to measures of their competence in the same domain. Several of the major biomedical and educational databases, including MEDLINE (2007) and the Research and Development Resource Base in CME (2006), were searched from the mid-1960s to 2005, to identify studies indexed with the keywords "self-directed learning," "self-assessment," and "self-reflection." From more than 700 studies identified, only a limited number of studies were selected for further analysis. Only those studies that reported clearly described self-assessments, along with independent measures of competence or performance, and that met criteria of methodological and statistical rigor were submitted to analysis.

The search yielded 17 studies that met all inclusion criteria and these studies reported 20 distinct comparisons of clinicians' self-assessments to outcome criteria. The studies possessed some methodological flaws; only seven demonstrated significant positive correlations. The majority of comparisons (13) demonstrated no correlation or reliably negative correlation between self-assessment measures and the target indicators. For example, Leopold et al. (2005) found a significant negative correlation ($r = -0.25$) between self-assessed confidence in knee injections and actual performance on a simulated knee for 93 surgeons practicing in the United States. Parker et al. (2004) tested 311 residents in family medicine and found reliable correlations between their anticipated performance and actual performance on their in-training examination, but the correlations were small and below 0.3. While findings from this review may perhaps be disappointing to some, they are not surprising: Other researchers have demonstrated similar problems with self-assessment confidence in college and graduate students (Falchikov & Boud, 1989; Kruger & Dunning, 1999) in the health disciplines (Gordon, 1991). Some studies have raised concerns for using expert ratings as the gold standard, as these often show low interrater reliabilities (Ward, Gruppen, & Regehr, 2002) and instead proposed studies in which students are asked to make judgments of their relative strengths and weaknesses. In a study Lynn, Holzer, and O'Neil (2006) found that medical residents were able to make such judgments better than chance; the average correlations were modest (around 0.3 and 0.4). These problems with self-assessment in residents and physicians should not be seen as inconsistent with the principles of self-directed lifelong learning, but they do suggest a need for increased emphasis on externally informed, directed self-assessments and evaluations.

COMPETENCY ASSESSMENT

A rich literature has developed these test measures, such as standardized patients, case vignettes, and so on, and has documented the reliability, validity, and reproducibility of these measurement variables (Norman, Neufeld, Walsh, Woodward, & McConvey, 1985; Peabody, Luck, Glassman, Dresselhaus, & Lee, 2000; Rushforth, 2007). For the most part, these tests have been tried and perfected in the undergraduate and graduate educational settings (medical school and residency education). In the past, these tests of competency have been used only in limited extent in the context of CME with practicing physicians.

One example of the use of objective testing in the world of practicing physicians is the McMaster University Physician Review and Enhancement Program (1999). This program was designed in the 1980s to help the provincial licensing body to assess the competence of clinicians that had been identified as performing below standard by their peer physicians (McAuley & Henderson, 1984). The program administers tests to these low-performing physicians, such as standardized patients, OSCE stations, chart stimulated recall, interviews, and other measures to determine the competency of physicians in a standardized testing environment (Cunnington, Hanna, Turnbull, Kaigas, & Norman, 1997). Interestingly, these competency tests have not been used to identify physicians with inferior knowledge and skills.

In recent years competency measures have been used in formal CME settings and are regularly used in training for advanced cardiac life support and related skills (American Heart Association, 2006; EEC Committee, Subcommittees and Task Forces of the American Heart Association, 2005). Perhaps, the most widely used competency measures are the programs of many of the nation's specialty societies (American College of Physicians, 2007; American College of Surgeons, 2007) to assess knowledge using multiple choice format tests with immediate feedback.

Most importantly, there is more to being a "good" physician than being able to respond correctly to knowledge questions and even to perform diagnosis and technical skills well during a test situation. There are real issues of translation of these competencies to everyday clinical performance.

The discovery of wide regional variation in the practice of medicine and measures of the outcomes of the treatment of physicians, discussed earlier in this chapter, clearly demonstrate the existence of a gap between actual and best medical practices. The variations in practice are reflected by workplace-based metrics that assess such activities as blood pressure measurements, ordering correct and appropriate diagnostic tests, criteria for referring patients to specialists, and criteria for prescribing appropriate medications and therapies. The variability of these measures clearly demonstrates differences, but they also pose some serious questions: What does "appropriate" mean? How can we determine which other factors (the presence of diabetes for example) should qualify a clinician's judgment criteria? Which routine measurements are collected (for insurance purposes, for example)?

SYNTHESIS: TOWARD A BROADER MODEL OF BEST PRACTICE

Measures of self-assessment abilities, medical competency, and everyday clinical performance and its health outcomes are critical for the development of a health-care system that implements the best available practices within the constraints of the available resources. In a subsequent section I will develop a model of what is needed to ensure physician competence and the monitoring of best practice in a seamless system based on the measurement of these three dimensions and their feedback to clinicians. This model can be generalized to a discussion of how competence and best practice can be attained within professions, outside of the health-care system. Before proposing the model, I first must review the history of the current system for CME credits.

BACKGROUND AND HISTORY OF CME: THE CURRENCY OF CREDIT

For more than 50 years, physicians in the US have been using CME credit to measure their participation in education.... The profession reasoned that engaging in lifelong learning would lead to a change in physician behavior and improved patient care. *(Davis & Willis, 2004)*

In the late 1940s the American Academy of Family Physicians[1] was the first organization to require each member to engage in at least 150 hours of approved CME over each three year period and they distinguished between "formal" and "informal" credits of CME. In 1955 the Academy[1] replaced this terminology to recognize two forms of learning, namely Category 1 and Category 2. Subsequently, in 1985, following the lead of the American Academy of Family Physicians (Davis & Willis, 2004), the American Medical Association's Council on Medical Education required a similar number of hours of credits and consolidated several categories of learning into two.

Several changes in the credit system have evolved over the subsequent years. First, while formal CME, such as lectures, seminars, and workshops, may be conveniently measured in hours, informal and self-directed activities, the categories described by Nowlen (1988), may not. This fact has increasingly led to the use of the term "credit" rather than credit hours. Second, problems with self-reporting and nonmeasurable qualities of self-directed learning had led regulators of CME credits to place limits on the number of credits for these self-monitored activities that can contribute toward the stipulated total amounts of CME credits.

The Use of CME Credits by State Medical Boards, Specialty Boards, and Others

While the CME credit system was never explicitly designed to monitor improvements in provided practices, assessments of current competency, or

---

[1]   At that time called the American Academy of General Practice.

measurement of performance, over the course of three decades there have been repeated proposals to use these required credits to achieve other regulatory objectives.

First, the maintenance of *licensure* to practice medicine is strongly linked to CME participation. Beginning in 1971, New Mexico adopted a policy of relicensure that was based on continued participation in sufficient number of CME activities (Derbyshire, 2003). Many states have followed suit. Currently, CME participation is mandated by the majority of state medical boards under the rubric of the states' medical practice acts (Johnson, Austin, & Thompson, 2005). Within these, however, there are wide variations in practice: Some of the boards require that all or part of these credits consist of education approved by the American Medical Association, and the number of hours required ranges from 20 to 50 hours per year.

Second, the *medical specialty boards*, such as the American Academy of Family Physicians, have had an important role in ensuring the competence of its members. The American Medical Association recognizes those physicians who have met the (re)certification requirements of any specialty medical board that is part of the American Board of Medical Specialties by giving them the Physician's Recognition Award (American Medical Association, 2007). Following its efforts to create standard methods to ensure competence in the trainees of graduate programs, the American Board of Medical Specialties has undertaken the creation of an extensive Maintenance of Certification Program, with four components (Miller, 2005). The physician needs to 1) maintain an unrestricted license to practice medicine; 2) have engaged in 10–50 hours per year of approved CME; 3) demonstrate cognitive expertise by passing a proctored, secure closed-book examination (p. 153); and 4) pass a practice performance assessment, which involves "determining what the physician actually does on the job, in the clinic, and what the physician is doing to keep improving his or her performance" (p. 153). Though these are seemingly disparate structures or domains of competence, the components are, in fact, heavily dependent on activities awarded CME credits.

Third, the American Medical Association's Physician's Recognition Award also meets the CME requirements of the Joint Commission on Accreditation of Health Care Organizations and thus allows the approved physicians the required accreditation to practice in hospitals (American Medical Association, 2007).

PREMISE OF CME CREDIT

Examination of this extensive and complex organizational structure reveals that it is built on several assumptions concerning how professional competence, performance, and health-care outcomes are maintained. The first assumption is that the physicians are able to self-assess their learning needs and to direct their own learning to be able to meet them. The second assumption is that formal CME or similar educational activities – such as clinical meetings, rounds, and conferences – are able to maintain and increase professional competence without augmenting these traditional categories of learning with new independent learning methods.

The Effect of CME Credits: Indirect Effects, Indirect Benefits

Recertification and related programs have focused to a large extent on the accumulation of formal CME credit hours as a means to ensure quality of care and to achieve the requirements of membership in medical specialty boards. Because of the marginal direct effect on patient outcomes and physician performance of formal CME, credit systems have come more recently to add categories of credit for other related learning activities such as self-directed learning, quality assurance and peer review activities, and other methods.

In medicine at least, the current process of acquiring or maintaining competence through current CME methods – and as vetted though the current CME credit system – is imperfect. A sizable gap frequently exists between what the physician knows or can do (his or her competence) and what he or she actually does in practice (his or her performance). Thus, rather than a seamless transfer of best evidence to patient outcomes, the picture is that of a poor connection, or maybe even a disconnect, between the entities.

In addition, systematic reviews of the effect of most CME efforts demonstrate that traditional educational methods such as conferences, meetings, and lectures are generally less effective than more proactive methods such as academic detailing, reminders at the point of care, audits and feedback, opinion leaders, interactive or case-based CME, and multiple methods. Traditional, even didactic lectures, may have a necessary role in improving factual knowledge acquisition and even retention, but they are not sufficient for performance change to occur (Davis et al., 1999). Finally, multiple methods, initially seen to effect more change than single interventions, perhaps produce roughly no more than 20 percent improvement in the effectiveness in clinical performance (Davis et al., 1999).

CME credit systems and the delivery of CME have been subjected to close scrutiny and substantial improvements have been made; some of these are detailed below.

Prior Attempts at Reform

Try again. Fail again. Fail Better.
(Samuel Beckett)

This chapter is not the first call to examine and reconfigure the CME system or even to link it more fully to patient care, triangulating self-learning, competence, and performance. Most recently, the Council on Medical Specialties has sponsored a collaborative and far-reaching initiative involving major stakeholders in CME to create a series of recommendations – the work of the Conjoint Committee on CME (Spivey, 2005).

There are several improvements to the CME system and its effect on health-care-related outcomes. First, physicians have long recognized the need to undertake CME activities; their professional societies and associations have adopted and formulated this activity into a series of activities and learning programs, which are designed to lead to recertification. Second, CME providers have been influenced by the evidence identifying the ineffectiveness of lectures and seminars and have shifted their educational activities toward interactive sessions (Accreditation Council for Continuing Medical Education, 2007; Society for Continuing Medical Education, 2007). They have also developed – with the support of health-services researchers and quality improvement experts – innovations in training and continuing education. For example, studies have shown that performance feedback by peers and audits of treatment records by external inspectors increases the adoption of guidelines, especially when the initial rate of adoption is low (Jamtvedt, Young, Kristoffersen, O'Brien, & Oxman, 2006). Further, Arnold and Straus (2005) found that interventions that combined education of physicians, patients, and the public "were the most successful in reducing antibiotic prescribing for inappropriate indications." More recent meta-analyses have evaluated the full range of methods used to increase implementation of guidelines, such as performance feedback, auditing, educational material, educational meetings, academic detailing, community-based opinion leaders, reminders, and patient-mediated strategies, as well as their estimated costs (Freemantle et al., 2000; Grimshaw et al., 2004; Grol & Grimshaw, 1999; Thomson-O'Brien et al., 2000; Vale, Thomas, Maclennan, & Grimshaw, 2007). CME providers also demonstrate a growing understanding of organizational issues influencing the adoption of best practices. Innovations that employ information and communication technologies have not been thoroughly studied and evaluated thus far. Internet-based tools provide the potential for reducing or even closing the evidence-to-practice gaps in medicine (Abdolrasulnia et al., 2004; Allison et al., 2005; Huis, Veld, van Til, Ijzerman, & Vollenbroek-Hutten, 2005; Rubin et al., 2006; Sintchenko, Iredell, Gilbert, & Coiera, 2005; Wall et al., 2005). This highly interdisciplinary field, termed "knowledge translation" by most scholars, studies interventions within their organizational context and their effects on health-care professionals' performance and their outcomes. Third, the regulation and accreditation of CME activities – the purview of organizations like the Accreditation Council for CME – has included criteria for the accreditation of CME activities that adhere to best educational principles and avoid commercial bias (Accreditation Council for Continuing Medical Education, 2007). Fourth, CME credits no longer apply only to participation in formal CME; CME providers encourage alternative methods of learning and training. The AMA's Physician Recognition Award, for example, has developed two new activities among its creditable activities – Performance Improvement Modules and the Internet Point of Care (Aparicio & Willis, 2005). These initiatives are in line with the development of CME based on just-in-time or point-of-care learning, in which physicians can learn based on issues generated by their everyday work with patients (Davis & Willis, 2004). Some studies suggest that many physicians would prefer this type of learning to traditional CME (e.g., Kahn, Ehlers, & Wood, 2006). There are developments to organize Internet resources and permit physicians to capitalize on the available resources for training with feedback (Boehm, in press). Both of these CME initiatives possess the potential to lead to practice-based learning opportunities that can be incorporated within a system for awarding CME credits.

PRESSURES FOR CHANGE

A dynamic health-care system needs to support initiatives for closing the gap between actual and best practices at both an individual and collective level. Some of these initiatives are generated externally to the system by sensational findings about problems with the current state of affairs, and these findings unleash forces of change. For example, in 2000 a medical doctor, Harold Shipman, was convicted of killing 15 of his patients. Subsequent investigation (The Shipman Inquiry, 2004) estimated that during his entire professional career, Shipman had killed about 250 patients. This deeply unsettling news led to discussions about necessary monitoring mechanisms (The Shipman Inquiry, 2004) that may, in the future, protect patients from the unlikely but apparently real possibility of abuse of the professional trust given to doctors (Baker, 2005). There are other recent examples of how patients are not receiving the best possible care due to financial and other logistical restraints in health-care systems. While we exist in a burgeoning information/technology explosion, there is limited individual capacity for knowledge retention and adoption due to age and prior training of physicians and to the volume, transient nature, and conflicting evidence of the information itself. In a recent review of quality of care and medical knowledge of physicians, Choudhry, Fletcher, and Soumerai (2005) reviewed articles linking these competencies and performances to physician age or years since graduation. Despite methodological difficulties, the review noted that over two-thirds of the studies reported decreasing performance or knowledge with increasing age for some or all outcomes and societal pressures for accountability. There is now a consensus for the need for enforced monitoring of physicians' performance. Patients agree with the concept of retesting physicians (Cain, Benjamin, & Thompson, 2005). A 2003 Gallup poll found 80 percent of Americans agreed with the concepts of reexamination with high success rates in those areas in which they specialize, periodic global examinations, and patient ratings (Brennan et al., 2004).

TOWARD A NEW BEST PRACTICE MODEL
FOR THE PROFESSIONS

The foregoing sections of this chapter argue for the creation of an idealized, triangulated "credit" system or model in which emphasis is placed on several key elements or criteria. This model would permit consideration of many elements and their potential interactions and influences. First, the concept of relative value of CME credit may be linked to health-care outcomes (Davis & Willis, 2004). Second, such a model would need to recognize and incorporate our current knowledge about the complex layering and dimensionality of physicians' competence and on-the-job performance. Third, there must be a clear commitment to the science of measurement. By using multiple measures, such as simulations, written examinations, on-the-job audits, and patient evaluations, it will be possible to establish and continually monitor reliability, validity, and generalizability of measurement methods. It is also important to develop measures that can provide the clinician with, ideally immediate, feedback. Finally and conceptually, this model needs to specify what organization is responsible for measurement of health outcomes and for determining the best practice for certain medical conditions. For example, licensing bodies that are responsible for quality of care may be the appropriate organization to measure performance outcomes.

The model consists of three major elements; their relationship is illustrated in Figure 8.1. The measurement of each element raises its own set of methodological issues and criteria for assessment, which have been discussed

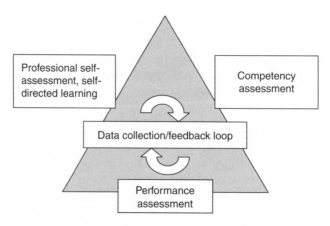

FIGURE 8.1. Triangulating the competence of professionals.

earlier in this chapter. Given that the work of the professionals is multifaceted and complex, the model focuses on three aspects of the professional's practice – his/her own self-assessment abilities and self-directed learning, his/her competence as assessed by tests, and his/her performance in the work environment. These aspects are clearly related phenomena that are measurable and instrumental to attaining best practice.

Two elements form the center of the triangle in Figure 8.1 as the data collection/feedback loop. The first of these is a mechanism to store and retrieve information about measurements at each level of the health-care system hierarchy. At the level of the physician, these measures include participation in CME activities, such as self-directed reading and literature reviews. Each physician would also have measures of his/her knowledge and other competency, such as scores on multiple choice examinations or achievement in simulated test environments (such as advanced cardiac life support courses). Finally, practice performance measures of each physician would include measures of their adherence to preventive guidelines (as determined by observation or chart reviews, for example), their success in inducing obese patients to reduce their weight, getting hypertensive patients to control their blood pressure, and attaining other desirable health-care outcomes for their current patients.

Davis and Willis (2004) propose that CME should document and focus on activities "that lead to actual change in practice and improved patient outcomes" (p. 142). They propose to rely on chart audits and other quality improvement data that verify an acceptable level of patient outcomes as well as improvements. They predict that in the near future, there will be computer-based tools that will automatically record and calculate these measures of patient outcomes. These data on ultimate health outcomes may be stored and retrieved for a variety of purposes – for self-analysis and measurement of progress toward self-set goals (achieving competence in a new field of study, for example), or for reporting to a regulatory or specialty body. The development of simulators of various medical procedures, such as surgery (Gallagher et al., 2005), are improving to the point where they can not only serve as training for students, but also provide a means to objectively measure the skills of physicians (Ericsson, 2004) – not such a small step!

SOME THOUGHTS ABOUT THE FUTURE

Always skate to where the puck is going to be. (Former hockey great, Wayne Gretzky)

Several trends noted in the preceding sections will shape the future of the issues related to the concept of best practice. There are three categories of ideas in this construct: new or expanded definitions of competencies, new technologies, and new methods for providing feedback. The chapter ends with a return to concepts proposed by Nowlen (1988) two decades ago, and paints a picture of an integrated model of triangulation.

New Competencies

New competency models in graduate programs have implications for the work of the Accreditation Council for Graduate Medical Education in their preparation for CME in the future (Accreditation Council for Graduate Medical Education, 2007). These new competencies include compassionate, appropriate and effective patient care; demonstration and application of knowledge; practice-based learning and improvement; interpersonal and communication skills; professionalism; and system-based practice (Nahrwold, 2005). The Institute of Medicine adds additional competencies: acquisition and use of information technology skills, and working within multidisciplinary teams (Institute of Medicine, 2001). While these new aspects of professional practice are highly clinical and thus physician-specific, they are generalizable to all professionals.

New Technologies

It is clear that information and communication technology will create new opportunities for access of knowledge during clinical practice, of learning activities, and of records for measurement of performance in practice. For example, the use of communication technologies such as personal digital assistants and web-based videoconferencing allow effective delivery of information to physicians in practice with clients. With the emergence of computer-based records of patients and their treatments, it will be possible to analyze the administered treatments and adherence to the guidelines for best practice.

The concept of the learning portfolio, which includes a record of a physician's learning activities, clinical measures, and health-care or practice outcomes has been significantly enhanced by models for knowledge management systems, computerized data collection systems related to CME participation, achievements in competency tests, and performance data. In the future, these systems may link to CME resources so that the practitioners can – once a gap in knowledge or in following practice guidelines is identified – actively seek out resources to fill the gap and provide access to the relevant evidence and procedures for acquiring the procedures and skills. In addition to such physician-specific tools, information and communication technologies have also evolved to include patient- or client-specific methods. In their simplest form, such methods remind the physician – at the point of care – about a specific action to be undertaken (a reminder that this patient's blood pressure has not been recorded in a period of time or that preventive measures have not been taken). More advanced versions will consist of integrated decision-support systems, enabling the physician to review clinical recommendations captured as clinical practice guidelines, to weigh alternatives, to review records, and to enable the formation of a clinical management plan (Garg et al., 2005; Wright, Goldberg, & Hongsermeier, 2007).

Methods of Feedback

Feedback on competence and performance to the physician is necessary given the documented difficulties of professionals to accurately self-assess. In medicine, such feedback is based on data. Rudimentary feedback is generated on an increasingly regular basis in the health-care system. For example, surgeons and other medical professionals receive data on length of hospital stay; primary care physicians receive data on preventive measure such as mammography and Pap smear rates; emergency department staff collect data on patient revisits with the same problem or on speed to appropriate treatment. While this type of feedback has been validated to show that they are at least marginally effective, they pose several problems that need to be resolved in the future. First, the performance measures do not always reflect situations in the control of the individual to whom the feedback is given. Patients may be instructed to take medication to treat their condition, but they may not – for a variety of reasons – do so. Second, and perhaps more importantly, feedback measures are often sterile and factual and require an understanding of the context of practice and the means and resources to correct the gap. As a partial solution to these problems the U.K.'s appraisal system relies on reviews by a trusted mentor. In this system a trained and respected peer reviews the physician's portfolio on a regular basis, noting areas of achievement or deficiencies, and providing more elaborate feedback and guidance about further CME and related activities.

A PICTURE OF THE FUTURE

Finally, this chapter ends where it began with Nowlen's (1988) view of the education of professionals. His work has added significantly to our understanding of the need to progress from simpler "update" models of learning to more complex and practice-grounded models achieving the goals of enhanced performance and competence. In addition, his efforts to characterize three types of learning – random and informal activities, self-directed activities, and formal learning – have been enhanced by our increasing attention to inadequate abilities to self-assess and the need for professions and professionals to be more accountable.

The layering of accountability and self-assessment abilities onto basic models of education and learning affords a picture of the future, recognizing

	What's not so effective	What works
Proposed scenario		Performance models: • More complete understanding and use of effective educational methods • Feedback on self-assessment based on objective, evidence-based information on self-, competency-, and performance-assessment; triangulation of "best practice"
Current picture	The update model • Reliance on generally ineffective educational, formal methods • Self-assessments without formal feedback; little attempt at competency assessment except in unusual circumstances; little or inadequate performance measurement or monitoring	

FIGURE 8.2. A 2×2 table outlining effect of CME interventions to current and proposed scenarios in CME delivery.

both the hubris and the folly of such activities. Nonetheless, it is clear that we will move from reliance on the update model and systems that count only formal activities, to a more performance- or outcome-driven model, in which feedback on objective measures of competence and performance are married to a better understanding of effective educational methods (Fig. 8.2).

I conclude the chapter with a comment about the place of medicine within its social-educational context. Most societies value health to the point that a large portion of the societal resources are dedicated to health care and medicine. The importance of medicine as a social value and the commitment of organized medicine to delivering the best health care to citizens have motivated medical educators to develop an advanced system for measurement and continued education. In medicine, unlike some other domains, there is a consensus and a scientific base for determining best clinical practices. In other professional domains, such as education, management, and leadership, there still exists (in some instances) considerable controversy about what knowledge and skills professional schools should teach, and how performance should be measured and evaluated (Pfeffer & Fong, 2002, 2004).

As their scientific bases and consensus emerge, these other professional domains should be able to learn from medicine, not just by its achievements, but perhaps equally important from the mistakes during its development toward improved CME.

REFERENCES

Abdolrasulnia M., Collins, B. C., Casebeer, L., Wall, T., Spettell, C., Ray, M. N., et al. (2004). Using email reminders to engage physicians in an Internet-Based CME intervention. *BMC Medical Education, 4*(1), 17.

Accreditation Council for Continuing Medical Education (ACCME). *Annual report data.* Retrieved March 20, 2007, from, http://www.accme.org/index.cfm/fa/home.popular/popular_id/127a1c6f-462d-476b-a33a-6b67e131ef1a.cfm.

Accreditation Council for Continuing Medical Education (ACCME). Retrieved March 20, 2007, from, http://www.accme.org.

Accreditation Council for Graduate Medical Education. *General competencies.* Retrieved March 20, 2007, from, http://www.acgme.org/outcome/comp/comp-Full.asp.

Allison, J. J., Kiefe, C. I., Wall, T., Casebeer, L., Ray, M. N., Spettell, C. M., et al. (2005). Multicomponent Internet continuing medical education to promote chlamydia screening. *American Journal of Preventive Medicine, 28*(3), 285–290.

American College of Surgeons. *Surgical education and self assessment program* (SESAP). Retrieved March 20, 2007, from, http://www.facs.org/fellows_info/sesap/sesap.html.

American Academy of Family Physicians. *CME accreditation.* Retrieved March 20, 2007, from, http://www.aafp.org/online/en/home/cme/cmea.html.

American Academy of Family Physicians. *Evidence-based CME.* Retrieved March 20, 2007, from, http://www.aafp.org/online/en/home/cme/cmea/ebcme.html.

American Academy of Family Physicians. *Producing quality CME activities.* Retrieved March 20, 2007, from, http://www.aafp.org/online/en/home/cme/cmea/quality-activities.html.

American College of Physicians. *Medical knowledge self assessment program (MKSAP).* Retrieved March 20, 2007, from, http://www.acponline.org/catalog/mksap/14/.

American Heart Association 2005 (2006). American Heart Association (AHA) guidelines for cardiopulmonary resuscitation (CPR) and emergency cardiovascular care (ECC) of pediatric and neonatal patients: Pediatric advanced life support [electronic version]. *Pediatrics, 117*(5), 1005–1028.

American Medical Association. *Physician resources for CME.* Retrieved March 20, 2007, from, http://www.ama-assn.org/ama/pub/category/2922.html.

American Medical Association. *Physician's recognition award.* Retrieved March 20, 2007, from, http://www.ama-assn.org/ama/pub/category/15889.html.

Aparicio, A., & Willis, C. E. (2005). The continued evolution of the credit system. *Journal of Continuing Education in the Health Professions, 25*(3), 190–196.

Arnold, S. R., & Straus, S. E. (2005). Interventions to improve antibiotic prescribing practices in ambulatory care. *Cochrane Database of Systematic Reviews, (4),* CD003539.

Asch, S. M., McGlynn, E. A., Hiatt, L., Adams, J., Hicks, J., DeCristofaro, A., et al. (2005). Quality of care for hypertension in the United States. *BMC Cardiovascular Disorders, 5*(1), 1.

Baker, R. (2005). Placing principle before expediency: The Shipman inquiry. *Lancet*, 365, 919–921.

Boehm, J. (in press). Best of the web in pathology: A practical guide to finding specific pathology resources on the internet. *Journal of Clinical Pathology* (Published on the Internet on May 11, 2007).

Brennan, T. A., Horwitz, R. I., Duffy, F. D., Cassel, C. K., Goode, L. D., & Lipner, R. S. (2004). The role of physician specialty board certification status in the quality movement. *Journal of the American Medical Association*, 292(9), 1038–1043.

Buhrmann, R., Assaad, D., Hux, J. E., Tang, M., & Sykora, K. (2003). Diabetes and the eye. In J. Hux, G. Booth, P. Slaughter & Laupacis, A. (Eds.), *Diabetes in Ontario: An ICES Practice Atlas*. Toronto: The Institute for Clinical Evaluative Studies, 10, 193.

Cabana, M. D., Rand, C. S., Becher, O. J., & Rubin, H. R. (2001). Reasons for pediatrician nonadherence to asthma guidelines. *Archives of Pediatrics & Adolescent Medicine*, 155(9), 1057–1062.

Cabana, M. D., Rand, C. S., Powe, N. R., Wu, A. W., Wilson, M. H., Abboud, P. A., et al. (1999). Why don't physicians follow clinical practice guidelines? A framework for improvement. *Journal of the American Medical Association*, 282(15), 1458–1465.

Cain, F. E., Benjamin, R. M., & Thompson, J. N. (2005). Obstacles to maintaining licensure in the United States. *British Medical Journal*, 330(7505), 1443–1445.

Chassin, M. R., & Galvin, R. W. (1998). The urgent need to improve health care quality. Institute of Medicine National Roundtable on Health Care Quality. *Journal of the American Medical Association*, 280(11), 1000–1005.

Choudhry, N. K., Fletcher, R. H., & Soumerai, S. B. (2005). Systematic review: The relationship between clinical experience and quality of health care. *Annals of Internal Medicine*, 142(4), 260–273.

Cluzeau, F. A., Littlejohns, P., Grimshaw, J. M., Feder, G., & Moran, S. E. (1999). Development and application of a generic methodology to assess the quality of clinical guidelines. *International Journal for Quality in Health Care*, 11(1), 21–28.

Craig, The OSCME, 1990s.

Craig, J. (1991). The OSCME (opportunity for self-assessment CME). *JCEHP*, 11 (1), 87–94.

Cunnington, J. P., Hanna, E., Turnbull, J., Kaigas, T. B., & Norman, G. R. (1997). Defensible assessment of the competency of the practicing physician. *Academic Medicine*, 72(1), 9–12.

Davis, D. A., Barnes, B. E., & Fox R. D. (Eds.). (2003). *The continuing professional development of physicians: From research to practice*. Chicago, IL: AMA Publications.

Davis, D. A., Mazmanian, P. E., Fordis, M., Van Harrison, R., Thorpe, K. E., & Perrier, L. (2006). Accuracy of physician self-assessment compared with observed measures of competence: A systematic review. *Journal of the American Medical Association*, 296(9), 1094–1102.

Davis, D. A., O'Brien, M. A., Freemantle, N., Wolf, F. M., Mazmanian, P., & Taylor-Vaisey, A. (1999). Impact of formal continuing medical education: Do conferences, workshops, rounds, and other traditional continuing education activities change physician behavior or health care outcomes? *Journal of the American Medical Association*, 282(9), 867–874.

Davis, D. A., Thomson, M. A., Oxman, A. D., & Haynes, R. B. (1992). Evidence for the effectiveness of CME: A review of 50 randomized controlled trials. *Journal of the American Medical Association, 268*(9), 1111–1117.

(1995). Changing physician performance: A systematic review of the effect of continuing medical education strategies. *Journal of the American Medical Association, 274*(9), 700–705.

Davis, N. L., & Willis, C. E. (2004). A new metric for continuing medical education credit. *Journal of Continuing Education in the Health Professions, 24*(3), 139–144.

Derbyshire, R. C. (2003). Relicensure for continued practice. *Journal of Medical License Discipline, 89*(1), 16–22.

Dombkowski, K. J., Cabana, M. D., Cohn, L. M., Gebremariam, A., & Clark, S. J. (2005). Geographic variation of asthma quality measures within and between health plans. *American Journal of Managed Care, 11*(12), 765–772.

Ecc Committee, Subcommittees and Task Forces of the American Heart Association (2005). 2005 American Heart Association Guidelines for Cardiopulmonary Resuscitation and Emergency Cardiovascular Care. *Circulation, 112*(24 Suppl), IV1–203.

Ericsson, K. A. (2004). Deliberate practice and the acquisition and maintenance of expert performance in medicine and related domains. *Academic Medicine, 79*, S70–S81.

Falchikov, N., & Boud, D. (1989). Student self-assessment in higher education: A meta-analysis. *Review of Educational Research, 59*, 395–430.

Freemantle, N., Harvey, E. L., Wolf, F., Grimshaw, J. M., Grilli, R., & Bero, L. A. (2000). Printed educational materials: Effects on professional practice and health care outcomes. *Cochrane Database of Systematic Reviews*, (2), CD000172.

Gallagher, A. G., Ritter, E. M., Champion, H., Higgins, G., Fried, M. P., Moses, G., et al. (2005). Virtual reality simulation for the operating room: Proficiency-based training as a paradigm shift in surgical skills training. *Annals of Surgery, 241*(1), 364–372.

Garg, A. X., Adhikari, N. K. J., McDonald, H., Rosas-Arellano, M. P., Devereaux, P. J., Beyene, J., et al. (2005). Effects of computerized clinical decision support systems on practitioner performance and patient outcomes. *Journal of the American Medical Association, 293*(10), 1223–1238.

Gordon, M. J. (1991). A review of the validity and accuracy of self-assessments in health professions training. *Academic Medicine, 67*, 672–679.

Grilli, R., & Lomas, J. (1994). Evaluating the message: The relationship between compliance rate and the subject of a practice guideline. *Medical Care, 32*(3), 202–213.

Grimshaw, J. M., Thomas, R. E., MacLennan, G., Fraser, C., Ramsay, C. R., Vale, L., et al. (2004). Effectiveness and efficiency of guideline dissemination and implementation strategies. *Health Technology Assessment, 8*(6), iii–iv, 1–72.

Grol, R., Baker, R., & Moss, F. (Eds.). (2004). *Quality improvement research: Understanding the science of change in health care.* London: BMJ Books.

Grol, R., & Grimshaw, J. (1999). Evidence-based implementation of evidence-based medicine. *The Joint Commission Journal on Quality Improvement, 25*(10), 503–513.

Huis in't Veld, M. H., van Til, J. A., Ijzerman, M. J., & Vollenbroek-Hutten, M. M. (2005). Preferences of general practitioners regarding an application running on a personal digital assistant in acute stroke care. *Journal of Telemedicine and Telecare,* *11*(1, Suppl), 37–39.

Institute of Medicine (U.S.), Committee on Quality of Health Care in America. (2001). *Crossing the quality chasm: A new health system for the 21st century.* Washington, DC: National Academy Press.

Jamtvedt, G., Young, J. M., Kristoffersen, D. T., O'Brien, M. A., & Oxman, A. D. (2006). Audit and feedback: Effects on professional practice and health care outcomes. *Cochrane Database Systems Review,* (2), CD000259.

Johnson, D. A., Austin, D. L., & Thompson, J. N. (2005). Role of state medical boards in continuing medical education. *Journal of Continuing Education in the Health Professions,* *25*(3), 183–189.

Kahn, C. E., Ehlers, K. C., & Wood, B. P. (2006). Radiologists' preferences for just-in-time learning. *Journal of Digital Imaging,* *19*, 202–206.

Kruger, J., Dunning, D. (1999). Unskilled and unaware of it: How difficulties in recognizing one's own incompetence lead to inflated self-assessments. *J Pers Soc Psychol.,* *77*, 1121–1134.

Leopold, S. S., Morgan, H. D., Kadel, N. J., Gardner, G. C., Schaad, D. C., Wolf, F. M. (2005). Impact of educational intervention on confidence and competence in the performance of a simple surgical task. *J Bone Joint Surg Am.,* *87*, 1031–1037.

Lynn, D. J., Holzer, C., & O'Neill, P. (2006). Relationships between self-assessment skills, test performance, and demographic varibles in psychiatry residents. *Advances in Health Sciences Education,* *11*, 51–60.

McAuley, R. G., & Henderson, H. W. (1984). Results of the peer assessment program of the College of Physicians and Surgeons of Ontario. *Canadian Medical Association Journal,* *131*(6), 557–561.

McMaster University: Physician Review and Enhancement Program (1999). *Enhancing physician competence.* Hamilton, ON: McMaster University, Faculty of Health Sciences.

MEDLINE. PubMed [database on-line]. (2007). Bethesda, MD: National Library of Medicine, http://www.pubmed.gov.

Miller, S. H. (2005). American Board of Medical Specialties and repositioning for excellence in lifelong learning: Maintenance of certification. *Journal of Continuing Education in the Health Professions,* *25*(3), 151–156.

Nahrwold, D. L. (2005). Continuing medical education reform for competency-based education and assessment. *Journal of Continuing Education in the Health Professions,* *25*(3), 168–173.

Norman, G. R., Neufeld, V. R., Walsh, A., Woodward, C. A., & McConvey, G. A. (1985). Measuring physicians' performances by using simulated patients. *Journal of Medical Education,* *60*(12), 925–934.

Nowlen, P. M. (1988). *A new approach to continuing education for business and the professions: The performance model.* New York: Macmillan.

Parker, R.W., Alford, C., Passmore, C. (2004). Can family medicine residents predict their performance on the in-training examination? *Fam Med.,* *36:* 705–709.

Peabody, J. W., Luck, J., Glassman, P., Dresselhaus, T. R., & Lee, M. (2000). Comparison of vignettes, standardized patients, and chart abstraction: A prospective study of 3 methods for measuring quality, *Journal of the American Medical Association,* *283*(13), 1715–1722.

Pfeffer, J., & Fong, C. T. (2002). The end of business schools? Less success than meets the eye. *Academy of Management Learning and Education, 1*, 78–95.

(2004). The business school "business": Some lessons from the US experience. *Journal of Management Studies, 41*, 1501–1520.

Pimlott, N. J., Hux, J. E., Wilson, L. M., Kahan, M., Li, C., & Rosser, W. W. (2003). Educating physicians to reduce benzodiazepine use by elderly patients: A randomized controlled trial. *Canadian Medical Association Journal, 168*(7), 835–839.

Research and Development Resource Base (RDRB) [database on-line] (Updated 2006, December). http://www.cme.utoronto.ca/search.

Rogers, E. M. (2003). *Diffusion of innovations* (5th ed.). New York: The Free Press.

Rubin, M. A., Bateman, K., Donnelly, S., Stoddard, G. J., Stevenson, K., Gardner, R. M., et al. (2006). Use of a personal digital assistant for managing antibiotic prescribing for outpatient respiratory tract infections in rural communities. *Journal of the American Medical Informatics Association, 13*(6), 627–634.

Rushforth, H. E. (2007). Objective structured clinical examination (OSCE): Review of literature and implications for nursing education. *Nursing Education Today, 27*, 481–490.

Schuster, M. A., McGlynn, E. A., & Brook, R. H. (1998). How good is the quality of health care in the United States? *Milbank Quarterly, 76*(4), 509, 517–563.

Shah, B. R., Mamdani, M., & Kopp, A. (2003). Drug use in older people with diabetes. In J. Hux, G. Booth, P. Slaughter, & A. Laupacis (Eds.), *Diabetes in Ontario: An ICES Practice Atlas*. Toronto: The Institute for Clinical Evaluative Studies.

Sintchenko, V., Iredell, J. R., Gilbert, G. L., & Coiera, E. (2005, July–August). Handheld computer-based decision support reduces patient length of stay and antibiotic prescribing in critical care. *Journal of the American Medical Informatics Association, 12*(4), 398–402.

Society for Continuing Medical Education (SACME). *Biennial survey*. Retrieved March 20, 2007, from, http://sacme.org/Biennial_survey/default.htm.

Spivey, B. E. (2005). Continuing medical education in the United States: Why it needs reform and how we propose to accomplish it. *Journal of Continuing Education in the Health Professions, 25*(3), 134–143.

The Shipman Inquiry. *Fifth Report – Safeguarding Patients: Lessons from the past – proposals for the future*. Published December 9, 2004. Command Paper Cm 6394. Retrieved March 20, 2007, from, http://www.the-shipman-inquiry.org.uk/fifthreport.asp.

Thomson-O'Brien, M. A., Oxman, A. D., Davis, D. A., Haynes, R. B., Freemantle, N., & Harvey E. L. (2000). Educational outreach visits: Effects on professional practice and health care outcomes. *Cochrane Database of Systematic Reviews*, (2), CD000409.

Vale, L., Thomas, R., Maclennan, G., & Grimshaw, J. (2007). Systematic review of economic evaluations and cost analyses of guideline implementation strategies. *The European Journal of Health Economics, 8*, 111–121.

Wall, T. C., Mian, M. A., Ray, M. N., Casebeer, L., Collins, B. C., Kiefe, C. I., et al. (2005). Improving physician performance through Internet-based interventions: Who will participate [electronic version]? *Journal of Medical Internet Research, 7*(4), e48.

Ward, M., Gruppen, L., & Regehr, G. (2002). Measuring self assessment: Current state of the art. *Advances in the Health Sciences Education, 7*, 63–80.

Wennberg, D. E., Kellett, M. A., Dickens, J. D., Malenka, D. J., Keilson, L. M., & Keller, R. B. (1996). The association between local diagnostic testing intensity and invasive cardiac procedures. *Journal of the American Medical Association, 275*(15), 1161–1164.

Wright, A., Goldberg, H., & Hongsermeier, T. (2007). A description and functional taxomomy of rule-based decision support content at a large integrated delivery network. *Journal of American Medical Informatics Association, 14,* 489–496.

9

Advances in Specifying What Is to Be Learned: Reflections on the Themes in Chapters 6–8

RICHARD E. MAYER

INTRODUCTION

Advances in Instructional Design

If you want to be successful in designing effective instruction, you need to begin with a clear specification of what is to be learned. This is a central premise underlying various instructional-design theories since their inception (Reigeluth, 1983, 1999; Reiser & Dempsey, 2007). The three chapters in this section provide a useful description of advances in the field of instructional design, focusing on techniques for specifying what is to be learned. In this review, after a brief analysis of the types of knowledge, I examine four phases in the evolution of instructional-design approaches. As summarized in Table 9.1, these phases involve different ways of characterizing what is to be learned – compartmentalized behaviors, compartmentalized knowledge, integrated knowledge, and individualized knowledge.

APPLYING THE SCIENCE OF INSTRUCTION

Learning is a change in the learner's knowledge due to experience (Mayer, 2001). Instruction is the systematic manipulation of the learner's experience in order to foster learning (Mayer, 2003). In short, learning involves a change in the learner's knowledge and the goal of instruction is to foster a change in the learner's knowledge. However, you can only infer a change in the learner's knowledge indirectly by observing a change in the learner's behavior, such as changes in the learner's performance on a specified task. An important contribution of the science of instruction is the specification of various types of knowledge that must be learned for success on complex cognitive tasks (Anderson et al., 2001; Gagné, 1965; Mayer, 2003):

I wish to thank Anders Ericsson for his useful suggestions.

Table 9.1. *Four approaches to specifying what is to be learned.*

Approach	What is to be learned	Exemplary tools	Exemplary methods
Compartmentalized behaviors	Behaviors in an isolated task	Task analysis	Behavioral objectives
Compartmentalized knowledge	Procedures and facts in an isolated task	Cognitive task analysis	Learning hierarchies
Integrated knowledge	Procedures, facts, strategies, concepts, and beliefs needed for performing a complex cognitive task in context	Cognitive task analysis	Guided simulations
Individualized knowledge	Procedures, facts, strategies, concepts and beliefs that the learner does not already know	Cognitive task analysis and learner modeling	Embedded assessment

- *Facts:* Factual knowledge consists of descriptions about the characteristics of elements, as indicated by being able to answer the question, "How many sides does a square have?"
- *Concepts:* Conceptual knowledge includes knowledge of categories, principles, models, theories, and schemas, as indicated by being able to distinguish between a word problem that requires using the time-rate-distance formula and one that requires using the Pythagorean formula for triangles.
- *Procedures:* Procedural knowledge involves knowing a list of steps, such as the procedure for multiplying 3-digit numbers.
- *Strategies:* Strategic knowledge involves knowing a general approach to a task, including strategies for devising a plan, and metacognitive strategies such as monitoring one's performance and assessing one's need for new learning.
- *Beliefs:* Attitudinal knowledge involves beliefs about self-efficacy, interests, attributions, values, and goals that affect task performance, such as believing that "I am not good in math."

In short, in describing "what is learned," it is useful to distinguish among the five kinds of knowledge – facts, concepts, procedures, strategies, and beliefs – as summarized in Table 9.2. Advances in the science of instruction allow for more precise and useful specifications of "what is to be learned" – that is, the change in knowledge that is targeted by instruction. In the remainder of this review, I outline four phases in the search for how to specify what is to be learned – each representing a significant advancement.

Table 9.2. *Five kinds of knowledge.*

Type	Short name	Description	Example
Factual knowledge	Facts	Knowing a characteristic of an object	A square has _____ sides
Procedural knowledge	Procedures	Knowing how to carry out a procedure	$312 \times 457 =$ _____
Conceptual knowledge	Concepts	Knowing principles, categories, models, theories, or schemas	Recognizing that a word problem is a distance-rate-time problem
Strategic knowledge (and meta-strategic knowledge)	Strategies	Knowing how to devise a plan or method, or how to monitor and manage cognitive processing	Breaking a problem into parts, recognizing that a plan is not working, or that new learning is needed
Attitudinal knowledge	Beliefs	Interests, self-efficacy beliefs, attributions, values, or goals	"I am not good in math."

PHASE 1: SPECIFYING COMPARTMENTALIZED BEHAVIORS

The first approach in Table 9.1 concerns specifying intended learning outcomes in terms of compartmentalized behaviors. Early attempts to specify "what is to be learned" focused on descriptions of desired behaviors, as exemplified in Mager's (1962) behavioral objectives. Using task analysis to break a task into its parts, instructional designers can specify each of the behaviors required for performance. Schraagen (Chapter 7) notes that "every instructional design will incorporate a task or content analysis" in which task analysis is "viewed as a decomposition of a complex task into a set of constituent subtasks."

Although task analysis is essential to the instructional system design (ISD) approach (Jonassen, Tessmer, & Hannum, 1999), Schraagen (Chapter 7) has noted "designers are often not convinced that task analysis is worth the effort." Schraagen reports that "task analysis requires a lot of time, effort, and expertise; it is more of an art than a science; and its usefulness is frequently doubted."

What is wrong with task analysis? Although task analysis represents a significant advance in specifying what is learning, its primary limitation is a focus on describing the learner's desired behavior. This approach is consistent with a behaviorist view of learning, in which "what is learned" is a change in behavior. The behaviorist approach has been effective in promoting learning of simple procedures and responses, mainly through instruction based on drill and practice with feedback (Mayer, 2003). However, when the goal of instruction is to promote performance on more complex tasks, the behaviorist approach is not as successful in suggesting effective instructional programs.

A particular problem involves what Schraagen calls "the gulf between the outcomes of task analysis" and the design of effective instruction. In short, having a list of to-be-learned target behaviors does not translate directly into a plan for how to provide effective instruction.

PHASE 2: SPECIFYING COMPARTMENTALIZED KNOWLEDGE

The second approach in Table 9.1 involves specifying the intended learning outcome in terms of compartmentalized knowledge. Schraagen notes an important transition from task analysis (in which a task is broken into subtasks) to cognitive task analysis (in which a task is analyzed in terms of the knowledge needed). In short, in task analysis we ask, "What does the learner need to do in order to perform the task?" and in cognitive task analysis we ask, "What does the learner need to know in order to perform the task?" Both approaches retain the emphasis on analysis into parts, but they differ in terms of what is analyzed. In cognitive task analysis, it is not a task that is learned, but rather, it is facts, procedures, concepts, strategies, and beliefs. For example, Schraagen (Chapter 7) notes that "from the early 1980s onward, the emphasis was placed more and more on the underlying knowledge and strategies required for expert performance."

What is wrong with cognitive task analysis? Although cognitive task analysis represents a crucial advance in specifying what is learned, it has challenges in implementation. Schraagen shows that cognitive task analysis is hard to complete when the goal is to specify what an expert knows. This is why early applications of cognitive task analysis tended to focus on discrete procedures, such as Brown and Burton's (1978) analysis of students' procedure for three-column subtraction or discrete facts such as in some of Gagné's (1968) learning hierarchies. However, Schraagen (Chapter 7) reports that learning about basic facts and procedures does not correlate highly with application of this knowledge in real-life situations.

When the goal is to support performance in a complex task such as troubleshooting, learners need more than procedures and facts. They also need the specialized strategies and concepts used by experts, so they can determine when to apply various procedures and when to modify what they are doing. For example, in Chapter 7 Schraagen reports a successful training program that helped learners develop strategies and concepts they needed for success in troubleshooting within the context of authentic troubleshooting problems. This leads to the next major phase as described in the next section.

PHASE 3: SPECIFYING INTEGRATED KNOWLEDGE

The next step in the evolution of instructional-design approaches to specifying what is to be learned is the integrated knowledge approach listed in Table 9.1. While retaining the previous approach's focus on analyzing the to-be-learned knowledge, in the integrated knowledge approach we add more complex types of knowledge – namely, strategies, concepts, and beliefs – and we focus on using knowledge in the context of complex authentic tasks, such as how to negotiate with someone from another culture or how to integrate multiple sources of information to make an immediate decision under stress.

The shift from approach 2 to approach 3 corresponds to aspects of what van Merriënboer and Boot (Chapter 6) call a "paradigm shift in military training," which includes a shift in goals from "a task, condition, standard paradigm to more open-ended goals," and a shift in approach from "atomistic linear approaches that teach specific instructional objectives one-by-one to holistic zigzag approaches that take real-life tasks and situations as a starting point." van Merriënboer and Boot (Chapter 6) also note that instructional technology can play a useful role, particularly by affording the opportunity for learners to practice within interactive simulations, which they call technology enhanced learning environments (TELEs).

When we shift to cognitively complex authentic tasks as the starting point for cognitive task analysis, it becomes necessary to consider all five kinds of knowledge listed in Table 9.2. In particular, the focus shifts from basic knowledge such as procedures and facts, to complex knowledge such as strategies (including meta-strategies), concepts (including principles, categories, and models), and beliefs. In approaches 1 and 2, van Merriënboer and Boot (Chapter 6) note "military training has been based upon a systems approach called Instructional Systems Design (ISD)" in which "uniform training requirements and assessments are established in task, condition, and standard (TCS) paradigm: which tasks should be executed, under which complicating conditions, and by which objective standard." This approach is particularly well suited to well-defined procedures that can be reduced to simpler elements. In contrast, the shift to approach 3 is motivated by van Merriënboer and Boot's assessment that "military training is currently transforming, instigated by the increasing shift of responsibility over task performance down the chain of command." According to van Merriënboer and Boot, these new tasks require "creative solutions in constantly changing environments and considerable cultural awareness" and "shared situational awareness." These new demands require more complex knowledge including strategies, concepts, and beliefs.

Increasingly, the goal of instruction is to help learners develop the knowledge they need for "decision making, creativity, imagination, and problem solving for dealing with local, unexpected situations" and for determining "what to do in new, unfamiliar, and unforeseen situations" (van Merriënboer & Boot, Chapter 6). In these cases, "it is becoming impossible to specify all goals of training in highly specific learning objectives." What is needed is not only specification of procedures and facts in isolation, but also a description of the strategies and concepts that are needed for authentic tasks, as well as metacognitive strategies for how to manage knowledge within what van Merriënboer and Boot call "whole tasks."

PHASE 4: SPECIFYING INDIVIDUALIZED KNOWLEDGE

The next approach listed in Table 9.1 is the individualized cognitive approach, in which instructional designers specify to-be-learned knowledge as well as which aspects of the knowledge that the learner already knows. In short, it is useful to specify the strategies, concepts, beliefs, procedures, and facts that are required for performing the target task, as well as which aspects of the knowledge that the learner already knows. To accomplish this goal requires that assessments be embedded within the instructional program, which determines the aspects of intended learning outcome remaining to be learned. In this way, assessment can be used as a tool to guide instruction.

For example, Davis (Chapter 8) notes that medical professionals may have significant gaps in their knowledge, but may lack the self-assessment strategies that would lead them to seek appropriate training through continuing medical education. Davis defines self-assessment as "the ability of the professional to determine his or her own gaps ... and thus assess needs for learning and changes in practice" and recognizes it as "the cornerstone of self-directed learning." In short, learners need to be able to assess what they need to know – which is listed as a metacognitive strategy in Table 9.2.

An important example of individualized knowledge is reflected in Davis's review of research on continuing medical education, showing that medical professionals are not effective in determining the gaps in their knowledge. Medical professionals need ways of assessing their current knowledge and comparing it against the knowledge needed for effective medical practice in their field. In short, professionals need assessments (including self-assessments) of the specific knowledge required for carrying out authentic professional tasks and any gaps they have in that knowledge.

WHERE DO WE GO FROM HERE?

An important step in the instructional-design process is to specify what is to be learned, that is, to describe the intended learning outcome. This review focuses on four approaches to specifying intended learning outcomes, beginning with a focus on compartmentalized behaviors, then compartmentalized pieces of knowledge, then integrated knowledge, and finally individualized knowledge. The first approach of research on instructional design focuses on specifying specific behaviors based on a task analysis of basic cognitive tasks. The second approach focuses on specifying specific pieces of knowledge to execute basic cognitive tasks. The third approach focuses on specifying collections of knowledge required for complex cognitive tasks. The fourth approach

Table 9.3. *Three steps in instructional design.*

1. Determining what the learner needs to know
2. Determining what the learner already knows
3. Determining how to teach

adds a focus on embedded assessment of what the learner knows, which can guide the instructional program.

Table 9.3 shows three steps in the instructional-design process – determining what to teach, determining what the learner already knows, and determining how to teach. This review has focused mainly on the first two steps, but a crucial link is to the third step.

However, a clear description of what the learner needs to learn (i.e., steps 1 and 2) does not necessarily suggest an instructional program for accomplishing this goal (i.e., step 3). What is needed is basic research on which features of technology-based learning environments improve learning which kinds of knowledge on which kinds of tasks for which kinds of learners under which kinds of conditions.

According to Ericsson's (2006) theory of deliberate practice, after years of individualized training with a teacher or a coach, the expert acquires refined representations for monitoring his or her performance as well as its mediating mechanisms. These representations allow the performer to modify and refine the mechanisms to permit elimination of mistakes and development of a higher level of skill. What the performer needs is to keep continually identifying specific aspects of performance that can be improved – typically with the help of a master teacher or coach, who can recommend or design a training task with appropriate immediate feedback and the opportunity to repeatedly modify and refine the performance to attain the training goal (deliberate practice). The improved aspect can then be transferred to tasks that are more closely representative of superior performance in the domain (Ericsson, Chapter 18). With increases in skilled performance, the professionals take responsibility for how their skills and the associated mechanisms should change. What they need is learning environments that permit the measurement of their representative performance and the design of training tasks with immediate feedback. The amount of deliberate practice has been shown to be closely related to increases in performance and thus differs qualitatively from merely gaining more experience of activities within the domain by playful interaction and professional experience (Ericsson, Chapter 18).

In searching for a link from the specification of intended learning outcomes to effective instructional practices, van Merriënboer and Boot (Chapter 6) discuss examples of three technology-based learning environments intended to foster constructivist learning: computer programming activities such as Papert's (1980) Logo Turtle Graphics environment, Computer Supported Collaborative Learning (CSCl) such as Kolodner's (Kolodner et al., 2003) learning by design, and electronic learning environments such as WebCT or Blackboard. However, in spite of many strong claims, there is no strong research evidence to support the implementation of any of these forms of educational technology. Concerning Papert's constructionist learning environment for Logo, there is consistent research evidence that learning Logo in a pure discovery environment is ineffective (Mayer, 1988, 2004). In a recent review of research on CSCI, Jonassen, Lee, Yang, and Laffey (2005) concluded there is not sufficient evidence for claiming that CSCI improves learning. Finally, there is no convincing research base to support the claim that using course management systems such as WebCT or Blackboard enhance learning (Mayer et al., 2006). In short, using technology per se does not improve student learning. Instead, as Clark (2001) has repeatedly shown, it is effective instructional methods that foster learning.

Overall, research is needed that specifies which instructional methods are most useful in fostering the kinds of intended learning outcomes described in this review. I call this research the search for the missing link – that is, the missing link between specifying intended learning outcomes and effective instructional methods that promote learning of the intended outcomes.

Training is a central mission of the U.S. military and is embedded within its culture (Blascovich & Hartel, 2008; Bratton-Jeffery, Hoffman, & Jeffrey, 2007). For example, van Merriënboer and Boot (Chapter 6) eloquently note the importance of training: "Before and after executing operational missions, the military is primarily a training organization." To better accomplish changing training needs in the 21st century, instructional designers should broaden how they specify "what is to be learned" and link their new specifications to effective instructional methods.

REFERENCES

Anderson, L. W., Krathwohl, D. R., Airasian, P. W., Cruikshank, K. A., Mayer, R. E., Pintrich, P., et al. (2001). *Taxonomy for learning, teaching, and assessing: A revision of Bloom's taxonomy of educational objectives.* New York: Longman.

Blascovich, J. J., & Hartel, C. R. (Eds.). (2008). *Human behavior in military contexts.* Washington, DC: National Academy Press.

Bratton-Jeffery, M. F., Hoffman, S. Q., & Jeffery, A. B. (2007). Instructional design opportunities in military education and training environments. In R. A. Reiser & J. V. Dempsey (Eds.), *Trends and issues in instructional design and technology* (2nd ed., pp. 185–196). Upper Saddle River, NJ: Pearson Merrill Prentice-Hall.

Brown, J. S., & Burton, R. R. (1978). Diagnostic models for procedural bugs in basic mathematical skills. *Cognitive Science, 2,* 155–192.

Clark, R. E. (Ed.). (2001). *Learning from media.* Greenwich, CT: Information Age Publishing.

Ericsson, K. A. (2006). The influence of experience and deliberate practice on the development of superior expert performance. In K. A. Ericsson, N. Charness, P. J. Feltovich, & R. R. Hoffman (Eds.), *The Cambridge handbook of expertise and expert performance* (pp. 683–703). New York: Cambridge University Press.

Gagné, R. M. (1965). *The conditions of learning.* New York: Holt, Rinehart, and Winston.

Gagné, R. M. (1968). Learning hierarchies. *Educational Psychologist, 6,* 1–9.

Jonassen, D. H., Tessmer, M., & Hannum, W. H. (1999). *Task analysis methods for instructional design.* Mahwah, NJ: Lawrence Erlbaum Associates.

Jonassen, D. H., Lee, C. B., Yang, C. C., & Laffey, J. (2005). The collaboration principle in multimedia learning. In R. E. Mayer (Ed.), *The Cambridge handbook of multimedia learning* (pp. 215–228). New York: Cambridge University Press.

Kolodner, J. L., Crismond, D., Frase, B. B., Gray, J. T., Holbrook, J., Ryan, M., et al. (2003). Problem-based learning meets case-based reasoning in the middle-school science classroom: Putting a learning-by-design curriculum into practice. *Journal of the Learning Sciences, 12,* 495–548.

Mager, R. F. (1962). *Preparing instructional objectives.* Belmont, CA: Fearon Publishers.

Mayer, R. E. (Ed.). (1988). *Learning and teaching computer programming.* Mahwah, NJ: Lawrence Erlbaum Associates.

(2001). *Multimedia learning.* New York: Cambridge University Press.

(2003). *Learning and instruction.* Upper Saddle River, NJ: Pearson Merrill Prentice-Hall.

(2004). Should there be a three strikes rule against pure discovery learning? The case for guided methods of instruction. *American Psychologist, 59*(1), 14–19.

Mayer, R. E., Almeroth, K., Bimber, B., Chun, D., Knight, A., & Campbell, A. (2006). Technology comes to college: Understanding the cognitive consequences of infusing technology in college classrooms. *Educational Technology, 46*(2), 48–53.

Papert, S. (1980). *Mindstorms.* New York: Basic Books.

Reigeluth, C. M. (Ed.). (1983). *Instructional-design theories and models.* Hillsdale, NJ: Lawrence Erlbaum Associates.

(1999). *Instructional-design theories and models: Volume II.* Mahwah, NJ: Lawrence Erlbaum Associates.

Reiser, R. A., & Dempsey, J. V. (Ed.). (2007). *Trends and issues in instructional design and technology* (2nd ed.). Upper Saddle River, NJ: Pearson Merrill Prentice-Hall.

SECTION 3

THE ASSESSMENT AND TRAINING OF SKILLED AND EXPERT PERFORMERS IN THE MILITARY

The third section of the book contains a discussion of the current and new evolving methods for training skilled professionals, such as fighter pilots, officers leading combat units, and submarine officers.

10

Toward a Second Training Revolution: Promise and Pitfalls of Digital Experiential Learning

RALPH E. CHATHAM

I begin, in the time-honored military lecture way, by telling you what I intend to tell you:

> Early results with language, convoy operations, and information technology troubleshooting suggest that, at their best, lightweight digital simulations can train superbly. However, the notion of training delivered on personal computers also gives rise, apparently by spontaneous generation, to a horde of 'games for training' fanatics whose products ensure that, at the median, such simulations are dreadful. Even the best of breed suffer because training individuals to perform as part of a larger military unit often forces the rest of the team and other echelons, above and below, to become expensive and difficult-to-schedule training devices. Moreover, current military operations require soldiers to spend most of their time doing exactly what they did not join the military to do: deal with very sticky situations involving human and cultural interactions. A successful second training revolution must deal with these new missions. To do so simulations will need 'people engines' to control characters in virtual cultural landscapes in the same way 'physics engines' control physical simulation objects. A handful of plausibility arguments suggest that this might be doable, but there are few existence proofs. Finally, and always, whatever we create will fail if training is not embedded from the beginning.

THE FIRST TRAINING REVOLUTION DOES NOT SCALE

In Chapter 2, I discussed a revolution in military training. While used principally by the U.S. Army and the three American air forces (Navy, Marine Corps, and Air Force), the process is not intrinsically bound to military training, as the example of currency arbitrage suggested. The key elements of this training revolution were the following:

1. Creating a large-scale simulation of the war du jour, with enough fidelity to exercise all the important elements of that conflict.

2. Playing that "war" out on an instrumented range that accurately measures what happens.
3. Providing a well-trained opposing force that uses enemy tactics and enemy equipment, an enemy so good that the forces being trained expect to be defeated.
4. Conducting no-holds-barred after-action reviews (AARs) where everyone is encouraged to think about what happened, when, why, and what might be done about it.
5. Dedication to using the process.

Recent Changes at the National Training Center

The flexibility and wide applicability of this process to multiple domains is illustrated by the dramatic changes that have occurred at the National Training Center (NTC) in the last few years. Throughout the 1980s and 1990s, the focus of the NTC was on large-scale maneuver warfare while a similar training center in Fort Polk, Louisiana took on training for stability and urban operations. The conflicts in Afghanistan and Iraq altered what our forces were asked to do. In response, the initial site of the Army's training revolution, under the leadership of Brigadier General Robert Cone, reinvented itself in dramatic ways to train large units in "nonkinetic operations." While there are today too many definitions of nonkinetic operations, I will use the phrase here to mean everything that a soldier did *not* join up to do: dealing not with bombs, bullets, tanks, and major battles, but with human and social interactions in a foreign culture.[1]

Now, instead of great tank battles, a unit is required to control a huge desert area filled with villages, roads, and over 250 Iraqi-Americans acting as the local population. The opposing forces (OPFOR) also include 750 Army soldiers acting as insurgents.

Complicated plots play out in this giant improvisational theater over a period of a few weeks (Filkins & Burns, 2006). If a unit finds out that fertilizer has been stolen from the factory, they can follow the trail into the hills and avert a large (simulated) bomb from disrupting the march from Medina Jubal to the Mosque-on-the-Hill the next week. If they fail to figure out that fertilizer

---

[1] Other people have different definitions of nonkinetic operations. Herein you are stuck with mine: All those things soldiers didn't think they would be doing, but are today. Not shooting, driving tanks, reacting violently, but what is sometimes viewed as "bunny-hugging." The list includes acting as: ambassadors; all-source intelligence collectors; forensic evidence custodians; health-care managers; civil engineers; auditors; contract specialists; public affairs officers; anthropologists; politicians; power brokers; lawyers; linguists; paramedics; negotiators; social workers; psychologists; police; diplomats; town managers; Machiavellian bureaucrats; liaisons with nongovernmental organizations, United States Agency for International Development, etc.

can be used to make explosives, they can still avert the disaster by tracking the bomb-building money or the vehicle that might deliver it.

If one of the OPFOR who is playing a local Iraqi hot dog vendor offers to provide his wares to the brigade's base, the trainees had better search the hot-dog truck for bombs *every* time he comes in. (In one case he was searched for the first few days and blew up the simulated bomb on the fourth day.) Every situation can be solved by talking, but it is not easy for the unit to figure that out in time. The NTC has changed from training maneuver warfare to nonki-netic operations by dint of dedicated effort, sometimes in the face of institutional resistance. Yet the *process* and its effectiveness remains the same.

The revolution, powerful and adaptable as it is, is episodic and never reaches some units, and the whole unit – bag and baggage, troops and tanks – must go to the center to get the benefit. Summarizing this in engineering shorthand: "NTC doesn't scale."[2] The Defense Science Board task forces on Training Superiority and Training Surprise and Training for Future Conflicts (Braddock & Chatham, 2001; Chatham & Braddock, 2003) recommended that we might make it scale by bottling the essential elements of the revolution and export it electronically to more people, more of the time and in more places. We wanted to fill in the "bathtub curve" of unit proficiency versus time, which shows that competence peaks every few years and then drops again rapidly (see Figure 2.8). We wanted to smooth out that curve and maintain proficiency continuously at a high level. One of the goals of the DARWARS program,[3] which I subsequently started at the Defense Advanced Research Projects Agency (DARPA), was to start down that path, but even as we did, the demands on our forces changed. This effort and its results are the subject of this chapter. Before I go on, however, I offer a few more observations on training processes and assessment.

Observations on Individual Training

Tutors work. There is good evidence that the best and best-retained training, military or otherwise, comes from (1) one-on-one tutoring (Bloom, 1984), and (2) letting students experience performing the specific tasks that will be required of them, even if only in simulation.

There are, unfortunately, never enough tutors and fewer still *good* tutors. Worse, as the pace of our new conflicts picks up, it is hard enough for the tutors themselves to remain current, let alone bring students up to date. As

---

[2] Anthony Tether, private communication, December, 2006. A useful phrase; I wish I had had it five years ago.

[3] DARWARS is an acronym for "DARpa's universal, persistent, on-demand, fill in-your-own-adjective-here, training WARS." I wanted there to be a hint that DARPA was inside of any training tool that resulted. You may now forget the origin; the program really didn't end up going in that direction anyway.

for experiential training, there is also the problem of scarcity. There are not enough opportunities to practice the range of skills that soldiers will be asked to exercise when deployed. Scaling is an issue here as well. When a large unit trains together, those events that help the unit's leaders learn are often counterproductive for the subordinate units and individuals. This results in the common aphorisms: "It takes 10 people to train one," and "Large-scale exercises result in the soldiers acting only as expensive training devices for their commanders."

What You Don't Measure Can Hurt You

As if that were not enough, there are substantial conflicts among achieving good training results, the acquisition of modern military hardware, and a personnel assignment system that was created a century ago. These issues are discussed in Braddock and Chatham (2001) and Chatham and Braddock (2003). A fundamental reason for these disconnects resides in the abysmal state of assessment and measurement of training results. What you can't measure, you find easy to ignore. "Numbers of aircraft" or "armor performance" have obvious measures. Training, and what is more important, proficiency do not have such simple measures.

Kirkpatrick's Assessment Categories

A convenient sorting of training assessment methods comes from Kirkpatrick, who described four categories (Kirkpatrick, 1987). They range from simply asking whether the students liked it (level 1), to tests administered at the end of a course (level 2), to assessment of how much the student retains by the time he or she arrives in the field (level 3), to what really counts: whether the training changed the unit's performance in some real mission (level 4). You are lucky if your training, military or any other kind, is measured sensibly at the end of the training encounter. This is bad enough for individual training; in multiple echelon training, the assessment problem rivals in difficulty the scaling problem of ensuring that training occurs at every level.

The Proximity Effect

One final observation on the process of guided experiential training at the NTC: They make a tacit assumption that putting a student or unit into an experience, guiding them through it, and then conducting the AAR is an effective way to train proficiency in similar real-world experiences. While this assumption is tacitly accepted today, it is not there by accident; it was the result of years of dedicated research that led up to the founding of the NTC.

In the DARWARS program we found the corollary to this for PC-based training, what I will coin here as the "proximity effect": training is enhanced when the learning and the experience requiring use of that learning come in close proximity in time. If you are introduced to the UNIX command "Ping" precisely when you need it to troubleshoot a network, or if the consequences of failure to bag evidence are brought to your attention at an AAR immediately after you dumped the contraband weapons loose in the bed of your HMMWV, you remember the lesson better than if it came in a lecture a day or week before. Moreover, as I will show anecdotally later, it is not just a case of better retention; proximity in time of the lesson to performing the task strongly influences motivation and immersion.

Although it is not often done well today, PC-based training has the potential to put the teaching and the experience very close together in time. The language and information technology (IT) troubleshooting digital tutors discussed below show how this can be done and demonstrate the motivational value.

TOWARD A SECOND TRAINING REVOLUTION

Simulation to the Rescue?[4]

Everything short of actual war is simulation.[5]

As foreshadowed by the last few paragraphs, electronic simulations of warfare situations appear to offer solutions to many of the military training problems cited. They can replace expensive forces or dangerous situations with virtual ones. They are easy to reset and run again. They are not usually interrupted by weather. It should even be possible to collect all the necessary data on performance needed for assessment; after all, everything that happens is mediated by the computers that facilitate the training.

In fact, a number of grand-scale, high-fidelity simulations have achieved that promise. Aircraft and submarine diving and attack simulators have been providing effective training for over half a century. More recently, the distant descendents of DARPA's SIMNET program, the Air Forces Distributed Mission Trainer/Operations trainers, and the Army's Close Combat Tactical Trainers, have shown that superb training transfer can be achieved with less than complete fidelity in the displays.

All these training tools, however, are still expensive, reside at large fixed sites, and serve only a special subset of the armed forces: pilots, maneuver-warfare vehicle crews, or submarine control teams. We cannot afford to use this kind of high-fidelity training simulation to train the brain behind *every* trigger finger and *every* steering wheel. We cannot even afford enough of the

---

[4] In the interests of full disclosure, this and the subsequent discussion of *DARWARS Ambush!* and the *Tactical Iraqi Language and Culture* training are an expansion of an article I wrote for Mike Zyda in the late summer of 2006. The working title was "Games for Training: The Good, the Bad, and the Ugly." When it finally saw the light of publication (Chatham, 2007) the subtitle had been lost.

[5] General Paul F. Gorman, U.S. Army (retired), private communication, but oft repeated.

airplane, tank, and submarine simulators to meet the real training needs of those special groups who man the expensive platforms, even though they usually have substantial funding available for training. Those who drive logistic convoys, however, don't have even those resources.

Lighter-weight simulations, however – those that could run on common personal computer hardware – might be accessible most of the time to most of the military personnel who are in need of training. If such training could be shown to transfer into proficiency in real-world tasks, then it might be able to fill in the "all users, all the time" gap that grand-scale simulations cannot affordably fill. It is more or less this observation that led me to create in 2002 DARPA's Training Superiority (DARWARS) program. I asked if we could create examples of a new class of PC-based training that could demonstrate effective and low-cost training for many. This led, inevitably, to the issue of "games for training."

Can Computer Games Help?

The prospect that lightweight training simulations might be finally ready for prime-time use in training arises chiefly from the astounding success of PC gaming simulations over the last decade or so. The game simulation market actually drove the PC hardware market to the point where a commodity graphics card today would have been considered a supercomputer five years ago. Since the simulation capability was created by the games market, there is a strong tendency in one's thinking automatically to include the game part along with the new simulation capability. This leads, far too often, to import into our training the "bathwater along with the baby.[6]

The uninitiated tend to think of existing games, from massive multiplayer online games (MMOG) down to first-person shooters, as instant training devices. After all, they are manifestly good at teaching people to play games. Shouldn't they, therefore, be good at training other things? The emerging answer is that this is true only sometimes. A major theme of this chapter comes from mangling another old metaphor: "a game unexamined is an empty trainer."

Common Assumptions About Games for Training

I, too, entered the realm of training games with a number of unstated, and therefore unexamined, assumptions about their value. Training games, I expected would be:

1. Cheap (inexpensive to create, deploy, and maintain)
2. Fast (could be developed quickly)

---

[6] My thanks to Dr. Harold Hawkins of the Office of Naval Research for this distortion of the old metaphor.

3. Effective (would train skills that matched those needed in the real world)
4. Trainer-less (give the disk to a user and she or he would automatically learn with no supervision)
5. Universal (they would be automatically accessible to anybody with a computer). (Chatham, 2007)

Unless the training developers take extreme care, these assumptions will prove false. Even as I explore below a few examples in which the above list rises above the level of myth, there is a serious danger that the wrong lessons will be drawn from the successes. Lightweight training simulations at their best can be superbly effective; at the median they are awful (Ferguson, 2006). Thus, it is incumbent upon the training developer who uses game technology to show what works, why it works, what is needed outside the game to make it work, and whether a student's learning actually translates to performance in the real world.

The games-for-training fanatics have so much influence at the moment that I will expend more than my allotted wordage to describe where game technology helps or hinders us to develop and deploy lightweight training simulations and to distinguish between *games,* which are in the final analysis irrelevant, and proficiency *gains,* which are what counts.

BAIT: SOME DARWARS TRAINING PROJECTS AND A TRANSFER STUDY

When we started the DARWARS program, one of the goals was to produce PC-based training systems over a range of applications that would serve as bait to the military training world. That is, they would show that lightweight simulations (although I did not use that phrase then) could work and cause training systems developers to realize, "If you could do that, then I could use a similar tool for my application." Two of the major DARWARS projects used game engines as their base simulation tool; two did not. I will describe the game-based projects and one project that, while it does not use a game engine, seems to be as immersive as the most addictive games. (The fourth failed more for military anthropological reasons than technical ones and I will not mention it further.) I will also describe an anecdote and a series of experiments that begin to make the case that learning derived from lightweight simulations transfers to real-world performance.

Tactical Language and Culture Trainer

I will start with an example where the developer used Epic Games' *Unreal* game engine essentially as an operating system for a complete digital training tool, although we did not start out with that intention. The project arose from my observation that, although advisory panels continued to say that the military needed more linguists, there would never be enough of them (linguists, not advisory panels). So, as a supplement to the doomed effort to create a massive corps of linguists in obscure languages, I asked if it would be possible to put a little bit of gesture, culture, and mission-specific vocabulary into the brain behind every trigger finger or behind every steering wheel. I realized that, given everything else that we would have to teach to those we send to foreign countries, we could count on no more than two weeks of contact time with the student, and that time was unlikely to come all in one block. Thus, my charge to the performer was to define "tactical language"; that is, the amount of militarily-relevant culture and language you could stuff into the brains of even foreign-language-impaired humans (like me), and then figure out how to teach it in two discontinuous weeks.

One of the products is the *Tactical Iraqi Language Training System*. There are others: Pashto, Levantine Arabic, and French. Like Gaul, *Tactical Iraqi* is divided into three parts (Figures 10.1 and 10.2). It comes as a single CD, free for government use,[7] and can be used on any game-playing PC. It delivers over 100 hours of training in three modes. A vocabulary and culture tutor, the "Skill Builder" provides instruction that listens to students' utterances, applying speech-recognition technology to identify disfluencies and assess their progress. A set of arcade games includes mazes through which a student's avatar navigates in response to his or her spoken Iraqi Arabic commands: directions (left, right, forward, back, north, south, toward the river, etc.), place names, color names, and military ranks. The arcade games include listening modes as well, where the trainee moves her or his avatar in response to commands delivered to the student by an Iraqi "voice from the sky." Finally, but possibly most important for practice producing foreign sounds in context, there is a Mission Environment. It works much like a computer game where the student must talk his way in Iraqi Arabic through many sticky situations and encounters with multiple characters. The student can shift from mode to mode as he or she chooses (Figure 10.2).

The use of a game was part of the developer's (University of Southern California's Center for Advanced Research in Technology for Education, CARTE) answer to the "two week" challenge. Initially the game engine only drove the mission environment. (In the early versions, in fact, it looked so much like a game that we had to remind the student that this was language and culture training. We arranged it such that if you pushed the left mouse button, which is weapon trigger in action computer games, a banner popped up and said, "You can't shoot in this game; you must talk your way out." You had to use the right mouse button to start the speech recognizer.)

---

[7]   As of this writing anyone with a ".mil" email address can download at no cost *Tactical Iraqi*, as well as Tactical Dari, Pashtoo, and French, after registering on the website of Tactical Language Training, LLC: support.tacticallanguage.com.

FIGURE 10.1. Three parts of the *Tactical Language* Trainers: a Skill-Builder screen shot, one of the *Tactical Iraqi* Arcade Games, and early scene from the *Pashto Mission* Mode.

(*Source:* Defense Advanced Research Projects Agency.)

FIGURE 10.2. Student learning basic Iraqi language and culture with TLCTS at the 7th Army Training Center, Grafenwoehr, Germany.

(*Source:* Defense Advanced Research Projects Agency.)

The decision to use an *existing* game engine, versus creating a new one from scratch, was driven by the time and cost of building a simulation engine. Moreover, we already had research-license access to the *Unreal* engine, which had proven itself to be adaptable to other applications, such as the *America's Army* recruiting game. The use of the *Unreal* engine allowed us to get prototypes up and running quickly to help us learn if it were even possible to teach some language to everyone. That spiral development approach also enabled us to show off intermediate products to users, funders, and the press throughout the development. Those demonstrations were vital to keeping the program alive and funded.

We quickly learned that the users often wanted to shift from the mission (game) mode to the skill builder (vocabulary and culture) and back again. This led to the first problem with using existing game systems for training: *The game wants the entire computer's resources* and leaves little computing power left to do things like language recognition or on-demand videos of a talking head. CARTE dropped some of these desirable features to allow the student to shift rapidly from one mode to the other. At that stage of development, the best way to do that was to use the game engine as the software basis for every feature of the trainer.

Some game engine tools were usefully adapted for alternate uses. For example, when we discovered that the students were finding it hard to perceive how the attitudes of the virtual characters in the mission (game) environment were changing, CARTE took the "ammunition status bar" and converted it directly into a "trust meter." They were able to use America's Army characters and uniforms for the initial versions, although little of that remains in the final version.

There were some features of the game engine, however, that were distinctly not useful. In creating the foundation for the arcade games, for example, a programmer found that once one's avatar reached a new point in the Pac-Man-like maze it would assume a random orientation, rather than keep pointing in the direction it had taken to travel there. The documented routine that should have solved this didn't; it reliably crashed when used to draw the overhead two-dimensional view of the maze. It took several weeks of poking down into the dusty, disused corridors of the *Unreal* engine to find a work-around.

A second problem was more serious and it took longer to detect even its existence, let alone its source. In the process of converting the training system from one created in compliance with a research license, to a system that used a newly purchased commercial license, it became necessary to use some different software tools. At the same time we were also developing a new language tutor for *Tactical Pashto*. It slowly dawned on the developers that the speech recognition of *Pashto* was not working as well as it should. Looking back at the new version of *Tactical Iraqi*, CARTE found that the even the *Arabic* recognition performance had degraded from previous versions. Eventually, all this was traced to a filter in the newly applied *Unreal* tools, which cut out all information above 8 kHz. That was perfectly satisfactory for speech in a game, and was probably used to decrease the amount of PC resources needed to handle sounds. For a foreign language speech recognizer, however, it was a disaster. It was also not documented.

The lesson from these examples is that one must always keep in mind that *the factors that drive the development of a game engine are not coincident with those that drive a training application.* The game developers stop fixing things when the game works well enough for their gaming customers. This leads to the existence of many dangling, undocumented software features that only appear when one uses the game engine for something other than playing a tested game.

The next set of traps into which the unwary games-for-training developer may fall are licensing issues. When you stop using a low-cost research license and seek to use the new training product for real, then the company who created the base game wants, justifiably, to have a cut of the revenue you obtain. After all, your revenue is, in part, based upon the game developer's original hard work. I will deal with more license issues later, but for this application, the license was expensive compared to the cost of a typical schoolhouse training curriculum development project. Many games-for-training hopefuls balk at paying several hundred thousand dollars just to be allowed to distribute a tool based upon a game engine. In the case of *Tactical Language*, however, the license was a bargain. It gave the government rights to use Epic's engine in any current and future tactical language tutor. The major caveats relating to that right are that the packaging must show that Epic's game engine is inside, and that a small percentage of new development costs be paid to the game company. For what the government got in return, it was money well spent.

An oft-cited alternative to paying for licensing is to use an open source game engine. Such developments often show promise early in their development, but since there is no revenue involved in such an effort, the early, usually competent, pioneers of the open source engine generally move on to other things. This leaves the game engine without resources to improve or maintain the software, fix bugs, or adapt to the rapid changes in PC hardware or software. While open source engines sometimes meet the need, in the end, it is often better to pay the license fee to get current software.

Game from the Start: *DARWARS Ambush!*

In the fall of 2003, the Director of DARPA expressed concern about the growing number of ambushes occurring in Iraq. He challenged the agency to find ways to control this problem. Since my portfolio concerned training, I asked myself whether there were a way to teach the voice in the back of the head of every service person to identify ambushes, to prepare for them, to deal with them, and to recover from them. When I was given the unexpected gift of new money for the DARWARS program, I decided to find out.

I chose a team that I knew would consider the training features of whatever they produced as their first priority, that is, they understood that my goal was *gains in performance, not necessarily games*. I gave them six high-level project goals and then I gave them freedom to do the work. Here are the starting requirements for the program that I dubbed *DARWARS Ambush!*:

1. Work with a respected early adopter who will embrace the technology and help us understand what is needed. I found Col. Robert Brown, United States Army, the commander of the 1st Stryker Brigade Combat Team. He enthusiastically adopted us and had my contractors (BBNT, Total Immersion Software, and Jason Robar, Inc.) marching in the mud with them at a training rotation to the Joint Readiness Training Center, Fort Polk, Louisiana within a week of the signing of the contract.

2. Build a training tool for the squad and its soldiers, not for the lieutenant colonel. It is the soldier and the Marine who are bearing the brunt of the ambushes and they need to learn how to deal with them.

3. Provide for easy and rapid field authoring. The character of attacks will change rapidly and I wanted it to be possible to change the scenarios to match what happened yesterday, not wait for months for some software expert to make the change at additional cost and confusion.

4. The opposing force (OPFOR) should be the squad next door, not software. The user, I expected, would learn as much building and executing the ambush as being ambushed. Moreover, there could be some sort of competition among squads, which might increase the likelihood that the training tool would actually be used continually, rather than being played once and put on the shelf.

5. Base the product on a game to be sure that play was compelling (but still insist that training was inside).

6. Develop and deliver to the early adopting unit in six months.

The result is a networked, multi-user, PC-game-based, convoy-ambush training tool that "allows Soldiers and Marines both to experience lessons learned by others and to construct their own scenarios based upon actual experiences. Trainees move about in a shared, immersive, first-person perspective environment where they carry out mounted and dismounted operations, operate ground and air vehicles, use small arms and vehicle-mounted weapons, and communicate over multiple radio nets" (Roberts, Diller, & Schmitt, 2006) (See Figures 10.3 and 10.4).

BBNT and their team met and then exceeded those goals. *DARWARS Ambush!* has become as widely used as I had hoped, training over 20,000 soldiers in 2006, but the range of applications to which the Army and Marines

FIGURE 10.3. Soldiers at Fort Lewis training with *DARWARS Ambush!* in summer 2004.
(Photograph by Jason Kaye in Wilkins, 2004. Used with permission.)

FIGURE 10.4. Screenshot from *DARWARS Ambush!*
(*Source*: Defense Advanced Research Projects Agency.)

have put it is far greater than I ever expected. I'll expand on this shortly, but the principal reason for the spread is the field authoring capability.

Note that the last four of the requirements make it very hard for those who did the training development to make a continuing business out of the product. I had envisioned that the developers would do the rapid authoring themselves in response to field requests, but somewhere during the six months of development their emphasis changed from *field authoring* to *user authoring*. The tools they created were easily learned by the users, empowering the soldiers themselves to author scenarios. As a result, all but the most complicated changes are made locally by the soldiers or their immediate support contractors – at no additional cost but their own labor. Similarly, home-grown OPFOR could adapt to any new roles without bringing in the developing contractor to make changes. The game engine, *Operation Flashpoint*, was already stable and cost as little as $10 per seat, an amount that the units themselves could easily absorb. None of the minimal cash used to create a new *DARWARS Ambush!* training facility or to create new kinds of training went to the training system developer. It all came from, and the benefits thereof returned directly to, the user. Finally, the six-month deployment goal held a tacit assumption that the government-developed product was free to the users and could be freely copied and distributed without further cost. Thus, there was only a minimal additional revenue stream available to the training developer after the initial deployment when DARPA's investment slowed.

At my request, BBNT created a set of alternative plans to see if they could make a viable business after the initial development was complete. We found that, once I ruled out charging the units for the software (and probably even had I not), the small size of the market made it unlikely that selling or supporting *DARWARS Ambush!* could be a particularly profitable business. DARPA, and others, now principally the Army, continue to send occasional time-and-materials contract additions to BBNT to add features, scenarios, or terrain, but the amounts are small. The major continuing business is providing training support via web and phone as well as train-the-trainer support. This, too, does not represent an enticing source of continuing revenue for a company like BBNT and the function has now been taken over by the Army itself.

The above does not mean that I recommend that training developers try to sell game-like training software on a per-seat basis, maintaining control over changes and charging for upgrades. Others have tried that business model with limited success. It often engenders user annoyance with the product when users are not allowed to make even minor, but important, changes. Moreover, the soldier market is still small compared to the civilian game market, and thus per-seat changes can become prohibitively expensive. In fact, one company that formerly used the per-seat model, in face of competition from *DARWARS Ambush!* (I believe, but cannot prove that this was the cause) now extols the virtue of user authoring and low-cost upgrades. The using units do not have the budget to pay the vendor for changes. What they do have available is their own labor.

Probably the best hope for a good product, satisfied users, and a modest profit for the developer is what we did: provide development money up front from a central source. Then it may be possible for the developer, or, perhaps, some other entity, to deliver set-up help, train-the-trainer training, and user support on a time-and-materials basis in chunks small enough to fit into individual user unit's budgets.

Why a Game, and Why That Specific Game

The requirement that a working training system be delivered in six months led to the decision to adopt an existing simulation engine. We considered eight or ten alternatives on the basis of the following criteria. Listening to our early adopter, we chose to emphasize convoy ambushes. This required the ability to create large-scale outdoor terrain. We also needed simple multiplayer capability. Further, we required that those multiple users be able to enter and operate vehicles. We also insisted on a user-tested, flexible, stable system. These needs, plus the requirement for easy and rapid field authoring of scenarios, pushed us toward a specific computer game to provide our trainer's simulation engine: *Operation Flashpoint*, a product of Bohemia Interactive Studios.[8]

Flashpoint was a good choice, as it turned out, for several more reasons. The game had been in use for several years and thus did not require a top-of-the-line PC, making it more accessible to more military customers who did not have hardware with the latest video and high-capacity memory cards. It had been well tested in similar kinds of applications by the gaming community. Moreover, that community had created a large number of simulation resources and objects that were available usually at the cost merely of acknowledging the person who had created them.

Flashpoint was also a *less* than optimal choice for two reasons, both of which we thought we understood when we chose to use it. First, it did not provide good tools for AARs, because our training developers had no access to the game source code. The developers worked around this problem with the tools they had or could create. More of a problem was the licensing situation.

Late in the development, a lengthy negotiation over licensing requirements erupted that took time and energy away from distribution and support activities. Part of the problem came from a mismatch between the business model for making money with a commercial game, which risks much money early in hopes of making it back on sales, versus the government's acquisition practice, where profit comes during a paid development period. The licensing issues were finally resolved with an agreement linking licensing fees to actual development costs. The usual legal wrangling was brightened when BBNT let their attorneys play *DARWARS Ambush!*, and the technical staff got to shoot the lawyers.

Distribution by Diffusion

DARPA is well outside the normal channels of U.S. military bureaucracy, so while the software was quickly embraced by our chosen early adopter, we had

---

[8] www.bistudio.com

no mechanism with which to distribute *DARWARS Ambush!* further, or even to deliver the knowledge that it existed. *Tactical Language* was in the same boat. Our solution was to engage the press, visit units with demonstrations, and conduct word-of-mouth campaigns. Knowledge and demand for both products spread rapidly and for the next six months, I received at least one email or phone call a day asking how to get the product. The mendicants received the software in the next day's mail. This would not have worked had we charged the units for the government-developed tools.

There are now sites at Army and Marine bases across the country and overseas with 64 or more computers dedicated to training with *DARWARS Ambush!* One site trains as many as 400 soldiers in a typical week. Another prepares non-commissioned officers (NCOs) to pass a handful of leadership field tests by running them through a simulation of those tests back-to-back in *DARWARS Ambush!* The number of failures in the field has dropped dramatically. (No, I don't have the numbers, only the anecdotal reports.) The "Semi-Permanent *DARWARS Ambush!* Training Facility" used by our forces in Germany makes similar use of our tools in a week-long NCO leadership course that trains almost 500 students each month.

Diffusion worked. From where we stood in DARPA, we could not have introduced the products from the top. Had we tried, we would still be awaiting approval. Bureaucracy is slow, but a government charge card in the hands of a major is fast.

Since its proliferation, the services have begun to pay for central maintenance of both *DARWARS Ambush!* and *Tactical Iraqi* software and user support. This is timely, since DARPA is the Attention Deficit Disorder poster-child of defense research. Once we have taken the technical rug out from under those who say something cannot be done, we abandon it.[9] Service logistic and training organizations are resistant, in most cases with good justification, to adopting the support burden of something pushed on them from the outside. Since that support cost was unplanned, it must come out of some other budget that is already tight. Without strong user demand, and demonstrable training performance, distribution by diffusion will ultimately lead to long-term failure.

Why DARWARS Ambush! Was a Success

First, it met an urgent and clearly perceived need so that users were willing to try it. Once they had tried it, they discovered that *training had been built into the product. DARWARS Ambush!* was not just an environment in which

---

[9]   My use of "we" to mean "DARPA" is perhaps unjustified. By the time this chapter sees print, I will be working elsewhere. DARPA has a strict term limit policy for program managers and I have been privileged to come right up to the edge of the six-year hard stop, not to mention a previous four-year tour at DARPA in the 1980s trying to make lasers in space talk to submarines under water and clouds.

training could take place; BBNT also delivered, right on the disk, training manuals, tactically representative scenarios with descriptions of how to use them for training, train-the-trainer information, simulation resources (such as buildings, bombs, and wandering civilians), and user authoring tools to let the soldiers and Marines make the training their own.

Military billets are often gapped (one person leaves before her or his relief arrives), so you cannot expect one user's enthusiasm to be transferred to the next. At one training facility the new director said that upon his arrival, he had a foot-high stack of CDs of game-like things all claiming to train. Only the *DARWARS Ambush!* CD told him how to train with it.

A key thing we did learn from the game community is the need for *extensive user testing before release* of a product. When distribution depends upon the acceptance of the users, not upon a bureaucracy that can force things down from above, then the tool had better appeal instantly to the customer who will be using it. Commercial testing practice is far more extensive than normal military R&D use testing. BBNT's game subcontractors, Total Immersion Software and Savage Entertainment, insisted upon commercial practice and, as a consequence, the initial (and subsequent) users had no petty annoyances to prejudice them against the product. We had no bug reports in the first year of use.

We have already mentioned that the low-cost per seat was a key factor in user adoption. The $10 to $20 cost per computer to purchase the base game fit well within a small unit's budget.

The third, and most important, reason for success was the provision for *user authoring*. We did not deliver an application that, once the students had run through the 24 scenarios provided, lost value and user interest. Instead, ordinary users could change scenarios and create new ones to meet changing circumstances. Lessons from deployed units were incorporated into training within days. Specific training needs identified by a commander were met by user modifications. Units encoded the terrain of their own bases for multiple uses.

The most amusing soldier-created use was in a disaster relief exercise where simulated tornado damage was generated by a platoon of virtual tanks in the simulation. They knocked down trees, flattened cars, and damaged buildings. Once the swath of destruction had been created, the disaster relief coordinator was elevated in a virtual helicopter to view the scene. A different user employed *DARWARS Ambush!* to create a training video of a real battle. The brigade commander used the video as a tool to discuss his intent with his officers and senior enlisted men and women, and to explore tactical options with them. As a trainer, however, my favorite use came from a unit who had returned from a rotation at the NTC, where they had found some holes in their performance. They created a new set of scenarios in *DARWARS Ambush!* at their home station, exercised with them and then, better prepared, they deployed overseas. Neither the contractor nor I were involved in developing or deploying the above user-created applications of the software. We found out about them by accident after the fact.

The flexibility for users to invent and implement new ways to use the tool without a contractor between them and their tactics, techniques, and procedures was the most important lesson of the project. When users can do this with no delay and no new costs but their own labor, they embrace the training system as their own and don't think of it as something imposed from above. They don't ask the developer whether it trains well; they see its value in their own AARs, and they build their application to match their own perceived need.

It is worth noting that the effort was well funded. We built the initial system in six months for about $1.5 million. This gave the developers adequate reserve so that they did not need to worry about the cost of a prospective feature, leaving only schedule and performance to be traded against each other. We spent very little after the initial development.

A last lesson: we listened to the users and engaged them early and often in the development cycle. We took draft systems on the road every month to discover what needed fixing. But, because we listened, we found that the very first alpha version trained important lessons about convoy ambushes even as the early testers showed us how to improve the training. One soldier told us, "It really made me think. I'll have to ask my chain of command about rules of engagement. I am no longer sure what 'hostile' really means." Using a game platform allowed us to get vital feedback early.

A Lesson or Two about Trainer-Less Training

DARWARS Ambush! Is an Environment, Not a Trainer
It is worth distinguishing between a tool like the *Tactical Language Trainer*, which has its curriculum embedded in the software itself, and *DARWARS Ambush!*, which does not train by itself. Alone, *Ambush!* is just a user-editable game – fun, full of resources, artwork, geo-typical terrain, etc. – but it is not a trainer. There are no tactics, techniques, or procedures, no mission plans, few artificial bad guys exercising current bad-guy behavior.

This is not to say that training was not part of the design. We delivered example scenarios, training manuals, and train-the-trainer documentation, but the actual, day-to-day training comes from what the soldiers themselves put inside. They plan for an operation. They brief it. They execute it. They play the bad-guy du jour and they use *DARWARS Ambush!* tools to help conduct AARs. What is said in the reviews, however, and what the soldiers or Marines learn comes from within themselves and their units. This is the power of user authoring. If the world changes, the users can make their training change in hours.

Fortunately for the Tactical Language and Culture Trainers, language does not change as fast as our enemies change their behavior, so user authoring was not vital to its initial success. Tactical Language Training, LLC, however, believes that continuing success will require rapid authoring tools for certain parts of the language and culture training process, and they have built authoring and editing tools for themselves and for limited end-user application.

Fortunately for *DARWARS Ambush!*, tactics are something soldiers and Marines know and can manipulate themselves, unlike obscure languages and cultures where user editing would be, to say the least, counterproductive. In either case, whether the pedagogy is *in* the software or enabled *by* the software, the products would not have worked if the creators of the systems had not been trainers first and simulation builders second.

There Is No Golden Disk

Taking the above lesson further, we derived another insight from *DARWARS Ambush!* and the Tactical Language tutor family: there is no "trainer-less training," at least not yet. The mere acquisition of a disk with the training software very seldom results in optimum training. *Ambush!* reduces very quickly to a free-for-all fight unless it is used in a setting with an instructor, training goals, and enforced AARs. We also found that the *Tactical Language and Culture Trainer*, while usable by the highly motivated individual, delivered much more useful training when done in a group setting with supervision.

Another lesson involved one pair of novice students working on the same computer and taking turns in the simulations (we had that week one too few stations for the number of students). They seemed to get more out of it than did most students in the same class who had a computer to themselves. This was surprising to us, for a major hypothesis in development of the tactical language trainers was that production of language – students speaking in context – was key to making it work in a short time for nonlinguists. We had thought that two students per computer would halve the production opportunities per student. Apparently the interchange between the two students hovering over one monitor not only provided an ample opportunity for both to produce foreign sounds, but also increased their motivation to use the tutor, and their test scores after use.

There is also value in having instructors present to ensure that any artificialities of the simulation do not lead to erroneous conclusions by the students. When challenged with this potential for "negative" transfer of training, several users of *DARWARS Ambush!* strongly countered that if it did happen, it would be because the trainers failed the students, not because of the software. In fact, in other parts of the DARWARS program, we saw very strong evidence of positive transfer from mental skills learned in computer simulation to combat-like situations (Widerhold & Widerhold, 2005).

INFORMATION TECHNOLOGY TROUBLESHOOTING
DIGITAL TUTOR: IMMERSIVE EXPERIENTIAL TRAINING
WITHOUT A GAME

The closest thing to a trainer-less training system that DARWARS produced is being built by Acuitus, Inc. Expanding upon Bloom's observations, they have built an artificial tutor to train information technology (IT) students in system operator (SYSOP) troubleshooting. Key to their approach is the insight that the state of the student's mind is not observable, but that the tutor-student interaction is. So they don't work to create a model of the learner, they build a model of the learning.

They originally thought they could do this by bottling a well-taught class through observation and conversion. They had done it once. They could probably do it again, but the task I set them off to do involved training in an area for which there was no good course available anywhere. There *were* courses, but there were no good ones. (We looked hard for one in both the military and commercial worlds.) Thus, they had to divert resources to create the content, provide opportunities for a good tutor to interact one-on-one with many students (more than 10 but less than 50), and *then* capture all those interactions to build a digital tutor.

In the process of observing the student-tutor interaction, Acuitus began, step-by-step, to take away the human-to-human parts of the interaction. First, the student and the human tutor were put in different rooms and only allowed to interact via keyboard and screen, although the human tutor could watch the student on a video link. In the end the video link was severed. Surprisingly this Turing-Test-like interaction did not degrade the learning achievements of the student. The human tutors reported that they *did* have to work harder as "Turing tutors" than when they had visual and audio contact with their tutees, but the measured progress was the same in either case.

The pilot effort delivered 4 to 5 hours of instruction on UNIX troubleshooting. The student, with minimal fanfare, was placed in front of one computer that acted as a tutor. Initially it started delivering a lecture on its screen, with text-to-speech if the user wanted. The digital lecture included exercises on UNIX that the student conducted on one of two other monitors representing separate computers, one monitor and keyboard on either side of the digital tutor's monitor and keyboard (Figure 10.5). Within 10 minutes or so, the tutor challenged the student to fix a failure in communications between the computers flanking the tutor. For example, the digital tutor would tell the student that their Commanding Officer had complained that his computer, the one on the left, could not open a web page. They were told that the computer on the right was the server. Then the student was let loose to troubleshoot.

The electronic tutor would sense what experiments the student performed on the networked computers and provided hints, encouragement, and instruction

FIGURE 10.5. Students learning on the UNIX troubleshooting tutor built by Acuitus, Inc.

(*Source*: Defense Advanced Research Projects Agency.)

as required. In prototype trials, half a day of working with the electronic tutor enabled the students to complete, unassisted, two to three hard challenge problems[10] in one hour, equal to the performance of students tutored one-on-one by the best human tutors we could find. Students provided with a day of classroom and human-instructed computer lab training could not solve any of them.

A remarkable characteristic of this prototype tutor was its ability to maintain student engagement over periods of 4 to 5 hours at levels unheard of for technical instruction. In an independent assessment, a Stanford University–developed motivation metric was applied to videos of 20 Navy IT apprentice students using the tutor. The students, who had widely varied initial levels of experience, scored at a level of 95 to 97 on a 100-point engagement scale. To put a human face on that measure, recall your response to the last computer-/web-based training you endured (in my case it was Office of the Secretary of Defense ethics training), and compare that to the case of one young sailor, training with the DARPA tutor on the night shift. He was head down and tail up in discovery, typing alternately on the keyboards of the two problem computers and interacting with the digital tutor, when the experiment monitor came in and announced that he had brought food and they could knock off learning. The student didn't even look up; he just kept on solving the problem.

Watching the students learning with Acuitus's tutor (and using it myself), I am reminded of the most engaging of computer games. It is not clear what the key to engendering that level of intense focus might be, but I speculate that it is related to the aforementioned lesson of proximity: the opportunity

---

[10] The challenge problems were called "CNN problems," because if a large company had one and didn't fix it within an hour, CNN would hear about it.

afforded students to practice immediately what they learn, and to the delivery of lessons exactly when they fit into the flow of the student's experience with the troubleshooting problems. The developers intentionally created the tutor to push their students to solve sub-problems that were just within their competence in a way reminiscent of what is experienced in computer games (Gee, 2007).

We also don't know if that level of intensity can be maintained by the student as the length of the instruction expands beyond 5 hours to 40. The power of computer games to hold their players offers some encouragement that it might.

In turn, we may be able to inform the game world something about engagement/immersion. Very preliminary data show that when we push the students to the point where they can no longer maintain the concentration, we find that the loss of focus is not gradual. It seems to occur as a step function after about 6 hours. This matches the finding with *Tactical Iraqi*; students get better results if they don't work for a whole day at a time with the tutor.

As noted above, when we emphasize modeling the interaction between the student and the teacher in order to abstract the learning process, one needs to observe a well-taught course. There do not seem to be very many of these. Moreover, the amount of material that a tutor can cover far exceeds what is possible to cover in a classroom. Thus Acuitus has had to spend much of their effort creating course material aimed at a deep understanding of computer operating system and troubleshooting principles (not a smorgasbord of disconnected facts), applying the new course with a very good human tutor, and *then* observing the interaction. This does not bode well for easy scaling of the process. Still, the learning gains appear to me to be worth the investment. Convincing those who have to pay the up-front costs, however, may be a difficult to impossible task, especially as poorly designed web- and computer-based products continue to give digital training a bad name.

Gorman's Gambit

In this transformed world of come-as-you-are conflicts, one of the few things upon which soldiers can depend is that whatever they prepare and train for will not be what they actually encounter. We tried a small experiment to explore new ways to train units to succeed in unusual, unanticipated, and unanticipatable situations (Hussain et al., 2005). The approach was suggested by retired Army General Paul Gorman, a pioneer of the Army training revolution.

Sitting in the back of an early DARWARS Service and Joint User meeting, General Gorman asked why so much emphasis was placed on making highly realistic simulation of a warfare situation when it was unlikely to match rapidly changing reality. Why, he asked, couldn't we just put a military unit in front of an existing commercial multiplayer computer game and let them experience how they work together in unfamiliar settings? The experience would teach the same class of communications, coordination, and unit cohesion lessons as a more obviously military simulation, but with far more incentive for the soldiers to continue training. We created the Gorman's Gambit project to find out if this were the case. Additional issues explored related to how multi-user *training* differed from commercial multiplayer *gaming*, and how to maximize the training value and time with digital simulations as the numbers of participants grew beyond a handful.

After several small-scale pilot trials, we gathered almost 50 Fort Benning soldiers into a room in late December, 2004. Divided into two teams, they fought against each other for three days in the virtual world of the computer game *Neverwinter Nights*. The process clearly delivered the lessons in unit coherence and problem solving for which we had hoped, although some of the observations were a bit surreal. A report came out of a cubicle hung over with camouflage netting, "There is a princess in there!" The harried army medic responding to a call for help reported on the voice-over-Internet protocol circuit: "I don't have any more healing spells. All I got's is resurrection." The soldiers found ways to use griffins, which were part of the virtual world, to perform reconnaissance. Within a few hours they stopped referring to them as "dragons" and started calling them UAVs (unmanned aerial vehicles).

Here are a few of the more formal technical lessons we took away from this exercise. It *is* possible to observe and measure teamwork skills of large groups performing in a multiplayer role-playing game/simulation. One cannot, however, naively take a commercial game and instantly deliver training. Targeted scenarios must be created, the training part of the product needs to be robust, and a capability for rapid scenario authoring should be provided to the training monitors. Nor can gaming technology be used effectively for training unless non-game assessment tools are developed and applied. Also required is some preliminary training on game play and character skills. "Digital Generation" hype to the contrary, not all soldiers understand computer games or how to play them.

While there are some obvious drawbacks to using a non-military simulation for training, the enthusiasm of the soldier and the level of involvement before, during, and after the simulation sessions convinced me that structured use of massive multiplayer games could help units learn how to deal with the unexpected, but I ran out of funds to pursue this further.

DOES TRAINING TRANSFER FROM LIGHTWEIGHT PC SIMULATIONS INTO REAL-WORLD COMPETENCE?

If one is to bottle the NTC process, some thought must be given to what kind of bottle to put it in. At the beginning of the DARWARS program, I decided that I didn't have the budget to build new training hardware, nor would the

Army have the budget to buy it. What they did have were PCs, CD drives, and the authority to make small purchases with their government credit cards. The question arises, then, "Can PCs teach us anything useful in the real world?" I will answer that with an anecdote and with data from a fairly large-scale experiment on training transfer from experiences in one kind of computer simulation to something close to real-world expertise.

First the anecdote. The recruiting game, *America's Army*, was created partly to show to those who might join the Army what the organizational culture really was. If you find that you don't like the idea that to gain privileges and do neat things, you must work and qualify for them, then it is better for you and for the Army if you learn that lesson as a result of playing *America's Army* rather than after you have been in the service for a year. One of the cool things you could do in the game was be a medic, but you had to go to a school to become qualified.

Having run out of money to create some sort of highly interactive training, the developers fell back on the actual course. They had a virtual instructor enter a virtual classroom, lecture to virtual PowerPoint slides, and give a multiple choice test on virtual paper. Surprisingly, players of *America's Army* tolerated this rather well and many qualified to play medics in the game.

In the fall of 2005, the mother of one of these called the *America's Army* team and said, "Thank you. Your game saved my son's life."[11] It turns out that she had two sons. One cut himself severely and his brother, a graduate of the *America's Army* medic course, applied the lessons he had learned in virtual PowerPoint, stopped the bleeding, and stabilized the situation until medical help arrived. The attending physician said that without his brother's rapid action, the other brother would have died.

Effective training transfer has also been shown under more controlled conditions (Widerhold & Widerhold, 2005). The Virtual Reality Medical Center and Strategic Operations, a military training branch of a San Diego TV and movie studio, showed in 2005 that a few minutes of PC-based virtual reality training can prepare teams of Marines to clear rooms in a hostile situation in unfamiliar buildings more effectively than could several practice sessions in a highly realistic environment. Strategic Operations built onto their studio back-lot, among other things, building interiors, an Iraqi village, a set of ship interiors, and the actual fuselage of a commercial airplane (Figure 10.6). Teams of Marines, soldiers, Special Forces, SWAT teams, and Coast Guard personnel can enter these areas and shoot Simunitions (soap bullets that hit with a 400 feet per second kick) from real weapons. Strategic Operations provides effective enemy OPFOR forces as well as creating highly

---

[11] See http://www.americasarmy.com/intel/makingof.php, which says: "In at least one case we know of, an America's Army veteran called upon these skills to save the life of his brother." The extra detail described here comes from discussions with Dr. Mike Zyda.

FIGURE 10.6. Strategic operations, part of a San Diego movie studio, provides a highly realistic training environment.

(*Source*: Photograph by Dr. Mark Widerhold, Virtual Reality Medical Center. Used with permission.)

realistic simulated wounds, explosions, and other dramatic special effects. Each area is instrumented to measure the progress of the mission, and individuals were instrumented to measure trainee physiological responses to the situations. Seven hundred Marines were training at the facility one day when I visited.

The Virtual Reality Medical Center recreated these training areas and situations in a virtual world using the common graphics tools. They then let soldiers or Marines experience them through a commercial PC game, *Unreal Tournament*, interface. In a series of exercises they tested the value of giving individuals experience in the virtual world before they were formed into teams and then performed a mission in the (almost) real one. While I fully expected improvements, what they found surprised me (Figure 10.7).

A 10-minute single-player familiarization session in the PC–virtual world proved more effective than several actual teamed practice missions as measured by four-person team room clearance times. First-time teams took 12 seconds to clear a room in the "shoot house." By the fourth session they could clear a room in 9 seconds. Marines who experienced one single-person, 10-minute session of virtual familiarization were able to clear a "real" room in the shoot house in four-person teams *the first time* in less than 9 seconds. Moreover, when they did enter the real room for the first time, the heart rate measures of

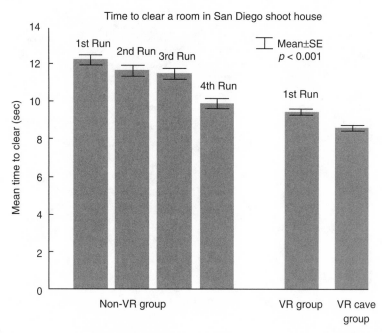

FIGURE 10.7. Training transfer. Teams of Marines who were exposed one-at-a-time to video familiarization were able to clear a room in a highly realistic combat simulation at a movie studio faster than teams who had practiced in the "almost real world" three times. Use of a large, projected video display gave a small additional boost.

(*Source*: Report to the Defense Advanced Research Projects Agency by the Virtual Reality Medical Center, San Diego, CA.)

those trained with virtual reality were like those of practiced teams, not those of first-time users. The same results were obtained with Coast Guard personnel who were tasked to conduct a ship search. A single session as individuals in a game-like PC familiarization improved team performance better than four team trials performing the actual task in the back-lot realistic training environment.

These experiments were conducted multiple times with groups of 20 Marines or Coast Guard sailors. This makes a strong case for the transfer of training from PC exercises to warfare skills. There has never been much question that PC/laptop training is considerably cheaper and easier to schedule than real exercises. Now there is evidence that, while it should not *replace* real exercises, its use should make the more realistic, but more costly, training more effective and decrease the time spent in the expensive training environments. Digital training can make the first day in the costly training environment like the third day used to be without the digital practice. Moreover, under some circumstances, PC mission rehearsal may be the only kind available. These results suggest that such rehearsals can be useful.

ENDING WITH A WHIMPER, NOT A BANG

The above is a description of a few things we did in the DARWARS program and lessons that arose from it. I end with a few random thoughts about other projects, research challenges, my hope for future work, caveats, and a warning to beware of cheap imitations. It is also probably too late to point out that, while my work was on military training, most of the lessons are equally applicable to any postsecondary training situations. Unfortunately, I suspect that those of you with a nonmilitary bent stopped reading this chapter long ago.

You Can't Do This Cheaply

The language and culture training had a budget of over $2 million per year for three years, as did the IT training project. *DARWARS Ambush!* cost over $1.5 million to create, test, deploy, and sell. Although the cost of all of these projects combined is *far* less than the cost of just one commercial console game to develop and market, this is still a lot of money for the military training world. Thus, one of the goals of all the projects was to create a process to make the next digital tutor easier and cheaper to build. Nevertheless, these kinds of products will always have substantial up-front costs that cannot be skimped on. These start-up costs will deliver large savings later in training time, travel costs, and improvements in learning, but there are bureaucratic impediments. Chiefly, this is a problem of fungability; the savings cannot be passed backward in time or shifted from one budgetary bucket to another to fund the initial development.

What Is Missing?

We have no understanding of what important things in the real world cannot be well simulated on a PC interface. For example, one's geographical relationship to a power line is persistently obvious in the real world, but that powerful navigational cue is hardly ever noticed by a user concentrating on a PC display. The power line may be there in the simulation, but it is just not as obvious on the small screen as it would be in real life. In the real, distant, world we perceive slopes as steeper and distances longer if we are tired or are carrying a heavy pack. The short-range vision circuits through which we view a PC screen are not similarly affected (Proffitt, 2006). (I surmise, but can't prove, that this is the reason that I can proofread this document when projected on my wall eight feet away from me, but can't do nearly as well on the monitor two feet from my eyes.) Computer games don't have to simulate the real world; training simulations do. We don't yet know the implications of this.

    Motivation and engagement are likely to be important features in this kind of training. I think proximity of tasks to training is a key to motivation in lightweight simulation, but don't have much more supporting evidence than finding that this seems to be the case in two very powerful digital tutors. We found, also anecdotally, that Marines are quite motivated by seeing a rating of their language progress that they can compare to the score of their buddies. In a similar vein, Microsoft discovered that awarding game points for achieving difficult tasks in each of their console games motivated gamers to buy new games to get more points so they could accrue prestige among their peers. The points are not redeemable for anything; they just give bragging rights (Hyman, 2007).

In fact, there is no sign of any engineering discipline of what works and doesn't work in PC-like simulations. What I wrote for the Defense Science Board five years ago is still true:

> There is no deep understanding in either the commercial game world or the psychology community of what makes games compelling and keeps users engaged so that lessons can be taught. There should be a catalog of sound, motion, color, visual effects, orienting response, levels, pacing, etc., and an understanding how each of these affects learning and user focus. There should be, but there isn't. Given the current incentive structure, nothing is likely to change: game developers can't afford the research and academics can't get grants for frivolous things like game dynamics and game assessment … neither the industry nor the academic community is likely to pursue research into the science of what makes games work without an external source of motivation [by which I meant: like somebody paying them to do so].
>
> Games will play a part, even a large part, in future training, given that they can provide practice with feedback that previously touted teaching revolutions could not, as well as provide strong motivation to practice. Nevertheless, without some research into how games actually work, the games-for-training fad may end up as peripheral to real training as did the education revolution once claimed for training films and for educational television. (Chatham & Braddock, 2003, p. 21)

Where We Might Go from Here: People Engines in a Simulation of a Mindscape

What's next? My choice would be to create something like *DARWARS Ambush!* to let soldiers train themselves how to behave in the sticky social and human interactions they encounter in vastly foreign cultures today. Lightweight simulations could teach complex new habits of thought to help our forces do things that are exactly what they didn't join the services to do, what I called above generalized nonkinetic operations. Moreover, they will need to be able to do those things *and* be able to shoot at a moment's notice, and then, before the adrenaline has drained from their systems, return to being nonkinetic. This change from nonkinetic behavior to kinetic and back is often called "transition operations" or "escalation/de-escalation of force."

The only way I can imagine to train our young (and older) soldiers and Marines to succeed in this kind of environment is to expose individuals and teams to such experiences over and over again, so they will have intellectual head-room to think (modestly) dispassionately about what is happening when the real event occurs. As noted at the start of this over-long chapter, the NTC is doing this today with giant improvisational theater performances in the Mojave Desert for 3,500 trainees. It doesn't scale.

To get this to scale, a new kind of computer simulation should be created that works, not only in a simulated landscape, but a simulated "mindscape."[12] Acting in this simulation would be "people engines"[13] that would serve the function that physics engines serve in current kinetic warfare simulations. The people engines would be like stock actors complete with characters, histories, and culturally correct behaviors, actions, words, and gestures. Users would be provided with a closet-full of these artificial characters and the social, religious, family, clan, and business connections among them. To give a slightly frivolous example, when the plot called for the author to pull out of his closet the character of the Grandfather in Peter and the Wolf, then out of that closet should come also the wolf, the huntsmen, the duck, bird, and Peter, too and all their social connections. The simulations would also need a library of stories and scenarios that are able to react to user actions and change their course as the trainees move through the experience.

There would have to be a set of tools, services, interfaces, and controls supporting the people engines and a sandbox in which they could play. One of these services would be a library of culturally determined actor-level behaviors upon which every people engine could call. If the people engine called for anger, the actor-level behavior for anger would be sent to the rendering engine so the character walked, talked, and looked angry for his or her own culture. If you have ever watched a computer game character or avatar "idle" you will appreciate the notion of idling with an attitude rather than just moving the features and limbs randomly. One could imagine an emotional dashboard where a user could enter his or her own emotional state and have his/her avatar reflect that to all involved, human and computer-generated alike.

The characters would have to be "rigged" so that they could show culture-specific gestures with articulated fingers and wrists. Similar rigging (not provided by today's computer games) would be needed to display facial gestures and allow lip-synching to American and foreign speech. Work done for

---

[12] My thanks to Bill Ferguson, Rich Lazarus, and Bruce Roberts of BBN Technology for inventing this term. The usage makes it easier to discuss human-interaction simulations.

[13] Ditto to the late Tom Armor who, when I was describing what I wanted to create, said, "Oh, what you want are *people engines*." And so I did.

me, while at DARPA, by a small company, VCom3D, Inc., to develop a digital library of over 500 culturally specific gestures and facial expressions suggests that this is now possible.

The physical landscape would need a cultural overlay of affordances in the mindscape. It would not be enough to have the interior and exterior structure of a building with all its doors and domes. The nonkinetic digital trainers would need to know that this building is a mosque and walking into it without taking off your shoes will have consequences, and then propagate the consequences to whomever (virtual or real) might reasonably get involved. This mindscape would be hard to build. Landscapes have watchers like Google Earth and are (relatively) easily captured by cameras, radars, laser radars, etc. There is no MapQuest for the mindscape. We would have to invent one.

There is more, but I hope you get the idea. This is something that the computer gaming world is unlikely to do in the near future. With costs to develop and market a single high end console game at $40 million and rising, seeming inevitably, to $100 million (80 percent of the cost going to artwork and graphics), they are not going to try risky things like moving out of the kinetic game to the nonkinetic. Non-player characters (NPCs) are today mostly vending machines and jousting dummies.[14] When a massive multiplayer game developer tried to create more human-behaving characters, they *were* able to make artificial characters with which a human player could hold conversation with three or four utterances back-and-forth before it became evident that the NPC was not human. The incensed reaction of the human players was, "I wasted all this time on something that was generated by the computer and not human." The effort was dropped.

I believe that there are plausibility arguments for each of the elements of such a people-engine simulation in a mindscape, but I will spare you the discussion. It will only be relevant if some organization with deep pockets and a willingness to take risks for high payoffs (like DARPA) would take it on. They might. Or they might not. As of this writing, the "might nots" are winning.

Oh, yes, and all the above must be user-authorable so that the soldiers could match their training to our current fiendishly reactive enemy. That, too, might be possible. See, for example, the computer game Façade and its descriptions of a fully realized interactive PC-based drama (Mateas & Stern, 2003).

Final Words and the Promised Whimper

There now exist proofs that lightweight experiential training works and can be monitored and assessed. There is mounting evidence that it transfers to improved performance in the real-world tasks for which it purports to train. The consumer PC and console gaming community has helped bring the

---

[14]   Thanks to Bill Ferguson of BBNT for pointing this out.

delivery hardware to a state where it is possible to create a wide range of training opportunities at an affordable price, and to bring it directly to a wide number of users almost anywhere, but games themselves are not trainers.

The next step, which the gaming industry is unlikely to fund by themselves, is to develop not "first-person shooters" but "first-person talkers for teams." There are plausibility arguments that the pieces necessary to start this are in place.

There is, however, a danger that many people will fail to perceive that it is the "proficiency gains" not the "games" that are responsible for the success of the DARWARS projects described. If these and the other reasons for success are missed, this will inevitably lead to a large number of cheap imitations. Those products, like the average computer-/web-based trainers that have literally driven some sailors to tears, will then start to proliferate faster than the more expensive, well-designed experiential trainers causing the whole business of lightweight training simulations to get a bad reputation. It is already hard to get institutional funding for commercial development of the projects described herein; the well has been poisoned (Newkirk, 2007).

I have great hope for the distributed experiential training revolution. We have given control of the soldier's training back to the soldier, now as locally authorable and locally useable digital individual and group simulations, but I fear for the future of the second training revolution in the hands of the lowest bidders.

REFERENCES

Bloom, B. S. (1984). The 2 sigma problem: The search for methods of group instruction as effective as 1-to-1 tutoring. *Educational Research, 13,* 3–15.

Braddock, J., & Chatham, R. (2001). *Training superiority and training surprise.* Report of the Defense Science Board, Washington, DC. Retrieved January 4, 2007, from, www.acq.osd.mil/dsb/reports.htm.

Chatham, R., & Braddock, J. (2003). *Training for future conflicts.* Report of the Defense Science Board, Washington, DC. Retrieved January 4, 2007, from, www.acq.osd.mil/dsb/reports.htm.

Chatham, R. E. (2007). Games for training. *Communications of the ACM, 50*(7), 36–43.

Filkins, D., & Burns, J. F. (2006). The reach of the war: Military; Deep in a U.S. desert, practicing to face the Iraq insurgency. *The New York Times,* section A, page 1 (May 1).

Gee, J. G. (2007). *What video games have to teach us about learning and literacy.* New York, and Houndsmills, Basingstoke, Hampshire, England: Palgrave Macmillan.

Hussain, T., Weil, S., Brunye, T., Frederick, D., Entin, E., Ferguson, W., et al. (2005). *Gorman's gambit: Assessing the potential of massive multi-player games as tools for military training.* Report from BBN Technologies and Aptima.

Hyman, P. (2007). Microsoft has gamers playing for points. *The Hollywood Reporter* [on-line article]. Retrieved January 4, 2007, from, http://www.hollywoodreporter.com/hr/content_display/features/columns/playing_games/e3i905026bcaa187b31cf6beffe4df27d9a#.

Kirkpatrick, D. L. (1987). Evaluation. In R. L. Craig (Ed.), *Training and development handbook* (3rd ed., pp. 301–319). New York: McGraw-Hill.

Mateas, M., & Stern, A. (2003). Façade, an experiment in building a fully-realized interactive drama. *Game Developers Conference*, San Jose, CA. Available from from: http://www.interactivestory.net/.

Proffitt, D. R. (2006). Embodied perception and the economy of action. *Perspectives on Psychological Science, 1*, 110–122.

Roberts, B., Diller, D., & Schmitt, D. (2006). *Factors affecting the adoption of a training game.* Paper presented at the 2006 Interservice/Industry Training, Simulation and Education Conference.

Widerhold, B., & Widerhold, M. (2005). *Physiological monitoring during simulation training and testing, Final Report.* Virtual Reality Medical Center report on contract DAAH01–03-C-R-301.

Wilkins, S. (2004, August 27). Video gaming aids combat training. *Northwest Guardian*, Authorized Newspaper of Fort Lewis, Washington, p. A1.

11

Evaluating Pilot Performance

BRIAN T. SCHREIBER, WINSTON BENNETT, JR.,
CHARLES M. COLEGROVE, ANTOINETTE M. PORTREY,
DAVID A. GRESCHKE, AND HERBERT H. BELL

Piloting an aircraft, especially in combat situations, requires a high level of performance. Air combat tactics involve dynamic, four-dimensional (x, y, z, and timing) maneuvering and positioning of the aircraft; done at high speed, often approaching or surpassing supersonic speed. Physical and cognitive capabilities and resources are frequently put to the test during flight. Poor performance in wartime can lead to death. Even peacetime military operations and civilian aviation are not incident or accident free. To best prepare our pilots, an understanding of their knowledge, skill competencies, and deficiencies is necessary. In order to accomplish this objective, their performance must be measured and their training progress tracked on various skills using objective outcome measures in both the training environment and in live-range exercises.

In many fields the benefits of task-specific and experiential training are beginning to experience investigation and consideration, with an integration of training and historically conventional methods of education (Boshuizen, Chapter 17; Ericsson, Chapter 18; Lajoie, Chapter 3; Schraagen, Chapter 7). This is not the case with the field of aviation, where the importance of task-specific training has been realized since the initiation of manned flight. As technologies within the aviation industry increased in complexity and sophistication over the past century, so did the demand for training and measuring pilot proficiency. This growing demand was the impetus for the development in flight simulation, within both the military and commercial industries. This development was to address the hazards of flying, the knowledge and skills required to pilot an airplane, and the need for a training aid to supplement pilot instruction (Mayer, 1981). Over the years, the need for assessing pilot performance has paralleled the simulation industry's development. In both cases, the needs have grown in number, type, and complexity.

A BRIEF HISTORICAL OVERVIEW OF FLIGHT SIMULATION

The use of flight simulation in pilot training is nearly as old as manned flight itself. The first flight simulator was developed around 1910, just seven years after

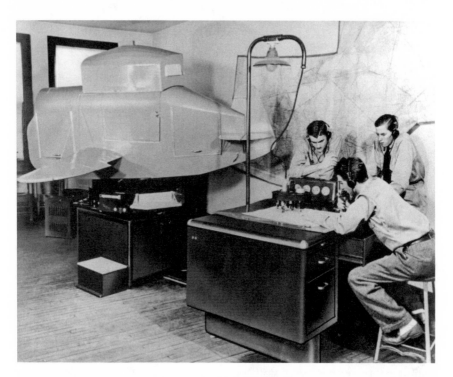

FIGURE 11.1. Link Pilot Trainer.
(*Source:* Photo courtesy of L-3 Link Simulation & Training.)

Orville Wright took his first flight in Kitty Hawk, North Carolina, in 1903. This low technology device, a barrel with short wings that was physically manipulated by the instructor to simulate pitch and roll, offered students the opportunity to practice basic flight control (Moroney & Moroney, 1999). During the following two decades, other attempts were made to design flight training devices; their usefulness, however, was limited. In 1929, the modern flight simulator was born with the development of the Link Pilot Trainer (Figure 11.1) by Edwin Albert Link to teach instrument flight rules. The Link Trainer was fitted with dummy instruments and the means for their actuation, allowing movement around all three axes: horizontal, vertical, and longitudinal. In 1934 after the United States Army Air Corps took over carriage of U.S. Air Mail from commercial airlines, 12 pilots were killed in a 78-day period due to their unfamiliarity with instrumentation flying. This loss of life prompted the Air Corps to look into various pilot trainers as a solution and acquiring the first six Link Trainer flight simulators as a result. In the late 1930s, the Army Air Corps and the U.S. Navy began using flight trainers to assess student pilot performance. As time progressed, Link Trainers became more advanced, including 360-degree rotation and various instruments that operated either mechanically or pneumatically. With these changes, another major focus was to measure the medical and physiological effects of flight on the pilot. The "blackout" problem encountered by pilots due to the accelerations produced by their aircraft during air combat and dive bombing maneuvers became a serious concern to aviation physiologists. In order to study the problem and to develop methods of protecting the pilots during these maneuvers, human centrifuges with cockpits were built to reflect the G-environments that pilots continuously faced (Crosbie, 1995).

During World War II, when airplanes became stronger, lighter, and more lethal due to weapon-based delivery system development, the use of trainers for pilot selection and training increased dramatically (Moroney & Moroney, 1999). The Army–Navy Trainer, ANT-18 Basic Instrument Training, known as the Blue Box, was standard equipment at every air training school in the United States and the Allied nations. Developments in aircraft design such as variable pitch propellers, retractable undercarriages, higher airspeeds, and radio navigational aids made training in cockpit drill essential. Pilot performance was evaluated through dual flights with instructor pilots using performance record sheets, or instrument procedures through trainers such as the Link Trainer.

From the end of World War II through the late 1950s, the increasing numbers and types of aircraft in service and under development prompted the design and deployment of simulators that replicated the characteristics of specific aircraft. During this period, simulator development branched out from the military into the commercial industry. In 1937, American Airlines was the first world airline to purchase a Link Trainer to train their pilots. The airlines began using the simulators for training and measuring flight crew performance for normal and emergency operating procedures. Many emergency operating procedures dealt with failures or malfunctions of aircraft systems such as electrics, hydraulics, pressurization, flight instruments, and flying in adverse weather. Furthermore, measurement research in simulators expanded to include the development of safety technologies and procedures to handle these situations. In the 1950s, commercial companies ventured into the pilot training and certification business to meet the growing demand for qualified pilots and aircrew. The advancements of computer processing power in the late 1960s and early 1970s led to the development of more sophisticated, high-fidelity simulators and the ability to obtain objective performance measures from the simulators along with instructor evaluation sheets (Dickman, 1982).

The most widespread use of modern military and commercial flight simulators is in flight crew training because of lower cost, increased safety for personnel and equipment, and more efficient use of resources. All major commercial airlines have extensive simulator complexes to meet various levels of Federal Aviation Administration (FAA) approval criteria (Dillard, 2002). Both military and commercial flight simulators have the advantage of being able to operate twice as many hours than that of an airplane with the possible faults and abnormal operational situations virtually unlimited, making it possible to train various levels of proficiency to accommodate the differing needs of students or businesses. Today, flight simulation is widely used in every aspect of pilot training, from simple emergency procedures on Cockpit Procedure Trainers (CPT), through advanced military exercises performed in distributed mission operations (DMO) in high-fidelity Multi-Task Trainers (MTT).

DISTRIBUTED MISSION OPERATIONS

DMO are currently the state-of-the-art means to facilitate distributed training exercises for operational, joint, and coalition military aircrew. The goal of DMO training is to use repetition of a particular set of scenarios designed to exercise specific skills and to provide specific experiences. DMO provide the trainee with the unique opportunity to operate in a team-oriented, multi-player environment and thereby train on higher-order and more varied skills than in a single-simulator environment. By incorporating many players and more mission-relevant features into the distributed exercise, today's trainee can receive training on more complex cognitive skills than would ordinarily be trained in a single-simulator environment, such as those prevalent throughout most of the 20th century. Single simulators afford training at lower-level cognitive tasks relevant to a single aircraft (e.g., emergency procedures), while DMO, by virtue of combining assets and people, can afford training higher-end cognitive skills. DMO can combine live (e.g., aircraft flying over training ranges), virtual (human in-the-loop simulators), and/or constructive (e.g., computer wargame models) training assets on a distributed network (Figure 11.2).

DMO are considered state-of-the-art training in the military. Just a few or several hundred entities can be "brought together" to conduct small-scale missions or entire battle-like experiences. Among the examples of skills that can be trained in a distributed environment are the opportunities to work on radar targeting and sorting, communication skills, and maintaining team formation and tactics throughout the engagement. DMO may involve a variety of aircraft types (e.g., fighters, bombers, tankers, command, and control aircraft) as well as non-aviation assets such as ground-based command and control centers, surface-to-air missile (SAM) sites, and ground vehicle simulators. With larger scale exercises, even higher-order cognitive functions can be trained, such as situation awareness, leadership, tactical decision making, etc. This complexity creates many challenges for assessing human performance. Some challenges are traditional experimental control, while others are purely technical; however, new challenges are showing up as a unique result of the emerging DMO community.

DISTRIBUTED SIMULATION DEVELOPMENT: CHALLENGES FOR ASSESSMENT

In traditional experimental psychology, variables of interest are purposefully manipulated to understand their effects (i.e., independent variables or IV),

FIGURE 11.2. Representation of assets involved in a DMO training exercise. (*Source*: Courtesy of the Air Force Research Laboratory.)

while variables not of theoretical interest or relevance in the study are "controlled" so as not to confound or complicate conclusions about the data. On the extreme end of the experimental control spectrum, *all* possible variables except the IV are controlled. This highest level of experimental control results in (usually) single-person or small-group interactions involving highly controlled tasks. The benefits of this control yields a more precise dependent variable (DV) measurement of the human participant, and the highest potential cause/effect inference the IV/DV relationship can achieve. The pilot training environments of today involve many more (uncontrolled) participants, changing scenarios, various technologies, and multiple performance objectives that may lead to measured DV trade-offs, either known or unknown to the researcher. The result of this intricate, uncontrolled environment is that our ability to assess performance becomes more complicated.

Certainly, technology presents many of the same challenges today as did yesterday's simpler systems, only today those same challenges exist on larger, more complicated systems. These technological issues transcend time (e.g., reliability, timing, compatibility, etc.), but they all have a common side effect for performance measurement – it is more difficult to assess performance if you do not get the raw data or if it is inaccurate. Another challenge is the pace at which technology changes, requiring the assessment methods to undergo adjustments at a corresponding pace (e.g., Kirschenbaum et al., Chapter 12).

Not so obvious, however, are the challenges that are an artifact of the DMO community itself. As a relatively new technology experiencing growing pains, much of the large, diverse professional community behind DMO voice their need for change based on engineering capabilities and limitations. Their concern is what can the system do or not do, or what does it replicate or not replicate faithfully, such as terrain or feature display generation, weapons model fidelity, or cockpit layout. What is rarely prioritized, and often directly compromised, is research on understanding human performance (and performance measurement) as a function of technology changes or improvements. This further complicates assessing performance in this complex domain. The development of distributed simulation networks historically has been viewed and prioritized in terms of two fundamental *engineering* capability questions: "What data need to be available on the network?," and "How can the simulation be made more effective, realistic, lifelike, etc.?" In 1992, the "what" question was addressed by the distributed interactive simulation (DIS) standard, which defined the data necessary for heterogeneous entities to maintain their own states on the network, and to communicate any changes in their internal states (location, velocity, orientation, articulated parameters, etc.) to other entities on the network. Having these data available allowed simulation entities to interoperate and thus create a distributed simulation network.

Recently, significant amounts of product design and development work have been done in the distributed simulation field, primarily on the previously stated "how" question. The engineering aspects of distributed simulation development have focused on how to improve the network quality of service (QOS) and how to improve the user experience by upgrading the fidelity of components such as computer-generated forces (CGF). Areas such as network data packet delivery and transmission reliability have been addressed by subsequent DIS standards. In addition, much work has been done in improving the quality and fidelity of image generators (IG) and terrain databases. All are very important efforts, but at times these efforts have taken on a life of their own. Origins of simulations, including DMO, exist because of the need to improve pilot performance. This often-forgotten purpose results in significant challenges to quantifying performance. Consciously or unconsciously, management and decision makers in the DMO community typically address the "what" and "how" engineering issues and questions at the expense of assessment efforts. As a result, assessing the warfighter has not become any simpler over the course of time.

The simulation community has invested substantial amounts of time and money into developing simulation networks aimed at providing a better user experience. However, the following question is more important than simply how the technology works: How does all of this affect the individuals who participate in man-in-the-loop simulations? Meaning, how do we measure and quantify the performance of an individual participating in DMO exercises? What is the improvement in human skill and on what tasks? Once performance can be assessed, we can measure differences as a function of new technologies – or, alternatively, new combat tactics – to provide data-driven recommendations for changes. After all, the purpose of DMO is not solely about how to develop a better simulation network; it is really about *how to make a better warfighter as a result of time in the distributed network environment*. Often, technology advancements are made without thought as to whether or not they should be made, let alone as a result of quantifiable data to support and/or validate the change. Emphasis and priority should be placed upon those environments and technologies that yield demonstrable improvement in warfighter skills. Though the environments provide immense training potential, *we must measure and quantify human performance* to understand its value and where and when to best use it to maximize the operational effectiveness of our warfighters.

THE DMO COMMUNITY'S ASSUMPTIONS

DMO facilities share a common primary purpose: to train warfighters to be better prepared to complete their missions. Most pilots, instructors, and subject matter experts (SME) will agree that when warfighters participate in DMO exercises, positive training is taking place. However, little effort has been made to objectively quantify the measure of improvement during DMO and resulting from DMO training.

The community makes two major assumptions regarding the effectiveness of warfighter training in distributed learning systems. First, the community assumes the training received in the simulated environment will be carried through to actual combat or combat-like missions. While subjective evaluations and warfighter feedback can verify this is happening, the simulation community has lacked a quantifiable method to verify that knowledge and skill transfer is taking place as a result of participation in the DMO environment. The challenge of an objective assessment of skill performance in expertly trained individuals is an issue extending to many areas of study (Ericsson, Chapter 18).

The second assumption is that the warfighters are increasing their skills, competencies, and knowledge, and that these increased abilities are demonstrated in subsequent training sessions. This shared assumption about simulated training, including other military simulation, is used at the Army's National Training Center (NTC) (Chatham, Chapter 10). For example, SME evaluators could observe a group of warfighters throughout a week-long training session, and note that by the end of the week the group, as a whole, is killing the adversary while spending less time within close proximity to the enemy, thereby implying the group is deploying their munitions more effectively and at longer ranges. While subjective observations appear to confirm these results, only recently have efforts resulted in objective analyses to confirm (and precisely measure) these differences in exact times and deployment ranges (Schreiber, Stock, & Bennett, 2006).

Unfortunately, until recently, the scientific and warfighting communities have not had standardized data collection and measurement tools available that could objectively measure human performance in a distributed network. An objective measurement platform needs to have a wide range of potential operating environments throughout the community. Such an application needs to be capable of listening to the network traffic on any DMO network and providing objective, quantitative results that indicate whether or not training is taking place. The future of training will greatly rely on DMO, but going forward, we need to understand how to assess performance so that we know how and when to best use DMO as a training tool. Comparing multiple methods of training across different environments and objectives becomes possible with standardized data collection and measurement, an important consideration for improving training (Mayer, Chapter 9.

PRIOR HUMAN PERFORMANCE DMO DATA

Since DMO capability is comparatively new (1990s), human performance data in DMO environments are relatively new, fairly scarce, and almost exclusively subjective. History provides simulator data of some relevance. A number of early studies investigated either in-simulator learning or transfer effectiveness, and all found simulator training beneficial (Gray, Chun, Warner, & Eubanks, 1981; Gray & Fuller; 1977; Hagin, Durall, & Prophet, 1979; Hughes, Brooks, Graham, Sheen, & Dickens, 1982; Jenkins, 1982; Kellogg, Prather, & Castore, 1980; Leeds, Raspotnik, & Gular, 1990; Lintern, Sheppard, Parker, Yates, & Nolan, 1989; McGuinness, Bouwman, & Puig, 1982; Payne et al., 1976; Robinson, Eubanks, & Eddowes, 1981; Wiekhorst, 1987; Wiekhorst & Killion, 1986; for reviews, see Bell & Waag, 1998, and Waag, 1991).

However, prior research has only involved measuring simple tasks representative of a small portion of a mission (e.g., manual bomb delivery, one-versus-one air combat maneuvering, etc.). Compared to predominantly stand-alone systems of the past, DMO not only afford the ability to train individual and team skills, but also to train larger and more complex portions of the mission. Given that DMO environments afford the ability to train more varied skills, what can be used from performance measurement methodological perspectives and/or conclusions are limited. Methods and measures to capture performance have been lacking for these complex DMO environments.

Ideally, assessments in DMO would include operator opinions, in-simulator learning, and transfer-of-training evaluations to the actual environment (Bell & Waag, 1998; Waag & Bell, 1997) using a variety of data sources, including objective measures for quantification. Popular opinion among the DMO community is that networked simulation training is highly beneficial, and significant performance improvement takes place within DMO exercises. While we do not doubt this widespread consensus, empirical evidence quantifying the warfighter performance and in-simulator learning improvement is, at best, scarce. In the short history of DMO, performance measurement has been limited largely to opinions or subjective ratings (e.g., Bennett, Schreiber, & Andrews, 2002; Crane, Robbins, & Bennett, 2000; Krusmark, Schreiber, & Bennett, 2004; Waag & Bell, 1997; Waag, Houck, Greschke, & Raspotnik, 1995). Published works using objective, quantifiable metrics for empirical investigations of performance transfer from multiplayer networked environments to the actual environment appear, for DMO, to be nonexistent. Hundreds of millions of dollars are being invested in these networked simulation training environments without routine, objective, and quantifiable metrics that assess performance and help generate clear evidence of learning, transfer effectiveness, and return on investment. In other words, the performance measurement for multiplayer networked simulation environments has historically rested upon operator opinions and expert evaluation ratings.

LIMITATIONS ON RELYING ON SUBJECTIVE ASSESSMENT IN COMPLEX ENVIRONMENTS

The DMO community at large can benefit from objective measurement, as subjective measures contain severe limitations. First, although it is possible to subjectively evaluate a number of skills, subjective evaluation does not provide the level of precision and detail in measurement that are obtained by using objective measurement software. Additionally, in the absence of objective measurements, there is no way to evaluate the raters, meaning the possibility exists for a SME rater evaluating a group of pilots to adjust ratings over time to account for proficiency gains. Or, the SME may (and often do) fall victim to one or more other well-known limitations often associated with subjective evaluations, such as anchoring, rater biases, different frames of reference, etc.

To illustrate the complications in relying upon subjective measures in a complex DMO environment, Krusmark et al. (2004) analyzed SME rating data for 148 pilots from 32 F-16 aircraft teams (Figure 11.3) participating in one-week DMO training research. The teams flew between seven and nine one-hour DMO missions (a total of 222 scenarios across the 32 teams). Due to understandable logistical constraints, it is not uncommon (Krusmark et al., 2004) for the SME to be employed by the DMO organization and make their rating judgments while observing the missions in real-time. Even though the authors found that the subjective ratings increased over the course of a week of training, suggesting learning and improvement in performance, it could be argued that the results were due to a vested interest in successful training and/or the lack

FIGURE 11.3. F-16 aircraft.
(*Source:* DoD photo by MSGT Michael Ammons, USAF.)

of using a blind rater methodology. Furthermore, although the overall trend suggested improvement, the authors employed a multilevel modeling approach and found little systematic variability among the 40 individual skill constructs rated. The authors also found that evaluators typically assign a passing grade to most training events, resulting in minimal variation across students within lock-step training progressions, an observation noted in other studies (e.g., Nullmeyer & Spiker, 2003). Krusmark et al. concluded that significant learning almost certainly took place, but that plausible alternative explanations for the rating changes existed and the subjective rating system did not appear sensitive enough to differentiate between specific knowledge or skill constructs.

For networked simulation, subjective evaluations have been the foundation for large-scale aggregate analyses. However, those subjective metrics are not solely sufficient for assessing human performance in DMO training environments, nor are they particularly useful for quantifying warfighter learning improvement translating directly to mission effectiveness. Even well-controlled scenarios and studies reporting significant improvements in average expert ratings for dozens of warfighters on a multitude of missions for constructs such as "situation awareness" or "tactical employment" still do not inform the warfighters, the instructors, or the scientific community what impact those changes have on specific and mission-essential knowledge or skills or mission performance, such as changes in kill ratios, bombing errors, missile hit ratios, time spent within various range rings, communication step-overs, precise angles/ranges for clear avenue of fire, etc. An objective measurement system directly assessing mission critical parameters validates and *quantifies* the opinion and subjective rating data, thereby providing the return on investment data justifying DMO training expenses (Schreiber & Bennett, 2006).

Though objective performance measurement in DMO has a very short history, objective data has not been neglected. Rather, the objective data intent has focused on *immediate warfighter feedback*. Many earlier automated assessment systems (from the 1970s and 1980s) captured aircraft system status data and flight parameters like airspeed and altitude (Brictson, Ciavarelli, Pettigrew, & Young, 1978; McGuinness, Forbes, & Rhoads, 1984; Wooldridge, Obermayer, Nelson, Kelly, Vreuls, & Norman, 1982). Polzella, Hubbard, Brown, and McLean (1987) surveyed over 100 Air Force C-130, H-53, E-3A, and B-52 simulator instructors concerning frequency of use and value of parameters and procedures monitoring tools designed to enhance instructor awareness in simulators, and found that the parameters provided value. More contemporary, but still in the same spirit of providing data as mission-specific feedback, a number of DMO facilities today demonstrate impressive debriefing capabilities with the ability to replay and/or show vast quantities of objective data [e.g., Nellis Air Force Base (AFB), Air Force Research Laboratory (AFRL), Mesa Research Site, Shaw AFB, etc.]. However, all of these systems are focused on the objective data for feedback on *a given scenario or live-fly event* – that is, focused on *debriefing* a particular mission. Certainly these debrief systems provide extremely useful feedback to the warfighter, but they do not (a) permit quantifying learning by assessing performance on a given skill (it is left up to instructor interpretation of raw system data), (b) store assessment data by individual or team, (c) use the same measures across sites and across different simulator vendors, or (d) use data to understand skill proficiency for training or other uses, such as training effectiveness evaluation or capability of force calculation. Given these shortcomings, a measurement system capable of automatically tagging, storing, and aggregating performance data over scores of missions and warfighters is strongly desired.

Some systems have been designed to capture complex objective measures from simulated systems and to use them to diagnose skill performance of individuals and store or track the aggregated data for later statistical analysis (e.g., Vreuls Research Corporation, 1987), but these idiosyncratic measurement systems were not designed to capture human performance in a standardized format across a diverse set of simulators and training sites, such as in DMO. Though DMO pose a significantly more challenging environment in which to attempt quantifying human performance, enabling processes and technologies for objectively measuring human performance have emerged over the past several years.

METRIC GENERATION AND VALIDATION

The fundamental engineering requirement of all distributed exercises – that of standardizing data transfer so that entities can interoperate – can also be used as the same foundation for science and quantifying human performance. Such engineering standardization enables standardizing data capture and human performance measurement across simulators and environments (Schreiber, Watz, Bennett, & Portrey, 2003). Additionally, we now have the ability to connect with instrument training ranges and record movement and exact timing during complex combat sequences. Currently, only policies prohibit the routine integration of data from complex avionics from the actual aircraft, which would provide even more new opportunities for on- and off-board data logging for human performance assessment (e.g., avionics management, sensor control, weapons employment, etc.). Having overcome major technological obstacles to quantifying human performance across systems and sites in a DMO environment, two critical questions still remain: what to measure and how best to measure it.

In order to define the criterion, the Air Force has developed a structure and methodology called Mission Essential Competencies or MECs. Mission Essential Competencies are defined as the "higher-order individual, team, and inter-team competencies that a fully prepared pilot, crew or flight requires for successful mission completion under adverse conditions and in a non-permissive environment" (Colegrove & Alliger, 2002). The MEC structure encompasses knowledge, skills, and developmental experiences. During the MEC process, operational warfighters define the list of critical knowledge, skills, and developmental experiences necessary for a warfighter to be fully prepared for combat. These warfighter-defined skills then provide the list of skills that must be measured in complex environments such as DMO. Examples of A-10 skills are provided in Table 11.1.

The Warfighter Readiness Research Division at AFRL has also developed a methodology to link these experiences to the knowledge and skills they support and then directly to the higher level MEC (Symons, France, Bell, & Bennett, 2005). Mission Essential Competencies define how the "what to measure" question is answered.

The second question – how measurement should be done – is really about deciding the best way to capture and use data to assess what we decide to measure. The ideal measurements would be very sensitive, capable of discerning high, medium, and low performance on experienced warfighters on the skills required in combat. A warfighter possessing all the MEC experiences and demonstrating high degrees of proficiency in the MEC skills will likely be very successful in combat missions. A principal function of distributed simulation training is increasing the pilots' MECs through experiences, and practicing the skills critical for successfully performing air combat missions. Mission Essential Competencies are scalable from individuals to teams and team of teams. Air-to-air and airborne warning and control system (AWACS) aircrew have an MEC related to Detection, an activity in which they must collaboratively succeed to be successful in a combat environment. Drawing

Table 11.1. *Examples of A-10 MEC skills (subset of A-10 skills provided).*

Fly at Low Level	Able to tactically maneuver aircraft at low level while using the terrain and prioritize terrain clearance tasks
Deconflicts	Able to create and adhere to plan to deconflict with flight members, other aircraft, mission members, weapons, artillery, and ground forces, etc.
Manages Survivor (CSAR)	Provides information, aid, support, protection to survivor(s) to increase their likelihood of survival; provides specific, clear guidance to survivor (e.g., ROE, handling stress/fear)
Locates Objective	Uses electronic and visual cues to find the survivor/target
Identifies Targets/Threats	Interprets the visual cues/system indicators that identify various targets/threats
Decides Course of Action	Determines how to approach target/objective; considers situation, threat, environment, and aircraft and weapons limitations
Weaponeering	Matches assets to targets; selects weapons to achieve desired goal; limits collateral damage; avoids fratricide
Positions Assets/Weapons Systems	Arranges assets for maximum impact and minimum threat exposure consistent with mission accomplishment
Maneuvers Defensively	Employs appropriate tactics (e.g., applies defensive aids – chaff flare, maneuvers) to negate or minimize enemy weapons effects
Provides Mutual Support	Uses communications, visual lookout, and firepower to provide mutual support
Battle Damage Assessment (BDA)	Interprets visual/sensor cues for determining extent of battle damage
Directs Assets (CSAR/FACA)	Directs assets as necessary to achieve mission (e.g., able to direct helicopters for CSAR)
Talk-On	Transforms what is seen on the ground from the air into words and confirms that it is understood by other parties

on that commonality we can design objectives for sensor-shooter training that emphasize the skills and knowledge associated with each team's portion of the mission, as well as provide an organizing structure for the combined team of teams.

To meet the objective measurement needs of distributed networks, researchers and engineers, using the MEC-defined skills as a framework and the measurement validation processes previously discussed, set out to develop and implement a measurement system, called the Warfighter Readiness and Performance Measurement Tracking System (WRAPMTS), to record and analyze data during distributed missions. There were three primary development goals for WRAPMTS. First, produce a software tool capable of objective measurements over multiple platforms, including live, virtual, and constructive simulators. Second, the tool must serve multiple purposes, such as human performance assessment and simulator technology validation. Finally, the tool should operate on multiple levels, including measurements designed for individuals, groups of individuals (teams), teams of teams (packages), and multiple packages (forces).

To derive the measures for the MEC skills and to input them into the WRAPMTS system, structured interviews were conducted with several SME. A minimum of three SMEs was used for independent interviewing and development of each metric. The Air Force began measurement development with the air superiority domain. Even before interviews commenced, it became immediately apparent that some skills (e.g., decision making) could only be assessed by developing behaviorally anchored subjective rating techniques, and parallel subjective assessment efforts were undertaken to include as part of WRAPMTS (Carolan et al., 2003). For the objective measurement development, the SMEs first were asked to identify outcome metrics, and then skill measures associated with good and poor performance on those outcomes. For the skill measures, SMEs were asked to describe observable behaviors or events that constituted examples of good and poor performance. Skill metrics and the associated rule sets for a number of measures were identified; the minor discrepancies found between SMEs during the independent interviews occurred only for a few metrics as the result of assumption differences and ideas that were overlooked. These differences were quickly resolved by bringing the SMEs together for concurrence. Finally, the measures were mapped to each of the MEC skills, programmed into the system, and validated according to the nine steps outlined in chronological order below:

1. Initial conceptual validity of each outcome and process metric was established through the structured SME interview process described above.
2. Each metric was transformed into software code and the rule sets were again presented to SME before beta data collection.
3. To ensure the capturing of unusual scenario events and capturing measures correctly, specific simulator scenario set-ups were designed and flown with very specific, out-of-the-ordinary trigger events in order to exercise all portions of software code (e.g., multiple simultaneous shots at same entity, fratricides, entities killed as a result of flying into the ground trying to evade munitions, etc.).

4. Initial beta testing of the software was performed, collecting "test" data on operational pilots in the DMO environment. Software engineers identified and corrected bugs, if any.

5. Researchers and SME observed individual beta testing engagements in real-time and examined output files to confirm that the proper values of metrics were taken.

6. Outcome and shot-related metrics were provided as feedback to the beta testing operational warfighters.

7. Researchers plotted large sample distributions of each metric to ensure not only that all values did indeed fall within bounds for that metric, but also that the distribution properties observed adhered to expected values for that platform, missile, tactic, etc.

8. Trend data were checked across high/low experience demographics for improvements in the expected directions.

9. As a final validity check, a formal database was created for outcome metrics and shots. A research assistant, following a blind protocol, observed and manually recorded these same measurements. In the case of the F-16 automated measure development, this process was followed for 163 scenarios. The human recorded data were then compared to the automatically collected objective data of the same scenarios. The resultant correlations were nearly perfect, and where deviations existed, it was later found that the human was more error-prone. (Schreiber, Stock, & Bennett, 2006)

One measure derived from this lengthy process was "controls intercept geometry." Intercept geometry is the range and angular relationships (e.g., aspect angle) between aircraft that are used to determine weapon launch boundaries. To illustrate the types of logic derived in the workshops and transformed into code, the following calculations are performed automatically via computer. In Figure 11.4, the performance measurement system needs to "know" the positions of the friendly aircraft in the center and the threat aircraft (top). The system will then calculate the aspect angle of the threat to the friendly aircraft. If the aspect angle is greater than 120 degrees, then the threat is potentially in a position to shoot. Then, assuming aspect angle condition is satisfied, and given the threat's altitude, weapon type, and quadrant, is the current range less than that of a configuration table value? If yes, then the friendly has violated the minimum abort range (MAR). This measure, as just one of many measurement examples, is the type of automated measurement that was derived from the whole process – initially performance measurement workshops, then mapped to the MEC, and finally subjected to validation.

Though the system, process, and example measures discussed above have had successes in assessing performance in a complex DMO environment, significant challenges nonetheless still remain. First, to capture standardized human performance data across systems and sites, the "raw network data"

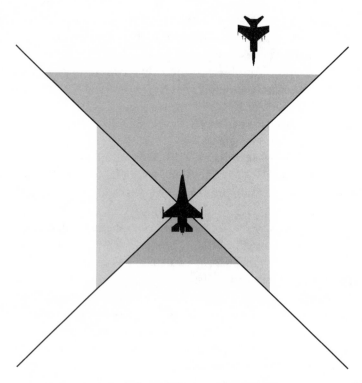

FIGURE 11.4. Controls intercept geometry.

used for human assessment calculations must be present on the DMO network
in standardized form. If the raw information is not present, an assessment
cannot be made. Additionally, as previously discussed, the DMO environment
can include a great number of simulators from a number of organizational
sites. The desire is to be able, using the same standardized method and measures, to capture human performance across all the sites and at various levels
of abstraction (individual, team, team of teams), as shown in Figure 11.5.

In Figure 11.5, the lowest level "tubes" represent individual pilots or aircrews, whereas the larger tubes represent a scaling of higher level grouping of
teams. A current challenge for performance measurement in DMO is that the
various players are represented by different simulators across different geographical locations. In theory, the standardized human performance assessment approach should scale from individuals to teams to teams of teams and
then to forces, and operate successfully across many organizational sites. In
practice, it has been discovered that the standardized human performance
assessment theoretical approach to DMO works well for single-site, mature,
DMO systems, but that the more players and the more organizational sites
involved, the greater the probability that the DMO environment will contain
raw data issues that create significant obstacles for assessing all players involved
in the network (Schreiber, Watz, & Bennett, 2007). Just a small sampling of the

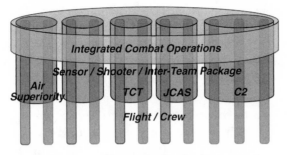

FIGURE 11.5. Abstraction levels of assessment.

problems arising from large-scale DMO events includes network data errors, latencies, and underlying low-fidelity models or system limitations that necessitate unusual "corrective" actions on the part of mission directors (e.g., "reincarnating" a player). On larger scale DMO events, data issues such as these make it an order of magnitude more difficult to assess outcome measures for the teams/forces (e.g., kills), or to accurately assess a skill for an individual. When quantifying individual proficiency, the numbers are rendered much less useful, although to some extent they can still be calculated, as they've been significantly contaminated by outside factors.

CONCEPTUAL APPLICATION/TRANSITION OF MEASURES FOR ADAPTIVE TRAINING

The gold standard for military pilots is simply stated, but difficult to achieve. The best possible performance is meeting all mission objectives while simultaneously minimizing risk (e.g., vulnerability exposure by not penetrating a missile envelope), mistakes (e.g., violating communication standards), and inefficiencies (e.g., unnecessary use of afterburner). With standardized human performance assessment data in place, adaptive training could occur, thereby further maximizing human performance potential. With adaptive training, continual assessment of an individual's skill proficiencies is conducted and the greatest skill deficiencies compared to a referenced standard are identified and fed back into the training system to most efficiently train that individual (i.e., a closed-loop system). In order to use standardized measures for adaptive training, a warfighter would initially accomplish a standardized core set of live and virtual missions. The intent is to build performance profiles and benchmark the applicable skills, the summaries of which provide the position on a proficiency or resource investment learning curve. After the initial position is established, the warfighter enters the adaptive maintenance/targeted training mode – maintaining those skills that meet or exceed standards and using the most efficient training media to execute customized training. Extended periods without live exercises require another series of core missions to re-benchmark. A centralized performance tracking system could make recommendations for the next training activity based on identified weaknesses and the "best value" training media. Moreover, the competencies serve to define the constructs of interest for evaluating training in the simulation environment and for examining the transfer of knowledge from the simulation to live operations (Colegrove & Bennett, 2005). This process is a clear example of matching the method of training with the material that ultimately should be trained, a fundamental challenge to instructional design (Mayer, 2007).

MEC-based syllabi designed for simulation training will develop proficiency sooner and more efficiently. Properly structured virtual training, applied when a unit member first arrives, has shown in a small sample size to accelerate those individuals ahead of their peers. For example, the AFRL designed a short virtual combat training syllabus of two versus two and two versus four tactical scenarios, based on identified knowledge, skills, and experiences, for pilots who were graduating from their formal training unit (FTU) and moving to their first operational posting. The goal of this quick look was to assess the likely impact of a principled, competency-based virtual training exposure on knowledge and skills identified as important for new combat pilots to possess. The results, which are based on a very small sample of six pilots, indicate that the graduates who were exposed to competency-based scenarios benefited substantially from the virtual training exposure. When compared to a cohort group of six pilots who graduated in the same time frame and were posted to a base with the same aircraft, the virtual trained pilots were rated by their new organizations as being substantially better at flight planning, maintaining communications standards, and working as wingmen. Finally, these preliminary results also point to the potential for developing a set of more fundamental or foundational knowledge and skills that could help not only to restructure how schoolhouse combat training is accomplished, but also to define the relationships and linkages from knowledge and skill proficiency in school to proficiency in the first posting after school.

ADDITIONAL AIR FORCE PERFORMANCE MEASUREMENT NEEDS AND USES

Since DMO environments present a great number and variety of performance assessment needs for the Air Force (current and future), this chapter has focused on performance measurement in regard to contemporary DMO environments. Of course a great number of other Air Force performance measurement needs and uses exist. A sampling of other key domains includes pilot selection, cockpit design and testing, and pilot training cost estimation.

Performance Measurement for Pilot Selection

Over a century of flight has shown many times over that some humans are better suited for aviation than others. Those professionals, schools, and agencies that have the responsibility for selecting pilot candidates from a large pool of potential candidates must accurately and validly measure the characteristics of those candidates and compare them to some standard for selection. Carretta and Ree (2003) provide an excellent review of past and current selection trends and issues and describe future research issues. They cite research reported by Dockeray and Isaacs (1921) about the first research program aimed at pilot selection measures. Those measures examined reaction time, emotional reaction, equilibrium, perception of muscular effort, and attention. Due to its complex nature, selecting pilots requires a multidisciplinary approach. Bailey and Woodhead (1996) describe aptitude tests for six aircrew ability domains (attentional capacity, work rate, psychomotor skills, numerical reasoning, verbal reasoning, and spatial ability). Carretta and Ree (2003) describe personality tests that are used to measure pilot candidates' personality variables (e.g., big five factors model of agreeableness, conscientiousness, extraversion, neuroticism, and openness to experience). Carretta and Ree finish their discussion by examining future pilot selection methods. Most notable are measures of general cognitive ability such as chronometric measures, neural conductive velocity, and cognitive components.

Performance Measurement for Cockpit Design and Testing

Wickens (2003) describes flying in terms of four "meta tasks," prioritized as "from highest to lowest, aviate (keeping the plane in the air); navigate (moving from point to point in 3-D space and avoiding hazardous regions of terrain, weather, traffic, or combat vulnerability); communicate (primarily with air traffic control and with others on board the aircraft); and manage systems" (p. 147). Good human performance measurement is crucial in designing and testing cockpit designs that facilitate all four meta tasks. Given the complex nature of aviation, modern aircraft designers have a variety of challenges as they balance the sometimes overwhelming amount of information that can be presented to the pilot with the perceptual and response limitations of pilots. How much information can be displayed at one time via aural, visual, and vestibular media and still allow the pilot to be able to sense and interpret in a timely manner? What response input mechanism will be least taxing on the pilot's resources? How far can input devices such as buttons and dials be placed from the pilot and still have the pilot reach them in an emergency? These and a plethora of other design questions must all be answered if the cockpit designer hopes to build an optimal device. Human performance data are crucial in this process. Physiological measures such as reaction times, cognitive measures such as memory storage and workload estimates, and communication measures such as intelligibility of speech are just a few examples of measurement types that can be used in cockpit design.

Performance Measurement for Cost Estimation for Trainee
in a Pilot Training Course

Training pilots is an expensive activity, even when simulators are heavily used
to augment actual flying. The current estimate to produce one military pilot
ready for operational duty easily exceeds one million dollars. For undergraduate pilot training in fiscal year 2006 alone, the U.S. Air Force spent approximately $809 million, the Army $635 million, and the Navy/Marine Corps $365
million (Bush, 2005).

CONCLUSION

As illustrated throughout this chapter, aviation mechanics is a complex human
performance task. Measurement of that performance is vital and presents
many of its own unique challenges. The aviation community's ability to accurately and validly measure the performance of pilot and aircrew trainees has
grown tremendously since the early days of flight. The use of advanced simulators for undergraduate and advanced pilots has opened many doors to better
performance measurement. The days of relying on instructor pilots to make
all of the judgments about trainee pilots based *solely* on their own subjective
observations are over. However, even with all of the automated simulation-
based performance measurement tools described in this chapter, an experienced instructor pilot will always be involved in the final instructional and
evaluative decisions about their trainees.

Good performance metrics can help make accurate estimates of how long
it will take to train a certain number of pilots, and how much it will cost to
make changes to those training programs. These metrics can be used in sensitivity studies to perform trade-offs with various pilot training resources such
as instructor pilots, time, training aircraft, and simulators. For instance, if a
nation enters a major war and has a need to increase the production of pilots
over a period of time, sound performance measures of current trainees can be
used to help determine if, and by how much, the training rate could be accelerated using existing and/or additional resources. Past attempts to make these
types of estimates have often been plagued with inaccuracies because the estimates for trainee throughput were based on invalid performance measures.

Historically, objective measurements resulting from customized applications for one simulation system were not always well suited to others. Now standardized engineering protocols not only allow geographically separated entities
to engage one another, but also allow standardized data to be shared on a common network – a valuable resource in trying to standardize human performance
assessment. If or when an objective performance measurement system capability can mature to overcome current challenges, *one* system with the same metrics could be used across all airframe simulators, military and commercial. The

resultant number and types of laboratory studies and field in-simulator assessments, ranging from the testing of safety and severe weather flying procedures to full DMO exercises, and the subsequent leveragability of results would be unprecedented. If that same human performance assessment system could also be employed for live-range activities, imagine the potential for cross-comparison of laboratory and field in-simulator learning, and transfer-of-training evaluations both within the military and commercial airline industry.

ACRONYMS

3-D	3-Dimensional
AFB	Air Force Base
AFRL	Air Force Research Laboratory
AWACS	Airborne Warning and Control System
CGF	Computer-Generated Forces
CPT	Cockpit Procedure Trainer
DIS	Distributed Interactive Simulation
DMO	Distributed Mission Operations
DV	Dependent Variable
FAA	Federal Aviation Administration
FTU	Formal Training Unit
IG	Image Generator
IV	Independent Variables
MAR	Minimum Abort Range
MEC	Mission Essential Competency
MTT	Multi-Task Trainer
QOS	Quality of Service
SAM	surface-to-air missile
SME	Subject Matter Expert
WRAPMTS	Warfighter Readiness and Performance Measurement Tracking System

REFERENCES

Bailey, M., & Woodhead, R. (1996). *Current status and future developments of RAF aircrew selection. Selection and training advances in aviation: AGARD conference proceedings 588* (pp. 8-1–8-9). Prague, Czech Republic: Advisory Group for Aerospace Research and Development.

Bell, H. H., & Waag, W. L. (1998). Evaluating the effectiveness of flight simulators for training combat skills: A review. *The International Journal of Aviation Psychology, 8*(3), 223–242.

Bennett, W., Jr., Schreiber, B. T., & Andrews, D. H. (2002). Developing competency-based methods for near-real-time air combat problem solving assessment. *Computers in Human Behavior, 18,* 773–782.

Brictson, C. A., Ciavarelli, A. P., Pettigrew, K. W., & Young, P. A. (1978). *Performance assessment methods and criteria for the Air Combat Maneuvering Range (ACMR):*

Missile envelope recognition (Special Report No. 78–4 (Confidential)). Pensacola, FL: Naval Aerospace Medical Research Laboratory.

Bush, G. W., President. (2005). *Budget of the United States government*. Fiscal Year 2006. Retrieved February 15, 2007, from, http://www.whitehouse.gov/omb/budget/fy2006/.

Carolan, T., MacMillan, J., Entin, E. B., Morley, R. M., Schreiber, B. T., Portrey, A. M., et al. (2003). Integrated performance measurement and assessment in distributed mission operations environments: Related measures to competencies. In *2003 interservice/industry training, simulation and education conference (I/ITSEC) proceedings*. Orlando, FL: National Security Industrial Association.

Carretta, T. R., & Ree, M. J. (2003). Pilot selection methods. In P. S. Tsang & M. A. Vidulich (Eds.), *Principles and practice of aviation psychology* (pp. 357–396). Mahwah, NJ: Lawrence Erlbaum Associates.

Colegrove, C. M., & Alliger, G. M. (2002, April). *Mission essential competencies: Defining combat mission readiness in a novel way*. Paper presented at the NATO RTO Studies, Analysis and Simulation (SAS) Panel Symposium. Brussels, Belgium.

Colegrove, C. M., & Bennett, W., Jr. (2005). *Competency-based training: Adapting to warfighter needs*. Paper presented at the meeting of the Royal Astronautic and Engineering Society, London, UK.

Crane, P. M., Robbins, R., & Bennett, W., Jr. (2000). Using distributed mission training to augment flight lead upgrade training. In *2000 Proceedings of the interservice/industry training systems and education conference*. Orlando, FL: National Security Industrial Association.

Crosbie, R. J. (1995). *The history of the dynamic flight simulator*. Washington, DC: Department of the Navy.

Dickman, J. L. (1982). Automated performance measurement: An overview and assessment. In *Proceedings of the 4th interservice/industry training equipment conference: Volume I* (pp. 153–165). Washington, DC: National Security and Industrial Association.

Dillard, A. E. (2002). Validation of advanced flight simulators for human-factors operational evaluation and training programs. In *Workshop on foundations for modeling and simulation (M&S) verification and validation (V&V) in the 21st Century* (Foundations '02 V&V Workshop). Laurel, MD: Johns Hopkins University, Applied Physics Laboratory.

Dockeray, F. C., & Isaacs, S. (1921). Psychological research in aviation in Italy, France, England and the American Expeditionary Forces. *Journal of Comparative Psychology, 1*, 115–148.

Gray, T. H., Chun, E. K., Warner, H. D., & Eubanks, J. L. (1981). *Advanced flight simulator: Utilization in A-10 conversion and air-to-surface attack training* (AFHRL-TR-80–20, AD A094 608). Williams Air Force Base, AZ: Air Force Human Resources Laboratory, Operations Training Division.

Gray, T. H., & Fuller, R. R. (1977). *Effects of simulator training and platform motion on air-to-surface weapons delivery training* (AFHRL-TR-77–29, AD A043 648). Williams Air Force Base, AZ: Air Force Human Resources Laboratory, Operations Training Division.

Hagin, W. V., Durall, E. P., & Prophet, W. W. (1979). *Transfer of training effectiveness evaluation: US Navy Device 2B35* (Seville Research Corporation Rep. No. TR79–06, ADA073669). Pensacola, FL: Chief of Naval Education and Training.

Hughes, R., Brooks, R. B., Graham, D., Sheen, R., & Dickens, T. (1982). Tactical ground attack: On the transfer of training from flight simulator to operational Red Flag exercise. In *Proceedings of the 4th interservice/industry training equipment conference: Volume I* (pp. 127–130). Washington, DC: National Security Industrial Association.

Jenkins, D. H. (1982). *Simulation training effectiveness evaluation* (TAC Project No. 79Y-OO1F). Nellis AFB, NV: Tactical Fighter Weapons Center.

Kellogg, R., Prather, E., & Castore, C. (1980). Simulated A-10 combat environment. In *Proceedings of the Human Factors Society 24th annual meeting* (pp. 573–577). Santa Monica, CA: Human Factors Society.

Krusmark, M., Schreiber, B. T., & Bennett, W., Jr. (2004). *Measurement and analysis of F-16 4-ship team performance in a simulated distributed mission training environment* (AFHRL-HE-AZ-TR-2004–0090). Mesa, AZ: Air Force Research Laboratory Human Effectiveness Directorate, Warfighter Readiness Research Division.

Leeds, J., Raspotnik, W. B., & Gular, S. (1990). *The training effectiveness of the simulator for air-to-air combat* (Contract No. F33615–86-C-0012). San Diego, CA: Logicon.

Lintern, G., Sheppard, D., Parker, D. L., Yates, K. E., & Nolan, M. D. (1989). Simulator design and instructional features for air-to-ground attack: A transfer study. *Human Factors, 31,* 87–100.

Mayer, G. B., Jr. (1981). *Determining the training effectiveness and cost-effectiveness of visual flight simulators for military aircraft* (AD A104627, Master's thesis). Monterey, CA: Naval Postgraduate School.

McGuinness, J., Bouwman, J. H., & Puig, J. A. (1982). Effectiveness evaluation for air combat training (ADP000203). In *Proceedings of the 4th interservice/industry training equipment conference: Volume I* (pp. 391–396). Washington, DC: National Security Industrial Association.

McGuinness, J., Forbes, J. M., & Rhoads, J. E. (1984). *Air combat maneuvering performance measurement system design* (AFHRL-TP-83–56). Williams Air Force Base, AZ: Operations Training Division, Armstrong Laboratory.

Moroney, W. F., & Moroney, B. W. (1999). Flight simulation. In D. J. Garland, J. A. Wise, & V. D. Hopkin (Eds.), *Handbook of aviation human factors.* Mahwah, NJ: Lawrence Erlbaum Associates.

Nullmeyer, R. T., & Spiker, V. A. (2003). The importance of crew resource management in MC-130P mission performance: Implications for training evaluation. *Military Psychology, 15*(1), 77–96.

Payne, T. A., Hirsch, D. L., Semple, C. A., Farmer, J. R., Spring, W. G., Sanders, M. S., et al. (1976). *Experiments to evaluate advanced flight simulation in air combat pilot training: Volume I.* Transfer of learning experiment. Hawthorne, CA: Northrop Corporation.

Polzella, D. J., Hubbard, D. C., Brown, J. E., & McLean, H. (1987). *Aircrew training devices: Utility and utilization of advanced instructional features. Phase 4. Summary report* (AFHRL-TR-87–21; ADA188418). Brooks Air Force Base, TX: Air Force Human Resources Laboratory.

Robinson, J. C., Eubanks, J. L., & Eddowes, E. E. (1981). *Evaluation of pilot air combat maneuvering performance changes during TAC ACES training.* Nellis Air Force Base, NV: U.S. Air Force Tactical Fighter Weapons Center.

Schreiber, B. T., & Bennett, W., Jr. (2006). *Distributed mission operations within-simulator training effectiveness baseline study: Summary report* (AFRL-HE-AZ-TR-2006–0015-Vol I, ADA461866). Mesa, AZ: Air Force Research Laboratory, Warfighter Readiness Research Division.

Schreiber, B. T., Stock W. A., & Bennett, W., Jr. (2006). *Distributed mission operations within-simulator training effectiveness baseline study: Metric development and objectively quantifying the degree of learning* (AFRL-HE-AZ-TR-2006–0015-Vol II, ADA461867). Mesa, AZ: Air Force Research Laboratory, Human Effectiveness Directorate, Warfighter Readiness Research Division.

Schreiber, B. T., Watz, E., & Bennett, W., Jr. (2007). DIS: Does interoperability suffice? A need to set a higher standard (07S-SIW-067, 2007 Spring SIWzie Award). In *2007 spring simulation interoperability workshop conference*. Norfolk, VA: SISO.

Schreiber, B. T., Watz, E., Bennett, W., Jr., & Portrey, A. (2003). Development of a distributed mission training automated performance tracking system. In *Proceedings of the 12th conference on behavior representation in modeling and simulation (BRIMS)*. Scottsdale, AZ.

Symons, S., France, M., Bell, J., & Bennett, W., Jr. (2005). *Linking knowledge and skills to mission essential competency-based syllabus development for distributed mission operations* (AFRL-HE-AZ-TR-2006–0014). Mesa, AZ: Air Force Research Laboratory, Warfighter Readiness Research Division.

Vreuls Research Corp. (1987). *Air combat maneuvering performance measurement system for SAAC/ACMI*, Volume II, Appendices 5 & 6. Wright-Patterson Air Force Base, OH: Air Force Systems Command.

Waag, W. L. (1991). The value of air combat simulation: Strong opinions but little evidence. In *The Royal Aeronautical Society flight simulator symposium: Training transfer – Can we trust flight simulation? Proceedings*. London: The Royal Aeronautical Society.

Waag, W. L., & Bell, H. H. (1997). *Estimating the training effectiveness of interactive air combat simulation* (AL/HR-TP-1996–0039). Armstrong Laboratory, AZ: Aircrew Training Research Division.

Waag, W. L., Houck, M., Greschke, D. A., & Raspotnik, W. B. (1995). Use of multiship simulation as a tool for measuring and training situation awareness. In *AGARD Conference Proceedings 575 Situation awareness: Limitations and enhancement in the aviation environment* (AGARD-CP-575). Neuilly-Sur-Seine, France: Advisory Group for Aerospace Research & Development.

Wickens, C. D. (2003). Aviation displays. In P. S. Tsang & M. A. Vidulich (Eds.), *Principles and practice of aviation psychology* (pp. 357–396). Mahwah, NJ: Lawrence Erlbaum Associates.

Wiekhorst, L. A., & Killion, T. H. (1986). *Transfer of electronic combat skills from a flight simulator to the aircraft* (AFHRL-TR-86–45, AD C040 549). Williams Air Force Base, AZ: Air Force Human Resources Laboratory, Operations Training Division.

Wiekhorst, L. A. (1987). *Contract ground-based training evaluation: Executive summary* (ADA219510). Langley Air Force Base, VA: Tactical Air Command.

Wooldridge, L., Obermayer, R. W., Nelson, W. H., Kelly, M. J., Vreuls, D., & Norman, D. A. (1982). *Air combat maneuvering performance measurement state space analysis* (AFHRL-TR-82–15; ADA121901). Brooks Air Force Base, TX: Air Force Human Resources Laboratory.

12

Contrasting Submarine Specialty Training: Sonar and Fire Control

SUSAN S. KIRSCHENBAUM, SHELLEY L. MCINNIS,
AND KEVIN P. CORRELL

Within the submarine environment, sonar technicians (ST) and fire control technicians (FT)[1] are the two largest groups of enlisted submarine specialists. The specialties, and therefore the training and performance metrics, differ in interesting ways. Sonar is largely a perceptual discrimination skill while fire control is more of a cognitive skill. The primary task of an ST is to detect and classify the signal (i.e., a sound wave) of a sonar contact; the FT's primary task is to localize (determine course, speed, and range) the sonar contact, using a set of tools, procedures, and algorithms. For both these submarine specialties, the training pipeline is changing with the addition of periodic, just-in-time, ashore classroom sessions interspersed with at-sea shipboard practice. Other significant changes include the development of more objective performance measurements that supplement the traditional qualification metrics. As a result, the STs and FTs of tomorrow should have far more systematic and comprehensive training and evaluation than even today's senior enlisted specialists.

The decision makers in the submarine environment, as everywhere, depend on sensory information that allows them to understand the state of the world. In many domains, much of that sensory information is readily available right before the eyes of the decision maker – the chess player can see the playing board and the golfer can see how the ball lies relative to the course. In contrast, there is no directly observable information about the non-static situation outside the submarine. The senior decision makers must depend on sophisticated systems and the skills of the sensor operators (STs) and the analysts (FTs) to interpret sonar sensor data and transform that data into useful information about the unseen world outside the hull. Consequently, the skill of these operators and analysts is critical to both the safety of the ship and the successful completion of the ship's military missions.

---

[1] It should be noted that "fire control" is not analogous to a "fire fighter" but rather weapons launch control.

Who are these critical links in the decision chain? STs and FTs are enlisted submariners with at least a high school education. By tradition and standards, submariners are among the best and the brightest of the Navy's recruits and they need to be for these technically demanding jobs. There are high standards for cognitive capability, emotional stability, and physical endurance. Submariners cannot be color-blind and must have 20/20 corrected vision. Sonar technicians have additional auditory perception standards that do not apply to FTs. The ST and FT designations denote that these men[2] must not only be able to operate the complex computer systems, but also repair them when needed. When a submarine is at sea, the ship must be entirely self-sufficient so as not to compromise one of its greatest advantages, stealth. Since this chapter is labeled "*contrasting submarine specialty training*," we will focus on the unique skills rather than the common computer technician elements of the ST and FT jobs.

While this chapter concentrates on the submarine world, there are many parallels with other dynamic and uncertain domains such as medicine or fire fighting. Medicine, for example, presents challenges that are analogous to those in the submarine world. The disease process continues, even while the medical team tries to diagnose and treat the problem. We might add that sonar, originally developed for undersea warfare, is now used as a diagnostic tool (ultrasound) in medicine. Like submarining, medicine is a team activity, in which the physician is supported by nurses, technicians, laboratories, and technology. Each of these specialties has its own training pipeline and certification process. In both medicine and submarining, apprenticeship (internship) plays a significant part in the training of novices and teaching is often part of the progression from novice to expert. The reader can probably think of many other domains that also fit all or part of this description.

THE SUBMARINE WORLD

Before we can begin to talk about the nature of expertise and the training of submariners, we need to understand a bit about the environment in which they work. There are a number of characteristics that make the world of the submarine very different from most of the domains in which expertise has been studied. The submarine is, of course a warship, but it is a special kind of boat because it gains military value from remaining stealthy. Thus submarines are careful about making excess noise and about when and where they surface and communicate. The submarine uses passive sonar as its primary sensor. There are several different sonar arrays that might be in use, including a towed array of hydrophones that cannot distinguish left from right because of the conical shape of its acoustic beams. (We will say more about sonar when we

---

[2]   As of this writing the U.S. submarine force is all male. Therefore, masculine pronouns will be used throughout.

describe the job of the ST.) Only when at periscope depth can a submarine use other sensors such as radar. Even at periscope depth, visual information is constrained – rather like looking at the world through a long tube – and thus can be misleading. Therefore, the submariner must work hard just to learn the state of the world using signals that are inherently noisy and uncertain.

Another thing that differentiates submarine decision makers from other experts is that submarining is a very dynamic world. Nothing happens while the chess Grand Master recognizes a game pattern (Chase & Simon, 1973) or while the golf champion lines up the shot (Ericsson & Lehmann, 1996) or even while the musician reads the score (Ericsson, 2002). In contrast, things keep happening regardless of what the submariner does; all the players are moving all the time. Not doing anything is also a decision.

And lastly, because of all these factors, the submarine is a dangerous environment where a wrong action, or failure to take action, can lead to disaster. Hitting a sea mount or a fishing boat is more than bad luck; it is poor performance by a highly experienced team.

Task Descriptions: ST and FT Expertise

Sonar Technicians

The process of searching, localizing, and classifying other objects in the unseen world outside the submarine's hull requires some explanation prior to discussion training and performance. When you drive your car down the road you are doing all these things simultaneously and by yourself. In a submarine, it takes many men to accomplish these same tasks because of the demanding nature of the undersea environment. Light in the atmosphere travels in a relatively straight line; sound undersea reflects, bends, and refracts, similar to the way the optical images in a funhouse mirror are bent and refracted (Urick, 1983). The ocean is a particularly harsh environment for detecting and classifying a sonar contact. For example, sound waves can have shadow-like areas where the contact cannot be heard because the sound waves cannot penetrate an ocean acoustics phenomenon known as a "thermal layer" that often separates the contact from the submarine. There are a host of other factors beyond the scope of this chapter that make detecting sonar contacts in the ocean very difficult. If ocean physics does not make the problem difficult enough, the ocean is a difficult and noisy environment, with loud merchant vessels, quiet sailboats, fishing boats trailing nets far behind, and biologics such as whales and snapping shrimp all generating sounds that can mask the sound from a potential sonar contact. For a description of an expert, albeit, fictional ST see Clancy's descriptions of "Jonesy" (Clancy, 1984).

Traditionally, STs used auditory (and visual) cues to both detect and identify (classify) the contacts. A noisy tanker sounds different from a noisy whale. A quiet submarine is difficult to pick out from the noisy background ocean sounds. The

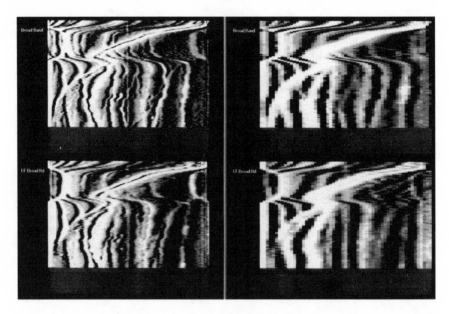

FIGURE 12.1. Sonar waterfall display.

auditory skill of an ST is akin to the auditory skill of a good orchestra conductor; he must be able to pick out all the players within the ensemble and make the most of each sound. Passive sonar is displayed in what is called a "waterfall" display with time "falling down" the *y*-axis and bearing represented on the *x*-axis. Where there is coherent noise, that is, a potential sonar contact, a line develops (Figure 12.1). Today, educated ears are augmented by many different kinds of sophisticated analysis tools and systems to help find and identify a sonar contact, but nothing, so far, can replace the eyes and ears of an ST. Thus, sonar detection and classification is a *human* sensory process, augmented by technology.

The tasks of detecting coherent sounds among the noise and identifying what made the sounds are supported by technology and sophisticated signal processing algorithms. This signal processing technology breaks the sound into its component parts the way a linguist takes speech apart into phonemes, syntax, signs, etc. The results of these analyses create well over a hundred different displays. The expert ST must put the signal back together by using the many displays of the details. One necessary skill, therefore, is the ability to "see" what goes with what and integrate the information from many displays into a coherent pattern. Efforts are now under way to aid the ST in this task by new and creative ways to visualize these data. Thus, sonar is a sensory process, augmented by technology.

Fire Control Technicians
Those are just some of the problems faced by STs in analyzing sonar data. In effect, the submarine is blind, so likewise, FTs face an equally daunting task (Jackson, 2006). One problem is that of determining course, speed, and

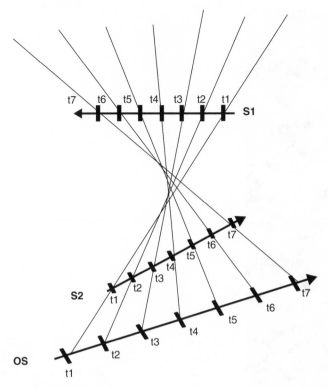

FIGURE 12.2. The bearing fan drawing illustrates the problem of locating a sonar contact with only bearings information. The arrows are submarine tracks. The bottom arrow (OS) is the user's own sub's track. The upper arrows (S1 and S2) are possible contact tracks. The tick marks are equal distances and hence indicate equal time intervals. The longer lines are lines of bearing drawn at equal time intervals. These lines must go through the contact's track, regardless of where the contact is. Only two (S1 and S2) of a large set of possible solutions are drawn. There are limits, of course, on both speed and range, but these limits do not reduce the set sufficiently.

range to the contact. This problem is known as target motion analysis (TMA) (Cunningham & Thomas, 2005; McKenna & Little, 2000). The distance between your eyes, occlusion, relative size, and several other cues give you a good idea about the distance to passing objects. Given the much longer distances that passing ships should maintain (like airplanes, it should be over a mile for safety), the distances are often too great for any analogue to binocular depth perception, so distances (ranges) are undetermined. Moreover, only two bits of information are known, bearing and bearing rate (change in bearing over time). The problem is that of establishing the course, speed, and range of the contact so that the decision maker can understand the situation. This is a mathematically under-determined problem, with two known values and three unknowns. The number of solutions is almost infinite. Figure 12.2 illustrates the problem.

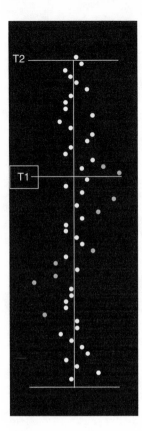

FIGURE 12.3. Representation of the MATE display. By adjusting the parameters of the solution the skilled operator can find a probable solution to the TMA problem. In this example, the gray "dots" have been suppressed by an expert FT.

Added to the problems faced by FTs is the need to keep track of many, many contacts and the noisy nature of the sonar data. Naturally, there are algorithms and automation to help him, but little guidance on which ones to use when. Thus, with many possible solutions and tools, the problem is less a sensory one and more of a cognitive one. For example, one such tool is called the Manual Adaptive/Aided TMA Estimator (MATE) (Figure 12.3), which was designed to input the parameters of a solution and examine the fit to the sonar data. The ever-inventive FTs quickly discovered that they could adjust the solution so that it fit better than the estimates that they were given. They learned to recognize key patterns that indicate particular kinds of errors. The goal is to "stack the dots" so that there is a minimal difference between the solution and sonar data. Today the dot stack is one of the primary tools supporting TMA.

Just having a straight dot stack does not guarantee the accuracy of the solution. As can be seen in Figure 12.2, many solutions might fit. Logic is required to verify that the solution makes sense and is congruent with all data (as, for example, before and after a contact makes a maneuver or when there is a periscope observation). One of the ways that the expert FT performs differently from the novice is by selecting the appropriate data to include in the

FIGURE 12.4. Line-of-sight diagram. The base ship is at the bottom with the target at the top. Vector direction represents course and length represents speed. Additional components would decompose the vectors into speed within the line of sight and speed across the line of sight.

analysis. Because sonar data are inherently noisy and there might be more than one tracker or sensor for the same contact, the decisions about how much and which data to use in the analysis are crucial to achieving an accurate and timely solution. In Figure 12.3, the operator has suppressed the gray dots. In a recent study we saw that the mean novice FT rate of editing data was 4.6 (SEM = 2.4) dots per minute, while the experts performed the same action at a rate of 2.0 (SEM = 1.2) dots per minute. As data editing was laborious, the experts reported "visually editing" (i.e., ignoring) noisy data. Moreover, the experts used data, selectively, from all available trackers while the novices used only one tracker at a time. The FTs must prioritize their efforts, keep their superiors informed as to the state of their solutions, be sure that the system is updated with the best current solutions, etc. These are skills that go well beyond the manual skills of operating the displays, as complicated as they are (Cunningham & Thomas, 2005).

One of the skills that sets the experts apart is their ability to mentally create and transform the "picture" of their own ship and the contact(s), including relative motion. If given a bearing and bearing rate (change of bearing over time), the expert can quickly draw the classic "line-of-sight" (LOS) diagram (Figure 12.4) with which all mariners are familiar, while novices struggle to make such translations (Kirschenbaum, 1992). These spatial transformations are complicated by the fact that sometimes bearing references true North and sometimes it is relative to one's own ship's head.

Due to relative motion illusions, some geometries are to be very difficult to understand. One of those is the over-lead problem. As you pass a slower car, you have no problem realizing that the other vehicle is going the same direction as you are, but drawing backwards, relative to your own vehicle. Now imagine that you can't see it, and only know the value of the bearing as it changes over time. The slow auto that you are passing and the oncoming traffic could look very much alike. To make the problem more complex, ships do not necessarily travel in fixed traffic lanes so that other vessel might be moving in almost any direction. Thus, the components of relative motion are direction and speed. This is a well-known physics problem that can be solved with vector math, but a difficult one to comprehend, the way experts do, with mental spatial transformations (Trafton & Trickett, 2001; Trafton et al., 2006).

In summary, the knowledge and skills required of the ST and the FT are different, not only in content, but also in the key processes required for success. However, they need one another just like the eyes and ears need the brain.

These are complex skills, required to solve complex problems, in a demanding and unforgiving world. As with other demanding domains, to do this effectively takes many years of training and practice (Ericsson, Krampe, & Tesch-Römer, 1993). That practice is achieved in two ways – by serving an apprenticeship under a skilled expert and by deliberate practice using simulated data. Both have their advantages and disadvantages. Apprenticeship is, obviously, a costly process involving the time of both the learner and the teacher. Moreover, the apprentice at sea rarely knows if he is correct, can't replay the events, and the particulars of any event are uncontrolled; that is they occur by chance, depending on what platforms and environmental conditions come along. Practice with simulated data, however, rarely has the noise, urgency, or difficulty of the real thing. Simulations are not inexpensive, either, because of the need to build elaborate trainers for every version of equipment. Below we address these twin challenges and some newly developed attempts at solutions.

THE PROBLEM WITH MILITARY TRAINING

One problem with military training is military equipment. Historically, military equipment has been designed for a special purpose and to rigorous standards of ruggedness that would not apply to commercial equipment. It would be economically counterproductive to design commercial equipment to withstand the shock of a torpedo hit, the mud of a foxhole, or the dust of the desert. Moreover, no commercial value is given to a passive sonar or an encrypting phone/radio. In many areas, the military led the way in the development of advanced technology, but at a price. Equipment built for the military and to military standards was expensive and often arcane. As a consequence, the new recruit had to learn to use equipment that was unlike anything in civilian life.

Moreover, the equipment (software and hardware) was designed by engineers, without user input. It was not only entirely new to these recruits, but it was not designed for usability – or for novices. Training under these circumstances took a long time and great effort.

Time allotted for training was never long enough, and so the majority of the training focused on how to maintain and use the equipment ("knobology"), rather than on understanding the concepts and processes that the equipment supported. The schools where these sailors were trained wanted and needed examples of the real equipment to use for training. Training meant learning where the functions were located and memorizing a sequence of actions to accomplish the goal. When the equipment changed, the sequence and the actions changed.

Things began to change as technology changed. Today commercial computers are ubiquitous and relatively inexpensive. Moreover, the standards for software usability have made even Navy engineers reconsider their designs with the user in mind. Users are involved in determining requirements and in testing new systems. Since commercial technology has caught up with military needs, the standard military system today often uses "commercial, off-the-shelf" (COTS) equipment. Although the software is still usually developed primarily for military use, the commercial world has found new uses for what were originally military products. Sonar is used in fish-finders and medicine; the Internet (originally the military-only Arpanet) is everywhere; and security solutions apply not only to the military, but to many different kinds of transactions including financial transactions, medical recordkeeping, and safeguarding the individual's personal information.

The amount of technology knowledge that the new recruit brings with him or her is another big change from the past. When the first author first began to work in this field, she had to train subjects to use a mouse before running an experiment. Today the only problem is that they critique the carefully controlled experimental displays as if they were intended to go to sea! All this has had a profound impact on training.

Training and Performance Measurement: Old Model

Under the old model of training, all submarine enlisted recruits begin their training with Basic Enlisted Submarine School (BESS). After BESS, submarine sailors went to specialized training in "A" (apprentice) schools for each job. Much of the "A" school curriculum was focused on computer training and maintenance of the specific equipment associated with their specialty. The schools were structured much like any traditional school, with lectures for content and labs for practice. Instructors were, and still are, men who have practical at-sea experience. In general, they are not trained educators, but are knowledgeable about the tasks they are teaching. They taught in the traditional model, using scripted and pre-prepared set of instructional lectures and PowerPoint slides. The training was augmented by laboratory exercises using as close to real equipment as possible. This equipment was stimulated and the training scenarios were pre-scripted or canned. Opportunities for training innovation were limited.

After approximately two years of general and specialized training, the novice was only minimally qualified in the new specialty when sent to sea for the first time. In truth, the novice was not able to perform more than the most basic functions independently and required significant on-the-job training to reach a level to be able to act independently. The new sailor's first shipboard assignment was often as cook's mate because he lacked the skills to actually perform any part of his job. Thus, by the time he began sitting watches in the role for which he had been trained, even that level of proficiency was seriously degraded and he was only beginning to be a competent part of the crew when his initial enlistment commitment was completed. One of the problems with this time line was that it required (and still does) more individuals aboard the ship because the newbie was just learning and the shipboard expert spent his time teaching. Neither was able to spend time actually performing the required task.

It is only aboard ship that the seaman apprentice can actually "qualify" for submarines and earn the right to wear dolphins. The qualification process is guided by a qualification (qual) card that specifies what knowledge and skills the recruit needs to master. The recruit generally has a mentor to guide him through this process, but then must prove mastery of all skills to a qualification board via an oral exam and a walk through the boat, answering questions about specific equipment and demonstrating learned skills.

Another problem is that the performance of the apprentice was not measured objectively so much as judged (subjectively) by superiors. What was considered acceptable on one sub might be superior performance or even unacceptable under another command.

After "A" schools, the now sea-experienced STs/FTs would attend "C" schools and eventually Master Level schools as they progress from novice/apprentice to journeyman to expert. The career path of the ST reflects this. There are several STs and one Sonar Supervisor on each watch. The best experts become Acoustic Intelligence (ACINT) specialists who are not assigned to specific crews, but ride boats as the mission requires. While there is no equivalent to the ACINT for FTs, there is a similar career path from novice/apprentice to supervisor.

This training pipeline is similar to medical training in that it is a mixture of classroom and supervised practical experience. As with the newly minted MD, the new submariner really needs an additional period of practice (apprenticeship or internship) before receiving full certification to practice the new profession. The significant difference is that the medical practitioner (physician, nurse, or medical technician) has significantly more theoretical education than the submariner gets under the old training model.

Training and Performance Measurement: Training Continuum Model

In recent years the Navy has undergone a "revolution in training" motivated by Chief of Naval Operations, Admiral Vern Clark (Clark, 2002) and instituted by Vice Admiral Harms and subsequently Vice Admiral J. Kevin Moran, Commander, Naval Education and Training Command. In the submarine world, this revolution was shepherded by then Submarine Learning Center Commander, Captain (now Rear Admiral) Arnold Lotring.

The first step in the revolution was to analyze the tasks that need to be trained. These task analyses led to building the detailed task descriptions that the Navy calls "skill objects." The skill objects were then validated in consultation with fleet experts. The task analysis showed both the overlap in required skills and the job specific skills. Thus, both FTs and STs must learn about computer maintenance, in general, but each group must also learn about the specifics of its own unique equipment. The third step in the revolution was to re-engineer the curriculum and associate performance measures. Lastly, the revised curriculum was incorporated into a career path that takes the sailor from raw recruit to expert.

After a job-task analysis, it was found that several jobs had the same tasks for the apprentice and the schools were combined into the Submarine Electronics Computer Field (SECF) course. This course introduces the recruit to submarine qualification, basic combat system operation, basic maintenance, basic sonar operations, and basic seamanship, and prepares the apprentice for the first sea tour. The training time line has been shrunk to about six months without significant impact on shipboard performance. The problem of the newly assigned sailor has not been completely resolved, but the sailor is now able to begin on-the-job training that much sooner.

The remainder of this chapter will focus on step three – the new, and still evolving, training model and associated performance measurement (Shobe, 2007). The Submarine Learning Center began the re-engineering of the course structure with the "A" school, which was transformed into the new Submarine Electronics Computer Field Apprentice course. Figure 12.5 illustrates the idea of shared and specific training for FTs and STs. Much of the core and shared training is on seamanship and computer skills. The specific skills are what differentiate the ST from the FT.

At the same time that the "A" school curriculum was changed, the measurement model was changed. The new model, called the Kirkpatrick Levels of Assessment framework (Kirkpatrick, 1994; Shobe, 2007), uses four levels to assess the student's perception of the course, examinations, laboratory performance metrics, and follow-up evaluation by the student's on-the-job

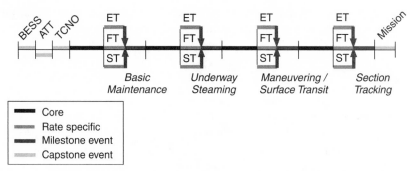

FIGURE 12.5. Generic training time line.

supervisor. We cannot definitively evaluate whether the new model produces better performance because the performance measurements are not comparable between the two models. Using Kirkpatrick's (Kirkpatrick, 1994) Levels of Assessment for Training, initial indications are that progress toward qualifications is as good or better than in the past (Shobe, 2007). The new model gets the recruit to the job faster and allows the recruit to spend more of his career actually doing the job. Judging by that metric, it is an unquestionable success.

The most radical changes in the training pipeline is a shortening of the training time before a sailor's first tour at sea and extensive, individual, computer-based training that can be done both ashore and aboard ship. Another radical change is that the sailor returns to the schoolhouse from the ship periodically for short (about two weeks) refresher/technology update training.

What, specifically, do the STs and FTs learn, beyond electronics and computers? STs learn both factual information about acoustics and learn to recognize the sounds of different kinds of sonar contacts. This is akin to the scientific knowledge acquired by medical practitioners and fills an important gap. While the factual training and the equipment operation skills fit nicely into the concept of "skill objects," it is more difficult to develop a neat description of the auditory skills that an ST needs. One might just as well ask for a task analysis for recognizing a voice over a poor telephone connection when the speaker has a bad cold. While there is automation and a large library of undersea sounds to aid the ST, the task is still daunting. ST training requires practice, practice, and more practice with sounds in isolation (e.g., a single pump) and amid the entire cacophony of sounds made by a ship at sea. A good ST can classify a contact as merchant or warship, surface or subsurface, friendly or hostile, and sometimes even name the ship "by nature of sound," and can also determine the speed of a ship by listening to the propeller and counting the turns.

There is no substitution for deliberate practice of the auditory skills that an ST needs. Automation and simulations facilitate that practice in new training systems. The Interactive Multisensor Analysis Training (IMAT) (Foret, Korman, Schuler, & Holmes, 1997; Wetzel-Smith, Ellis, Reynolds, &

Wulfeck, 1995) system is the first of the new simulation-based training tools to actually show an impact on learner skills, using realistic auditory inputs and visualizations to teach acoustics. It builds skill by teaching students about the components of the sounds that they will hear, just as medical personnel learn about the parts of the body and how they function. Thus, they learn to identify the regularities of a 60-Hz engine noise or a three-bladed propeller as they build their own sound library. It also teaches about the impact of the environment on the sonar signal. Using a pre-test/post-test evaluation, IMAT has shown that it improves skills and increases the interactions between instructors and students. Today IMAT is used both in the schoolhouse and at sea.

Auditory skills are not the only ones an ST needs. An ST must also be able to operate the complex sonar system effectively and efficiently, and analyze the signals. The complexities of employing the equipment effectively as well as the subsequent analyses are both technical and context dependent. They also differ depending on the exact equipment on any boat and the operation area where that boat is going. Again, practice under a variety of conditions is essential. For these skills the computer-based Sonar Basic Operations Trainer (SBOT) can augment or facilitate training. It simulates a variety of conditions and equipment. Training in the older model depended upon practice on the actual equipment that would be aboard the individual boat. In the new model, simulation makes it possible to practice on a simulated version of the expected equipment and ocean environment. This trainer and the associated simulations can be used in the classroom or by an individual sailor and can be linked to provide sub-team and team training.

The ST's most challenging learning task is to identify the myriad of sounds heard. The FT's biggest challenge is to translate the numeric data on that contact into a moving picture of the unseen world outside the hull. An expert can easily translate bearing and bearing rate into a mental picture that can be analyzed for the components of a solution. One such depiction is the line-of-sight diagram (see Figure 12.4) that has been used by mariners for centuries. He can also translate between true (North up) and relative bearing.

The Common Basic Operator Trainer (CBOT) addresses these and other concepts that the FT needs to learn. The CBOT provides training to the FT in key concepts for analysis and matching bearing and bearing rate to develop target motion analysis solutions, thus deriving range, course, speed, and bearing to the contact of interest. Like the SBOT, CBOT provides an emulation of the majority of the system configurations currently deployed and emulates the FT core competencies necessary to localize any contacts providing bearing data to the FT operator.

The SBOT and CBOT are part of a network of training tools and courses incorporated into the e-learning SkillsNet catalog. Shipboard, the Submarine on Board Training (SOBT) system can provide both refresher courses and training for advancement. The Submarine on Board Training (SOBT) Performance

Evaluation tool provides several selectable, dynamic displays that are useful for monitoring a training exercise in progress, or after the exercise, for debriefing a crew or class on how they performed. It will also replay an exercise that has been completed.

One of the goals of the new model is to provide as good or better training in a shorter time frame; to send better qualified sailors to the boats; and to lower the cost of training. Data on the success of this goal are still being collected. There is no question that time from selection to qualification is shorter, but the performance metrics on these new training systems are not yet in. The training has changed and therefore the performance measurement is changing. The impact on the fleet will be seen in the future.

No two days are the same and there is no ground truth available (except when something goes wrong). This makes deliberate practice difficult. Training goes on continually – for individuals, teams, and entire battle groups. Some of it employs simulators, some uses "real" equipment in ashore stimulated with simulated data, and some of it takes place in exercises at sea against friendly ships playing the role of enemies.

CONCLUSIONS

The development of expertise in the submarine world, like the development of expertise in similar complex, dynamic, and uncertain domains, is a combination of formal training, on-the-job training, and experience. Formal training includes classroom activities and deliberate practice in laboratory or simulation environment. Submariners practice on simulated versions of their equipment using simulated data (environment, contacts, etc.); medical personnel practice on simulated patients using real or simulated equipment. On-the-job training is somewhat more formal for medical personnel, including internships and residency requirements. For submariners, it is less formal but no less important. The time length, however, is not fixed, but depends on progress toward completing the requirements for qualification. As with medical personnel, submariners must pass a rigorous qualification exam for certification. Training, however, never ends, with each qualification leading to the next. The third class of training in both fields involves lifelong deliberate practice that is characteristic of the growth of expertise. In both domains, the demands of technological change play a part in the need for continual training, as does the need to maintain certification and acquire additional qualifications. Thus, in both of these domains, as in many others, qualification and expertise are tied to continual deliberate practice.

While submarining is an exotic domain, training to develop expertise follows the same path as in other dynamic, uncertain, and complex domains. The differences between novices and experts are both quantitative and qualitative. The route from newbie to expert is paved with continual deliberate practice in classrooms, laboratories/simulators, and real-world exercises.

REFERENCES

Chase, W. G., & Simon, H. A. (1973). Perception in chess. *Cognitive Psychology, 4*(1), 55–81.

Clancy, T. (1984). *The hunt for Red October.* Annapolis, MD: Naval Institute Press.

Clark, V. (2002). Sea power 21: Projecting decisive joint capabilities. *U.S. Naval Institute Proceedings, 128*(196), 32–41.

Cunningham, A., & Thomas, B. (2005). *Target motion analysis visualisation.* Paper presented at the Asia Pacific Symposium on Information Visualisation (APVIS 2005), Sydney, Australia.

Ericsson, K. A. (2002). Attaining excellence through deliberate practice: Insights from the study of expert performance. In M. Ferrari (Ed.), *The pursuit of excellence through education* (pp. 21–55). Mahwah, NJ: Lawrence Erlbaum Associates.

Ericsson, K. A., Krampe, R. T., & Tesch-Römer, C. (1993). The role of deliberate practice in the acquisition of expert performance. *Psychological Review, 100*(3), 363–406.

Ericsson, K. A., & Lehmann, A. C. (1996). Expert and exceptional performance: Evidence of maximal adaptation to task constraints. *Annual Review of Psychology, 47,* 273–305.

Foret, J. A., Korman, M. S., Schuler, J. W., & Holmes, E. (1997). Design and development of pc-imat: Teaching strategies for acoustical oceanography. *The Journal of the Acoustical Society of America, 101*(5), 3097–3098.

Jackson, C. (2006). *Development of human performance measures for analyzing design issues in submarine tactical control systems.* Undersea Human Systems Integration Symposium (p. 8). Mystic, CT.

Kirkpatrick, D. (1994). *Evaluating training programs: The four levels.* San Francisco: Berrett-Koehler Publishers, Inc.

Kirschenbaum, S. S. (1992). Influence of experience on information-gathering strategies. *Journal of Applied Psychology, 77*(3), 343–352.

McKenna, I. H., & Little, S. (2000). *Developing tactics using low cost, accessible simulations.* Paper presented at the 2000 Winter Simulation Conference.

Shobe, K. K. (2007). *The Navy's revolution in training: A trining effectivness assessment of a new submarine "A" school.* Paper presented at the 2007 Human Systems Integration Symposium, Annapolis, MD.

Trafton, G., & Trickett, S. B. (2001). *A new model of graph and visualization usage.* Paper presented at the Twenty-Third Annual Conference of the Cognitive Science Society.

Trafton, J. G., Trickett, S. B., Stitzlein, C. A., Saner, L., Schunn, C. D., & Kirschenbaum, S. S. (2006). The relationship between spatial transformations and iconic gestures. *Spatial Cognition and Computation, 6*(I), 1–29.

Urick, R. J. (1983). *Principles of underwater sound* (3rd ed.). New York: McGraw-Hill.

Wetzel-Smith, S. K., Ellis, J. A., Reynolds, A. H., & Wulfeck, W. H. (1995). *Interactive Multisensor Analysis Training (IMAT) system: An evaluation in operator and tactician training* (Technical Report No. TR-96-3). San Diego, CA: Navy Personnel Research and Development Center.

https://www.cnet.navy.mil/sobt/web/subskillsnet_slides_files/frame.htm.

13

Training Complex Cognitive Skills: A Theme-Based Approach to the Development of Battlefield Skills

SCOTT B. SHADRICK AND JAMES W. LUSSIER

Professionals face unexpected challenges every day. The sector of our society that has had the most experience preparing for unexpected crises situations is the military. As a result of the contemporary operational environment, soldiers have experienced the need to adapt to virtually continuous changes in technical equipment and skills, as well as unique radical changes resulting from differences in conventional war and guerilla war. This has led to an increased need to develop adaptability skills in Army leaders (e.g., Barnes, 2005; Wong, 2004). For example, Barnes (2005) wrote, "Iraq has deeply challenged the soldiers who serve there, sometimes forcing them to perform duties far different from those they trained for. As a result, the Army has come to believe that teaching its soldiers how to think is as important as teaching them how to fight" (p. 72). Due to the complexity and uncertainty of the modern battlefield, Army leaders will need to be skilled at making rapid battlefield decisions under the most difficult conditions (Johnston, Leibrecht, Holder, Coffey, & Quinkert, 2002).

To address the needs described above, researchers at the U.S. Army Research Institute (ARI) for the Behavioral and Social Sciences investigated new methods designed to train complex cognitive behaviors. The result of the work was a theme-based training approach (Lussier & Shadrick, 2006) that could be used to train soldiers in expert mental models using an explicit set of behaviors or "themes." The training method has been used to train leader adaptability skills in tactical and non-tactical environments, crisis management skills, and battle command thinking skills. This chapter documents a series of research efforts embodied in the theme-based method to develop the U.S. Army's Think Like a Commander (TLAC) training program (Lussier, Shadrick, & Prevou, 2003; Shadrick, 2004; Shadrick & Lussier, 2002a). The TLAC program structures a deliberate practice of military thinking to develop habits consistent with those of expert tacticians. In addition, use of the method in civilian organizations is discussed.

ADAPTIVE PERFORMANCE AND ADAPTIVE THINKING

Pulakos, Arad, Donovan, and Plamondon (2000) reported that "adaptability, flexibility, and versatility are elusive concepts that have not been well defined in the psychological literature and therefore difficult to measure, predict, and teach effectively" (p. 612). They identified eight behavioral dimensions of adaptability. The dimensions identified were: (1) handling emergencies or crisis situations; (2) handling work stress; (3) solving problems creatively; (4) dealing with uncertain and unpredictable work situations; (5) learning work tasks, technologies, and procedures; (6) demonstrating interpersonal adaptability; (7) demonstrating cultural adaptability; and (8) demonstrating physically oriented adaptability. Pulakos et al. (2000) provided support for the taxonomy and linked the dimensions to several predictors of performance. With regard to the U.S. Army, their research showed that military jobs exhibited high scores on all eight behavioral dimensions, illustrating the adaptability requirements for junior officers. While all eight dimensions are relevant to military jobs, "dealing with uncertain and unpredictable work situations" was most related to the type of adaptation outlined by the U.S. Army leadership. Pulakos et al. (2000) defined that dimension as:

> Taking effective action when necessary without having to know the total picture or have all the facts at hand; readily and easily changing gears in response to unpredictable or unexpected events and circumstances; effectively adjusting plans, goals, actions, or priorities to deal with changing situations; imposing structure for self and others that provide as much focus as possible in dynamic situations; not needing things to be black and white; refusing to be paralyzed by uncertainty or ambiguity. (p. 617)

The cognitive task to which our research efforts have been applied is what has come to be called "adaptive thinking" by the U.S. Army. Adaptive thinking is a specific component of adaptability under a set of conditions similar to those described by Pulakos et al. (2000). Adaptive thinking describes the "cognitive behavior of an officer who is confronted by unanticipated circumstances during the execution of a planned military operation" (Lussier et al., 2000, p. 2). It can also be defined as the ability of a leader to respond effectively under complex and rapidly changing conditions when a multitude of events compete for a leader's attention. According to Lussier et al. (2000) and Ross (2000), adaptive thinking skills are based on domain-specific cognitive behaviors that have become automatic. The automaticity of the cognitive behaviors – or thought habits – structures the thinking of officers during times of stress to free the mind to work at higher cognitive levels, to assess a situation in more depth, to cope with complex issues, and to collaborate with other team members. Developing adaptive and responsive leaders is "a difficult process, but one that must be undertaken" (Dostal, 2002, p. 12). What was needed is an effective and efficient means for training adaptive thinking behaviors (e.g., Army Training and Leader Development Panel, 2001; Brown, 2000; Freakley, 2004; Toomey, 2001).

TRAINING ADAPTIVE PERFORMANCE AND MENTAL MODELS

Hatano (1982) noted that experts displayed a high level of performance in activities for which they had years of training and actual experience. However, performance of some experts decreased as the task became less typical and routine. That is, they were unable to adapt to the situation. Other experts, however, were able to adapt to the changing conditions by understanding the situation and inventing new procedures. Feltovich, Spiro, and Coulson (1993) showed individuals that display cognitive flexibility performed better than experts who did not demonstrate flexibility in thinking. The disparity reflects the differences between routine and adaptive expertise (Crawford, Schlager, Toyama, Riel, & Vahey, 2005; Hatano, 1982; Hatano & Inagaki, 1986; Hatano & Oura, 2003). Both routine and adaptive experts may have the same fundamental knowledge of basic tasks in the domain, but adaptive experts have the ability to think more flexibly about applications. With reference to military tactics, Brown (2000) reported that the "essence of adaptive learning is development of the ability to understand the how and why across the variables of warfare, as much as the what that is learned through repetitive performance to standard" (pp. IV-3). Brown (2000) continued by stating that "adaptive learning develops the leader's ability to understand, then anticipate, change in a world of increasing complexity – highly complex, ambiguous, simultaneous change" (pp. IV-3–IV-4).

Norman (1983) wrote that "in interacting with the environment, with others, and with the artifacts of technology, people form internal, mental models of themselves and of the things with which they are interacting. The models provide predictive and explanatory power for understanding the interaction" (p. 7). Mental models provide a foundation that allows individuals to predict and explain behavior in novel situations (Norman, 1988), understand the relationship between events, and develop expectations for what will happen next (Johnson-Laird, 1983). In applying the concept of mental models to tactical thinking, Serfaty et al. (1997) noted that expert commanders develop models that are different and better than the models developed by novice commanders. Expert commanders develop mental models that allow them to assemble large amounts of information into meaningful patterns that can be quickly retrieved when situations require. Thus, the recognition and retrieval of information is an automatic, non-conscious process that is "stimulated by the situation" (Ross, Battaglia, Hutton, & Crandall, 2003, p. 9). The retrieved information can, if time permits, be evaluated to see if it is appropriate or to decide if a new approach is needed. Once explored, the expert can then match the feasibility of the potential courses of action to the specific mental model of the current situation.

Reference to cognitive flexibility as an attribute of mental models as thinking structures can be used to describe the differences between individuals who show adaptive performance and those who do not, but the concepts do not really help the task of those who aim to improve adaptive thinking. Various researchers have found that training people to develop mental models is not easy. A mental model is, by its very nature, a simplified representation of the body of knowledge. For this reason, it is often difficult for individuals to directly verify that updates applied to a mental model are appropriate (Goodwin & Johnson-Laird, 2005) – which means that training the correct behavior is not a straightforward affair. Even when training is successful, the performance gains often appear only across multiple interventions (Ellis & Davidi, 2005).

The approach most commonly used previously by the Army to develop adaptive thinking was to use standard educational practices – for example, classroom lectures, writing assignments, case studies – to develop the knowledge structures needed to form tactical mental models. Then officers were placed in highly realistic, simulated performance environments. It was hoped that the officers would learn through realistic experiences to apply the knowledge in an adaptive and flexible manner. That process, relying greatly on individual officers to develop the adaptive thinking skills on their own, worked fairly well for some, but overall was slow, inefficient, costly, and unreliable in the sense that many officers did not develop adequately. The approach described in this chapter, which we termed a theme-based approach, is an attempt to improve the efficiency and effectiveness of that approach.

The theme-based approach – evidently a successful one – seemingly runs counter to some of the beliefs about training adaptability. For example, it is thought that training adaptability and adaptive thinking skills require training strategies and methods that are somewhat different than the methods traditionally employed (Smith, Ford, & Kozlowski, 1997). Typical training methods are inappropriate and may even impede performance in novel and ambiguous situations. For example, Charney and Reder (1987) noted that a critical component in the acquisition of cognitive skill is the ability to understand and recognize the conditions under which a particular approach should be used. If the training program always makes it obvious which approaches are required and practiced, "then an important element of the skill – the ability to recognize when to use each procedure – is not trained" (Druckman & Bjork, 1994, p. 32). Traditional training methods also rely heavily on developing procedural skills. Traditional methods are appropriate for training routine expertise (Holyoak, 1991) and are designed to develop automatic behavioral responses to performance requirements that are familiar to the performer (Holyoak, 1991; Kozlowski, 1998). However, as task and job demands become less predictable the "traditional … perspective to training design has diminishing relevance" (Smith, Ford, & Kozlowski, 1997, p. 89). As an alternative approach, Holyoak (1991) stated that the focus needs to be on the development of adaptive expertise. Adaptive expertise is the ability to apply knowledge flexibly and adaptively to novel and ambiguous situations (Brophy, Hodge, & Bransford, 2004; Hatano, 1982).

While the above authors are likely correct in many regards, we do not believe that training in general thinking skills or in general adaptive skills is particularly effective, especially in the stressful, demanding, and attention-focusing tactical environments in which our officers must operate. Additionally, we believe that traditional training methods *can* be productively applied. The difference is that the training is not focused only on how to solve problems in the domain, but also on how to think about problems in the domain.

TRAINING THINKING BEHAVIORS

The notion that thinking can be trained as a behavior has a precedent in practice. For decades, the Soviet chess machine thoroughly dominated all competition (Johnson, 2005). Chess players around the world assumed the Soviets achieved their success solely by extra effort in selecting, developing, and supporting promising players. Few, however, imagined that the Soviets had some new and secret training methods that the rest of the world did not (Alburt, 2003). With the breakup of the U.S.S.R., Soviet chess academies became publishing houses. The release of such books as Mark Dvoretsky's *Secrets of Chess Training* (1996) and *Positional Play* (1997) surprised the chess world. It seemed that the Soviets did have methods they had not revealed.

Researchers at the ARI saw a parallel between the problem of training battlefield commanders to think adaptively in tactical situations and that of training chess grandmasters, and they analyzed the Soviet training manuals to understand their methods. The difference between the Soviet methods and traditional chess instruction is, in a sense, the difference between education and training. The rest of the world studied the game of chess, its strategies and tactics, and tried to understand why one move was better than another. As students studied the game, they acquired knowledge about chess and understanding of its principles. They educated themselves about the game of chess. The Soviets did that as well, but also studied the human processes of finding good moves and avoiding errors, of searching and evaluating chess positions, and of controlling emotion and fighting a psychological battle with one's opponent. The Soviets described principles of expert play that reflected the thought patterns of grandmasters. While many of these expert principles were familiar to the rest of the world, the Soviet trainers went one critical step further. They created exercises that trained these principles, ingraining them in their students.

After sufficient training, the Soviet students employed the expert thought patterns not simply because they understood the principles or because they were consciously directing their thinking by using the expert patterns as a checklist. Rather, the cognitive behaviors were retrieved and controlled without effort. As a result of the exercises, the students followed the principles without thinking about them, freeing their limited conscious resources to focus on the novel aspects of the contest and to think more deeply and creatively at the board. The Soviet chess trainers in essence treated the thinking that the player does during a game as a behavior – something a player does with chess knowledge as opposed to the knowledge itself – and then developed exercises to train that thinking performance to conform to that of an expert.

THE EXPERT THEMES OF BATTLEFIELD THINKING

In order to apply traditional training techniques to non-observable cognitive behavior, there are two essential problems that must be solved. The first is to identify what is to be trained. After all, you cannot directly observe an expert's thoughts to see if there are any consistent patterns typical of most experts. The second is to reveal the student's thoughts during the training process – these must be made clear in order to provide focused corrective feedback. In this section, we describe how we approached the first problem, the development of the themes.

The themes need to be behavioral, albeit cognitive behaviors, that are at the right level of generality – neither too general nor too specific. By way of illustration, a very general thinking skill, which is applicable to a wide variety of situations, could be phrased "take a different perspective." A more specific instance, tailored to battlefield situations would be embodied in a rule such as "if the enemy does something you didn't expect, ask yourself what purpose he hopes to achieve by the act" – a behavior that inclines one to take the enemy's perspective. A yet more specific instance would be "when you see an enemy-emplaced obstacle, ask yourself why he put it in that exact location and what he intends to achieve by it." Recall that these thought acts – these cognitive behaviors – are not part of a large checklist that one continually seeks to proactively apply to the environment, rather they are thought habits that operate within complex structures (i.e., mental models) and must be triggered by some stimulus event. When the triggering event is very specific and identifiable such as an enemy-placed obstacle, the training may proceed readily but has a limited applicability. Achieving the desired effect of improving adaptive thinking in tactical situations would require training for an enormous number of such habits. At the other end of the spectrum, the mandate to "take a different perspective" is so vaguely triggered, and the act of taking the different perspective so broadly flexible, that a tremendous and thorough training effort must be required to achieve any lasting effect, especially when one considers the attention-demanding and focus-narrowing environment in which we seek to affect behavior. Thus, we believe the course taken in this effort to be the most efficacious one – to place the themes at just such a level of generality that they represent thinking behaviors that are as specific as possible while remaining relatively consistent over a wide range of tactical situations. Because of that consistency, the access and/or generation of plans for action will occur more quickly, and because of the specificity they will more likely operate in the desired conditions.

The themes were developed (Lussier, 1998; Ross & Lussier, 2000) by observations, interviews, and experiments in a wide variety of tactical conditions. A particularly significant contribution was made by research with very high-level tactical experts (Deckert, Entin, Entin, MacMillan, & Serfaty, 1994). The behaviors consist of eight "themes of the battlefield thinking" and have been determined to be common elements in the thinking framework or mental model of a number of successful tactical thinkers. Table 13.1 lists each of the themes and a brief description.

We believe the eight tactical thinking behaviors are a good set for the following reasons. First, the behaviors are characteristic of high-level expert tactical decision makers. On observing acknowledged experts, we can clearly see that these elements guide their actions and conclusions. Second, the concepts are familiar to most officers. They have been taught to do these things and generally are able to do them with some degree of proficiency. Third, observations of officers in realistic tactical performances indicate that they typically do not perform according to these norms; the more intense the exercise, the less likely are the officers to exhibit these behaviors. Fourth, the set describes thinking actions that can be loosely characterized as "what to think about" rather than "what to think." Fifth, and very importantly, the themes represent thinking behaviors that are relatively consistent over a wide range of tactical situations. Because of that consistency, the formation of automatic thought habits will occur more quickly at this level of generality than it will for the unique and specific aspects of each situation, that is, the inconsistencies of tactical thinking.

Ross et al. (2003) and Phillips, Shafer, Ross, Cox, and Shadrick (2005) later applied these eight themes to develop a cognitive model of tactical thinking expertise that was used in the analysis of tutorial sessions and tactical thinking mental models. Ross et al. (2003) noted that the "themes comprise the mental models that a learner must construct and learn to use in practice to achieve the status of an expert tactical thinker" (p. 9). Based on their analysis and previous research by Lussier (1998), these researchers expanded the eight themes to reflect stages of development from novice to expert.

It is not sufficient to simply memorize the eight tactical thinking themes and learn the questions that commanders must ask. In fact, as has been indicated, the eight themes are already well known in one form or another to

Table 13.1. *Themes of battlefield thinking.*

Theme	Description
Keep a focus on the mission and higher intent	Commanders must never lose sight of the purpose and results they are directed to achieve – even when unusual and critical events may draw them in a different direction.
Model a thinking enemy	Commanders must not forget that the adversaries are reasoning human beings intent on defeating them. It's tempting to simplify the battlefield by treating the enemy as static or simply reactive.
Consider effects of terrain	Commanders must not lose sight of the operational effects of the terrain on which they must fight. Every combination of terrain and weather has a significant effect on what can and should be done to accomplish the mission.
Use all assets available	Commanders must not lose sight of the synergistic effects of fighting their command as a combined arms team. They consider not only assets under their command, but also those that higher headquarters might bring to bear to assist them.
Consider timing	Commanders must not lose sight of the time they have available to get things done. Experts have a good sense of how much time it takes to accomplish various battlefield tasks. The proper use of that sense is a vital combat multiplier.
See the big picture	Commanders must remain aware of what is happening around them, how it might affect their operations, and how they can affect others' operations. A narrow focus on your own fight can get you or your higher headquarters blind-sided.
Visualize the battlefield	Commanders must be able to visualize a fluid and dynamic battlefield with some accuracy and use the visualization to their advantage. A commander who develops this difficult skill can reason proactively like no other. "Seeing the battlefield" allows the commander to anticipate and adapt quickly to changing situations.
Consider contingencies and remain flexible	Commanders must never lose sight of the old maxim that "no plan survives the first shot." Flexible plans and well-thought out contingencies result in rapid, effective responses under fire.

officers at the tactical level. The themes are not intended to be a checklist either. Difficulty with adaptive thinking is a performance problem, not a knowledge problem, and it will not be solved by the acquisition of additional declarative knowledge. What is needed is an effective method for training the *behaviors* that represent expert mental models.

DELIBERATE PRACTICE

In complex activities such as tactical decision making, expert performance levels cannot be attained without relying on the effortless access resulting from the acquisition of skilled performance. To develop the immediate accessibility characteristic of expert performance, it takes deliberate practice with opportunities for performance improvement (Ericsson, Krampe, & Tesch-Römer, 1993).

The cornerstone of developing expertise is the use of deliberate practice (or deliberate training). A main tenet of the deliberate practice framework is that expert performance is acquired during extended periods of intense training and preparation (Ericsson et al., 1993). Describing the structure of deliberate practice activities, Ericsson et al. write

> subjects ideally should be given explicit instructions about the best method and be supervised by a teacher to allow individualized diagnosis of errors, informative feedback, and remedial training.... Deliberate practice is a highly structured aim; the specific goal of which is to improve performance. Specific tasks are invented to overcome weaknesses, and performance is carefully monitored to provide cues for ways to improve it further. (pp. 367–368)

Traditionally, the training of tactical thinking in the U.S. Army has not employed deliberate practice concepts. Instead, officers are placed in realistic simulations and are asked to perform in a whole-task environment to the best of their ability. The maxim "train as you fight" has risen to such a level of familiarity in the U.S. Army that the value of the notion goes almost unquestioned. Yet studies of the development of expertise clearly indicate that "as you fight," meaning performing in fully realistic simulated battles, is neither the most effective nor efficient method of developing expertise. Such "performances" can help a novice become acquainted with applying military knowledge and can reinforce existing knowledge in an experienced person, but will not in and of themselves lead to the development of expertise. In many fields where expertise has been systematically studied (e.g., chess, music, sports), development beyond intermediate level requires large amounts of deliberate practice (Ericsson, et al., 1993) and good coaching (Charness, Krampe & Mayr, 1996; Ericsson, 1996).

How does deliberate practice differ from exercises based on full-scale realistic performance? Table 13.2 provides a description of some characteristics that distinguish deliberate practice (Lussier & Shadrick 2003; Ross & Lussier, 1999).

Table 13.2. *Characteristics of deliberate practice.*

Characteristic	Description
Repetition	Task performance is induced by presenting designed tasks rather than waiting for these task demands to occur naturally. A goal of deliberate practice is to develop skills that operate expertly and efficiently.
Focused feedback	Task performance is evaluated by the coach or learner during performance. There is a focus on elements of form, critical parts of how one does the task.
Immediacy of performance	After corrective feedback on task performance there is an immediate repetition so that the task can be performed to better match the processes of experts.
Stop and start	Because of the repetition and feedback, deliberate practice is typically seen as a series of short performances rather than a continuous flow.
Emphasis on difficult aspects	Deliberate practice will focus on more difficult aspects. For example, when flying an airplane normally only a small percentage of one's flight time is consumed by takeoffs and landings. In deliberate practice simulators, however, a large portion of the time will be involved in landings and takeoffs and relatively little in steady-level flight. Similarly, rarely occurring emergencies can be exercised regularly during deliberate practice.
Focus on areas of weakness	Deliberate practice can be tailored to the individual and focused on areas of weakness. During "train as you fight" performances the individual will avoid situations in which he knows he is weak, and rightly so as there is a desire to do one's best.
Conscious focus	Expert behavior is characterized by many aspects being performed with little conscious effort. During skill acquisition individuals acquire mental models that trigger immediate access to relevant actions and situational factors. In fact, if the expert had to attend to a few elements of the situation rather than the overall situation their performance is degraded. During deliberate practice the learner may consciously attend to a particular element of the situation in order to improve some special aspect of task performance. After a number of repetitions attending to the desired element to ensure that it is performed as desired, the learner resumes performance while focusing on the overall situation rather than the particular element.

(continued)

Table 13.2. *(continued)*

Characteristic	Description
Work versus play	Characteristically, deliberate practice feels more like work and is more effortful than casual performance. The motivation to engage in deliberate practice generally comes from a sense that one is improving in skill.
Active coaching	Typically a coach must be very active during deliberate practice, monitoring performance, assessing adequacy, and controlling the structure of training.

TLAC TRAINING

TLAC training develops adaptive expertise by using a series of highly complex and unpredictable tactical situations, or vignettes, that focus on a wide range of military problems. The training program utilizes the eight themes of battle-field thinking to develop a learner's mental model. The goal of the training is to reduce the amount of time to achieve a certain competency level in adaptive thinking behavior. The training uses cognitive drills to apply deliberate practice training concepts to thinking skills, and allows students to apply the behavioral themes to model their thinking, understandings, plans, visualizations, and decisions after expert thinking patterns (Lussier et al., 2003). Thus, the training utilizes a deliberate training approach to train thinking skills (cf., with Soviet chess training methods and deliberate practice).

We will now briefly describe the design of the TLAC training product. A more extensive description is available in *Think Like a Commander Prototype: Instructor's Guide to Adaptive Thinking* by Lussier et al. (2003). The central component of TLAC is a set of vignettes based on tactical situations drawn from a single over-arching scenario. Each vignette begins with a short – typically two to four minutes in duration – video that presents a complex tactical situation (see Figure 13.1).

While each vignette has no officially sanctioned solution, each does have a set of unique *indicators* that represent important considerations of expert battlefield commanders. These are the elements of the situation – the key features – that should play a role in the decision-maker's thinking. While the themes are consistent across all vignettes, each vignette has unique indicators that represent what an expert commander should consider in that specific situation if the commander were to engage in the thinking behavior represented by the theme. The indicators are designed to indicate to what extent each theme was represented in the student's thinking.

Once the presentation is completed, the student is asked to think about the situation presented and to list items that should be considered before making a

1. Student received training on the expert Themes of Battlefield Thinking and reviews and example.

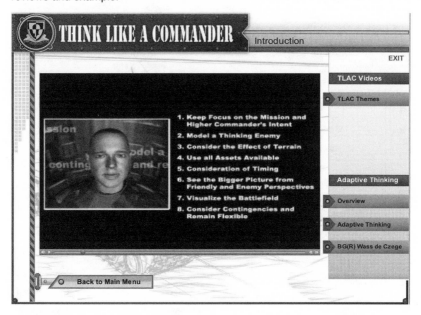

2. Students view and a 3-5 minute theme-based vignette that presents a complex and rapidly changing tactical situation.

FIGURE 13.1. Think Like a Commander (TLAC) training overview. (Example taken from *Captains in Command*, an instructor-less version of TLAC.)

3. Students are then asked apply their tactical knowledge to think adaptively and list their key considerations.

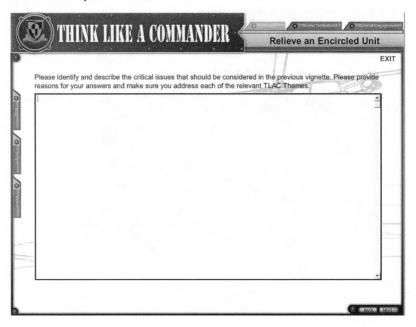

4. Students then view a 3D caoch discussing expert considerations pertaining to each of the battlefield thinking skills.

5. The students are prompted to evaluate their response based on an expert solution and respond to a coach's questions.

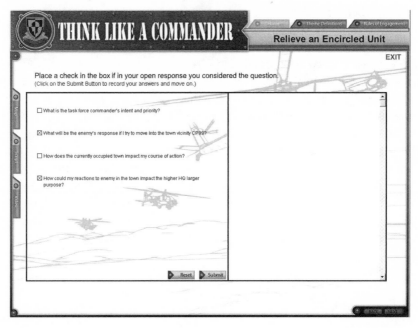

6. After covering each of the eight themes, the student is provided feedback to his or her responses.

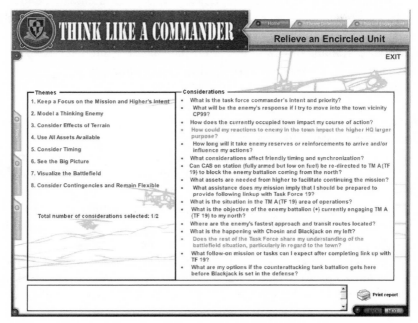

decision. Over time, the instructor decreases the amount of time students are allowed, forcing them to adapt to increased time pressure. After the students complete their lists, the instructor leads a discussion. Class members discuss the second- and third-order effects related to the actions suggested by the students. Students are required to discuss and/or defend considerations relevant to the vignette. Such coaching by a subject matter expert is a key part of the learning process to enable the student to develop expert habits.

In the final phase of each vignette, the students see the list of considerations that experts believed were important, along with the list they initially made, and they mark the indicators they have in common with the experts. Once the students rate their performances, they are given feedback linked to the general themes (e.g., 25% for the "Model a Thinking Enemy" theme). This individual feedback supplements and complements the feedback given by the instructor during the class discussion phase of the training. The students are then able to focus their future thinking on subsequent vignettes and place additional attention on themes for which they scored low.

Evaluation of the TLAC Training

The first empirical test of the method evaluated whether or not the theme-based method utilized in the TLAC training resulted in a significant change in performance (Shadrick & Lussier, 2002b). A group of Army captains participated in the training and completed seven vignettes. The design provided a way to determine if identification of key tactical considerations, a component of adaptive thinking, increases with repeated use of the training. The mean amount of considerations (i.e., indicators) identified by the captains for each of the vignettes is displayed in Figure 13.2. On average, student performance increased as training progressed. That is, students learned to identify significantly greater numbers of indicators as the training progressed.

Such findings are even more impressive in light of the increasing time constraints imposed by the instructors. This trend becomes clearer when performance is expressed as average number of considerations identified per unit of time. Figure 13.3 illustrates the average number of critical indicators identified as a function of the amount of time provided to participants to complete each vignette. For example, for vignette one, participants were allowed 15 minutes to complete the exercise and they identified an average of six considerations for the whole exercise, or a total of .41 considerations per minute. For vignette seven, participants were allotted 3 minutes to complete the exercise and participants identified just over 10 indicators, a rate of 3.4 considerations per minute.

Although Shadrick and Lussier (2002b) demonstrated significant performance gains via the TLAC training, it remains to be demonstrated that what is being learned is adaptable thinking. That is, of course, a question of construct validity. Construct validity is used to indicate that "scores are to be interpreted

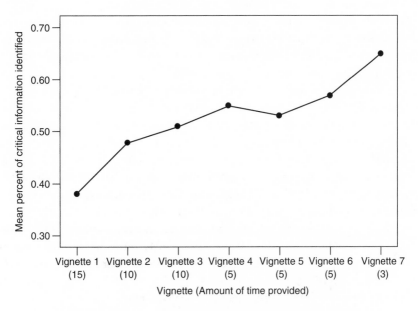

FIGURE 13.2. Mean percent of critical information identified.

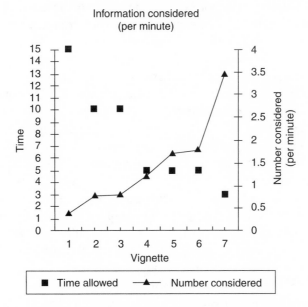

FIGURE 13.3. Information considered by time allowed.

as indicating standing on the psychological construct" (American Psychological Association, 1999, p. 174). One way to establish construct validity is by comparing measures of the given construct to other measures or indicators of performance (e.g., Bommer, Johnson, Rich, Podsakoff, & MacKenzie, 1995; Lance,

Teachout, & Donnelly, 1992; Vance, MacCallum, Coovert, & Hedge, 1988). If measures of the construct converge and diverge in a predicable manner, then the construct validity of the measures will be apparent (Cook & Campbell, 1979; Horan, 1987; McNamara & Horan, 1986).

Adaptable thinking is assumed to increase as a function of either length of experience, type of experience, or deliberate training (i.e., TLAC). If this is true, then higher-ranking individuals (used as a proxy for length of experience) should perform better on the TLAC measures. Likewise, those who have been in active combat zones (e.g., Iraq, Afghanistan) should also perform better, especially since it has recently been argued that these deployments are increasing the adaptivity of our leaders (e.g., Wong, 2004). Such patterns would support the construct validity of the TLAC approach.

Shadrick, Lussier, and Fultz (2007) collected data from officers of the ranks lieutenants, captains, majors, and lieutenant colonels from nine U.S. Army installations. Participants were categorized based on whether or not they had been deployed to Iraq (Operation Iraqi Freedom [OIF]) or Afghanistan (Operation Enduring Freedom [OEF]). The analysis revealed a statistically significant effect for deployment – officers with deployments to OIF/OEF identified significantly more indicators than officers without OIF/OEF deployments. The results also indicated a significant effect for rank – performance improved as a function of rank. Captains, majors, and lieutenant colonels all outperformed lieutenants significantly, but performed similarly to each other. Within each level of rank, there were significant effects for deployment status. This is illustrated in Figure 13.4.

Figure 13.4 also illustrates the differences for each group for those officers with and without deployments to OIF/OEF. For non-OIF/OEF officers, performance differences were clearly observed by order of rank. That is, captains performed better than lieutenants, majors better than captains, and lieutenant colonels better than majors. For deployed officers, the results are not as clearly observed. Lieutenants with OIF/OEF deployments performed slightly better than lieutenants with non-OIF/OEF deployments. However, captains, majors, and lieutenant colonels with OIF/OEF deployments performed noticeably better than those without. The performance of the three groups converged. This pattern of results is consistent with the proposition that certain "crucible experiences" (Wong, 2004) can accelerate the development of adaptable thinking that would otherwise require long experience.

In establishing the construct validity, Shadrick, Lussier, and Fultz (2007) also developed baseline measures of performance for officers with and without deployment experience. Figure 13.5 illustrates the baseline measures for percent of indicators identified for non-OIF/OEF captains without training, deployed captains without training, and a TLAC training group. As the figure indicates, the average percent of indicators identified for the training group was higher than the baseline measures. In fact, captains receiving the training (who had *not* been deployed in either OIF or OEF) outscored even a sample of lieutenant

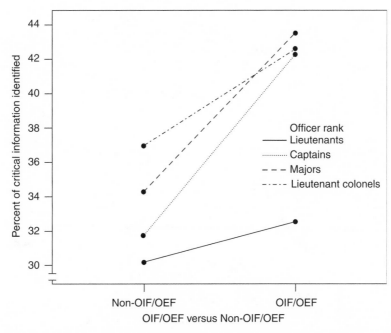

FIGURE 13.4. Mean percent of critical information identified for each rank by deployment.

colonels *with* OIF/OEF deployment experience but no adaptive thinking training. Captains trained using the TLAC training program show levels of adaptive thinking consistent with officers of more senior rank. Note, of course, that we are not claiming that we measure all that is learned during a deployment, but it is compelling evidence of a capability to accelerate learning in this domain. The main point here is that the experiential learning that takes place over a long period in the real environment can be gained in a much shorter time using a more deliberate focused training approach and research-based scenario development, such as those employed in the theme-based method.

The TLAC training has met the challenge of teaching the underlying structures or themes that can relate to the varying and complex job demands and stresses encountered by military commanders. Furthermore, it has been shown that the training does train adaptive thinking skills. What is still unknown is whether or not the training can be transferred to tasks outside of the vignettes. Transfer of training can be defined as the degree to which trainees effectively apply the skills, knowledge, and/or attitudes gained in a training context to a new context (Baldwin & Ford, 1988). Transfer thus occurs when an individual applies previously learned knowledge to solve a novel problem.

Shadrick, Crabb, Lussier, and Burke (2007) attempted to determine if TLAC training demonstrates transfer by investigating how training affected students' performance in the Armor Captains Career Course (ACCC). Specifically, the

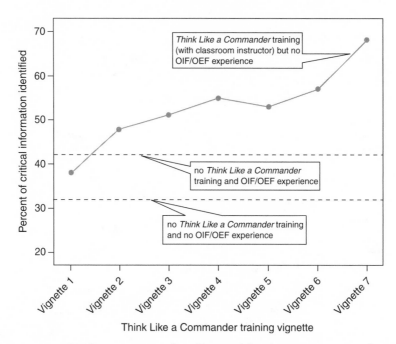

FIGURE 13.5. Baseline measures of performance for the mean percent of critical information identified for each group of captains.

researchers compared the performance of students who received TLAC training with those who did not in the writing of a company-level operational order (OPORD). This can be considered a *far* transfer task with relatively *low* surface similarity to the scenarios used during training (cf., Gick & Holyoak, 1987). Laboratory research has shown that transferring knowledge from one context to a new context can be very difficult, particularly for far transfer with low surface similarity (e.g., Gick & Holyoak, 1980).

Pre-test scores indicated that there were no significant differences between the groups before TLAC training began. Post-test scores, however, indicated that there were significant differences between the groups – groups that had undergone the training outscored those without the training but that received traditional tactical decision-making games. In fact, there was strong evidence that the training compensated for areas of weakness in certain aspects of the course.

APPLYING THE THEME-BASED TRAINING METHOD
TO CRISIS RESPONSE TRAINING FOR MILITARY
AND CIVILIAN ORGANIZATIONS

The theme-based method has been successful in training adaptive thinking skills in the U.S. Army. The method provides a way of providing a learner with a mental model that can be used during decision making – whether in a military setting or in a civilian environment. To examine the generalizability of the theme-based method, training was developed for civilian and military crisis response training.

Crisis response operations require that relevant local, state, and federal agencies effectively collaborate with one another. However, recent events such as Hurricane Katrina have made it clear that attained levels of collaboration are often sub-optimal. Effective interagency collaboration in crisis response efforts is a difficult undertaking for several reasons. First is the inevitably different manner in which specialized terms are developed. Quite simply, each organization tends to have its own culture and "language," thereby making clear and concise communication difficult. Second is the different, and sometimes contradictory, standing operating procedures (SOPs) employed by different organizations (Dixon, 2006). Third is the fact that the dynamic nature of crisis response situations dictates that leadership responsibilities often rotate throughout the course of a mission. (For example, a crisis may initially appear to be an accidental explosion, which would be led by the local fire departments. Subsequently it may be determined to be a deliberate act, which would be led by law enforcement agencies. Finally, there is the inevitable cleanup of an explosion event, which would be led by other agencies, such as the Departments of Environmental Management or Natural Resources.) Fourth is the distributed nature of expertise: Any interagency effort requires the understanding of expertise that is scattered across individuals with different specialist backgrounds. Most important, however, is the lack of opportunity to train and practice these activities.

To address the need to develop training for crisis response, a cognitive task analysis (utilizing the Flexible Method for Cognitive Task Analysis [Shadrick, Lussier, & Hinkle, 2005]) was conducted on the domain of crisis response. The distributed nature of expertise in crisis response situations can be seen by the makeup of the expert sample. The cognitive task analysis included experts from different organizations, including the Army National Guard, Weapons of Mass Destruction Civil Support Teams, the Department of Environmental Management, the Department of Transportation, the Department of Homeland Security, Emergency Management Agencies, fire rescue, and local, county, and state police among others. Care was taken to sample experts from both rural and urban agencies, because such agencies differ greatly in terms of available resources and response styles.

Based on the cognitive task analysis, a list of behavioral themes that consistently appeared throughout the interviews was developed along with a series of high-level training scenarios. The scenarios included events that experts judged likely to occur in the near future, but ones for which their respective agencies were particularly ill-prepared to handle. When designing the scenarios, care was taken to ensure that each scenario required extensive coordination among multiple civilian groups. In addition, the scenarios were dynamic, requiring individuals to critically analyze each situation to determine whether or not it was an accident, natural disaster, or homeland security incident. For each scenario, a set of behavioral indicators that could be used to assess performance in each training scenario was developed. These indicators serve as benchmarks of expert performance unique to a given scenario.

Following the capturing of distributed expertise, the resulting information provided the content for a prototype crisis response training program. The program was designed to train Army leaders and their civilian counterparts in the crisis response behaviors required for effective performance in homeland security and natural disaster scenarios using the theme-based method.

Content validation procedures are used to evaluate how well important aspects of a domain are represented. Research in test content validation has also found a correlation between these indices of content validity and criterion validity (Carrier, Dalessio, & Brown, 1990; Dubois & Dubois, 2000). The leveraging of such procedures is arguably even more important in tasks wherein the costs of inferior performance are high; that is, when improper training can lead to damaged property or lost lives. Schaefer, Shadrick, and Beaubien (2007) conducted a content validation of the training program. The results strongly support the content validity of the training program. In examining the behavioral themes, experts unanimously viewed them as essential.

The training has been implemented in both military and civilian organizations. Schaefer, Shadrick, and Crabb (in preparation) have shown that the training produced gains in performance similar to those observed in the TLAC training program. That is, participant performance improved as they complete the training exercise. Moreover, the qualitative participant feedback gathered so far is promising. Many of the comments elicited from participants focused upon how realistic the scenarios were (e.g., several participants stated that "these scenarios could easily happen"). Perhaps the most beneficial aspect of the training, however, is the interagency discussions that take place after a scenario has been assessed at the individual level. Many participants highly praised this aspect of the training. For example, participants stated that "the training opened my eyes to areas in which I have little experience" and "the discussion ... encouraged all to think outside the box."

CONCLUSION

Contemporary Army operations require high levels of adaptive performance in Army officers. The well-documented need to develop adaptive leaders remains an area of focus to the U.S. Army senior leadership (Harvey & Schoomaker, 2006). There is a corresponding need for a more adaptive civilian workforce. The theme-based training method was developed to address the need to develop an effective method for training complex, cognitive skills.

Rouse and Morris (1986) suggest that learners must be provided with a mental model for training to be most effective and generalizable. Officer mental models – and hence, adaptability – are typically developed over the course of a long career, which is obviously inefficient from a time and resource standpoint. The theme-based method utilized in the TLAC training hastens the development of adaptability by training officers to better operate their mental models based upon behaviors exhibited by acknowledged experts. This type of training also provides the officers with the opportunity to apply the expert patterns to their own thinking process across a range of dynamic situations. In so doing, the officers become able to more rapidly assess tactical situations and identify the key features and tactical considerations more thoroughly, in less time, and in a more deliberate, controlled fashion.

The application of deliberate instructional methods is equally important to the theme-based method and TLAC training program. Deliberate practice (or, more appropriately, deliberate training) requires the individual to apply the behavioral themes to a wide range of situations through cognitive drills (e.g., vignettes). The drills pair repetitive application of the themes across different situations with coaching and feedback. Such deliberate practice maximizes cognitive adaptation and increases performance (Ericsson, Krampe, & Tesch-Römer, 1993). Unfortunately, the Army has not routinely applied deliberate practice training methods to instill cognitive skills (Lussier et al., 2003). Rather, the Army has focused upon experiential learning and live, virtual, and constructive simulations.

Taken as a whole, results have supported the effectiveness of the theme-based training method, which uses behavioral themes and deliberate training techniques to develop cognitive skills in training participants. The theme-based method has been implemented as a training tool in the development of cognitive behaviors. The method has also been shown to improve performance in anti-terrorism, leadership, and crisis response situations and can be applied to a wide range of other cognitive skills.

REFERENCES

Alburt, L. (2003). *Secrets of the Russian chess masters: Fundamentals of the game,* Volume 1. W. W. Norton & Company.

American Psychological Association. (1999). *Standards for educational and psychological testing.* Washington, DC: Author.

Army Training and Leader Development Panel. (2001) Officer study: Report to the Army. Washington, DC: Department of the Army.

Baldwin, T. T., & Ford, J. K. (1988). Transfer of training: A review and directions for future research. *Personnel Psychology, 41,* 63–105.

Barnes, J. E. (2005, October 31). An open mind for the new army. *U.S. News & World Report, 139*(16), 72–74.

Bommer, W. H., Johnson, J. L., Rich, G. A., Podsakoff, P. M., & MacKenzie, S. B. (1995). On the interchangeability of objective and subjective measures of employee performance: A meta-analysis. *Personnel Psychology, 48,* 587–605.

Brophy, S., Hodge, L., & Bransford, J. (2004). *Work in progress – adaptive expertise: Beyond applying academic knowledge.* Paper presented at the 34th ASEE/IEEE Frontiers in Education Conference, Savannah, GA.

Brown, F. J. (2000). *Preparation of leaders* (IDA No. D2382). Washington, DC: Institute for Defense Analysis.

Carrier, M. R., Dalessio, A. T., & Brown, S. H. (1990). Correspondence between estimates of content and criterion-related validity values. *Personnel Psychology, 43* (1), 85–100.

Charness, N., Krampe, R. T., & Mayr, U. (1996). The role of practice and coaching in entrepreneurial skill domains: An international comparison of life-span chess skill acquisition. In K. A. Ericsson (Ed.), *The road to excellence: The acquisition of expert performance in the arts, sciences, sports, and games* (pp. 51–80). Mahwah, NJ: Lawrence Erlbaum Associates.

Charney, D. H., & Reder, L. M. (1987). Initial skill learning: An analysis of how elaborations facilitate the three components. In P. Morris (Ed.), *Modelling cognition* (pp. 135–165). Chichester, UK: John Wiley & Sons.

Cook, T. D., & Campbell, D. T. (1979). *Quasi-experimentation: Design and analysis issues for field settings.* Boston: Houghton Mifflin Company.

Congressional Report No. 109-396 (2006). *A failure of initiative final report of the bipartisan committee to investigate the preparation for and response to Hurricane Katrina.* Washington DC: Government Printing Office.

Crawford, V. M., Schlager, M., Toyama, U., Riel, M., & Vahey, P. (2005, April). *Characterizing adaptive expertise in science teaching.* Paper presented at the Annual Conference of the American Educational Research Association, Montreal, Canada.

Deckert, J. C., Entin, E. B., Entin, E. E., MacMillan, J., & Serfaty, D. (1994). *Military decision-making expertise* (ARI Research Note 96–15). Fort Leavenworth, KS: U.S. Army.

Dixon, R. G. (2006). *Systems thinking for integrated operations: Introducing a systematic approach to operational art for disaster relief.* Fort Leavenworth, KS: School of Advanced Military Studies (DTIC No. ADA448434).

Dubois, D. A., & Dubois, C. L. Z. (2000). An alternate method for content-oriented test construction: An empirical evaluation. *Journal of Business and Psychology, 15*(2), 197–213.

Dostal, B. C. (2002). *Adaptive leaders and the IBCT: Initiative within intent.* Retrieved September 27, 2005, from http://www.globalsecurity.org/military/library/report/.

Druckman, D., & Bjork, R. A. (1994). Transfer: Training for performance. In D. Druckman & R. A. Bjork (Eds.), *Learning, remembering, believing* (pp. 25–56). Washington, DC: National Academy Press.

Dvoretsky, M. (1996). *Positional play.* London: Batsford, B.T., Ltd.

(1997). *Secrets of chess training.* London: Batsford, B.T., Ltd.

Ellis, S., & Davidi, I. (2005). After-event reviews: Drawing lessons from successful and failed experience. *Journal of Applied Psychology, 90*(5), 857–871.

Ericsson, K. A. (1996). The acquisition of expert performance: An introduction to some of the issues. In K. A. Ericsson (Ed.), *The road to excellence: The acquisition of expert performance in the arts and sciences, sports, and games* (pp. 1–50). Mahwah, NJ: Lawrence Erlbaum Associates.

Ericsson, K. A., Krampe, R. T., & Tesch-Römer, C. (1993). The role of deliberate practice in the acquisition of expert performance. *Psychological Review, 100,* 363–406.

Fallows, J. (2006). Declaring victory. *The Atlantic, 298*(2), 60–75.

Feltovich, P. J., Spiro, R. J., & Coulson, R. L. (1993). Learning, teaching, and testing for complex conceptual understanding. In N. Frederiksen & I. Bejar (Eds.), *Test theory for a new generation of tests* (pp. 181–217). Hillsdale, NJ: Lawrence Erlbaum Associates.

Freakley, B. C. (2004, April 1). Commandant's note: Training adaptive leaders and units. *Infantry Magazine, 2,* 1–2.

Gick, M., & Holyoak, K. (1980). Analogical problem solving. *Cognitive Psychology, 12,* 306–365.

(1987). The cognitive basis of knowledge transfer. In S. M. Cromier & J. D. Hagman (Eds.), *Transfer of learning: Contemporary research and applications* (pp. 9–46). San Diego, CA: Academic Press Inc.

Goodwin, G. P., & Johnson-Laird, P. N. (2005). Reasoning about relations. *Psychological Review, 112*(2), 468–493.

Harvey, F. J, & Schoomaker, P. J. (2006). *A statement to the posture of the United States Army 2006.* Washington, DC: Office of the Chief of Staff, U.S. Army, Executive Office of the Headquarters Staff Group.

Hatano, G. (1982). Cognitive consequences of practice in culture specific procedural skills. *The Quarterly Newsletter of the Laboratory of Comparative Human Cognition, 4,* 15–18.

Hatano, G., & Inagaki, K. (1986). Two courses of expertise. In H. Stevenson, J. Azuma, & K. Hakuta (Eds.), *Child development and education in Japan* (pp. 262–272). New York: W. H. Freeman.

Hatano, G., & Oura, Y. (2003). Commentary: Reconceptualizing school learning using insight from expertise research. *Educational Researcher, 32*(8), 26–29.

Holyoak, K. J. (1991). Symbolic connectionism: Toward third-generation theories of expertise. In K. A. Ericsson & J. Smith (Eds.), *Towards a general theory of expertise* (pp. 301–335). Cambridge: Cambridge University Press.

Horan, J. J. (1987, April). *Paradigms for establishing experimental construct validity in counseling and psychotherapy.* Invited address at the annual meeting of the American Educational Research Association, Washington, DC.

Johnson, D. (2005). Cold war chess. *Prospect Magazine, 111.* Retrieved from http://www.prospect-magazine.co.uk/article_details.php?id=6901.

Johnson-Laird, P. (1983). *Mental models.* Cambridge, MA: Harvard University Press.

Johnston, J. C., Leibrecht, B. C., Holder, L. D., Coffey, R. S, & Quinker, K. A. (2002). *Training for future operations: Digital leaders' transformation insights* (ARI Special Report No. 53). Alexandria, VA: U.S. Army Research Institute for the Behavioral and Social Sciences.

Kozlowski, S. W. J. (1998). Training and developing adaptive teams: Theory, principles, and research. In J. A. Cannon-Bowers & E. Salas (Eds.), *Decision making under stress: Implications for training and simulation* (pp. 115–153). Washington, DC: American Psychological Association.

Lance, C. E., Teachout, M. S., & Donnelly, T. M. (1992). Specification of the criterion construct space: An application of hierarchical confirmatory factor analysis. *Journal of Applied Psychology, 77*(4), 437–452.

Lussier, J. W. (1998, May). *Developing expertise in battlefield thinking: Models of battlefield thinking.* (Unpublished briefing.) Fort Leavenworth, KS: U.S. Army Research Institute for the Behavioral and Social Sciences.

Lussier, J. W., & Shadrick, S. B. (2006, April). *Integrating new technologies into warfighting operations.* Paper presented at the 13th ROK-US Defense Analysis Seminar, Seoul, South Korea.

Lussier, J. W., Ross, K. G., & Mayes, B. (2000, December). *Coaching techniques for adaptive thinking.* Paper presented at the Interservice/Industry Training, Simulation, and Education Conference, Orlando, FL.

Lussier, J. W., Shadrick, S. B., & Prevou, M. (2003). *Think Like a Commander prototype: Instructor's guide to adaptive thinking* (Research Product 2003-02). Alexandria, VA: U.S. Army Research Institute for the Behaviour and Social Sciences.

McNamara, K., & Horan, J. J. (1986). Experimental construct validity in the evaluation of cognitive and behavioral treatments for depression. *Journal of Counseling Psychology, 33*, 23–30.

Norman, D. A. (1983). Some observations on mental models. In D. Gentner & A. L. Stevens (Eds.), *Mental models* (pp. 7–14). Hillsdale, NJ: Lawrence Erlbaum Associates.

(1988). *The design of everyday things.* New York: Doubleday.

Phillips, J. K., Shafer, J., Ross, K. G., Cox, D. A., & Shadrick, S. B. (2005). *Behaviorally anchored rating scales for the assessment of tactical thinking mental models.* Alexandria, VA: U.S. Army Research Institute for the Behavioral and Social Sciences.

Pulakos, E. D., Arad, S., Donovan, M. A., & Plamondon, K. E. (2000). Adaptability in the workplace: Development of a taxonomy of adaptive performance. *Journal of Applied Psychology, 85*(4), 612–624.

Ross, K. G. (2000). Training adaptive leaders: Are we ready? *Field Artillery Journal,* Sept.–Oct., 15–19.

Ross, K. G., & Lussier, J. W. (1999). A training solution for adaptive battlefield performance. Proceedings of the 1999 Interservice/Industry Training, Simulation, and Education Conference, Orlando, FL.

Ross, K. G., & Lussier, J. W. (2000). *Adaptive thinking seminar.* (Available from the Armored Forces Research Unit, U.S. Army Research Institute, Building 2423, 121 Morande St., Fort Knox, KY 40121–4141.)

Ross, K. G., Battaglia, D. A., Hutton, R. J. B., & Crandall, B. (2003). *Development of an instructional model for tutoring tactical thinking* (Final Technical Report for Subcontract No. SHAI-COMM-01; Prime Contract No. DASW01-01-C-0039 submitted to Storrler Henke Associates INC., San Mateo, CA). Fairborn, OH: Klein Associates.

Rouse, W. B., & Morris, N. M. (1986). On looking into the black box: Prospects and limits in the search for mental models. *Psychological Bulletin, 100*(3), 349–363.

Schaefer, P., Shadrick, S. B., & Crabb, B. (in preparation). *Assessment of the red cape: Crisis action planning and execution training.* Alexandria, VA: U.S. Army Research Institute for the Behavioral and Social Sciences.

Serfaty, D., MacMillan, J., Entin, E. E., & Entin, E. B. (1997). The decision-making expertise of battle commanders. In C. Zsambok & G. Klein (Eds.), *Naturalistic decision making* (pp. 233–246). Mahwah, NJ: Lawrence Erlbaum Associates.

Shadrick, S. B. (2004). *Think like a commander: Mission to Azerbaijan.* (Available from the Armored Forces Research Unit, U.S. Army Research Institute, Building 2423, 121 Morande St., Fort Knox, KY 40121–4141.)

Shadrick, S. B., Crabb, B. T., Lussier, J. W., & Burke, J. T. (2007). Positive transfer of adaptive battlefield thinking skills (ARI Research Report 1873). Alexandria, VA: U.S. Army Research Institute for the Behavior and Social Sciences.

Shadrick, S. B., & Lussier, J. W. (2002a). *Think Like a Commander: Captain's Edition – Prototype 1.0.* (Available from the Armored Forces Research Unit, U.S. Army Research Institute, Building 2423, 121 Morande St., Fort Knox, KY 40121–4141.)

(2002b, December). *The application of Think Like a Commander in the Armor Captains Career Course.* Presented at the Interservice/Industry Training, Simulation and Education Conference, Orlando, FL.

Shadrick, S. B., Lussier, J. W., & Fultz, C. (2007). Accelerating the development of adaptive performance: Validating the Think Like a Commander training (ARI Research Report 1868). Alexandria, VA: U.S. Army Research Institute for the Behavior and Social Sciences.

Shadrick, S. B., Lussier, J. W., & Hinkle, R. (2005). *Concept development for future domains: A new method of knowledge elicitation* (Technical Report 1167). Alexandria, VA: U.S. Army Research Institute for the Behavioral and Social Sciences.

Shadrick, S. B., Schaefer, P. S., & Beaubien, J. (2007). *Development and content validation of crisis response training package red cape: Crisis action planning and execution.* Alexandria, VA: U.S. Army Research Institute for the Behavioral and Social Sciences.

Smith, E. M., Ford, J. K., & Kozlowski, S. W. J. (1997). Building adaptive expertise: Implications for training design. In M. A. Quinones & A. Dudda (Eds.), *Training for a rapidly changing workplace: Applications of psychological research* (pp. 89–119). Washington, DC: American Psychological Association.

Toomey, C. J. (2001, May). The adaptive engineer leader. *Engineer: The Professional Bulletin for Army Engineers, 5,* 49–51.

Vance, R. J., MacCallum, R. C., Coovert, M. D., & Hedge, J. W. (1988). Construct validity of multiple job performance measures using confirmatory factor analysis. *Journal of Applied Psychology, 73*(1), 74–80.

Wong, L. (2004). *Developing adaptive leaders: The crucible experience of Operation Iraqi Freedom.* Carlisle Barracks, PA: Strategic Studies Institute of the U.S. Army War College.

14

Structuring the Conditions of Training to Achieve Elite Performance: Reflections on Elite Training Programs and Related Themes in Chapters 10–13

ROBERT A. BJORK

There can be arguments as to what training revolution we are in the midst of currently (Chatham, Chapters 2 and 10; Hunt, Chapter 5), but what does not seem debatable is that our society now confronts social, technological, and cultural conditions that require a revolution in training. Personnel in industry, health, military, and the public sector have more to learn in less time. Increasingly sophisticated and rapidly changing electronic and other technologies impose additional training demands at the same time that they offer the potential to make training more effective and more portable. The chapters in this section focus on these problems from the perspective of the military, which has always tried to be at the cutting edge of research and knowledge of learning and mastery. The United States Army, for example, requested that the National Academy of Sciences commission a National Research Council Committee study on the techniques for the enhancement of human performance (Druckman & Bjork, 1991, 1994; Druckman & Swets, 1988).

From the perspective of the military, changes in technology, types of wars, and the social/cultural contexts of warfare require that training must continue after military personnel are deployed, including in combat zones. Such changes also require that an elite performer possess a high level of interpersonal and cultural skills and sensitivities, as well as a high level of traditional warfighter skills. To optimize training, given these changes and challenges, requires new perspectives and new technologies, as well as capitalizing on progress in the science of learning.

BASIC CONSIDERATIONS IN STRUCTURING TRAINING TO ACHIEVE ELITE PERFORMANCE

My charge is to comment on the four chapters that comprise the section of this volume on the training of elite performers in the armed forces. The following considerations provide a framework for my comments.

The Need to Distinguish Between Learning and Performance

One of the most time-honored distinctions in research on learning is the distinction between learning and performance. Basically, what we can observe during training is *performance*, whereas *learning* – conceived of as relatively permanent changes in cognitive, perceptual, and motor representations that will support long-term retention and transfer of knowledge and skills to the post-training contexts that are the target of training – must be inferred. The distinction is important because performance during training is often an unreliable guide to whether the desired learning has actually happened. Considerable learning can happen across periods when performance is not improving and, conversely, little or no learning can happen across periods when performance is improving markedly.

Learning Without Performance

That learning can happen without improvements in performance was demonstrated decades ago by both animal- and human-learning researchers. Latent-learning experiments with animals (e.g., Tolman & Honzik, 1930), for example, demonstrated that a period of free exploration, without systematic changes in performance, could nonetheless result in considerable learning as evidenced by an animal's performance once reinforcement was introduced. With humans, research on the acquisition of motor skills demonstrated that training trials structured so that a buildup of fatigue prevented any further improvement in performance nonetheless resulted in further learning, as evidenced by subsequent performance after fatigue had dissipated (see Adams & Reynolds, 1954).

Such findings led learning theorists – whatever their other arguments and differences – not only to distinguish, empirically, between learning and performance, but also to distinguish, theoretically, between *habit strength* (learning) and *momentary action potential* (performance), to use Hull's (1943) terms, for example, or between *habit strength* and *response strength*, to use Estes's (1955) terms. More recently, Elizabeth Bjork and I have resurrected such a distinction in the context of a "new theory of disuse" (Bjork & Bjork, 1992), which distinguishes between the *storage strength* of the memory representation corresponding to a skill or knowledge, versus the *retrieval strength* of that representation. Storage strength is assumed to reflect how entrenched or interassociated the memory representation is with respect to related knowledge and skills that exist in memory, whereas retrieval strength is assumed to reflect the current activation or accessibility of that representation, which is a product of factors such as current situational cues and recency. Importantly, current performance is presumed to be solely a product of current retrieval strength, but storage strength acts to retard the loss of retrieval strength and enhance the gain of retrieval strength, given practice or further study.

Performance Without Learning

That the converse is true as well – namely, that little or no learning, as measured by long-term post-training retention or transfer, can result from training during which there are pronounced improvements in performance – is demonstrated by a wide range of more recent studies (for reviews, see Bjork, 1994, 1999 ; Christina & Bjork, 1991; Schmidt & Bjork, 1992). Manipulations such as blocking or massing practice on a given subtask of what is to be learned can result in rapid apparent learning, but not support post-training retention or transfer, whereas conditions that introduce difficulties and challenges for learners, slowing the rate of apparent learning, can optimize retention and transfer (see Shea & Morgan, 1979 ; Simon & Bjork, 2001). Such "desirable difficulties" (Bjork, 1994a, 1994b) include spacing rather than massing study sessions; interleaving rather than blocking practice on separate topics or tasks; varying how instructional materials and tasks are presented or illustrated; reducing feedback; and using tests rather than presentations as learning events.

It is important to emphasize, first, that many of the difficulties one can create for learners are undesirable during learning, at the end of learning, and forever after, and second, that desirable difficulties can become undesirable if such difficulties cannot be overcome. Such difficulties are desirable because responding to them engages processes that foster the understanding, linkages, and elaboration that support long-term retention and transfer, but they become undesirable if learners, by virtue of their prior learning and current motivation, are unable to overcome those difficulties. Having learners generate to-be-learned skills and knowledge, for example, versus presenting such knowledge and skills for observation and study, is a desirable difficulty, but if learners are not in a position to succeed at such generation, it can become an undesirable difficulty (see McNamara, Kintsch, Songer, & Kintsch, 1996). For that reason and perhaps others, it becomes a matter for research to determine whether and when such difficulties should be introduced. (See Wulf & Shea, 2002 , for evidence that the procedures for optimizing simple skills and complex skills may differ.)

The Potential for Instructors and Learners to Be Misled

That performance during training is an unreliable index of learning, as measured by post-training retention and transfer, has important implications. To the extent that instructors and trainees interpret current performance as learning, instructors become susceptible to choosing less effective conditions of training over more effective conditions, and trainees become susceptible to preferring – and evaluating more highly – poorer instruction over better instruction. Said differently, to the extent that current retrieval strength is assumed to reflect storage strength – that is, learning – instructors and learners are susceptible to being misled. As several of the chapters in this section stress, especially the chapters by Chatham (Chapter 10) and by Schreiber,

Bennett, Colegrove, Portrey, Greschke, and Bell (Chapter 11), good assessment and measurement of performance is critical to the evaluation of training, but good measures of performance in the post-training contexts that are the target of training are usually lacking. Additionally, when such measures do exist, they may not get back to training personnel at all or not in a way that they can be related to a given trainee's conditions of training.

Without such post-training assessments and measures, it is natural to assume that performance *during* training indexes learning and provides a basis for distinguishing between and choosing among instructional practices. In fact, that assumption is so compelling that it is unlikely to even be questioned. As a consequence, however, the potential exists for training personnel to be shaped into choosing conditions of training that make performance improve rapidly and not choosing the kind of desirable difficulties that might enhance performance by military personnel when it matters most – that is, after trainees are deployed. The motivation to choose conditions that enhance trainees' performance – and apparent learning – is fueled by another consideration: Individuals responsible for the conditions of training are likely themselves to be evaluated by the performance of their trainees during training.

The problem can be exacerbated when trainees' evaluations of their ongoing training are used as a basis for choosing among alternative conditions of training. There is evidence from laboratory studies (see Kornell & Bjork, 2008; Simon & Bjork, 2001) that learners, too – in predicting their future performance on a post-training criterion test – are fooled by their own current performance, even when that performance is a product of local conditions, such as blocking and massing of practice, that result in poor long-term retention and transfer. Aside from the potential for trainees to evaluate less-than-optimal training very highly, training conditions that are made artificially easy – by keeping conditions of practice constant and predictable, for example, or by massing practice on a given subtask of a more complex task – can create illusions of comprehension and competence. As my colleagues and I have emphasized elsewhere (e.g., Bjork, 1999; Jacoby, Bjork, & Kelley, 1994), there is something far worse than individuals not possessing critical skills and knowledge – namely, not possessing such skills and knowledge, but thinking they do. Illusions of comprehension and competence become especially hazardous in settings, such as military settings, where mistakes and miscommunication can be so costly not only to one's self, but also to so many others.

The Potential to Misunderstand the Meaning and Role of Errors

As I emphasized in a final epilogue (Bjork, 1994b) to the third of three reports by a National Research Council Committee on Techniques for the Enhancement of Human Performance (Druckman & Bjork, 1994), a committee commissioned by the National Academy of Sciences on behalf of the United States

Army, one of the "institutional impediments to effective training" in military settings is a misunderstanding of the meaning and role of errors. To the extent that optimizing training requires introducing desirable difficulties and simulating, during training, the complexity, variety, and unpredictability of combat conditions, errors and mistakes by trainees during training will be frequent. Within military cultures, however, there remains a tendency to view errors and mistakes as evidence of a less-than-optimal training, rather than as opportunities for learning and a necessary component of maximally effective training. Expressions such as "we do it right the first time" and "we don't practice mistakes" reflect and contribute to that tendency.

The meaning of errors can be misunderstood, too. Within both the military and our society more generally, in my view, differences in innate ability between individuals tends to be over-appreciated, whereas the power of training, effort, and experience tends to be under-appreciated. As a consequence, differences in individual performance tend to be over-attributed to differences in innate ability – meaning that errors, rather than being interpreted as an opportunity for learning, are seen as evidence of the inadequacies of trainees, trainers, or both.

A final important consideration is that efforts to avoid errors and mistakes being made during training – by providing artificial supports, such as creating constant and predictable conditions; providing cues that would not be present in actual combat; encouraging imitation; and so forth – will *not* tend to eliminate such errors being made when such supports are absent. Rather, the effect can be to delay such errors being made until after training, possibly in circumstances where such errors really matter.

Top Gun, the National Training Center (NTC), and Similar Programs as Counterexamples

Having said that there is a "tendency" in the military to misunderstand the meaning and role of errors, I must now hasten to add that there are striking exceptions to that generalization. The fact that people learn by making and correcting mistakes is not only well understood by many individuals in the military, training programs such as the Navy's Top Gun program and Army's NTC have provided among the most compelling, real-world examples of that principle. General Paul Gorman, now retired, who served as a consultant to the National Research Council Committee on Techniques for the Enhancement of Human Performance (see Druckman & Bjork, 1994), and who was a principal architect of the NTC, provides an especially good example of a key individual who understands, rather than misunderstands, the meaning and role of errors during training. (For more on General Gorman, see Chatham, Chapter 2.)

After-Action Reviews

If people are to learn by making and correcting errors during training, then it is crucial that performance is measured in a rigorous and accurate way, that there be feedback – bottom up as well as top down – to individuals and units that is informative, and that there is an opportunity to discuss and analyze why errors were made. To the military's credit, after-action reviews (AARs) typically have all of those properties.

The Prevalence of Forgetting and Its Role in Relearning

Finally, before turning to comments on the individual chapters in this section, I cannot resist chiming in on the discussion (Chatham, Chapter 2; Hunt, Chapter 5) on the importance of understanding the nature of forgetting and the interaction of forgetting and learning. Chatham rightly emphasizes the importance of acknowledging that skills and knowledge, once apparently acquired, will often not remain accessible over time – that is, they will be forgotten – and often at a rapid rate. It is, in fact, a fundamental – and even adaptive – property of human memory that skills and knowledge, with disuse, become inaccessible.

Forgetting, of course, is often frustrating to us, but it is arguably as important to our day-to-day functioning as is remembering. To be efficient requires that we continually update procedures, facts, and episodes in our memories: We need to remember, for example, how the current version of a given software program works, or how it works on a new computer, not how the old program worked on our old computer; we need to remember current names and numbers, not the names and numbers they replaced; we need – as military personnel – to remember the details of a current military engagement or how a new piece of military hardware works, not the details of an earlier and similar engagement, or how the old hardware worked; we need to remember where we parked the car today, not yesterday or a week ago; and on and on. Any efficient information-processing system, whether living or non-living, needs some means to set aside or erase information that is no longer relevant and a possible source of confusion. In human memory, forgetting plays that role.

Research on forgetting, tracing back more than 120 years, has demonstrated that forgetting, rather than being a process of decay, analogous to footprints fading in the sand, is a consequence of interference and competition among memories (for a brief history of research on forgetting, see Bjork, 2003). Learning new information and using that information renders inaccessible information that is no longer being used. The acceleration of forgetting that accompanies disuse is an especially pertinent consideration in military contexts. Much of military training focuses on procedures, skills, and knowledge that – under typical conditions – are accessed only rarely and intermittently, such as in actual combat situations. Without systematic relearning and rehearsal procedures, much of what has been "learned" during military training will be inaccessible when needed.

The Importance of Overlearning and Relearning

Hunt (Chapter 5) is also right when he mentions that the efficiency of learning must be measured not simply by whether a learning curve has appeared to plateau, but also – or even especially – by the forgetting curve that follows various degrees of practice and training. As he mentions, overlearning procedures that appear to be inefficient, as measured by the small or nonexistent improvements in performance across overlearning trials, can be efficient as measured by the subsequent forgetting rate (e.g., Krueger, 1929; for a review, see Christina & Bjork, 1991). In terms of the distinction between storage strength and retrieval strength mentioned earlier, overlearning can continue to build storage strength – and, hence, slow the rate of subsequent forgetting – even though retrieval strength is no longer increasing, or increasing only slightly.

Forgetting as a Necessary Condition for Optimal Relearning

One of the misconceptions laypeople have about how they learn and remember, or fail to learn and remember, is that learning is a matter of building up something in memory, and forgetting is then a matter of losing some or all of what has been built up. In fact, a variety of conditions that increase forgetting (two examples being changing contextual cues or increasing a retention interval) also enhance learning. Thus, after instruction, individuals who are later tested in a context that differs from the context of instruction will tend to exhibit more forgetting than do individuals who are tested back in the context of instruction (see, e.g., Smith, 1988), but if both groups are re-instructed, rather than tested, the relationship tends to reverse (see Smith, Glenberg, & Bjork, 1978). Similarly, as exemplified by the well-known "spacing effect" (see Dempster, 1996; Glenberg, 1992), increasing the retention interval from an initial study episode to a test or second study episode decreases performance in the test condition, but increases the effectiveness of the repeated-study condition, as measured by long-term retention. Increasing the difficulty (Bjork & Allen, 1970) or similarity (Cuddy & Jacoby, 1982) can produce similar pattern.

Basically, conditions that induce forgetting, rather than undoing learning, create the opportunity for additional learning, over and beyond the level achieved earlier, when skills and knowledge are rehearsed or relearned. Forgetting, in effect, can enable learning. A discussion of *why* that is the case would take this commentary too far afield, but within the context of Bjork and Bjork's (1992) new theory of disuse it comes about because increments in storage strength (learning) are assumed to be smaller the higher the current retrieval strength of a given memory representation. Said differently, when some skill or knowledge is maximally accessible from memory, given local conditions, little or no learning results from additional instruction or practice.

Implications for Sustaining Elite Performance

From the perspective of traditional research on learning and skill acquisition, it is important to distinguish between the phase of training and its distinct environment from the subsequent phase of performance in a target environment. The problem for a training organization is to maximize performance when it matters, that is, *after* training and, especially, when individuals are deployed. To achieve that goal requires not only that initial training be designed in ways that foster durability and flexibility of to-be-learned skills and knowledge, but also that – following initial training – there be well-designed schedules of relearning and rehearsal of critical skills and knowledge.

More considerations go into such relearning being "well designed" than appropriate for me to discuss here, but two considerations merit emphasis. First, it is crucial for there to be a kind of task analysis that sorts needed skills and knowledge into those that are simpler versus those that are more complex and those that are, in the normal course of an individual's job, accessed more frequently and less frequently. The more complex the skill or knowledge in question and the less frequently it is accessed on a day-by-day, week-by-week, and month-by-month basis, the more it needs to be the target of relearning/ refresher procedures. Second, it needs to be recognized that the potency of relearning procedures will be enhanced by such factors as the delay from initial learning and changes in situational and interpersonal contexts – that is, by factors that produce forgetting and enhance learning.

It must also be recognized, though, that in many – perhaps most – training situations in professional and military contexts, the line between the training phase and the after-training phase is blurred. Graduates from professional schools or military training facilities end up spending a long period in on-the-job-training before they become proficient (see Lajoie, Chapter 3) and some of them eventually reach expert levels of performance (see Ericsson, Chapter 18). During the on-the-job-training, the trainees engage in a majority of the representative daily activities and, thus, the period of delay (and the associated forgetting) between successive executions is often short.

SPECIFIC COMMENTS ON THE PRECEDING CHAPTERS

Quantifying Warfighter Performance in Distributed SimulationEnvironments

In this chapter, Schreiber, Bennett, Colegrove, Portrey, Greschke, and Bell (Chapter 11) provide a brief history of the use of simulators in flight training, which they point out has a history nearly as long as manned flight itself. Their primary focus is on the current state of distributed mission operations (DMO), technologically demanding simulations that provide learners an opportunity "to operate in a team-oriented, multiplayer environment, and thereby train higher-order and more varied skills than would normally be trained in a single-simulator environment."

The authors provide a compelling argument for the potential of distributed/team simulations, but they couple that argument with an even more compelling argument that quantitative measurements of the improvements in performance owing to such simulations is sorely lacking. Without measuring and quantifying performance and improvements in performance, they argue, we cannot test the actual effectiveness of such simulations, which are complex and expensive, nor do we have a basis for refining such simulations over time. They assert that "for networked simulation, subjective evaluations have been the foundation for large-scale aggregate analyses" and that "published works using objective, quantifiable metrics for empirical investigations of performance transfer from multiplayer networked environments to the actual environment appear, for DMO, to be nonexistent."

With respect to the "basic considerations" I provided as a framework for my comments, there are several points that merit emphasis. First, the authors' emphasis is on measuring *performance* – and mostly on measuring performance during simulation exercises. Given the unreliability of performance *during* training as an index of learning, as measured by post-training retention and transfer of skills and knowledge, there is a risk of developing simulations that maximize performance during training, but are not optimal for the post-training performance that is the target of training. To be fair to the authors, however, they emphasize that improvements in performance must be measured in objective, quantifiable ways both during DMO and "resulting from" DMO training. The following are other points that warrant emphasis.

Introducing Desirable Difficulties

A considerable virtue of distributed simulations, in my view, is that they have the potential to incorporate, in a natural way, a number of the conditions of learning and practice that I have labeled desirable difficulties. By the very fact that they are interactive, for example, they incorporate generation activities in a natural way – unless, of course, they are structured so that most of what trainees do is to observe and/or imitate. In addition, because they involve multiple players, the conditions of practice depend on the responses of other individuals, meaning that those conditions will incorporate variation, versus being constant and predictable.

Those intrinsic benefits of distributed simulations notwithstanding, however, I believe that certain types of desirable difficulties should be designed into such simulations. The emphasis by Schreiber et al. on "repetition" is important, for example, but it is important that such repetitions be spaced or interleaved, versus massed or blocked. The authors' emphasis on providing feedback seems well advised, too, but their emphasis on providing "immediate warfighter feedback" after each complex trial may not be optimal. In research on the learning of relatively simple motor skills (e.g., Schmidt & Bjork, 1992; Schmidt, Young, Swinnen, & Shapiro, 1989), providing intermittent or summarized feedback rather than constant/immediate feedback has been found to enhance long-term retention. Whether those findings would extend to more complex simulations remains to be seen, but I think it is non-controversial to say, given those findings, that research is needed to explore how the acquisition of different types of skills can be optimized by design about the amount, content, and timing of the feedback.

Engineering Fidelity Versus Psychological Fidelity

Designing distributed simulations in a way that even comes close to simulating the real-world dynamics they are designed to simulate is an impressive technological achievement. It also tends to be the case that each additional increment in such engineering fidelity tends to multiply the development costs of such simulations. From that perspective, it is important to remember that in research on simulators it has frequently been the case that low-tech simulators have often produced training outcomes that are as good or better than high-tech simulators. What is crucial in simulations is not engineering fidelity, per se, but the psychological fidelity of a simulation – that is, does it exercise the processes that will be needed later, when it matters? Early in training, for example, a simpler representation of the task and environment might be more effective than representing fully the complexities that characterize the actual real-world task. (For a review of the considerations in the context of optimizing transfer of training, see Reder & Klatzky, 1994.)

Learning Versus Relearning

Finally, it is important to emphasize that the optimal way to design such distributed simulations – or single-simulator environments, for that matter – is likely to depend on whether the goal is to optimize the original learning of skills and knowledge, or to refresh existing skills and knowledge. Stated in terms of the new-theory-of-disuse framework, when the problem is to build storage strength (learning), as in the case of original learning, the considerations are different than when storage strength already exists but retrieval strength has been lost owing to disuse. In the latter case, relearning will tend to be very rapid, practice can be more massed in time, and a high level of engineering fidelity may be very desirable.

Contrasting Submarine Specialty Training: Sonar and Fire Control

In this chapter, Kirschenbaum, McInnnis, and Correll (Chapter 12) focus on the training of the two largest groups of enlisted submarine specialists, sonar technicians (STs) and fire-control technicians (FTs). The authors assert and demonstrate that the skills necessary to excel in each specialty differ and, hence, that training and "performance metrics" must differ, as well, if training is to be optimized in each case. More specifically, they argue that STs must develop a high level of perceptual skills, whereas FTs must develop skills that are more cognitive in nature, including mastering a "set of tools, procedures, and algorithms." They describe and illustrate the tasks confronting each type of specialist; they characterize the unique environment in which submariners must work; they summarize the problems that confront current military training, such as inadequate time for training; and they contrast what they refer to as the "old model" of training with the new "training continuum model."

The focus of the authors' analysis is on two specialties in submarine training, but the implications of their analysis are quite general, in my opinion. The following are some observations.

The Old Training Model Versus the New Training Model

Among the problems the authors identify with the old training model are that inadequate time for training resulted in an emphasis on maintaining and using equipment, rather than on understanding concepts and processes; that when trainees went to sea the first time, they were not able to perform basic functions independently, meaning that extensive on-the-job training was required; and that such on-the-job training consumed the time of shipboard experts, meaning their time to focus on their own tasks was reduced.

The new training model reflects what the authors refer to as a revolution in training within the Navy. The components of the revolution include a careful and validated specification of the "skill objects" associated with the tasks that characterize a job within the Navy; a re-engineering of the training curriculum to focus on those tasks; and incorporating the curriculum within a "career path that takes a sailor from raw recruit to expert." The new "training continuum model" results in a shortening of the training before a sailor goes out to sea and includes individual computer-based instruction that can be completed both on shore and on ship. Another "radical change" is that sailors periodically leave the ship and return to the classroom for refresher and technology training stints of about two weeks' duration.

Learning Versus Performance

The basic goals of the new training program include "providing as good or better training in a shorter timeframe." Analyzed in terms of basic principles of learning and memory, the new program would seem to have many desirable characteristics. An early exposure to the realities of submarine life and tasks has to be good in terms of motivating and framing subsequent training; going back and forth between the classroom and the ship must introduce variation, spacing of practice, and an integration of higher-order and lower-order learning and concepts; and the interspersing of individualized computer-based training seems both efficient and potentially effective.

But is the new program an improvement? According to the authors, an assessment is ongoing, but documenting that the new model is better in any rigorous way "cannot be evaluated" because performance measurements are not, for some reason, comparable between the two models, a fact that again supports the arguments of Schreiber et al. that agreed-to and quantifiable measures of performance are essential if programs of training are to be evaluated and optimized. From the description given by Kirschenbaum et al., it also seems to be the case that the ongoing assessment rests heavily on measures of performance *during* training and on sailors' "perception of the course," both of which are, as I emphasized earlier, likely to be unreliable indicators of whether the long-term learning that is the target of training has been achieved. One of the measures included, however, is a "follow-up evaluation by the student's on–the-job supervisor." Although perhaps not as valuable as rigorous measures of actual on-the-job performance, this measure should at least reflect the longer-term consequences of training.

Career-Long Learning

The description and analysis by Kirschenbaum et al. provide a nice example of a trend in military training that is likely to become pervasive. It may have been true many years ago – though perhaps it was never entirely true – that military training largely preceded and was isolated from individuals actually going to war. If that were ever true, it clearly is no longer true. Because training capabilities are more transportable than ever before, because equipment and technologies are changing more rapidly than ever before, and because new types and contexts of combat pose new challenges, the training of military personnel needs to be viewed as a career-long process. Continuing medical education is an interesting example of how the domain of medicine has developed methods for maintaining and advancing the skills of its practitioners (Davis, Chapter 8).

Training Complex Cognitive Skills: A Theme-Based Approach

In their chapter, Shadrick and Lussier (Chapter 13) provide a report on a program designed to train adaptive thinking skills. They argue that being able to think adaptively, which has always been important in military conflicts, has become more important than ever given the complexities and non-traditional nature of recent conflicts, such as the current war in Iraq. Dimensions of adaptive thinking include being able to respond effectively when confronted with unanticipated situations and responding effectively to rapidly changing conditions when multiple events and inputs compete for one's attention.

The authors refer to their approach to training thinking as "theme based." Broadly, the idea is to identify the cognitive behaviors and habits – or themes – that contribute to flexible thinking and problem solving. Examples might be learning to adopt a different perspective or modeling how an enemy is thinking and how that thinking might be changing as a function of battlefield events. The approach is embodied in a Think Like a Commander (TLAC) training program that, among other things, incorporates deliberate-practice (Ericsson, Krampe, & Tesch-Römer, 1993) techniques in an effort to develop expert mental models and understanding of presented tactical scenarios. In an analogy with how chess masters analyze chess positions from games and then obtain feedback on the correctness of their move selection and their analyses, Shadrick and Lussier assume that military officers can be trained to think by being presented with tactical situations that require them to analyze those situations before taking action and then, later, to obtain feedback on their analyses and thoughts.

To the authors' great credit, they have evaluated the TLAC training program not via testimonials or some kind of face validity, but by well-designed research. The results of the four experiments they report not only provide strong support for the effectiveness of the TLAC program, but are also interesting and provocative with respect to some broader considerations in training. The following are some observations.

The Generality of Training Principles

The authors argue that traditional training methods, such as those applied to the learning of motor skills and verbal and spatial information, can also be applied to train thinking skills. In contrast to other opinions in the literature, the authors do not think that training adaptability and adaptive thinking require training paradigms that are uniquely suited to higher-order cognitions and to people being able to perform appropriately in novel or ambiguous situations.

I, personally, share the authors' opinion. I believe the principles and methods that optimize learning – such as that generating information and skills leads to better, later production of that information or those skills than does studying and observing such information or skills – are very general indeed. My opinion in that regard has been shaped by a range of experimental findings, but also by an experience co-teaching a graduate seminar with my colleague, Richard Schmidt. The goal of the seminar was to identify how the techniques that optimize the learning of motor skills (his area) differ from the techniques that optimize the learning of verbal and conceptual information (my area). Somewhat to our surprise, we were able to identify far more principles that were common to motor and verbal learning than we could unique principles, which led us to write an article entitled "New conceptualizations of practice: Common principles in three paradigms suggest new concepts for training" (Schmidt & Bjork, 1992).

The Interaction of Experience and Training

Among the most striking aspects of the findings the authors report is that the effectiveness of TLAC training interacts with whether participants in their studies did or did not have deployment experience in Iraq or Afghanistan.

The training program was effective for both groups, but having been deployed increased the effectiveness of the training for all ranks – from lieutenants, to captains, to majors, to lieutenant colonels. The authors' findings in that respect may illustrate a broad and important generalization with respect to military training: Whenever it proves feasible to have personnel go back and forth between deployment settings and training settings, the effectiveness of training is likely to be enhanced. One can think of motivational reasons why such a generalization may hold, but there may be other reasons as well having to do with deployment experiences yielding an interpretive framework for the content of training. The new program for training submarine specialists, described by Kirschenbaum et al., may profit from that standpoint by interleaving classroom training ashore with training aboard ship.

Deliberate Practice and Learning Versus Performance Revisited

The TLAC program includes deliberate practice as a component of training (see Ericsson , Chapter 18). On the surface, aspects of deliberate practice, especially practicing one tactical scenario after another with analysis and feedback after each scenario, appear to be at odds with my earlier arguments that one should introduce desirable difficulties, such as spacing versus massing, and intermittent or summarized feedback versus immediate/continuous feedback, to enhance learning. Ericsson, however, would – and has – argued that sampling scenarios from a large collection of challenging tactical situations introduces variation and spacing of key concepts in an intrinsic, natural way.

Aside from any arguments as to whether deliberate-practice routines could be made even more effective by a planned introduction of spacing, variation, and summarized feedback, it is important to emphasize that if the focus is on performing at one's best when it matters (as would often be the goal, say, in a high-level athletic competition), then my earlier assertions need to be modified. That is, if the goal is not learning, but preparing one's self to perform some learned skill or procedure at the highest possible level, the considerations are different. There may, for example, be an important role for massed repetition, partly to keep a skill or routine maximally activated, but also to build confidence. Continuous feedback from a coach or expert may be important, too, once a skill has been acquired, if the fine-grain adjustments necessary for maximal performance are to be made.

From the standpoint of manipulating confidence and motivation, it can also be important, in some circumstances, to start with practice conditions that are *not* optimal with respect to long-term learning, such as massed practice and constant conditions, and then gradually withdraw such crutches and introduce desirable difficulties. Such a combination has the virtue of encouraging the learner via inducing early rapid improvement while still incorporating conditions of instruction that can be expected to foster learning (storage strength) versus performance (retrieval strength).

Toward a Second Training Revolution: Promise and Pitfalls of Digital Experiential Training

In his chapter on digital experiential training, Chatham (Chapter 10) argues strongly, if with occasional caveats, for the training potential of "light-weight digital simulations" – that is, training on personal computers (PCs). He sees the potential of the lessons learned from what he refers to as the "first training revolution," which led to training programs and settings such as the NTC, to be incorporated into PC training. As a kind of background for his comments, he observes that one-on-one tutoring can be remarkably effective, but is impossibly expensive and impractical for other reasons as well; that the state of assessment and measurement of training results is "abysmal" (he adds the cynical comment, "what you can't measure, you can ignore"); and that proximity in time between training and experience in the context in which that training is needed is one key to making training maximally effective.

Chatham argues that "grand-scale, high-fidelity simulations" can, at their best, be superb trainers, but they are very expensive, have fixed sites, and tend to serve specialized needs of some subset of military personnel. By contrast, he sees lighter weight, PC-based simulations as being accessible to "most of the military" who are in need of training "most of the time." In the remainder of his chapter, Chatham explores the potential of existing and future computer games as training platforms. In that analysis, he draws on examples such as *DARWARS Ambush!, Operation Flashpoint,* and *America's Army.*

Games as Tools for Training

The success of PC games, whether measured by their global market, their increasing sophistication, or by the hours that people, especially young people who otherwise have short attention spans, spend immersed in such games, has suggested to many individuals – including individuals at military training sites, such as Fort Monroe, and at non-military sites, such as the Institute for Education Sciences – that such games might be harnessed for science learning and other types of learning. Chatham argues that games may or may not be effective and that any game that is "unexamined" – that is, not tested for the training gains it produces – is an "empty trainer."

In that assessment, I wholeheartedly concur. Games as possible tools for learning often seem to be evaluated – and positively – in terms of their novelty, their whiz-bang technological features, and their attractiveness to users. The truth, though, is that – as tools – they can be used poorly or well. If a game is not structured to exercise the processes that support comprehension, understanding, and the production of to-be-learned procedures or knowledge, it will not be effective as a learning platform, however glitzy and attractive it may seem.

Performance Gains Versus Learning Gains

I am inclined to give the author the benefit of the doubt, because he refers to the "results" of training in one or two places, but his emphasis on "performance gains" as the criterion by which simulations should be evaluated, suggests that he is referring to performance across and during simulation sessions. If so, then my earlier cautions with respect to performance during training being misleading as an index of learning are relevant to his analysis. If versions of the simulation are evaluated by rate of improvement across experience with the simulation, as opposed to long-term post-training retention and transfer, then designers of the simulation will be susceptible to including massing, predictability, and other conditions that act to prop up current performance but not support learning.

User Authoring, Generation Effects, and Cooperative Learning

The author cites *user authoring* as a very important factor in the success of the *DARWARS Ambush!* program. Because the program could be altered, students' experience was not limited to the initial 24 scenarios, and the author cites this property as a reason that students did not lose interest in the simulation. Students could both change scenarios and create new scenarios. I am sure user authoring was a very important feature in exactly that way, but it was probably also important because doing such authoring constitutes a kind of generation that no doubt had a powerful learning effect. That is, the kind of learning that results from modifying or creating a scenario is going to be powerful and long lasting, far more so than simply playing through an existing scenario.

Finally, the author mentions – in the context of the Tactical Language and Culture trainer – that the simulation, "while usable by the highly motivated individual, delivered much more useful training when done in a group setting." More specifically, the author mentions that, to his surprise, a pair of novice students working at the same computer seemed to gain more from the simulation than did students who had a computer to themselves. Such a finding, which is consistent with the voluminous evidence that cooperative learning, structured appropriately, can enhance individual learning (e.g., Aronson, 1978; Dansereau, 1987; for a review, see Druckman & Bjork, 1994), suggests it could well be profitable, in simulations designed to train individual skills, to design the games as a two-person interaction.

CONCLUSION

The dominant reaction I have after working through the chapters in this section is optimism. The training challenges faced by our society – in educational, medical, and industrial contexts, as well as military contexts – are daunting in their complexity, their novelty, and their sheer scope, but the chapters in this section illustrate that new technologies, informed by the science of learning, have unprecedented potential to create and sustain elite performers.

REFERENCES

Adams, J. A., & Reynolds, B. (1954). Effect of shift in distribution of practice conditions following interpolated rest. *Journal of Experimental Psychology, 47,* 32–36.

Aronson, E. (1978). *The jigsaw classroom.* Beverly Hills, CA: Sage.

Bjork, R. A. (1994a). Memory and metamemory considerations in the training of human beings. In J. Metcalfe & A. Shimamura (Eds.), *Metacognition: Knowing about knowing* (pp. 185–205). Cambridge, MA: MIT Press.

(1994b). Institutional impediments to effective training. In D. Druckman & R. A. Bjork (Eds.), *Learning, remembering, believing: Enhancing human performance* (pp. 295–306) Washington, DC: National Academy Press.

(1999). Assessing our own competence: Heuristics and illusions. In D. Gopher & A. Koriat (Eds.), *Attention and performance XVII. Cognitive regulation of performance: Interaction of theory and application* (pp. 435–459). Cambridge, MA: MIT Press.

(2003). Interference and forgetting. In J. H. Byrne (Ed.), *Encyclopedia of learning and memory* (2nd ed., pp. 268–273). New York: Macmillan Reference USA.

Bjork, R. A., & Allen, T. W. (1970). The spacing effect: Consolidation or differential encoding? *Journal of Verbal Learning and Verbal Behavior, 9,* 567–572.

Bjork, R. A., & Bjork, E. L. (1992). A new theory of disuse and an old theory of stimulus fluctuation. In A. Healy, S. Kosslyn, & R. Shiffrin (Eds.), *From learning processes to cognitive processes: Essays in honor of William K. Estes* (Vol. 2, pp. 35–67). Hillsdale, NJ: Lawrence Erlbaum Associates.

Christina, R. W., & Bjork, R. A. (1991). Optimizing long-term retention and transfer. In D. Druckman & R. A. Bjork (Eds.), *In the mind's eye: Enhancing human performance* (pp. 23–56). Washington, DC: National Academy Press.

Cuddy, L. J., & Jacoby, L. L. (1982). When forgetting helps memory: Analysis of repetition effects. *Verbal Learning and Verbal Behavior, 21,* 451–467.

Dansereau, D. F. (1987). Transfer from cooperative to individual studying. *Journal of Reading, 30*(7), 614–619.

Dempster, F. N. (1996). Distributing and managing the conditions of encoding and practice. In E. L. Bjork & R. A. Bjork (Eds.), *Memory: Vol. 10. Handbook of Perception and Cognition* (pp. 317–344). New York: Academic Press.

Druckman, D., & Bjork, R. A. (Eds.). (1991). *In the mind's eye: Enhancing human performance.* Washington, DC: National Academy Press.

(1994). *Learning, remembering, believing: Enhancing human performance.* Washington, DC: National Academy Press.

Druckman, D., & Swets, J. A. (Eds.). (1988). *Enhancing human performance: Issues, theories, and techniques.* Washington, DC: National Academy Press.

Ericsson, K. A., Krampe, R. T., & Tesch-Römer, C. (1993). The role of deliberate practice in the acquisition of expert performance. *Psychological Review, 100,* 363–406.

Estes, W. K. (1955). Statistical theory of distributional phenomena in learning. *Psychological Review, 62,* 369–377.

Glenberg, A. M. (1992). Distributed practice effects. In L. R. Squire (Ed.), *Encyclopedia of learning and memory* (pp. 138–142). New York: Macmillan.

Hull, C. L. (1943). *The principles of behavior.* New York: Appleton-Century-Crofts.

Jacoby, L. L., Bjork, R. A., & Kelley, C. M. (1994). Illusions of comprehensions and competence. In D. Druckman & R. A. Bjork (Eds.), *Learning, remembering, believing: Enhancing human performance* (pp. 57–80). Washington, DC: National Academy Press.

Kornell, N., & Bjork, R. A. (2008). Learning concepts and categories: Is spacing the "enemy of induction"? *Psychological Science, 19,* 585–592.

Krueger, W. C. F. (1929). The effect of overlearning on retention. *Journal of Experimental Psychology, 12,* 71–78.

McNamara, D. S., Kintsch, E., Songer, N., & Kintsch, W. (1996). Are good texts always better? Interactions of text coherence, background knowledge, and levels of understanding in learning from text. *Cognition and Instruction, 14*(1), 1–43.

Reder, L. M., & Klatzky, R. L. (1994). Transfer: Training for performance. In D. Druckman & R. A. Bjork (Eds.), *Learning, remembering, believing: Enhancing human performance* (pp. 25–56). Washington, DC: National Academy Press.

Schmidt, R. A., & Bjork, R. A. (1992). New conceptualizations of practice: Common principles in three paradigms suggest new concepts for training. *Psychological Science, 3,* 207–217.

Schmidt, R. A., Young, D. E., Swinnen, S., & Shapiro, D. C. (1989). Summary knowledge of results for skill acquisition: Support for the guidance hypothesis. *Journal of Experimental Psychology: Learning, Memory, and Cognition, 15,* 352–359.

Shea, J. B., & Morgan, R. L. (1979). Contextual interference effects on the acquisition, retention, and transfer of a motor skill. *Journal of Experimental Psychology: Human Learning and Memory, 5,* 179–187.

Simon, D. A., & Bjork, R. A. (2001). Metacognition in motor learning. *Journal of Experimental Psychology: Learning, Memory, and Cognition, 27,* 907–912.

Smith, S. M. (1988). Environmental context-dependent memory. In D. M. Thomson & G. M. Davies (Eds.), *Memory in context: Context in memory* (pp. 13–33). New York: Wiley.

Smith, S. M., Glenberg, A. M., & Bjork, R. A. (1978). Environmental context and human memory. *Memory & Cognition, 6,* 342–353.

Tolman, E. C., & Honzik, C. H. (1930). Introduction and removal of reward and maze performance of rats. *University of California Publications in Psychology, 4,* 257–275.

Wulf, G., & Shea, C. H. (2002). Principles derived from the study of simple skills do not generalize to complex skill learning. *Psychonomic Bulletin & Review, 9*(2), 185–211.

SECTION 4

THE DEVELOPMENT OF EXPERTISE
AND EXPERT PERFORMANCE

The fourth and final section of the book focuses on how we can describe and explain the acquisition of skilled and expert performance.

15

The Influence of Learning Research on the Design and Use of Assessment

EVA L. BAKER

In the education and training worlds, the term "assessment" is on everyone's agenda – from classroom instruction to local schools, to on-the-job training, to international comparisons of education, both at high school and college levels. Although the term has technical variations in meaning, the ascriptions of assessment dramatically shift according to the education and training settings in which the terms are used. In the clinical psychology realm, assessment usually denotes the use of specific procedures to examine and interpret patient status as well as the results of these procedures. In the military and in business sectors, assessment applies to a broader range of activities and purposes that can include the evaluation of a program's effectiveness, an individual's productivity, and even the estimate of future status of an entire area, as in "technology assessment." In this discussion, I will use the term assessment and its functional synonym, "test," to refer both to (1) the procedures designed and used, and (2) the criteria and judgments made, which together estimate the proficiency of an individual or group with respect to a domain of desired behaviors, achievements, or performances. Assessment procedures within this interpretation may vary with respect to their purposes, design, surface features, methods of analysis, and reporting approaches. They also may explicitly favor uniform or adaptive performance. Assessment can also be used as part of the dependent variables for efforts such as research studies or program evaluations.

Acknowledgments: The work reported herein was supported under the Educational Research and Development Centers Program, PR / Award Number R305B960002 and Award Number R305A050004, as administered by the Institute of Education Sciences, U.S. Department of Education, and by the Office of Naval Research, Award Number N00014–02–1–0179.

The findings and opinions expressed in this report do not reflect the positions or policies of the National Center for Education Research, the Institute of Education Sciences, the U.S. Department of Education, or the Office of Naval Research.

I wish to thank Greg Chung and Girlie Delacruz for their findings, and David Westhoff and Katharine Fry for their assistance.

Although a tight, functional relation of assessment to the learning it measures would seem to be obvious, the reality in everyday practice is much different. This chapter will consist of a dialectic to (1) explore the current relationship between measurement and student learning, and (2) briefly describe a set of methods intended to make the relationship of formal assessments and learning more explicit and transparent, and ultimately to restore the planning for learning and its integrated assessments. If such recommendations were followed, assessment validity would be designed into assessments. Results from such measures would be trustworthy influences on both the proximal redesign of instructional systems and the formulation of needed accountability policies.

At the outset, I will identify some historical traditions that may undermine our goals of integration of learning and measurement. Then, I intend to frame the linkage between learning and measurement, in part through describing attributes of models of learning, including cognitive demands, their classification or description, and frameworks for explicating the knowledge to be learned and measured, their integration into content frameworks and the development of scoring criteria. Integrated within this discussion will be concerns for feasibility, usability, cost, and renewal.

REVIEW OF ASSESSMENT PARAMETERS

To begin, I will briefly review some basic truths in assessment (Table 15.1). The described claims are well known to measurement experts but may have fuzzier connotations for readers with other backgrounds. A brief review, therefore, is in order. First, tests or assessments are only a sample of the possible tasks, questions, or test items in the domain of interest. Domains may be explicit (e.g., extract a particular tooth, such as the lower left bicuspid), which limits the domain to oral surgery, but still involves a wide range of considerations, such as anesthesia options given the patient's health, the anxiety of the patient, the tools available to the surgeon, and the degree of disease on the target tooth and surrounding tissues and structures. Obviously a task either in simulation, in real life, or via written procedures describing the strategy and procedures

Table 15.1. *Basic truths in assessment.*

- Tests or assessments are always only samples of domains of interest.
- The purposes of tests vary and imply different approaches to ensuring quality.
- Without documented validity, we may be basing training inferences on weak and unreliable results.
- In rapidly changing environments, tests or assessments must measure both the automatic (mindless) application of skills and the (mindful) transfer and generalization of complex performance adjusted to unforeseen circumstances.
- If adaptation is a goal, then transfer needs to be trained and systematically measured.

to accomplish this performance would require an explicit description of what is critical and tangential to performance, as well as explicit criteria to judge adequacy of the outcome. Although this example from dental surgery is somewhat grisly, there are other cognitive domains that can be more or less specific as "universes" within which assessment should be directed and sampled (see Hively, Patterson, & Page, 1968, for a referent discussion). Specifications of domains may be defined by rules, such as adding any combinations of three four-digit numbers, such as 2496+7231+4780, or specified by a list by enumeration (as was the case in my graduate English literature classes, e.g., all works by Ezra Pound, T. S. Eliot, Gerard Manley Hopkins, and Dylan Thomas). In cases of domain specification by either rule or enumeration, only those tasks or test items that fall within the boundaries of the rules or enumerations can be used for assessment. It is still possible to massively underrepresent in the test the domain of interest, such as assuming analysis of a novel such as *Ulysses* is equivalent to another, such as *Gone With the Wind*, where the literature differs in complexity, allusion, evolution of character, transparency, and linguistic complexity. But at a minimum, learner/examinee/test designer and instructor understand what is a fair (within bounds) task for the examination and consequently for instruction.

Traditional measurement focuses on constructs that generalize across specific domains, often unidimensional descriptions of a broad set of performances, such as math ability, rather than specific performances that meet particular rules for inclusion. The difficulty with test design involving general abilities is the need for a strategy for generating tasks for examinations. There are myriads of different ways to interpret a specification (or a state standard) that describes the ability to read, understand, and solve problems in plane geometry.

A second important element noted in Table 15.1 is the notion that different goals for assessing students' knowledge and abilities have far-reaching implications for quality and validity studies. Newer approaches to validity attempt to demonstrate that the measurement works in the way intended (see American Educational Research Association (AERA), American Psychological Association (APA), & National Council on Measurement in Education (NCME), 1999). For example, many tests are justified by their stated purposes: to measure how much has been learned; to provide an index of the rate of learning to measure the effectiveness of institutions (schools); to compare individual students or groups on their performance; and to guide instructors, teachers, and learners by providing detailed feedback and pointing the direction for improvement-oriented experiences. At the National Center for Research on Evaluation, Standards, and Student Testing (CRESST) we have found that assessments may often be designed to meet all these purposes; however, for the most part, the administered tests are adaptations of old tests that are retrofitted to match the range of desired purposes. Tests designed for some particular purposes may even be misleading for other purposes. For example, tests that measure student growth will re-test the same domains year-to-year, so that growth components can be directly compared. On a practical level, assessments of growth will not provide enough unique detail to assist learners and teachers to use test results as specific feedback and guidance in order to improve the mastery of the domain. In the first case, validity studies would address the extent to which growth modeling follows trajectories that differ for students of different prior knowledge, or other measurable characteristics. In the improvement model, the key validity evidence concerns whether teachers, for example, could make inferences from assessment results to design and instruct the students so that observed improvements can be causally related to the assessment. Unfortunately, current tests and measures used in assessment of educational systems do not rise to the minimum standards set forth in the *Standards for Educational and Psychological Testing* (AERA, APA, & NCME, 1999).

The third point of Table 15.1 underscores the obvious: If appropriate validity evidence is not assembled for the purpose(s) of the desired assessments, then inferences and actions based on test results may be wrong. For example, if assessments of students' performance were shown to be inadequate to help teachers improve their instruction, penalizing teachers for lack of improvement would be inappropriate.

The fourth point of Table 15.1 concerns what should be measured. If assessments are designed to measure students' or trainees' future performance, it is clear that the students need to be able to adapt their performance to different settings and contexts. This type of performance requires, in my judgment, that students need to be well trained in the proficient or automatic performance of given procedures, so that they will be able to reinstantiate them without much cognitive effort and that they can discern the conditions to which they apply. This set of future outcomes can be taught via guided practice with varied content and across different domains of activity. Yet students also need to be able to adapt their learning of principles to new requirements and to unforeseen combinations of content and constraints. To estimate students' proficiency, measures of transfer should be included in original tests. This is not the old time transfer of teach *x* and measure *y*, but rather a systematic analysis of constraints that might change between the trained domains and the new unfamiliar contexts and domains – ideally expressed as a metric of distance from the original focused tasks. The failure to transfer with traditional education is nicely illustrated when students are asked to compute arithmetic with vertically arrayed columns and then fail dismally when asked to do the same tasks, sometimes with the same numerals, in a horizontal format. Genuine transfer requires, however, much more than switching between graphical formats, or even among symbolic representations, such as charts, numbers, and words. It mostly focuses on the students' deep understanding of principles and their ability to identify and classify new problems or tasks appropriately and then adapt learned principles to the newer constraints.

Table 15.2. *Common limitations found in tests and assessments for training.*

1. Measured domains are usually not well described.

2. Construct-based tests are less relevant in training.

3. Test content typically addresses only common errors to be remedied, or tasks directly related to only subsets of jobs.

4. Key attributes and contexts may be omitted and serious problems skipped.

5. Technical quality (validity, reliability, and fairness) is usually poor or remains uninvestigated for the range of purposes intended for the measure.

The last point of Table 15.1 is also a truism. Transfer does not spontaneously "happen" for most people with traditional training, and thus needs to be assessed longitudinally with measures that document its acquisition and improvement.

Let me now turn to the deficiencies of current training that need to be overcome by improved design (Table 15.2), implied by the discussion about Table 15.1. Currently, little time and energy are invested in the specification of domains for instruction and assessment of particular educational outcomes. There are a few exceptions, but in these cases the tasks are procedural and the exact outcomes are of known value (e.g., marksmanship in the army with their assigned weapons). In most educational contexts, discussion and intellectual capital are primarily expended on the political side of generating goals and objectives. Do we want to train and educate well-rounded professionals? What are college readiness skills? Should all students complete algebra? While these decisions are important road signs for the curriculum, teaching, and measurement of domains, the step that is almost always short-changed is the careful statement of cognitive demands, content representations, and criteria expected to guide test developers. The consequence of this deficiency is that test developers are influenced by their somewhat arbitrary preferences in the design of measurement of curriculum and learning.

As corollary, it is also clear that the less well-described the outcomes (i.e., constructs rather than explicit domains), the less well-fit the goals are for training, where measurable outcomes are expected within time and costs constraints. In other words, tidy and clear objections can be measured in only limited ways, whereas vaguely described domains lend themselves any number of instructional and assessment approaches.

A third point is that test questions may focus primarily on tasks that elicit common errors of students rather than infrequent mistakes that uncover failures to understand revealed by unusual errors. This focus inevitably locks instruction into a do-this/don't-do-that niche, rather than providing a platform to diagnose students' misunderstanding of the domain.

Almost all these deficiencies can be attributed to time and cost constraints. With ever-shorter cycles of reform, and expectations for improvement and change, there has been no parallel breakthrough in the conduct of validity.

Furthermore, when budgets are tight and becoming tighter, research assessing validity is the first thing to be cut – a false economy.

CHALLENGES TO THE INTEGRATION OF LEARNING AND MEASUREMENT

A Brief History of Testing: So How Did We Get Here?

We know that assessment (and its half sister, testing) has roots in psychology. Early work by Thorndike (1904) for example, emphasized measures related to learning goals. However, the dominant influence on the measurement of achievement has been the process of classifying individuals into relatively durable descriptions or types based on their test performance. Thus, most assessments in education or psychology trace their history to a search for stable traits, personality types, ability levels, or aptitudes. These traits have been studied to ascertain the degree to which scores and resultant standardized classifications of examinees predict performance in other measurement situations or in applied settings where one would expect the trait to operate. Again, these are general traits applied to general situations. For example, tests of mathematics aptitude should predict some years later a student's performance on mathematics achievement tests in college, or a test of trait anxiety should predict the examinee's stress response to future situations.

THE CONFLICT BETWEEN MEASURING STABLE CONSTRUCTS AND LEARNING

During the extended history of assessments, the intuitive understanding of a test score, has been based on the underlying stable normal distribution of psychological characteristics. Stability is the assumption underlying most of the psychometric analyses of achievement used to describe samples of learned behavior, a practice with a long and well-documented history (Cronbach & Suppes, 1969). It is also at the core of almost all commercial achievement tests, whatever they may be called for marketing purposes. Reporting techniques commonly use normative interpretations, for it is easy to grasp a score as a rank compared to scores of other examinees. Nonetheless, the value of this approach is questionable when learning is measured. It is true that some people may retain their relative rank in a distribution even after extended instruction, school experience, or substantial learning. Yet, we know that the process of learning leads to uneven change rather than generalized and equal improvement, which would be required to preserve the rank order of the tested students. There are many instances where people go from zero to very proficient, independent of their initial rank (see Bachman & Palmer, 1996; Bloom, 1964; Bruner, 1977 ; Harris, 1963). Predictions of learning should vary based not only on the stable traits of the learner, but also on the *effects* of levels of exposure to and interaction with different content, engagement, and goals of instruction. Students' or trainees' performance will also depend on their willingness to put forth serious effort in the learning situation and to manage their own attention during acquisition (O'Neil & Chuang, 2005). In other words, individual differences in the intensity of the learning of the trainees or students will influence the learning outcomes. Nonetheless, in designing conceptual or problem-solving assessments, particularly those given on a large scale and often interpreted with significant consequences for individuals and institutions, the operational connection among learning, instruction, and assessment is not usually exhibited. This finding is supported by studies of alignment, which, at best, cover superficial aspects of instruction and testing (Baker, 2005).

LEARNING FROM PROCEDURES

For procedural tasks that specify sequential execution (e.g., replacing a HEPA filter in a specific vacuum cleaner according to the manual) there is a clearly perceived functional relation between learning, instruction, and assessment. This tight connection is almost exclusively limited to psychomotor tasks (e.g., shooting an arrow or vaulting above a certain height). In fact, most conceptual or strategic learning takes place in a messier context, with unclear problems (Spiro, Feltovich, Jackson, & Coulson, 1991) and distractions such as stress (Cannon-Bowers & Salas, 1998). If change, or learning, depends on the dynamic interaction between the learner and various objects, people, or systems, our assessment designs must attend to the cognitive processes underlying deep understanding of declarative knowledge, acquisition of patterns or schema, problem solving, planning, and communication. The careful representation of the knowledge to be learned is also essential, despite a complex context. This is closely related to the issues discussed by van Merriënboer and Boot (Chapter 6), Schraagen (Chapter 7), and Mayer (Chapter 9) about the importance of describing learning goals for instructional design intended to promote the acquisition of the complex integrated skills desired in professional settings. Unfortunately, instead of even approximating the complexity of learning as it progresses, many widely administered, nominal measures of learning continue to be based on the assumption of stability and only analysis of technical quality of the tests, such as reliability and validity. There are, however, several attempts in this volume to develop such objective assessments of complex performance as described, in particular, by Davis (Chapter 8), Shadrick and Lussier (Chapter 13), and Ericsson (Chapter 18).

There are harmful effects of the mismatch between dynamic learning and outcome measures reflecting the assumed stability of abilities in the traditional school system. These effects go far beyond the mechanical notions of targeted changes specified in policy doctrine (No Child Left Behind Act of 2001, 2002). One unnerving concern is that inappropriately designed and interpreted measures have served as dependent measures for much research in education, psychology, and training. Results based on these measures may have significantly misrepresented the effects of research treatments, and biased interpretations of the science of learning itself. How important is the "right" assessment? While it is true that most measures of cognitive abilities are correlated, one would expect these correlations would diminish when an appropriate dependent measure was selected – one that was properly measuring the core effects of the adaptive instruction (Glaser, 1977). So the measure matters.

ASSESSMENT PURPOSES (OR CLARIFYING FUNCTIONS OF RESULTS)

There is a raft of common intentions or purposes for assessment. As described in Table 15.3 and alluded to in the previous discussion, these intentions or purposes have different implications for the conception, design, interpretation, and validation of assessments. Table 15.3 lists purposes in two columns. The first focuses on the individual student and the use of his or her test results: *certification* of successful completion of a course or set of competencies; *admission* to a program or institution; *selection,* which is closely allied to admission that may evaluate or place students in different courses or programs depending upon prior achievement or on other relevant criteria; *diagnosis,* where test results are used to identify particular strengths or needs of the student in order to attain a particular set of goals; *progress,* where the goal is to understand the rate of acquisition of proficiency by the student; *process,* where the assessment generates information on how the student engages in learning tests either during instruction or the test itself; and *completion,* which is based on typically minimal requirements for performance and participation

Table 15.3. *Common purposes for assessments and tests.*

Individual	Group
Certification	Certification
Admission	Evaluation
Selection	Accountability
Diagnosis	System monitoring
Progress	Feedback
Process	Team processes
Completion	Progress

that certifies a student without the claim of a particular attainment of proficiency level. Notice that the first three listed – certification, admission, and selection – have life consequences for the student and are often called "high stakes" purposes.

The second column in Table 15.3 shows how data on an individual's learning can provide evidence and conclusions about the status and effectiveness of teachers and institutions of learning. For example, the average performance of students at a given point in time, or as a slope (increases and growth), may be used to determine *certification* of teachers or doctors. *Evaluation* of training or interventions may often depend upon the measured impact on students, when extraneous factors are statistically controlled. An example might be the effects of a particular reading program on third grade learners. A related use of group measures is in the realm of *accountability,* where student performance – again current achievement or rate of growth, including the participation and performance of identifiable subgroups that are on target – not only evaluates the quality of proficiency, but may classify it into predetermined categories (e.g., Below Basic, Advanced), and use the proportions of students' performances falling in desired categories as a measure of the success of the accountability system. Key to accountability for learning is the explicit assignment of responsibility for performance to the appropriate personnel. For example, in the U.S. state accountability systems, the school as an institution is typically assigned as the "responsible party," and sanctions associated with inferior performance are attributed to the institution or its supervising authority, such as a school district. In some districts, responsibility is assigned to teachers, who receive rewards or sanctions based on attainment of their groups of students. Note that often in the United States, unlike in some other countries, accountability for students may be "low stakes." In these cases, the students take the state exam without any personal consequences. In other states and countries, students themselves may be advanced or held back based directly on their individual test performance. The use of examinations to hold students, teachers, and principals, or institutions directly accountable for their test performance must influence the development of the measures, their validation. *System monitoring* is generally a form of comparative assessment that keeps track of the global level of progress made by school districts, states, or regular training programs (e.g., Basic Training in the Army). Sometimes system monitoring is used in international comparisons to see which countries' test performances are falling back or moving ahead. Obviously, the measures used should be relevant and fair to the learning systems monitored. Furthermore, some of the administrators of the monitored systems may attempt to directly affect performance on these measures, as they represent a diverse mix of measures relevant to explicit goals and to transfer options. *Feedback* is another use of group assessment data that provides members of the learning community, policy makers, and the public information of current performance trends. Although typically perceived to be low stakes, as is system monitoring, successive waves of feedback without the desired progress can lead to political action and accountability.

Those purposes especially pertinent to this discussion include certification, criteria of completion, process and progress monitoring, diagnosis, personal and institutional feedback, and accountability, with the caveat that program evaluation may be relevant if the programs have desired learning outcomes. Most importantly, is the argument presented by Messick (1989) and his followers, which argued that validity of a measure has a conditional meaning relative to its particular purpose(s). Validity assessment entails the practice of interpreting test results and making use of these results for decisions and actions rather than merely to report a computed coefficient in a manual. Not too long ago a "cut score" such as a correlation coefficient of .90 or larger, conveyed an acceptable level of validity, even though a validity argument should be made based on a range of evidence directly related to the purposes of the assessment. Today, validity evidence, both qualitative or quantitative types, should be assembled and interpreted for every purpose to which a given test is used.

A STATUS CHECK ON ASSESSMENT DESIGN

The great difficulty with test design is that through testing or assessment, one intends not only to sample the examinee's current performance, for instance, preceding or following instruction, but also to make inferences about future performance typically in the same domain but in a wider set of situations than those tested. In other words, we want to assess transfer. The idea of random sampling from this broader domain of situations makes intuitive sense, if the universe of possible content and skill combinations can be fully or even partially specified with precision. In reality, this type of specification is usually incomplete both in education and training. *The specification shortfall derives in part from constraints in the measurement time and setting, from the lack of seriousness with which the learning opportunities for task acquisition and promotion of transfer are designed, from an incomplete understanding of the future, and from traditional approaches used to conceive and realize the test.* In this volume several past and current proposals for measuring the target performance are discussed. In Chapter 1, Ericsson et al. reviewed projects in the armed forces to measure job performance of military recruits after training by giving them tasks with representative work samples. Shadrick and Lussier (Chapter 13) and Ericsson (Chapter 18) proposed how to present challenging representative situations with demands for immediate action that capture expertise in the associated domains of expertise.

In the remainder of this chapter, I will draw attention to desired characteristics of specification. Although much of the following will be very familiar to researchers in learning, these ideas will appear far more radical to many scholars or practitioners schooled in the mainstream measurement tradition.

COGNITIVE DEMANDS AND DOMAIN DESCRIPTION

A central task of assessment is the careful description of the domain to be measured. Because much testing and assessment seem to have purposes attending to both learning outcomes and the process of learning, the full range of learning tasks needs to be described via specifications as well as their relationships to one another. Along with the clarity of purpose of the assessments, attention must be given to the features that guide their design, for both elements are essential to establishing the validity of the measures. The key activity in preparing for the construction of a test involves the specification of the range and depth of cognitive complexity that is intended to be sampled. This approach differs from traditional test design, which lets empirical difficulty of test items – obtained in field trials – substitute for complexity assessed by task analysis (Schraagen , Chapter 7).

In the scientific study of complex learning, there is no shortage of hierarchical or practical analytical frameworks to characterize learning (Anderson, 1983; Anderson & Krathwohl, 2001; Bloom, 1956; Gagné, 1985; Gagné, Briggs, & Wagner, 1992; Merrill, 2000). How well do these approaches capture performance in an actual job or profession, such as medicine?

These analytical frameworks are based on classification of tasks in terms of processes, or observable performances, or both. While some are built with the focus of analyzing performance outcomes (i.e., Bloom, 1956), others emphasize the design of instruction (Gagné et al., 1992). In all of these frameworks there are underlying assumptions about the structure of tasks, the role of prior declarative and procedural knowledge, the aids and interventions necessary to help the learner achieve criterion levels of achievement, and the generalizability of the performance to similar or further removed situations (see Table 15.4).

All the frameworks propose differing accounts of acquisition, maintenance, retention, and transfer of learning at different levels of explicitness. They also differ in the suggested behavioral or neurobiological mechanisms to support and mediate learning. For the purpose of this chapter, the key is to select a framework that is sufficiently rich to permit the modeling of information, processes, and criterion performance. The construction of this model is a necessary step for designing assessment tasks that follow the "nap of the earth," or match closely to both educational objectives and instructional methods. Of growing interest is understanding and measuring examinees' ability to perform complex, interactive steps, and to use immediately available data to adjust instruction, context, information, or performance changes. (See the analyses of the performance of medical doctors described by Davis [Chapter 8] and

Table 15.4. *Models of learning informing testing.*

• Bloom et al.	• Knowledge, comprehension, application, analysis, synthesis, evaluation
• Gagné, Briggs, and Wagner	• Verbal learning, discrimination, procedures, cognitive strategies
• Glaser	• Expertise, patterns, automaticity, rich content
• Merrill	• Activation, demonstration, application, integration, problem solving
• Anderson and Krathwohl	• Declarative, factual, conceptual, procedural, and metacognitive
• Mayer; Sweller; Chi	• Schema support, working memory conservation
• CRESST Compilation, Baker	• Content explanation, problem solving, communication, teamwork, metacognition

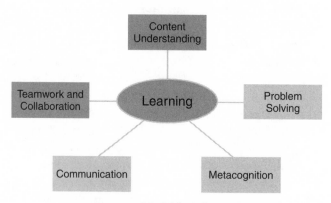

FIGURE 15.1. Model-based assessment.

Boshuizen [Chapter 17].) Additional attention should be given to team performance (Cannon-Bowers & Salas, 1997) in the measurement setting.

My own work at CRESST has derived from many of these analyses. What I have tried to do in what I've termed "model-based assessment" (Baker, 2007) is to recombine cognitive demands into somewhat more accessible categories related to learning outcomes. The approach first identifies five major families of achievement or performance: content understanding, problem solving, communication, metacognition, and teamwork. Although presented in Figure 15.1 as if they were separate, these families of achievement are obviously interactive, especially on complex tasks. The purpose of this array is to create measures that map to the families as listed. The idea is to first take whatever domain-independent knowledge there is (for instance, Bransford and Johnson's [1973] work on comprehension, or the corpus of work on expertise [see Ericsson, 2003]), and embed them in a carefully explicated network, which represents the core knowledge in the area. The idea is that to create a test, assessment, or learning system, we should use our most generalizable research knowledge about cognition and apply it to subject matter. Then, by analyzing the particular subject area, we should employ domain-specific strategies (i.e., best ways to solve equations), where the research is clear (*Knowing What Students Know*, National Research Council, 2001). Combining elements from the continuum of domain-independent to domain-specific knowledge in the design of assessments also provides a corpus of knowledge, models, templates, or objects that may be partially reused in other content. Note that this strategy inverts the usual process of test design, starting with the subject matter and making a test that optimizes its measurement. If one believes that transfer has to be explicitly taught (Bassok & Holyoak, 1989 ; Bjork & Richardson-Klavehn, 1989), then providing optimized assessments in a range of subject matters will further that goal. This proposal is consistent with the emphasis of specifying the complex target performance and then working backwards from this performance toward a specification of the practice activities that can induce these desired mechanisms and representations (Mayer, Chapter 9; van Merriënboer & Boot, Chapter 6; Schraagen , Chapter 7).

CONTENT REPRESENTATION

To depict content or subject matter knowledge, we at CRESST have used ontologies to represent fully the domain of interest including the major ideas, the links among them, and the supporting knowledge and task demand (represented by a subsection of the full ontology in Figure 15.2). Therefore, an analysis of these networks allows us to identify predicted conceptual difficulties. For example, if the similarity of a concept to other elements is great, then its learning will require discrimination between them. If a concept is far removed from key nodes that define mainline principles to be learned, then difficulties can be predicted. In addition, these learning tasks need to be designed to minimize problems with verbal explanations. Difficulty can inhere in structural and usage aspects of verbal stimulus materials to a degree that often swamps content knowledge. While it is important that academic language be appropriately involved (Bailey & Butler, 2004), language-based, construct-irrelevant variance affecting difficulty levels is a common characteristic of many available tests. It is important, then, that difficulty of assessments and the inferences made from lower performance is attributable to performance in the task domain of interest and is not confounded by language syntax that pose additional hurdles for the examinee.

As suggested, we have found that using very complete representations of knowledge in the form of networks allow us to create measures of mastery of the material efficiently and comprehensively (Chung, Niemi, & Bewley, 2003). We can identify the major external relationships and, based on our

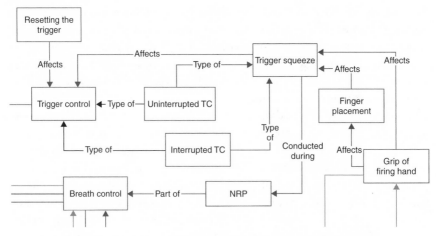

FIGURE 15.2. Ontology of M-16 marksmanship (subsection).

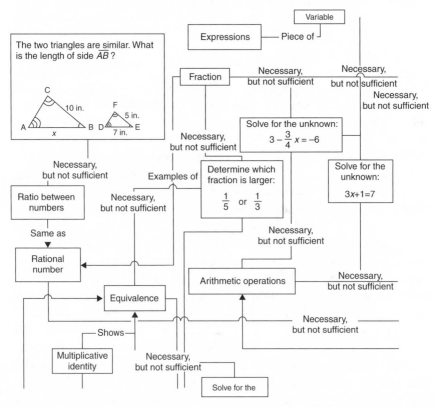

FIGURE 15.3. Knowledge map of teachers' understanding of algebra (subsection).

research experience, we can infer the corresponding cognitive schema as well. Presented below are ontologies used to design assessments and instruction for aspects of M-16 rifle marksmanship and algebra (see the subsections of the full ontologies in Figures 15.2 and 15.3; Chung, Delacruz, Dionne, & Bewley, 2003; Delacruz, Chung, Heritage, Vendlinski, Bailey, & Kim, 2007). This representation includes content nodes and processes (in links) to yield a map of relationships.

EXAMPLES OF ASSESSMENT DESIGN METHODOLOGY

Although it is clear to our CRESST team how principles derived from cognitive and computer science research apply to and improve the process and quality of assessments of learning, we also grant that making the translation to particular fields may be difficult. To provide concrete referents, consider major phases of development of assessment in a given domain. Our efforts begin with specifying cognitive demands and embedding them in content through use of detailed knowledge representations or ontologies. The design process is similar to knowledge-acquisition approaches used to develop expert databases. The ontology for M-16 rifle marksmanship (Figure 15.2) was developed from data that included interviews of marksmen at different levels of expertise, including snipers and experienced marksmanship coaches. We also examined the training doctrine for fixed distance shooting in three positions – sitting, standing, and prone – along with the analysis of performance records kept by experienced shooters. These shooters kept records following any practice situation, where the weather conditions (e.g., wind velocity and direction, visibility, additional constraints and challenges, and the shooters' adjustments) were described. These records could be viewed as a personally developed, longitudinal set of after-action reviews (AARs; Chatham, Chapter 2; Hunt, Chapter 5) that would permit self-reflection and the generation of ideas for improvement.

Our goal in the R&D program was to develop specific assessment architecture and tasks that would tap into key cognitive and procedural tasks. We realized that we needed to go beyond the procedural requirement (e.g., don't breathe when pulling the trigger), and capture other aspects, such as knowledge (what factors cause shot groupings to cluster in specific ways?), propensities (self-assessment, self-correction), and analysis of interim outcomes for self-improvement. By observing the standard training process, we found that the trainee needed to be able to observe and correct the positions of other shooters, to analyze shot groupings, to understand the relationship of precision of sighting and distance, and to control physical performance under a variety of situations. We designed measurement procedures for these tasks to support the training of the desired expert shooter designation. The ontology in Figure 15.2 was developed and then reviewed by a set of experts to ensure that it emphasized (through nodes with multiple links) the major components of expert marksmanship and that it was comprehensive and did not omit any important elements. In addition to this review, other experts completed their own representation (using CRESST software) to individually externalize their mental representation of the cognitive and behavioral requirements of the marksmanship suite of thinking and performance skills.

The developed ontology then is used to yield an integrated system of learning, instruction, formative assessment, and certification. Software provides practice of key tasks, for example, correcting positions of a three-dimensional virtual Marine to the expected standard. The design also provides guidance and job performance aids for the shooters, and coaches them to emphasize essential elements during training. The ontology also forms the basis for the design of assessments. Our experience with the ontology has led to further research questions and technology development. At present, we are conducting studies of coaching practices where we compare groups randomly assigned to receive our training to control groups (no results are yet available; Delacruz, in preparation). In addition, a simulated rifle has been developed with sensors providing physical data on breath control and the precise timing and pressure of trigger pull (Chung, Dionne, & Elmore, 2006). As well, our team is using neurological and psychophysiological measures of brain and attentional functions in the Accelerated Learning Program sponsored by Defense Advanced Research Projects Agency (DARPA) to determine whether results from these indicators can influence our training processes and result in faster learning curves with the same or higher attained proficiency. The work, in its early stages, has examined differences between experts (USMC marksmanship coaches) and novices on a rifle simulator on measures of shooting skill and performance, anxiety, engagement, and workload (Berka et al., 2008). As expected, experts performed higher on shooting performance and skill. During the three seconds prior to the shot, experts compared to novices were "in the zone" and had lower engagement levels. Both groups showed similar levels of workload. While exploratory, these results suggest that experts remained calm during the task, screened out external sensory stimuli, and exerted high mental effort. Subsequent work with larger samples has confirmed these general findings.

DEVELOPED ONTOLOGIES IN OTHER DOMAINS

Another ontology has been created for the domain of algebra. This ontology was created by mathematicians and validated by middle school teachers to depict a less dense structure (see Figure 15.4, which presents a subsection of the full ontology). This format was developed to facilitate teacher-led instruction and formative assessment (Niemi, Vallone, & Vendlinski, 2006), and is being used in the CRESST middle school initiative in pre-algebra, POWERSOURCE. We also have developed mapping software targeted to the creation of content

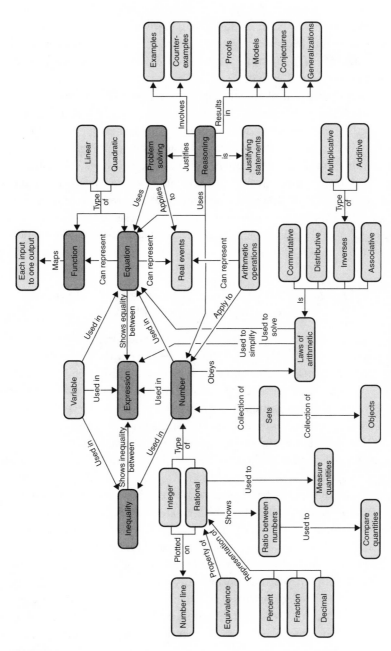

FIGURE 15.4. Algebra ontology for teacher and student use (subsection).

maps by experts, teachers, or students. This software is used to achieve consensus, identify differences in perceived subject matter structure, or to measure the outcomes of instruction of a topic on deep structural understanding (Chung, Baker, Niemi, Delacruz, & O'Neil, 2007).

Clear representation of subject matter relations allows us to select content systematically in terms of its importance, criticality, and confusability. The ontology guides the design of difficulty of measurement tasks applied in new settings, in other words, to demonstrate transfer, by controlling their complexity, discrimination, and constraints. In using ontologies, we have obviously extrapolated from procedures in artificial intelligence knowledge acquisition, as well as from the design of intelligent tutoring systems. In these fields, knowledge for expert systems and tutors is first represented in a network that can be used to guide individualized instructional sequences. Our intention is to broaden the impact of these procedures to the realm of testing.

CRITERIA NEEDED FOR EXCELLENT PERFORMANCE: MORE VALIDITY BUILT IN

It is often common practice in constructing open-ended or multi-step problems to ask teachers or instructors to tell the test designer what the "right" answer is. We have found, for instance, in tasks that seemed to be asking for complex analytical thought around particular literary pieces, that the "right" answer was framed by an expert as a particular inference about a character, rather than the process of inferring and justifying a plausible answer by the student. Even if a question may seem to tap higher order processes (e.g., what was the deep motivation for Antony's eulogy in "Julius Caesar"), if the answer were directly given in instruction, the task is transformed to one of simple memory. Thus, direct instruction could obviate what appears to be a complex task. In our own work with complicated tasks in literature, history, and science, we have employed a procedure to develop scoring criteria that are based on the expert–novice literature (Chi, Glaser, & Farr, 1988; Ericsson, 1996; Larkin, McDermott, Simon, & Simon, 1980). We asked experts in the field to solve target test questions themselves rather than to invent scoring criteria. Invariably, their thoughts generating the answers reflect processes similar to those reported in the expertise literature. They focused on central principles or themes, used a wealth of prior knowledge, and presented their responses in the mode of argument or expression that is a standard part of the discipline. As we have used expert–novice contrasts as the procedure for identifying scoring criteria, we have found both efficiency and empirical success, measured by factor analysis (Baker, Abedi, Linn, & Niemi, 1996). Differences between experts and novices in their use of principles to organize their analysis, in the appropriateness of examples and evidence of misconceptions, generated scoring rubrics used to judge secondary school performance in history, science, and literature. Two factors were found, one represented the experts' pattern and was highly related to judged performance, whereas the attributes of essay that related to "novice" approaches were judged to be lower in an overall impression score. Obviously, experts for the identification of scoring practices may be subject matter experts (SMEs) in the military. Not all performance should be compared to "experts," for example. For young or less-experienced people, the criteria may be derived from well-instructed performers, so that the distance in proficiency between respondent and expert journeyman may be too extreme.

VALIDATION AND MEASURES OF TECHNICAL QUALITY

Although most traditional measures depend upon many test items to achieve adequate levels of reliability, different approaches to measurement are needed when performance is measured by only four or five simulations. In these cases, replicated validity studies provide both validity and reliability information appropriate for assessments of instruction or training. These studies should demonstrate that the test can discriminate between trained, less well-trained, and novice performers. A second study can compare aspects of the task (i.e., prior knowledge) to other measures of relevant topical information by the same examinees, a common strategy called concurrent validity. A third set of studies will attempt to ensure that the test is sensitive to instructional impact (Linn, Baker, & Dunbar, 1991), rather than simply replicating performance that is determined by their background characteristics. With regard to fairness, an important aspect of validity (see, e.g., *Standards for Educational and Psychological Testing* , American Educational Research Association, American Psychological Association, and National Council on Measurement in Education, 1999), it should also be demonstrated that the relation of performance and background variables, such as socioeconomic status, changes as a result of the instruction, and that the test detects such changes. Is this, in part, a circle of inference? Yes, but if one is making a validity argument that the assessment adequately serves its intentions, multiple lines of evidence must be assembled to make the case for validity.

Despite adequate specification and sampling, tasks and items will, nonetheless, differ in difficulty, sometimes on bases that are hard to determine. It is desirable, whenever possible, to identify the features of complex tasks, for instance, in simulations that will be represented so that conceptual equivalence is attained. These features may include critical aspects of the tasks to be learned, the settings in which the task is likely to be performed, common distractions such as speed or multi-tasking, requirements for obtaining and verifying information, and so on. Although it is true that there will remain puzzling differences in difficulty, it is also true that differences in experience and relevant prior knowledge can reduce disparities in complex performance.

In conclusion, it is tempting, in a brief period, to revert to recipe-like guidance for assessment development but that approach is neither achievable nor

Table 15.5. *Tasks for improvement of the measurement of complex cognition.*

1. Specifications of tasks including content and probable contest variations.

2. Full models of criterion performances(s).

3. Expert performance or other empirical standard setting (not what is said, but what is done by experts).

4. Multiple templates or combinations of objects to create tests.

5. Process and progress monitoring.

6. Credible, timely, affordable validation on-the-fly.

7. Demonstration of impact.

my goal. There are a set of procedures, each requiring complex subroutines and sometimes sophisticated understanding that should be considered. For the sake of closure, I list them in Table 15.5.

CONCLUSION

Most of this chapter has been about procedures intended to improve the quality and appropriateness of measures of instruction and to integrate what we know about learning into their design. Yet, quality outcomes must be both credible and affordable to replace those measures already in use. Credibility can be obtained by displaying expert performance and using expertise as sources of scoring criteria rather than the traditional cut scores, described earlier in this chapter. Affordability can be attained if a development approach is used that creates a reusable content ontology, and identifies assessment objects and templates that can be reused for new tasks. It is essential to invest in a procedure to allow the rapid creation of new measures of high quality at reduced costs. In addition, these ontologies also have instructional value to instructors and students.

The new realities of change in civilian and military environments require that assessment not only keep up but actively anticipate future requirements. It is obvious that the new instructional contexts in the military will be different. Requirements will continue to rapidly change, and increasingly complex decisions will be decentralized and made by individuals of relatively low rank (and therefore of average intellectual performance). These challenges are complicated by the inevitability of surprise or multiple concurrent missions that will require the skills of split attention, rapid readjustment of concentration, and strong self-management. These skills will need to be applied in the face of multiple deployments, fatigue, anxiety, and rapidly changing threat. Certainly, high-powered and wonderful assessment won't reduce the stresses of these new environments. But to the extent that one needs confidence in people's readiness to use a given set of skills and their adaptability to new situations, our measures of training must integrate the best knowledge we have about learning, and provide core principles and strategies that, together with relevant knowledge, will support the new expectations of adaptation and transfer.

REFERENCES

American Educational Research Association, American Psychological Association, & National Council on Measurement in Education. (1999). *Standards for educational and psychological testing.* Washington, DC: American Educational Research Association.

Anderson, J. R. (1983). *The architecture of cognition.* Cambridge, MA: Harvard University Press.

Anderson, L. W., & Krathwohl, D. R. (Eds.). (2001). *A taxonomy for learning, teaching, and assessing: A revision of Bloom's taxonomy of educational objectives.* New York: Longman.

Bachman, L. F., & Palmer, A. S. (1996). *Language testing in practice.* Oxford, UK: Oxford University Press.

Bailey, A. L., & Butler, F. A. (2004). Ethical considerations in the assessment of the language and content knowledge of English language learners K-12. *Language Assessment Quarterly, 1*(2&3), 177–193.

Baker, E. L. (2005). Aligning curriculum, standards, and assessments: Fulfilling the promise of school reform. In C. A. Dwyer (Ed.), *Measurement and research in the accountability era* (pp. 315–335). Mahwah, NJ: Lawrence Erlbaum Associates.

——— (2007). Model-based assessments to support learning and accountability: The evolution of CRESST's research on multiple-purpose measures. *Educational Assessment* (Special Issue), *12*(3&4), 179–194.

Baker, E. L., Abedi, J., Linn, R. L., & Niemi, D. (1996, March/April). Dimensionality and generalizability of domain-independent performance assessments. *Journal of Educational Research, 8*(4), 197–205.

Bassok, M., & Holyoak, K. J. (1989). Transfer of domain-specific problem solving procedures. *Journal of Experimental Psychology: Learning, Memory, and Cognition, 16*, 522–533.

Berka, C., Chung, G. K. W. K., Nagashima, S. O., Musacchia, A., Davis, G., Johnson, R., et al. (2008, March). *Using interactive neuro-educational technology to increase the pace and efficiency of rifle marksmanship training.* Paper presented at the annual meeting of the American Educational Research Association, New York, NY.

Bjork, R. A., & Richardson-Klavhen, A. (1989). On the puzzling relationship between environment context and human memory. In C. Izawa (Ed.), *Current issues in cognitive processes: The Tulane Flowerree Symposium on Cognition.* Hillsdale, NJ: Lawrence Erlbaum Associates.

Bloom, B. S. (Ed.). (with Engelhart, M. D., Furst, E. J., Hill, W. H., & Krathwohl, D. R.). (1956). *Taxonomy of educational objectives: The classification of education goals. Handbook 1: Cognitive domain.* New York: David McKay.

——— (1964). *Stability and change in human characteristics.* New York: John Wiley.

Bransford, J. D., & Johnson, M. K. (1973). Consideration of some problems of comprehension. In W. Chase (Ed.), *Visual information processing* (pp. 383–438). New York: Academic Press.

Bruner, J. S. (1977). *The process of education.* Cambridge, MA: Harvard University Press.

Cannon-Bowers, J. A., & Salas, E. (1997). A framework for developing team performance measures in training. In M. T. Brannick, E. Salas, & C. Prince (Eds.), *Team performance assessment and measurement: Theory, methods, and applications* (pp. 45–62). Mahwah, NJ: Lawrence Erlbaum Associates.

Cannon-Bowers, J., & Salas, E. (1998). *Making decisions under stress: Implications for individual and team training.* Washington, DC: American Psychological Association.

Chi, M. T. H., Glaser, R., & Farr, M. (Eds.). (1988). *The nature of expertise.* Hillsdale, NJ: Lawrence Erlbaum Associates.

Chung, G. K. W. K., Dionne, G. B., & Elmore, J. J. (2006). *Diagnosis and prescription design: Rifle marksmanship skills* (Deliverable to the Office of Naval Research). Los Angeles: University of California, National Center for Research on Evaluation, Standards, and Student Testing (CRESST).

Chung, G. K. W. K., Baker, E. L., Niemi, D., Delacruz, G. C., & O'Neil, H. F. (2007). *Knowledge mapping* (CRESST white paper). Los Angeles: University of California, National Center for Research on Evaluation, Standards, and Student Testing.

Chung, G. K. W. K., Delacruz, G. C., Dionne, G. B., & Bewley, W. L. (2003). *Linking assessment and instruction using ontologies.* Proceedings of the I/ITSEC, 25, 1811–1822.

Chung, G. K. W. K., Niemi, D., & Bewley, W. L. (2003, April). *Assessment applications of ontologies.* Paper presented at the annual meeting of the American Educational Research Association, Chicago, IL.

Cronbach, L. J., & Suppes, P. (Eds.). (1969). *Research for tomorrow's schools: Disciplined inquiry for education.* Stanford, CA/New York: National Academy of Education, Committee on Educational Research/ Macmillan.

Delacruz, G. C. (in preparation). *Moving closer to the target: Investigating the impact of an evaluation tool on the training process.* Unpublished doctoral dissertation, University of California, Los Angeles.

Delacruz, G. C., Chung, G. K. W. K., Heritage, M., Vendlinski, T., Bailey, A., & Kim, J-O. (2007, April). *Validating knowledge elicitation techniques: Examining the relation between measures of content knowledge and knowledge of teaching algebra.* Paper presented at the annual meeting of the National Council on Measurement in Education, Chicago, IL.

Ericsson K. A. (Ed). (1996). *The road to excellence: The acquisition of expert performance in the arts and sciences, sports, and games.* Hillsdale, NJ: Lawrence Erlbaum Associates.

 (2003). The search for general abilities and basic capacities: Theoretical implications from the modifiability and complexity of mechanisms mediating expert performance. In R. J. Sternberg & E. L. Grigorenko (Eds.), *Perspectives on the psychology of abilities, competencies, and expertise* (pp. 93–125). Cambridge, UK: Cambridge University Press.

Gagné, R. M. (1985). *The conditions of learning* (4th ed.). New York: Holt, Rinehart & Winston.

Gagné, R. M., Briggs, L. J., & Wagner, W. W. (1992). *Principles of instructional design* (4th ed.). Fort Worth, TX: Harcourt Brace Jovanovich.

Glaser, R. (1977). *Adaptive education: Individual diversity and learning.* New York: Holt, Rinehart and Winston.

Harris, C. W. (Ed.). (1963). *Problems in measuring change.* Madison: The University of Wisconsin Press.

Hively, W., Patterson, H. L., & Page, S. H. (1968). A "universe-defined" system of arithmetic achievement tests. *Journal of Educational Measurement, 5,* 275–290.

Larkin, J. H., McDermott, J., Simon, D. P., & Simon, H. A. (1980). Expert and novice performance in solving physics problems. *Science, 208,* 1335–1342.

Linn, R. L., Baker, E. L., & Dunbar, S. B. (1991). Complex, performance-based assessment: Expectations and validation criteria. *Educational Researcher, 20*(8), 15–21.

Mayer, R. E. (2003). *Learning and instruction.* Upper Saddle River, NJ: Merrill Prentice-Hall.

Merrill, M. D. (2000). Knowledge objects and mental models. In D. A. Wiley (Ed.), *The instructional use of learning objects* [on-line version]. Retrieved August 13, 2007, from, http://reusability.org/read/chapters/merrill.doc.

Messick, S. (1989). Validity. In R. L. Linn (Ed.), *Educational measurement* (3rd ed., pp. 13–103). New York: Macmillan.

National Research Council. (2001). *Knowing what students know: The science and design of educational assessment.* Committee on the Foundations of Assessment. J. Pelligrino, N. Chudowsky, & R. Glaser (Eds.). Board on Testing and Assessment, Center for Education, Division of Behavioral and Social Sciences and Education. Washington, DC: National Academy Press.

Niemi, D., Vallone, J., & Vendlinski, T. (2006). *The power of big ideas in mathematics education: Development and pilot testing of POWERSOURCE assessments* (CSE Rep. No. 697). Los Angeles: University of California, National Center for Research on Evaluation, Standards, and Student Testing (CRESST).

No Child Left Behind Act of 2001, Pub. L. No. 107–110, § 115 Stat. 1425 (2002).

O'Neil, H. F., & Chuang, S.-H. (2005). Self-regulation strategies. In H. F. O'Neil (Ed.), *What works in distance learning. Guidelines* (pp. 111–121). Greenwich, CT: Information Age Publishing.

Spiro, R. J., Feltovich, P. J., Jackson, J. J., & Coulson, R. L. (1991). Cognitive flexibility, constructivism, and hypertext: Random access instruction for advanced knowledge acquisition in ill-structured domains. *Educational Technology, 31*(5), 24–33.

Sweller, J. (1999). *Instructional design in technical areas.* Camberwell, Australia: ACER Press.

Thorndike, E. L. (1904). *An introduction to the theory of mental and social measurement.* New York: Science Press.

16

Acquiring Conceptual Expertise from Modeling:
The Case of Elementary Physics

KURT VANLEHN AND BRETT VAN DE SANDE

In many domains, the real world is modeled with systems of equations. Such a model uses variables to represent domain properties and equations to represent applications of domain principles. Given a set of true domain relationships expressed as equations, one can deduce new equations from them using only the rules of mathematics, and the new equations will also be true domain relationships. The latter step, wherein mathematical implications are derived from the initial model, can often be done mechanically, for example, by mathematical symbol manipulation programs, spreadsheets, calculators, etc.

Given a real-world situation that is amenable to such analysis, experts and novices understand them quite differently. Whereas novices must go through the whole modeling process by writing equations on paper and solving them, experts can generate many conclusions about the same situations without having to commit anything to paper. For the expert, many domain relationships are just "obvious" or can be easily inferred "by inspection."

There are limits to the experts' abilities. Although experts usually cannot mentally infer *quantitative* relationships, such as the exact numerical value for an energy or a velocity, they can infer *qualitative* relationships, such as whether a quantity is zero, increasing or greater than some other quantity. Thus, it is often said that expertise in such domains is characterized by a *conceptual* or *qualitative* understanding of real world situations (VanLehn, 1996). It is sometimes said that they have developed domain-specific *intuitions* (Simon & Simon, 1978). This ability of the experts is called *conceptual expertise*, and it is the focus of this chapter.

Interest in conceptual expertise has increased in recent years with the discovery that in some surprisingly simple situations, novices have intuitions that

Acknowledgments: This work is supported by NSF under grants 0325054 and 0354420. We thank Anders Ericsson, Robert Shelby, Tim Nokes, Robert Hausmann, and Jodi Davenport for their comments on drafts.

conflict with the experts' intuitions (McCloskey, Caramazza, & Green, 1980). For instance, suppose a bowling ball and a golf ball are dropped from 2 meters above the Earth's surface. An expert will know immediately that the two balls strike the earth at exactly the same time, whereas novices usually say that the balls land at slightly different times. Novice intuitions about such situations are often quite systematic, leading to the view that novices have alternative beliefs about how the world works, often called *misconceptions*. In the last few decades, such misconceptions have been documented in almost every branch of science (Pfundt & Duit, 1998).

Scientists and educators have been appalled at the ubiquity of misconceptions, which appear in the responses of even the best students. That such misconceptions survive high school and university science courses has been viewed as a crisis in science education. Preventing and/or overcoming misconceptions is the explicit goal of countless educational research and development projects. One step toward achieving that goal is understanding conceptual expertise. In short, interest in understanding conceptual expertise has increased with the discovery of ubiquitous, systematic misconceptions among students who have already taken appropriate courses.

In this chapter, we analyze conceptual expertise and propose an account for its acquisition. Our claim, which is not surprising in the context of this book, is that this kind of conceptual expertise arises from extensive practice of a certain kind. Moreover, there is a natural developmental sequence that occurs with every domain principle: from a *superficial* understanding, to a *semantic* understanding, and finally to a *qualitative* understanding. Novices often have too little practice of the right kind, so they never reach the semantic stage of understanding, which appears to be the key.

Although we believe this account will hold true in many domains, this chapter discusses it in the context of just one domain: elementary physics – the kind of physics taught in first-year college courses and in advanced high school courses. Elementary physics is a small and well-defined domain compared to others in the expertise literature, which makes it tractable for laboratory study. Indeed, early in history of expertise research, elementary physics emerged as the premier domain with a number of very influential studies discovering characteristics of expertise that were later found to be general (Chi, Feltovich, & Glaser, 1981 ;Chi, Glaser, & Rees, 1982; Larkin, McDermott, Simon, & Simon, 1980).

Apart from its small, well-defined knowledge base, elementary physics is a domain with excellent access to participants at many levels of expertise. In pioneering studies (e.g., Chi et al., 1981; Simon & Simon, 1978), the concepts and the performance of novices were contrasted with those of experts, where the *experts* were college instructors who had been teaching elementary physics for many years, and the *novices* were recent graduates of such physics courses. Some studies reached further back and tested students just beginning a college physics course (*pre-novices*).

Problem:
A bomber is flying at 1000 km/hr at an altitude of 500 m. If the bomber releases a 1000 kg bomb, what is its impact speed? What would the impact speed of a 500 kg bomb be?

Solution:
Let m be the bomb's mass, so m = 1000 kg.
Let v1 be the bomb's initial velocity, so v1 = 1000 km/hr = 278 m/s.
Let h be the height of the bomb when it is released, so h = 500 m.
Let v2 be the bomb's final velocity. We need to solve for this.
The initial total mechanical energy of the bomb is KE1 + PE1 = ½*m*v1^2 + m*g*h.
The final total mechanical energy is KE2 = ½*m*v2^2.
Because we can ignore air friction, mechanical energy is conserved,
so we can equate the initial and final total mechanical energies.
Thus, ½*m*v2^2 = ½*m*v1^2 + m*g*h.
Solving, we have v2 = sqrt[v1^2 + 2*g*h] = sqrt[(278 m/s)^2 + 2*(9.8 m/s^2)*(500 m)].
So, v2 = 295 m/s.
Because m cancels, a 500 kg bomb would have the same impact speed.

FIGURE 16.1. A quantitative elementary physics problem and its solution.

Another reason to study expertise in elementary physics is that the task domain has been thoroughly analyzed in order to develop artificially intelligent physics problems solving software (Bundy, Byrd, Luger, Mellish, & Palmer, 1979; de Kleer & Brown, 1984 ; Forbus, 1985; Larkin, 1981; Larkin, Reif, Carbonell, & Gugliotta, 1988; McDermott & Larkin, 1978; Novak & Araya, 1980); intelligent tutoring systems (Jordan, Makatchev, Pappuswamy, VanLehn, & Albacete, 2006; Loftin, Mueller, Way, & Lee, 1991; Murray, Schultz, Brown, & Clement, 1990; Reif & Scott, 1999; VanLehn et al., 2002; VanLehn et al., 2005); computational models of learning (Elio & Scharf, 1990; Jones & Fleischman, 2001; Lamberts, 1990; Reimann, Schult, & Wichmann, 1993; VanLehn & Jones, 1993b; VanLehn, Jones, & Chi, 1992); and qualitative accounts of learning (M. T. H. Chi, 2005 ; di Sessa, 1993; Sherin, 2001, 2006).

Still another reason for studying physics expertise is that it permits us to study two different indices of mastery of the domain. The first type is *quantitative* problem solving, which involves writing equations and solving them, usually over a period of several minutes. Figure 16.1 shows a quantitative problem and its solution. The second index of expertise is solving problems that involve little math, little writing, and brief solution times. These are called *conceptual* problems or sometimes *qualitative* problems, and they are often devised to display differences between expert and novice intuitions. Figure 16.2 shows some conceptual problems.

On the face of it, the conceptual problems should be the easier of the two because they take less time, involve no math, and so on. A consistent finding in the literature of physics expertise is, however, that even novices who approach experts in their ability to solve quantitative problems are often more like pre-novices in their ability to solve conceptual problems (Hake, 1998; Hestenes, Wells, & Swackhamer, 1992).

1. A steel ball rolls along a smooth, hard, level surface with a certain speed. It then smoothly rolls up and over the hill shown below. How does its speed at point B after it rolls over the hill compare to its speed at point A before it rolls over the hill?

A. Its speed is significantly less at point B than at point A.
B. Its speed is very nearly the same at point B as at point A.
C. Its speed is slightly greater at point B than at point A.
D. Its speed is much greater at point B than at point A.
E. The information is insufficient to answer the question.

2. Two steel balls, one of which weighs twice as much as the other, roll off a horizontal table with the same speeds. In this situation:
   A. Both balls impact the floor at approximately the same horizontal distance from the base of the table.
   B. The heavier ball impacts the floor at about half the horizontal distance from the base of the table than does the lighter.
   C. The lighter ball impacts the floor at about half the horizontal distance from the base of the table than does the heavier.
   D. The heavier ball impacts the floor considerably closer to base of the table than the lighter, but not necessarily half the horizontal distance.
   E. The lighter ball impacts the floor considerably closer to base of the table than the heavier, but not necessarily half the horizontal distance.

FIGURE 16.2. Two qualitative physics problems.

(*Source:* Problem 1 courtesy of Prof. David Hestenes, Arizona State University.)

Most physics education researchers assume that current physics instruction is at fault, and they have invented and sometimes evaluated many instructional innovations. Although there have been improvements, Hake (1998) and others conclude that after decades of instructional innovation, the problem is still not solved.

Our hypothesis is that conceptual expertise is comprised of a qualitative understanding of domain principles, and that extensive practice is needed for a learner to develop through the stages of superficial understanding and semantic understanding before finally arriving at a qualitative understanding. Instructional innovations that fail to provide sufficient practice of the right kinds take students only part of the way toward conceptual expertise.

This chapter will expand upon this hypothesis by presenting a cognitive task analysis and learning mechanisms that are consistent with findings from the elementary physics literature. Because the chapter presents no new findings, it is purely theoretical.

The chapter has several sections, one for each of these questions:

1. What knowledge comprises conceptual expertise in physics?
2. What happened to novices' misconceptions?
3. How does expertise affect quantitative problem solving?
4. How can conceptual expertise be learned?

The first three sections develop an account for the existing body of expert–novice findings. The key idea is that experts have acquired a class of knowledge, called *confluences*, that novices lack. The fourth section proposes an explanation for how conceptual expertise can be learned, based on two well-known learning mechanisms, induction from examples and EBL. The key idea is that learners go through three stages of understanding per principle: superficial, semantic, and qualitative.

This chapter does not attempt to argue systematically for the generality of its claims beyond elementary physics. However, many of the expert–novice phenomena observed in physics have also been observed in other task domains, which increases the plausibility that elementary physics will again prove prototypical of other task domains. As an example of such an expert–novice finding, consider the Chi, Feltovich, and Glaser (1981) discovery that physics novices classify problems by surface features, whereas physics experts prefer to classify problems by deep features. This expert–novice difference has been found in other task domains as well, such as chemistry (Kozma & Russell, 1997), management organizational problems (Day & Lord, 1992), genetics (Smith, 1992), programming (Weiser & Shertz, 1983), counseling (Mayfield, Kardash, & Kivlighan, 1999), and fishing (Shafto & Coley, 2003). As a second example, consider Priest and Lindsay's (1992) finding that experts could mentally generate and orally explain a plan for solving an elementary physics problem, but novices could not. This expert–novice difference has been found in other task domains as well (Ericsson, 2006; Ericsson & Lehmann, 1996; Heyworth, 1999). In short, although parts of this proposal for conceptual expertise are clearly specific to physics alone, it is likely that other parts are more general and apply to mastery of several different domains of knowledge-based expertise. Some speculations on generality are included in a final discussion at the end of the chapter.

WHAT KNOWLEDGE COMPRISES CONCEPTUAL EXPERTISE IN PHYSICS?

In order to uncover the knowledge that comprises conceptual expertise, this section works backward from the problems used to assess it. It asks: What knowledge is needed in order to correctly solve these problems? This section is a summary of a computer model, Cascade, that Ploetzner and VanLehn (1997) showed could correctly solve many problems on the widely used Force Concept Inventory (Hestenes et al., 1992). However, the basic categorization of knowledge presented here appears in many other accounts of physics knowledge, including both those backed by computer modeling (Bundy et al., 1979; Elio & Schart, 1990; de Kleer & Brown, 1984; Forbus, 1985 ; Jones & Fleischman, 2001; Lamberts, 1990; Larkin, 1981; Larkin et al., 1988; McDermott & Larkin, 1978; Novak & Araya, 1980; Reimann et al., 1993; VanLehn & Jones, 1993b; VanLehn et al., 1992) and others (M. T. H. Chi, 2005; di Sessa, 1993; Hestenes, 1987; Sherin, 2001, 2006).

Concept inventories are usually multiple-choice tests with questions such as those in Figure 16.2 and the following one (from Prof. Robert Shelby, personal communication):

A dive bomber can release its bomb when diving, climbing, or flying horizontally. If it is flying at the same height and speed in each case, in which case does the bomb have the most speed when it hits the ground?

A. Diving
B. Climbing
C. Flying horizontally
D. It doesn't matter. The bomb's impact speed is the same in all three cases.
E. More information is needed in order to answer.

Most novices and pre-novices choose A as their answer. The experts prefer D, as they recognize this as an application of Conservation of Mechanical Energy. Now consider this problem (from Hestenes et al., 1992):

A book is at rest on a table top. Which of the following force(s) is (are) acting on the book?

1. A downward force due to gravity.
2. The upward force by the table.
3. A net downward force due to air pressure.
4. A net upward force due to air pressure.

Experts would answer 1, 2, and 4, whereas novices tend to answer 1 and 3. Although the dive bomber problem requires applying a principle, the book problem only requires identifying forces.

These problems illustrate two aspects of conceptual expertise. The book problem illustrates what Hestenes (1987) calls the "description phase" of modeling. The expert decides how to describe the physical world in terms of ideal objects, relationships, and quantities, such as point masses, forces, energies, accelerations, etc. Likewise, solving the dive bomber problem begins with a description phase, where the expert constructs an idealized model by deciding whether to neglect friction, ignore rotation of the Earth, treat the bomb as a point object, and so on. At the end of the description phase, the stage is set for applying principles, but no principles have been applied.

Let us coin the term "description phase knowledge" and agree that conceptual problems, such as the book problem, test whether students have such knowledge. Such knowledge appears as a distinct type in several computational models of physics problem solving (e.g., Bundy et al., 1979; Ploetzner & VanLehn, 1997 ; VanLehn et al., 1992), whereas in other models, it is represented in the same formalism as other knowledge. All these models interleave the application of description phase knowledge with other knowledge in order to be consistent with human data. When problems are exceptionally tricky, experts verbalize applications of description phase knowledge and the applications are intermingled with application of other knowledge rather than being done as a distinct phase (Larkin, 1983).

Although description phase knowledge alone suffices for solving some problems, it does not suffice for the dive bomber problem. For the dive bomber problem, experts must both recognize that Conservation of Mechanical Energy can apply and draw conclusions from its application. In the Hestenes (1987) terminology, these comprise the formulation and ramification stages of modeling. It is widely believed, and consistent with much work on the modeling of expertise (VanLehn, 1996), that the knowledge driving these stages is organized into principle *schemas* (Chi et al., 1981; Dufresne, Gerace, Hardiman, & Mestre, 1992; Larkin, 1983; VanLehn, 1996). Thus, we use "principle schemas" to refer to it.

Schemas have three important parts: applicability conditions, bodies, and slots (Russell & Norvig, 2003). The information for deciding whether a schema applies is called the *applicability conditions* of the schema, and the information that draws conclusions comprises the *body* of the schema. A schema also has *slots*, which are filled with objects from the problem situation and indicate how the principle is mapped onto the situation. Applicability conditions determine which objects can fill the schema's slots. For instance, in applying Conservation of Mechanical Energy to the dive bomber problem, the schema's applicability conditions decide that the principle should be applied to the bomb, not the plane; that is, the bomb should fill one of the slots of the principle's schema. Let us examine applicability conditions a bit further, then consider the bodies of schemas.

Verbal protocols taken as experts read ordinary problems suggest that they recognize the applicability of schemas rapidly, sometimes after reading just a few words of the problem (Hinsley, Hayes, & Simon, 1977). This suggests that their knowledge includes simple applicability conditions for recognizing commonly occurring special cases. For instance, one such applicability condition is:

> If there is a moving object, and we have or need its velocity at two time points, time 1 and time 2, and there are no non-conservative forces acting on the object between those two time points, then we can apply Conservation of Mechanical Energy to the object from time 1 to time 2.

This applicability condition could be used for the dive bomber problem, and expert verbal protocols suggest that it is indeed used for many Conservation of Mechanical Energy problems (Chi et al., 1981).

Applicability conditions delineate only the *possible* principle applications. This would suffice if the question merely asked, "Which principles apply when a dive bomber drops a bomb?" (cf., Owen & Sweller, 1985; Sweller, Mawer, & Ward, 1983). However, the dive bomber question did not ask about principle applications, but about the speed of the bomb when it reached the ground. To answer such questions, the expert must use knowledge from the *body* of the principle's schema. For this example, the expert might use this knowledge component:

> If Conservation of Mechanical Energy is applied to two objects, A and B, and the mass, initial velocity, initial height, and final height have the same values for object A as for object B, then objects A and B must have the same final velocity as well.

The second type of knowledge component is a rule inferred from the principle's equations, $KE_1 + PE_1 = KE_2 + PE_2$, where KE stands for kinetic energy and PE stands for potential energy, and the numbers distinguish the two time points. A rule inferred from a qualitative interpretation of an equation is called a *confluence* (de Kleer & Brown, 1984). A confluence is stated in terms of a qualitative value system, such as {positive, negative, zero, non-zero} or {increasing, decreasing, constant, non-constant}. For instance, if the **algebraic** form of a principle is $X = Y + Z$, then a confluence based on the value system {increase, decrease, constant} is "If X increases and Y is constant, then Z increases." Another confluence for the same equation and same value system is, "If Z decreases and Y decreases, then X decreases." There are 19 more such confluences. For any equation and any qualitative value system, there are a finite number of confluences, and it is straightforward to work them all out.

To summarize, the hypothesis is that experts solve conceptual problems by applying three types of knowledge component: (1) description phase knowledge, (2) *applicability conditions*, which have the form, "if <condition> then <principle application>," and (3) *qualitative confluences*, which have the form, "if <principle application> and <quantity has qualitative value>, <quantity has qualitative value>, … then <quantity has qualitative value>." The latter two are parts of principle schemas. Experts have a great deal of knowledge besides these three types, but for answering simple conceptual problems, they probably only need these three.

Although concept inventories are convenient and widely used to assess conceptual expertise, there are other methods as well. Thus, we need to check that the three types of knowledge mentioned above will succeed on these less-common assessments as well.

Several assessments involve showing participants some ordinary *quantitative* problems, such as the one shown in Figure 16.1, and asking them *not* to solve the problems but instead to:

1. Sort the problems into clusters of similar problems (Chi et al., 1981; Chi et al., 1982),
2. Describe their basic approach or plan for solving the problem (Chi et al., 1982; Priest & Lindsay, 1992), *or*

3. Pick which of two other problems is similar to the given problem (Hardiman, Dufresne, & Mestre, 1989).

The common finding among all these studies is that experts can mentally generate a plan for solving a problem. The plan identifies the major principle applications, which are then used for problem clustering and problem similarity judgments. When the experts explain their choices in these tasks or their basic approach to solving a problem, they nearly always mention principles.

On the other hand, novices' basic approaches seldom mention application of principles. According to Chi et al. (1981, p. 142):

> when asked to develop and state "a basic approach," [novices] did one of two things. They either made very global statements about how to proceed, "First, I figured out what was happening ... then I, I started seeing how these different things were related to each other ... I think of formulas that give their relationships and then ... I keep on relating things through this chain....." or they would attempt to solve the problem, giving the detailed equation sets they would use.

This suggests that experts' schemas include *planning confluences*, where a planning confluence is a confluence (a non-numerical interpretation of an equation) that uses the value system {known, sought}. For instance, generic planning confluences for $X = Y + Z$ include "if X and Y are known, then Z is known," and "if X is sought and Y is known, then Z is sought." As another example, a planning confluence useful for Figure 16.1 is:

> If the definition of kinetic energy applies to an object at time 1, and the velocity of the object at time 1 is sought, then its kinetic energy at time 1 should be sought.

In summary, the principle schemas of experts, but not novices, have planning confluences of the form, "if <principle application> and <quantity is known/sought>, <quantity is known/sought>, ... then <quantity is known/sought>."

There is evidence that these confluence are actually used by experts. Chi et al. (1981, p. 124) found that their experts took longer than novices to choose a cluster for a problem (45 seconds per problem versus 30 seconds). This is consistent with experts using the extra time to plan a solution to some problems. Moreover, Larkin (1983) found that when experts are given unfamiliar problems, their verbal protocols are peppered with statements of the form "<quantity> is known, so ..." and "we need <quantity>, so ...." When students' principle schemas have correct applicability conditions but lack planning confluences, then certain kinds of quantitative problem can fool them into applying principles that are irrelevant to solving the problem (M. Chi & VanLehn, 2008).

The question addressed by this section is, "what knowledge comprises conceptual expertise in elementary physics?" and the proposed answer is, "description phase knowledge, and for each principle, mastery of its applicability conditions, its qualitative confluences, and its planning confluences." This claim should be understood as an approximation. There are other knowledge components that do not fit these categories and yet they are part of conceptual expertise.

For instance, experts tend to know which quantities typically cancel out during calculations. It turns out that simple reasoning with confluences is incomplete – there are solutions to systems of confluences that cannot be found by the simple algorithm (Forbus & de Kleer, 1993). One method, called "plunking" (Forbus & de Kleer, 1993), for increasing the number of solutions found, is to assume that a quantity will cancel out and then check (somehow!) that it does. This appears to be what experts do, but the evidence is only anecdotal at this time.

Finding sound and complete algorithms that solve large systems of confluences is just one of the problems studied in the field of qualitative reasoning (QR) about physical system. The field has an extensive literature, a textbook (Forbus & de Kleer, 1993), and periodic conferences (http://www.cs.colorado.edu/~lizb/ qr08.html is the web site for the 22nd conference, which occurred in 2008). For the QR community, this whole section is old news. For them, it is axiomatic that conceptual expertise includes at least qualitative principle schemas and description phase knowledge. Moreover, QR applies to a wide variety of science and engineering domains. The default assumption is that if one can model something with differential equations, then it can probably also be modeled with QR.

WHAT HAPPENED TO THE NOVICES' MISCONCEPTIONS?

On conceptual problems, many different novices give the same incorrect answer. For instance, on the dive bomber problem, most novices think that releasing the bomb when the dive bomber is diving will maximize the final velocity of the bomb. Such systematic, incorrect responses have been collected and codified as *misconceptions* (also called alternative conceptions). A common misconception is: "If an object is moving in a certain direction, there is a force acting on it in that direction." Many misconceptions have been inferred (Pfundt & Duit, 1998) and there has been much research on their epistemology and ontogeny (e.g., Chi, in press; di Sessa, 1993; Vosniadou & Brewer, 1992).

Presumably, physics experts once had misconceptions, which have disappeared as the experts achieved conceptual expertise. Because graduate student teaching assistants still hold many misconceptions (Hestenes & Wells, 1992; Hestenes et al., 1992), the disappearance of misconceptions may occur somewhat late in development. If we nonetheless assume that experts lack misconceptions, we can speculate as to the reasons for their demise.

A key observation, made by many (e.g., Hestenes et al., 1992; Ranney & Thagard, 1988) is that abstract, general misconceptions are incompatible with conceptual expertise. For instance, suppose someone who believes that motion always implies force in the direction of motion gradually acquires a qualitative confluence of Newton's Second Law, that a zero acceleration (i.e., constant velocity) implies a zero net force. These two beliefs produce contradictory predictions about many familiar situations. As budding experts begin to master such confluences, they may notice the contradictions. This probably weakens their belief in the misconceptions and narrows the situations where the misconceptions' predictions are preferred. Figuratively speaking, misconceptions don't ever die, they just get beaten in so many situations by confluences that they retire.

Increasing conceptual expertise may also modify misconceptions and/or the conditions under which they are retrieved or believed. As an example of modification, Sherin (2006) suggests that his students' vague belief that force implies motion (di Sessa's [1993] force-as-mover p-prim) was specialized to become the correct belief that "force implies change in velocity."

HOW DOES EXPERTISE AFFECT QUANTITATIVE PROBLEM SOLVING?

As mentioned earlier, science educators use two common indices of mastery: quantitative problem solving (Figure 16.1) and conceptual problem solving. So far, we have discussed only conceptual problem solving as it occurs either during concept inventories whose multiple-choice problems do not involve quantities (Figure 16.2), or during laboratory tasks where subjects sort, compare, or discuss, but do not solve, quantitative problems. Are there also differences between experts and novices on the second indicator, the solving of quantitative problems, such as the one in Figure 16.1?

An early finding in the expert–novice literature was that as experts solved quantitative problems, they wrote down or mentioned equations in different order than pre-novices. At first, this phenomenon was characterized as forward (experts) versus backward (pre-novices) problem-solving strategies (Larkin et al., 1980 ; Simon & Simon, 1978). However, later analyses characterized the orderings as grouped by principle schemas (experts) versus algebraic chaining (pre-novices) (Larkin, 1983). For instance, Larkin (1983, p. 89) says of the experts that, "in all cases, the work associated with one schema is completed before work associated with another is begun."

However, these early studies used pre-novices, that is, students who were just beginning their study of college physics. The pre-novices made so many errors that it was often difficult to compare their work to the work of experts. Moreover, the pre-novices averaged about 40 seconds per equation, whereas the experts averaged about 5 to 10 seconds per equation (Larkin, 1981), which gives one an idea of just how different their behaviors are.

On the other hand, several studies of *novices* (i.e., students who had just finished a physics course) showed that their behavior on quantitative problems was remarkably similar to expert behavior. Chi et al. (1981) found no difference in speed between experts and novices, and only a small difference in accuracy. More tellingly, Priest and Lindsay (1992) found no difference between experts and novices in the *order* in which equations were written.

This suggests that both experts and novices have well-developed knowledge components for the equations associated with principles, whereas prenovices are still struggling to learn the equations. As computer modeling has shown (Klenk & Forbus, 2007 ; Larkin, 1981), many physics problems can be solved quite efficiently given only a thorough knowledge of the equations, which would explain why novices behave so much like experts despite their lack of conceptual knowledge.

On the other hand, although experts and novices display similar equation ordering, speed, and errors, their mental processes seem quite different. When participants describe their reasoning either during or after problem solving, experts display clear plans for solutions whereas novices do not (Priest & Lindsay, 1992). This makes sense, given that experts, but not novices, tend to succeed at the planning tasks discussed earlier. All these findings are consistent with the assumption that experts have mastered many planning confluences and novices have not.

HOW CAN CONCEPTUAL EXPERTISE BE LEARNED?

The preceding sections argued that all the expert–novice findings can be explained by assuming that novices lack the expert's description phase knowledge, confluences, and applicability conditions. This section indicates possible methods of learning each of these three types of knowledge. It draws on machine learning and more specifically on the Cascade model of physics learning (VanLehn, 1999; VanLehn & Jones, 1993b; VanLehn et al., 1992). It describes how conceptual expertise *can* be learned, in that it presents machine-learning methods that can output the appropriate knowledge when given the appropriate training. It also compares the prescribed methods to current practices in physics education. In particular, it describes what would need to be changed in order to increase the number of college students who achieve conceptual expertise by the end of a year-long introductory course.

Learning Description Phase Knowledge

Description phase knowledge is essentially a set of classifications or categories. They recognize instances of categories such as forces, magnetic fields, pressure, etc. A piece of description phase knowledge says that if certain conditions exist, then a certain object or property exists as well. In machine learning, a piece of knowledge in the form "if <conditions> then <instance of class exists>" is called a classifier (Russell & Norvig, 2003).

A simple way to learn classifiers is by induction from labeled examples. For physics, an example is just a physical situation, such as a block sliding down an inclined plane. The label indicates whether the classifier applies (positive example) or does not apply (negative example). For instance, the conditions under which a normal force exists can be induced from situations where the learner is told that a normal force is present (positive examples) or told that it is absent (negative examples). Many cognitive mechanisms suffice for performing classifier induction, which is also called concept formation or category learning in the psychology (Ashby & Maddox, 2005; Medin & Ross, 1989).

Learning a classifier can take hundreds of examples, but an instructor can dramatically decrease the number of examples required via several pedagogical methods. One is to teach just one classifier at a time and to use the simplest examples possible. For instance, when teaching students to recognize forces, instructors should ideally show a situation with just one force and as few distracting details as possible. If the situation physically requires multiple forces, then the instructor should explicitly indicate which parts of the situation support the existence of each force. Students should also practice identifying concepts in isolation, and they should get feedback on their performance. By drawing forces (Heller & Reif, 1984) and energies (Van Heuvelen & Zou, 2001) in isolation, and not as part of solving a larger problem, students could probably induce those key description phase concepts with only a few dozen situations. Unfortunately, such exercises were uncommon (Hestenes, 1987), so most students may have to acquire description phase concepts by analysis of feedback on their solutions to larger problems, which could slow their learning significantly.

A second way to speed up induction is to include ample negative examples. Textbooks seldom present a situation where there are no forces, then ask the student to identify all forces. Such exercises should help.

A particularly useful technique is to present minimally contrasting pairs of examples: One example is positive, the other is negative, and they differ in only one critical feature. For instance, one can contrast a projectile moving along a curved constant speed path with one moving at constant speed along a straight path, and ask students to identify accelerations. Another contrasting pair shows two situations, both positive, but differing in a critical feature. For instance, students often believe that only animate agents can exert forces, so one can show a situation where a person's hand (animate agent) supports a motionless book, versus a situation where a table (inanimate agent) supports a motionless book. The instructor points out that there is a normal force acting on the book in both situations despite the fact that one agent is animate and the other is not. Minimally contrasting pairs are only moderately common in current physics instruction.

Learning Applicability Conditions

Applicability conditions determine when a principle schema can be applied. They also determine its possible slot fillers, for example, whether to apply Conservation of Mechanical Energy to the bomb or the dive bomber.

Applicability conditions are also classifiers, so they too can be induced from labeled examples. For instance, the dive bomber problem is a positive example for Conservation of Mechanical Energy, but a negative example for Newton's First Law. Because applicability conditions must also fill slots, they are first order categories, so more intricate induction methods may be needed (Muggleton, 1992).

Learning such applicability conditions would be simple if students were given isolated training examples instead of examples of quantitative and qualitative problem solving, which include application of schemas as only a small part of their solution. That is, given a situation, students would be shown which principles applied to which object. Later, they would be asked to list all the principle applications for a given situation and would get feedback on their choices. When Dufresne, Gerace, Hardiman, and Mestre (1992) added classification training to quantitative problem solving, conceptual expertise increased.

Learning Confluences

In contrast to the two types of knowledge discussed so far, which can be acquired by simple mechanisms, confluences can be acquired in moderately complex three-stage process. The stages correspond to three different ways of understanding the fundamental equations behind the principles: *superficially*, *semantically*, and *qualitatively*.

The learning process starts with the students acquiring a *superficial* understanding of the principle's equations. This is what novice students do now, much to the chagrin of instructors. For Conservation of Mechanical Energy, students might literally encode $KE_1 + PE_1 = KE_2 + PE_2$ as a string of characters. Indeed, when asked to state the principle, they may say, "Kay ee one plus pea ee one equals...." Moreover, when such students are asked, "But what is kay ee one?" they do *not* say, "kinetic energy at time one" but instead would probably reply, "Kay ee equals one-half em vee squared." Students with a superficial understanding of the principles' equations have not integrated the semantics of the generic variables into the equation.

Explanation-based learning (EBL; see Russell & Norvig, 2003) can be used to construct an equation containing expressions that refer to quantitative properties of the objects, times, etc., to which the principle is being applied. That is, the terms inside the equations are not symbols or character strings, but are instead referring expressions similar to the mental representations of noun phrases. Moreover, embedded inside these referring expressions are references to the slots of the schemas. Thus, an equation like $KE_1 + PE_1 = KE_2 + PE_2$ is now understood by the student as:

> "The kinetic energy of <the object> at <time 1> + the potential energy of <the object> at <time 1> = ..."where <the object> and <time 1> slots.

When the principle is applied to the dive bomber problem, <the object> is filled by "the bomb" and <time 1> is filled by "the moment that the bomb is released" so that the a problem-specific semantic equation reads:

"The kinetic energy of the bomb at the moment it is released + the potential energy of the bomb at the moment it is released = …"

It should be easy for students to acquire semantic equations since they are usually given all the information they need in the text. For instance, a statement of Conservation of Energy might include:

… $KE_1 + PE_1 = KE_2 + PE_2$, where KE_1 denotes the kinetic energy of the object at time 1, and PE_1 denotes ….

All the student has to do is to integrate the phrase "where <symbol> denotes <expression>" into the equation. This is just what EBL would do.

However, physics students can solve quantitative problems via purely algebraic, shallow, analogical methods (Klenk & Forbus, 2007; Larkin, 1981 VanLehn, 1998; VanLehn & Jones, 1993a, 1993b). If this is the only training they get, then they have no incentive to formulate semantic equations. The superficial versions will do just fine.

In short, although students have opportunities to construct semantic equations, ordinary homework does not encourage or require it. This may explain why at the end of the semester, only some students have reached a semantic stage of understanding on some principles.

Semantic equations would be simple to learn if students were given exercises that required use of semantics. For instance, Corbett et al. (2006) gave students a problem and an equation that applied to that problem, then had students type in English descriptions for variables and expressions in the equation. Here is one of the Corbett et al. problems:

The Pine Mountain Resort is expanding. The main lodge holds 50 guests. The management is planning to build cabins that hold six guests each. A mathematical model of this situation is $Y = 6X + 50$. What does X stand for? What does Y stand for? What does $6X$ stand for? What does 50 stand for?

Answering each question with a menu or typing should cause students to construct semantic versions of equations, and that may explain why the Corbett et al. instruction was successful compared to ordinary quantitative problem-solving practice.

The third and last stage of learning principle schemas is to construct *confluences* from the semantic equations. Again, this can be done via EBL, but it requires some background knowledge, called a generic confluence (Forbus & de Kleer, 1993). A *generic confluence* matches the form of a semantic or algebraic equation but has no domain content itself. For instance, one such generic confluence is,

> Given that the equation $?W + ?X = ?Y + ?Z$ applies to two objects, if $?W$, $?X$, and $?Z$ are the same for both objects, then so is $?Y$,

where $?W$, $?X$, $?Y$, and $?Z$ are intended to match semantic (or algebraic) expressions. For instance, they would match terms in the semantic equation of Conservation of Mechanical Energy:

> The kinetic energy of <the object> at <time 1> + the potential energy of <the object> at <time 1> = the kinetic energy of <the object> at <time 2> + the potential energy of <the object> at <time 2>

and produce a confluence, which is part of the qualitative understanding of the principle:

> If the kinetic energies of <the two objects> are the same at <time 1>, and the potential energies of <the two objects> are the same at <time 1>, and the potential energies of <the two objects> are the same at <time 2>, then the kinetic energies of <the two objects> are the same at <time 2>.

This confluence provides the key step for solving the dive bomber problem when <the two objects> is filled by the bomb from the diving plane and the bomb from the climbing plane.

In order to do such learning, students should solve qualitative problems, such as the dive bomber problem. However, they must already know the semantic equations for principles and the appropriate generic confluences. The generic confluences can either be taught explicitly or induced from experience in mathematics. When the student has both semantic equations and generic confluences, they can be applied to solve qualitative problems. EBL can then abstract the problem-specific parts away, leaving a physics-specific confluence, which is added to the principle's schema. In other words, the desired principle-specific confluences are probably acquired by specialization of generic confluences, which are themselves acquired from mathematics practice.

A similar proposal was articulated by Sherin (2001, 2006), who points out that certain knowledge components exist midway between physics-rich, principle-specific confluences and physics-free, generic confluences. He calls these knowledge components *symbolic forms*. For instance, one symbolic form, called "balancing," says that if a situation can be analyzed as two opposing force-like entities, X and Y, that are in balance, then $X = Y$, where the "=" should be understood as both a qualitative and algebraic relationship. This knowledge component has some physics content, but not as much as, say, the confluences for Newton's First Law. If students possess knowledge of symbolic forms, they may be able to use EBL to specialize them to principle-specific confluences. According to Sherin, symbolic forms develop out of di Sessa's (1993) p-prims, which are components of intuitive physics possessed even by young children. Generic confluences and symbolic forms provide two routes to the same destination: the confluences that comprise a qualitative under-standing of principles.

EBL essentially just moves knowledge around, combining parts of two knowledge components to form a new knowledge component. Machine learn-ing of one confluence is easy and requires just one example. However, there are many possible confluences to learn. For instance, given an equation with three terms (e.g., A = B*C) and a number system with two values (e.g., {zero, non-zero}), there are 24 different possible confluences such as "If B is zero and C is non-zero then A is zero" and "If A is zero and B is non-zero then C is zero." It is not clear how many qualitative physics confluences need to be constructed for a student to achieve conceptual expertise, so it is not clear how many con-ceptual problems they need to solve.

They probably do not need to practice each confluence separately, as there can be hundreds of confluence *per principle*, and not even experts have solved that many conceptual problems. It is more likely that experts only possess con-fluences for a few common cases. When they lack the appropriate confluence, they just use the semantic equation and the generic confluence instead.

Indeed, when Dee-Lucas and Larkin (1991) taught students using seman-tic versions for equations written in English, the students did better on con-ceptual problems than students taught the same material with mathematical equations. This suggests that the students already had generic confluences (which is likely, given that they were students in a highly selective technical university), and that they constructed confluences on-the-spot while answer-ing the conceptual questions.

If learning a confluence is so easy, why don't today's students acquire con-ceptual expertise? Although a likely response would be that students may not be getting enough conceptual problem-solving practice, the prevalence of conceptual problems increased dramatically since 1980 and this does not seem to have cured the problem. It seems likely that students are getting concep-tual problems but are solving them by some method that avoids conceptual learning. Because conceptual problems have such simple answers, it is rela-tively easy to memorize them. For instance, students may learn that "when two objects are dropped from the same height, they hit the ground together." This is just a slight generalization of a common conceptual problem (posed earlier with a bowling ball and a golf ball), so it is often called a *problem* schema. A problem schema suffices only for a very narrow set of problems, whereas a *principle* schema is more general. Indeed, students often answer one problem on a concept inventory correctly but miss another that, to a physicist, seems nearly identical. For instance, even if a student gets the bowling ball and golf ball problem right, they may give an incorrect answer on:

> Suppose a bowling ball and a golf ball are released at the same time from around shoulder height, but the bowling ball is somewhat higher than

the golf ball when they are released. Will the bowling ball catch up to the golf ball before they hit the ground?

The problem schema is too specific to apply to this problem.

To prevent memorization of conceptual problems as conceptual problem schemas, students should probably only be given such practice *after* they have mastered the relevant semantic equations. Many instructors feel that because conceptual problems are easier (for them), they should come before quantitative problem solving. Indeed, many high school courses teach only conceptual problem solving. The claim here is that students should get conceptual problems only after achieving a semantic stage of understanding, which can be done with the training outlined above.

This section addressed the question, "What learning mechanisms suffice for acquiring conceptual expertise?" The proposed answer is that two learning mechanisms are involved. Induction (also called concept formation or category learning) suffices for learning description phase knowledge and applicability conditions. EBL (a form of partial evaluation or knowledge compilation) suffices for learning confluences. Both learning mechanisms can be sped up by giving learners specific types of training. Such training is not currently part of college instruction, although most of it was successful in laboratory experiments. A key experiment would be to assemble all these types of training into a multi-week experimental curriculum, and compare it to standard instruction over the same period of time.

CONCLUSION

We have argued that conceptual expertise in elementary physics consists of mastery of description phase knowledge, applicability conditions, and confluences. Description phase knowledge and applicability conditions can be induced from certain types of examples. Confluences can be learned from equations during a three-stage process: Learners first acquire a *superficial* understanding of the equation; then they construct a *semantic* version of the equation via EBL; and finally they construct a *qualitative* version via EBL, which is comprised of multiple confluences.

Because current physics instruction does not contain the right sort of training, only a few students acquire a semantic understanding of some principles, and very few attain a qualitative understanding of any principle. The training that students currently receive is mostly practice in solving quantitative and conceptual problems. Quantitative problems can be solved with only a superficial understanding of equations, and conceptual problems can be solved by memorizing problem schemas. An interesting experiment would be to replace most of the conventional problem-solving practices with the training recommended above and see if that allows more students to achieve conceptual expertise with no increase in training time.

In what other task domains is this basic path to conceptual knowledge likely to be similar? A key feature of physics is that it is mostly concerned with constructing mathematical models of situations. Such modeling occurs in many other task domains as well, because modeling is such a powerful cognitive tool. One converts a situation into a mathematical model, then "turns the crank" to produce mathematical implications, and these implications turn out to be true of the situation. In elementary physics, the models are systems of algebraic equations. In other task domains, they can be differential equations, causal networks, rule-based systems, etc., The point is that once a situation is represented in a model, it is mechanical to produce implications. However, qualitative approximations to the implications can be produced with simpler methods. That is the major finding of the QR community, a subfield of artificial intelligence. The claim here is simply that conceptual expertise consists of such QR. This is hardly a surprise to the QR community, but perhaps novel to others.

However, the power of modeling is seductive to students. They focus on the "turn the crank" parts of modeling exclusively. They find ways to circumvent the model-construction and model-interpretation processes. In particular, they find ways to solve quantitative exercises by working only with a superficial understanding of the model (e.g., the names of the variables, causal network nodes, etc., and not their meanings). Consequently, many students fail to develop a semantic understanding of the models. Without this semantic understanding, they have no way to deal with conceptual questions. Such questions are constructed so that one cannot write down a mathematical model. The only way to answer them properly is to use semantic understandings of the domain, which these students lack. Since they can't reason properly, they answer using their naïve misconceptions or their memory of previously solved conceptual questions. So the irony is that the power of mathematical modeling to produce important domain conclusions with purely mathematical, non-domain reasoning seduces learners into trying to ignore the semantics of models. Such superficial reasoning works surprisingly often on conventional analysis problems, but fails utterly on conceptual problems. Hence, conceptual expertise indicates mastery of a semantic understanding of models, which in turn can be used for both qualitative and quantitative problem solving.

Our suggestions for increasing conceptual expertise focus on increasing semantic understanding of the models. The suggested training focuses on individual pieces of a quantitative model, such as a vector, a variable, a term, an applicability condition, etc., and drills students on the denotations of each in isolation. Once a semantic understanding of the models has been mastered, it should take only a few conceptual problems to build the requisite qualitative knowledge. Current instructional practices give them too early, before students have the semantic understanding of models that will allow them to construct appropriate qualitative knowledge.

On an even more general level our work suggests that mastery and conceptual knowledge are not passively attained as a function of students' typical activity in the task domain. In particular, the development of mastery and QR within a wide range of domains, such as medicine (Boshuizen, Chapter 17; Davis , Chapter 8), law (Boshiuzen, Chapter 17), military tactics (Shadrick & Lussier, Chapter 13), music, sports, and chess (Ericsson, Chapter 18) do not emerge as automatic consequences of experience, but require engagement in designed learning environments relying on reflective thinking and deliberate practice. To think and reason in an insightful and expert manner in a domain is, therefore, the fruit of extended efforts and is an observable characteristic of attained mastery in the relevant domain.

REFERENCES

Ashby, G. F., & Maddox, W. T. (2005). Human category learning. *Annual Review of Psychology, 56,* 149–178.

Bundy, A., Byrd, L., Luger, G., Mellish, C., & Palmer, M. (1979). *Solving mechanics problems using meta-level inference.* In Proceedings of the Sixth International Joint Conference on AI (pp. 1017–1027). San Mateo, CA: Morgan Kaufmann.

Chi, M., & VanLehn, K. (2008). Eliminating the gap between the high and low students through meta-cognitive strategy instruction. In B. P. Woolf, E. Aimeur, R. Nkambou, & S. P. Lajoie (Eds.), *Intelligent tutoring systems: 9th International Conference: ITS2008* (pp. 603–613). Amsterdam, NL: IOS Press.

Chi, M. T. H. (2005). Common sense conceptions of emergent processes: Why some misconceptions are robust. *Journal of the Learning Sciences, 14,* 161–199.

(in press). Three types of conceptual change: Belief revision, mental model transformation, and categorical shift. In S. Vosniadou (Ed.), *Handbook of research on conceptual change.* Mahwah, NJ: Lawrence Erlbaum Associates.

Chi, M. T. H., Feltovich, P., & Glaser, R. (1981). Categorization and representation of physics problems by experts and novices. *Cognitive Science, 5*(2), 121–152.

Chi, M. T. H., Glaser, R., & Rees, E. (1982). Expertise in problem solving. In R. J. Sternberg (Ed.), *Advances in the psychology of human intelligence,* vol. 1 (pp. 7–75). Hillsdale, NJ: Lawrence Erlbaum Associates.

Corbett, A., Wagner, A. Z., Lesgold, S., Ulrich, H., & Stevens, S. M. (2006). The impact of learning of generating vs. selecting descriptions in analyzing algebra example solutions. In S. A. Barab, K. E. Hay, & D. T. Hickey (Eds.), *The 7th International Conference of the Learning Sciences* (pp. 99–105). Mahwah, NJ: Lawrence Erlbaum Associates.

Day, D. V., & Lord, R. G. (1992). Expertise and problem categorization: The role of expert processing in organizational sense-making. *Journal of Management Studies, 29*(1), 35–47.

de Kleer, J., & Brown, J. S. (1984). A qualitative physics based on confluences. *Artificial Intelligence, 24,* 7–83.

Dee-Lucas, D., & Larkin, J. (1991). Equations in scientific proofs: Effects on comprehension. *American Education Research Journal, 28*(3), 661–682.

di Sessa, A. A. (1993). Towards an epistemology of physics. *Cognition and Instruction, 10*(2 & 3), 105–225.

Dufresne, R. J., Gerace, W. J., Hardiman, P. T., & Mestre, J. P. (1992). Constraining novices to perform expert-like problem analyses: Effects on schema acquisition. *The Journal of the Learning Sciences, 2*(3), 307–331.

Elio, R., & Scharf, P. B. (1990). Modeling novice-to-expert shifts in problem-solving strategy and knowledge organization. *Cognitive Science, 14*, 579–639.

Ericsson, K. A. (2006). Protocol analysis and expert thought: Concurrent verbalizations of thinking during experts' performance on representative tasks. In K. A. Ericsson, N. Charness, P. Feltovich, & R. R. Hoffman (Eds.), *The Cambridge handbook of expertise and expert performance* (pp. 223–241). Cambridge, UK: Cambridge University Press.

Ericsson, K. A., & Lehmann, A. C. (1996). Expert and exceptional performance: Evidence of maximal adaptation to task constraints. *Annual Review of Psychology, 47*, 273–305.

Forbus, K. D. (1985). The role of qualitative dynamics in naive physics. In J. R. Hobbes & R. C. Moore (Eds.), *Formal theories of the commonsense world* (pp. 185–226). Norwood, NJ: Ablex.

Forbus, K. D., & de Kleer, J. (1993). *Building problem solvers*. Cambridge, MA: MIT Press.

Hake, R. R. (1998). Interactive-engagement vs. traditional methods: A six-thousand student survey of mechanics test data for introductory physics students. *American Journal of Physics, 66*(4), 64–74.

Hardiman, P. T., Dufresne, R. J., & Mestre, J. P. (1989). The relation between problem categorization and problem solving among experts and novices. *Memory & Cognition, 17*(5), 627–638.

Heller, J. L., & Reif, F. (1984). Prescribing effective human problem-solving processes: Problem descriptions in physics. *Cognition and Instruction, 1*(2), 177–216.

Hestenes, D. (1987). Toward a modeling theory of physics instruction. *American Journal of Physics, 55*, 440–454.

Hestenes, D., & Wells, M. (1992). A mechanics baseline test. *The Physics Teacher, 30*, 159–166.

Hestenes, D., Wells, M., & Swackhamer, G. (1992). Force concept inventory. *The Physics Teacher, 30*, 141–158.

Heyworth, R. M. (1999). Procedural and conceptual knowledge of expert and novice students for the solving of a basic problem in chemistry. *International Journal of Science Education, 21*(2), 195–211.

Hinsley, D. A., Hayes, J. R., & Simon, H. A. (1977). From words to equations: Meaning and representation in algebra word problems. In P. Carpenter & M. A. Just (Eds.), *Cognitive processes in comprehension*. Mahwah, NJ: Lawrence Erlbaum Associates.

Jones, R. M., & Fleischman, E. S. (2001). Cascade explains and informs the utility of fading examples to problems. In *23rd Annual Conference of the Cognitive Science Society* (pp. 459–464). Mahwah, NJ: Lawrence Erlbaum Associates.

Jordan, P., Makatchev, M., Pappuswamy, U., VanLehn, K., & Albacete, P. (2006). A natural language tutorial dialogue system for physics. In G. Sutcliffe & R. Goebel (Eds.), *Proceedings of the 19th International FLAIRS Conference*. Menlo Park, CA: AAAI Press.

Klenk, M., & Forbus, K. D. (2007). Cognitive modeling of analogy events in physics problem solving from examples. In D. S. McNamara & J. G. Trafton (Eds.), *Proceedings of the 29th Annual Cognitive Science Society* (pp. 1163–1165). Austin, TX: Cognitive Science Society.

Kozma, R. B., & Russell, J. (1997). Multimedia and understanding: Expert and novice responses to different representations of chemical phenomena. *Journal of Research in Science Teaching, 34*(9), 949–968.

Lamberts, K. (1990). A hybrid model of learning to solve physics problems. *European Journal of Cognitive Psychology, 3*(2), 151–170.

Larkin, J. (1981). Enriching formal knowledge: A model for learning to solve textbook physics problems. In J. R. Anderson (Ed.), *Cognitive skills and their acquisition.* Mahwah, NJ: Lawrence Erlbaum Associates.

Larkin, J. (1983). The role of problem representation in physics. In D. Gentner & A. Stevens (Eds.), *Mental models.* Mahwah, NJ: Lawrence Erlbaum Associates.

Larkin, J., McDermott, J., Simon, D. P., & Simon, H. A. (1980). Models of competence in solving physics problems. *Cognitive Science, 4,* 317–345.

Larkin, J., Reif, F., Carbonell, J., & Gugliotta, A. (1988). Fermi: A flexible expert reasoner with multi-domain inferencing. *Cognitive Science, 12*(1), 101–138.

Loftin, B. R., Mueller, S., Way, B., & Lee, B. (1991). An intelligent tutoring system for physics problem solving. In *Proceedings of the contributed sessions 1991 conference on intelligent computer-aided training* (p. 127).

Mayfield, W. A., Kardash, C. M., & Kivlighan, D. M. (1999). Differences in experienced and novice counselors' knowledge structures about clients: Implications for case conceptualization. *Journal of Counseling Psychology, 46,* 504–514.

McCloskey, M., Caramazza, A., & Green, B. (1980). Curvilinear motion in the absence of external forces: Naive beliefs about the motion of objects. *Science, 210*(5), 1139–1141.

McDermott, J., & Larkin, J. H. (1978). Re-representing textbook physics problems. In *Proceedings of the second national conference of the Canadian society for computational studies of intelligence.* Toronto, Ontario.

Medin, D. L., & Ross, B. H. (1989). The specific character of abstract thought: Categorization, problem solving and induction. In R. J. Sternberg (Ed.), *Advances in the psychology of human intelligence,* Vol. 5 (pp. 189–223). Mahwah, NJ: Lawrence Erlbaum Associates.

Muggleton, S. (1992). *Inductive logic programming.* New York: Academic Press.

Murray, T., Schultz, K., Brown, D., & Clement, J. (1990). An analogy-based computer tutor for remediating physics misconceptions. *Interactive Learning Environments, 1*(2), 79–101.

Novak, G. S., & Araya, A. A. (1980). Research on expert problem solving in physics. In *Proceedings of the first national conference on Artificial Intelligence.* Menlo Park, CA: AAAI Press.

Owen, E., & Sweller, J. (1985). What do students learn while solving mathematics problems? *Journal of Educational Psychology, 77*(3), 272–284.

Pfundt, H., & Duit, R. (1998). *Bibliography: Students' alternative frameworks and science education,* 5th ed. Kiel, Germany: Institute for Science Education.

Ploetzner, R., & VanLehn, K. (1997). The acquisition of informal physics knowledge during formal physics training. *Cognition and Instruction, 15*(2), 169–206.

Priest, A. G., & Lindsay, R. O. (1992). New light on novice-expert differences in physics problem solving. *British Journal of Psychology, 83,* 389–405.

Ranney, M., & Thagard, P. (1988). Explanatory coherence and belief revision in naive physics. In V. Patel & G. J. Groen (Eds.), *The Tenth Annual Conference of the Cognitive Science Society* (pp. 426–432). Mahwah, NJ: Lawrence Erlbaum Associates.

Reif, F., & Scott, L. A. (1999). Teaching scientific thinking skills: Students and computers coaching each other. *American Journal of Physics, 67*(9), 819–831.

Reimann, P., Schult, T. J., & Wichmann, S. (1993). Understanding and using worked-out examples: A computational model. In G. Strube & K. F. Wender (Eds.), *The cognitive psychology of knowledge* (pp. 177–201). Amsterdam: Elsevier.

Russell, S., & Norvig, P. (2003). *Artificial intelligence: A modern approach*, 2nd ed. Upper Saddle River, NJ: Prentice-Hall.

Shafto, P., & Coley, J. D. (2003). Development of categorization and reasoning in natural world: Novices to experts, naive similarity to ecological knowledge. *Journal of Experimental Psychology: Learning, Memory, and Cognition, 29*, 641–649.

Sherin, B. L. (2001). How students understand physics equations. *Journal of the Learning Sciences, 19*(4), 479–541.

(2006). Common sense clarified: The role of intuitive knowledge in physics problem solving. *Journal of Research in Science Teaching, 43*(6), 535–555.

Simon, D. P., & Simon, H. A. (1978). Individual differences in solving physics problems. In R. S. Siegler (Ed.), *Children's thinking: What develops?* Mahwah, NJ: Lawrence Erlbaum Associates.

Smith, M. U. (1992). Expertise and the organization of knowledge: Unexpected differences among genetic counselors, faculty, and students on problem categorization tasks. *Journal of Research in Science Teaching, 29*(2), 179–205.

Sweller, J., Mawer, R. F., & Ward, M. R. (1983). Development of expertise in mathematical problem solving. *Journal of Experimental Psychology: General, 112*, 629–661.

Van Heuvelen, A., & Zou, X. (2001). Multiple representations of work-energy processes. *American Journal of Physics, 69*(2), 184–194.

VanLehn, K. (1996). Cognitive skill acquisition. In J. Spence, J. Darly, & D. J. Foss (Eds.), *Annual Review of Psychology*, Vol. 47 (pp. 513–539). Palo Alto, CA: Annual Reviews.

(1998). Analogy events: How examples are used during problem solving. *Cognitive Science, 22*(3), 347–388.

(1999). Rule learning events in the acquisition of a complex skill: An evaluation of Cascade. *Journal of the Learning Sciences, 8*(2), 179–221.

VanLehn, K., & Jones, R. M. (1993a). Better learners use analogical problem solving sparingly. In P. E. Utgoff (Ed.), *Machine Learning: Proceedings of the Tenth Annual Conference* (pp. 338–345). San Mateo, CA: Morgan Kaufmann.

(1993b). Learning by explaining examples to oneself: A computational model. In S. Chipman & A. Meyrowitz (Eds.), *Cognitive models of complex learning* (pp. 25–82). Boston, MA: Kluwer Academic Publishers.

VanLehn, K., Jones, R. M., & Chi, M. T. H. (1992). A model of the self-explanation effect. *The Journal of the Learning Sciences, 2*(1), 1–59.

VanLehn, K., Jordan, P., Rose, C. P., Bhembe, D., Bottner, M., Gaydos, A., et al. (2002). The architecture of Why2-Atlas: A coach for qualitative physics essay writing. In S. A. Cerri, G. Gouarderes, & F. Paraguacu (Eds.), *Intelligent Tutoring Systems, 2002, 6th International Conference* (pp. 158–167). Berlin: Springer.

VanLehn, K., Lynch, C., Schultz, K., Shapiro, J. A., Shelby, R. H., Taylor, L., et al. (2005). The Andes physics tutoring system: Lessons learned. *International Journal of Artificial Intelligence and Education, 15*(3), 147–204.

Vosniadou, S., & Brewer, W. F. (1992). Mental models of the Earth: A study of conceptual change in childhood. *Cognitive Psychology, 24*, 535–585.

Weiser, M., & Shertz, J. (1983). Programming problem representation in novice and expert programmers. *International Journal of Man-Machine Studies, 14*, 391–396.

17

Teaching for Expertise: Problem-Based Methods in Medicine and Other Professional Domains

HENNY P. A. BOSHUIZEN

The daily train trip between my small hometown and the university city where I used to work has always provided me with lots of unexpected opportunities to receive feedback about students' perceptions of their education. In all those years I have overheard them talking about their studies, teachers, lectures, peers, but also about parties and village gossip. One conversation among three students of a beauty course in one of the community colleges struck me because of the sensible things they were saying about their curriculum. One of the girls was trying to read a chapter in a book about health for their assignment of that week. The book was meant for care and wellness courses, which was their course, taught by a young physician who – as they grumbled – "was not even handsome." Apart from the appearance of their teacher, which might have been some compensation, their main complaint was that they did not have a clue about the use of this kind of knowledge for their future practice as beauticians.

The girls' complaint is very similar to the situation students in discipline-organized and teacher-centered academic curricula find themselves in. These kinds of curricula have many problems; among them are lack of horizontal and vertical integration of the subjects taught, an absence of apparent practical relevance to the students' perception of their future profession, a constant overload with too many courses, and an emphasis on the principles and practices of the separate academic disciplines instead of the practices of their future profession. As a consequence, the students themselves must find out what and how they can ultimately use the knowledge they are building up during a specific course. More importantly, they must fill in the gaps between the discipline knowledge and the professional application and practice themselves. Just like our future beauticians, can we expect our students to apply

---

Acknowledgment: I thank the department of educational research and development of Maastricht University for their hospitality in the month of January 2007. Discussions with Cees van der Vleuten, Hetty Snellen-Balendong, Arno Muijtjens, Lambert Schuwirth, and Albert Scherpbier inspired me when writing this chapter.

what they have learned about tumors or immune processes to anti-aging or acne therapy? No wonder that many students learn just for the exam and never again think about the topic, let alone integrate it with other learning.

These problems were recognized by Barrows in the 1960s when he started to work with simulated patients integrated in his neurology courses (Barrows, 1968); later this initiative developed into a complete method (Barrows, 1971). From this work the famous McMaster problem-based learning (PBL) method was developed (Barrows & Tamblyn, 1980). Another, simultaneous movement was the call for community-based education, so important because much of the work of a physician is done in the community and not in the hospital. Though countries differ a great deal in their reliance on community-based medical practice (so no generally applicable recipe can be given), the necessity for a community view on the curriculum is generally recognized. Developing countries especially have strongly advocated and developed this approach. Although PBL and CBL (community-based learning) can be implemented independently, one without the other, in practice we see that new medical curricula include both. Harden, Sowden, and Dunn (1984) have described developments in medical education in six dimensions: (1) student-centered versus teacher-centered, (2) integrated versus discipline-based, (3) systematic versus apprenticeship-based, (4) problem-based versus information-gathering, (5) community-based versus hospital-based, and (6) elective versus uniform. I have already discussed four of these dimensions in my introduction but the third might need some clarification. The dimension contrasting systematic and apprenticeship-based education distinguishes training programs where the training problems must be selected and developed by well-informed teachers, or found in the actual situations that confront students during medical practice. Stated another way: What provides a better learning environment – the ward and community with its rich supply of patients and situations students can learn from, or the well-planned curriculum of cases and problems that have been carefully selected to provide good coverage in terms of diseases, patient groups, severity, epidemiology, treatments, and approaches? Harden et al. concluded that the established schools tended to be more on the right-hand or traditional side of these dimensions, while the newer ones were more often on the left-hand side, although theoretically speaking all kinds of combinations are possible.

These curriculum reforms based on PBL can be redefined at a more abstract level. They are integrated, planned, and geared toward the actual encountered problems of the field involved, focusing the competencies required for continued professional success as defined by the needs of the community served.

This is in a nutshell the development of PBL in medicine. In this chapter I will further elaborate several steps in this process, starting with a description of the problems with traditional education for the learned professions. Next "traditional" PBL will be described at an instructional and curriculum level, and some new developments will be presented. Finally, the key question will be raised – that is, whether it works or not. To answer this question, attention will be given to the measurement of performance in the professions. Medicine will be used as a prototype for PBL. Where necessary and available, I will give examples from other domains to illustrate the diversity in implementations and to show the reader that the cognitive and practical characteristics of the different professional fields have their implications for educational design.

TRADITIONAL PROFESSIONAL ACADEMIC EDUCATION

Academic professional education is as old as the universities themselves. An example is the University of Bologna (Italy), which is the oldest existing European university dating back to the 11th century. At that time it taught the liberal arts and law. In the 14th century other academic professions were included as well – medicine and the clergy, whose education and training so far had been the privilege of the monasteries. The most famous medical faculty at that time was Padua, also in Italy, where famous scientists such as Vesalius and Falloppio taught. The curriculum structure that was developed at that time has remained the norm for many centuries. Basic sciences such as anatomy, herbology, and later physiology and pathology were taught in the first years; in the clinical phase of training, bedside teaching was the dominating work form. Da Monte may be considered the founder of the clinical sciences in the 16th century. He introduced ward rounds with the medical staff and students, followed by discussions on diagnosis and treatment. Boerhaave brought this system to perfection in Leiden, The Netherlands, in the early decades of the 18th century. He emphasized the connection between biomedical knowledge and clinical observations, and systematically used post-mortems to check the analyses and conclusions based on history and physical examination (Kidd & Modlin, 1999).

Other curricula for professional education share the emphasis on a thorough introduction into the basic sciences of the field, but deviate from this approach in the sense that a systematic introduction to the practical sciences is missing. Instead, graduates work as trainees or volunteers to build up practical experience and skill.

An exception is legal education in the United States. By the end of the 19th century it was recognized that neither a systematic, lecture-based introduction nor the apprenticeship method was very effective. To solve this problem, Christopher Langdell of Harvard Law School introduced the case method in 1870, a method that still dominates legal education in the United States (Williams, 1992).

Let us return to the basic sciences curricula. Problems with this kind of curricula are not confined only to problems of "not-seeing-the-use-of-it," as expressed by our future beauticians, and with lack of integration; issues concerning changed opinions in society about professional accountability and risk avoidance, curriculum overload, changed opinions about tasks, and the role of the professional also play a part (Dornan, Scherpbier, & Spencer, 2008).

Horizontal and Vertical Integration

Horizontal and vertical integration regard the links between basic science knowledge (horizontal) and between basic and clinical or other applied sciences (vertical). Integration as a cognitive process is not automatic. Connections between parts of the knowledge bases will only be constructed when they are activated at the same time. This can be due to simple reminding processes, when reading or hearing about one concept or principle in one context is reminiscent of something else studied earlier. For instance, studying the production of bile and its storage and transport through the gallbladder may remind one of anatomic knowledge of the gallbladder and upper abdomen. Later, both knowledge parts can again be activated when studying a patient case about gallstones. More intensive cognitive operations such as elaboration, critical processing, or application will result in more and stronger links between the knowledge parts.

The utility of knowledge integration is not self-evident for students. Especially during secondary education, students may have been confronted with teachers who ridicule them for asking questions about the link between topics in history and economics, or about the difference between how different disciplines use a term such as "capital" or "elasticity." Integration in medicine is not self-evident either. Some experiments with co-teaching by a clinician and a bioscientist have only been successful when organized bottom-up by colleagues who know and trust each other and value each others' work.

Another reason why organizing a curriculum that promotes integration can be difficult is that the different groups do not always agree about the level of detail that should be reached. Koens, Custers, and Ten Cate (2006) found that basic scientists and clinicians agreed on the inclusion of concepts at the clinical, organ, and cellular level. However, they strongly disagreed about the importance of knowledge at the molecular level. Together with the cellular level, this is the area where tremendous scientific progress is being made at this moment.

Curriculum Overload

The diverse sciences and academic disciplines that inform professional knowledge and practice have their own dynamics and their own development. For instance, recently the nanotechnology, genetics, and proteomics areas have made quantum leaps, affecting the fields of pharmacology and medicine, but also engineering. Also, the legal field is changingbecause of international

changes and treaties overruling national legislatures. For instance, the establishment and growth of the European Union has resulted in an abundance of
articles and analyses in most legal domains about the consequences for national
(now 25 nations) legislation and jurisdiction. The dynamics in economics and
business administration is strongly related to economic change. Uncritically
incorporating all these developments in a curriculum will inevitably lead to
overload. However, in most such situations new scientific knowledge does not
replace old knowledge.

Overload is a problem that especially afflicts the traditional professional
curricula. The disciplines in such curricula have their own independent place
and make their own independent decisions about content. Teachers who find
themselves in a situation where they have a semester of two lecture hours and
two hours of practical training and lab available to teach their discipline do not
have many selection criteria. One is time. The second is based on the systematic approach to their discipline: its basic findings, systems, theories, methods,
and recent developments. The third is their own appreciation of their domain –
the things that make them tick and that they want to convey to their students.
Every year new methods, theories, and findings require an addendum to the
syllabus. There is no need to point out that the connection with practice and
other disciplines is not guaranteed this way.

Accountability and Risk Avoidance

Professions differ in the inherent risks and dangers. Lawyers may lose their
court cases, surgery may result in unforeseen complications, investment decisions may lead to substantial losses, an architectural construction may not
be resistant to strong winds or may collapse under its own weight, etc. But
also less costly errors, sometimes made in a split second, can have long-lasting effects on a client's health or financial well-being. There is a big difference
between Europe and the United States in the way professional mistakes are
legally dealt with. The number of lawsuits against professionals is much larger
in the United States. Yet, also for Europeans, the tendency toward a greater
transparency of professional services and accountability of professionals is
unmistakable where professional bodies or the state require that they are competent and certified. This affects both the content of undergraduate training as
well as the position of the student or the apprentice on the work floor. It also
affects the perception of practice as a learning situation.

Task and Role of the Professional

In recent years, many professional bodies have attempted to describe the profile of the future professional. Their explorations of future developments and
scenario studies were based on trends in the profession and in society. These

studies have resulted in advice regarding both work and education of the professional-to-be.

For instance, the General Medical Council (1993, 2002) has published several books and articles on the changing roles and duties of physicians in the United Kingdom. Similarly, the Royal College of Physicians and Surgeons of Canada has published its "The CanMEDS 2005 Physicians Competence Framework," in which it has inventoried and analyzed the roles of the physician with the intent to improve the practice standards, train better physicians, and provide better care (Frank, 2005). It describes roles that only partly overlap the prototype of the medical doctor many generations grew up with, and that still underlies many undergraduate, graduate, and specialist training programs. It discerns the medical expert as being the central role, integrating and forming the basis for the other roles of communicator, collaborator, manager, health advocate, scholar, and professional. Some of these roles are relatively new (e.g., communicator, collaborator, and manager); other roles date back to Hippocrates but have accumulated new content.

Implications

The combination of more accountability and risk reduction on the one hand, and renewed descriptions and prescriptions of the role of the professional in society on the other, has led to a trend to train undergraduates so that they are well prepared for practice, or at least have the key competencies at the level of independent though supervised practice. Yet, professions vary along this dimension. It is the danger of harm being done to the clients or to the professional him- or herself in the practical situation that defines how "complete" the graduate must be on entering the workplace (Boshuizen et al., 2008). Yet, although this is true in many professions, it does not apply to all. At the 2008 AERA meeting, Division I organized a panel discussion regarding how different professions deal with mistakes and errors. Wim Gijselaers showed that, unlike law, nursing, medicine, and engineering, the fields of finance, economics, and business administration did not have prescribed ways of dealing with these issues. The whole financial profession still struggles with defining ethical and sustainable practices (Thrush, 2008).

For instance, a newly trained pilot must be able to do all procedures on all occasions under all circumstances with all aircraft for which he or she is certified. There is no second chance for wrong solutions, and skills cannot be trained while in the air. Medical graduates, nurses, operators in process industry, or teachers are much like pilots. Their jobs have a real-time character; routinized, unreflective actions are based on instant responses to immediate recognition; errors made can have very negative or long-lasting effects on the people in their care. At the other end of the spectrum, we find professions such as engineering design or law trainees who can do much of their work off-line and have the possibility to discuss their proposals with their supervisors before bringing things into effect. Eraut (1994) analyzed the time characteristics of different workplaces and professions. He characterized the latter type as deliberative analysis and decisions, and actions following a period of deliberation. The characteristics of the workplace graduates prepare for affect the amount of practical training that has to be included in these curricula in real or simulated settings.

As a consequence of these developments, many professional academic curricula adopted PBL as their instructional and curriculum format. Well-chosen, authentic problems provide the context in which basic and applied sciences are studied and integrated. The same problems also provide the key for selection of relevant subject matter, and are a means for integrating relevant skills training.

PROBLEM-BASED LEARNING AS AN INSTRUCTIONAL METHOD AND AS A CURRICULUM STRATEGY

Problems

As an instructional method, PBL is based on authentic problems, which students analyze in small groups. These groups are chaired by a student and supported and supervised by a tutor. By doing so, students suggest explanations of and solutions to the problem, but more importantly, they recognize gaps and inconsistencies in their knowledge. This leads to the identification of a set of learning goals that, in turn, spark the students' learning. Many PBL implementations require that students themselves identify the learning resources and materials that best fit their goals and their own preferences. This does not mean that students do not have lists of selected handbooks or web-portals, but a one-to-one relationship between learning goals and resources (up to the precise page numbers) will not be provided. Typically, two or three PBL sessions per week are held, chaining activities of problem analysis and learning goal identification one day, and discussion of what has been learned and problem solutions a few days later, with independent learning activities taking place in between. After having completed one problem, the analysis of a new one immediately starts off.[1] Table 17.1 gives typical examples of PBL problems from different faculties of Maastricht University.

Problems are chosen to serve specific goals. Schmidt and Moust (2000) have developed a classification system that is based on these different cognitive

---

[1]   Actually, implementations of PBL in community colleges will often deviate from this format by giving the students more structural and content support and working in a different time frame. In this case, a day may start with a problem analysis and close with discussion of what has been learned, while the learning resources may be pre-selected or even transformed to a more digestible format.

Table 17.1. *Four PBL problems.*

What a mess!	Faculty of Health Science, 1999–2000

The ladies at the university's switchboard, Lidy, Elly, Carla, and Ingrid, are having a terrible time at their work. This week a new telephone system has been put into operation and everything goes wrong. Prior to its installation, it had been explained to them in depth how the new system worked, and they also had the opportunity to practice with it. Everybody felt well prepared. But things are not running as smoothly as they had thought. The ladies have to keep their mind closely on what they are doing. This is hard to manage because other employees also run into problems and start to phone them: the telephone is ringing all the time. Especially Lidy, the oldest and most experienced of them all, is having a hard time. Normally she could always do something extra, such as knitting, but not today. They all hope and expect that it will be going better in a few weeks and consider the problems of today as typical starting problems. Only Lidy is worried and wonders whether she is getting too old and slow to adapt herself to new situations, and whether she will ever be able to work with this new telephone system. Of course, she does not show it, but she has her doubts.

The Company	Faculty of Economics and Business Administration, 1999–2000; Arts, Gijselaers and Segers (2002)

Context: The Company problem consists of a description of the firm, and links to different pages with information about the consumers, production, research, market position, etc.

The Company's strategy can be characterized as fast-paced globalization of their business. It aims for total coverage of international markets.

The Company group now generates 96 percent of sales in four segments its covers for over 50 years, and has concentrated its efforts on ten major global brands, which are responsible for 87 percent of its sales. Kelly Kreuger, Chair and CEO of The Company, is planning a strategic meeting with the management committee to discuss implications of potential strategic alliances with current competitors.

Melena	Faculty of Medicine, 1996–1997

A 64-year-old accountant presents to his GP's office with weakness and epigastric pain. He has a 20-year history of mild dyspepsia. He has a long history of cigarette smoking, drinks alcohol moderately, and has been taking aspirin for two weeks for lower back pain. For two days he noticed "jet-black, sticky stools that looked like tar."

On physical examination he looks pale; his blood pressure is 130/70 mmHg, pulse is regular (110 beats/min). There is tenderness in the epigastrium to the right of the midline. Further physical examination reveals no abnormalities except for the presence of tar-like stool by rectal examination.

Laboratory:

Hb 6.5 mmol/L

Thrombocytes 421 $*10^9$/L

Table 17.1. *(continued).*

Alkaline phosphatase 98 U/L	
Gamma-GT 40 U/L	
Urea 12.2 mmol/L	
Creatinine 84 μmol/L	

Will You Defend Me?	Faculty of Law, 1985–1986
	Schmidt and Moust (2000, p 60)

"You are staring aimlessly into the fire of your cigarette. Your client has just told you about the crimes he has committed. His story was awkward. Numerous serious sexual assaults were described in detail. He described incidents of drug trafficking and severe physical abuse. In the same breath, he told you about his bitter childhood experiences: his stepfather, who mistreated him; his mother, who neglected him; his brothers and sisters, who made life miserable for him. He concluded his story with a desperate gesture and asked, "Please, will you defend me?"

All problems have been translated and adapted from UM course material. "The Company" is an abbreviated and anonymized description of a real PBL problem, based on descriptions in Arts, Gijselaers, and Segers (2002). "Will you defend me?" is from Schmidt and Moust (2000). "What a mess!" and "Melena" are reproduced by courtesy of the Faculty of Health, Medicine and Life Science.

goals; that is, the kind of knowledge to be built. They discerned three kinds of academic and professional knowledge (descriptive, explanatory, and procedural) and personal, normative knowledge. Progress toward each cognitive goal can be made by working on particular kinds of problems: Descriptive knowledge is often addressed with fact-finding problems, explanatory knowledge with explanation problems, and procedural knowledge with strategy problems. Personal, normative knowledge is mostly acquired through moral dilemma problems. Problems can be presented in a pure form, but mixes are possible as well. Also, students can choose learning goals that emphasize something other than what the planning group intended, depending upon their own interests and on the gaps and inconsistencies they may have identified.

For instance, "What a mess" in Table 17.1 is typically an explanation problem meant to build explanatory knowledge, bringing together theories on expertise development, neuropsychology, and work psychology. These theories and the supporting evidence may partly contradict. The key problem in this vignette underlies Lidy's worries: Does older age or alternatively overtraining of one's skill set prevent or impede learning a new, similar, but different skill set? If so, how? If not, how? To find answers to these questions, students first discuss their pre-existing knowledge and identify strategies to find and evaluate additional information, both in terms of validity and reliability of the source and the content of the information, and in terms of the case with which they are dealing. In this case, students must weigh two phenomena described in the literature: On one hand, high levels of skills mastery enable learning new knowledge and skills in the same domain, also at old age (e.g., VanLehn, 1996); on the other hand, experience concentration may result in very rugged skills profiles with combinations of very well-trained and neglected areas, with skills obsolescence lurking in the future if the content and context of work may change (Thijssen & van der Heijden, 2003). These neglected areas in particular may hinder new learning. The students' learning in this specific case not only requires learning theories plus supporting evidence, but also critical evaluation of information according to scientific rules, and weighing and combining of the results in order to formulate an answer for Lidy's problem.

"Melena" also regards explanatory knowledge, but probably the planning group also intended procedural knowledge goals. It is very possible that the students take this task as an opportunity to revise descriptive knowledge and find out all about specific kinds of lab values, what normal and abnormal values are and what they indicate. Students often formulate a problem like this in a general way: "What is the diagnosis? And explain the findings." In this case they have to explain how black stools, high pulse rate, low Hb, elevated thrombocytes, and epigastric tenderness are related. A further evaluation of the case does not only entail the diagnosis (plus possible alternatives plus their plausibility, and how they can be differentiated), but also an evaluation of the severity of the situation and possible progression. Based on this analysis they may also discuss what a doctor should do.

"The Company" is a strategy problem meant to build descriptive and procedural knowledge in the domain of business administration. In this problem the focus is on the analysis of the company itself, as an example of a specific kind of company as opposed to other companies (e.g., manufacturing and marketing cosmetics versus a fast food chain), and as a player in a dynamic environment. Finally, "Will you defend me?" is a moral resolution problem, aimed at building personal, normative knowledge. The issue here is the alignment of personal emotions, norms and value, and professional standards.

There is some debate about the role and required competencies of the tutor. In the early years of PBL it was thought that everyone with good social and group skills could be a tutor. So even secretaries and lab personnel acted as tutors. Most of them were not very successful and students had a clear preference for domain experts, that is, for doctors in case of a medical faculty. Moust (1993) tested a model of tutor achievement in a law school, using several instruments including a tutor observation scale, a group functioning questionnaire, and some outcome variables: hours spent on self-directed learning, grade, and interest in the course topic at the end of the module. Outcomes were accumulated at the group ($N = 38$) level; tutor expertise varied from master students to domain experts. A path-analysis showed that a combination of (use of) domain expertise and social congruence (active and personal involvement with students) leading to cognitive congruence of the tutor (the skill of tutors to put themselves in the place of students, and to express themselves in terms understandable for students) is the key to successful tutoring. This had a direct positive effect on group functioning and, through that, on both student grades and interest in the topic. Tutors also play a role helping students to determine whether they have covered the intended material, gone deep enough into that material, and applied scientific reasoning skills the right way.

Courses and Curricula

Apart from a description at the problem level, PBL can also be depicted at the course and at the curriculum level. To reach the ultimate goals described above, more is needed than working with authentic problems. Apart from these problems, such a course can consist of a set of lectures, skills training, integrated knowledge application, and learning in real or simulated practice sessions. The resulting course is the product of a careful analysis of the knowledge, attitude, and skills goals and the required mastery level to be reached, combined with an analysis of the most suitable work forms. Course planning groups must take care that teachers are not left to their old reflexes but are well prepared for their new role. Lectures are a telling example. Many teachers love to lecture. Left to themselves they could fill the whole course with lectures on their topics, disrupting all the careful planning. Lectures should be used only for those topics that students cannot easily read in the standard books: new developments, topics that are known to be difficult for students and that easily lead to misconceptions, introductions to disciplines with which students have not yet become acquainted (examples are sociology or ethics for medical or law students), and demonstrations (e.g., patient demonstrations for medical students).[2]

Finally, student evaluation and assessment must fit the type and level of the goals of the course and the curriculum. Saying this is in itself almost a platitude. Yet, practical PBL implementations have shown a myriad of exams that contradict this basic principle of educational testing. Reasons of efficiency, but also perceptions of validity, reliability, and of what is good educational testing, may underlie these choices. For instance, it is easier to secure good content coverage using multiple-choice questions, but the disadvantage is that such exams tend to be superficial and fact oriented. However, the most important

---

[2]   Remarkably, even very well-planned courses from the problem and training perspective can be very sloppy regarding lecture planning and communication. H. A. M. Snellen-Balendong, personal communication January 29, 2007, Maastricht, NL.

reason is probably that exam construction always comes last and suffers from the planning group's tailing energy. Under optimal conditions the design of student evaluations should be an integrated part of course and curriculum design. Early planning of the content and format of assessments will contribute to the relevance and representativeness of the assessments in relation to the domain being taught. Good exams require students to show their mastery of the domain in terms of factual knowledge, critical analysis, and evaluation, as well as application in relevant contexts at the level that can be expected of students in this stage of expertise development.

At the curriculum level, decisions must be made about the organizing principles within and over years. An example of such an organizing principle – again from medicine – is organ systems: gastrointestinal, neurological, respiration, reproductive, etc. For the structure within modules, similar decisions must be made. One may choose to work starting from the relevant biomedical structures, and its processes, growth, and regulation, followed by disease and malfunction as expressed in different cases. Again principles for choosing these cases must be agreed upon; for example: Do we prefer frequent problems over severe? Will typical cases be chosen or atypical cases? Should we use authentic or pre-processed cases? Furthermore, decisions must be made about integration between courses, practical experience, etc. This is also the level in organizations where gaps in the curriculum and duplication of topics across several courses should be identified.

Different Goals and Different Implementations of Problem-Based Learning

Problem-based learning, from its inception, has had many different implementations at different levels. For instance, PBL in McMaster has traditionally consisted of long patient cases. The goal was that, apart from knowledge, students should develop good problem-solving and management skills. At this moment a profound curriculum reform (Neville & Norman, 2007; Norman et al., 2004) is taking place in which the information-seeking skills of the students are de-emphasized and information-processing skills are prioritized. The curriculum is reorganized around critical concepts; problems in a course is ordered in such a way to help students further refine their knowledge base and differentiate between diseases and clinical manifestations. Finally, the role of information and communication technology (ICT) is redefined. Also, in clinical rotations, new formats are developed, in which mobile ICT will play a prominent role to capture individual experience. The reasons for this reform are very diverse, ranging from the normal wear and tear of the curriculum, to new requirements because of changes in the role of the physician (see above), to the present emphasis on evidence-based practices, and the ever-increasing availability of relevant information, which requires different information skills than before.

Problem-based learning in the medical school of Maastricht University has always given much attention to the integrated study of the basic and clinical sciences, aiming for a well-developed and well-integrated knowledge base. More recently it concluded that academic competencies should receive more attention and that the strict divide between the four-year, pre-clinical period and the clinical period should be diminished. This change had immediate effects on knowledge acquisition, which was shown in the analyses of the progress test results of different batches of students before, during, and after the curriculum change. A progress test is a periodical test pitched at the end of curriculum level. Each student takes parallel forms of the test 24 times before graduation. The results from Maastricht students were compared with the results of students taking the same tests in two other medical schools in which such a curriculum change had not taken place (Muijtjens, Schuwirth, Cohen-Schotanus, & Van der Vleuten, 2008).

Manchester University Faculty of Medicine more recently changed into PBL, at first in the two-year pre-clinical phase only, but later also in the clinical period. Reason for the latter change was mainly curriculum coverage (Patel, David, Boshuizen, & Wolfhagen, 1998). To integrate PBL and experiential learning, self-directed learning in between the two discussion sessions should not only include printed and electronic materials, but also practical learning resources that are available in the clinical context. Examples are clerking a relevant patient, observation in a specific clinic, or participating in community activities. It was soon recognized that students needed a lot of support to identify relevant activities. They had problems finding out what was going on in the clinic, but even more so to recognize what could be important for their learning goals and to get access to these activities. Hence, a sign-up system was developed that included a database containing all activities in which students were welcome to participate, the number of students allowed and – most importantly – the learning goals that could be achieved through that activity. Part of the requirement for participation was that the students evaluate the activity and report on their learning before they could sign up for a new activity (Dornan, Hadfield, Brown, Boshuizen, & Scherpbier, 2005).

Bringing the concept of PBL to other professional areas requires a careful analysis of the structure of practice in that field and of the relation between basic and applied sciences. For instance, the typical PBL structure in medical faculties largely resembles the situation in the outpatient clinic in which several patients presenting different complaints and having different backgrounds enter the office within an hour and cooperation with other physicians or other health professionals is not very prominent. The tempo and structure of work in software engineering, law, or marketing do not fit this very well. Tasks and projects do not only take longer, but teamwork of cooperating specialists may be an essential quality of the work. Adaptation of PBL tasks to such features may greatly improve students' learning and knowledge application, as was shown by Arts and colleagues (2004, 2006) when they redesigned "the Company" case and course, shown in Table 17.1. This task was expanded to several weeks, and restructured to facilitate the different levels of system analysis described above. An analysis of what makes learning in that domain difficult can also be of help, and should actually be part of all educational design (see Nievelstein, Van Gog, & Prins, 2008, and Williams, 1992, for the domain of law).

PBL AND EXPERTISE RESEARCH

For many years education and educational psychology had no relation whatsoever with expertise research, not even with knowledge. Only in the last decade could the first break with this long tradition be witnessed, when *How People Learn*, the book by Bransford, Brown, and Cocking (1999), was published. The professional fields were faster with their recognition of the importance of expertise development research for the design of their curricula. Examples of domains where curriculum change was not only inspired by changes in the profession and the society, but also by expertise development research, are law (due to the work by Crombag, de Wijckersloot, & Cohen, 1977), economics (see Gijselaers, Tempelaar, & Keizer, 1994), and medicine (see below).

Medical Expertise Development Research

Medicine is the professional field most intensively researched as far as expertise development is concerned. The first studies were by Elstein, Shulman, and Sprafka (1978), who investigated clinical reasoning by students, subexperts, and experts. It was generally expected at that time that there would be a big difference among these groups in their processes of clinical reasoning. However, research showed no significant differences; as well, these authors could find no differences between top experts nominated by their peers and mediocre physicians. I myself started my research in this domain about the time their book had just been published, and I could only conclude that it was a period of strong convictions about the nature of expert reasoning that could not be supported by empirical evidence. For instance, when trying to find experts who were willing to participate in my studies, I was more than once informed that there was no need at all for an experiment like this, because, they said, everyone already knew how clinical reasoning worked, and how it should be done and taught. Another telling example was a family physician who participated in my first think-aloud study (reported in Boshuizen & Schmidt, 1992). He carefully read all presented information aloud as requested but showed no thinking. My standard question "Please keep thinking aloud" resulted in the remark: "Well, I don't think yet, I try to postpone thinking to keep my mind open, but actually I thought that he might have ... [and several hypotheses were formulated]." This physician showed strong adherence to the ideology that good clinical reasoning is characterized by an open mind and postponement of hypothesis generation until all information has been gathered to prevent premature closure. The outcome that groups differing in expertise level did not differ in reasoning style or strategy was very disappointing, though we found that the more expert groups (experienced family physicians compared to fifth, fourth, and second year medical students) had better diagnoses and better diagnostic hypotheses. And it was recognized that these non-findings were, in fact, very telling, and that the outcomes so far showed great resemblance to de Groot's 1946/1965 chess findings.

To quote Elstein, Shulman, and Sprafka (1978 , p. 276):

> Thus investigations of problem solving in chess, in logic, and in medicine are converging on the same conclusion. The difference between experts and weaker problem solvers are more to be found in the repertory of their experiences, organized in long-term memory, than in differences in the planning and problem-solving heuristics involved.

Once it was recognized that findings in medical expertise research were so similar to de Groot's (1946/1965) findings, many researchers followed in his footsteps to find out whether de Groot's measurements would also lead to interpretable results in medicine. de Groot's key findings were that experts did not think better but thought better things, and that experts could better remember elaborate, mid-game board positions than less expert players. In medicine, the latter findings could only be partially replicated. Boshuizen (1989 ; later extended by Van de Wiel, 1997) could demonstrate that many articles showed a positive, monotonic relationship between levels of expertise and recall measures. However, researchers constructed these results by reporting amount of recall divided by the total amount of time spent on reading a case or by dividing it by amount of time taken for reproduction. At the basic level, the relationship consistently turned out to be an inverted U-shaped relationship. This means that when given ample time, intermediates remember more of a case than novices and experts. However, when time is seriously constrained (from 3 minutes 30 seconds down to 30 seconds), experts perform better than medical students, in recall and again in diagnostic accuracy (Schmidt & Boshuizen, 1993).

This outcome and other phenomena in the recall (e.g., interpreted versus uninterpreted recall) were taken as an indication that experts' knowledge structure allows processing of information in a different way than intermediates (advanced medical students) and novices (beginning medical students). Other, more direct methods such as priming (Rikers, Schmidt, & Boshuizen, 2001) could corroborate these conclusions. Also, think-aloud, self-explanation, and post-hoc explanation studies showed how the quality and organization of basic and applied science knowledge changed with increasing expertise levels. Table 17.2 summarizes the conclusions derived from these studies.

Table 17.2. *Knowledge restructuring, clinical reasoning, and levels of expertise.*

Expertise level	Knowledge representation	Knowledge acquisition and (re)structuring	Clinical reasoning	Control required in clinical reasoning	Demand on cognitive capacity	Clinical reasoning in action
Novice	Networks	Knowledge accretion and validation	Long chains of detailed reasoning steps through pre-encapsulated networks	Active monitoring of each reasoning step	High	Difficulty to combine data collection and evaluation and clinical reasoning
Intermediate	Networks	Encapsulation	Reasoning through encapsulated network	Active monitoring of each reasoning step	Medium	
Expert	Illness scripts	Illness script formation	Illness script activation and instantiation	Monitoring of the level of script instantiation	Low	Adjust data collection to time available and to verification/falsification level of hypotheses

(*Source:* From Boshuizen & Schmidt, 2008.) Reprinted with permission from Elsevier.)

Does It Work?

Though theory and practice of PBL are scaffolded by the outcomes of expertise research, it does not relieve PBL schools of the requirement to show that their approach indeed has the desired effects. That is, can the following questions be answered with "yes": Do students learn better? Have they learned better? Do graduates have better fitting jobs? And do they do a better job? Before we try to answer these questions some caveats are needed. Assessing the effects of PBL can be done in two ways: historical comparison within one school or one course (before and after the innovation), and comparison between schools or courses. Both approaches have inherent design flaws related to the general quality of faculty and content of the curriculum, and to selection and self-selection of students. Rarely do we see studies in which students have been randomly allocated to a PBL or a traditional version of one course or a whole curriculum. The aspect of selection and self-selection is less problematic in PBL studies in the domain of medicine conducted in The Netherlands. Here, a national committee selects students on the basis of their grades on the national exams at the end of secondary education, and allocates them to one of the medical schools based on availability and student preference.[3] Colliver, Kucera, and Verhulst (2008) have pointed out that these biases and errors may accumulate in systematic review studies since there are reasons to assume that they are correlated to educational format. Some researchers doubt whether comparisons among institutions are worth the effort. They have reservations regarding the value from the perspective of curriculum improvement. The huge amount of bias and error in these studies make them ineffective in that respect, they say.[4] They expect more from process-oriented research especially dedicated to the affective and learning processes and the related instructional measures.

Comparisons made between PBL and non-PBL schools and courses in medicine mostly regard the first two questions. In the final part of this chapter, I will review research that can answer these questions.

Do Students Learn Better?

The question whether students learn better regards effects on instructional and educational parameters, as well as cognitive and affective processes and content; for example: Do students learn better in terms of process and outcomes? Are they better motivated? Are the attrition rates lower? Hmelo, Goterer, and Bransford (1997) have argued that to assess the effect of PBL, not just knowledge should be taken into consideration, but also the theoretical goals of PBL

---

[3] This situation has changed recently when medical schools were allowed by the ministry of education to admit students on basis of specific experience or motivation. Only a few schools use this option.

[4] Cees van der Vleuten, Maastricht, January 8, 2007. Also see Visschers-Pleijers (2007).

(clinical reasoning, integration of clinical and biomedical knowledge, lifelong learning skills), and that cognitive measures derived from expertise research should be used.

Many of such investigations have been done since the early 1970s. A couple of review studies have summarized the outcomes. The first burst of reviews was in 1993 (Albanese & Mitchell, 1993; Berkson, 1993 ; Vernon & Blake, 1993), followed by a new burst about 10 years later (Colliver, 2000; Dochy, Segers, Van den Bossche, & Gijbels, 2003 ; Gijbels, Dochy, Van den Bossche, & Segers, 2005; Hmelo-Silver, 2004 ; Schmidt, 2006). The first and most famous (narrative) review was by Albanese and Mitchell (1993). They concluded the following (p. 52):

> Compared with conventional instruction, PBL (...) is more nurturing and enjoyable; PBL graduates perform as well, and sometimes better, on clinical examinations and faculty evaluations; and they are more likely to enter family medicine. Further, faculty members tend to enjoy teaching using PBL. However, PBL students in a few instances scored lower on basic sciences examinations and viewed themselves as less well prepared in the basic sciences than were their conventionally trained counterparts.

Vernon and Blake (1993) reviewed the same studies but used a statistical meta-analysis. They found that PBL was superior regarding students' appreciation of their program and clinical performance. No differences could be detected regarding knowledge outcomes. However, PBL students did slightly worse on the National Board of Medical Examiners (NBME) Step 1 test. Berkson's (1993) study in the same year was again a narrative synthesis of almost the same set of studies. Her conclusion was that there were no differences between graduates of the two kinds of curricula, but that the costs in terms of stress and money were too high. Colliver's (2000) conclusion, several years and several studies later, contradicted this. He found no convincing evidence – or evidence of a relevant magnitude – regarding knowledge and clinical performance, but concluded that PBL was more challenging, motivating, and enjoyable for the students.

Later, methodologically more rigorous analyses by both Dochy et al. (2003) and Gijbels et al. (2005) built again on these previous reviews, extending the database and doing more dedicated analyses. Hmelo-Silver (2004) did a narrative, theory-driven analysis. Dochy et al. (2003) extended the database with other articles from refereed journals or book chapters of health-related curricula, written in English. Their statistical meta-analyses searched for main effects of curriculum on knowledge and skills, and for moderating effects for possible differences among curricula, such as the empirical design of the study and the kind of assessment instrument used. These instruments were very diverse: multiple-choice questions, modified essay questions, long and short essay questions, progress tests, free recall, performance-based testing (ratings), standardized simulated patients, long and short cases, etc. Dochy et al.

concluded that there was a robust and positive effect of PBL on cognitive and sensorimotor skills, and a tendency toward negative results on knowledge, which was mainly due to two outliers. They also concluded that the more trustworthy research designs were associated with less negative results regarding knowledge acquisition, that is, the most negative outcomes were found in studies using historical comparisons. Furthermore, students' expertise levels were related to effect, size, and direction of knowledge outcomes, but these differences disappeared when knowledge application is tested in the context of diagnostic tasks. Effects of retention period suggested that PBL students might have acquired slightly less knowledge but retained that knowledge better, while their skills were superior at immediate tests and were also better retained. Finally, the assessment method used in the studies affected the outcomes. The more an instrument required the integrated use of knowledge in representative contexts, the larger the positive effect of PBL was.

Gijbels et al. (2005) investigated the effect of assessment methods identified by Dochy et al. (2003) more deeply. They did not only include studies in medicine and the health fields, but also a few other domains. They differentiated between knowledge tests regarding concepts, principles, and application. Results showed that the more complex knowledge tests favored PBL students, while the simple test items on concepts did not yield overall significant differences between PBL and traditional curricula.

Hmelo-Silver (2004) reviewed the PBL research literature trying to formulate lessons for other educational fields than medicine. Her conclusion about knowledge and skills are similar to Dochy et al. (2003). She also concluded that self-directed and self-regulated learning is not learned automatically in PBL. In the beginning, all students struggled in directing their own learning to attain success with PBL. However, students lacking solid skills in self-directed learning had problems with PBL. Current programs do not provide instructional means to help students to develop these skills. At the other part of the spectrum, a similar problem can negatively influence learning of highly competent and experienced self-directed learners. PBL theory and practice does not provide guidelines for reduced teacher control (Vermunt, 2000). Hmelo-Silver also concluded that only a few studies have been done that focus on the effect of one distinctive feature of PBL, that is, cooperative learning. Similarly, the effect of PBL on motivation and of PBL as a whole has been hardly investigated.

Finally, Schmidt (2006) reviewed 16 studies in which PBL and other medical curricula in The Netherlands were compared. He also included studies published in the Dutch language. Again it was found that different curricula did not yield positive effects on knowledge outcomes, but that PBL students scored higher on skills and skill-related tasks. Schmidt (2006) also reported consistently lower attrition rates for PBL curricula. When we take the outcomes of expertise research into account, we may indeed conclude that PBL curricula lead to better learning.

Table 17.3. *Results of final-year students and graduates from PBL and more traditional schools on knowledge and skills test.*

	N subjects	Measurement	Results	
	PbL | comparison		Effect size	p-value
Studies of knowledge				
Saunders et al., 1990	45 | 243	MCQ	–0.716	< 0.0001
Van Hessen & Verwijnen, 1990	179 | *	MCQ		< 0.05
Albano et al., 1996	120 | 181	MCQ	=	
Verhoeven et al., 1998	135 | 122	MCQ	–0.385	< 0.01
Studies of skills				
Schmidt et al., 1996	100 est.	30 cases	+ or =	
Schuwirth et al., 1996	32 | 25	60 cases	+ 1.254	< 0.001

(*Source*: Based on Dochy et al., 2003.)

Reported information per study if available: Number of subjects in the PBL and comparison groups (* is compared with a national standard); kind of measurement used; direction and size of the effect (+ means that the PBL group did better, – did worse, = no difference); and p-value.

Have Students Learned Better?

The question whether students have learned better relates to effects on outcome at the graduate level. Outcome criteria can be formulated in terms of key competencies reached, but many professions judge their new entrants in terms of knowledge only. An example of such an entrance test is the NBME Step 3 examination of the U.S. Medical Licensing Examination. This test takes two days. One and one-half days are spent doing multiple-choice questions; the rest of the time is spent in solving computer-simulated patient management problems.

The analyses made by Dochy et al. (2003) reveal that only 8 of the 43 studies that had been done included this level of competence. No comparisons were based on NBME Step 3 results. Five studies included comparisons based on knowledge tests using students in their final year; three studies did the same using skill-related tests. Only six of these studies reported information about the numbers of participants involved and/or the basis for comparison of their findings (Table 17.3). The findings of graduates are not much different from those of students. PBL graduates do better than those from traditional school on skills, but not on knowledge tests.

Do Graduates Have Better Fitting Jobs?

Not many PBL schools will claim that their graduates will get better jobs. Yet, assuming that PBL graduates are better prepared for the job implies that they should end up at least having better fitting jobs, or have built competencies that better fit the jobs they have.

Studies that directly address this question could not be found. However, Meng (2006) investigated how well problem- and project-based education had prepared graduates for generic and domain-specific competencies required in their jobs about three or four years after graduation. His research deviates in many ways from the usual PBL-evaluations presented above. He compared about 25,000 graduates of higher education institutes in nine countries in different parts of the world and with different educational systems and labor market dynamics, using graduates' self-ratings and estimates of the necessity of the rated competencies in their jobs. Furthermore, he distinguished between activating (problem- and project-based) curricula and non-activating (laissez-faire or teacher-centered) schools. Meng found that, in general, students in activating study environments ended up with an academically oriented competence mix, perhaps a bit deficient in domain-related specific competencies. He also found that students who spent more time on the acquisition of discipline-specific competencies through self-study or by study-related employment did that successfully. Since his study dealt with graduates from a huge variety of studies and schools, it is hard to say whether this specific finding would also be found when the professional schools are analyzed as a separate group. His finding that dedicated training on discipline-related specific competencies yields positive outcomes can be taken as an indicator for that. Another indication might be that the same analyses done for tertiary vocational education again show that the activating environments result in better general academic competencies, while these groups of students did not show negative effects on domain-specific competencies.

Do Problem-Based Learning Graduates Do a Better Job?

Another consequence of the claim that PBL graduates are better prepared for their jobs is that they should also make a difference in the practice they join. For instance, medical graduates of a school that promotes integrated care for the elderly should show more collaboration with other allied health workers and work for more preventive actions. After a couple of years their actions and the results of their actions should be detectable in the health statistics. From the viewpoint of the public served, the most important question is whether PBL graduates perform better.

This question is only rarely investigated. An exception is a study by Tamblyn, Abrahamowicz, Dauphinee, Girard, Bartlett, Grand'Maison, and

Brailovsky (2005). These authors used four health administrative databases to derive indicators for the graduates' preventive care, continuity of care, precision of the diagnoses (this was derived from the prescription rate of dedicated medicines versus symptom relieving medicines), and quality of patient management (which was derived from the prescription rate of contraindicated drugs for a specific age group). These criteria reflect the changed tasks of the physician but they mainly concern the medical expert role. Tamblyn et al. compared health care effects of graduates before and after a curriculum reform at Sherbrooke Medical School (historic controls). They also compared them with graduates in the same years of three other Canadian medical schools where no curriculum reform had taken place. The findings showed that introducing PBL resulted in improvements on preventive care, continuity of care, and precision of the diagnoses as expressed by the improved prescription rate of disease-specific drugs. No improvement was found on the prescription rate of age-contraindicated drugs. These health care indicators of graduates from traditional schools were stable over the same period. Despite the considerable improvement on three indicators, the PBL graduates only performed best at the preventive and continuity of care indicators, and were second best on the two medication indicators.

CONCLUSION

Can we conclude that PBL is indeed a good way of teaching for expertise? This overview suggests that it is, although a couple of remarks have to be made. The first is the use of measures that can capture expert performance. We have seen that most knowledge tests used in the comparisons do not meet this requirement. Only some of the skills measures used can be characterized as addressing the core competence of the medical profession, but even these can be criticized. For instance, the short case tests used by Schmidt, Machiels-Bongaerts, Hermans, Ten Cate, Venekamp, and Boshuizen (1996), and by Schuwirth, Verhoeven, Scherpbier, Mom, Cohen-Schotanus, Van Rossum, et al. (1996) were rather prototypical in nature and pre-processed in the sense that they were formulated in encapsulating terms. Both features facilitate relevant knowledge activation. Furthermore, the tasks asked only for diagnosis; patient management and treatment were not included. Research by Harasym, Papa, and Schumacker (1997) suggests that the higher expertise levels are able to make finer discriminations exactly on these dimensions. Research into expert performance and effects of education and training misses such an instrument that is sensitive to these differences. Second, PBL in its present format needs better concepts regarding support and development of self-directed and self-regulated learning. The attention given in the new McMaster curriculum to information skills may help students to monitor more complex kinds of learning. Third, careful course and curriculum planning is needed based on knowledge of stages and characteristic difficulties in expertise development in the specific field. Similarly, monitoring the curriculum in action is the best way to prevent wear and tear. A well-designed and maintained PBL learning environment is the best way we have at the moment to prepare for professional practice. Improvement of the triad – learning task/learning process/learning outcome – and its evolvement over a period of several years require attention to all aspects alike. Implementations that neglect parts of it will be affected in all respects. The first three conclusions formulated here require further research. A better alignment of measurement instruments and procedures and expertise level in particular might have both theoretical and practical value.

REFERENCES

Albanese, M. A., & Mitchell, S. (1993). Problem-based learning: A review of literature on its outcomes and implementation issues. *Academic Medicine, 68*, 52–81.

Albano, M. G., Cavallo, F., Hoogenboom, R., Magni, F., Majoor, G., Mananti, F., et al. (1996). An international comparison of knowledge levels of medical students: The Maastricht Progress Test. *Medical Education, 30*, 239–245.

Arts, J. A. R., Gijselaers W. H., & Segers, M. S. R. (2002). Cognitive effect of an authentic computer supported, problem-based learning environment. *Instructional Science, 30*, 465–495.

(2004). Fostering managerial problem-solving: From cognitive research to instructional design to expertise. In H. P. A. Boshuizen, R. Bromme, & H. Gruber (Eds.), *Professional learning: Gaps and transitions on the way from novice to expert* (pp. 97–119). Dordrecht, The Netherlands: Kluwer Academic.

(2006). Enhancing problem solving expertise by means of an authentic, collaborative, computer supported and problem-based course: An effect outcome comparison of a traditional and a refined PBL course. *European Journal for Psychology of Education, 21*(1), 71–90.

Barrows, H. S. (1968). Simulated patients in medical teaching. *Canadian Medical Association Journal, 98*(14), 674–676.

(1971). *Simulated patients (programmed patients): The development and use of a new technique in medical education.* Springfield, IL: Thomas.

Barrows, H. S., & Tamblyn, R. M. (1980). *Problem-based learning: An approach to medical education.* New York: Springer.

Berkson, L. (1993). Problem-based learning: Have the expectations been met? *Academic Medicine, 68*(10), S79–S88.

Boshuizen, H. P. A. (1989). *De ontwikkeling van medische expertise; een cognitief psychologische benadering* [The development of medical expertise; A cognitive psychological approach]. PhD thesis, Maastricht University, The Netherlands.

Boshuizen, H. P. A., Phythian-Sence, C., Wagner, R. K., Gravemeijer, K., van der Aalsvoort, G. M., Nievelstein, F., et al. (2008). Instructional models in domains and professions. In J. M. Spector, M. D. Merrill, J. Van Merriënboer, & M. P. Driscoll (Eds.), *Handbook of research on educational communications and technology* (3rd ed., pp. 537–566). New York: Erlbaum/Routledge.

Boshuizen, H. P. A., & Schmidt, H. G. (1992). On the role of biomedical knowledge in clinical reasoning by experts, intermediates and novices. *Cognitive Science, 16*, 153–184.

(2008). The development of clinical reasoning expertise. In J. Higgs, M. Jones, S. Loftus, & N. Christensen (Eds.), *Clinical reasoning in the health professions* (3rd ed.). Amsterdam: Elsevier.

Bransford, J. D., Brown, A. L., & Cocking, R. R. (Eds.). (1999). *How people learn: Brain, mind, experience, and school.* Washington, DC: National Academy Press.

Colliver, J. A. (2000). Effectiveness of problem-based learning curricula: Research and theory. *Academic Medicine, 75*(3), 259–266.

Colliver, J. A., Kucera, K., & Verhulst, S. J. (2008). Meta-analysis of quasi-experimental research: Are systematic narrative reviews indicated? *Medical Education, 42*(9), 858–865.

Dochy, F., Segers, M., Van den Bossche, P., & Gijbels, D. (2003). Effects of problem-based learning: A meta-analysis. *Learning and Instruction, 13*, 533–568.

Crombag, H. F. M., de Wijkersloot, J. L., & Cohen, M. M. J. (1977). *Een theorie over rechterlijke beslissingen* [A theory of judicial decision making]. Zwolle: Tjeenk Willink.

de Groot, A. D. (1946). *Het denken van den schaker: Een experimenteel-psychologische studie.* Amsterdam: Noord-Hollandsche Uitg. Mij.
 (1965). *Thought and choice in chess.* The Hague: Mouton.

Dornan, T., Hadfield, J., Brown, M., Boshuizen, H., & Scherpbier, A. (2005). How can medical students learn in a self-directed way in the clinical environment? Design-based research. *Medical Education, 39*, 356–364.

Dornan, T., Scherpbier, A. J. J. A., & Spencer, J. (2008). Learning medicine. A continuum from theory to practice; In J. M. Spector, M. D. Merrill, J. J. G. van Merriënboer, & M. P. Driscoll (Eds.), *Handbook of research on educational communications and technology* (3rd ed., pp. 537–566). New York: Erlbaum/Routledge.

Elstein, A. S., Shulman, L. S., & Sprafka, S. A. (1978). *Medical problem solving: An analysis of clinical reasoning.* Cambridge, MA: Harvard University Press.

Eraut, M. (1994). *Developing professional knowledge and competence.* London: Routledge Falmer.

Frank, J. R. (Ed.). (2005). *The CanMEDS 2005 physician competency framework. Better standards. Better physicians. Better care.* Ottawa, Canada: The Royal College of Physicians and Surgeons of Canada.

General Medical Council. (1993). *Duties of a doctor.* London: General Medical Council.
 (2002). *Tomorrow's doctors.* London: General Medical Council.

Gijbels, D., Dochy, F., Van den Bossche, P., & Segers, M. (2005). Effects of problem-based learning: A meta-analysis from the angle of assessment. *Review of Educational Research, 75*(1), 27–61.

Gijselaers, W. H., Tempelaar, D., & Keizer, P. (Eds.). (1994). *Educational innovation in economics and business administration: The case of problem-based learning.* Dordrecht, The Netherlands: Kluwer Academic.

Harasym, P. H., Papa, F. J., & Schumacker R. E. (1997). The structure of medical knowledge reflected in clinicians' estimates of the probabilities of signs/symptoms within diseases. In A. J. J. A. Scherpbier, C. P. M. van der Vleuten, J. J. Rethans, & A. F. W. van der Steeg (Eds.), *Advances in medical education* (pp. 602–607). Dordrecht, The Netherlands: Kluwer Academic.

Harden, R. M., Sowden, S., & Dunn, W. R. (1984). Educational strategies in curriculum development: The SPICES model. *Medical Education, 18*(4), 284–97.

Hmelo-Silver, C. E. (2004). Problem-based learing: What and how do students learn? *Educational Psychology Review, 16*(3), 235–266.

Hmelo, C. E., Gotterer, G. S., & Bransford, J. D. (1997). A theory-driven approach to assessing the cognitive effect of PBL. *Instructional Science, 25*, 387–408.

Kidd, M., & Modlin, I. M. (1999). The Luminati of Leiden: From Bontius to Boerhaave. *World Journal of Surgery, 23*, 1307–1314.

Koens, F., Custers, E. J., & Ten Cate, O. T. (2006). Clinical and basic science teachers' opinions about the required depth of biomedical knowledge for medical students. *Medical Teacher, 28*(3), 234–238.

Meng, C. (2006). *Discipline-specific or academic? Acquisition, role and value of higher education competencies.* PhD thesis, Maastricht University, The Netherlands.

Moust, J. (1993). *De rol van tutoren in probleem-gestuurd onderwijs; Contrasten tussen student- en docent-tutoren* [The role of tutors in problem-based learning: Contrasts between student and staff tutors]. PhD thesis. Maastricht University, The Netherlands.

Muijtjens, A. M. M., Schuwirth, L. W. T., Cohen-Schotanus, J., & Van der Vleuten, C. P. M. (2008). Differences in knowledge development exposed by multi-curricular progress test data. *Advances of Health Sciences; Education, Theory and Practice, 13*(5), 593–605. DOI 10.1007/s10459–007–9066–2.

Nievelstein, F., van Gog, T., & Prins, F. J. (2008). Learning law. In J. M. Spector, M. D. Merrill, J. J. G. van Merriënboer, & M. P. Driscoll (Eds.), *Handbook of research on educational communications and technology* (3rd ed., pp. 537–566). Mahwah, NJ: Erlbaum/Routledge.

Norman, G., Neville, A. and the Task Force on the MD Program Curriculum (2004, November). *A new curriculum for the information Age: A concept- and practice-based approach.* McMaster University.

Neville, A. J., & Norman, G. R. (2007). *PBL in the undergraduate MD program at McMaster University: Three iterations in three decades. Academic Medicine, 82*(4), 370–374.

Patel, V. L., David, T. J., Boshuizen, H. P. A., & Wolfhagen, H. A. P. (1998). Implementation, students' perceptions and students' performance in problem-based and traditional paedriatic clerkships. *Education for Health, 11*, 215–223.

Rikers, R. M. J. P., Schmidt, H. G., & Boshuizen, H. P. A. (2001). Effects of clinical case priming on the activation of encapsulated knowledge: Differences between medical experts and subexperts. *Advances in Psychology Research, 4*, 1–31.

Saunders, N. A., Mcintosh, J., Mcpherson, J., & Engel, C. E. (1990). A comparison between University of Newcastle and University of Sydney final-year students: Knowledge and competence. In Z. H. Nooman, H. G. Schmidt, & E. S. Ezzat (Eds.), *Innovation in medical education: An evaluation of its present status* (pp. 50–54). New York: Springer.

Schmidt, H. G. (2006). Effecten van probleemgestuurd medisch onderwijs; 16 Nederlandse curriculum vergelijkingen [Effects of problem-based medical education; 16 Dutch curriculum comparisons]. *Nederlands Tijdschrift voor de Geneeskunde, 150*, 1085–1089.

Schmidt, H. G., & Boshuizen, H. P. A. (1993). On the origin of intermediate effects in clinical case recall. *Memory and Cognition, 21*, 338–351.

Schmidt, H. G., Machiels-Bongaerts, M., Hermans, H., Ten Cate, T. J., Venekamp, R., & Boshuizen, H. P. A. (1996). The development of diagnostic competence: Comparison of a problem-based, an integrated, and a conventional curriculum. *Academic Medicine, 71*, 658–664.

Schmidt, H. G., & Moust, J. H. C. (2000). Towards a taxonomy of problem used in problem-based learning curricula. *Journal of Excellence in College Teaching, 11*(2), 57–72.

Schuwirth, L. W. T., Verhoeven, B. H., Scherpbier, A. J. J. A., Mom, E. M. A., Cohen-Schotanus, J., van Rossum, H. J. M., et al. (1996). An inter- and intra-university comparison with short-case testing. *Advances in Health Science Education, 4*, 233–244.

Tamblyn, R., Abrahamowicz, M., Dauphinee, D., Girard, N., Bartlett, G., Grand'Maison, P., et al. (2005). Effect of a problem-based learning curriculum on quality of primary health care delivered by graduates: A historical cohort comparison study. *British Medical Journal, 331*(7523), 1002.

Thijssen, J. G. L., & van der Heijden, B. I. J. M. (2003). Evaporated talent? Problems with talent development during the career. *International Journal of Human Resources Development and Management, 3*(2), 154–170.

Thrush, C. R. (2008). *Bridging our knowledge about errors across the professions.* Panel discussion held at the Annual Meeting of the American Educational Research Association. New York, March 24–28.

Van Hessen, P. A. W., & Verwijnen, G. M. (1990). Does problem-based learning provide other knowledge. In W. Bender, R. J. Hiemstra, A. J. J. A. Scherpbier, & R. P. Zwierstra (Eds.), *Teaching and assessing clinical competence* (pp. 446–451). Groningen: Boekwerk Publications.

Van de Wiel, M. W. J. (1997). *Knowledge encapsulation; Studies on the development of medical expertise.* PhD thesis, Maastricht University, The Netherlands.

VanLehn, K. (1996). Cognitive skill acquisition. *Annual Review of Psychology, 47,* 513–539.

Verhoeven, B. H., Verwijnen, G. M., Scherpbier, A. J. J. A., Holdrinet, R. S. G., Oeseburg, B., Bulte, J. A., et al. (1998). An analysis of progress test results of PBL and non-PBL students. *Medical Teacher, 20*(4), 310–316.

Vernon, D. T. A., & Blake, R. L. (1993). Does problem-based learning work? A meta-analysis of evaluative research. *Academic Medicine, 68,* 550–563.

Vermunt, J. D. (2000). *Studeren voor nieuwe geleerden; Over de kwaliteit van het leren* [Learning for new scientists; About the quality of learning]. Inaugural address Maastricht University, The Netherlands.

Visschers-Pleijers, A. (2007). *Tutorial group discussion in problem-based learning: Studies on the measurement and nature of learning-oriented student interactions.* PhD thesis, Maastricht University, The Netherlands.

Williams, S. (1992). Putting case-based instruction into context: Examples from legal and medical education. *The Journal of the Learning Sciences, 2*(4), 387–427.

18

Enhancing the Development of Professional Performance: Implications from the Study of Deliberate Practice

K. ANDERS ERICSSON

Sources of large individual differences in professional achievement are still inadequately understood. Experience in a domain of activity appears to be necessary to perform adequately, but extensive experience does not invariably lead people to attain superior (expert) performance. When individuals are first introduced to a professional domain after completing their training, preparation, or education, they are often confused and must rely on advice from more-experienced colleagues to complete their responsibilities. After months or even years of mentored experience, their independent work reaches an acceptable level. Virtually everyone in a given domain of activity tends to improve with experience during this initial phase. After this point there are, however, considerable individual differences in development. Some professionals continue to improve steadily during many years or even decades, and are eventually recognized by their peers as having attained the highest levels as experts or masters. In contrast, most professionals in a domain reach a stable, average, undistinguished level of achievement within a relatively short time frame and maintain this mediocre level for the rest of their careers.

The nature of these individual differences in attained achievement is still controversial. The most common and traditional explanation is that individuals' achievements in any domain are limited by innate factors that cannot be changed through experience and training; hence, limits of attainable performance are determined by the person's basic endowments, such as physical and anatomical characteristics, mental capacities, and inborn talents. This traditional view of professional development had led to reduced emphasis on trainability and continued improvement of job performance. Several recent reviews and special issues debating the role of deliberate practice and innate talent have presented evidence showing that most aspects of human characteristics, excepting height and body size, can be modified through intense training

Acknowledgments: This research was supported by the FSCW/Conradi Endowment Fund of Florida State University Foundation. The author wants to thank Len Hill, for the helpful comments on earlier drafts of the chapter.

over extended periods of time (Ericsson, 2006a, 2007a, 2007b; Ericsson & Lehmann, 1996; Ericsson, Roring, & Nandagopal, 2007a, 2007b). The documented trainability is consistent with several findings about the development of expert levels of professional performance. First and foremost, it is very difficult to predict which individuals will attain expert levels of achievement. In spite of extensive screening and selection of applicants to professional schools and jobs, the levels of achievement of the trainees attained after years of on-the-job experience reveal striking individual differences. Given that everyone at the initial exposure of the domain of expertise is unable to perform at even acceptable levels implies that skilled and expert performance must be acquired through learning and skill acquisition. Only by accurately measuring the detailed structure of the increased professional performance are we likely to be able to assess the differences among those professionals who keep improving their performance and those who stagnate in their professional development shortly after the start of their professional careers.

In this chapter, I will discuss the difficult issues of measuring the development of socially constructed expertise, and review the new emerging insights into the practice activities that are related to objectively measured improvements in performance. First I will trace some of the historical ideas of innate characteristics and practice to Plato and its more modern conception developed by Sir Francis Galton (1869/1979). I will then discuss our emerging knowledge about how to measure very high levels of performance and how to identify factors related to its attainment in many types of domains, such as sports, music, and chess. Finally, I will discuss how these insights can be extrapolated to development in a wide range of professional domains.

THE TRADITIONAL VIEW OF SKILL ACQUISITION AND PROFESSIONAL DEVELOPMENT: HISTORY AND SOME RECENT CRITICISMS

In early civilizations, children learned the customs, language, and skills from their parents in a highly interactive manner. As cities grew, the diversity of professional paths increased and some adolescents had a choice between different professions and types of work. Philosophers such as Plato started to speculate about how one could design a city where every citizen was assigned to the type of work that best suited their temperaments and abilities. Plato (1954 , p. 233) argued that there are three definite classes of people whose personality types fit the roles of soldiers, workers, and leaders. No amount of training could overcome these basic personality differences. Plato believed in the power of occupational training, advocated the importance of early training, and recommended a lifelong theoretical learning of society's leaders. He wanted to identify the individual who was "a lover of all sorts of hard labour" (p. 335) and wanted "both to work hard with his body and to complete all that study and practicing as well" (p. 335).

Much later during the Middle Ages, as crafts became more specialized, craftsmen formed guilds to pass on their special knowledge of production methods, such as for lace, barrels, and shoes, to their students (apprentices). Apprentices would typically start at around age 14 and commit to serve and study with their master for around 7 years (Epstein, 1991). The guild system concerned crafts where the primary job involved production of observable products, such as shoes, tables, and jewelry, where inspection of adequate quality was relatively easy.

With the more recent development of public education, it is no longer necessary for students to make an early decision about their vocations and they can acquire knowledge through their teachers rather than having to discover the relevant knowledge and methods by themselves. There have been very important developments in our understanding of designing basic instruction in a wide range of domains based on instructional design (van Merrienboer & Boot , Chapter 6), task analysis (Schraagen, Chapter 7), and cognitive analysis (VanLehn & van de Sande, Chapter 16). General training in basic mathematical and verbal skills, along with general knowledge about sciences, history, and foreign languages, may have reduced but did not eliminate the need for professional training and development. Even the development of advanced schools for engineering, medicine, business, and law could only provide theoretical training up to a point, from which there has always been a clear transition from theoretical learning to the transition into a real job and to establishing a professional career. Some students have very successful professional careers; however the large majority have more modest ones. Surprisingly, success in professional schools (grades) seems to be almost unrelated to professional success as measured by salary. Roth and Clarke's (1998) meta-analysis found a correlation of 0.15 with starting salary and only a correlation of 0.05 with salary growth. These findings raise questions about the nature of the factors that lead to professional success.

The traditional views of professional success hold that individuals have certain types of inborn abilities and capacities that cannot be changed through training and cause only some of them to be more successful. Sir Francis Galton is often cited as the primary advocate of this view, described in his book *Hereditary Genius* (Galton, 1869/1979). According to Galton, relevant heritable capacities determine the upper boundary for the performance an individual can attain through practice, and reflect the immutable limit that "Nature has rendered him capable of performing" (p. 16). Galton argued convincingly that the characteristics that limit maximal performance, after all benefits of training have been gained, must, by definition, be innately endowed. On the other hand, if individuals' performances can still be improved through some type of training, then other types of explanations for the attainment of a sub-maximal level are possible.

In most professional domains it is difficult to measure individuals' levels of attained performance with objective methods. Most people's levels of expertise and achievements are assessed based on social judgments by supervisors and peers. Some scientists typically viewed expertise as an orderly progression from novice to intermediate and then to expert, where the primary factors mediating the progression through these stages were instruction, training, and experience. Thus, the primary criteria for identifying experts were social reputation, completed education, accumulated accessible knowledge, and length of experience in a domain (over 10 years) (Chi, 2006; Chi, Glaser, & Farr, 1988).

Several reviews over the past decade (Bédard & Chi, 1992; Ericsson, 2006a, 2006b; Ericsson & Lehmann, 1996; Ericsson & Smith, 1991) have raised issues about this definition of expertise. Most importantly, when individuals, based on their extensive experience and reputation, are nominated by their peers as experts, their actual performance is occasionally found to be unexceptional. Ericsson and Lehmann (1996) reported on research showing that highly experienced computer programmers' performance on programming tasks is not always superior to that of computer science students, and physics professors from the University of California at Berkeley were not always consistently superior to students on introductory physics problems. Furthermore, Ericsson and Lehmann (1996) reviewed evidence that the level of training and experience frequently has only a weak link to objective measures of performance. For example, the length of training and professional experience of clinical psychologists is not related to their efficiency and success in treating patients. In a recent review of political judgment, Philip Tetlock (2005) compared predictions from hundreds of experts in different fields with well-informed, nonexperts and were able to dispel the myth that experts' forecasts are superior.

The traditional study of experts identified by social and experience-based indicators will not allow us to understand the structure and acquisition of superior performance. In their chapter, Mumford and his colleagues (Mumford, Friedrich, Caughron, & Antes, Chapter 4) discussed several different measures of leadership ranging from subjective ones, such as peer and supervisor ratings, to objective ones, such as verifiable biodata and problem solving for a series of presented scenarios (Connelly et al., 2000). The focus should not be on examining the socially recognized experts, but rather on reproducibly superior performance on representative, authentic tasks in their field (Ericsson & Smith, 1991); for example, on the processes of diagnosis and treatment of patients in a superior manner, on the consistent selection of the best moves for chess positions, and on superior performance in music and sport competitions. The first step in a science of expert performance requires that scientists be able to capture the reproducibly superior performance on some consistently administered critical tasks of the domain of expertise, and then be able to examine this performance with laboratory methods, as will be described in the next sections.

CAPTURING REPRODUCIBLY SUPERIOR PERFORMANCE UNDER STANDARDIZED CONDITIONS

In everyday life, experts encounter unique challenges under different conditions, which makes it nearly impossible to compare levels of performance of different experts. For example, one doctor may treat two clients with complex and difficult treatment problems, whereas another may treat six clients with relatively routine treatment problems. One manager has to resolve several serious interpersonal conflicts during a restructuring of a firm, and another manager merely has to guide an enthusiastic team. Unless professionals encounter the same or comparable situations, it will be very difficult to measure individual differences in performance in a meaningful manner.

In a pioneering study, de Groot (1978) was able to design representative tasks that captured the superior performance of world-class chess players. The ultimate criterion for success in chess is success at chess tournaments, where players match their chess skills in matches that last for several hours. There are statistical methods for estimating a chess player's rating on an interval scale of chess ability based on outcomes from 20 to 50 tournament matches with different opponents (roughly 40 to 100 hours of play). Using an innovative approach, de Groot (1978) found a way to elicit the critical processes distinguishing chess expertise that avoided an analysis of extended chess-playing behavior. He identified particular chess positions in past games between chess masters, where the accurate selection of the next move was critical. He then presented the selected positions to chess players during an individual testing session and asked them to "think aloud" while they generated the best possible next move for each of the positions. de Groot (1978) demonstrated that world-class players reliably found the best moves for these positions, whereas skilled club players only found the best chess moves for some them. Subsequent research with large groups of chess players differing widely in skill level has shown that the selection of the best move for selected chess positions is correlated with the tournament ratings (Ericsson, Patel, & Kintsch, 2000; van der Maas & Wagenmakers, 2005). When performance on 20 selection tasks is aggregated, the resulting score is highly correlated with chess ratings – thus, it is possible to measure a chess player's skill after less than 15 minutes of testing. Of particular interest, de Groot (1978) was able to identify how the thought processes of world-class players differed from highly skilled club players by analyzing their think-aloud protocols from the selection tasks.

In the early 1990s, Ericsson and Smith (1991) proposed a new approach to the study of expertise based on a generalization of de Groot's paradigm, which was later elaborated as the *expert-performance approach*. In this approach the expert's performance in a given domain of expertise, such as music, sports, or medicine, is examined to identify naturally occurring situations in a given domain of expertise that require immediate action, and that capture the essence of expertise in the associated domain of expertise. For example, in the everyday life of a doctor or a nurse, they will encounter situations where they have to assess the symptoms of a patient for immediate diagnosis and treatment. Similarly it is possible to film soccer game situations where a given player is required to elicit an action without any delay (Ward & Williams, 2005). Once

Domain	Presented information	Task

Chess

Select the best chess move for this position

OVERVIEW--NATURE AND NURTURE OF EXPERTISE

The central challenge for any account of expertise is to explain how some individuals attain the highest levels of achievement in a domain and why so few reach that level. However, given the continuing struggle in Psychology to explain every day (lower) levels of achievement, it may appear presumptuous to attempt to explain even more advanced levels. Consequently, the accounts of expertise have been focusing on the general characteristics of the mechanisms. In order to be able to achieve at very high (expert) levels in domains of expertise both nature and nurture are nessary. Hence, everyone agrees that experts need to have acquired the necessary domain-specific knowledge and skills (nurture). Furthermore, the expert's performance often looks effortless and their most refined and insightful behavior is generated rapidly and naturally rather than the result of prolonged deliberation. It would thus appear that experts must excel in general basic characteristics, such as intelligence, memory, speed and flexibility, which have been assumed to be impossible to train and thus must be determined to a large degree by genetic factors (nature). Over the last couple of centuries, the arguments of the relative importance of nature versus nurture for expert achievement have been intricately linked to the theories of the actual processes that mediate the achievement of experts and to the conceptions of which aspects of human characteristics could be modified through development and training. Hence, this entry will briefly review the most important conceptions during the last century and then turn to a summary of our current knowledge and in conclusion the implications and connections of expert performance for creativity and genius will be outlined.

Typing

Type as much of the presented text as possible within one minute

Music

Play the same piece of music twice in the same manner

FIGURE 18.1. Three examples of laboratory tasks that capture the consistently superior performance of domain experts in chess, typing, and music.

(*Source*: From Ericsson, K. A., & Lehmann, A. C., 1999. Expertise. *Encyclopedia of Creativity*. Copyright by Academic Press.)

these situations have been selected and appropriate courses of action identified, it is then possible to reproduce them with appropriate context and an immediate demand for action under standardized conditions for all tested participants. In a controlled environment, such as a laboratory with a video screen or a simulator, it is possible to present these representative situations to participants differing in skill level. For each situation it is possible to record the time prior to initiation of action and the correctness/appropriateness of the action, along with process-tracing data, such as eye-fixations and concurrent or retrospective verbal reports, which allow for the determination and explication of mechanisms that can account for the reproducible differences in performance.

The representative tasks are designed in such a manner that individuals exhibiting superior performance under everyday conditions (experts) should exhibit superior performance on the tasks, since the tasks are designed to simulate task demands and situations that a performer might encounter. For example, if a chess master consistently selects the best move for a set of presented positions, then that individual would be able to select the best moves during chess games and thus beat most opponents. Figure 18.1 illustrates representative tasks in three domains that have been found to capture the essence of the associated expertise. The measured performance is closely related to the naturally occurring performance in each case. To study chess expertise, players at different skill levels are asked to generate the best move for identical positions where a single superior move is available (as determined by new chess-playing programs that are superior to the best human players for tactical problems). Different typists are presented the same text and asked to copy as much of the presented material as possible during a fixed time period. Musicians, who specialize as accompanists, are instructed to play unfamiliar pieces of music without being given time to practice and prepare. When skilled accompanists perform unfamiliar music at a prescribed tempo, their accuracy and performance quality is far superior to other pianists (Lehmann & Ericsson, 1996).

When the empirical evidence is restricted to only the observable superior performance, obtained under comparable conditions, a couple of relationships between expert performance and experience generalize across domains of expertise. First, greatly superior performance is only attained after extensive experience in a given domain. Second, improvements in performance are only associated with engagement in some restricted types of experience. In fact, many thousands of hours of specific types of practice and training are necessary for reaching the highest levels of performance.

The Necessity of Domain-Specific Experience for Attaining Reproducibly Superior Performance

Expert performance is only attained after extended engagement in domain-related activities in the corresponding domain (Ericsson, 2006a, 2006b; Ericsson & Lehmann, 1996). The level of performance of experts during development can be summarized and sketched as a function of years of experience, as follows. First, longitudinal assessments of performance of experts reveal that all individuals improve gradually, as illustrated in Figure 18.2. When performance is assessed by the same adult standards, there appears to be no objective evidence that a child or adult is able to exhibit a high level of performance without any relevant prior experience and practice (Ericsson, Roring, & Nandagopal, 2007a, 2007b). When the performances of child prodigies in music and chess are measured against adult experts, they show gradual, steady improvement over time. Second, elite performance keeps improving beyond the age of physical maturation – the late teens in industrialized countries (Ulijaszek, Johnston, & Preece, 1998) – and these increases are, thus, not limited by the normal development of the body and brain. Peak performance of experts is nearly always attained in adulthood – many years, and even decades, after initial exposure to the domain, as illustrated in Figure 18.2. The age at which performers typically reach their highest level of performance in many vigorous sports is the mid to late 20s. For the arts and sciences, it is one or two decades later, in the 30s and 40s (see Schulz & Curnow, 1988, and

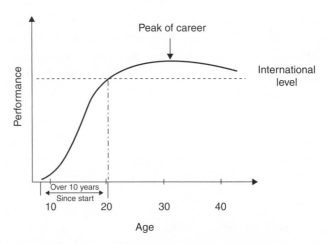

FIGURE 18.2. An illustration of the gradual increases in expert performance as a function of age, in domains such as chess. The international level, which is attained after more than 10 years of involvement in the domain, is indicated by the horizontal dashed line.

(*Source:* From Ericsson, K. A., & Lehmann, A. C., 1999. Expertise. *Encyclopedia of Creativity.* Copyright by Academic Press.)

Simonton, 1997, for reviews). The continued increases of expert performance during adulthood show that the highest level of performance must reflect further learning and physiological adaptation due to training and experience.

Finally, most findings supporting the necessity of vast experience in attaining expert performance come from investigators who have shown that everyone, even the most talented individuals, need to invest 10 years of active engagement in a domain (10-year rule) to become an expert (Bryan & Harter, 1899) and to win at an international level (Simon & Chase, 1973). Subsequent reviews have shown that these findings extend to international level success in music composition (Hayes, 1981), as well as to sports, science, and the arts (Ericsson, Krampe, & Tesch-Römer, 1993). Further, outstanding scientists and authors normally publish their first work at around age 25, and their best work follows around 10 years later (Raskin, 1936).

FROM EXPERIENCE TO DESIGNED PRACTICE

Many individuals seem satisfied with reaching a merely acceptable level of performance, such as amateur tennis players and golfers, and they attempt to reach such a level while minimizing the period of effortful skill acquisition. Once an acceptable level has been reached, they need only to maintain a stable performance, and often do so with minimal effort for years and even decades. For reasons such as these, the length of experience has been frequently found to be a weak correlate of job performance beyond the first two years (McDaniel,

Schmidt, & Hunter, 1988). More generally, length of professional experience is not systematically related to superior performance (Ericsson & Lehmann, 1996). Recent reviews of the performance of doctors and nurses show that extended experience (beyond the first couple of years) since graduation is not associated with continued improvements, as most people had thought, but rather continued decrements in performance are more common (Choudhrey, Fletcher, & Soumerai, 2005; Ericsson 2004; Ericsson, Whyte, & Ward, 2007). Davis (Chapter 8) reviews the research showing that physicians have poor abilities to assess their own weaknesses and level of professional performance. The critical variable for performance improvement is identifying areas of desired goals of achievement and engaging in effective training and practice to attain the associated improvement.

From retrospective interviews of international-level performers in the arts, sciences, and sports, Bloom (1985a) and his colleagues (1985b) demonstrated that these performers have a fundamentally different developmental history than their less-accomplished peers. The parents of the future elite performers helped their children from an early age to get help from teachers, spent large sums of money for teachers and equipment, and devoted considerable time to escorting their child to training and weekend competitions. In some cases, the performers and their families even relocate to be closer to the chosen teacher and superior training facilities. Based on their interviews, Bloom (1985a) argued that access to the best training resources was necessary to reach the highest levels.

At the same time, the best training environments are not sufficient to produce the very best performers, and there are substantial individual differences even among individuals in these environments. Can differences in the amount and type of domain-related activities in which individuals engage explain individual differences in music performance even among the best performers? Expert violinists at the music academy in Berlin kept a weekly diary on how much time they spent during a week on different activities (Ericsson et al., 1993). All groups of expert violinists were found to spend about the same amount of time (over 50 hours) per week on music-related activities. However, the best violinists were found to spend more time per week on activities that had been specifically designed to improve performance, which we named "deliberate practice." Expert musicians working in a solitary setting in order to master specific goals determined by their music teacher at weekly lessons, is a good example of goal-directed efforts to reach a higher level of performance. At a given lesson, the musicians are told by their teachers to improve and attain a level of playing that they are unable to reach at that time. A week later, and after considerable amount of solitary practice, the musicians are now able to play at the requested level. When the same groups of expert violinists were interviewed to estimate the amount of solitary (deliberate) practice in which they had engaged during their musical development, most accomplished

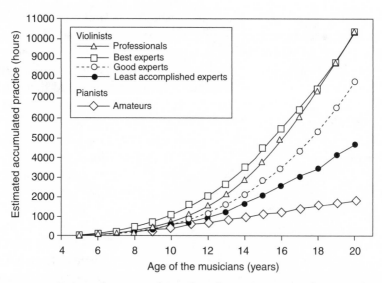

FIGURE 18.3. Estimated amount of time for solitary practice as a function of age for the middle-aged *professional* violinists (triangles), the *best* expert violinists (squares), the *good* expert violinists (empty circles), the *least-accomplished* expert violinists (filled circles), and *amateur* pianists (diamonds).

(*Source:* From Ericsson, K. A., Krampe, R. Th., & Tesch-Römer, C., 1993. The role of deliberate practice in the acquisition of expert performance, *Psychological Review, 100*(3), 379, 384. Copyright 1993 by American Psychological Association. Adapted with permission.)

musicians were found to have spent more time in deliberate practice during their development. Figure 18.3 shows that these differences were reliably observable before their admittance to the academy at around age 18. By the age of 20, the best musicians had spent over 10,000 hours practicing, which averages 2,500 and 5,000 hours, respectively, more than two less-accomplished groups of musicians at the same academy (Ericsson et al., 1993). In comparison to amateur pianists of the same age (Krampe & Ericsson, 1996), the best musicians from the academy and the professionals had practiced 8,000 more hours.

The central assumption of the framework of expert performance (Ericsson, 1996, 2002, 2004; Ericsson et al., 1993) is that expert performance can be described as a sequence of states associated with increasingly higher levels of performance as shown in Figure 18.4. In the case of acquisition of music performance, pianists acquire playing techniques in consecutive fashion, with the most difficult techniques acquired last. As shown in Figure 18.5, these techniques are closely associated with the number of years of playing. For example, after a few years of studying piano, teachers would start to assign music pieces that require complex movement with the non-dominant hand.

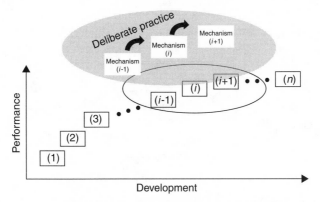

FIGURE 18.4. A schematic illustration of the acquisition of expert performance as a series of states with mechanisms for monitoring and guiding future improvements of specific aspects of performance.

(*Source:* Adapted from Ericsson, K. A., 2003. The development of elite performance and deliberate practice: An update from the perspective of the expert-performance approach. In J. L. Starkes and K. A. Ericsson (Eds.), *Expert performance in sport: Recent advances in research on sport expertise* (p. 70). Copyright 2003 by Human Kinetics.)

After nine years of piano instruction, the student starts with polyrhythms, where the musicians' hands have to play with a different rhythm; for example, for every two beats in one hand, the other hand has to complete three beats or other ratios of rhythms such as 4:5 and 5:6. Composers for the piano invented the techniques shown in Figure 18.5 in the 18th and 19th centuries but had to wait until professional pianists acquired the necessary skill levels to master the new techniques if they ever wanted to hear the music pieces performed. It is, therefore, not surprising that the invented techniques keep increasing in complexity over historical time, as is demonstrated in Figure 18.5. Similar findings have been made in sports, where the performances of individual athletes, such as the maximum weight lifted or the running time for the marathon, are improving over their careers (Ericsson, 2007a). The central point is that the aspiring expert performer needs to be able to find ways to go beyond their current state of maximal performance (Figure 18.4) and find a way through training to improve the mediating mechanisms. The key challenge to motivated performers is to identify aspects of performance that can be improved within a reasonable time and the associated training activity that will incrementally increase that aspect as well as the overall performance. Coaches and teachers can observe students' performances and recommend training tasks with explicit goals that will allow the students to improve on the training task as well as their performance. For example, students who need to increase their speed for executing particular finger combinations are often encouraged to execute particular finger exercises and etudes with increasing

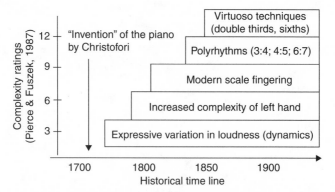

FIGURE 18.5. Introduction of new pianistic techniques since the early development of the piano. (Adapted from The historical development of domains of expertise: Performance standards and innovations in music, by A. C. Lehmann and K. A. Ericsson, in A. Steptoe (Ed.), *Genius and the mind* (p. 70). Copyright 1998 by Oxford University Press).

speed. According to the concept of the acquisition of expert performance as a sequence of states of performance, improvements will correspond to the acquisition of new methods, increased speed, or greater control over performance. To engage in deliberate practice (Ericsson, 2006a) requires that the performers need to work on tasks that are initially outside their current realm of reliable performance. Furthermore, it must be possible to improve on the targeted characteristic within a limited number of hours of practice or else the performer will become discouraged.

Deliberate practice tasks will depend on the particular training goals and the individuals' pre-existing skills for monitoring and controlling their performance (Ericsson, 2006a, 2006b, 2007a). For example, a chess player that is presented with the task of finding the best move for a specific chess position will engage in planning to find it, and then will engage in analysis to figure out why he/she did not find the best move to avoid any similar mistakes in the future. Similarly, an athlete attempting to increase strength in a movement will repeat the movement with appropriate weights and until exhaustion of muscles. The central assumption is that an individual's performance on a training task will vary as a function of focus of attention, type of strategy, and many other situational factors. If one wants to reach one's highest performance consistently or even go beyond one's initial maximal performance, one has to identify the optimal factors. Consequently, any type of deliberate practice is designed to maximize gains to performance by allowing the performer to be fully rested at the start of the activity. The performers should also be fully prepared for initiation of the task, be given immediate feedback from the outcome, and then be allowed to repeat the same or similar task with gradual modifications. Performing the task under these optimal conditions is more effective than performing the associated task only when it occurs within the natural context of performance. Hence, part of the practice is to gradually embed the trained task in its natural context with regular time constraints and less predictable occurrences. For example, imagine an amateur tennis player who misses a volley at the net. The play will go on until some time later a similar situation emerges unexpectedly with a similar problem for the player. Contrast this type of on-the-job learning with a session with a tennis coach. The tennis coach would set up situations where the player would stand at the net and be ready to execute the volley. With mastery of the easy volleys, the coach can increase the difficulty of the shots and eventually embed volley shots into the rallies. It is easy to see that a few hours of this type of training would improve the player's volley more than 10s or 100s of hours of regular tennis play against other amateurs.

Hence, the focus on changing and improving performance sets deliberate practice apart from both mindless, routine performance and playful engagement. The latter two types of activities would, if anything, merely strengthen the currently inadequate cognitive mediating mechanisms rather than modify them to allow increases in the level of performance. In learning everyday activities such as driving a car, typing, or playing golf, a person's primary goal is to reach an acceptable level of performance. During the first phase of learning of everyday skills (Anderson, 1982; Fitts & Posner, 1967), beginners try to understand the activity and focus their attention on completing their first attempts for successful actions, as is illustrated in the first part of the lower arm of Figure 18.6. With more experience (the middle phase of learning), gross mistakes become increasingly rare, sequences of performance steps are elicited more smoothly, and learners can elicit their performance without the need to actively deploy their attention to control their performance as they had to do in the beginning. After a limited period of training and experience – frequently less than 50 hours for most recreational activities – learners attain an acceptable standard of performance, which can be elicited with much reduced concentration. At this advanced point, most individuals no longer attempt to make further modifications and improvements, which typically lead to a stable plateau of performance that can be maintained with regular activity for months, years, and decades. In direct contrast, the individuals aspiring to reach expert performance never allow their performance to be fully automated. They continue to seek out, with the help of their teachers, new training activities where they need to engage in problem solving to alter their cognitive representations that allow them to keep improving the mechanisms mediating performance, as illustrated by the upper arm in Figure 18.6. Some aspiring performers will eventually stop pushing their limits after months or even years of training. The performance level at the end of training will be eventually automated and their development will be prematurely arrested at that intermediate level as illustrated by the middle arm in Figure 18.6.

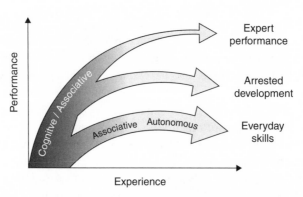

FIGURE 18.6. An illustration of the qualitative difference between the course of improvement of expert performance and of everyday activities. The goal for everyday activities is to reach as rapidly as possible a satisfactory level that is stable and "autonomous." After individuals pass through the "cognitive" and "associative" phases, they can generate their performance virtually automatically with a minimal amount of effort (see the gray/white plateau at the bottom of the graph). In contrast, expert performers counteract automaticity by developing increasingly complex mental representations to attain higher levels of control of their performance, and will therefore remain within the "cognitive" and "associative" phases. Some experts will at some point in their careers give up their commitment to seeking excellence and thus terminate regular engagement in deliberate practice to further improve performance, which results in premature automation of their performance.

(*Source:* Adapted from Ericsson, K. A., 1998. The scientific study of expert levels of performance: General implications for optimal learning and creativity. *High Ability Studies, 9,* 90. Copyright 1998 by European Council for High Ability).

Recent reviews (Ericsson, 2006a, 2007a, 2007b; Ericsson, Roring, & Nandagopal, 2007a, 2007b) have found that individuals do not attain expert and exceptional levels of performance without deliberate practice. Even the well-entrenched beliefs that that more "talented" children improve faster during the first phase of their music development than normal children appears to be in large part due to the fact that these children spend more time in deliberate practice each week (Sloboda, Davidson, Howe, & Moore, 1996). Field studies of how normal children practice with their musical instruments show that practice that meets the criteria for deliberate practice is rare (Renwick & McPherson, 2002). Consistent with this observation, Lehmann (1997) found that the correlation between number of hours of "practice" and performance was rather low for beginners, but increased for advanced students committed to a professional music career (Ericsson, 2002). Furthermore, Grape, Sandgren, Hansson, Ericsson, and Theorell (2003) found that professional singers had increased levels of physiological and psychological indicators of concentration and effort during a singing lesson compared to amateur singers. The professional singers reported focusing on improving their performance during the lesson, whereas the amateur singers experienced the lesson as self-actualization and an enjoyable release of tension. It is relatively easy to identify deliberate practice in music and some sports because the coaches and teachers frequently guide the continued attempts for mastery. The designed activities require that the performer always try, by stretching performance beyond its current capabilities, to correct some particular weakness while preserving other functional aspects of performance. This type of activity (deliberate practice) requires full attention (concentration) on the performance of the activity, but even with extreme effort, failures are virtually inevitable. However, gradual improvements occur through frequent corrections of methods and increasingly refined repetitions. By instructing advanced musicians to think aloud during practice, the normally covert cognitive processes are externalized and one can observe their monitoring of performance and their sustained focus on mastering new challenges through problem solving and specialized training techniques (Chaffin & Imre, 1997; Ericsson, 2002; Nielsen, 1999). In chess, Charness and colleagues (Charness, Krampe, & Mayr, 1996; Charness, Tuffiash, Krampe, Reingold, & Vasyukova, 2005) have found that the amount of solitary chess study was the best predictor of chess skill, and when this factor was statistically controlled, there was only a very small benefit from the number of games played in chess tournaments. During solitary study, aspiring chess experts study published games and try to predict each move by the masters. If they successfully predict the next move, then they match the level of play of the masters. If they fail to predict the move, they study the position more closely to discover the reasons for the master's move. By this type of immediate feedback players are able to make corrections to their representations and their search for alternative combinations of chess moves, so they can avoid that mistake as well as mistakes for other related chess positions. Similar findings have been made in other domains. For example, in a study of district, national, and professional dart players, Duffy, Baluch, and Ericsson (2004) found that solitary deliberate practice was closely related to performance, whereas the amount of social dart activities did not predict performance. In another example, Urena (2004) compared the developmental history of professional ballet dancers, including dancers from the Russian Bolshoi Company, to ballet dancers at universities. She found that the estimated amount of deliberate practice accumulated by age 17 predicted the level of professional achievement even among the professional female dancers. The development of ballet performance tends to start early and can be described in a predictable series of stages (van Rossum, 2001) or milestones, such as first public solo performance (Urena, 2004).

There is also an impressive body of evidence showing that the training volume and intensity is related to competitive performance among athletes (Ericsson, 2003a, 2003b, 2007a, 2007b). It has been more difficult to isolate practice activities that meet all the criteria for deliberate practice in team sports, where most of the practice time is not directed toward eliminating specific weaknesses of individual players, that can be measured objectively. Nonetheless, several studies have found a consistent relationship between attained levels of performance and the total amount of estimated practice. For example, the amount of time spent in team-related deliberate practice activities correlates reliably with the level (local, national, and international) of a player's skill in team sports (Ward, Hodges, Williams, & Starkes, 2004). Also, the elite-level youth soccer players spent significantly longer periods per week and accrued more total time in deliberate practice, while less-skilled players spent the majority of their time with soccer in "play."

Deliberate practice has also been found to permit maintenance of high levels of performance among older expert musicians and chess players (see Krampe & Charness, 2006, for a comprehensive review). Krampe and Ericsson (1996) found that musicians over 60 years old showed a normal age-related decline for traditional laboratory measures of cognitive abilities, such as the speed of substituting digits for symbols. In direct contrast, those pianists who continued spending around 10 hours a week on practice did not exhibit any reliable decline on representative tasks that captured their ability to play the piano after preparation. Similarly master athletes in their 50s and 60s are able to maintain very high levels of performance, though lower than elite young athletes, by maintaining a regular training schedule (Starkes, Weir, & Young, 2003). In fact, when the training schedules are matched to young athletes very few differences in physiological variables can be detected (Ericsson, 2000). Similar findings on maintained cognitive abilities within their domain of expertise have been demonstrated in a very interesting series of studies by Masunaga and Horn (2001) for professional and less skilled GO-players. Charness et al. (2005) found that solitary deliberate practice is an even more potent predictor of performance for older chess players compared to younger ones. The evidence on maintained levels of high performance of expert performers has led me to propose (Ericsson, 2000) that the primary reason for age-related decline in healthy, older performers is their reduction or elimination of regular practice, and that reduced deliberate practice can explain a very large portion, perhaps even most, of age-related decline in the performance of experts in their 50s, 60s, and early 70s.

Deliberate practice is typically a separate activity that differs from actual work activities. When a surgeon performs surgery on a patient, this is not the time to try out an alternative method or focus on improving some particular weakness. During work, public performance, and competitions, the performer should be fully focused on achieving the best possible result given their attained level of skill. This does not mean that the time associated with competition or work cannot be used to improve performance. The performer can often invest a lot of preparation time prior to actual performance, such as planning the surgery or preparing to play a set of music pieces or facing specific athletic opponents. It is even possible to simulate actual performance conditions during practice sessions (performance practice) in anticipation of the actual (often public) performance. Even more important, after the end of a performance it is possible for the individuals to reflect on their memory for the immediately preceding performance and identify problems and weaknesses that can be targeted in subsequent practice sessions. In some sports, like soccer and tennis, there may often be enough time between ball possessions and active play for the performers to consider alternative methods of attack that will be more successful.

More generally, deliberate practice is closely connected to actual measurable performance and it is thus during performance of representative tasks under typical conditions, such as weather problems, noisy audiences, and technical/equipment problems, that the performer can accurately identify weaknesses or areas for further improvement. In some cases, deliberate practice will therefore be similar to actual work and performance. For example, the best way to increase one's typing speed is to set aside 10 to 20 minutes each day, when one is most alert, and then attempt to type 10–20 percent faster than one's normal reliable speed of typing (Dvorak, Merrick, Dealey, & Ford, 1936). During these efforts to push beyond one's reliable speed, the typists realize which key stroke combinations are creating problems and causing hesitations. Once these combinations have been identified, the typists can target these problems with special practice and then work on special texts where these problems are relatively frequent, to incorporate the modifications into their integrated typing skill. Then the cycle starts over with identifying new problems that are holding the typists' elevated speed back.

APPLYING THE FRAMEWORK TO PROFESSIONAL TRAINING AND PRACTICE

There are several initiatives in education that have constructed bridges between traditional learning and professional practice. Two of the most influential developments have been cognitive apprenticeships (Lajoie, Chapter 3) and problem-based learning (Boshuizen, Chapter 17). In both cases, the focus is on providing help so that the student is able to handle representative problems, whether they concern diagnoses of avionics of airplanes or of patients with medical problems. For example, in medical schools with problem-based curricula, students' learning is to a large extent focused around typical medical problems, such as upper respiratory problems, that a doctor might encounter when dealing with real patients. The mastery of knowledge and techniques is more closely tied to their use in practice for helping patients with specific medical problems than the traditional education based on mastery of the scientific knowledge and its general principles. In a related trend, medical students are now regularly trained as well as tested in simulated clinical settings by attempting to diagnose patients, who have been trained to simulate the symptoms of a particular disease (Boshuizen, Chapter 17; Davis, Chapter 8).

Most professionals – such as doctors, nurses, stockbrokers, and accountants – do not receive the constant feedback or pressure from performing in front of an audience of paying ticket holders, like actors, musicians, and athletes. The lack of scrutiny and perhaps feedback may be an important difference that explains why many doctors do not spontaneously adopt the best practice methods for treating their patients (Davis, Chapter 8), and spend a rather modest amount of time engaged in deliberate practice and effortful training to improve and maintain their skills. It is interesting to compare these doctors and other professionals to professional musicians and soccer players, who spend vastly more time in training and the acquisition of new music repertoire or tactics than they spend in public performance.

The lack of paid time to practice raises interesting challenges for professionals who want to improve their performance. It is possible for individuals to spend time in addition to their paid time on practice-related activities, such as additional time in planning and subsequent review of one's performance. The greatest obstacle for deliberate practice during work is the lack of immediate objective feedback. Frequently, the accuracy of decisions about medical treatments or stock investments may not be apparent for weeks or months as consequences of the decisions are realized. In work environments, typically a more-experienced individual, such as a supervisor, will give feedback. This feedback is unfortunately only as good as the objective performance of that individual, which raises the issues of subjective criteria of expertise. In many domains, such as medicine, the trainees will make decisions about treatments while being monitored by experienced doctors. If the trainees' decision differs from their supervisor, the "correct" decision will be explained. For example, the training of new radiologists lets medical interns make their diagnoses of incoming mammograms and then receive feedback on their diagnoses by the senior radiologists reviewing the same X-rays. However, the accuracy of the senior radiologists is only around 70 percent for correctly diagnosing malignant growths, so the radiology interns can only slowly reach a level matching their best teachers. In radiology, it is theoretically possible to provide immediate and highly accurate feedback about diagnostic decisions about mammograms with malignancies in an educational setting. It is possible to collect a library of old mammograms with either known malignancies (validated by subsequent surgery) or healthy breast tissue (validated by no symptoms in the following two years). Radiology interns could then be given detailed feedback about their diagnoses immediately following their diagnostic decision for a given mammogram. If they made a mistake, they could be presented with a series of mammograms illustrating the gradually diminishing differences between healthy and malignant tissue. Given the modest accuracy of senior radiologists, this type of training facility could serve as a means of maintaining and improving diagnostic performance by radiologists at all levels. More generally, it is possible to develop similar collections of training situations for a wide range of professional tasks if the resources were available. Collections of representative tasks with verifiably correct answers cannot only be used to measure the objective performance of individual experts, but they can also be used for training new recruits as well as for maintenance testing and continued training of experienced professionals.

All types of professional experience involve the experience of new situations, and this experience is more common for beginners, novices, and less-experienced individuals. In many professional contexts, the novice will assist and observe the more-experienced individual and eventually take over while their performance is monitored by an experienced professional, such as a submarine commander (Kirschenbaum, Chapter 12), a master mechanic (Lajoie, Chapter 3), a flight instructor, and a master surgeon. These training and learning activities involving apprentices are relatively costly and time consuming, and cannot be extended into training large groups of beginners, such as military recruits in the army and salespeople in companies. Chatham (Chapter 10) provides an inside view of the design of computer games that familiarize potential recruits with the situations encountered in the military – of particular interest is the case of linking of instruction to qualifying to be a medic in the game. Schreiber et al. (Chapter 11) give a very nice account of the historical developments of general purpose and special purpose flight simulators, and the issues of measuring performance in the simulators and under real flight missions. Recent reviews of the effectiveness of flight simulators have found surprisingly few significant transfer effects on targeted performance in the real environment, when one excludes new procedural skills that can be learned in a low-fidelity trainer (Allerton, 2000; Rantanen & Talleur, 2005; Roessingh, 2005; Ward, Williams, & Hancock, 2006).

Within the last few years there have been major advances in the study of the effects of training with surgical simulators. In medicine, technical advances have allowed surgeons to use advanced technical tools (including video taken from inside the body) to perform laparoscopic surgery with a very small opening of the skin. Early research showed that there was no observable transfer from traditional open surgery, so both novice and highly experienced traditional surgeons increased their efficiency and reduced complications from surgery markedly with the number of procedures that each individual completed (see Ericsson, 2004, for a review). A recent review (Issenberg, McGaghie, Petrusa, Gordon, & Scalese, 2005) showed that effective learning was achieved in simulation studies primarily when certain elements were present. The most important factor was that feedback was provided; the second most important factor was that repeated practice was required. In a more selective review, McGaghie,

Issenberg, Petrusa, and Scalese (2006) examined 32 studies that incorporated the effective factors and found a strong relationship between the number of hours of training and the standardized educational outcomes (η^2 = .46). They proposed that effective medical training should incorporate the elements of deliberate practice, and that extended training in the simulator is necessary to reach a plateau in the learning curve (cf. Benner et al., 2004). Based on studies of skilled surgeons' performance of tasks in simulators, researchers have now developed proficiency levels based on speed and accuracy that educators are now using as guidelines for training students with virtual reality simulators in laparoscopic surgery (Van Sickle et al., 2007). New studies are trying to refine the effectiveness of simulation studies by timing and designing feedback (Van Sickle, Gallagher, & Smith, 2007), as well as distributing training across days (Verdaasdonk, Stassen, van Wijk, & Dankelman, 2007). Most of the research has focused on preparing medical students and interns for their first procedures with human patients. There is a growing interest in helping surgeons improve during their first two hundred or so procedures, when there is a marked improvement in speed and outcomes of treated patients (Hollenbeck et al., 2007; Vickers et al., 2007). Research on training in medicine, especially surgery, has emerged as one of the leaders in developing effective learning environments for students and continuing professional development.

There are several very interesting research efforts attempting to assess deliberate practice activities among professionals. Sonnentag and Kleine (2000) analyzed the professional activities of salespeople and were able to find a reliable, albeit modest, relationship between their sales performance and the estimated time the salesperson spends engaging in activities referred to as deliberate practice. Medical teams with the best performance for new types of surgical (laparoscopic) procedures were found to spend a lot more time than less successful teams on deliberate learning and reflections on how to improve as a team (Pisano, Bohmer, & Edmundson, 2001).

Several of the chapters in this volume describe efforts to design learning environments with deliberate practice activities. A particularly spectacular example was the establishment of the Top Gun training school (Chatham , Chapter 2) where pilots were allowed to train against the simulated enemy by fighting against trained instructors flying the enemy aircrafts. Instead of using live ammunition in their guns and shooting missiles, the planes used film cameras and radar information to determine whether a given plane would have been shot down. During the debriefing the trained pilots were able to learn from their mistakes and generate alternative methods of attack rather than being irrevocably terminated from future combat due to a premature death.

Another challenge in professional domains is that difficult and challenging situations occur very infrequently. It is commonly observed that frequent problems are often handled reasonably well by most professionals, but the key individual differences arise when dealing with infrequent and urgent problems, such as emergency situations for airline personnel and emergency room staff. To train personnel for such situations that will never be experienced by most professionals, it is necessary to conduct training in simulators where emergency situations can be generated. McKinney and Davis (2004) analyzed a large database on actual airplane emergency situations and training records of similar emergency situations in the simulator. They found that if the expert pilots had practiced the same emergency situation in the simulator prior to the emergency event, they were reliably more successful dealing with an actual event and thus the specific training reduced the probability of negative outcomes for pilot and plane.

With an increased interest in the lifelong development of professional performance, there should be an increase in studies examining deliberate practice in many different types of professional activities, as well as designing training environments with challenging relevant situations that require immediate action and that can provide feedback and opportunities for repeated encounters of the same and similar tasks.

CONCLUSION

Once professionals have reached an acceptable level of performance, improvements in performance of adult experts do not occur automatically or without discernable causes. Continued improvements in performance can be linked to changes in cognitive mechanisms mediating how the brain and nervous system control, and how physiological mechanisms execute, the performance. However, it is difficult to attain stable changes that allow performance to be incrementally improved. The general Rule (or Law) of Least Effort predicts that the human body and brain have been designed to carry out activities at the minimum cost to the metabolism. When physiological systems, including the nervous system, are significantly strained by ongoing activity, such systems initiate processes that lead to physiological adaptation and mediation of simpler cognitive processes to reduce the metabolic cost. This phenomenon is evident in most types of habitual professional and everyday activities such as driving a car, typing, or carrying out familiar tasks, in which individuals tend to automate their behaviors to minimize the effort required for execution of the desired performance.

Merely performing the same practice activities repeatedly on a regular daily schedule will not lead to further improvement, once a physiological adaptation to the current demand has been achieved. The key attribute of deliberate practice is that individuals seek out new challenges that go beyond their current level of reliable achievement – ideally in a safe and optimal learning context that allows immediate feedback and gradual refinement by repetition. These learning environments can be viewed as scaffolds that facilitate attainment of a higher level of performance that later need to be gradually eliminated so performance can be embedded and elicited in the natural environments in the domain of expertise.

Once we realize that superior levels of performance are mediated by complex integrated systems of representations for the execution, monitoring, planning, and analyses of performance, it becomes clear that acquisition of skilled performance requires an orderly and deliberate approach. Deliberate practice focuses on improving a specific aspect of performance. By designing training tasks that capture conditions of representative situations, the performer will engage the complex cognitive mechanisms that mediate (generate) superior performance. The same mechanisms and representations also allow the expert to monitor, evaluate, and reason about their performance.

Improvements are always conditional on the performers' pre-existing mechanisms and entail modifications of their own specific representations. The tight interrelationship between representations that monitor and generate performance minimizes the risk of unwanted side effects from modifications. However, the complex integration of the mechanisms mediating superior expert performance makes it impossible to isolate distinct processes of problem solving, decision making, and reasoning. In fact, the principal challenge of professional skill acquisition appears to be in developing representations that coordinate each of the following: selection of actions, monitoring, control of ongoing performance, and incremental improvements to performance.

The research on expert levels of achievement in professions and other domains of expertise will need to focus on the mechanisms mediating the superior domain-specific performance. There is, however, an accumulation of generalizations across many domains about the acquisition of these mechanisms during an extended period of deliberate practice. These general insights range from the characteristics of ideal training environments, to the methods for fostering motivation by providing both emotional support and attainable training tasks of a suitable difficulty level. Furthermore, research indicates that professionals developing skills in one domain, such as laparoscopic surgery, can benefit by relying on the knowledge about the best training methods developed in domains with longer traditions of developing elite performance, such as training violinists. There is a new partnership emerging among scientists, coaches, and expert performers interested in reaching higher levels of performance by making systematic changes to practice methods and training environments. The knowledge has implications for education and professional training of performance for all the preliminary levels that lead up to the expert levels in professional domains of expertise. By examining how the prospective expert performers attained each level of achievement, we should be able to develop practice environments and foster learning methods that help large groups of people to attain the fundamental representations and the self-regulatory skills that would give them the ability to continue to increasingly higher levels of achievement.

REFERENCES

Abernethy, B. (1991). Visual search strategies and decision-making in sport. *International Journal of Sport Psychology, 22,* 189–210.

Allerton, D. J. (2000). Flight simulation: Past, present and future. *Aeronautical Journal, 104,* 651–663.

Anderson, J. R. (1982). Acquisition of cognitive skill. *Psychological Review, 89,* 369–406.

Bédard, J., & Chi, M. T. H. (1992). Expertise. *Current Directions in Psychological Science, 1,* 135–139.

Benner, W. C., Korndorffer, J. R., Sierrra, R., Massarweh, N. N., Dunne, J. B., Yau, C. L., & Scott, D. J. (2004). Laparoscopic virtual reality training: Are 30 repetitions enough? *Journal of Surgical Research, 122,* 150–156.

Bloom, B. S. (1985a). Generalizations about talent development. In B. S. Bloom (Ed.), *Developing talent in young people* (pp. 507–549). New York: Ballantine Books.

Bloom, B. S. (Ed.). (1985b). *Developing talent in young people.* New York: Ballantine Books.

Bryan, W. L., & Harter, N. (1899). Studies on the telegraphic language: The acquisition of a hierarchy of habits. *Psychological Review, 6,* 345–375.

Chaffin, R., & Imreh, G. (1997). "Pulling teeth and torture": Musical memory and problem solving. *Thinking and Reasoning, 3,* 315–336.

Charness, N., Krampe, R. Th., & Mayr, U. (1996). The role of practice and coaching in entrepreneurial skill domains: An international comparison of life-span chess skill acquisition. In K. A. Ericsson (Ed.), *The road to excellence: The acquisition of expert performance in the arts and sciences, sports, and games* (pp. 51–80). Mahwah, NJ: Lawrence Erlbaum Associates.

Charness, N., Tuffiash, M. I., Krampe, R., Reingold, E., & Vasyukova, E. (2005). The role of deliberate practice in chess expertise. *Applied Cognitive Psychology, 19,* 151–165.

Chi, M. T. H. (2006). Two approaches to experts' characteristics. In K. A. Ericsson, N. Charness, P. Feltovich, & R. R. Hoffman (Eds.), *Cambridge handbook of expertise and expert performance* (pp. 21–38). Cambridge, UK: Cambridge University Press.

Chi, M. T. H., Glaser, R., & Farr, M. J. (Eds.). (1988). *The nature of expertise.* Hillsdale, NJ: Lawrence Erlbaum Associates.

Choudhrey, N. K., Fletcher, R. H., & Soumerai, S. B. (2005). Systematic review: The relationship between clinical experience and quality of health care. *Annals of Internal Medicine, 142,* 260–273.

Connelly, M. S., Gilbert, J. A., Zaccaro, S. J., Threlfall, K. V., Marks, M. A., & Mumford, M. D. (2000). Exploring the relationship of leadership skills and knowledge to leader performance. *Leadership Quarterly, 11,* 65–86.

de Groot, A. (1978). *Thought and choice and chess.* The Hague: Mouton. (Original work published 1946).

Duffy, L. J., Baluch, B., & Ericsson, K. A. (2004). Dart performance as a function of facets of practice amongst professional and amateur men and women players. *International Journal of Sport Psychology, 35,* 232–245.

Dvorak, A., Merrick, N. L., Dealey, W. L., & Ford, G. C. (1936). *Typewriting behavior.* New York: American Book Company.

Epstein, S. A. (1991). *Wage labor and guilds in Medieval Europe.* Raleigh, University of North Carolina Press.

Ericsson, K. A. (1996). The acquisition of expert performance: An introduction to some of the issues. In K. A. Ericsson (Ed.), *The road to excellence: The acquisition of expert performance in the arts and sciences, sports, and games* (pp. 1–50). Mahwah, NJ: Lawrence Erlbaum Associates.

(2000). How experts attain and maintain superior performance: Implications for the enhancement of skilled performance in older individuals. *Journal of Aging and Physical Activity, 8,* 346–352.

(2002). Attaining excellence through deliberate practice: Insights from the study of expert performance. In M. Ferrari (Ed.), *The pursuit of excellence in education* (pp. 21–55). Hillsdale, NJ: Lawrence Erlbaum Associates.

(2003a). The development of elite performance and deliberate practice: An update from the perspective of the expert-performance approach. In J. Starkes & K. A. Ericsson (Eds.), *Expert performance in sport: Recent advances in research on sport expertise* (pp. 49–81). Champaign, IL: Human Kinetics.

(2003b). How the expert-performance approach differs from traditional approaches to expertise in sports: In search of a shared theoretical framework for studying expert performance. In J. Starkes & K. A. Ericsson (Eds.), *Expert performance in sport: Recent advances in research on sport expertise* (pp. 371–401). Champaign, IL: Human Kinetics.

(2004). Deliberate practice and the acquisition and maintenance of expert performance in medicine and related domains. *Academic Medicine, 10,* S1–S12.

(2006a). The influence of experience and deliberate practice on the development of superior expert performance. In K. A. Ericsson, N. Charness, P. Feltovich, & R. R. Hoffman (Eds.), *Cambridge handbook of expertise and expert performance* (pp. 685–706). Cambridge, UK: Cambridge University Press.

(2006b). Protocol analysis and expert thought: Concurrent verbalizations of thinking during experts' performance on representative task. In K. A. Ericsson, N. Charness, P. Feltovich, & R. R. Hoffman (Eds.), *Cambridge handbook of expertise and expert performance* (pp. 223–242). Cambridge, UK: Cambridge University Press.

(2007a). Deliberate practice and the modifiability of body and mind: Toward a science of the structure and acquisition of expert and elite performance. *International Journal of Sport Psychology, 38,* 4–34.

(2007b). Deliberate practice and the modifiability of body and mind: A reply to the commentaries. *International Journal of Sport Psychology, 38,* 109–123.

Ericsson, K. A., Krampe, R. Th., & Tesch-Römer, C. (1993). The role of deliberate practice in the acquisition of expert performance. *Psychological Review, 100,* 363–406.

Ericsson, K. A., & Lehmann, A. C. (1996). Expert and exceptional performance: Evidence on maximal adaptations on task constraints. *Annual Review of Psychology, 47,* 273–305.

Ericsson, K. A., Patel, V. L., & Kintsch, W. (2000). How experts' adaptations to representative task demands account for the expertise effect in memory recall: Comment on Vicente and Wang (1998). *Psychological Review, 107,* 578–592.

Ericsson, K. A., Roring, R. W., & Nandagopal, K. (2007a). Giftedness and evidence for reproducibly superior performance: An account based on the expert-performance framework. *High Ability Studies, 18,* 3–56.

(2007b). Misunderstandings, agreements, and disagreements: Toward a cumulative science of reproducibly superior aspects of giftedness. *High Ability Studies, 18,* 97–115.

Ericsson, K. A., & Smith, J. (1991). Prospects and limits in the empirical study of expertise: An introduction. In K. A. Ericsson & J. Smith (Eds.), *Toward a general theory of expertise: Prospects and limits* (pp. 1–38). Cambridge, UK: Cambridge University Press.

Ericsson, K. A., Whyte, J., & Ward, P. (2007). Expert performance in nursing: reviewing research on expertise in nursing within the framework of the expert-performance approach. *Advances in Nursing Science, 30,* E58–E71.

Fitts, P., & Posner, M. I. (1967). *Human performance*. Belmont, CA: Brooks/Cole.

Galton, F., Sir (1869/1979). *Hereditary genius: An inquiry into its laws and consequences* (Originally published in 1869). London: Julian Friedman Publishers.

Grape, C., Sandgren, M., Hansson, L.-O., Ericson, M., & Theorell, T. (2003). Does singing promote well-being?: An empirical study of professional and amateur singers during a singing lesson. *Integrative Physiological & Behavioral Science, 38*, 65–71.

Hayes, J. R. (1981). *The complete problem solver*. Philadelphia, PA: Franklin Institute Press.

Hollenbeck, B. K., Dunn, R. L., Miller, D. C., Daignandt, S., Taub, D. A., & Wei, J. T. (2007). Volume-based referral for cancer surgery: Informing the debate. *Journal of Clinical Oncology, 25*, 91–96.

Issenberg, S. B., McGaghie, W. C., Petrusa, E. R., Lee Gordon, D., & Scalese, R. J. (2005). Features and uses of high-fidelity medical simulations that lead to effective learning: A BEME systematic review. *Medical Teacher, 27*, 10–28.

Krampe, R. Th., & Charness, N. (2006). Aging and expertise. In K. A. Ericsson, N. Charness, P. Feltovich, & R. R. Hoffman (Eds.), *Cambridge handbook of expertise and expert performance* (pp. 723–742). Cambridge, U.K.: Cambridge University Press.

Krampe, R. Th., & Ericsson, K. A. (1996). Maintaining excellence: Deliberate practice and elite performance in young and older pianists. *Journal of Experimental Psychology: General, 125*, 331–359.

Lehmann, A. C. (1997). Acquisition of expertise in music: Efficiency of deliberate practice as a moderating variable in accounting for sub-expert performance. In I. Deliege & J. A. Sloboda (Ed.), *Perception and cognition of music* (pp. 165–191). Hillsdale, NJ: Lawrence Erlbaum Associates.

Lehmann, A. C., & Ericsson, K. A. (1996). Music performance without preparation: Structure and acquisition of expert sight-reading. *Psychomusicology, 15*, 1–29.

(1998). The historical development of domains of expertise: Performance standards and innovations in music. In A. Steptoe (Ed.), *Genius and the mind* (pp. 67–94). Oxford, UK: Oxford University Press.

Masunaga, H., & Horn, J. (2001). Expertise and age-related changes in components of intelligence *Psychology and Aging, 16*, 293–311.

McDaniel, M. A., Schmidt, F. L., & Hunter, J. E. (1988). Job experience correlates of job performance *Journal of Applied Psychology, 73*, 327–330.

McGaghie, W. C., Issenberg, S. B., Petrusa, E. R., & Scalese, R. J. (2006). Effects of practice on standardized learning outcomes in simulation-based medical education. *Medical Education, 40*, 792–797.

McKinney, E. H., & Davis, K. J. (2004). Effects of deliberate practice on crisis decision performance. *Human Factors, 45*, 436–444.

Nielsen, S. (1999). Regulation of learning strategies during practice: A case study of a single church organ student preparing a particular work for a concert performance. *Psychology of Music, 27*, 218–229.

Pisano, G. P., Bohmer, R. M. J., & Edmondson, A. C. (2001). Organizational differences in rates of learning: Evidence from the adoption of minimally invasive cardiac surgery. *Management Science, 47*, 752–768.

Plato (1954). The republic. In E. H. Warmington & P. G. Rouse (Eds.), *Great dialogues of Plato*. New York: Penguin Putnam.

Rantanen, E. M., & Talleur, D. A. (2005). Incremental transfer and cost effectiveness of ground-based flight trainers in University aviation programs. *Proceedings of the 49th Annual Meeting of the Human Factors and Ergonomics Society* (pp. 764–768).

Raskin, E. (1936). Comparison of scientific and literary ability: A biographical study of eminent scientists and letters of the nineteenth century. *Journal of Abnormal and Social Psychology, 31,* 20–35.

Renwick, J. M., & McPherson, G. E. (2002). Interest and choice: Student-selected repertoire and its effect on practising behaviour. *British Journal of Music Education, 19,* 173–188.

Roessingh, J. J. M. (2005). Transfer of manual flying skills form PC-based simulation to actual flight – Comparisons of in-flight measured data and instructor ratings. *International Journal of Aviation Psychology, 15,* 67–90.

Roth, P. L., & Clarke, R. L. (1998). Meta-analyzing the relation between grades and salary. *Journal of Vocational Behavior, 53,* 386–400.

Schulz, R., & Curnow, C. (1988). Peak performance and age among superathletes: Track and field, swimming, baseball, tennis, and golf. *Journal of Gerontology: Psychological Sciences, 43,* 113–120.

Simon, H. A., & Chase, W. G. (1973). Skill in chess. *American Scientist, 61,* 394–403.

Simonton, D. K. (1997). Creative productivity: A predictive and explanatory model of career trajectories and landmarks. *Psychological Review, 104,* 66–89.

Sloboda, J. A., Davidson, J. W., Howe, M. J. A., & Moore, D. G. (1996). The role of practice in the development of performing musicians. *British Journal of Psychology, 87,* 287–309.

Sonnentag, S., & Kleine, B. M. (2000). Deliberate practice at work: A study with insurance agents. *Journal of Occupational and Organizational Psychology, 73,* 87–102.

Starkes, J. L., Weir, P. L., & Young, B. W. (2003). Retraining expertise: What does it take for older athletes to continue to excel? In J. L. Starkes & K. A. Ericsson (Eds.), *Expert performance in sport: Recent advances in research on sport expertise* (pp. 252–272). Champaign, IL: Human Kinetics.

Tetlock, P. E. (2005). *Expert political judgment.* Princeton, NJ: Princeton University Press.

Ulijaszek, S. J., Johston, F. E., & Preece, M. A. (Eds.). (1998). *The Cambridge encyclopedia of human growth and development.* Cambridge, UK: Cambridge University Press.

Urena, C. (2004). *Skill acquisition in ballet dancers: The relationship between deliberate practice and expertise.* Unpublished PhD dissertation, Florida State University.

van der Maas, H. L. J., & Wagenmakers, E. J. (2005). A psychometric analysis of chess expertise. *American Journal of Psychology, 118,* 29–60.

Van Rossum, J. H. A. (2001). Talented in dance: The Bloom stage model revisited in the personal histories of dance students. *High Ability Studies, 12,* 181–197.

Van Sickle, K. R., Gallagher, A. G., & Smith, C. D. (2007). The effects of escalating feedback on the acquisition of psychomotor skills for laparoscopy. *Surgical Endoscopy, 21,* 220–224.

Van Sickle, K. R., Ritter, E. M., McClosky, D. A., Lederman, A., Baghai, M., Gallagher, A. G., & Smith, C. D. (2007). Attempted establishment of proficiency levels for laparoscopic performance on a national scale using simulation: The results from the 2004 SAGES Minimally Invasive Surgical Trainer – Virtual reality (MIST_VR) learning center study. *Surgical Endoscopy, 21,* 5–10.

Verdaasdonk, E. G. E., Stassen, L. P. S., van Wijk, R. P. J., & Dankelman, J. (2007). The influence of different training, schedules on the learning of psychomotor skills for endoscopic surgery. *Surgical Endoscopy, 21,* 214–219.

Vickers, A. J., Bianco, F. J., Serio, A. M., Eastham, J. A., Schrag, D., Klein, E. A., et al. (2007). The surgical learning curve for prostate cancer control after radical prostatectomy. *Journal of National Cancer Institute, 99,* 1171–1177.

Ward. P., Hodges, N. J., Williams, A. M., & Starkes, J. L. (2004). Deliberate practice and expert performance: Defining the path to excellence. In A. M. Williams & N. J. Hodges (Eds.), *Skill acquisition in sport: Research, theory and practice* (pp. 231–258). London: Routledge.

Ward, P., & Williams, A. M. (2005). Perceptual and cognitive skill development in soccer: The multidimensional nature of expert performance. *Journal of Sport & Exercise Psychology*, 25, 93–111.

Ward, P., Williams, A. M., & Hancock, P. A. (2006). Simulation for performance and training. In K. A. Ericsson, N. Charness, P. Feltovich, & R. R. Hoffman (Eds.), *Cambridge handbook of expertise and expert performance* (pp. 243–262). Cambridge, UK: Cambridge University Press.

19

It Takes Expertise to Make Expertise: Some Thoughts About Why and How and Reflections on the Themes in Chapters 15–18

JOHN D. BRANSFORD AND DANIEL L. SCHWARTZ

We have been asked to discuss the chapters in Section 4, which focus on descriptions and measurements of the acquisition of skilled and expert performances. The chapters in this section (and the book in general) make it clear that the field has built upon, yet gone beyond, the classic research studies that compared expert and novice performances (Chi, Feltovich, & Glaser, 1981; NRC, 2000). The emphasis has turned to the *development* of expertise, and to objective approaches to its measurement. The progress in moving from retrospective to prospective assessments of expertise development is truly exemplary and critical to defining effective learning conditions.

As we considered what we might say about this book's discussions of expertise development, we were reminded of a graduate student in the learning sciences who once asked us to complete the following statement: "*Practice makes per_____.*" Expecting a possible trick question we paused for a moment. Eventually we said "*perfect*"; it seemed like the only choice.

The graduate student chuckled. He had taught kindergarten and explained "Practice makes permanent, not perfect." For example, if you let young children hold their pencils incorrectly when they write, they can easily become efficient at doing the wrong kinds of things.

This simple example suggests that "it takes expertise to make expertise," and this idea fits well with the theory and research discussed in this volume. For example, Ericsson (Chapter 18) and Baker (Chapter 15) make the important argument that fixed psychological traits are not sufficient for predicting expertise, so contextual supports must be important. VanLehn and van de

Acknowledgments: This work was supported in part by a grant from the National Science Foundation (NSF#0354453). Any opinions, findings, and conclusions expressed in the paper are those of the authors and do not necessarily reflect the views of the National Science Foundation. We are indebted to our colleagues in the LIFE Center (Learning in Informal and Formal Environments) for many ideas that have enriched our thinking and research.

Sande (Chapter 16) and Boshuizen (Chapter 17) explicitly discuss instructional conditions that develop expertise.

The idea that "it takes expertise to make expertise" becomes clear to anyone who has been highly motivated to learn something new, yet lacks access to experts who can help them. For example, one of us (Bransford) has written about an experiment where, after moving to a house on a river, he tried to learn to fish for bass through "discovery learning," then by consulting some books, then by consulting local experts (Bransford, Slowinski, et al., in press). Without access to expertise, his rates of success (catching bass) would have been so low that he would undoubtedly have soon given up.

TWO KINDS OF EXPERTISE

There are two different kinds of expertise involved in the idea that "it takes expertise to make expertise." There is learning expertise and teaching expertise.

Learning Expertise

Learning expertise involves the degree to which would-be experts continually attempt to refine their skills and attitudes toward learning – skills and attitudes that include practicing, self-monitoring, and finding ways to avoid plateaus and move to the next level. Ericsson's studies of "deliberate practice" provide powerful examples of the kinds of activity individuals engage in to get better. These ideas resonate with the work of Hatano and Inagaki (1986) on "adaptive" rather than routine experts (Lin, Schwartz, & Bransford, 2007).

In the work of both Ericsson and Hatano and Inagaki, effective learners make use of existing resources to help them improve. They read books (on chess, for example), seek help from others, experiment with their environments, and "try on" new ideas to see if they help them make progress (e.g., in fishing, playing music, and playing chess). Over time, effective learners presumably internalize many resources from their culture (Vygotsky, 1987) and become better at knowing how to gauge and improve their progress.

There seems to be a strong social component to the learning process that appears worthy of further articulation by expertise researchers. For example, Tiger Woods hired a coach to help him rebuild his swing (e.g., http://sports-centeraustin.blogs.com/the_view/2005/05/tiger_woods_why.html). Had he failed to do so he would probably be one of Ericsson's examples of "very competent but not great." But without the coach, this change in behavior would undoubtedly have been very difficult and, most probably, impossible. What it means for a student or player to be "coachable" probably depends greatly on social issues of identity and affect as much as cognitive issues (e.g., Barron, 2004).

Teaching Expertise

Teaching expertise represents the second kind of expertise involved in the idea that "it takes expertise to make expertise." Teaching expertise can involve a variety of forms including coaches (sometimes a set of coaches with different kinds of expertise), well-written strategy books, designed videos, school curricula, and computer programs such as intelligent tutors. There is a sizeable literature demonstrating that simply being an expert in an area does not guarantee that one is good at teaching that expertise to others (e.g., Nathan & Petrosino, 2003; Schoenfeld et al., 2007).

We had the opportunity to talk with a Tissu expert who also coaches young people in the practice (personal communication, Feb. 1, 2008). The art of Tissu, originating in France and named for the fabric that is integral to this aerial dance form, involves the dexterity of a gymnast, the grace of a dancer, and the strength of an athlete (see Figure 19.1 and www.silkaerial.com).

The Tissu expert notes the following about her teaching:

> The work is so challenging I like to give them positive feedback, incentive. If it's too hard, they will give up if they don't get some success. I like to start easy to get experience and some success. I can see that for some students it hurts or they are scared when they drop. Others want to learn trick after trick and that's great but what about pointing your toes?

The teacher's experiences have taught her about individual differences.

> Some people need to see it done. Some students like me showing, some like telling, some like looking, watching. I know they won't be able to hear me when they are upside down. They won't know where right is when they are hanging upside down so I have to send them up knowing what to do.

It is also noteworthy that the expert is continually developing her expertise as a teacher:

> The more I teach a move, the more I learn how to deconstruct it into smaller bites that are learned much more quickly. My communication becomes more efficient and effective creating greater student success.

We asked the teacher if she regularly interacted with other Tissu teachers to improve her coaching. She explained:

> I do continue my own training with other Tissu artists which definitely informs my teaching. I have not taken a formal teacher training in the fabric. However, I also work with a community of aerial performers. I was a dancer, a gymnast, an actress and I have taught in these areas as well.

(b)

(a)

FIGURE 19.1.   A student learning the art of Tissu (a), and her teacher (b).
(*Source:* Photos courtesy of Teasha Feldman [the student], Esther Edleman [the teacher], and Sue Feldman [the photographer].)

FEEDBACK FOR BI-DIRECTIONAL LEARNING

Ideally, learners learn from teachers and teachers learn from learners. This adds a dynamic element to the idea that "it takes expertise to make expertise"; namely, that we need to develop systems that allow the continual development of both kinds of expertise.

Central to this goal is the need to examine different types of feedback cycles. We especially emphasize bi-directional cycles that are important not only for learners but also for teachers (including mentors and coaches) so that they can improve their abilities to help others learn.

Each of the chapters in this section highlights different types of feedback cycles. Chapter 15 by Baker directly asks what types of knowledge can be measured by high-stakes tests that are diagnostic of expertise development. The feedback generated by these measures tends to go to decision makers, but not necessarily the learner. In our experiences in schools, feedback from these tests comes too late to serve as classroom-based formative assessments that can guide teachers. Even when schools create their own formative assessments, they are often used by the teachers to gauge student progress but not used to help *students* learn to self-assess (Partners in Learning, 2006).

Boshuizen (Chapter 17) explores whether problem-based medical curricula affect subsequent medical expertise. He uses the feedback from research studies and their measures to inform curricular design. VanLehn and van de Sande (Chapter 16) consider how measures of learning can inform instruction in physics. Their innovative proposal is that physics expertise involves the development of a finite space of qualitative knowledge that captures the main "inflection" points of mathematical formulas. In this work, the feedback cycle guides instructional decisions by the computer.

Ericsson (Chapter 18) points to feedback cycles that go directly to the learner. He convincingly argues that expertise development is characterized by deliberate practice where people work on problems that are hard and new, rather than business as usual. So, by this account, if we want to see who is on a trajectory to expertise, we can see who is engaging in deliberate practice and gaining useful feedback. However, for younger students, especially those in the early stages of learning, we also need to explore the social conditions that allow them to connect with people who can help them along the way.

If we were to place a bet on where to measure and enable expertise development, we would bet on bi-directional learning experiences that provide rich feedback to both learners and teachers (including coaches, computer systems, etc.). The feedback may be cognitive in nature, but as Boshuizen's (Chapter 17) review of the literature indicates, conditions of feedback have broad affective implications as well. We explore additional issues of feedback below.

PROBLEMS WITH LOW-QUALITY FEEDBACK CYCLES

Baker (Chapter 15) discusses feedback as a prime example of the many different roles that measurement has played in the educational arena. One role of measurement is to predict who will be good at learning something; for example, mathematics or flying an airplane. Another role of measurement is to use it as a source of feedback to support learning. Baker notes that early work by Thorndike (1904) focused on this latter issue. One of our favorite Thorndike examples involves a study where he gave students hundreds of trials of practice drawing four-inch lines, but none of them improved. The reason was that they were blindfolded and received no feedback on their performances. Once the blindfolds were removed the students improved dramatically.

Thorndike's example focuses on the effects of *students* being blindfolded. We have emphasized the importance of bi-directional feedback, and teachers can also be blindfolded. Bickman and colleagues (Sapyta, Riemer, & Bickman, 2005) discuss this point in the context of wanting to learn archery:

> If you are learning by yourself or with an instructor and are blindfolded, you have no information about where the arrow lands…. Intuitively, hiring a coach seems to be a better method than depending on trial and error to learn any number of different tasks. However, if neither the coach nor the student can see the target, improvement is limited because of the lack of feedback. (p. 147)

Note that this situation is different from the earlier example of helping students learn to hold a pencil properly, or the Tissu expert working with high school students. In both of these cases, the teachers' distances between what was being taught and what was being learned were very close. And the performance measures (writing, performing the tissue routines) were highly authentic as well. However, as Baker notes, often this is not the case. Many measures of learning are weak proxies for the actual performances and abilities that we hope students will exhibit outside the classroom. This can provide both the students and the teachers with a false sense that they are performing well. VanLehn and van de Sande (Chapter 16) provide examples from physics, where students and teachers emphasize feedback from quantitative problems that do not reveal the lack of qualitative understanding necessary for expertise.

The Top Gun fighter training discussed by Chatham (Chapter 2) presents an excellent example where low-fidelity feedback of successful learning had dire consequences. The failure of pilots in actual fights eventually led trainers to employ mock battles with a "red team" that was equipped with the same airplanes and tactics as the enemy that the pilot trainees would eventually face. The high-fidelity feedback provided by this new training situation helped a great deal. Several examples of the effects of high-fidelity feedback on teaching for expertise are provided below.

Research with Clinicians

Bickman and colleagues (Sapyta, Riemer, & Bickman, 2005) have explored the degree to which clinical therapists learn to get better over time, and they argue that most of them quickly hit a plateau of relatively moderate performance and stay there. Their argument is that the clinicians' opportunities for high-quality feedback limit their abilities to improve.

> In essence, therapists are trained, are supervised, and practice in the absence of information about client treatment response from objective sources. Examples of limited clinician ability to make accurate judgments without feedback are plentiful. Despite [this evidence], professionals are typically very confident of their ultimate clinical decisions (Garb, 1998). The accuracy of clinical judgments, even for those clients who stay in treatment for considerable periods, has also been called into question on the basis of the general human tendency to overvalue one's own work ... Providing feedback that the client is doing well only confirms to the clinician that the treatment plan is working well. This finding is not surprising; in fact it is consistent with theories that describe feedback induced behavior change as the consequence of a discrepancy between the feedback information and some standard (p. 147).

Note that the lack of learning affects both the clinicians and the clients. It amounts to a double failure to learn.

Research with Language Therapists

Ann Michael is a language therapist who served for several years as a clinical supervisor of college students who were beginning a practicum in therapy for language-delayed children. The college students had all passed the required pre-clinical college courses including theories of language and their implications for therapy. Many had done extremely well in their course. Nevertheless, in the clinical setting, Michaels' saw almost no evidence that the students used their classroom knowledge in the therapy sessions. Instead they tended to fly by the seat of their pants. Michaels' concluded that the college course must have been very poorly taught.

Michaels' was later asked to teach that college course herself. She did what she thought was a highly competent job and was pleased with the general performance of the students on her tests. A year later, she encountered a number of her students once again – this time in the clinical practicum on language therapy. Much to her surprise and dismay, these students also showed almost no evidence of applying anything they had learned in their language course. Many could remember facts when explicitly asked about them, but they did not spontaneously draw on that knowledge to help them solve problems in the clinic.

This time around, Michaels' was reluctant to conclude that her college students performed poorly because of unmotivated or less-than-clinically knowledgeable instructors. Instead, she decided to explore problems with traditional approaches to instruction and to study ways to overcome them. She did this successfully in her doctoral thesis (using video cases in a special way; see Michael, Klee, Bransford, & Warren, 1993). For our purposes, the important point is that she would not have realized the need to change her teaching without the opportunity to see the students attempt to use what they had learned to do something "real." She had moved from experiencing low-fidelity to high-fidelity feedback. The effects on her learning as a teacher, and eventually on her students' learning, were profound.

Problem-Based Learning in Medicine

Several years after Michael conducted her study, one of us had the opportunity to visit Howard Barrows at the medical school in Springfield, Illinois, where he had brought his work on problem-based learning (PBL) that he had begun in Canada. Boshuizen (Chapter 17) provides an excellent overview of PBL and the kinds of innovative thinking and research that it has spawned.

Upon meeting Dr. Barrows we asked how the idea for PBL had emerged, and we discovered a story very similar to Michael's (although Barrows's discoveries had begun considerably earlier). Barrows noted that he taught a clinical assessment course and was shocked to find how ill-prepared medical students were for this experience, even though they had passed very rigorous courses. One way to characterize the situation from a cognitive perspective is that the medical students had learned many facts and procedures but had not acquired the kinds of organized knowledge and understandings that prepared them for strategic action. As Whitehead (1929) would have said, the students' knowledge tended to remain inert (see also Bransford, Franks, Vye, & Sherwood, 1989). VanLehn and van de Sande (Chapter 16) discuss similar discoveries about physics teaching and learning. They note that students are often more adept at mathematical computations than they are at understanding the conceptual foundations needed for flexibility and accelerated future learning.

In all the cases noted above, the major point we emphasize is that none of these teaching and learning problems would have been discovered unless people had begun to create settings for high-fidelity feedback that went beyond typical tests of piecemeal knowledge. These discoveries helped both the teachers and the students improve.

Work in Education

Teachers in schools of education and teachers in K–12 classrooms also face challenges of dealing with weak feedback proxies. Colleagues in education have often made tongue-in-cheek comments about "teachers with 20 years of experience and those who have 1 year of experience 20 times." Ideally, teachers and teacher educators would see their students in action post-graduation. Like the experiences of Michael and Barrows, they could get a better sense of which aspects of their instruction worked and which aspects need improvement. But typical teachers teach many students. In practice, this kind of feedback can be difficult to gather.

Many researchers in teacher preparation institutions recognize this problem and are beginning to devise ways to create high-fidelity feedback loops that give faculty a much clearer indication of what their students are taking away from the classroom and using in practice (Peck, Gallucci, & Sloan, 2006). This includes a variety of activities such as visits by students who have graduated, responses by graduates to written teaching cases, and feedback from groups of professionals (e.g., local principals and superintendents) who provide valuable information about ways that graduates are and are not being prepared for the workplace.

One of the present authors (Bransford) made a significant change to his classes for prospective teachers after receiving feedback from a group of local principals who serve as an advisory board for the teacher preparation program at his university. The principals noted that the learning course, as well as subject matter methods courses, frequently appeared to use contrasting cases of "good" versus "less good" ways to teach particular kinds of subject matter. They liked this, but they also pointed out that it caused a problem. A case they pointed to was that many of the examples of *poor ways* to teach middle school science came from a textbook that the district was mandated to use! When former students from the teacher preparation program saw this text being used in their schools they reacted negatively and did nothing but criticize. The principals explained that they were not fans of this text either, but since it was mandated they had no choice at the present point in time. They explained that they tried to help teachers find ways to use strong teaching strategies (e.g., teaching for understanding) even within the confines of this textbook. Ever since this session, the author who heard this feedback has emphasized to his students that they need to become "effective teachers in an imperfect world, hence they need to learn to innovate."

The work cited earlier by Peck and colleagues (Peck, Gallucci, & Sloan, 2006) provides illustrations of implementations of feedback cycles for teacher educators that are more systemic and elaborate than the simple example noted above. Similarly, Bickman and colleagues (Sapyta, Riemer, & Bickman, 2005) discuss computerized systems that provide feedback to clinicians about key patient outcomes. The present authors are also working with an entire school system that is using the web to make teaching, learning, and assessments (without student identification) public (Bransford et al., in press); unfortunately, discussing the details of these innovations is beyond the scope of this chapter.

However, they all point to efforts to create the kinds of bi-directional feedback systems that can help both teachers and students continue to learn.

STANDARDS OF EXPERT PERFORMANCE

The idea that feedback must be compared to some "standard" is crucial for discussions of its usefulness. To return to our kindergarten students who are learning to hold a pencil, the standard used as a basis for feedback plays a crucial role in helping them learn. Recent studies of expertise, especially by Ericsson and colleagues (Ericsson, Charness, Feltovich, & Hoffman, 2006), have paid careful attention to finding authentic tasks that allow repeatable assessments of skilled performances. In golf, for example, attempting to sink a long putt is a frequently encountered part of play, and Ericsson and colleagues have been able to measure this skill under standardized and controlled conditions.

The work by VanLehn and van de Sande (Chapter 16) in physics also has important implications for performance standards by focusing attention on key qualitative ideas that are assumed to serve as much better foundations for future learning than the typical "mile wide and inch deep" (or kilometer wide and centimeter deep) content and formulaic coverage that we see in many courses and texts (e.g., NRC, 2000; Wiggins & McTighe, 1997). In a similar manner, work in areas such as PBL is guided by standards for performance that go beyond mere declarative knowledge and involve the kinds of interview and assessment activities with patients that represent key aspects of professional medical work.

Knowledge of Performance Conditions

Having clear knowledge of performance conditions seems to be extremely important for both teachers and learners. *Teachers* who have this knowledge can create conditions that allow them to continually assess students' progress toward authentic tasks. Of course, this knowledge will not necessarily lead to these kinds of assessment behaviors. The early examples by Michaels' (who knew what it was like to be a language therapist) and Barrows (who knew what it was like to be in his area of clinical practice) demonstrate that they needed to experience a sense of disequilibria about their students' learning before rethinking how they taught and assessed.

Learners can also benefit from clear knowledge of performance conditions. They can better monitor their own understanding and hence take a "metacognitive" approach to learning, including knowing when to ask questions of clarification (e.g., NRC, 2000; Vye, Schwartz, Bransford, Barron, Zech, & CTGV, 1998). Some times it can be valuable to let students experience performance conditions before demonstrating standards of expert performance. Research has demonstrated that there are often advantages to first letting students experience the complexities of a situation and then providing information that helps them understand expert techniques in light of their earlier successes, difficulties, and questions (e.g., Schwartz & Bransford, 1998).

Ideally, *both teachers and learners* have a strong sense of the performance conditions they are working toward and can continually inform one another about the degree to which their current experiences are leading to increased learning. Often this does not happen, especially in school. To illustrate the issue, imagine a Top Gun red team training where the instructors were aware of the tactics of the enemy but did not make this information explicitly available to the pilots being trained. The pilots would presumably learn something from the experience, but probably not as much as they would learn when the red team's tactics were made explicit to them. To draw an analogy to Judd's (1908) classic studies on transfer, one can imagine that the "implicitly trained" pilots would not do as well as the "experience plus explicitly trained pilots" if the enemy later changed some key tactics and these could be analyzed and taken into account.

Stable and Variable Performance Conditions

It seems useful to ask how different conditions of performance might affect ideal approaches to teaching and assessment. For example, in a circus act like Tissu, the rope and the equipment remain constant from performance to performance, and there is no opponent (as in chess and many other settings) that tries to knock one off the rope.

The importance of being able to rely on well-specified performance arenas is illustrated by the 2000 Olympics held in Sydney, Australia. After a number of gymnasts experienced great difficulty in the women's vault competition, it was discovered that the vault had been set 5 centimeters too low (see http://www.youtube.com/watch?v=q7bxa77ccmQ). In gymnastics, as in Tissu, the performance apparatus is assumed to be stable and fit very strict standards. Even slight deviations from these standards can cause deleterious effects.

In many areas of expertise, performers cannot count on stable conditions. Preparing for rapidly changing conditions seems to be quite different than preparing for the (usually) predictable layout of the equipment to be used at a gymnastics meet or a Tissu exercise. The introduction to this book makes a strong statement about rapidly changing conditions:

> Developments in technology and software engineering are making many types of traditional jobs, such as bookkeeping, accounting, routine design, and document indexing, virtually obsolete (Rasmussen, 2000).... Today's work conditions require ongoing adaptations by employees and entrepreneurs to new demands and competitive opportunities through continuing education and training.... the competitive advantage of any country aspiring to economic prosperity is increasingly dependent on the capability of both its research and development groups and its skilled

workforce, not only to create and develop new and improved products that are at the cutting edge, but also to quickly react and adapt to market forces. The shift from the industrial to the technological age clearly motivates increased efforts to support the development of existing and future professionals with these skill sets; to identify existing experts and high-performers; and to provide suitable learning environments. (Ericsson et al., Chapter 1)

This quotation focuses on flexibility and innovation, a focus that others have also emphasized (Bransford, 2007; Mead, Stephens, Richey, Bransford, & Weusijana, 2007; Spiro et al., 1987). The premium on flexibility and innovation in variable environments does not mean that learners and teachers should give up on efficiency in the pursuit of adaptability. When structured appropriately, they compliment one another (e.g., Schwartz, Bransford, & Sears, 2005). A balance between the two supports what Hatano and Inagaki (1986) have called "adaptive expertise" rather than "routine expertise."

Are there standards of performance that can help us develop the kinds of adaptive expertise that seem necessary for the coming century? Our conjecture is that the answer is "yes," but these standards look different from those that are typically used as test items. Baker's chapter (Chapter 15) on measurement makes similar arguments about the need to assess flexible abilities to learn. Our argument (see Schwartz, Bransford, & Sears, 2005) is that typical test items retrospectively assess previously acquired schematized knowledge. This is important, of course, but more is needed for fast changing environments. People also need to adapt to new innovations or environmental changes that can cause momentary implementation dips and force them to move away from their existing comfort zones. And people also need to learn to innovate on their own. An important aspect of developing expertise is learning to notice and look for new standards of expert performance, which is amplified in changing environments.

Our view is that measures of expertise must include measures of learning that ask how prepared people are to learn new information, develop new standards of performance, and to invent new tools and procedures that can help them "work smarter." If we care about learning in everyday environments, we need to move beyond "sequestered problem solving" (SPS) assessments, where people solve problems shielded from opportunities to learn. Instead, it is more useful to look at how people use resources around them to support their learning. This includes the ability to experiment with objects in one's environment, to use technology to find and test information, and to work with others in "distributed expertise" teams. From this perspective, the development of social networks of expertise becomes an important aspect of learning that is extremely important to encourage and assess (O'Mahony et al., submitted).

The idea of assessing peoples "preparation for future learning" (rather than only assessing what was learned previously and is now being applied) brings us back to the issue of feedback and its importance for human adaptation. Most tests are feedback free while people take them; there is no chance to explore, see what happens, and then invent a new strategy for trying again. We have argued elsewhere (Schwartz, Bransford, & Sears, 2005) that sequestered feedback-free assessments can create both false positives and false negatives. They can make some people look much better than they are because they received special instruction that aligned closely with the test items. Or, they can make people look worse than they are because they are excellent learners but did not have the specific learning opportunities necessary to do well on the sequestered test.

Non-interactive assessments in an interactive world can fail to reveal the different types of interactions that people use to support learning and the potentials for opportunities to further support learning and interaction. Nasir (in press), for example, examined learning in the context of playing dominos. She describes the rich interactive repertoires that children and experts use to help learn and teach the game of dominos. Children can make partial moves that experts finish; experts can bluff to help children think ahead, children can directly ask for help, and so forth. While Nasir made her assessments of learning and interaction through careful observation, she concluded that there are ways to make interactive assessments that are less labor intensive but still allow students and teachers to respond and adjust to feedback. Interactive assessments that depend on unaided observation can be difficult, but with technology, assessments can become interactive and we can begin to look at how students and teachers respond and adjust to feedback. For example, Lin has developed technology-driven assessments that help students and teachers in diverse classrooms recognize and manage differences in their educational values (e.g., Lin, Schwartz, & Hatano, 2005). The main value of these assessments does not lie in the scores that people get on them, but in the productive, interactive discussions that allow new learning to occur.

A friend of ours, Dr. Bror Saxborg, kindly wrote us about an interactive assessment where he was allowed to ask questions, receive feedback, and use this information to learn so that he could craft his answer. He is an M.D. and a Ph.D., who also wanted to gain business experience. He learned that a major management firm was hiring people "out of field" (they were running short of good candidates from business schools), and went for an interview. Here is the account that he wrote for us:

> I was interviewing with McKinsey and Co., a very well-known interna-
> tional management consulting company that had become interested in
> what they termed "non-traditional hires," people who did not have tra-
> ditional business or MBA backgrounds, but who could learn. I think I
> stretched the edge of their definition: at the time I was being interviewed,
> I knew almost nothing about business – I was an M.D./Ph.D. research
> type, who's first idea about "bonds" were chemical, and who'd assume that
> a "warrant" had something to do with the legal system.

They had clearly instructed their interviewers to try to use non-business examples so as not to frighten off non-traditional folks like me. So this very nice partner at McKinsey who interviewed me gave me a case example of a ballet company, thinking this would surely be something that I could think about out loud. He began by asking me to help him think about the different factors that would go into the profit of a ballet company. My response to his question was, "I'll be glad to help you think this through, but you first need to give me a little help. Is profit the number you have AFTER you take away the costs, or before you take away the costs?" There was, admittedly, a longish pause, and he then said, "The number AFTER costs are taken away," and off I went – that's all I needed to know. They did, indeed, hire me, and ever after I looked back in wonder at the patience of this extremely senior and talented business consultant, who took the time to interview a complete know-nothing and, without batting an eye, helped fill in a little but important detail to let me show what I was likely to be able to do. (Saxborg, personal communication, 2007)

A number of members of the LIFE Center (Learning in Informal and Formal Environments, http://life-slc.org/) are currently working to compare students' performances in non-interactive (SPS) test situations (i.e., typical tests) with those that provide opportunities to seek information and feedback for new learning. For example, the team is designing interactive game-like environments (using Second LIFE, for example), that explore how prepared people are to design and continually improve "smart tools," protocols, and strategies for accomplishing important tasks involving STEM disciplines (i.e., science, technology, engineering, and mathematics). The assessments are interactive and hence provide opportunities for students to learn as they explore.

The studies are revealing many strengths that students bring to these tasks (including technology skills *and* content knowledge that guide their question asking as they use the technology). The studies also reveal some of the students' common misconceptions, and this is rather good. It creates the kinds of bi-directional high-quality feedback loops (between teachers and students) that help everyone learn more effectively.

These kinds of "preparation for future learning" assessments are clearly useful for formative assessments, but could they also be used for summative assessments? We think that the answer is yes and are working in this direction. Examples of early work along this line are discussed in Bransford et al. (1999) and further explored in Partners in Learning (2006).

CONCLUSION

To summarize, the chapters in this section of the book, and also in the entire volume, provide rich discussions of issues of expertise *development*. From our perspective, a principle underlying all these lines of work can be summarized by the notion that "it takes expertise to make expertise." This helps emphasize that the process of expertise development is a social process where one's success is affected by (1) peoples' motivations to learn something that is important to them; (2) access to relevant teaching expertise; (3) the fidelity of the feedback cycles available to both teachers and learners; and (4) the management of affect that accompanies struggles to truly improve.

Under the right set of configurations, both teachers (coaches, etc.) and learners will continue to improve throughout their lifetimes and avoid reaching premature plateaus in their performances. High-quality feedback cycles seem to play highly important roles in this process; we have discussed several examples of changes in teaching and learning that accompanied changes from "low-fidelity" to "high-fidelity" glimpses of what students know and were able to do. Ultimately, we believe that high-quality feedback cycles also need to include new kinds of assessment that better illuminate existing potentials of learners and teachers, and provide new ways to define learning successes that go beyond traditional assessment practices. Efforts to more directly assess how prepared people are to tackle new *learning challenges* (i.e., how prepared they are for future learning) seems to be a useful avenue to pursue.

REFERENCES

Barron, B. (2004). Learning ecologies for technological fluency: Gender and experience differences. *Journal of Educational Computing Research, 31*(1), 1–36.

Bransford, J., Copeland, M., Honig, M., Nelson, H. G., Mosborg, S., & Gawel, D., et al. (in press). Adaptive people and adaptive systems: Issue of learning and design. In A. Hargreaves, M. Fullan, D. Hopkins, & A. Leiberman (Eds.), *The second international handbook of educational change*. Dordrect, The Netherlands: Springer.

Bransford, J., Slowinski, M., Vye, N., & Mosborg, S. (in press). The learning sciences, technology and designs for educational systems: Some thoughts about change. In J. Visser & M. Visser-Valfrey (Eds.) *Learners in a changing learning landscape: Reflections from a dialogue on new roles and expectations*. Dordrecht, The Netherlands: Springer.

Bransford, J. D., Brown, A. L., & Cocking, R. R. (2000). *How people learn: Brain, mind, experience, and school*. Washington, DC: National Academy Press.

Bransford, J. D., & Darling-Hammond, L. (2005). *Preparing teachers for a changing world: What teachers should learn and be able to do*. San Francisco, CA: Jossey-Bass.

Bransford, J. D., Franks, J. J., Vye, N. J., & Sherwood, R. D. (1989). New approaches to instruction: Because wisdom can't be told. In S. Vosniadou & A. Ortony (Eds.), *Similarity and analogical reasoning* (pp. 470–497). New York: Cambridge University Press.

Bransford, J. D., Zech, L., Schwartz, D., Barron, B., Vye, N., & Cognition and Technology Group at Vanderbilt. (1999). Designs for environments that invite and sustain mathematical thinking. In P. Cobb (Ed.), *Symbolizing, communicating, and mathematizing: Perspectives on discourse, tools, and instructional design* (pp. 275–324). Hillsdale, NJ: Lawrence Erlbaum Associates.

Bransford, J. D. (2007). Preparing people for rapidly changing environments. *Journal of Engineering Education, 96*(1), 1–3.

Carver, C. S., & Scheier, M. F. (1981). *Attention and self-regulation: A control theory approach to human behavior.* New York: Springer-Verlag.

Chi, M. T. H., Feltovich, P., & Glaser, R. (1981). Categorization and representation of physics problems by experts and novices. *Cognitive Science, 5*, 121–152.

Ericcson, K. A., Charness, N., Feltovich, P. J., & Hoffman, R. R. (2006). *The Cambridge handbook of expertise and expert performance.* New York: Cambridge University Press.

Garb, H. N. (1988) Comment on "The study of clinical judgment: An ecological approach." *Clinical Psychology Review, 8*, 441–444.

Hatano, G., & Inagaki, K. (1986). Two courses of expertise. In H. Stevenson, H. Azuma, & K. Hakuta (Eds.), *Child development and education in Japan* (pp. 262–272). New York: Freeman.

Judd, C. H. (1908). The relation of special training to general intelligence. *Educational Review, 36*, 28–42.

Lin, X. D., Schwartz, D. L., & Bransford, J. D. (2007). Intercultural adaptive expertise: Explicit and implicit lessons from Dr. Hatano. *Human Development, 50*, 65–72.

Lin, X. D., Schwartz, D. L., & Hatano, G. (2005). Towards teacher's adaptive metacognition. *Educational Psychologist, 40*, 245–256.

Mead, P. F., Stephens, R., Richey, M., Bransford, J. D., & Weusijana, B. K. A. (2007, April). *A test of leadership: Charting engineering education for 2020 and beyond.* Paper presented at the American Institute of Aeronautics and Astronautics Conference, Hawaii.

Michael, A. L., Klee, T., Bransford, J. D., & Warren, S. (1993). The transition from theory to therapy: Test of two instructional methods. *Applied Cognitive Psychology, 7*, 139–154.

Nasir, N. (in press). Individual cognitive structuring and the sociocultural context: Strategy shifts in the game of dominoes. *Journal of the Learning Sciences.*

Nathan, M. J., & Petrosino, A. J. (2003). Expert blind spot among preservice teachers. *American Educational Research Journal, 40*(4), 905–928.

NRC/National Research Council. (2000). *How people learn: Brain, mind, experience, and school* (Expanded edition). Washington, DC: National Academy Press.

O'Mahony, T. K., Vye, N. J., Bransford, J. D., Richey, M. C., Dang, V. T., Lin, K., et al. (submitted). Creating environments for continuous learning: Adaptive organizations and adaptive expertise. *Cognition & Instruction.*

Partners in Learning. (2006). *School leader development: Assessing 21st century learning.* [compact disk]. Redmond, WA: Microsoft Corporation.

Peck, C., Gallucci, C., & Sloan, T. (2006). Negotiating dilemmas of teacher education reform policy through self study. In L. Fitsgerald, M. Heston, & D. Tidwell (Eds.), *Collaboration and community: Pushing the boundaries of self study.* Proceedings of the Sixth International Conference on Self-Study of Teacher Education Practices. East Sussex, U.K.

Sapyta, J., Riemer, M., & Bickman, L. (2005). Feedback to clinicians: Theory, research and practice. *Journal of Clinical Psychology, 61*(2), 145–153.

Schwartz, D. L., & Bransford, J. D. (1998). A time for telling. *Cognition & Instruction, 16*, 475–522.

Schwartz, D. L., Bransford, J. D., & Sears, D. L. (2005). Efficiency and innovation in transfer. In J. Mestre (Ed.), *Transfer of learning from a modern multidisciplinary perspective* (pp. 1–51). Charlotte, NC: Information Age Publishing.

Spiro, R. J., Vispoel, W. L., Schmitz, J., Samarapungavan, A., & Boeger, A. (1877). Knowledge acquisition for application: Cognitive flexibility and transfer in complex content domains. In B. C. Britton & S. Glynn (Eds.), *Executive control processes in reading* (pp. 177–199). Hillsdale, NJ: Lawrence Erlbaum Associates, 1987.

Thorndike, E. L. (1904). *An introduction to the theory of mental and social measurement.* New York: Science Press.

Vye, N. J., Schwartz, D. L., Bransford, J. D., Barron, B. J., Zech, L. K., & Cognition and Technology Group at Vanderbilt. (1998). SMART environments that support monitoring, reflection, and revision. In D. Hacker, J. Dunlosky, & A. Graesser (Eds.), *Metacognition in educational theory and practice* (pp. 305–346). Mahwah, NJ: Lawrence Erlbaum Associates.

Vygotsky, L. S. (1987). *The collected works of L. S. Vygotsky.* New York: Plenum.

Wiggins, G., & McTighe, J. (1997). *Understanding by design.* Association for Supervision and Curriculum Development, VA.

Whitehead, A. N. (1929). *The aims of education.* New York: Macmillan.

20

The Value of Expertise and Expert Performance:
A Review of Evidence from the Military

J. D. FLETCHER

Intuitively we seek expertise in all areas of human activity as observers, beneficiaries, and performers. Beyond intuition, however, can we justify the resources we expend in developing expertise and expert performance? This chapter concerns the value of expertise and expert performance in a high stakes area: military operations. It provides some quantitative evidence of this value and its relation to themes that appear to be common to the development of expertise across many areas and are raised in the chapters of this book.

THEMES

This book addresses the development, measurement, and assessment of expertise from many directions and in many contexts. Findings and conclusions from its chapters may be summarized and organized around a number of "themes." These themes apply to the development, measurement, and assessment of expertise in the military. They help crystallize and focus the ways individuals and groups prepare for the exigencies that inevitably arise in the performance of many activities, including military operations. These themes may be summarized and described, in no particular order, as the following.

Self-Assessment and Self-Directed Learning

Learners at all levels of development are increasingly expected to take responsibility for their professional growth. This trend has been accompanied by an increasing emphasis on techniques, capabilities, and tools that help them become more self-directed and self-assessing. Related issues include: (1) the use and value of distributed learning – available anytime and anywhere, to remote locations as well as to residential classrooms (Chatham, Chapters 2 & 10; Ericsson, Chapter 18; Kirschenbaum, McInnes, & Correll, Chapter 12); (2) the need to integrate assessment and learning (Baker, Chapter 15; Davis, Chapter 8; Hunt, Chapter 5); (3) the importance of developing metacognitive skills and allowing for reflection and reasoning (Davis, Chapter 8; Ericsson, Chapter 18; VanLehn & van de Sande, Chapter 16); and (4) the accessibility of tools for local authoring, editing, and navigation within instructional environments (Chatham, Chapter 10; van Merriënboer & Boot, Chapter 6).

Deliberate Practice in Developing Expertise

As Ericsson (2006) has pointed out, people who achieve unusually high levels of expertise may be distinguished by their efforts to seek training and experience in areas where they perceive weaknesses or gaps in their capabilities. Chapters in this book that touch on this theme emphasize: (1) the need for professional growth after initial learning (Ericsson, Chapter 18; VanLehn & van de Sande, Chapter 16); (2) the deliberate search for desirable (not too hard and not too easy) difficulty (Bjork, Chapter 14; Ericsson, Chapter 18); and (3) the need to tailor learning experiences to the specific needs of individual learners (Davis, Chapter 8; Ericsson, Chapter 18).

Agility in Expertise and Professional Performance

A key component of expertise and professional performance is the ability to recognize and deal with unforeseen circumstances and events. Chapters that discussed this theme emphasized: (1) preparation for the unexpected (Mumford, Friedrich, Caughron, & Antes, Chapter 4; Shadrick & Lussier, Chapter 13); (2) developing backup plans (Mumford et al., Chapter 4); and (3) generalization from case-based learning (Boshuizen, Chapter 17; Davis, Chapter 8; Mumford et al., Chapter 4).

Assessment of Professional Growth Toward Expertise

Assessment was widely recognized and frequently discussed as essential in managing learning and developing expertise. It was discussed in chapters concerning: (1) the use of performance versus process in assessing expertise (Bjork, Chapter 14; Davis, Chapter 8; Schreiber et al., Chapter 11; (2) the need to better understand the psychometric properties of simulation used in assessment (Schreiber et al., Chapter 11); (3) increasing capabilities for modeling and assessing learners and learner progress using data from routine interactions and responses (Baker, Chapter 15; Boshuizen, Chapter 17; Schreiber et al., Chapter 11); and (4) the need for early identification of individuals capable of very high levels of expertise (i.e., "aces") (Boshuizen, Chapter 17; Chatham, Chapter 2; Ericsson, Chapter 18).

Centrality of Cognition in Expertise

The central, sometimes surprising, role played by cognition in all forms of expertise and expert performance is mentioned frequently in this book. However well we may provide for motivation, social structure, measurement, and practice, we still need to understand what human cognition brings to the table. Discussions of cognitive issues concerned: (1) the cognitive basis of expert performance (Baker, Chapter 15); (2) essentiality of cognitive task analysis (Lajoie, Chapter 3; Schraagen, Chapter 7; Shadrick & Lussier, Chapter 13; VanLehn & van de Sande, Chapter 16); (3) the need to train cognitive capabilities (Mayer, Chapter 9; Shadrick & Lussier, Chapter 13); (4) the need for competent cognitive performance at every level of organizational hierarchies (Mumford et al., Chapter 4; van Merriënboer & Boot, Chapter 6); (5) the need to consider general mission competencies in addition to capabilities for performing discrete critical tasks (Schraagen, Chapter 7; Schreiber et al., Chapter 11; van Merriënboer & Boot, Chapter 6); (6) forgetting (as well as learning) curves (Bjork, Chapter 14; Hunt, Chapter 5); (7) the role of mental models in developing expertise (Baker, Chapter 15; Boshuizen, Chapter 17; Mumford et al., Chapter 4; VanLehn & van de Sande, Chapter 16); (8) the role of visualization and "situation awareness" (Schreiber et al., Chapter 11; Shadrick & Lussier, Chapter 13); and (9) cognitive apprenticeships (Lajoie, Chapter 3).

Design of Learning Environments to Promote Expertise

The need for techniques and procedures for designing and developing environments that reliably produce necessary levels of performance received considerable attention. Mayer (Chapter 9) emphasized the common, core issues of explicitly determining where we are (models of the learner), where we want to go (models of the performance we seek), and how to get from here to there (models of learning and learning environments). Points raised include (1) the criticality of the analysis stage of design, which establishes the objectives of instruction (Schraagen , Chapter 7); (2) the paradox of training – that to promote outcomes such as retention and transfer, we must tolerate less efficient training (Bjork, Chapter 14); (3) the need to develop designs for self-directed learning (Ericsson , Chapter 18; Mayer, Chapter 9; van Merriënboer & Boot, Chapter 6); (4) the need to incorporate non-cognitive goals in design (Hunt, Chapter 5); (5) the need for individualization in prescribing activities to develop high levels of expertise (Davis, Chapter 8; Ericsson , Chapter 18); (6) the need to develop more comprehensive and better designed environments for case-based learning (Davis, Chapter 8; Mumford et al., Chapter 4); (7) the need to allocate and blend learning activities between classrooms and job or duty stations (Kirschenbaum et al., Chapter 12); (8) the need to balance abstract principles with reasoning about specific examples (VanLehn & van de Sande,

Chapter 16); and (9) the need to balance academic knowledge with practical skill training (Hunt, Chapter 5; VanLehn & van de Sande, Chapter 16).

The themes proposed here help provide a foundation for this chapter, which concerns human performance in military operations and keys on the many substantive findings reported elsewhere in this book.

MILITARY VALUE

There is one more organizing theme that arises frequently in this book. It is the basis for the remainder of this chapter. It concerns the military value of expertise.

Education and training in the military are not undertaken for their own sake. The ultimate goal is to ensure availability of the human expertise needed to successfully perform military operations (Fletcher & Chatelier, 2000; Schreiber et al ., Chapter 11). Training and education – along with recruiting, selection, job classification, career development, ergonomic design, job and decision aiding, and all other efforts to enhance human performance – are means to a single end, namely, the successful execution of military operations. They have value only to the extent that they contribute to this end.

In this context, then, we are approaching Kirkpatrick's "Level Three" and "Level Four" assessments. Kirkpatrick (e.g., 1987)[1] did the training community a great service by articulating and systematizing some long-standing ideas about assessment. He identified four levels of assessment:

- *Level One: Surveys.* Level One assesses the opinions and beliefs of the people involved. It is similar to assessments of face validity in psychometrics. It is not without value, but it tells us much more about what people thought of the instruction than the instruction itself.[2]
- *Level Two: Performance on Training Outcome Measures.* Level Two assessments are carried out to see if the training achieved its objectives – if it produced abilities to perform targeted tasks to specified standards under specified conditions.
- *Level Three: Transfer to Job (or Duty Station) Performance.* Level Three assessments begin to tell us if, in addition to doing things right, we are doing the right things – to see if increases in knowledge and skills acquired by individuals and teams through training improve their performance in duty station tasks and military operations.
- *Level Four: Benefits to the Sponsoring Organization.* Level Four assessments are intended to determine if the human performance and expertise

---

[1] And in various other re-statements, occasionally with five levels rather than four. Four should suffice for our purposes.

[2] As an aside, we might recall the finding reported by Rodin and Rodin (1972) that students liked most the teachers from whom they learned least.

attained through training enhance overall organizational effectiveness, productivity, and the likelihood of success. Assessment at this level, then, concerns the fundamental reasons for providing the training in the first place. In business, did it produce and/or enhance productivity and profitability? In the military, did it improve readiness and operational effectiveness? Did it, in the ultimate test, do the right things?

HUMAN ABILITY AND MILITARY TASK PERFORMANCE

There is evidence that basic human ability as measured by the standardized tests used to select individuals for the military is related to better military performance. For instance, Winkler, Fernandez, and Polich (1992) investigated the relationship between ability, measured by the Armed Forces Qualification Test (AFQT),[3] and operationally critical task performance, measured using a high-fidelity, tactical communications simulator. They examined success in establishing a communications network and troubleshooting faults in it. After controlling for demographic background, education, and military experience of the three-member teams that operate and troubleshoot the network, Winkler et al. found that teams with higher average AFQT scores performed better than those with lower average AFQT scores. More specifically, they found that raising the average AFQT score in these teams by 18 points increased the probably of successful equipment setup by about 16 percent and increased troubleshooting performance by about 17 percent.

Similar results were found by Orvis, Childress, and Polich (1992) who examined the relationship between ability, again measured by the AFQT, and performance of Patriot air defense system operators, again measured in a simulator. After controlling for the independent variables of experience, training, location, and unit assignment, Orvis et al. found that performance by Patriot system operators in simulated air defense battles improved 5–10 percent with every category improvement (16–21 percentile points) in AFQT scores.

In studying the cognitive ability of tank commanders and gunners, Scribner, Smith, Baldwin, and Phillips (1986) found a statistically significant relationship between AFQT scores and performance in tank gunnery simulators. Scribner et al. found that tank commanders from AFQT Category III scored about 20 percent more hits in gunnery practice than did tank commanders from Category IV. Similarly, tank gunners in AFQT Category III outscored tank gunners in Category IV by 34 percent.

---

[3] The AFQT is a measure of general mental ability. Its scores are grouped in "mental categories." Category I covers AFQT percentiles 99–93; Category II covers percentiles 92–65; Category IIIA covers percentiles 64–50; Category IIIB covers percentiles 49–31; and Category IV covers percentiles 30–10. Category V personnel are generally excluded from military service.

Holz, O'Mara, and Keesling (1994) examined success rates in force-on-force exercises at the instrumented National Training Center (NTC).[4] They found that the success of platoons with more than one-third of their personnel with low AFQT scores was about half that of platoons with less than one-third of their personnel with low AFQT scores.[5] Given the findings discussed above, this result is not surprising. However, this difference in success rate vanished completely among platoons in which most personnel had more than 20 months' experience in the Army. Evidently, experience may compensate for lower levels of AFQT-measured ability.

In an early study, Jones (1974) found that the ability of individuals in sports teams could account for team success better in some sports than others. It appeared that the more coordination and collaboration were required in a team, the less well its overall success was predicted by the separate abilities of its team members.

Tziner and Eden (1995) pursued Jones's (1974) finding by experimentally varying the composition of three-member tank crews, which are characterized by high levels of coordination and collaboration. Ability in their experiment was a composite measure of cognitive capabilities such as overall intelligence and level of education. Over a two-month period, commanders and deputy commanders each ranked the proficiency of eight crews made up of individuals whose ability and motivation had been varied for this study. Overall, the rankings of 208 tank crews were included in the analysis. At the extremes, Tziner and Eden (1995) found the average rank of crews consisting of all high-ability individuals was 6.1 (out of 8.0 at the maximum) compared to 3.0 for crews consisting of all low-ability individuals. They also found that each crew member's ability contributed to crew performance differentially depending on the ability levels of the other crew members and that ability is better used when concentrated in teams than when spread around. Notably, they found that the rankings of crews composed entirely of high-ability individuals far exceeded that expected simply from the additive affects of their abilities, and that teams composed of uniformly low-ability individuals received performance rankings far lower than expected. In brief, Tziner and Eden (1995) found the whole of team performance to be more than a simple sum of its parts.

More specific measures of ability may enhance development of more specific areas of expertise. The "aces" concept calls for early identification of potentially high performers in critical positions, as was mentioned in other chapters in this book (Boshuizen , Chapter 17; Chatham , Chapter 2). Smith and Graham (1987) examined the effect of more finely tuned selection and personnel job classification procedures on performance in anti-armor

[4] The NTC, the key training range for armor units, is about the size of Rhode Island.
[5] They do not define "low AFQT scores."

gunnery simulators. They investigated the selection of gunners based on spatial ability (orientation, location, and shape of objects) and psychomotor ability (hand–eye coordination), both of which appear to be at a premium in anti-armor gunnery. They found that a battalion with anti-armor gunners who score in the upper third of ability for these measures performs as though it had 29 percent more tanks than a battalion with gunners who score in the lower third.

EXPERTISE AND MILITARY TASK PERFORMANCE

The above studies all used simulation (including combat engagement simulation) to measure the military value of human mental ability. What about expertise and performance? Beyond native mental ability and/or aptitude, what can we say about the value of expertise, whatever its source, to operational effectiveness? What is a pound of expertise worth? Evidence-based answers to these questions are much needed but rare. Some are shown in Table 20.1.

There is evidence that operational experience contributes to success. As shown in Table 20.1, Weiss (1966) reported that a single success as a World War II submarine commander increased by a factor of three the chances of further success over other not-yet-successful commanders. Also Tillson and Canby (1992) found that maneuver battalions commanded by officers with more than six months of battle experience in Vietnam suffered one-third fewer combat deaths than those commanded by less-experienced officers.

One striking and more recent example of the contribution of human expertise to the performance of military operations arises from development and use of the Interactive Multisensor Analysis Training (IMAT) system (Naval Studies Board, 1997 ; Wetzel-Smith, Ellis, Reynolds, & Wulfeck, 1995; Wulfeck & Wetzel-Smith, 2007). IMAT was developed jointly by the Navy Personnel Research and Development Center and the Naval Surface Warfare Center. It provides training in sensor employment and tactics (e.g., environmental analysis, sensor selection and placement, search rate and threat detection, multisensor crew coordination, multisensor information integration). It combines newer curriculum design technologies, such as cognitive modeling, situation learning, and elaborated explanations, with sophisticated computer graphics. These capabilities allow sensor operators to rapidly acquire the complex skills needed in anti-submarine warfare (ASW) for visualizing in three dimensions the structural and spatial interrelationships existing among sensors, platforms, submarine systems, and ocean environments.[6]

---

[6] Wulfeck and Wetzel-Smith (2007) use and then describe at some length the term "incredibly complex tasks" to characterize these skills.

Table 20.1. *Predictors of operational effectiveness.*

Readiness measure	Effectiveness measure	Source
Command experience	World War II submarine commanders with one successful engagement increased the chances of further success by a factor of three	Weiss, 1966
Command experience	Battalions commanded by officers with more than six months experience in Vietnam suffered one-third fewer battle deaths than those commanded by officers with less experience	Tillson and Canby, 1992
Sonar detection	IMAT training produced a 10 dB tactical gain	Naval Studies Board, 1997
Flying hours	A 10 percent increase in flying hours is associated with a 5.2 percent decrease in average bombing miss distance	Cavalluzzo, 1984
Flying hours	A 10 percent increase of career flying hours decreases the probability of defeat in air-to-air combat by 6.3 percent A 10 percent increase of recent (one week) flying hours decreases the probability of defeat in air–to–air combat by 2.9 percent A 10 percent increase in career flying hours decreases average bombing miss distance by 1.5 percent A 10 percent increase in recent (one week) flying hours decreases average bombing miss distance by 1 percent	Hammon and Horowitz, 1990
Flying hours	A 10 percent increase in career flying hours decreases average bombing miss distance by 1.2 percent A 10 percent increase of recent (one week) flying hours decreases average bombing miss distance by 0.6 percent • A 10 percent increase in career flying hours by co-pilots and navigators decreases tactical air-drop miss distances by 0.5 percent • A 10 percent increase in recent (one week) flying hours by co-pilots and navigators decreases tactical air-drop miss distances by 2.3 percent	Hammon and Horowitz, 1992
Flying hours	A 10 percent increase in career flying hours increases torpedo attack scores of patrol aircraft by 0.6 percent	Hammon and Horowitz, 1996
Tank miles driven	Number of miles driven is correlated with offensive mission performance ($r = 0.68$) and defensive mission performance ($r = 0.80$)	Holz, O'Mara, and Keesling, 1994

Some of the findings regarding IMAT effectiveness listed by the Naval Studies Board (1997) are:

- IMAT graduates scored significantly higher on oceanography knowledge and skills tests than did fleet personnel with 3 to 10 years experience.
- Apprentice aviation ASW operators who were trained using IMAT scored higher on acoustic problem solving than journeyman fleet personnel.
- IMAT produced a four- to six-year equivalent experience gain in search planning for ASW officers.

Additionally, IMAT provides a significant example of the cost-effective value of human expertise in enhancing hardware performance. It has been estimated that every decibel (dB) gain in sensor performance costs about $100 million in research and development (Naval Studies Board, 1997). The human expertise produced by IMAT achieved a 10-dB tactical gain in at-sea trials. That is to say that IMAT-trained operators detected undersea objects with the same probability that other operators would if the sound source were 10 times more intense or less than half as far away – or if a billion dollars had been spent in research and development to upgrade the physical capabilities of the sensor systems. This contribution is of substantial value to naval operations from both an operational and economic standpoint.

It is expensive to fly tactical military aircraft and, despite impressions to the contrary, defense budgets are not unlimited. The question then arises: What do we get for the flying hours we pay for? A series of studies were undertaken to help answer this question. They related flying hours to bombing (Cavalluzzo, 1984), air-to-air combat (Hammon & Horowitz, 1990), tactical air-drop (Hammon & Horowitz, 1992), and aircraft torpedo attack scores (Hammon & Horowitz, 1996).

Cavalluzzo's results are drawn from aircraft dropping live bombs on a naval bombing range. She found that a 10 percent increase in flying hours is associated with a 5.2 percent decrease in average bombing miss distance. As she says, these data represented the best peacetime proxy of warfighting capabilities for medium attack aircraft.

Hammon and Horowitz (1990) suggest that flying enhances proficiency in two ways: through the short-term honing of skills and the long-term development of mastery. They examined associations between flying experience and both bombing accuracy and success in air combat maneuvering exercises. In general, they found (echoing findings by Ericsson 2006), that while both short- and long-term experiences are important, long-term experience was more strongly related to expertise than recent massed practice experience. More specifically they found, as Table 20.1 shows, that:

- A 10 percent increase of Navy pilot career flying hours decreases the probability of defeat in air-to-air combat by 6.3 percent.

- A 10 percent increase of Navy pilot recent (one week) flying hours decreases the probability of defeat in air-to-air combat by 2.9 percent.
- A 10 percent increase in Marine Corps pilot career flying hours decreases average bombing miss distance by 1.5 percent.
- A 10 percent increase in Marine Corps pilot recent (one week) flying hours decreases average bombing miss distance by 1 percent.

The difference between short-term cramming (hours spent flying in the week before assessment) and long-term flying hours is notable. It suggests that in an emergency it would be difficult to remedy inadequate levels of expertise arising from insufficient career flying hours. As a practical matter, the limited availability of aircraft and training ranges – among other training resources – for massed practice further constrains our ability to improve effectiveness quickly.

Hammon and Horowitz (1990) also included data from automated delivery of bombs. These data are basically flat and unaffected by numbers of flying hours. They suggest that an increase by a factor of about five in career flying hours produces "manual" bombing accuracy that is about as accurate as automated delivery. Hammon and Horowitz also found that an increase by a factor of about five in previous-week flying hours produces "manual" bombing accuracy that can exceed automated delivery accuracy. Given studies (e.g., Simon & Bjork, 2002) of short- versus long-term performance, it may be reasonable to expect short-term performance to equal and perhaps exceed performance built up over the long term, but that it may also fade more quickly. More empirical examination of investment in short-term surges over long-term development appears needed to better understand this trade space and its cost and effectiveness implications for military operations.

In 1992, Hammon and Horowitz reported findings from a study investigating the relationship between flying hours by members of aircrews and parachute air-drop miss distances. They found, as Table 20.1 shows, that:

- A 10 percent increase in Marine Corps pilot career flying hours decreases average bombing miss distance by 1.2 percent.
- A 10 percent increase of Marine Corps pilot recent (one week) flying hours decreases average bombing miss distance by 0.6 percent.
- A 10 percent increase in Air Force military airlift career flying hours by co-pilots and navigators decreases tactical air-drop miss distances by 0.5 percent.
- A 10 percent increase in Air Force military airlift recent (one week) flying hours by co-pilots and navigators decreases tactical air-drop miss distances by 2.3 percent.

As in their 1990 study, Hammon and Horowitz again found that, compared to short-term surges in flying hours, the most important determinant of proficiency was total flying hours. And they again concluded that it would be difficult to correct long-term experience deficiencies with short-term surges.

In 1996 Hammon and Horowitz shifted their focus to anti-submarine warfare. They collected data from an instrumented range in which Navy patrol aircrews detect, classify, track, and launch exercise torpedoes against a submerged target submarine. They were not able to make detailed career versus recent flying hour comparisons but, as shown in Table 20.1, they found that a 10 percent increase in career flying hours of both aircraft pilot-commanders and Tactical Action Coordinators (TACCO) increases the torpedo attack scores of a patrol aircraft by 0.6 percent.

Tank miles driven may be roughly similar to aircraft miles in the development of expertise. This possibility is reinforced by the 73 Easting experience (described later in this chapter) involving the operational success of a cavalry (tank) troop after it had far exceeded its formal training allocation of fuel for tank miles driven. As shown in Table 20.1, Holz, O'Mara, and Keesling (1994) found that number of tank miles driven was correlated with force-on-force offensive mission performance ($r = 0.68$) and with live fire defensive mission performance ($r = 0.80$) at the NTC instrumented range.

The results reported in this section are mixed, and many are keyed to the assumption that expertise reliably arises simply from experience and/or time in training without regard to what occurs during the experience or training. Some, such as IMAT's dramatic 10-dB improvement in detection and the strong correlations found by Holz, O'Mara, and Keesling (1994) between tank miles driven and mission performance, suggest the value of cultivating expertise. Other results, however, are modest and, in some cases, flat. Evidently, cognitive ability, team composition, training design, and types of practice all affect the development of expertise. The value of deliberate practice tailored to the specific needs of individuals and teams is emphasized by these tepid results, which highlight the need for training that is not limited to repetitive practice on capabilities already mastered, but that concentrates on specific knowledge and skills that are insufficiently mastered by individuals and teams. Finally, the issue is not simply native ability versus expertise, but the relationship between them – a relationship that appears to remain a relevant and necessary target for research leading to cost-effective development of human performance.

SUCCESS IN MILITARY OPERATIONS

Assessment of combat success linked to human performance is close to Kirkpatrick's Level Four and essential in the development of military readiness and effectiveness. However, such assessment often requires the exigencies of combat, which exceed those that, for practical and, certainly, ethical reasons, can be provided in training.[7]

Hiller (1987) has described this issue as the "criterion problem" of military training. In effect, we must train individuals and groups of individuals without the benefit of criterion-referenced assessment. Instead we measure and evaluate units for their "readiness." These assessments are relevant and helpful, but they only indirectly address the ultimate effectiveness we seek. Given the dangerous and destructive nature of combat operations, we can be glad the criterion problem exists. Still, assessing the preparedness of military forces for combat engagements remains a compelling and nationally significant challenge for students of human behavior.

As an aside it should be noted that not all military operations directly involve combat – only about 14 percent of residential military training courses concern direct preparation for combat duties (Fletcher & Chatelier, 2000). However, the bedrock of military operational preparedness remains the ability to successfully perform combat operations. The examples that follow, then, draw from data relating human performance to the combat capabilities that are the raison d'etre for military organizations.

Top Gun

One example of the military value of expertise may be found in the Top Gun experience. A naturally occurring experiment involving Top Gun was described in more detail by Chatham in Chapter 2, Gorman (1990), and Fletcher (1999). It is only briefly discussed here, but this chapter would be incomplete were it not mentioned. Top Gun concerned the development of expertise and professional performance through the use of simulation and, specifically, the simulation of combat engagements in which units are trained in free-play exercises by facing a well-prepared opponent on an instrumented range.

Top Gun is frequently cited in discussions of the military value of developing human competence for military engagements. During the air war over North Vietnam, roughly 1965–1973, the U.S. Navy and U.S. Air Force flew aircraft of comparable capabilities. In fact, many of the aircraft used were exactly the same, armed with the same weapons. During the first four years of air-to-air combat, both the Navy and the Air Force experienced an identical, and disappointingly low, ratio of North Vietnamese to U.S. aircraft lost – 2.2 to 2.4 North Vietnamese aircraft for every U.S. aircraft downed, as shown in Table 20.2.

There was a halt in air-combat operations over North Vietnam from 1968 to 1970. During this period, the U.S. Navy initiated a training program using simulated, well-instrumented, force-on-force combat engagements to enhance pilot performance in air-to-air combat. Navy student pilots were pitted against

---

[7] In military training, it is assumed that everything other than actual combat is simulation.

Table 20.2. *Loss ratios in air-to-air engagements: 1965–1973.*

	Years	
	1965–1968	1970–1973
MIG to US Air Force loss ratio	2.25	2.00
MIG to US Navy loss ratio	2.42	12.50

"enemy" pilots – other, highly proficient Navy pilots trained in enemy tactics and flying MIG-type aircraft. Engagements were played and re-played until the Navy student flyers got them right.

This activity appeared to have significant military value, but verification of its validity remained. Did success in engagement simulation predict success in combat operations? The question was answered in 1970 when the air war resumed. As Table 20.2 shows, Navy pilots, still flying the same aircraft as their Air Force counterparts but trained using engagement simulation, performed about six times better than Air Force pilots whose training had remained unchanged. The new loss-exchange ratios were 2.0 for Air Force pilots and 12.5 for Navy pilots.[8]

These results demonstrated the value of force-on-force, free-play engagement simulation. Expertise in such simulation is developed through practice with feedback using objective data obtained through various forms of instrumentation, and concentration on scenarios that provide deliberate practice featuring problems of "desirable difficulty" as discussed by Ericsson (Chapter 18) and Bjork (Chapter 14). Because of its free-play nature, engagement simulation also enhances the "cognitive readiness" of individuals to recognize and deal effectively with the multitude of unexpected events that inevitably accompany military operations (Fletcher, 2004).

However, this approach is costly. It requires use of actual equipment (airplanes in the Top Gun exercises, but tanks on the ground and ships at sea in other areas of operation). Large numbers of individuals are also needed (e.g., exercise and scenario developers, battle masters, exercise operator/controllers, and logisticians) for the training. The exercise range and equipment used are instrumented (with position locators, lasers, laser sensors, and extensive play-back capabilities) to provide participants with sufficiently accurate and objective feedback on their performance to diagnose and improve it. Despite the costs and complexity of the approach, it has been expanded and enthusiastically adopted by all four U.S. military services because of its demonstrated value. A more recent example of the value of this approach and the expertise it produces can be seen in results from the Battle of 73 Easting.

---

[8] Given these results, the Air Force adopted a similar form of engagement simulation in 1974 for training its fighter pilots.

73 Easting

The Battle of 73 Easting provides a unique opportunity for analysis because it was captured in moment-to-moment, high-resolution detail by a Defense Advanced Research Projects Agency (DARPA) simulation. Design and development of the simulation have been documented and described by Christianson and Zirkle (1992) and Orlansky and Thorpe (1992). Commanders and soldiers on each side of the engagement were interviewed extensively with cross-reference checks. Additionally, fire direction logs, radio net recordings, reconnaissance imagery data, diagrammed platoon battles, tracks of wire-guided missiles, shell craters, and the like, were all examined (Bloedorn, 1992). As described by Thorpe (1992), the final simulation allows examination of the action at different levels of resolution ranging from overhead "God's eye" views to those from inside vehicle turrets.

McMaster (2005) provides a compelling, ground-level account of the battle itself. During the first Gulf War on February 26, 1991, the Second Armored Cavalry Regiment had raced north from Kuwait into Iraq and was wheeling to the east in order to seek out forces of the elite Iraqi Republican Guard. Its task was to locate and assess these units so that forces from VII Corps, which followed the Regiment, could then engage the Iraqis to best advantage. The Regiment itself was preceded by three reconnaissance troops moving east, in parallel (north to south). Each troop consisted of about 9 tanks, 12 armored personnel carriers, and 2 motorized mortars. The troops were to locate Republican Guard units and report their position(s) back to the Regiment so that VII Corps could deploy its larger forces effectively in planned, deliberate attacks.

Rain during the night of February 25th left heavy ground fog, limiting visibility to about 200 meters on the morning of the 26th. The fog gradually lifted, only to be replaced by a day-long sandstorm, which continued to limit both visibility and possibilities for air cover. At 1607 hours (4:07 P.M.), the middle troop encountered forward elements of what turned out to be the 18th Brigade of the Republican Guard's Tawakalna Division. The Brigade consisted of 58 tanks, 35 armored personnel carriers, and various artillery, trucks, and supply vehicles. The Brigade was dug into well-prepared defensive positions waiting for the Americans to appear.[9]

Having made this contact, the middle U.S. troop commander had a decision to make. He had completed his mission. He had located the enemy and had arrived at 70 Easting, which was supposed to be the easternmost limit of his advance. Instead, however, he led his troop into immediate, aggressive action against a force that greatly outnumbered his own.

---

[9] The Republican Guard commander had attended the Infantry Officer Advanced Course at Ft. Benning, Georgia.

His response was in accord with the training his regiment had received in Germany before deployment. Soldiers of the regiment had been told that centralized control was neither possible nor desirable. Junior leaders were to be trained to do the right things and then trusted to do them.

The middle troop subsequently crested a small rise, discovered the enemy in its well-prepared defensive positions, and proceeded to destroy about 50 T-72 tanks, 25 armored personnel carriers, 40 trucks, and a variety of other vehicles in a period of 23 minutes. The troop took no casualties.

This was the first major engagement of the Gulf War and the first battle ever fought by soldiers in the troop. When asked why he chose to pursue an attack, the middle troop commander replied directly that this was not the first time he had fought a battle. He had fought in force-on-force engagements at the NTC. He had taken platoons through tank tables, combined arms live-fire exercises, and simulations. He stated that he and his crews had simply carried out the correct drills automatically and completed them before realizing fully that they were not in a simulation (McMaster, 1992).

The offensive spirit that accounted for so much of this engagement's success did not occur without deliberate effort and practice. The troops' parent regiment had expended far more than its official allocations of fuel and ammunition in training (McMaster, 2005; Orlansky & Thorpe, 1992). Not only could the troop crews hit with almost perfect accuracy anything they could see, they knew that they could. They were confident in attacking an enemy that was numerically superior and, as often happens in combat, unhesitating, aggressive action prevailed (cf., Keegan, 1976, 1993).

Despite its disproportionate loss-exchange ratio, 73 Easting was a serious and challenging engagement. The Republican Guard soldiers fought determinedly, but without the depth of training the Americans had received. Further, their defensive deployment was better suited to a massed Iranian Infantry attack than a challenge from American cavalry.[10] Their vehicles and bunkers were too close together. Once the first positions were located, the Americans had the full Iraqi force in their sights.

CHAPTER THEMES REVISITED

What, on the basis of 73 Easting, is there to say about expertise and the themes that are found in this book?

Deliberate Practice

Seeking deliberate practice of difficult and challenging matters seems, not surprisingly, as important for crews, teams, and units as it is for individuals. As

---

[10] Liddel Hart quote, "After 7,000 years of warfare, one conclusion is clear, the only thing harder than getting a new idea into the military mind is getting an old one out."

the competence of 2nd Cavalry Regiment crews grew, the level of desirable difficulty also increased. Instead of resting on their achievements in training, 2nd Cavalry units were highly motivated to continue seeking professional growth after their baseline levels of performance were reached. Units deliberately sought out opportunities for practice in maneuver, gunnery, and crew drills under the most difficult of conditions – for example, in storms at night, with severely limited illumination (McMaster, 2005 ; Orlansky & Thorpe, 1992). Such practice prepares individuals and units to deal with the many expected challenges and situations they may encounter in combat and other military operations. It may also enhance their capabilities to recognize unexpected situations and, by establishing standard operating procedures, free up the cognitive processes needed to deal effectively with them (Fletcher, 2004; Tillson, et al., 2005).

Assessment and Self-Assessment

A key component of the free-play, force-on-force engagement training Americans receive in combat training centers such as the NTC, is the after-action review (AAR). These reviews are the Army's primary method for providing performance feedback after unit training exercises. They stem from oral history techniques, the "interviews after combat," developed by S. L. A. Marshall in World War II (e.g., Marshall, 1978). Over the years, the Army has developed specific principles for the conduct of AARs based on information feedback, performance measurement, cognition and memory, group processes, communication theory, and principles of instructional design (Morrison & Meliza, 1999).

Causal connections between actions and outcomes are as shrouded in the fog of action during unit training exercises as they are in combat. Correct decisions can lead to disaster, and wrong decisions can be favored with success by pure luck. How well a unit performs in an exercise may not be immediately obvious to participants and observers, even on well-instrumented ranges. An AAR is intended to be "a professional discussion ... that enables soldiers to discover for themselves what happened, why it happened, and how to sustain strengths and improve on weaknesses" (U.S. Army Combined Arms Center, 1993 , p. 1).

A "professional discussion" in an Army AAR consists of a rigorous, collective, self-examination of events, their causes, and ways to improve unit performance. It is not a critique conducted by a commanding officer, senior umpire, or a group of observers. Instead it is a facilitated, free-flowing discussion in which all exercise participants – young officers, experienced sergeants, and new privates alike – have full access to all objective performance indicators, instrumented data, results, and findings. All are expected to contribute actively. It is a combination of self-assessment and guided discovery learning.

AARs have been lauded as the single most important event in unit training (U.S. Army Training and Doctrine Command, 1997). Morrison and Meliza (1999) emphasize the findings and concepts arising from research on human behavior, many of which are discussed elsewhere in this volume, that underlie the development of AARs. In them we can observe at work such behavioral concepts as social facilitating; need for guidance in discovery learning; models of constructive feedback; active participation and problem solving; principles of situated, experimental learning; development of shared mental models; product and process assessment; minimizing delay of feedback; and enhancing the assessment capabilities of simulation. Because of their cooperative and open nature, AARs may be a uniquely American institution. They have proven difficult to replicate in the military organizations of other countries. They were a key component in the training received by the Americans who participated in 73 Easting.

Agility

The Regiment deliberately prepared for the unexpected by enhancing unit expertise in dealing with unforeseen consequences (Gorman, 1990 ; McMaster, 2005). Such expertise was viewed as a way to turn potential problems into opportunities. The action of the forward cavalry troops demonstrated a balanced interplay between automaticity in carrying out the well-practiced procedures needed for a successful attack, and judgment in choosing consciously and decisively to disregard orders from an earlier plan and advance to attack.

Centrality of Cognition

It also seems notable that cognitive capability and individual judgment were sought at all echelons. Swift, essential, and correct decision making, too detailed to include in this chapter (but see Gorman, 1990, and McMaster, 2005, for examples) was found in the history of 73 Easting from regimental command through junior officers to tank and armored personnel carrier drivers, gunners, and ammunition loaders. That the decisions so often turned out to be correct was attributed to the confidence individual soldiers had, not just in their own psychomotor, task-performance skills, but in their capabilities, proven in training, to choose and make the right mission-critical decisions at the right time.

Design of Learning Environments

Many suggestions concerning the design and structure of learning environments made by chapters in this book can be seen applied during training for the Second Armored Calvary Regiment (McMaster, 2005 ; Orlansky & Thorpe, 1992). Deliberate difficulty and repeated practice with feedback were chosen as the Regiment increased its capabilities. Mission competencies were emphasized to blend and integrate training on discrete, essential tasks into a coherent encompassing focus. Realistic knowledge of Iraqi culture and capabilities was included along with practical gunnery, driving, and maneuver skills, with the result that Iraqis who attempted to surrender were able to do so without misinterpretation by U.S. forces. Non-cognitive goals of confidence, pride, and morale were integral to the Regiment's training objectives.

Military Value of Training

Extra training in terms of experience in the field, extra ammunition, and extra fuel that the regiment received produced value. The crews trained not just to satisfy a formal program of instruction, but went beyond that to achieve measured levels of performance that exceeded formal, process-oriented training requirements. Beyond demonstrating superior performance, members of the regiment knew that they were proficient. They were confident that if they sighted the enemy and fired first, they would prevail. Again, the value of including non-cognitive training objectives, as recommended by Hunt (Chapter 5) among others, was recognized and emphasized.

CONCLUSION

The findings presented in this chapter along with the Top Gun and 73 Easting examples indicate the value if not the essentiality of expertise and professional performance in military operations. In retrospect these results should not be surprising. Combat-like sparring between individuals has traditionally been applied to develop military operational expertise. Its systematic use to develop the proficiency of military units, large and small, seems a natural extension.

Challenges to behavioral researchers remain. How much is a pound of expertise worth? How much ammunition, fuel, spare parts, extra equipment, and so forth should we give up to get it? Without rational, quantifiable answers to this question, investment in human performance and the development of expertise is likely to continue taking a back seat to the business of buying and supplying aircraft, ships, and tanks.

What should we do to get the expertise we need? Should we buy it off the shelf through recruiting, selection, and, perhaps, programs of lateral entry? Continue producing it through training and education, or finesse the issue entirely through the provision of performance and decision aids? What optimal combination of all these possibilities should we aim for? What can and should behavioral researchers tell defense decision makers that will help establish the proper trade-offs needed to resolve these issues?

Can we solve the paradox of training – that to ensure adequate transfer and retention of knowledge and skills we must tolerate less efficient progress toward achieving readily measurable, end-of-instruction goals? What balance should we set among efficiency in achieving these goals, providing "refresher" training, ensuring retention and transfer of knowledge and skill, and providing performance and decision aids?

The rapidly increasing capabilities of technology for distributing human knowledge, information, and learning on-demand, anywhere, and anytime (e.g., Dodds & Fletcher, 2004) appear to offer significant promise for enhancing human performance in all sectors, including the military. But these capabilities are themselves disruptive to current education and training institutions, policies, and practices, which are heavily based on in-place, on-time classroom learning. What can we do to ease the necessary transitions and make palatable the necessary changes?

Given the centrality of cognition in all expertise – skilled, psychomotor, and otherwise – can we produce reliable processes for cognitive analyses and valid measures of cognitive readiness? How can we best provide for and integrate non-cognitive objectives like ensuring motivation to pursue higher levels of expertise? How should we promote the development not just of adaptability but creativity, innovation, and operational improvisation as well?

The list of issues to be settled by behavioral research could, of course, go on. Many issues appear to be hardy perennials. But they are not without interest or challenge. Other issues will arise as the operational environment evolves. Resolving them will advance the state of the art and practice in the military and any other organization concerned with the development of human capabilities and expertise. As this book suggests, there remains plenty of work to be done – or, as people in the military might say, ample opportunities to excel.

REFERENCES

Bloedorn, G. (1992). Presentation of the fight (troops). In J. Orlanksy & J. Thorpe (Eds.), *73 Easting: Lessons learned from Desert Storm via advanced distributed simulation technology* (IDA Document D-1110) (pp. I-119–I-152). Alexandria, VA: Institute for Defense Analyses.

Cavalluzzo, L. (1984). *OPTEMPO and training effectiveness* (Professional Paper, 427). Alexandria, VA: Center for Naval Analyses.

Christianson, W. M., & Zirkle, R. A. (1992). *73 Easting battle replication – a Janus combat simulation* (IDA Paper P-2770). Alexandria, VA: Institute for Defense Analyses (DTIC/NTIS No. ADA 257 266).

Dodds, P. V. W., & Fletcher, J. D. (2004). Opportunities for new "smart" learning environments enabled by next generation web capabilities. *Journal of Education Multimedia and Hypermedia, 13*(4), 391–404.

Ericsson, K. A. (2006). The influence of experience and deliberate practice in the development of superior expert performance. In K. A. Ericsson, N. Charness,

P. J. Feltovich, & R. R. Hoffman (Eds.), *The Cambridge handbook of expertise and expert performance* (pp. 683–703). New York: Cambridge University Press.

Fletcher, J. D. (1999). Using networked simulation to assess problem solving by tactical teams. *Computers in Human Behavior, 15*, 375–402.

(2004). *Cognitive Readiness: Preparing for the Unexpected* (IDA Document D-3061) Alexandria, VA: Institute for Defense Analyses (DTIC/NTIS No. ADA 417 618).

Fletcher, J. D., & Chatelier, P. R. (2000). Military Training. In S. Tobias & J. D. Fletcher (Eds.), *Training and retraining: A handbook for business, industry, government, and the military* (pp. 267–288). New York: Macmillan.

Gorman, P. F. (1990). *The military value of training* (IDA Paper P-2515). Alexandria, VA: Institute for Defense Analyses (DTIC/NTIS No. ADA 232 460).

Hammon, C. P., & Horowitz, S. A. (1990). *Flying hours and aircrew performance* (IDA Paper P-2347). Alexandria, VA: Institute for Defense Analyses (DTIC/NTIS No. ADA 228 582).

(1992). *Relating flying hours to aircrew performance: Evidence for attack and transport missions* (IDA Paper P-2609). Alexandria, VA: Institute for Defense Analyses (DTIC/NTIS No. ADA 253 988).

(1996). *The Relationship Between Training and Unit Performance for Naval Patrol Aircraft – Revised* (IDA Paper P-3139). Alexandria, VA: Institute for Defense Analyses (DTIC/NTIS No. ADA 328 922).

Hiller, J. H. (1987). Deriving useful lessons from combat simulations. *Defense Management Journal, 23*, 29–33.

Holz, R. F., O'Mara, F., & Keesling, W. (1994). Determinants of effective unit performance at the National Training Center: Project overview. In R. F. Holz, J. H. Hiller, & H. McFann (Eds.), *Determinants of effective unit performance: Research on measuring and managing unit training readiness.* Alexandria, VA: US Army Research Institute for the Behavioral and Social Sciences (DTIC/NTIS No. ADA 292 342).

Jones, M. B. (1974). Regressing groups on individual effectiveness. *Organizational Behavior and Human Performance, 11*, 426–451.

Keegan, J. (1976). *The face of battle.* New York: Viking Press.

(1993). *A history of warfare.* New York: Alfred A. Knopf.

Kirkpatrick, D. L. (1987). Evaluation. In R. L. Craig (Ed.), *Training and development handbook* (3rd ed., pp. 301–319). New York: McGraw-Hill.

Marshall, S. L. A. (1978). *Men against fire: The problem of battle command in future wars.* Glouster, MA: Peter Smith.

McMaster, H. R. (1992). May 21, 1992 testimony before the United States Senate Armed Services Committee.

(2005). The Battle of 73 Easting. In F. Kagan (Ed.), *Leaders in war: West Point remembers the 1991 Gulf War (Cass Military Studies)* (pp. 103–117). London: Frank Cass Publishers.

Morrison, J. E., & Meliza, L. L. (1999). *Foundations of the after action review process.* Alexandria, VA: US Army Research Institute for the Behavioral and Social Sciences.

Naval Studies Board. (1997). *Technology for the United States Navy and Marine Corps, 2000–2035*: (Vol. 4), Human Resources. Washington, DC: Naval Studies Board, National Research Council, 1997.

Orlansky, J., & Thorpe, J. (Eds.). (1992). *73 Easting: Lessons learned from Desert Storm via advanced distributed simulation technology* (IDA Document D-1110). Alexandria, VA: Institute for Defense Analyses (DTIC/NTIS No. ADA 253 991).

Orvis, B. R., Childress, M. T., & Polich, J. M. (1992). *Effect of personnel quality on the performance of Patriot air defense system operators.* Santa Monica, CA: RAND.

Rodin, M., & Rodin, B. (1972). Student evaluations of teachers. *Science, 177*(4055), 1164–1166.

Scribner, B.L., Smith, D. A., Baldwin, R. H., & Phillips, R. L. (1986). Are smart tankers better? AFQT and military productivity. *Armed Forces & Society, 12*, 193–206.

Simon, D. A., & Bjork, R. A. (2002). Models of performance in learning multi-segment movement tasks: Consequences for acquisition, retention and judgments of learning. *Journal of Experimental Psychology: Applied, 8*, 222–232.

Smith, E. P., & Graham, S. E. (1987). *Validation of psychomotor and perceptual predictors for armor officer M-1 gunnery performance* (Technical Report 766). Alexandria, VA: U.S. Army Research Institute for the Behavioral and Sciences.

Thorpe, J. (1992). Background and objective. In J. Orlansky & J. Thorpe (Eds.), *73 Easting: Lessons learned from Desert Storm via advanced distributed simulation technology* (IDA Document D-1110) (pp. I-63–I-79). Alexandria, VA: Institute for Defense Analyses (DTIC/NTIS No. ADA 253 991).

Tillson, J. C. F., & Canby, S. L. (1992). *Alternative approaches to organizing, training, and assessing Army and Marine Corps units, Part I. The active component* (IDA Paper P-2791). Alexandria, VA: Institute for Defense Analyses (DTIC/NTIS No. ADA 261 943).

Tillson, J. C. F., Freeman, W. D., Burns, W. R., Michel, J., LeCuyer, J. A., Scales, R. H., & Worley, D. R. (2005). *Learning to adapt to asymmetric threats* (IDA Document 3114). Alexandria, VA: Institute for Defense Analyses (DTIC/NTIS No. ADA 442 427).

Tziner, A., & Eden, D. (1995). Effects of crew composition on crew performance: Does the whole equal the sum of its parts? *Journal of Applied Psychology, 70*(1), 85–93.

U.S. Army Combined Arms Center. (1993). *A leader's guide to after-action reviews* (Training Circular 25–20). Fort Leavenworth, KS: Author.

(1997). *The standard Army after-action review system (STAARS): After-action review (AAR) handbook* (Version 2.1, 9 May 1997). Fort Leavenworth, National Simulations Center: Author.

Weiss, H. K. (1966). System analysis problems of limited war. In *Proceedings of Fifth Annual Reliability and Maintainability Conference.* New York: American Institute of Aeronautics and Astronautics.

Wetzel-Smith, S. K., Ellis, J. A., Reynolds, A. M., & Wulfeck, W. H. (1995). *The Interactive Multisensor Analysis Training (IMAT) systems: An evaluation of operator and tactician training* (NPRDC Technical Report TR-96-3). San Diego, CA: Navy Personnel Research and Development Center.

Winkler, J. D., Fernandez, J. C., & Polich, M. (1992). *Effect of aptitude on the performance of Army communications operators.* Santa Monica, CA: RAND.

Wulfeck, W. H., & Wetzel-Smith, S. K. (2007). Use of visualization techniques to improve high-stakes problem solving. In E. Baker, J. Dickieson, W. Wulfeck, & H. F. O'Neil (Eds.), *Assessment of problem solving using simulations* (pp. 223–238). Florence, KY: Taylor & Francis-Lawrence Erlbaum Associates.

21

Expertise in the Management of People: A New Frontier for Research on Expert Performance

SUSAN E. F. CHIPMAN

Charged with the assignment of reflecting on the conference and volume as a whole, and following the contributions of so many other distinguished discussants, I have chosen to step back for a broader perspective and comment on what is not well represented in this volume or in the research from which it draws: expertise in the management of people. Expertise of this type is critical to the military services and to civilian society, in contexts ranging from school classrooms to large commercial organizations. Most studies of expertise focus on some form of technical expertise in an individual. It is rare to study expertise that involves a complex social context and interaction with many other people. In this volume several chapters discuss experts leading their teams, while commanding a military combat unit (Shadrick & Lussier, Chapter 13), conducting surgery (Ericsson, Chapter 18), or teaching introductory physics (VanLehn & van de Sande, Chapter 16). Only the chapter by Mumford, Friedrich, Caughron, and Antes (Chapter 4), focuses directly upon these issues. The reason that the conference and the associated book emphasized individual expert performance is that this is the type of superior objective performance that has been confirmed. Mumford et al. (Chapter 4) report that studies with demonstrations of leaders' influence on their teams' objective performance, such as productivity, are very rare and have conflicting results. The current research base on expertise in the management of people is minimal. Consequently, I am drawing heavily upon my own experience as a basis for discussing this topic. If I have an expertise, it is in a certain specialized form of management. Furthermore, I have experienced various efforts at training management skill: a Harvard Business School MBA as well as numerous, much shorter, government training courses.

Ideally, as others such as Mayer (Chapter 9) have described, education or training for a particular form of expertise, would be founded on a good description of what characterizes expert performance in the domain, a description that extends in depth to the analysis of cognitive knowledge, skills, and strategies required to support that expert performance. Education and training can then be designed in a way that would reasonably be expected to develop that expertise, and the description also provides a basis for evaluating both performance and the success of instruction in fostering expert performance. However, this ideal is rarely realized. More usually, education and training in most areas have evolved as a folk tradition. Few elements of instruction have been formally evaluated for their effectiveness, and specifying what should be measured in order to do such evaluations remains a challenge. The historical tradition of management training is relatively short, so it is still possible to uncover what people were thinking as they developed instruction in management.

In this chapter, I will be discussing the dominant tradition of management training, case-based instruction. Case-based instruction is widely used in law, where cases form part of the law and are used in legal arguments by practicing professionals, quite a different situation. Case-based instruction is also used more experimentally in medical training (Boshuizen, Chapter 17; Jarrell, 2003), but my discussion is limited to case-based instruction in management training. This leads to a discussion of teaching in case-based instruction as a form of people management, and then to university-level teaching expertise in general as people management. In these discussions, the teachers' mental models of students emerge as a critical dimension of expertise. One common form of brief management training experience in both government and private sector business seems to aim at developing managers' mental models of people, so a section of this chapter discusses that tradition. Finally, the chapter concludes by sketching a research agenda for the future and some suggestions about the research methods that need to be employed.

THE TRADITION OF MANAGEMENT TRAINING

One of the few available books about case-based instruction, *Teaching and the Case Method* (Barnes, Christensen & Hansen, 1994, a revision of a book first developed in 1975) contains a short, illuminating history of the Harvard Business School (HBS) and the development and evolution of the case method of instruction (pp. 38ff). In 1908, the president of Harvard noted that more than half of Harvard graduates were going on to employment in business and decided that they should be offered some appropriate preparation for that type of work in a graduate professional school. However, it seemed that no one had a good idea concerning what should be taught. The early faculty settled on a practice-oriented, problem-solving approach to instruction. One of the early professors wrote that businesspeople must be able to "meet in action the problems arising out of new situations of an ever-changing environment. Education, accordingly, would consist of acquiring facility to act in the presence of new experience. It asks not how a man may be trained to

know, but how a man may be trained to act." (Dewing, 1931, quoted on p. 41)
There has been a great emphasis on having students understand the specifics of a certain concrete, complex situation, to discern the important issues
in that complex context, and not to generalize. Students, these authors say,
are supposed to develop an *administrative point of view*, which is not a well-
defined concept. Definition is almost resisted. The point that each class is
also an experience in the benefits of group discussion for solving business
problems is also made here.

Notice that the instructional objectives were (and remain) both ambitious
and ill-defined. The chosen instructional approach was novel and unconven-
tional for formal education but also in some ways very conventional – aiming
for as close an approximation to practice of the desired skills as possible. Even
to this day, little has been said about evaluating either the overall success of
management training or the effectiveness of the chosen training approach.
Even less well-defined but recognized as important is the informal curriculum
of the intensive experience of the two-year MBA program itself, all those discussions and interactions with faculty and other students in the case-discussion
approach to management training. How can that be evaluated? In these days
of night school courses and distance learning approaches, it would be important to know how important this other dimension of the management training
experience might be.

CASE-BASED INSTRUCTION FOR MANAGEMENT
AND LEADERSHIP

The preferred method of instruction for management at the HBS, widely
imitated elsewhere, is the case method. The primary notion behind the case
method appears to be that it provides surrogate experience, compressed and
diverse (Lundeberg, 1999; Merseth, 1999). HBS thinks of itself as teaching
people to be general problem solvers by giving them a great deal of practice
in confronting diverse management problems. Consistent with that goal,
HBS cases are very long and complex – book chapter–length stories. Unlike
some much shorter instructional cases, these present greater challenges in
identifying the problem, separating relevant information from irrelevant in a
complex context. They strive for as much realism as possible, although selective editing of experience in the reporting of the case is inevitable. Students
read the case and then participate in a class discussion that brings out the
important issues and leads to a recommendation of possible actions. This
form of instruction contrasts strongly with a more theoretical statement of
general principles that might be applied to solve many problems in a variety
of situations. MBA programs do vary in the extent to which they use the case
method, as contrasted to more conventional didactic technical courses, but
selling its case materials is a big business for HBS.

How Effective Is Case-Based Instruction?

As a student at HBS, fresh from the most theoretical of undergraduate studies (the purest of pure math and physics), I was extremely frustrated by the failure to generalize. To me, it seemed that all, or at least many, of the cases in a given course were alike. Yet comparisons and generalizations were never made during the case discussions. The faculty did not encourage them. In my student days, however, I did not realize that the failure to compare and generalize was a deliberate feature of the ideology of case-based instruction. Apparently it is, as will be discussed below. Over the years, my opinion of case-based instruction has changed somewhat. At least a few times over the years, many years later, I found that work situations reminded me of cases that I had studied at the business school. For example, at the National Institute of Education, serious conflict arose between a secretary serving as a timekeeper and some members of the professional staff, doctoral-level professionals primarily drawn from academic working environments. This reminded me of business school cases where circumstances made lower status employees the de facto supervisors or controllers of high status employees: waitresses of chefs, bag boys of supermarket checkers. In general, this type of situation causes trouble. Notice that in describing these cases, I have stated a generalization about what all these situations have in common.

I do not know how many others have had such experiences. To my knowledge, such questions have not been studied. There is reason to believe that they may not be common. In the past few years, Dedre Gentner's program of research on learning from analogies, including research on reminding, has been extended to studying learning from business school cases (Loewenstein, Thompson, & Gentner, 2003; Thompson, Gentner, & Loewenstein, 2000). The results have been striking. The experiments were conducted in the context of a short course on negotiation skills at Northwestern University, recognized as a top business school. The students have been highly motivated, with several years of working experience in business, hoping to improve their negotiation skills and related job performance. The key experiment explored the effect of reading two cases describing a negotiation strategy, as opposed to reading and also comparing the same two cases, contrary to the usual business school practice. The outcome measure was use of the target negotiation strategy in a role-playing negotiation. The effects of making comparisons proved dramatic (Figure 21.1), of a size rarely seen in education and training research. When Thompson, the business school professor in this collaboration, presented these results at the HBS, the audience became quite upset. Later, however, HBS offered a faculty job to Loewenstein. Further experimentation has shown that reading cases without comparison provides little or no improvement over no cases at all. Theoretical statements are equally ineffective. Comparing a theoretical statement with a case also provides some instructional value. The

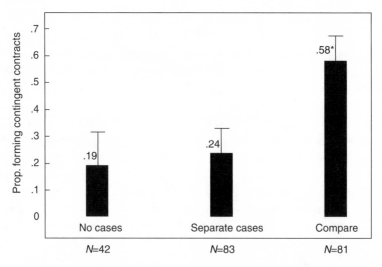

FIGURE 21.1. Comparing cases yields dramatic improvement in learning from case-based instruction.

obvious implication of these results is that most business school students, however motivated, are not making comparisons spontaneously. With my strong tendencies for comparisons and generalizations, I was unusual. Therefore, the reminding I experienced in later life may have been unusual also. Obviously there is reason to question whether case-based instruction is effective in attaining its goals. The cases used in the Northwestern courses and research were very short and sketchy compared to HBS cases, but the complexity of the HBS cases might make it even more difficult to see the common structure.

Because these results were so strikingly large, they were followed up by the announcement of a Small Business Innovation Research (SBIR) topic through the Office of the Secretary of Defense, calling for the development of an authoring tool for case-based instruction that would guide authors in using cases with case comparisons to maximize training effectiveness. The military services are very large bureaucratic organizations, so management training is of great interest. In addition, case-based instruction may be used to train specifically military decision making, drawing upon past military warfare experiences (e.g., Frame & Lussier, 2000). The contract was awarded to Stottler-Henke Associates and was successfully completed (Domeshek, 2006), although the degree of authoring ease that was desired was not achieved in this contract. Hopefully the company will use it in developing case-based courses, and further development will make it more accessible to less technically expert authors. An authoring tool specifically for case-based instruction was also an innovation in training technology.

Case-based instruction and its effectiveness need much more research investigation. It appears that there was no research, or virtually none, until teacher educators began to try case-based instructional methods in teacher education (Lundeberg, Levin, & Harrington, 1999). This brought case-based instruction to the attention of educational researchers. Mumford et al. (Chapter 4) endorse the idea of case-based instruction for organizational leadership. They believe that leadership decision making is often based on analogous cases, the process that Gary Klein has made famous under the name "recognition-primed decision making" (Klein, 1998; Nutt, 1984; Ross, Lussier, & Klein, 2005). In his commentary on the chapter by Mumford et al., Hunt (Chapter 5) also makes the point that successful leadership often seems to depend on having a substantial case library derived from the leader's own prior experience. Mumford et al. (Chapter 4) also present some ideas concerning the way that case-based instruction should be done that probably are not currently in practice, and argue that there is evidence that leadership training programs in general are effective, at least as measured by performance ratings by their supervisors. Reviews of evaluations of a somewhat similar type of training, team building, have revealed that there is little solid evidence that such training is effective in improving performance, despite the popularity and large monetary investments in such training (Salas, Mullen, Rozell, & Driskell, 1997).

EXPERTISE IN CASE-BASED DISCUSSION TEACHING

The two very disparate examples mentioned at the outset of this chapter – classroom management and the management of people in commercial business operations – come together in efforts to characterize the expertise of outstanding teachers of business using the case method of instruction with its reliance on classroom discussion. *Education for Judgment* (Christensen, Garvin, & Sweet, 1991) is a prime example of such an effort, especially the chapters by Christensen (1991a,b), the acknowledged master expert at discussion teaching. (There is now a Christensen Center for Teaching and Learning at HBS. A large percentage of the current faculty have now received training in the case-discussion method of instruction through this center.) As is true for most forms of expertise, most expert teachers find it difficult to articulate their expertise. At best, we are told about certain aspects of their expertise of which they are consciously aware. Christensen places great emphasis on getting to know each and every student in some depth, in a context where discussion classes are held in sections of 90 students! The HBS provides professors with cards having a picture, name, home address, and undergraduate college, much more information than a college professor is usually given. Beyond that, Christensen describes asking students for voluntary information statements covering such questions as their background preparation for, interest in, and goals for the course, as well as critical incidents in their past experience and why they chose those incidents. He also describes coming early to class for the opportunity to chat with early arriving students. It is obvious that he invested a large amount of effort in developing detailed models of each individual student. He describes the need to know students as people, their ambitions, uncertainties, blind spots, and areas of excellence (p. 111).

In addition, he describes using that information to make decisions on the fly about which student to call upon in what way, and at what point in the discussion: "In what fields does Ms. Petersen feel confident, have the knack of explaining, and the interest, patience, and ingenuity to state her message in a variety of ways?" (p. 109). He describes continual experimentation, over more than 40 years of experience, with the details of discussion management: experimenting with questioning students in different areas of the classroom, with asking the same question of two students in succession, with giving students a question that allows a delay for thinking before answering, with questioning by gesture as opposed to direct speech, and so on (p. 104). After every class, he kept notes on the success or failure of that day's tactics (p. 162). This seems an outstanding example of Ericsson's *deliberate practice* (Ericsson, Krampe, & Tesch-Römer, 1993) as the mark of a true expert. In fact, Christensen says, "sophisticated teaching is the product of study and practice – seasoned with a liberal dash of trial and error," even though it may come to seem so automatic as to be instinct (p. 153). He also describes coming to understand that a crucial role for the instructor in discussion teaching is making connections among remarks made in the discussion at different times, or even across different days, because the important points come out rather haphazardly in discussion, "presiding over disorder without disorientation," he called it (p. 105). Encouragement of comparisons and generalizations seems to have been part of his repertoire (pp. 160–161), even though I did not see much of it in my classes at HBS. (Although Christensen was teaching the required second-year course in Business Policy when I was at HBS, I was not fortunate enough to be in one of his sections.) Finally, Christensen also came to realize that part of what students were learning was participation in effective discussion itself, listening to and learning from the perspectives and contributions of others, an important element of management skill in later life (p. 110).

There are a number of paradoxes in the book *Education for Judgment*. It is lecturing in print about how to do a form of teaching that is based on the assumption that discussion of realistic problems is the best way to learn. Although case-method instruction at HBS seemed to me to glorify "gut feel" and its development, this book contains a number of warnings about the assumption that excellent teaching is instinctive and unconsciously produced. Abby Hansen, another author, warns that even effective pros can forget how to perform (p. 135). Christensen repeats that warning that the magic can wear off, with the specific example of a professor who chose to retire early because his classes were no longer working as well as they had in the past. Observers felt that the professor's style had changed and that he was no longer listening to his students (p. 155). Also, an important aspect of teaching expertise is very much in the background, apparently taken for granted. There are numerous brief comments indicating that the cases in a course are carefully selected and sequenced to make or "cover" certain points that represent the point and purpose of the course. This is not surprising. However, there is no description of the way a professor manages the coverage of the course objectives in the context of this type of teaching. Certainly the objectives are not spelled out for the students in the manner mandated by instructional systems design. Although it is difficult to say for sure 40 years later, I doubt that I could have stated the objectives of the courses I took at HBS. To an extent, these paradoxes are clarified and resolved by the earlier mentioned book, *Teaching and the Case Method* (Barnes et al., 1994). This book contains teaching problems, drawn from a variety of subjects, not just business, to be used in case-method discussion teaching of how to do case-method discussion teaching.

Some further insights can be taken from the investigations of Susanne Luperfoy (personal communications), a contractor who was working on the project aiming to design an authoring tool for computerized case instruction. She both took a short course at HBS and interviewed the instructors about their teaching methods. This brought out the fact that the neglect of case comparison was not just an oversight; it was part of the ideology of case-based instruction at HBS – consistent with the remarks above about responding to the unique circumstances of the case. Her interviews also revealed somewhat more about the nature of instructional planning than do the books cited above. Instructors do come in with an agenda of points they want to see made, and they manipulate the discussion subtly by such tactics as writing those points (and not others) on a blackboard as they emerge. Obviously it is necessary to be very subtle about this. In *Education for Judgment,* there are numerous critical remarks about professors who are too obvious or heavy-handed about their agendas. It may be that case-based instruction has evolved over time to have a more deliberate curriculum of points to be covered, as scholarship on business issues has developed, generating theoretical ideas to be drawn upon and conveyed to students, such that there is now more to it than relatively unguided practice in addressing a variety of business problems.

EXPERTISE IN COLLEGE AND GRADUATE LEVEL TEACHING, GENERALLY

Another recent book, *What the Best College Teachers Do* (Bain, 2004), reports an effort to characterize what a large sample of outstanding professors, using a variety of methods to teach a wide variety of different subjects, do that makes them effective. The professors who were studied were selected because there was some sort of convincing evidence that their students consistently achieve outstanding performance. Again, having a well-informed model of the students and focusing on their thinking and their developmental needs emerges as a common factor. Teaching them to think as it is done in the field of study is more important to these professors than conveying or covering the subject matter, certainly more important than displaying the professor's knowledge in a dazzling performance. Bain states (p. 75), "We found professors who took great pains to explore their students' learning, to analyze their work carefully, to think extensively about how and what different people could learn, and even to design particular assignments to fit the needs, interests and current abilities of each student. Even in large classes where it became impossible to know every single student, they explored composite pictures that could help them think about the types of students populating their classes." Bain found that these effective professors all appreciate that students must construct their own understanding, that professors cannot simply present or transmit their knowledge to the student. On the other hand, he did not find common patterns of personality, style, or appearance among effective professors (p. 137).

TOWARD A RESEARCH AGENDA FOR THE FUTURE

Teachers' Mental Models of Students

There are some obvious areas that call for further information. First of all, and perhaps easiest to investigate, is the nature of the mental models of students that expert teachers build. Such investigations seem to be rare. Work in intelligent tutoring has made it evident that most teachers do not construct the sort of detailed cognitive models of student knowledge and skill that characterize the most sophisticated artificially intelligent tutoring systems. Undoubtedly that is true even for outstanding teachers. On the other hand, human teachers undoubtedly model many aspects of student motivation and other human characteristics as yet unknown in artificial systems. In conjunction with a project building an intelligent tutor for remedial adult math training, a modest exploratory investigation was done of the way in which human tutors working in the context of the computer environment, as well as a couple of teachers working in a remedial basic skills training program, modeled their students (Derry & Potts, 1998). A knowledge engineering technique was used in which the tutors/teachers were presented with triads of individual students with whom they had worked. They were asked to identify the two students who were most similar and to say how they differed from the third student, revealing the concepts they used to characterize students and their individual differences. Cognitive and motivational constructs were about equally prevalent. The results for the most experienced tutor working in the computer environment, who also had about 10 years of classroom teaching experience, are perhaps the most relevant. He used 28 bipolar concepts in describing students, quite a complex system. His self-report concerning the constructs that most affected his tutoring behavior identified: interest in math theory, general competence, depth of thinking, concept mastery, and level of concentration (p. 75). Another tutor was heavily affected by working in the computer environment. His most important constructs influencing tutoring were: tolerance for frustration, degree of concept mastery, reflectiveness versus non-reflectiveness, meticulousness about diagram labeling, and interest in the use of graphics. A third tutor had worked primarily in an experiment with pairs of students and therefore identified many characteristics that had to do with the character of the interaction between the members of the pairs. His most important characteristics for tutoring were: degree of struggling, degree of motivation, extent of mentoring of partner, degree of involvement, and slow versus fast learner.

The math teacher from the remedial program identified these characteristics as most important: degree of persistence, voluntary participation, desire for help, ability level, and degree of motivation. The writing teacher from the remedial program differed from all other participants in not seeming to see any students as low in ability, attributing differences to effort or degree of motivation. However, this teacher did categorize students as learning disabled or not, which could be seen as another terminology for ability. This teacher characterized students as tending to be on or off task, by their degree of engagement, staying in a talking mode versus getting into writing, synthesizing or not synthesizing course materials, and being self-directed versus needing to be pushed.

It is notable that these teachers and tutors seem to be treating motivation as if it were a stable characteristic of the student. One might question whether that is appropriate or useful. Presumably a teacher or tutor should have a more complex and dynamic view of a student's motivation that would guide actions that motivate the student to learn more effectively in the particular situation. When an attempt was made to evaluate a version of Derry's math tutor in the remedial adult math course, it turned out that many of the students were taking the course because their employer would increase their pay if they took the course, not because they had a real need for the specific skills taught or an intrinsic interest in learning them. This had implications, for example, for how students behaved when given control over the instruction they received in an automated system. The instructors in the program had wanted to give the students a great deal of control within the computer tutor, but the students abused that control to click through the program at maximal speed, rather than engage extensively with its tutored problem-solving experiences.

Other interesting insights into the way human tutors moderate their tutoring behavior as a result of their perceptions of student characteristics can be found in Evens and Michael's 2005 book, *One-on-One Tutoring by Humans and Computers*. In this case, the students came from a high ability adult population, medical students.

Characterizing Skill in Discussion Teaching

Much more challenging for researchers would be to capture and characterize skill in discussion teaching of the type that Christensen describes, and the integration of the teacher's student models with the teacher's discussion-leading skills and their adaptation to the needs of the individual. Still more elusive, perhaps, is the way in which the teacher's curricular agenda and knowledge of the subject matter are coordinated with seemingly free-flowing group discussions. All of the discussions of expert teaching that I have cited assume that the teacher has expert knowledge of the subject matter; of course, that is not always true, especially in school rather than university environments.

Evaluating whether teachers who are outstanding by reputation actually have exceptional effects on the accomplishments of their students is an extremely challenging problem. Bain (2004) claims to have done so, and to have dropped many of those nominated by reputation, from the eventual study, but the nature of the evidence varied and remains a bit fuzzy after one reads the description. Inspiring as it is to read what he says, one does not know if Christensen, for example, would have met Bain's criteria. There is no doubt that he was a consummate expert by reputation, but did the instructional behavior he describes actually add value to the students? It is hard to know. He provides a few anecdotes about students to whom he gave special attention. The large size of the classes, however, puts definite limits on the number of students who could receive such attention, however dedicated the teacher.

The descriptions in *Education for Judgment* are very idealized. A little calculation shows, for example, that each student in a class of 90 cannot be doing much talking. It must be difficult for the instructor to have any basis for judging the quality of most students' contributions in a grading system that gives great weight to student contributions to discussion, let alone making finely adapted adjustments to the needs of those students. Looking back on my own experience at HBS, I cannot recall ever receiving any useful individual attention from a faculty member, even though I was quite conspicuous because there were no more than three women in these classes. As Bain writes, HBS professors must rely on models of student *types* in order to deal with large classes. While reading the chapter on teaching technical material via case discussion (Greenwald, 1991), I was startled to realize that in many of my classes, I was most likely classified as a common type of problematic student – one of those with relevant technical expertise: As an undergraduate at Harvard, I had been a math major. *Technical* courses at HBS would generally be those with some significant mathematical aspect, such as statistical decision theory.

Interestingly, *Education for Judgment,* published in 1991, says nothing about the special issues that might be presented by women students or other atypical business students, although one notices the frequent use of women's names in describing hypothetical students. This is a significant omission.

There was a great deal that was special and difficult about being a woman in one of the first classes at HBS to which women were admitted. I was one of 10 women in a class of 700. I was reminded of one of the major difficulties when Christensen discussed (pp. 22ff) the importance of managing discussions so that students' contributions are treated respectfully and built upon, making students feel that they are valued. Gradually, in my first year, I came to realize that when I did say something in class, the discussion often went on as if I had never spoken. A few years later, with the rise of the women's movement, this would be recognized as a common phenomenon in the way women were treated, as if they did not quite exist. It is likely that members of many minority groups have had similar experiences.

This experience was not as destructive for me as it might have been for many. The fact that I became consciously aware of what was going on helped. Also, I am sure that my prior experiences as an undergraduate at Harvard, where my contributions were better respected, provided some protection, as did my technical expertise. I was not that easy to ignore, and I did not stop talking. (After all, contributions to class discussion were a major component of grading at HBS.) One of the critical incidents I remember from my HBS experience was this: One day a classmate in an operations research course, part of my major in Managerial Economics, Decision and Control, an older student who was a military officer came up to me. He said, "I can take it, you understand; I can take it, but it is very difficult for some of these guys to be in a class with a girl younger than their daughters who is so much better at this than they are." One of the things that I learned from the informal curriculum of HBS was that if I pursued a business career, I would be spending a large fraction of my energy dealing with the special emotional reactions that the men surrounding me might have to competing with a women. This would be a significant handicap. Even today, women are scarce in the upper ranks of business management. They remain under-represented at HBS, and some recent articles in the alumni magazine suggest that many women are finding their careers in business management unrewarding. The magazine articles tend to blame the women for choosing to drop out of the business world, but my interpretation is that it is more likely that they are still experiencing glass ceiling effects.

Thus, the picture of HBS teaching that Christensen gives is over-idealized. When I was a student, either no one noticed or no one cared that I was becoming a very alienated student, even though the school had invested in me by giving me full fellowship support. Christensen surely would have noticed because my doodling became a major art form during that period, and Christensen regarded doodling as a very bad sign about the way the class was going. I also remember doing a lot of rotating in my swivel chair, an even more conspicuous behavior. It is quite possible that many faculty in those days felt that women did not belong at HBS and expected us to fall by the wayside. It is also possible that I was not noticed because I did well academically: Christensen's most extended anecdote of individual attention concerns a student who was failing his course and in danger of not getting the MBA.

Evaluating the Effectiveness of MBA Training

Regardless of apparent quality, it is difficult to know whether educational institutions like HBS truly add value to the students because of the role that such institutions play in the structure of our society and the business world. I myself chose to apply to HBS because I felt it would help me get a better job, help me to escape the secretarial ghetto that still awaited even female graduates of Radcliffe/Harvard in those days. Although I and other women in my class experienced strikingly overt sex discrimination in our job hunts, I think that expectation was justified. Some interviewers did say that they would never hire a woman, or never promote her if they did, but no one asked if we could type. Male students had comparable if less dramatic expectations for better job opportunities. On the other side of the employment relationship, I remember the father of a friend, a vice president of a large commercial bank, commenting that HBS and other elite business schools were just a recruiting convenience, performing a service in sorting through potential job applicants. Neither students nor employers had specific expectations about useful knowledge and skill that would be taught. General problem-solving ability is difficult to measure and difficult to differentiate from the general intellectual ability that partially determines admission to these institutions. Although it is possible to assess shorter-term instructional goals, as in the work of Gentner and her colleagues, measuring long-term career performance is much more difficult. It is, however, reasonable to conclude that if one does not get immediate transfer to a negotiation situation, for example, it is extremely unlikely that the training will show its effects years later. Although one might attempt to compare the career outcomes of individuals with comparable individual characteristics (intellectual ability, SES background, ethnicity, gender) who went into business with and without MBA training, it would be necessary to attempt to factor out the effect of possibly better access to early job opportunities. Comparable efforts to estimate the value of attending a highly selective college have cast doubt on the idea that there is any added value (Dale & Krueger, 2002).

The Role of Mental Models in the Management of People

Only a small fraction of the HBS curriculum dealt with the management of people. There was a required course in personnel management that was the source of the case-reminding experience I mentioned earlier. There was a second-year required course in organizational behavior that was taught by organizational psychologists – former military officers interestingly, but they were rather atypical of military officers in style and behavior. These instructors promoted the idea that problems in the superior–subordinate relationship would go away if only people understood each other. I disagreed, and still do, because I felt that when superiors and subordinates truly understood each other, they might find that their interests were at odds. The year following my experience, this course was scheduled to evolve into a mandatory *sensitivity training* experience. The major assignment in the organizational behavior course was to interview an individual in depth and write a paper about that person. It seemed that the ideal paper involved interviewing someone cracking up because of personal problems.

I do not recall anything being said at HBS about what one might do as a result of understanding a subordinate or superior. Bain describes outstanding college teachers as adapting student assignments to individual need, interests, and abilities. In education, this is a nice thing to do, but when one is a supervisor whose own performance is effectively a function of how well one's subordinates perform, it is truly vital to adapt assignments as much as possible to what those people will be willing and able to do. Of course, there is much less freedom about the nature of assignments in an organizational context than in a college course. Perhaps the discussions in the HBS courses simply served to reveal important individual differences in thinking, beliefs, and values. My father also attended HBS for one year before joining the Navy during World War II. The one comment I remember his making about the HBS experience was the amazing things that some of his fellow students said – things they would have better sense than to say in later life. The experience of hearing such thoughts expressed may enrich the ability to model other people who differ greatly from oneself in beliefs and values.

During a period when I was a supervisor of other research managers, I did operate with very complex mental models of each person, containing a great deal of diverse information about that individual. I do not know if there was any generic model or template behind those models of individuals. I am inclined to think not. Assignments were very much adapted to the abilities and experiences of the individual staff members. One person, for example, might get an assignment in very general terms to conduct a competitive RFP procurement on a given topic. Another might also get detailed scaffolding of what was involved in such a task – all its parts and the expected time requirements for each phase. Our secretaries were very poorly educated products of the Washington, D.C. public schools. One could get them to do useful work by being very specific about what needed to be done. Supervisors who came with expectations formed by their experiences with university secretaries (who were often the wives of male graduate students without other employment opportunities and much more capable than typical government secretaries), tended to be very frustrated by what happened when they did not give very specific instructions or delegated tasks that required considerable independent thinking.

In the odd form of management that made up most of my career, the distant and loose management of researchers in a research program funding researchers in other organizations in distant locations, detailed mental models of individual researchers, their strengths and weaknesses, and their motives also played an important role.

To the extent that I know how to be an effective manager of people, it was not, I think, due to anything I was taught at the HBS or in the government training courses to which I was sent. Aside from learning the hard way from my own experience, I think I learned useful things from my own parents. During my high school years, my father was a government contract officer who supervised about 200 people and regularly received awards for being an outstanding supervisor. My mother was a high school teacher of English, generally recognized as a very good teacher. Our dinner conversations often focused on their analyses and their efforts to think through problems with problem employees or problem students.

The Myers-Briggs Cult: A System for Mental Modeling of Employees

For at least the last couple of decades, there have been many government training courses that do attempt to teach one particular way of forming mental models of other people in the workplace. I first encountered this in 1980 when I was sent to a session at the Federal Executive Institute. It offers three- to seven-week residential programs. In the Department of Defense, the Federal Executive Institute (FEI) has established itself as a nearly mandatory *rite du passage* into the Senior Executive Service (SES), the upper echelons of the civil service. Although its status is not so strong in other agencies, eligible participants are GS-15 civil servants who might be expected to be promoted into the SES and others who are already in an SES position. I was sent as a minimally eligible substitute for another, more typical participant who proved to be too busy to go when the time for the program rolled around. (Since all potential participants are perceived to be very busy, the agencies are required to pay well in advance, and there are no refunds.) The prototypic participant was a white male, approximately 55 years of age. Each session had about 70 participants. Four of the participants in my session were women.

Prior to arrival, all participants were required to complete the Myers-Briggs personality test (Myers & McCaulley, 1990) and send it in for scoring. This test proved to have a rather central role in the program. At the opening session, the leader of our session, who also happened to be the director of FEI, went on at some length about personality types as given by the Myers-Briggs results. He made stronger statements about the immutability of personality characteristics than I believed to be generally accepted by experts in the field of personality psychology. He also said things that I believed would lead managers to hire and evaluate people on the basis of their personality types, contrary to civil service rules. This latter fear proved justified by remarks my co-participants made during later discussions. In a much more recent government training session, I found that the claims that were being made about the significance of the Myers-Briggs personality types were much less extreme than they had been at FEI. Inquiring about that, I was told that there had been a number of successful lawsuits brought against the uses that were being made of the Myers-Briggs in decisions that affected people's careers.

Eventually I came to the view that the Myers-Briggs activities were largely designed to convey the message to people like engineers that: (1) people exist, (2) they differ from each other, and (3) they don't have to be exactly like you in order to be effective employees. (The last part of the message tended to be undermined by repeated claims that federal managers typically had just one Myers-Briggs personality type. This claim was in fact true of the participants in my session. What I noticed about my co-participants – in a different dimension than the Myers-Briggs ones – was that they seemed to be very solid, stable personalities. Very few had been divorced. This may say something about what makes for success in the civil service.) Many of the participants from the Department of Defense were, in fact, engineers who had risen to high civil service rank as individual workers, without having to supervise other people, because of organizational efforts to pay competitive salaries to engineers. In an SES position, they were being confronted with the problem of supervising other people for the first time. Other participants, however, were highly experienced supervisors of large numbers of people. Research on the factors that determine field and career selection (Chipman & Thomas, 1987) shows that stereotypes of engineers are true: Interest in things as opposed to people is a strong predictor of becoming an engineer (Dunteman, Wisenbaker, & Taylor, 1979).

In general, I found the curriculum of the FEI sessions to be rather peculiar, not at all what I would have imagined as the content of a nearly mandatory training experience for entry into the SES. For example, I might have imagined sessions of training on the problems involved in dealing with political appointees and political administrations. When one reaches the upper echelons of the civil service, this becomes a problem. But there were no such sessions. It is hard to imagine that any sensible analysis led to the curriculum being what it was. The curriculum was made up of a lot of little modules, some required and some optional. Many of these modules were touchy-feely activities. Some of them dealt with the male mid-life crisis. The rooms at FEI were equipped with a small library of popular psychology books on the male mid-life crisis, a major pop psych topic at the time. Perhaps this focus met the personal needs of many participants, but it did not make a 34-year-old woman (all two of us) feel at home, nor did it seem clearly related to SES job responsibilities. It is important to remember that this training experience is a very expensive one, involving high costs in the salaries of participating executives as well as the costs of the travel, housing, and instructors.

Some modules appeared more substantive, but hardly content that everyone in the SES needed to know. For example, I enrolled in a little mini-course about Nicaragua, just because it seemed to have some substance. Participants in longer seven-week sessions might have made a field trip there, or some other place. As a member of the Vietnam War generation, I was somewhat appalled by what my fellow participants had to say in this course, but I was consequently not surprised when the United States later became involved in the activities there that we all know about now. Modules of this type seemed haphazardly selected and relevant to the jobs of only a few participants. In summary, the objectives of this training experience were rather obscure, the training experiences of doubtful effectiveness, and the cost-effectiveness even more in doubt.

HOW ADEQUATE ARE MYERS-BRIGGS MODELS OF PEOPLE?

When I returned from the FEI, the boss who had sent me was shocked to hear about the Myers-Briggs testing. She had once had a job, during her graduate school years, administering psychological tests and knew that the Myers-Briggs did not meet accepted standards of psychological test development. A relatively recent review (Boyle, 1995) concluded that, "Routine use of the MBTI is not to be recommended, and psychologists should be cautious as to its likely misuse in various organizational and occupational settings" (p. 71). Yet, the use of this test in business, counseling, and education is very widespread, to the extent that a *New Yorker* article (Gladwell, 2004) was written about it recently. It is an old test based on Jungian personality theory and not built with currently accepted psychometric methods. Its most evident shortcoming arises from its Jungian basis. Like biological traits in general, one would expect personality traits to be normally distributed, with most people in the middle of the scale. But no middle is allowed in the Myers-Briggs: People are forced into "types," leading to low reliability of the assigned types (Stricker & Ross, 1963). More professional personality tests do place most people in the middle of the scales. However, they also tend to have pejorative sounding terms labeling one end of some scales, such as *neuroticism*. The absence of such pejorative terms may well account for the popularity of the Myers-Briggs. One of the contrasts in the Myers-Briggs, introversion versus extroversion, invariably emerges as the most important dimension of personality when tests are constructed by accepted methods. This lends credibility, but surely most of us lie somewhere in the middle of that dimension. The other contrasts drawn by the Myers-Briggs (sensing versus intuiting, thinking versus feeling, and judging versus perceiving) do not have the same sort of general acceptance. Digman (1990), among others, reviews professional thinking about personality measurement. Not surprisingly, the more intellectual-sounding contrasts have some relationship with general intellectual ability (Crawley, Pinder, & Herriot, 1990), a salient and important dimension of individual differences.

Regardless, the models of people that the Myers-Briggs gives seem very simplistic compared to the information about individual students that Christensen describes himself as having and as providing guidance in very detailed actions he took. They seem very simplistic compared to the models I had of my subordinates when I was a supervisor. One can imagine them leading to legally dubious decisions that a person does not have the right personality type to be a high-level manager but not as providing detailed guidance in how to design an assignment or what to say in order to motivate a person. Research is needed to reveal the way in which successful supervisors actually do model people. Despite the emphasis on the Myers-Briggs at the FEI, the curriculum did not seem to include any discussion of what to do with personality information in managing people. The Myers-Briggs training experience includes a booklet entitled, "Please Understand Me." As a government employee and subordinate, I often felt misunderstood, but not in terms of Myers-Briggs dimensions – rather I felt that what motivated me in my job was not well understood. That is, the government's official systems for performance assessment and related rewards presume (or at least hope) that one will be highly motivated by rather small monetary rewards. But if monetary rewards had been my primary motivator, I would never have left the HBS career path and would never have been a government employee at all. This is true for many of the best government employees; one needs to appeal to what is actually motivating employees, often some aspect of the agency mission.

STUDYING MANAGEMENT AND LEADERSHIP BEHAVIOR

We do not know enough about the actual behavior of effective managers and leaders. If we are going to develop training for management and leadership, and evaluate the effectiveness of that training, we need to know what behavior we are aiming to develop. Organizational psychologists are surprisingly dependent upon questionnaire methods; study of actual human behavior is extremely rare. One can easily imagine that people could know all the right answers to one of Sternberg's measures of tacit knowledge of leadership (Hedlund et al., 2003), but be unable to successfully execute that right answer in their behavior. Studying actual human behavior is much more time consuming, tedious, and difficult to arrange than passing out questionnaires. Outside the field of organizational behavior, however, there have been research studies that use ethological methods or so-called ethnographic methods. For example, there have been a few developmental studies of the establishment of dominance relationships among children or adolescents, parallel to more common studies of dominance relationships among groups of animals (Savin-Williams, 1976; Strayer & Strayer, 1976; Zivin, 1977). Zivin described detailed observational studies of interactions among groups of children using videotapes that were then subjected to very detailed analyses. She identified what she called a "win predicting" facial expression. The expression was defined by the simultaneous presence of a raised brow, a direct stare toward someone's eye, and a raised chin. Because of the effect of talking on the position of the mouth, mouth position was not part of the coding scheme. However, the one photographic example of the expression in the article shows what I would call a look of determination to which the position of the mouth contributes greatly. I believe that the *Washington Post* once captured this expression in a front page photo of President Jimmy Carter, the day before he won an important treaty vote in the Senate.

These expressions were related to a ranking of individuals by perceived *toughness*, as rated by the children themselves. It was shown that the children interpreted toughness as meaning strong in fighting or in getting what one wants from someone else. There were very few physical fights in the study population. According to Zivin, in the older of the two age groups she studied (7 to 10 years of age), this expression tended to become very swift and fleeting and was used as a sort of haughty emphasis to conversational points. Not surprisingly, there were obvious sex differences in the rankings of the children – girls tended to be in the middle or lower ranks at both age groups studied, although one or two girls were in the top quarter of each group, and the earlier study by Strayer and Strayer found that the top ranking child was a girl. Such politically incorrect results may have made such research unpopular in recent years.

Detailed behavioral analysis has also been used to study the classroom management behavior of schoolteachers to provide guidance for teacher training (Thomas, Becker, & Armstrong, 1968). We have all encountered those few teachers and school administrators who seem to have outstanding command and control over even difficult student groups. Similar behavioral analysis of managers and leaders in action would, I believe, have great value.

When I was attempting to understand the behavior of my fellow students at the HBS, I came to believe that a lot of it was about struggling to establish a dominance hierarchy. For example, their behavior in small group discussion activities differed strikingly from what I had been used to seeing among Harvard undergraduates. Whether or not they actually cared about the topic of the discussion, HBS students would struggle to take charge of the discussion. Harvard undergraduates would not bother with a discussion that they did not care about. It also seemed to explain the strange behavior of a student who once clearly lost to me in a classroom discussion. It seemed to me that he overreacted to this loss in a very extreme way: Ever afterward, he was out to get me in the classrooms. The product of elite private schools, he had never been in a classroom with female students before; this, I believe, allowed him to maintain the belief that all females were inferior to all males. Therefore, I think, losing to me was equivalent to losing to all other males, explaining the overreaction. However, even stranger, he was also a Southern gentleman and behaved very graciously toward me in outside social situations.

The prototypic goal of the HBS student is to become the boss, the CEO, the person who gets other people to do what he wants. To be "the decider," as President George W. Bush, also a graduate of the HBS, puts it. This is very much about social dominance. Of course, social dominance is not simply determined by characteristics of the individual. It also depends upon support from the social environment, such as the social class status of the individual or the very clearly defined factor of military rank, or the low status generally assigned to females or members of various minority groups. Even among monkeys, Suomi (2005) has shown that social connections can override biological characteristics that usually predict social rank: It is a great help if a young male monkey has a high ranking mother.

It would be interesting to analyze what features of behavioral demeanor – similar or perhaps even identical to those Zivin described – predict success in attempts at leadership behavior in the military. One might call those *win faces* expressions of confidence. The role of confidence or feelings of entitlement or similar factors may explain another feature of the HBS that I found surprising. The professors often inflated the egos of the students, often by denigrating undergraduate academic professors. On the average, HBS students had not been particularly successful as undergraduate students. Christensen describes working on improving student confidence. The professors in arts and sciences at Harvard definitely did not behave that way, even though the average ability of Harvard undergraduates was noticeably higher than that of HBS students.

Once we have begun to learn more about these aspects of human behavior, it will be interesting to ask whether management differs significantly from leadership, the term so popular in the military context. *Leadership* is the glamour word; *management* is more mundane but perhaps practically more important. Interestingly, the word *leadership* does not seem to appear in the books about teaching at HBS, except in the context of discussion leadership, as in the subtitle of *Education for Judgment*. Perhaps this just reflects the emergence of leadership as a buzzword in recent years. Only against the background of effective management can leadership have real success. Underlining the glamour element in leadership, Mumford et al. (Chapter 4) suggest that leadership makes a difference in situations of organizational crisis and change, when organizations face complex and ill-defined problems.

REPRISE

In this chapter, I have identified a number of interesting research questions, the pursuit of which would certainly improve our understanding of the nature of expertise in the management of people. Relatively neglected as a topic of research, expertise in the management of people is highly important for all types of organizations. We need good, refined descriptions, in cognitive depth, of this type of expertise before we can meaningfully assess performance in this domain, sensibly develop education and training for this expertise, or assess the effectiveness of our training efforts.

Sophisticated mental models of other people are undoubtedly a key element in this expertise, but we know very little about the detailed nature of these models. What information do they typically contain? Available cognitive research methods should be able to provide the answer to this question. Then, one can begin to explore deliberate efforts to teach that mental modeling skill, going well beyond the current Myers-Briggs–based training efforts in this domain. Perhaps there could be useful interaction with the *theory of mind* research that has become prominent in developmental research, as well as in efforts to understand autism and Asperger's syndrome – where understanding of other people is notably deficient.

However, understanding of other people is only one aspect of management skill. We need to know much more about how these models function in guiding actual managerial or leadership behavior. For this purpose, very detailed observation and analysis of behavior will be needed. Can one, in fact, observe and describe the kind of fine adaptation of discussion-teaching behavior to individual student needs that Christensen describes doing? Although teaching may be quite different from other forms of people management, it may be a good initial focus for research because the behavior of interest is continuously available for observation, and obtaining the necessary permission for study is likely to be easier than in other organizational contexts.

Especially as we move away from the educational context, we need to ask how big a factor these mental models are in determining successful management or leadership of people. How much weight do they carry as compared to other factors such as the organizational support provided by military rank and its civilian counterparts? How important is the sense of confidence or entitlement of the individual attempting to manage and lead? Providing answers to such questions will certainly challenge our available research methods and call for creativity.

Even when we understand the nature of such management skills, devising ways to teach those skills remains a major creative challenge. One of the major approaches used today in management training is case-based instruction. But is it effective? The research by Gentner and her colleagues that was discussed in this chapter both casts doubt on the effectiveness of existing practices and points the way to possibly improved effectiveness. There should be much more research of this kind.

Many of the chapters in this book have tried to measure improved performance of individual professionals that results from training. However, measurement of expertise in the management of people is a much more complex, challenging matter because of the many variables inherent in the individual people being managed. Bain's study of outstanding college teachers tried to determine whether the teacher's students were unexpectedly successful and productive, but how this was done and the nature of the evidence remained obscure. It is not that this problem has lacked intelligent attention. Most organizations attempt to measure such performance in their management compensation systems, and a great deal of thought and effort has gone into developing those systems. It is inherently an extremely difficult problem.

It is important to ask whether there is evidence that this type of training truly adds value to the individuals trained, as discussed by Fletcher (Chapter 20). This is a difficult type of question to study when it comes to management training, but such research is not without precedent (cf. Dale & Kruger, 2002). The costs of such training are often high both for organizations and for individuals. The direct financial costs and the indirect opportunity costs of an MBA program for the individual student are often very high. Would that individual be better off spending those two years earning a salary, learning from business experience, and progressing in a career path? Quite possibly. If such training is ineffective, there is a great deal of money to be saved. Correspondingly, of course, there are conflicting interests of those who make a business of providing such training.

The issue of the effectiveness and value of management training will not be resolved by discussions and exchange of opinions. We need to extend the scientific methods that have been successfully used to measure differences in objective performance for individuals and to measure the differences between the sustained productivity and innovation of groups and teams. Once we are able to identify reproducible effects and differences we can control for group members' initial abilities to measure the influence of leaders' characteristics, behavior, and actions. We need to begin doing serious research to pinpoint the causal factors mediating the successful manager's effects on performance on groups and teams. Knowing what the causal factors are, we should be able to develop effective training in this socially vital domain of expertise so we can monitor and support the development of management expertise during life-long careers in the military services and in civilian society, in contexts ranging from school classrooms to large commercial organizations.

REFERENCES

Bain, K. (2004). *What the best college teachers do.* Cambridge, MA: Harvard University Press.

Barnes, L. B., Christensen, C. R., & Hansen, A. J. (Eds.) (1994). *Teaching and the case method: Text, cases and readings* (3rd ed.). Boston, MA: Harvard Business School Press.

Boyle, G. J. (1995). Myers-Briggs Type Indicator (MBTI): Some psychometric limitations. *Australian Psychologist, 30,* 71–74.

Chipman, S. F., & Thomas, V. (1987). The participation of women and minorities in mathematics, sciences, and technology. *Review of Research in Education, 14,* 387–430.

Christensen, C. R. (1991a). Every student teaches and every teacher learns: The reciprocal gift of discussion teaching. In C. R. Christensen D. A. Garvin, & A. Sweet

(Eds.), *Education for judgment: The artistry of discussion leadership* (pp. 99–122). Boston, MA: Harvard Business School Press.

(1991b). The discussion teacher in action: Questioning, listening and response. In C. R. Christensen D. A. Garvin, & A. Sweet (Eds.), *Education for judgment: The artistry of discussion leadership* (pp. 153–174). Boston, MA: Harvard Business School Press.

Christensen, C. R., Garvin, D. A., & Sweet, A. (Eds.). (1991). *Education for judgment: The artistry of discussion leadership*. Boston, MA: Harvard Business School Press.

Crawley, B., Pinder, R., & Herriot, P. (1990). Assessment centre dimensions, personality and aptitudes. *Journal of Occupational Psychology, 63,* 211–216.

Dale, S. B., & Kruger, A. B. (2002). Estimating the payoff to attending a more selective college: An application of selection on observables and unobservables. *The Quarterly Journal of Economics, 117,* 1491–1527.

Derry, S. J., & Potts, M. K. (1998). How tutors model students: A study of personal constructs in adaptive tutoring. *American Educational Research Journal, 35,* 65–99.

Digman, J. M. (1990). Personality structure: Emergence of the five-factor model. *Annual Review of Psychology, 41,* 417–440.

Domeshek, E. (2006). Phase II final report on analogical reasoning for authors and students of case-method instruction. Stottler Henke Associates, Inc. Final Report for Contract N00014–03–C-0453, 3/31/2006.

Dunteman, G. H., Wisenbaker, J., & Taylor, M. E. (1979). Race and sex differences in college science program participation. Research Triangle Institute: Report submitted to the National Science Foundation under Contract No. SED77–18728 (ERIC Document Reproduction Service No. ED 199034).

Ericsson, K. A., Krampe, R., & Tesch-Römer, C. (1993). The role of deliberate practice in the acquisition of expert performance. *Psychological Review, 100,* 363–406.

Evens, M., & Michael, J. (2005). *One-on-one tutoring by humans and computers.* Mahwah, NJ: Lawrence Erlbaum Associates.

Frame, A., & Lussier, J. W. (Eds.). (2000). *66 Stories of Battle Command.* Army Command and General Staff College, Ft. Leavenworth, KS: Report # A156644.

Gladwell, M. (2004). *Personality plus: Employers love personality tests. But what do they really reveal. New Yorker,* September 20. (Available on gladwell.com)

Greenwald, B. (1991). Teaching technical material. In C. R. Christensen, D. A. Garvin, & A. Sweet (Eds.), *Education for judgment: The artistry of discussion leadership* (pp. 193–214). Boston, MA: Harvard Business School Press.

Hedlund, J., Forsythe, G. B., Horvath, J. A., Williams, W. M. Snook, S., & Sternberg, R. (2003). Identifying and assessing tacit knowledge: Understanding the practical intelligence of military leaders. *Leadership Quarterly, 14,* 117–140.

Jarrell, B. E. (2003). *Surgery casebook.* Baltimore: Lippincott, Williams & Wilkins.

Klein, G. (1998). *Sources of power: How people make decisions.* Cambridge, MA: MIT Press.

Loewenstein, J., Thompson, L., & Gentner, D. (2003). Analogical learning in negotiation teams: Comparing cases promotes learning and transfer. *Academy of Management Learning and Education, 2*(2), 119–127.

Lundeberg, M. A. (1999). Discovering teaching and learning through cases. In M. A. Lundeberg B. B. Levin, & H. L. Harrington (Eds.), *Who learns what from cases and how? The research base for teaching and learning with cases* (pp. 3–23). Mahwah, NJ: Lawrence Erlbaum Associates.

Lundeberg, M. A., Levin, B. B., & Harrington, H. L. (1999). *Who learns what from cases and how? The research base for teaching and learning with cases.* Mahwah, NJ: Lawrence Erlbaum Associates.

Merseth, K. K. (1999). Foreword: A rationale for case-based pedagogy in teacher education. In M. A. Lundeberg, B. B. Levin, & H. L. Harrington (Eds.), *Who learns what from cases and how? The research base for teaching and learning with cases* (pp. ix–xv). Mahwah, NJ: Lawrence Erlbaum Associates.

Myers, I., & McCaulley, I. (1990). *Manual: A guide to the development and use of the Myers-Briggs type indicator.* Palo Alto, CA: Consulting Psychologists Press.

Nutt, P. C. (1984). Types of organizational decision processes. *Administrative Science Quarterly, 29,* 414–450.

Ross, K. G., Lussier, J. W., & Klein, G. (2005). From the recognition primed decision model to training. In T. Betsch & S. Haberstroh (Eds.), *The routines of decision making* (pp. 327–341). Mahwah, NJ: Lawrence Erlbaum Associates.

Salas, E., Mullen, B., Rozell, D., & Driskell, J. E. (1997). *The effects of team building on performance: An integration.* Paper presented at the 1997 annual conference of the Society for Industrial and Organizational Psychology, St. Louis, MO.

Savin-Williams, R. C. (1976). An ethological study of dominance formation and maintenance in a group of human adolescents. *Child Development, 47,* 972–979.

Strayer, F. F., & Strayer, J. (1976). An ethological analysis of social agonism and dominance relations among preschool children. *Child Development, 47,* 980–989.

Stricker, L. J. & Ross, J. (1963). Intercorrelations and reliability of the Myers-Briggs Type Indicator Scales. *Psychological Reports, 12,* 287–293.

Suomi, S. J. (2005). Mother-infant attachment, peer relationships, and the development of social networks in rhesus monkeys. *Human Development, 48,* 67–79.

Thomas, D. R., Becker, W. C., & Armstrong, M. (1968). Production and elimination of disruptive classroom behavior by systematically varying teacher's behavior. *Journal of Applied Behavior Analysis, 1,* 35–45.

Thompson, L., Gentner, D., & Loewenstein, J. (2000). Avoiding missed opportunities in managerial life: Analogical training more powerful than individual case training. *Organizational Behavior and Human Decision Processes, 82,* 60–75.

Zivin, G. (1977). Becoming subtle: Age and social rank changes in the use of a facial gesture. *Child Development, 48,* 1314–1321.

NAME INDEX

Page numbers in **bold** indicate full reference citations.

Abboud, P. A., 184, **198**
Abdolrasulnia, M., 190, **197**
Abedi, J., 350, **353**
Abernethy, B., **427**
Abrahamowicz, M., 399, **406**
Acchione-Noel, S. C., 164, 165, **176**
Accreditation Council for Continuing Medical
    Education, 190, **197**
Accreditation Council for Graduate Medical
    Education, 194
Ackermann, P., 139, **152**
Adams, J., 185, **197**
Adams, J. A., 313, **328**
Adhikari, N. K. J., 195, **199**
Airasian, P. W., 203, **210**
Albacete, P., 363, **376**
Albanese, M. A., 396, **401**
Albano, M. G., **401**, 409
Alburt, L., 290, **307**
Aleong, P., 76, **81–82**
Alexander, P. A., 62, 63, **80**
Alimo-Metcalfe, B., 87, **102**
Allen, N., 135, **153**
Allen, T. W., 318, **328**
Allerton, D. J., 423, **427**
Alley, W. E., 62, 66, 71, **82**
Alliger, G. M., 86, **105**, 258, **268**
Allison, J. J., 190, **197**
American Academy of Family Physicians, 188,
    190, **197**
American Board of Medical Specialties, 188, 191
American College of Physicians, 186
American College of Surgeons, 186, **197**
American Educational Research Association,
    335, 336, 351, **353**
American Heart Association, 186, **197**

American Medical Association, 187, 188, 191, **197**
American Psychological Association, 301, **307**,
    335, 336, 351, **353**
Amirault, R. J., 163, **176**
Ammeter, A. P., 86, **106**
Anderson, J. R., 113, 114, 115, **127**, 143, **152**, 343,
    353, 424, **427**
Anderson, L. W., 203, **210**, 344, 350, **353**
Anderson, Th., 140, **154**
Andrews, D. H., 255, **267**
Annett, J., 158, 159, **176**
Antes, Alison L., 11, 12, 84, 108, 120, 121,
    122, 123, 125, 126, 450, 451, 470,
    475, 489
Aparicio, A., 191, **197**
Arad, S., 287, 291, **310**
Araya, A. A., 358, 360, **377**
Armor, Tom, 243
Armstrong, M., 488, **493**
Army Training and Leader Development Panel,
    288, **307**
Army Training Circular, 32, **59**
Arnold, S. R., 190, **197**
Arocha, J. F., 62, **82**
Aronson, E., 327, **328**
Arroba, T., 98, **104**
Arthur, M. B., 86, **106**
Arthur, W., 88, **102**
Arts, J. A. R., 387, 392, **401**
Asch, S. M., 185, **197**
Ashby, G. F., 368, **375**
Assaad, D., 185, **198**
Atwater, L. E., 87, **102**
Audet, M., 90, **103**
Austin, D. L., 188, **200**
Austin, J. T., 6, **20–21**

SUBJECT INDEX

A (Apprentice) schools, 279
A-10 skills, 258, 259
AARs. *See* After Action Reviews (AARs)
ability, 453, 454, 459
ability of individuals, 454
ability to learn, assessing flexible, 443
abnormal behavior, 170
abstract principles, 451
academic and professional knowledge, 387
academic curricula, 375
academic disciplines, 382
academic knowledge, 452
academic professional education.
    See professional academic education
Accelerated Learning Program, 348
accompanists (pianists), 411
accountability, 195, 341, 384
Accreditation Council for Graduate Medical
    Education, 194
accreditation of CME activities, 190
aces, 49–53, 450, 454
achievement tests, 338
acoustic analysts. *See* sonar operators
Acoustic Intelligence (ACINT) specialists, 280
acquired skills, decay of, 34
ACT*-model, 143
action learning techniques, 98
action reviews (AARs). *See* After-Action
    Reviews (AARs)
activated cases, 92
activating (problem- and project-based)
    curricula, 399
active coaching, 295
actor-level behaviors, culturally determined, 243
Acuitus, Inc. 234
adaptability, 287
adaptable thinking, 302
adaptive aiding, 162

adaptive expertise, 290, 443
adaptive experts, 63, 285, 433
adaptive instruction, 74, 340
adaptive leaders, 306
adaptive learning, 285
adaptive thinking, 287, 289, 291, 294
adaptive thinking skills, 289, 303, 323
adaptive training, 263
administrative point of view, 472
admission, of an individual, 340
adult education, 181–182
adult math course, 479
adulthood, increasing expert performance
    during, 412
Advanced Instructional Design Advisor (AIDA)
    project, 134
affordability, of quality outcomes, 352
affordances, 135
Afghanistan (Operation Enduring Freedom),
    302
AFQT (Armed Forces Qualification Test), 453
After Action Reviews (AARs), 316
    all ranks encouraged to speak out, 110
    conducting, 32
    in engagement simulation training, 52
    Flashpoint not providing good tools for, 229
    key component of force on force engagement
        training, 464
    lauded, 465
    at Navy Fighter Weapons School, 30
    personally developed, longitudinal
        set of, 347
    soldiers subjecting everything to, 32
    specific principles for the conduct of, 464
    stressed by Chatham, 110
    as a uniquely American institution, 465
Age of Information Processing
    (1973–now), 159